Numerical Methods of Statistics
Second Edition

This book explains how computer software is designed to perform the tasks required for sophisticated statistical analysis. For statisticians, it examines the nitty-gritty computational problems behind statistical methods. For mathematicians and computer scientists, it looks at the application of mathematical tools to statistical problems. The first half of the book offers a basic background in numerical analysis that emphasizes issues important to statisticians. The next several chapters cover a broad array of statistical tools, such as maximum likelihood and nonlinear regression. The author also treats the application of numerical tools; numerical integration and random number generation are explained in a unified manner reflecting complementary views of Monte Carlo methods. Each chapter contains exercises that range from simple questions to research problems. Most of the examples are accompanied by demonstration and source code available on the author's Web site. New in this second edition are demonstrations coded in R, as well as new sections on linear programming and the Nelder-Mead search algorithm.

John F. Monahan is a Professor of Statistics at North Carolina State University, where he joined the faculty in 1978 and has been a professor since 1990. His research has appeared in numerous computational as well as statistical journals. He is also the author of *A Primer on Linear Models* (2008).

CAMBRIDGE SERIES IN STATISTICAL AND PROBABILISTIC MATHEMATICS

This series of high-quality upper-division textbooks and expository monographs covers all aspects of stochastic applicable mathematics. The topics range from pure and applied statistics to probability theory, operations research, optimization, and mathematical programming. The books contain clear presentations of new developments in the field and also of the state of the art in classical methods. While emphasizing rigorous treatment of theoretical methods, the books also contain applications and discussions of new techniques made possible by advances in computational practice.

1. *Bootstrap Methods and Their Application*, by A. C. Davison and D. V. Hinkley
2. *Markov Chains*, by J. Norris
3. *Asymptotic Statistics*, by A. W. van der Vaart
4. *Wavelet Methods for Time Series Analysis*, by Donald B. Percival and Andrew T. Walden
5. *Bayesian Methods*, by Thomas Leonard and John S. J. Hsu
6. *Empirical Processes in M-Estimation*, by Sara van de Geer
7. *Numerical Methods of Statistics*, by John F. Monahan
8. *A User's Guide to Measure Theoretic Probability*, by David Pollard
9. *The Estimation and Tracking of Frequency*, by B. G. Quinn and E. J. Hannan
10. *Data Analysis and Graphics Using R*, by John Maindonald and John Braun
11. *Statistical Models*, by A. C. Davison
12. *Semiparametric Regression*, by D. Ruppert, M. P. Wand, and R. J. Carroll
13. *Exercise in Probability*, by Loic Chaumont and Marc Yor
14. *Statistical Analysis of Stochastic Processes in Time*, by J. K. Lindsey
15. *Measure Theory and Filtering*, by Lakhdar Aggoun and Robert Elliott
16. *Essentials of Statistical Inference*, by G. A. Young and R. L. Smith
17. *Elements of Distribution Theory*, by Thomas A. Severini
18. *Statistical Mechanics of Disordered Systems*, by Anton Bovier
19. *The Coordinate-Free Approach to Linear Models*, by Michael J. Wichura
20. *Random Graph Dynamics*, by Rick Durrett
21. *Networks*, by Peter Whittle
22. *Saddlepoint Approximations with Applications*, by Ronald W. Butler
23. *Applied Asymptotics*, by A. R. Brazzale, A. C. Davison, and N. Reid
24. *Random Networks for Communication*, by Massimo Franceschetti and Ronald Meester
25. *Design of Comparative Experiments*, by R. A. Bailey
26. *Symmetry Studies*, by Marlos A. G. Viana
27. *Model Selection and Model Averaging*, by Gerda Claeskens and Nils Lid Hjort
28. *Bayesian Nonparametrics*, by Nils Lid Hjort, Peter Müller, Stephen G. Walker
29. *From Finite Sample to Asymptotic Methods in Statistics*, by Pranab K. Sen, Julio M. Singer, and Antonio C. Pedroso de Lima
30. *Brownian Motion*, by Peter Mörters and Yuval Peres
31. *Probability: Theory and Examples*, fourth edition, by Rick Durrett

Numerical Methods of Statistics

Second Edition

JOHN F. MONAHAN

North Carolina State University

CAMBRIDGE
UNIVERSITY PRESS

CAMBRIDGE
UNIVERSITY PRESS

University Printing House, Cambridge CB2 8BS, United Kingdom

One Liberty Plaza, 20th Floor, New York, NY 10006, USA

477 Williamstown Road, Port Melbourne, VIC 3207, Australia

314-321, 3rd Floor, Plot 3, Splendor Forum, Jasola District Centre, New Delhi - 110025, India

103 Penang Road, #05-06/07, Visioncrest Commercial, Singapore 238467

Cambridge University Press is part of the University of Cambridge.

It furthers the University's mission by disseminating knowledge in the pursuit of
education, learning and research at the highest international levels of excellence.

www.cambridge.org
Information on this title: www.cambridge.org/9780521139519

© Cambridge University Press 2001, 2011

First published 2001
Second edition published 2011

A catalogue record for this publication is available from the British Library

Library of Congress Cataloging in Publication data
Monahan, John F.
Numerical methods of statistics / John F. Monahan.
p. cm. – (Cambridge series in statistical and probabilistic mathematics)
Includes bibliographical references.
ISBN 978-0-521-19158-6
1. Mathematical statistics – Data processing. 2. Numerical analysis. I. Title.
II. Cambridge series in statistical and probabilistic mathematics.
QA276.4.M65 2001
519.5–dc21 00-031269

ISBN 978-0-521-19158-6 Hardback
ISBN 978-0-521-13951-9 Paperback

Contents

Preface to the Second Edition

In the ten years since the first edition of this book went to press, the field of statistical computing has exploded with innovations in many directions. At one time my goal was to write a comprehensive book on the subject. At this moment, however, my goals for a second edition must be more modest. Because the field has grown so much, the scope of this book has now become the core for a subset of this field. To fill in some gaps in this new core, a few sections have been added (e.g., linear programming) and others have been expanded. Many corrections have been made; I can only hope that just a few errors remain.

A second change in this timespan is the rapid widespread adoption of R in the field of statistics. As language and culture shape each other, my own views on computing have changed from teaching this material using R. Small changes scattered throughout reflect this change in viewpoint. Additionally, most of the demonstrations and examples – all that seemed appropriate – have been translated to R and are available on my Web site for this book (http://www4.stat.ncsu.edu/~monahan/nmos2/toc.html).

Thanks are due to Lauren Cowles of Cambridge University Press for encouraging this second edition. Karen Chiswell deserves recognition for finding numerous typos and providing other corrections. I would like to also thank Jerry Davis and Wendy Meiring for pointing out others. Bruce McCullough provided invaluable feedback, comments, questions, and suggestions. Thanks are also due to the many students who, perhaps unknowingly, provided feedback with their questions. And this second edition would not be possible without the love, support, and patience of my wife Carol.

Preface to the First Edition

This book grew out of notes for my Statistical Computing course that I have been teaching for the past 20 years at North Carolina State University. The goal of this course is to prepare doctoral students with the computing tools needed for statistical research, and I have augmented this core with related topics that through the years I have found useful for colleagues and graduate students. As a result, this book covers a wide range of computational issues, from arithmetic, numerical linear algebra, and approximation, which are typical numerical analysis topics, to optimization and non-linear regression, to random number generation, and finally to fast algorithms. I have emphasized numerical techniques but restricted the scope to those regularly employed in the field of statistics and dropped some traditional numerical analysis topics such as differential equations. Many of the exercises in this book arose from questions posed to me by colleagues and students.

Most of the students that I have taught come with a graduate level understanding of statistics, no experience in numerical analysis, and little skill in a programming language. Consequently, I cover only about half of this material in a one-semester course. For those with a background in numerical analysis, a basic understanding of two statistical topics, regression and maximum likelihood, would be necessary.

I would advise any instructor of statistical computing not to shortchange the fundamental topic of arithmetic. I have found that most students resist the idea that computers have limited precision and employ many defense mechanisms to support that denial. Until students are comfortable with finite precision arithmetic, this psychological obstacle will cripple their understanding of scientific computation. As a result, I urge the use of single precision arithmetic in the early part of the course and introduce numerical linear algebra using a low-level language, even though students may eventually use software or languages that completely hide the calculations behind operators and double precision. These operators will continue to be mysterious black boxes until the fundamental concept of finite precision arithmetic is understood and accepted.

Early in this effort, I faced the dilemma of how to describe algorithms. The big picture is easier to present or to understand with pseudocode descriptions of algorithms. But I always felt that skipping over the details was misleading the reader, especially when the details are critical to the success of an implementation. Furthermore, there is no better challenge to one's understanding of a topic than to take a big-picture description and program it to the smallest detail. On the other hand, writing one's own implementation of an algorithm often seems like a futile reinvention of the wheel.

And so my response to this dilemma is to have it both ways: to present algorithms in pseudocode in the text, but also to supplement the pseudocode with Fortran programs and demonstrations on the accompanying disk.

These programs provide the basic tools for extending the realm of statistical techniques beyond the bounds of current statistical software. But my primary goal in providing this code is instructional. Some exercises consist of implementing a particular algorithm, and occasionally I have intentionally included my implementation for the reader to compare with, or, perhaps, improve upon. I encourage the reader to examine the details of the code and to see how the algorithms respond to changes. A secondary goal is to include as many realistic problems as practicable, having endured the frustration of failing to get code to work on anything but toy problems.

I would like to express my appreciation to the many sources of support behind this effort. First of all, three heads of the Department of Statistics have supported my work in statistical computing: Tom Gerig, Dan Solomon, and the late Dave Mason. Some of the work included here is the result of collaborations with many colleagues over the years; especially notable are Al Kinderman on random number generation and Alan Genz on numerical integration. In particular, I would like to thank Sujit Ghosh and Dave Dickey for contributing invaluable advice on Chapter 13. Dennis Boos deserves special acknowledgment as a friend, colleague, and collaborator, and most importantly, for supplying me with many interesting problems over the years. I would like to thank all of the colleagues and students who brought interesting problems to me that have become material in this book. Finally, I appreciate the feedback that students have given me each semester on earlier versions of this manuscript, including their blank stares and yawns, as well as insightful questions.

1

Algorithms and Computers

1.1 Introduction

Discussing algorithms before computers emphasizes the point that algorithms are valuable mathematical constructs in themselves and exist even in the absence of computers. An *algorithm* is a list of instructions for the completion of a task. The best examples of algorithms in everyday life are cooking recipes, which specify how a list of ingredients are to be manipulated to produce a desired result. For example, consider the somewhat trivial recipe for cooking a three-minute egg. The recipe (or algorithm) for such a task exemplifies the need to take nothing for granted in the list of instructions.

Algorithm Three-Minute Egg
Put water in a pan.
Turn on the heat.
When the water boils, flip over the egg timer.
When the timer has run out, turn off the heat.
Pour some cold water in the pan to cool the water.
Remove egg.

Although this algorithm may appear trivial to most readers, detailed examination further emphasizes (or belabors) how clear and unambiguous an algorithm must be. First, the receiver of these instructions, call it the actor, must recognize all of the jargon of food preparation: water, pan, egg, egg timer, boil, and so forth. The actor must recognize constructions: "put ____ in ____"; "when ____, do ____." Some parts of these instructions are unnecessary: "to cool the water." If the actor is an adult who understands English, this may be a fine algorithm. To continue to belabor the point, the actor can only do what the instructions say. If the instructions failed to tell the actor to put an egg in the pan (as I did in writing this), then the actor may be stuck trying in vain to complete the last instruction.

The actor must also interpret some instructions differently in different environments. Even if the actor is working in a standard household, "Turn on the heat" has the same intent – but different implementations – for gas versus electric ranges. Moreover, in some environments, the heat may never be sufficient to boil the water, or be so hot that the water boils away in less than three minutes, and so the actor following this algorithm will fail to complete the task. Lastly, if the actor is not an adult, then the instructions must be much more specific and must reflect foresight for contingencies that a parent can imagine a child to encounter. This precision and foresight become even more important when considering instructions to be given to a machine.

Knuth (1997) listed five properties that algorithms must possess:

(1) finiteness – execution can be done with finite resources;
(2) definiteness – instructions are completely defined and unambiguous;
(3) input;
(4) output;
(5) effective – the instructions can be executed (my words).

To gain a general view of algorithms, consider that every statistical procedure must also abide by these requirements. Of course, the input is the data and the output the decision, test result, or estimator. But the steps of a statistical procedure must be as clearly defined, finite, and effective as any algorithm. If the desired estimator is the sample median, then the definition of the estimator must clearly state that if the sample size is an even number then the median is defined to be the average of the two middle values. How do you define a maximum likelihood estimator when the algorithm to compute it fails with some positive probability? What are the properties of such an estimator, such as consistency, efficiency, or mean square error? A statistical procedure is often clearly defined only by the algorithm used to compute it.

Most effective algorithms are repetitive: do these instructions and when you're done go back and do them again. The route of the instructions executed inspired the name *loop,* and the list of instructions to be completed is the *range* of the loop.

Algorithm Scramble(*n*)
Do these statements *n* times:
    take an egg out of the refrigerator;
    crack the egg's shell on the edge of the counter;
    pull the egg apart above the bowl;
    let the contents of the egg fall into the bowl;
    throw the egg shell in the waste basket.
Stir egg contents in the bowl.
Pour contents of bowl into frying pan.
  ⋮

In this algorithm, the range of the loop consists of five instructions. Notice that the number of repetitions is specified by *n* as an argument to the algorithm.

Iterative algorithms may use a condition to control the number of times a loop is to be executed.

Algorithm Cup-of-Water
  ⋮
Do these statements until it's exact:

if the level is above the line then pour a little water out;
if the level is below the line then pour a little water in.

⋮

Iterative algorithms are common and effective, but they hold the potential for danger. In this case, an actor with great eyesight and poor hand coordination may never be able to get the water level exactly on the line. If the condition is impossible to satisfy (in this case, "exact" may not be possible) then the algorithm may repeat indefinitely, becoming stuck in the black hole of computing known as an *infinite loop*. Good programming practice requires that – unless it is computationally provable that the algorithm is finite – all iterative algorithms should have a stated limit on the number of repetitions.

One personal experience may emphasize the need for care in constructing iterative algorithms. In constructing a fast algorithm for the Hodges–Lehmann location estimator (see Section 14.4), I used the average of the maximum and minimum of a set of real numbers to partition the set. Even if the set was weird and if this average separated only one number from the rest, the partitioning would eventually succeed at cutting the size of the set by one each time and eventually down to one element and finish. To my surprise, for one set of data the algorithm never finished because the algorithm was stuck in an infinite loop. Working on a computer with base-16 arithmetic, it is possible (see Exercise 2.9) that the computed average of max and min will be smaller than every number in the set. The set was never made smaller and so continued until I intervened to stop the program.

Some algorithms use a version of themselves as a subtask to complete their work and are called *recursive* algorithms. Consider the following algorithm for computing factorials.

Algorithm Factorial(n)
If $n = 1$ then Factorial $= 1$
    else Factorial $= n * $ Factorial$(n - 1)$

Recursive algorithms are extraordinarily effective in many problems, and some of the great breakthroughs (FFT, sorting; see Chapter 14) in computing rely on recursion. Although some software and computer languages do not permit explicit recursion, clever coding can often implement a simply stated recursive algorithm.

1.2 Computers

Many of the ideas in statistical computing originated in an era where a computer was a person, but the world of scientific computing now looks quite different. The visible equipment, or hardware, usually consists of a processor box, video screen, keyboard, mouse, and connections to other devices (e.g., a printer or modem). In spite of tremendous changes in computing equipment over the last thirty years, the underlying model for computing remains unchanged. The model for computing for this book consists of a central processing unit (CPU), memory, mass storage, and input and output devices. The CPU is a collection of semiconductor devices that controls the unit. Memory, usually referred to as RAM (random access memory), is so named because the time to access (write or read) any part of it does not depend on any order – a random order takes as long as a consistent sequence. Mass storage refers to any source of slower memory, which may be an internal disk drive, a floppy disk, magnetic tape, or a disk drive on the other side of the world connected by the Internet. These memory devices are slower to access and are designed to be accessed sequentially, at least in the small scale. Input and output devices may refer to the tangible ones – such as the keyboard, mouse, or printer – but could also include mass storage devices.

This general-purpose computer can only earn its name through the software designed to run it. At its furthest abstraction, software is a list of instructions to operate the machinery of a computer. The most fundamental software for a computer is its operating system. Other software – such as word processors, spreadsheets, games, compilers, and, yes, statistical software – are written in a very general framework and are designed to work within the framework that the operating system provides. Whereas a user may give instructions to a spreadsheet to add one number to another and put the sum in a third place, the software will give instructions that may look like the following:

get the first number from memory location x and put it here;
get the second number from memory location y and put it there;
add the two numbers stored in here and there, leaving the sum here;
store the number here to the memory location z.

The software's instructions are, in their executable form, machine-level instructions such as fetch, store, and add, but the storage locations are only relative. The operating system specifies the physical locations for x, y, and z, manages the list of instructions, and coordinates the input and output devices.

Computers operate most efficiently with both the data and instructions residing in memory. But some software, including the operating system, is very complicated and takes an enormous amount of space to store it. Some problems, such as simulating the weather system of the earth, have so much data that no computer has enough memory to hold all of it. These problems are managed by the operating system through *paging*. While the fundamental tools of the operating system reside permanently in memory, other pieces of the operating system, other pieces of the software, and other pieces of data reside in mass storage, usually an internal disk. As these pieces are needed, the operating system swaps space with other pieces, writing pieces residing in memory in mass storage, making room for the needed pieces in memory. Imagine a person doing calculations on a desk that doesn't have enough room for all of the pieces of paper. When this Computor needs more space, he takes some sheets of paper off the desk to make room and puts them in a file cabinet. When a sheet in the file cabinet is needed, he takes something else off the desk and exchanges sheets of paper from the file cabinet to the desk. This method allows incredibly large problems to be done with finite memory, at the cost of slower computation due to the swapping. More memory can allow some problems to run much faster by reducing the swapping, as if the Computor's desk were made much bigger. Poorly written software can aggravate the situation. Problems with enormous amounts of data improperly stored may require a swap for every computation; "spaghetti code" software can continually shift code around instead of

keeping some core routines constantly resident in memory and using compartmental-
ized auxiliary routines.

1.3 Software and Computer Languages

Most computer software is written for completing a specific task. For example, as complicated as the U.S. income tax laws may be, tax preparation software can satisfy the
needs of the vast majority of citizens every April. To satisfy the statistical needs of all
scientists, however, the range of tools available extends from very specific software to
general computer languages. Many standard office products, such as word processors
and accounting software, include tools for simple statistical analysis, such as t-tests or
simple linear regression. These tools are embedded in the main product and are limited in their scope. A step more general are spreadsheets – themselves more general
than, say, accounting software in that they are designed to do a variety of mathematical
tasks – with which the user has complete control over the arrangement of the calculations. At the far end of the spectrum are computer languages. Although most computer
languages are designed to solve a great variety of problems, some languages are better
at some tasks than others.

To assess the appropriate software needs in statistics, consider first the mathematical
tools of statistics. Statistical theory may rely on calculus for maximizing likelihoods or
computing posterior probabilities, but most statistical methods can be well explained
using linear algebra. Clearly, the main computational needs in statistics are implementing the tools of linear algebra. On the simple side, these are sums and sums of
squares for computing t-tests and doing simple linear regression. The more complex
needs then extend to solving systems of linear equations in positive definite matrices. Derivatives are occasionally needed, but numerical approximations will suffice
for most applications. Similarly, integration is sometimes required, but often numerical
approximations are the only route. Linear algebra encompasses most of the mathematical needs for statistical applications. Even though some mathematical software can
do calculus through symbolic manipulation, most calculus needs in statistics can be
implemented numerically.

In short, any software that can do sums and inner products can do a certain level of
statistical computing. Even sophisticated statistical techniques can be implemented in
spreadsheets. Some statistical software lies at this level of sophistication for the user:
the data take the form of vectors or rows or columns, and the more sophisticated tools
operate on these. Indeed, if most of the mathematics of statistics can be written in linear
algebra, then most statistical computing can be done with software designed to ma-
nipulate vectors and matrices. Of statistical software, Minitab and SAS's IML operate
with vectors and matrices, and have special ("canned") routines to do more sophisticated mathematical and statistical analysis beyond the view (and control) of the user.
An early computer language designed to do linear algebra is APL, which was once
quite popular in spite of its use of special symbols; its legacy can be seen in IML and R.
SAS's DATA step also can perform many of the required linear algebraic manipulations
and then tie into canned routines for more sophisticated analyses. Both R and S-Plus are
designed to do most linear algebraic manipulations using native operations, with a few

special canned routines and a structure (objects) for doing increasingly sophisticated manipulations. At all points along the way, there is a compromise between generality and control in one direction and a canned, special-purpose routine in the other.

Computer languages are needed to gain the full advantage of the "general" in general-purpose computing. These languages resemble human languages and consist of a set of instructions with a functional syntax – perhaps not a complete one, but then few human languages have one either. The grammar of subject-predicate-object works due to the recognizability of the structure through a complete categorizing or *typing* of the pieces. In deciphering spoken or written language we can recognize the predicate as the action word in a sequence of words, and (in English) the actor precedes the action as the subject and the object succeeds the action. Recognizing the parts of speech (nouns, adjectives, adverbs, etc.) limits their function in a sentence. The order of the words describes their function; for example, the adjectives "quick" and "brown" describe the noun and subject "fox" in the following sentence:

The quick brown fox jumped over the lazy dog.

Computer languages work in much the same way: (a) words are typed; (b) the type of a word limits its possible functions; and (c) the structure of the sentence determines the meaning. In comparison with human languages, computer languages must be more rigid in typing and structure, since a computer does not have the intelligence of a human. In using computer languages, an important skill is to recognize how the computer "thinks." Using certain rules, the computer interprets the input by *parsing* the text (or *code*) to determine the "parts of speech" for the language. The structure of the text then further clarifies the list of commands. Many languages parse text into four types: operators (such as $+$, $*$), constants (such as 2.7, 64), reserved words, and variables. Constructs such as "put ____ in ____" would have "put" and "in" as *reserved words* (i.e., text with special meaning). Often everything that is not an operator, a constant, or a reserved word is considered to be the name of a variable.

Once the text has been parsed, computer languages follow two routes for execution: interpreted or compiled. Interpreted code is set up for immediate execution. If the operator is (say) "norm" and the operand is a vector, then the command is to compute the norm of the accompanying vector. In further detail, the vector is stored as data, and the interpreted code passes the vector's pointer to a list of instructions that computes the norm. However, in some computer languages the code is first *compiled,* or translated into a single body of instructions. The difference between the two methods is a trade-off of effort. Interpreted code is intended to be executed just once for the particular arrangement of operator and operand. For example, we may compute the norm of a particular vector just once. Compiled code is designed to be used many times. The language itself dictates which route will be taken. In general, languages with more sophisticated operators will be interpreted whereas more general-purpose languages, which operate with lower-level commands, will be compiled.

The hierarchy of languages puts the array of software into perspective. At the base level of all computing is machine-language instructions. Only the basic steps of computing are written in machine language: usually just the basic commands to start the computer. At the next level are assembler commands. These are usually in a language with commands that directly translate to machine commands. At the next step are the low-level general-purpose computer languages, such as Pascal, C, Fortran, Lisp, and Cobol. Writing at this level gains access to certain machine-level operations, but the code can be written in a style that avoids most of the repetitive steps that assembler-language level would require. The gains with using these languages are (a) the great generality that is available and (b) the ability to rewrite tasks in terms of subtasks whose code can be accessed in a wide variety of other tasks. For example, a routine can be written to compute the norm of a vector that can be used by a variety of other routines. Once compiled, the code need never be written again and is simply accessed by its name. The strength of these languages is this foundation of subtasks, each one solidly written and tested, so that extensive structures can rest on these building blocks. These languages are quite general, and the same task can be written in any of them. The reason for the variety of languages is a variety of purpose; each language has its own features or constructs that make certain tasks easier.

At the next level of languages, the operands available are much more sophisticated and the details are hidden from the user. Notice the clear trade-off between power and control: more powerful constructs will limit the control of the user. If the user wants the usual Euclidean norm of a vector, then using a higher-level language saves time and worry about coding it correctly. However, if the user wants the $p = 4$ norm of a vector then the lower-level language will be needed. The higher-level languages are often interpreted, with the specific operands actually accessing the compiled code of a routine written in a lower-level language. For example, R and most of SAS are written in C.

Higher-level interpreted languages (e.g., R, SAS's IML, and GAUSS) have some strong advantages. Primarily, the languages are designed to operate with the same basic mathematical tools common in statistics: vectors and matrices. As a result, the code resembles familiar mathematical analysis and is easily read and understood without extensive documentation. Moreover, the user is seldom bothered by the details of the more sophisticated operations: solving linear equations, computing eigenvalues, and so on. This removes a strong distraction if these tools are soundly implemented, but it creates severe problems if they are not or if they are pushed to their limits. The disadvantages follow from their one-time interpretive nature. These languages often do not have a natural looping structure, and if looping is possible then the structures are clumsy. The one-time operation leads to the use of extensive dynamic storage allocation – that is, in the middle of computation, more storage is needed on a temporary basis. The problem of creating and using this temporary storage has been solved, yet often this temporary storage cannot be fully recovered and reused. This problem is known as "garbage collection," and the failure to solve it adequately leads to a continual demand for memory. As a result, these languages eat up memory and sometimes grind to a halt while trying to find more space.

As mentioned previously, many general-purpose computer languages have been written, often designed for specific purposes. Over the years, Fortran has been the dominant language for scientific computation. The strength of general-purpose languages lies in the formation of building blocks of subtasks, and Fortran does this particularly well. Fortran has often been considered an inferior language with byzantine syntax, but recent (1990, 1995) changes in the standard have cast off its worse parts and added a few really useful structures. The revised language now permits strong typing of variables; that is, all variables must have their type (integer, real, character) declared. This avoids silly errors such as misspellings and requires more disciplined coding. The use of local and global scoping, subprogram interfaces, and variable dimension declarations obviates any need for poor programming practices long associated with the language, such as spaghetti coding and circumlocutions for passing arguments to subprograms.

One of the more recent advances in software design is object-oriented programming. Instead of the traditional paradigm of flow charts, the focus is on *objects,* which are fundamentally containers for data with attendant software (for operating on the data) and communication tools (see e.g. Priestly 1997). In statistical applications, objects are primarily collections of data. For example, in a regression scenario an object may consist of the response vector $\mathbf{y}$ and design matrix $\mathbf{X}$, as well as least-squares estimates $\hat{\boldsymbol{\beta}}$ and residuals $\hat{\mathbf{e}}$.

1.4   Data Structures

Although most data in statistics are stored as vectors or matrices, a brief introduction to some more sophisticated structures – together with some details on the more common ones – provides some perspectives on the potential tools for problem solving. The fundamental data structure is a *linear list,* which is natural for storing a vector. Internally, a vector $\mathbf{x}$ is merely referred to by a pointer to the storage location of its first element. Any element of the vector, say x_j, is found by adding $(j - 1)$ to the pointer for $\mathbf{x}$. Matrices (and any higher-dimensional arrays) are still stored as a linear list. In some computer languages (e.g. Fortran), if the matrix $\mathbf{A}$ has dimensions m and n, then its pointer is the location of A_{11} and the element A_{ij} is stored $(j - 1) * n + (i - 1)$ locations away. As a result, A_{11} is next to A_{21}, which is next to $A_{31}, \ldots, A_{m1}$; then A_{12} through to A_{m2} and then A_{13}. As you traverse the list of elements, the leftmost index varies fastest. Higher-dimensional arrays follow the same rule. In other languages (e.g. C), the reverse convention is followed, with the order $A_{11}, A_{12}, \ldots, A_{1n}, A_{21}$, etc.

One type of linear list permits changes, additions, or deletions of elements only at the end of the list or at the top of a "stack." The most common scientific application of stacks is for counting in nested situations. For example, if we have j nested within i (say, days within months), then j or days are at the top of the stack and only *after* the cycling through j is completed do we drop to the lower level (i or months) and make a change there. Stacks are commonly used in computer systems to handle similar situations: nested loops or nested calls to subprograms.

Most data take the form of vectors, matrices, and other arrays; however, two other structures are occasionally useful in scientific programming: the linked list and the binary tree. Each element of a linked list consists of the body and pointers. The elements of a linked list are not stored in consecutive locations. The body of each element holds the data and, in the simplest case of a singly linked list, the pointer holds the address of the next element of the list. As a result, traversing a linked list requires going through the list from the front to the back – there is no way of knowing where the jth element is stored without traversing the first, second, third, to the $(j - 1)$th element. So what can be gained? The biggest gain is the ability to add or delete an element from the list without moving the body of information stored in that element of the list; all that needs to be done is to change the pointer. For example, in order to delete the third element, replace the pointer to "next" in the second element with the pointer to the fourth element (stored in "next" of the third element). To add a new element between the second and third, have "next" in the second point to the new one with the new one's "next" pointing to the third element. To overcome some of the problems in traversing the list, other pointers can be added. A doubly linked list has pointers both to the next and previous elements.

Linked lists are more commonly used in commercial applications for databases, sorting, and information retrieval. Moreover, they also permit simple dynamic storage allocation and garbage collection. Creating space means deleting elements from a linked list called FREESPACE, and garbage collection means adding elements to FREESPACE.

In a binary tree, elements are linked to pairs in a top-down fashion that resembles an upside-down tree. The first element, usually named the *root,* is at the top of the tree and is linked to two other elements or *children* (or the right and left child). These elements are then parents to the next generation of children. A special form of binary tree known as a "heap" is used in Chapter 14 for sorting. Other forms of a binary tree arise from time to time. A binary tree can be implemented in a fashion similar to a linked list, as long as the tree is traversed from top to bottom. Certain types of balanced trees can be implemented as linear lists.

1.5 Programming Practice

For whatever purpose the reader will be using this book – whether devising new statistical procedures or delving deeper into how codes for certain algorithms work – the author has considerable advice to offer. After over thirty years of programming, in many languages at different levels and throughout many changes in the computing environment, it is clear that the pitfalls at the interface between human and computer have not changed.

The appropriate attitude toward programming should be a healthy skepticism. Confidence in the results of a new routine can grow only from its proving itself in small steps. The envelope of trust opens as more and more difficult problems are attempted and successfully completed. Only after considerable successful testing does confidence become an appropriate attitude.

All big programming problems must be broken down into small component tasks. Then each subtask is resolutely tested until the user is confident in having established the envelope of proven reliability for that subtask. The great advantage of higher-level languages is that many of these subtasks have been taken care of, and only the bigger picture remains. Nevertheless, when starting out the user should be skeptical even of these fundamental subtasks and test them also. Testing involves creating a battery of test problems that are appropriate for the range of usage. The first test problems should be simple ones: there's no need to waste time on subtle problems when the easy ones don't work. Subsequent test problems should include some troublesome cases to ensure that the program does the right thing when the problem is beyond its capabilities. In other words, the program should unmistakably fail on an impossible task. For example, can a routine for solving a system of linear equations recognize and properly react when the system is singular?

Another lesson learned over many years is KISS, or "keep it simple, stupid." The great value of simple programs with simple, unambiguous steps is that if a mistake is made then it will be a big one and easy to recognize. As a program becomes more complicated, it becomes more difficult to find the "bugs" or mistakes in the code. Unnecessary features that increase complexity and potential for error are known as "bells and whistles"; they should be avoided until the main part of the program has been thoroughly tested and debugged.

The hardest lesson for this author to learn has been *documenting* the program – and I am still learning. All programs should be thoroughly documented with comments. The need for the comments follows from breaking down the large task into subtasks. As each subtask is completed, it must be fully documented as well as tested. This allows the programmer to then forget the details of one subtask when working on another. In commercial settings, this permits a programming team to divide up the effort and work in parallel. But when an error is encountered in a poorly documented program, only the person who wrote that part of the code will know how it works and what went wrong. In the case of a single person writing the whole thing, this means that the person who wrote the code a month ago can't remember how it works. Or in my case, there's no way I could remember what I was thinking ten or twenty years ago when writing some poorly documented code. The only solution may be to start all over, with considerable waste of time and energy.

The final lesson learned after many years of experience is that if you are not certain of your results then you have absolutely nothing. Hence, the only way to be sure of the whole task is to be sure of each piece. In working on some joint research several years ago, I observed some simulation results that were contrary to a theorem I thought we had proved. My colleague kept telling me that the program was wrong. Thinking he was right and that I was at fault, I started examining more than a thousand lines of Fortran code, looking for errors. After two weeks of checking each piece, I confidently told my colleague that no, the program is right; I am sure of each and every piece; the theorem must be wrong. The point is that it is possible to confidently write large programs that are entirely correct. It does take a lot of careful, disciplined checking, but the reader should be undaunted.

1.6   Some Comments on R

In the last ten years, the software system R has spread throughout the statistics community. Due to its flexibility and the powerful nature of its functions, a great deal of recent statistical research has been done in R. To those for whom R is not a native language, some of its peculiarities may not be obvious at first glance.

R and its predecessors were not designed with efficient computation as a primary goal. The author has often heard the rationale that computers will always be getting faster and faster with more and more storage. As a result, often multiple copies of data are stored at one time, and certain operations have considerable overhead that would be unthinkable with other languages or software systems. Vector/matrix operations are natural and efficient in R; looping is not so natural, although recent versions of R show considerable improvement.

One characteristic of R that may be surprising is known as *coercion*. R is very comfortable at converting from one data type to another. This may take the form as something as simple as the following code:

```
x <- 5
3 + (x > 3)
c(x,(x>3),"maybe")
```

The first statement is a simple assignment; the snippet:

```
( x > 3 )
```

produces a logical result. When we ask to add this logical to the numeric value 3, R will coerce the logical to a numeric (with value 1) and then add. This is not uncommon, as other languages allow such a conversion. However, in the next line, where we try to make a vector out of a numeric variable, a logical, and a character string, R converts them all to the "lowest" form, which is character – and makes a character vector of length 3. Good programming style would use explicit coercion with functions such as *as.numeric* or *as.character*, because unintended coercion is a major source of programming errors. Operations with vector and matrices often involve coercion and *recycling* where coercion may not have enough values to make a sensible result. The details of a simple operation:

```
1/(3:6)
```

is that we are asking R to divide a vector by a vector, which is fine but done element by element. But R sees 1 as a vector of length 1, mismatched with the (3:6), which is a vector of length 4; so, in trying to coerce them to match, R will recycle the value 1 four times to give the expected result. If we multiply a matrix times a vector with the matrix multiplication operator, R will coerce the vector to a conformable matrix and produce a matrix result. Although the dimension of this matrix is one, it is still a matrix. Recycling is ubiquitous in vector/matrix computations – and potentially dangerous indeed. A warning only arises when the recycling does not complete a cycle. If we make the simple change to:

```
c(1,2)/(3:6)
```

then we again get coercion to a vector of length 4 by recycling values producing the same as c(1,2,1,2), and the computation of (1/3,2/4,1/5,2/6). Only with:

```
(1:3)/(3:6)
```

will we get an incomplete cycle and a warning. Many R programmers use coercion and recycling all of the time without realizing it.

The power of R is in its functions. In many ways, the function definition in R does not look very different from a function definition in other languages. One big difference in R is that the result of a function can be more than just a scalar. The result of a function can be a vector, a matrix, or even a function – or even a list consisting of any combination of those three – even a list of . . . ad infinitum. A second important difference is that default values can be assigned for arguments that may be superfluous for certain instances. If the function is designed to compute normal tail probabilities, values for options such as left or right tail, or a flag for a log transformation can be dropped from the argument list if the default values are requested. A third difference is that R follows *call-by-value* rather than *call-by-name*. In languages that follow call-by-name, invoking a function or subprogram with an argument x with $func(x)$ really just passes the address of x to the function $func$. In R with call-by-value, the value of the variable x is passed to the function $func$. In languages with call-by-name, a function/subroutine/subprogram $update(A, how)$ may update a matrix **A** in place; in R, this might need to be recoded by taking the current value of the matrix **A** as an argument, computing the updated matrix, and then assigning its value back to **A**. Because at least two matrices are used at one time, the original **A** and the result of $update(.)$, storage efficiencies may be lost unless some clever alternatives are available.

The fourth important difference with functions in R deals with *environments*. Many languages have an external function that is a black box, taking arguments and producing results. The variables in the argument list are dummy variables that are replaced with an address (call-by-name) or value when the function is invoked. Within that black box, an assignment to a variable x not in the argument list is a local assignment, not related to any variable named x elsewhere. Any variable used in that black box aside from the argument list is a local variable that only exists in that function, so all information that the function needs must be passed through its arguments. (Some languages have awkward ways around this, e.g., modules in Fortran.) Some languages also have an internal function within a calling program that allows access to variables within the calling program; however, this function is not available outside the calling program. Functions in R have aspects of both internal and external functions through the use of *environments*. At the top level or command-prompt level lies the *global* environment. When a function is invoked, R creates a local environment for it and the values of the variables in the argument list are assigned. Within the function, R resolves the value of the other variables by looking first at the local environment and then at the global environment. If the function is nested within other functions, their environments are nested as well. If a variable in an expression is 1) not in the argument list or 2) not assigned as a local variable, then R will look through its nested environments looking for a value. If the user forgot to list x as an argument or forgot its assignment earlier in the function, then R will look for something called x. This approach for resolving values of variables in functions is called *lexical scoping* and allows for external and internal functions and all levels in between.

References

Robert Gentleman and Ross Ihaka (2000), "Lexical Scope and Statistical Computing." *Journal of Computational and Graphical Statistics* 9: 491–508.
Donald E. Knuth (1997), *The Art of Computer Programming* (vol. 1: Fundamental Algorithms), 3rd ed. Reading, MA: Addison-Wesley.
Mark Priestly (1997), *Practical Object-Oriented Design*. London: McGraw-Hill.

2

Computer Arithmetic

2.1 Introduction

Most of the time, we wish to be blissfully ignorant of the inner workings of any complicated machine. When we drive an automobile, traffic and road conditions demand our concentration, and we would prefer that our attention wander to a favorite song on the radio than to the oil pressure gauge. Only when trouble arises need we concern ourselves with the internal combustion engine, air pressure in the tires, the lever arms in the steering system, or a lug wrench. With as complicated a machine as a computer, most of the time we can likewise treat its inner workings as a collection of black boxes. However, researchers regularly operate a computer at its limits in the same way a race-car driver takes an automobile to the limits of its capabilities. In order to drive safely bumper-to-bumper at 200 mph, a race-car driver must understand the operation of every system of the machine. A researcher must understand the inner workings of the arithmetic of the computer; otherwise, Overflow and Underflow become mysterious demons. Knowledge will not only dispel the fears brought on by ignorance, it will also permit the researcher to control his or her computational destiny and not fall victim to "roundoff error" any more than to "racing luck."

The first three sections of this chapter present a brief overview of the mechanics of computer arithmetic. Although necessary for ground-level knowledge, they should be skimmed at first reading because the interesting details of the problems can easily sidetrack the reader. The more traditional numerical analysis topics, roundoff error and conditioning, are discussed in Sections 2.4 and 2.6. The limits of floating point arithmetic and techniques for surpassing those limitations are discussed in Section 2.5. Sprinkled throughout this chapter are pieces of Fortran code to demonstrate the implementation of various techniques.

Computers really cannot do arithmetic. They merely recognize two states: on (1) and off (0). Numbers on a computer are collections of these binary digits, or bits, whose values exist only by established human conventions. We often work with the abstraction of real numbers in mathematics, but only a small set of numbers – those that can be represented on the computer – constitute reality for arithmetic on a computer. The set of representable numbers is but a small subset (and not a very dense subset) of the real numbers.

Numbers are represented on a computer in two ways: fixed point numbers for representing the integers, and floating point numbers for the real numbers. While conversion from one to the other is common and sometimes automatic, they are quite different animals, and the same mathematical value will be represented by a different collection of bits. Wild behavior and catastrophic errors often result when a number written as a fixed point number is then read through floating point–colored glasses.

2.2　Positional Number Systems

By using their fingers, people can count very easily up to ten. In most languages, people created words for groups of ten, then hundreds, as far as their needs required. In English, the vestiges of other number systems remain in the language. The cup–pint–quart–gallon system used base 2; dozen–gross counters used base 12. The base-60 second–minute system remains in the language as part of mixed radix systems, with hours (base 12) for measuring time and degrees (base 360) for measuring angles. Since the eighteenth century, however, the trend has been toward the use of decimal measurement systems. In Europe, this metric system has been universally adopted, even for counting money.

Because binary digits are natural for the computer, the common human decimal convention has been abandoned for collections of binary digits. Thus, the base for arithmetic is not the human 10 but the more natural 2 or a power of 2, such as 16, which is often viewed as a collection of 4 bits. (All numbers written here are decimal unless otherwise noted.) Since any positive number z can be written as a base-B number using the set of digits $\{0, 1, \ldots, B - 1\}$ in the convergent infinite series

$$z = a_k B^k + \cdots + a_2 B^2 + a_1 B + a_0 + a_{-1} B^{-1} + a_{-2} B^{-2} + \cdots, \tag{2.2.1}$$

where the coefficients a_j are integers in the set $\{0, \ldots, B - 1\}$, it follows that the number z can be simply represented by the list of digits

$$z = (a_k \ldots a_2 a_1 a_0 . a_{-1} a_{-2} \ldots)_B, \tag{2.2.2}$$

where the period in this representation is called the *radix* point. In particular, for base 10, the usual decimal point name is used, "hexadecimal" for base or radix 16, and "binary" for base 2. Note that with base 2 the set of digits is just $\{0, 1\}$; with base 8, the set is $\{0, 1, \ldots, 7\}$. For base 16, the common Arabic symbols are not sufficient. Unimaginative as they may be, the letters $A = 10$, $B = 11$, through $F = 15$ effectively serve as symbols for the needed digits. The reader should be constantly mindful of the meaning of a number (e.g., the number of players on an American football team) versus the symbols used to write that number – whether on paper, such as 11 or 13_{eight}, or on a computer, $B_{\text{hex}} = 11_{\text{ten}} = 1011_{\text{two}}$.

The terms "fixed point" and "floating point" refer to the position of the radix point in the representation of a number as a list of base-B digits. Fixed point numbers are analogs to integers, with the radix point placed to the right of the list, either explicitly or implicitly. What is usually called "scientific notation" is the most common form of floating point representation of a number. The number of atoms in a mole suggests an integer, but Avagadro's number is usually written as

$$N = 6.023 \times 10^{23}.$$

Floating point representation usually takes the form of a sign S, the (integer) exponent E, and the fraction F, which could be written as the triple (S, E, F). The translation from the written (S, E, F) to the value implied by some convention requires explicit definition of that convention. The informal route taken here for demonstration purposes uses S as $+$ or $-$, E as a signed integer, and F as the list of base-B digits with the implicit radix point on the left, so that

$$N = (+, +24, .6023)$$

using base $B = 10$ and $d = 4$ digits. The contrast between fixed and floating point is clearest in considering financial transactions, which are performed not in whole dollars but in exact cents. The radix point is fixed, as two positions from the right of the list of numbers; the calculations are often done as integer cents on the computer and then written out in the more common dollars-and-cents form.

Let's get out the dustpan and clean up what was swept under the rug earlier. In floating point arithmetic, only a finite number (say, d) of digits can be used to represent a number, and so the mathematician's debate about the infinite expansions $(.37500000...)$ or $(.37499999...)$ is dismissed as a philosophical quibble. If the exponent E is bounded, then only a finite number of values are achievable using floating point notation. This means that any real number is approximated by an element of the (finite) set of representable numbers $\mathcal{F}$. Several issues now arise, the first of which is "rounding" versus "chopping." Suppose we are trying to represent the real number z that lies between the two consecutive representable numbers (S, E, F) and $(S, E, F + B^{-d})$. Avagadro's number is more precisely 6.02257×10^{23}, so for $d = 4$ and $B = 10$ the choices are $(+, 24, .6022)$ and $(+, 24, .6023)$. The method of chopping selects (S, E, F) or $(+, 24, .6022)$ and will bias numbers downward. Rounding to closest, here $(+, 24, .6023)$ is preferred, but still a detail remains if z is in the middle. Knuth (1997b, p. 237) discussed the merits of rounding to the nearest even or odd number, with a minor edge attributed to even. The rounding versus chopping issue has important consequences in the analysis of accuracy. If we define the function $\text{fl}(z) : \mathcal{R} \to \mathcal{F}$, mapping a real number z to its floating point representation, then the following bound can be established:

$$|\text{fl}(z) - z| \le U|z| \quad \text{for all } z \tag{2.2.3}$$

(see Exercise 2.17). Here U is called the *machine unit,* which takes the value B^{1-d} for chopping and half that for rounding to nearest. One expected implication is that the machine unit U bounds the relative error $|(\text{fl}(z) - z)/z|$ for the floating point representation. The reverse form of (2.2.3),

$$\text{fl}(z) = z(1 + u) \quad \text{where } |u| \le U, \tag{2.2.4}$$

will prove extremely useful in the analysis of floating point arithmetic in Section 2.4.

A second issue arises over multiple representations for the same number in $\mathcal{F}$. For example, the value 5 can be represented by $(+, 1, .5000)$ or $(+, 2, .0500)$, or $(+, 4, .0005)$. The first representation $(+, 1, .5000)$ is preferred, since it connotes correctly the accuracy of number, where the last could be representing any number in the interval $(4.5, 5.5)$. Representations where the most significant digit is nonzero are called *normalized.* Most computer systems rely on the normalized representation of floating point numbers. Clearly, the normalized floating point representation of Avagadro's number $(+, 24, .6023)$ is more accurate than the unnormalized $(+, 25, .0602)$ or $(+, 26, .0060)$. In Section 2.3, the use of "subnormalized" numbers in the IEEE floating point arithmetic standard will be discussed.

Methods for converting a number from its representation in one base to another depend on which base is available for arithmetic. In hand calculation (or most calculators), the arithmetic must be done in base 10. Computers regularly do two conversions – on input a list of decimal digits to the computer's native base, and back to decimal for output – both done in the native arithmetic. A positive number z written in base B or in base C as

$$z = (a_k \ldots a_1 a_0 . a_{-1} a_{-2} \ldots a_{-m})_B = (d_j \ldots d_2 d_1 d_0 . d_{-1} d_{-2} \ldots d_{-n})_C$$

can be converted in either direction using the arithmetic in base B. For the first case, the easiest route is to convert a number in base C to base B, from $\{d_i\}$ to $\{a_i\}$, just by following the definition (2.2.1):

$$z = d_k C^k + \cdots + d_2 C^2 + d_1 C + d_0 + d_{-1} C^{-1} + d_{-2} C^{-2} + \cdots .$$

The integer part is found by multiplying and adding,

$$((\ldots((d_j * C) + d_{j-1}) * C \ldots) * C + d_1) * C + d_0, \qquad (2.2.5)$$

and the fractional part is similar:

$$((\ldots((d_{-n}/C) + d_{1-n})/C \ldots)/C + d_{-1})/C. \qquad (2.2.6)$$

The multiply–add formulation for the evaluation of polynomials in (2.2.5) and (2.2.6) is known as Horner's rule, as will be discussed further in Chapter 7. The other direction, from $\{a_i\}$ to $\{d_i\}$, is a little more complicated but still follows the modulo arithmetic inherent in positional notation. Begin with the value $H_0 = a_k \ldots a_1 a_0$, the integer part in base B; then compute

$$H_{i+1} = \lfloor H_i/C \rfloor \quad \text{and} \quad d_i = H_i \bmod C = H_i - C H_{i+1}, \qquad (2.2.7)$$

where $\lfloor \cdot \rfloor$ denotes the floor or integer part for a positive number, and proceed until $H_i = 0$. For the fractional part, begin with $L_0 = .a_{-1} \ldots a_{-m}$ and then compute

$$d_{-i} = \lfloor C L_{i-1} \rfloor \quad \text{and} \quad L_i = C L_{i-1} - d_{-i} \qquad (2.2.8)$$

and proceed to the accuracy of z. The result is represented in base C as

$$z = (d_j \ldots d_2 d_1 d_0 . d_{-1} d_{-2} \ldots d_{-n})_C.$$

Conversion between two bases that are both powers of 2, say 8 and 16, involves merely bookkeeping. The first step is to unbundle each digit into blocks of bits, such as $3F8_{\text{sixteen}} = 0011\,1111\,1000$, and then recollect the bits in groups $001\,111\,111\,000_{\text{two}} = 1770_{\text{eight}}$. Often hex (Z) or octal (O) formats are used to print out the internal representation of a number as a list of bits. Knuth (1997b, sec. 4.4) has discussed special algorithms for base conversion, in particular for converting to and from bases 8 and 10. Documentation for most computers includes tables to assist in conversion from base 10.

Example 2.1: *Base Conversion – Decimal to Binary*

Convert $\pi = 3.14159265_{\text{ten}}$ to base $C = 2$. First the integer part: $H_0 = 3$, $H_1 = 1$, and $H_2 = 0$, so that $d_0 = d_1 = 1$. For the fractional part, $L_0 = .14159265$ and $2L_0 = .2831853$, so that $d_{-1} = 0$ and $L_1 = 2L_0$. Also, $L_2 = 2L_1 = .5663706$ so $d_{-2} = 0$, but $2L_2 = 1.1327412$ so $d_{-3} = 1$ and $L_3 = .1327412$. The next step has $2L_3 = .2654824 = L_4$ and $2L_4 = .5309648 = L_5$ so $d_{-4} = d_{-5} = 0$, but $2L_6 = 1.0519296$ so $d_{-6} = 1$. So far we have $\pi = 11.001001_{\text{two}}$. Recall the approximation of $22/7$, which in base 2 has the repeating expansion $11.001001001\ldots$. Converting back, say $\pi = 3.1104_{\text{eight}}$ looks easier. The fractional part is $(1 + (1 + (0 + 4/8)/8)/8)/8 = (1 + (1.0625/8))/8 = 1.1328125/8 = .1416015625_{\text{ten}}$, which is on the money for the number (5) of octal digits given.

Example 2.2: *Base Conversion – Octal to Decimal*

Convert $x = 10.1_{\text{ten}}$ to octal $C = 8$. Begin with $H_0 = 10$ and $H_1 = 1$, so $d_0 = 2$, $H_2 = 0$, and $d_1 = 1$. Turn then to the fractional part: $L_0 = .1$ and $L_1 = .8$, so $d_{-1} = 0$; multiplying again by 8 gives 6.4 or $d_{-2} = 6$ and $L_3 = .4$. The next step brings 3.2 (so $d_{-3} = 3$ and $L_4 = .2$), followed by 1.6 giving $d_{-4} = 1$ and $L_5 = .6$. One more step gives 4.8 ($d_{-5} = 4$ and $L_6 = .8 = L_1$); we now have a repeating pattern: $d_{-j-4} = d_{-j}$ for $j \geq 2$, and $10.1_{\text{ten}} = 12.063146314\ldots_{\text{eight}}$. Solving the repeating pattern gives $8^5 x = 1206174_{\text{eight}} + 8x$.

2.3 Fixed Point Arithmetic

The arithmetic of integers is comparatively simple, although there are three common conventions for the representation of integers: signed integer, one's complement, and two's complement. Each has its merits and drawbacks, although two's complement is by far the most popular today. For illustrative purposes, the examples will be given for 8-bit representations and the mathematical results for the general M-bit case.

The *signed integer* notation is the simplest for representing an integer. The first (leftmost) of a string of M bits is used to represent the sign of the number ($0 = $ positive), and the remaining $M - 1$ bits hold the magnitude of the number in base 2. The advantages are that the range of possible numbers is symmetric,

$$-2^{M-1} + 1 \leq x \leq 2^{M-1} - 1, \tag{2.3.1}$$

and division or multiplication by a power of 2 is easy – just shift. One disadvantage is that zero is not unique (10000000 and 00000000); more seriously, the operations of addition and subtraction are more difficult than with the other approaches. As a consequence, this method is not commonly used.

A more common method, *one's complement*, uses a different notation for negative numbers: complement each bit of the positive. In this case, $+21$ is written as 00010101 and -21 is obtained by complementing each bit to yield 11101010. Again zero has two representations (11111111 and 00000000) and the range of numbers is the same as in

(2.3.1), but the arithmetic for addition and subtraction is easier. This will become clear in our discussion of the third method.

The *two's complement* notation has its similarities and differences to one's complement. In two's complement, a negative number is found by complementing each bit and then adding one, so -21 is written 11101011. Notice that zero is now unique, but the range is no longer symmetric:

$$-2^{M-1} \le x \le 2^{M-1} - 1,$$

so that one number (viz., -2^{M-1}) does not have a negative. In fact, an attempt to negate this number $-x$ usually has no effect. The advantages of two's complement are simpler methods for addition and subtraction. First of all, note that the negation of a positive x can be viewed as

$$[(2^M - 1) - x] + 1 = 2^M - x,$$

since $(2^M - 1)$ produces a string of ones and subtraction of x complements each bit. The rules of addition and subtraction can be followed with two exceptions: first, the results are done modulo 2^M; second, overflows need to be tracked.

Before deciphering the overflow rules, note the placement of points on the real line and take care to distinguish the list of bits and the value implied by the convention. Positive integers are where they would be expected, and the largest positive integer is at $2^{M-1} - 1$. The next number looks like 2^{M-1}, but since it has a 1 bit in the leftmost position it actually has the value -2^{M-1}. As we proceed up the line we have larger numbers (although negative and decreasing in magnitude) until we reach the largest integer that we can write with M bits, $2^M - 1$, which has the value -1. The next number marks the other important boundary, 2^M, which cannot be written in M bits and is the modulus for the arithmetic. The overflow–underflow rules keep track of crossing the boundaries at 2^{M-1} and 2^M and, because of the modulo 2^M arithmetic, any multiple of these. The rule is that crossing one boundary indicates an overflow; crossing both kinds 2^{M-1} and 2^M in the same step is all right. In terms of bit positions, one boundary is a carry into the sign bit while the other is a carry out of the sign bit.

Example 2.3: *Subtraction by Adding the Negation Modulo* 2^M

$$
\begin{aligned}
+48 &= 00110000 = 48 \\
\underline{-21} &= \underline{11101011} = 235 = 2^8 - 21 \\
+27 &= 1\,00011011 = 283 = 256 + 27 \equiv 27 \bmod 2^8 = 00011011 \bmod 2^M.
\end{aligned}
$$

Notice that an apparent overflow occurred in computing a number (283) that cannot be stored. However, both the $2^{M-1} = 128$ boundary and the $2^M = 256$ boundary were crossed. If we added two large positive numbers, we would cross one boundary (at 128) but not the other (at 256):

$$
\begin{aligned}
+48 &= 00110000 \\
\underline{+96} &= \underline{01100000} \\
144 &= 10010000 = 256 - 112 \equiv -112 \bmod 256.
\end{aligned}
$$

If we added two large negative numbers, we would cross one boundary (at 256) but not the other (at 384):

$$-48 = \quad 11010000 = 208$$
$$-96 = \quad 10100000 = 160$$
$$-144 = 1\ 01110000 = 368 \equiv 112 \text{ mod } 256;$$

again a true overflow occurs. True overflows can thus be easily detected by following these rules.

Returning momentarily to one's complement, subtraction is also done by adding the negative, with the same overflow rules. The exception is that the nonoverflow carry – both into the sign bit and out of it – is not simply dropped, as it is in two's complement. Dropping this would be equivalent to modulo 2^M. In one's complement, this carry out bit is instead added to the first bit. Recalling $48 - 21$ from Example 2.2, -21 in one's complement would be $11101010_{two} = 234$, and the sum would be $282 = 1\ 00011010$. Taking the overflow bit around would give $00011011_{two} = 27$.

Overflow is not a major problem in integer arithmetic, except that sometimes it is not flagged and negative products arise from multiplying positive numbers. Usually, either the range of possible numbers is sufficient to solve the problem or the problem is combinatorial in nature, when limits are reached very quickly and floating point approximations are introduced (see Exercises 2.4 and 2.20). The more common pitfall in integer arithmetic is integer division. When an integer dividend is divided by an integer divisor, the usual mathematical result is the integer pair of quotient and remainder. However, the usual result on a computer is just the integer quotient; the fractional part (remainder/divisor) is truncated to leave the integer quotient. Whenever the divisor is larger than the dividend the result is zero. Reasonable care is sufficient to overcome this pitfall. For example, as long as we do the computations in the right order, we can compute combinatorials without difficulty:

```
IBICOF = 1
DO J = 1,K
IBICOF = ( IBICOF * (N-J+1) ) / J
ENDDO
```
(2.3.2)

In many applications, both the quotient and remainder are needed. One route is to compute the quotient and then get the remainder by multiplication and subtraction:

```
IQUOT = IDVDND / IDVSOR
IREMDR = IDVDND-IQUOT * IDVSOR
```

Another is to replace the last line with the modulo arithmetic intrinsic function MOD:

```
IREMDR = MOD( IDVDND, IDVSOR )
```

On many machines, the machine instruction for fixed point division produces both quotient and remainder. A good optimizing compiler should translate either of these methods to a single fixed point divide instruction.

The reader should be aware that not all machines have instructions for multiplication and division. The earliest computers did not, and a few special-purpose computers and many microcomputers currently implement multiplication and division by using software instructions. The algorithm is known as "shift and add" and is purely an adaptation of the elementary multiplication method using the trivial table of binary arithmetic:

11	0000 1011	
×10	×0000 1010	
00	1 011*	shift left one
11	101 1***	shift left three
110	0110 1110	add.

Alternatively, envision the multiplier as a sum of powers of 2. Thus a multiplication is the sum of the multiplicands shifted left by the power of 2. The analogous software divide follows a "shift and subtract" scheme. Here we do $115 \div 10 = 11$ with a remainder of 5:

$$
\begin{array}{ll}
00001011 & \text{quotient} \\
1010\,)\,01110011 & \text{compare 1010 and 1110, since smaller, subtract} \\
01010 & \\
0010001 & \text{compare 1010 and 1000, too big, try 10001, subtract} \\
0001010 & \\
00001111 & \text{compare 1010 and 1111, subtract} \\
00001010 & \\
00000101 & \text{left with remainder of 5.}
\end{array}
$$

In conclusion, fixed point arithmetic has two great advantages over floating point arithmetic. One advantage is that the results are exact, in contrast to the approximate results obtained with floating point arithmetic. The other advantage is that fixed point arithmetic is much faster. The disadvantages are that both the applicability and the range of numbers are limited.

2.4   Floating Point Representations

The positive real number z described in (2.2.2) by a list of digits a_j must be represented on a computer by a finite list of digits that is (say) d in length. The floating position of the radix point with respect to this list gives the name to this notation. As remarked in Section 2.2, floating point numbers are commonly written in three parts: (S, E, F), where S is the sign ($+$ or $-$), E is the exponent, and F is the fraction. The term "fraction" connotes the imaginary (or implied) placement of the radix point, usually to the left of the list of digits F. To simplify the instructions for addition and multiplication, the true position of the radix point is given by the difference between E and what is called the *excess* or *bias*. When the sign is stored in one bit ($0 = +$), the value of the number represented by (S, E, F) is given by

$$(-1)^S \times \text{Base}^{(E-\text{excess})} \times .F_{\text{Base}}. \tag{2.4.1}$$

To represent a number in the most accurate way, the leading (leftmost, most signifi-cant) digit in F should not be zero. A nonzero number represented so that the leading digit is not zero is called "normalized." Zero is usually written with the smallest possi-ble exponent and zero fraction. Most computers follow this convention or some minor variation for representing floating point numbers, each with its own base, number of digits, excess, and so forth.

In recent years, most microcomputers and workstations follow the IEEE binary float-ing point standard. The adoption of this standard is a milestone in computer arithmetic, since the standard extends to rounding rules and overflow–underflow handling. The word "binary" in the name denotes that the base is 2, and 32 bits are used to represent a single precision number. The (S, E, F) notation applies but with a subtle twist due to the normalization of base-2 numbers. Since normalization moves the radix point so that the most significant digit is nonzero, the first digit of a normalized number in base 2 must be 1. Following this fact, the value of a normalized number stored as (S, E, F) is

$$(-1)^S \times 2^{E-\text{excess}} \times 1.F,$$

so that the implied leading digit 1 is actually placed to the left of the decimal, oops, binary point. As before, the sign bit is 0 for positive numbers, but now eight bits are used for the exponent, so that E ranges from 0 to 255. The excess is 127 so that the true exponent range is -126 to $+127$, since the endpoints are treated as special cases. For very small numbers, the smallest exponent $E = 0$ denotes a minor change in the value of a number represented by (S, E, F). That is, for $(S, 0, F)$, the value is given by

$$(-1)^S \times 2^{-126} \times 0.F,$$

and these numbers are called "denormalized" since they do not follow the same nor-malization scheme. The motivation for such denormalized numbers is to provide a smoother drop from the smallest normalized number to zero, using numbers that can be represented in the system. These denormalized numbers allow for a "soft underflow." Zero is unnormalizable and is represented by $(0, 0, .0)$. At the other end, the exponent $E = 255$ provides other convenient features. The notation $(S, 255, .0)$ represents $+\infty$ for $S = 0$ and $-\infty$ for $S = 1$. For any other fractional part F, $(S, 255, F)$ represents a creature called "not-a-number" that is usually written as "NaN." The main purpose of such a creature is to represent the result of an undefined or illegal operation, such as $0/0$ or the square root of a negative. An alternative use is as an initialization value. Most variables are not initialized at the beginning of a program, and conventional practice uses zero or whatever was left at the end of the last program as the default values. How-ever, one of the most common errors is using a variable that has yet to be given a value. Initialization to NaN ensures that such an occurrence would be flagged as an error.

The last two rows in Table 2.1 show the smallest normalized number and the largest representable number in the single precision floating point system. The last column shows the internal representation in groups of four bits. In many computer languages, instead of writing a number as a decimal constant and using the compiler to convert, the internal representation of a number can be written directly by preceding the eight hex digits by the letter Z. Thus, to assign -1 to a variable V, the code is

```
V = Z'BF800000'
```

Table 2.1. *IEEE binary floating point representation (single)*

Number	Conversion	Sign, Exponent	Fraction	Z Format
1	$1.0_{two} \times 2^0$	0 011 1111 1	000 0000 0000 0000 0000 0000	3F800000
1/16	$1.0_{two} \times 2^{-4}$	0 011 1101 1	000 0000 0000 0000 0000 0000	3D800000
0	$0.0_{two} \times 2^{-127}$	0 000 0000 0	000 0000 0000 0000 0000 0000	00000000
-15	$-1.111_{two} \times 2^3$	1 100 0001 0	111 0000 0000 0000 0000 0000	C1700000
1.2E $-$ 38	$1.0_{two} \times 2^{-126}$	0 000 0000 1	000 0000 0000 0000 0000 0000	00800000
1.4E $-$ 45	$1.0_{two} \times 2^{-149}$	0 000 0000 0	000 0000 0000 0000 0000 0001	00000001
3.4E $+$ 38	$(2 - 2^{-23}) \times 2^{127}$	0 111 1111 0	111 1111 1111 1111 1111 1111	7F7FFFFF
$+\infty$		0 111 1111 1	111 1111 1111 1111 1111 1111	7FFFFFFF

– although very dependent on language, compiler, and operating system. For input and output, often Z can also be used as a format code to access the internal representation for both fixed and floating point numbers.

In order to gain greater accuracy, most languages offer "double precision" arithmetic. However, taking this route to avoid the perils of floating point arithmetic and roundoff error is really like whistling in the dark. The dangers are still there – they have merely been pushed farther away. In most of this chapter, four-digit decimal arithmetic has been used to illustrate some of the difficulties. The usual single precision arithmetic is equivalent to six or seven decimal digits but the problems are still there, as they remain even for arithmetic with 48-bit fractions. Confidence in the results of extensive computation comes only with the knowledge of where perils lie.

The use of double precision is a common source of errors in using mixed arithmetic. Usually a machine will use twice the storage (or two words) to store a double precision number. Yet because the formats for storing single and double precision numbers are different, the errors are similar to those of viewing a fixed point number through floating point–colored glasses. On most machines using the IEEE standard format, the double precision numbers have a different arrangement than the single precision numbers. Usually the sign and exponent are allotted 12 bits (3 more than the single's 9), and the fraction takes 52 bits, with 18 at the end of the first word and the remaining 32 bits in the second. As a result, the range of double precision numbers is much greater in the IEEE standard. On IBM mainframes, a double precision number follows exactly the same format as the single but with a longer 14-hexadecimal-digit fraction, so that the range of numbers is nearly identical. The first word holds 8 bits for sign and exponent, and the first 6 digits of the fraction fill the next 24 bits, so the last 8 digits take up all 32 bits of the second word. Woe to those who read the second word as a single precision floating point number! On the Cray machines, the exponent field of the second word is filled with zeros, while the fraction field contains the second 48 bits of the 96-bit fraction. In all three cases, reading under the wrong convention leads to big trouble.

A similar but different problem can arise in the retrieval of numbers stored in internal format. If we read off the 32 bits of 2π in single precision bit by bit from the floating point register and wrote it as 8 hexadecimal digits, we would have $40c90fd5$. Whereas most machines access storage by bytes, some would store 2π internally in *little endian* format (e.g., Intel) with the first byte as $d5$ and the fourth (most significant) byte as 40. However, *big endian* machines would store the first byte as 40 and the fourth (least significant) byte as $d5$. A problem arises when data may be stored in this internal format from one machine, to be read by another machine with a different internal format. In Fortran, the bytes just have to be reversed in order using some awkward equivalences; in R, *readBin* and *writeBin* have an 'endian=' argument; SAS supplies formats and informats for endianness writing/reading.

Finally, floating point multiplication and division are typically the slowest instructions on a computer, with their double precision versions even three or four times slower. In the analysis of algorithms, where floating point arithmetic dominates the workload, it is customary to measure work in "flops" – floating point operations. A *flop* consists of a floating point multiply (or divide) and the usually accompanying addition, fetch, and store. Other calculations, comparisons, and fixed point arithmetic for address calculations are much faster; their effect on the total workload is considered less important and often can be safely ignored.

In computers with more modern floating point architecture, especially those known as "supercomputers," a clever sequencing of these operations, called *pipelining,* is exploited. For problems where the main effort lies in floating point operations (e.g., vectors and matrices), pipelining leads to much faster execution. The principle of pipelining is to schedule the ancillary instructions for floating point operations so that no part of the operation is waiting. For example, for adding a multiple of one vector to another, $z_i = ax_i + y_i$, several similar steps are involved. Two sequences of values $\{x_i\}, \{y_i\}$ must be retrieved from storage and, for each step, two numbers are multiplied (ax_i), the product added to another, and the sequence of these sums $\{z_i\}$ stored. In its simplest form, the fetches for x_{10} and y_{10} are initiated long before the multiplication is scheduled. While the product ax_{10} is being computed, z_5 may be being stored and the summation $ax_8 + y_8$ computed. As a result, the slowest step – usually the floating point multiply – determines the execution time for the task. In earlier machines and in some contemporary PCs and workstations, only fetches and stores are pipelined and so the scheduling depends on memory retrieval speed, which – in big problems or small machines – can extend to disk.

2.5 Living with Floating Point Inaccuracies

Earlier we discussed the abstract world of real numbers and the real world of numbers that can be expressed on a computer. Because a number such as z in (2.2.2) cannot be written exactly on a computer, a floating point approximation of it, $\mathrm{fl}(z)$, is used and an approximation error must be endured. *Numerical analysis* is the study of this error and similar approximations necessary for practical computation. Since the purpose of this book is the computation of statistics, I will endeavor to limit the discussion to practicalities. We begin by reviewing some introductory material.

One measure of the accuracy of the approximation of a real number z by $\mathrm{fl}(z)$ is absolute error, $|\mathrm{fl}(z) - z|$. Although useful in some problems, most would agree that 6.023×10^{23} is a more accurate approximation of Avagadro's number than 3 is an approximation of the ratio of the circumference of a circle to its diameter. The more common measure of accuracy is relative error,

$$|fl(z) - z|/|z| \quad \text{for } z \neq 0.$$

To compute the relative error of our floating point approximation $fl(z)$ to the real number z, it is helpful to use a mild generalization of the floating point systems previously discussed. That is, a floating point number is represented by d digits in base B, where the true exponent lies between $-L$ and M. Thus the largest representable number is

$$f_{max} = (1 - B^{-d}) \times B^M$$

and the smallest positive number is

$$f_{min} = B^{1-L}.$$

The relative error of the floating point representation depends on whether we round to the nearest available number or chop; that is, whether 3.1415926535... is written as $(+, 1, .3142)$ (rounding) or $(+, 1, .3141)$ (chopping). The upper bound on the relative error is called the machine unit U, expressed as

$$|fl(z) - z| \leq U|z| \quad \text{for all } z,$$

where

$$U = \begin{cases} \frac{1}{2}B^{1-d} & \text{if rounding is used,} \\ B^{1-d} & \text{if chopping is used.} \end{cases}$$

The machine unit is more useful when this bound is rewritten backwards as $fl(z) = z(1 + u)$, where $|u| \leq U$. Analysis of the accuracy of floating point arithmetic is based on similar bounds for each of the four arithmetic operations, $\{+, -, *, /\}$. Avoiding the elegant, let's get to the practical and use $B = 10$ and $d = 4$ for these examples.

The first thing to learn is that floating point arithmetic does not obey the laws of algebra – more specifically, the associative law. That is, if a list of numbers is added in a different order, a different sum may be computed. For the simplest case with all positive numbers, take $a = 4 = (+, 1, .4000)$, $b = 5003 = (+, 4, .5003)$, and $c = 5000 = (+, 4, .5000)$. Adding one way is a high $(a + b) + c = (+, 5, .1001)$, but the other gives a low $a + (b + c) = (+, 5, .1000)$. This may look trivial, but suppose the list is just 54,321 numbers all equal to 1. If we go through the list adding a 1 to the current sum, then the sum will be $(+, 5, .1000)$ or 10,000. Why? Well, since $d = 4$, everything is fine for the first 10,000 additions. Now the next addition of 1 to 10,000 should give 10,001, but to write it as a floating point number the best that four decimal digits can do is $(+, 5, .1000)$ and so the sum doesn't increase. In fact, adding a million ones would yield the same result. This example becomes a serious problem in numerical integration, where more computational effort can lead to a less accurate result. Most such problems can be avoided by following these two principles: first, always add numbers of like magnitude together. The second principle is to add small numbers together before adding the larger ones (see Exercises 2.10 and 2.12). More sophisticated addition algorithms are discussed in Section 2.5.

The more serious violation of the associative law occurs when the signs of the numbers are mixed. Catastrophic cancellation arises when subtraction of two nearly equal numbers eliminates the most significant digits. Consequently, the small errors in rounding that were hiding so innocently are uncovered to become glaring errors. Using the same numbers as before, $(b-c)-a = b-(c+a) = (-, +1, .1000)$, which looks fine, but now double all three numbers: $2a = (+, +1, .8000)$, $2b = (+, +5, .1001)$, and $2c = (+, +5, .1000)$. Then the sign flips for one sum, $(2b-2c)-2a = (+, +1, .2000)$ whereas the other gives zero, $2b - (2c + 2a) = (+, -L, .0000)$. Here both the associative and distributive laws are violated.

In statistics, the most surprising cancellation problems occur in computing a difference of squares. The usual one-pass method for computing the sample variance of n numbers is to (a) find the sum and the sum of squares and then (b) take the difference of the sum of squares and n times the square of the mean. If the sample is just five numbers $(356, 357, 358, 359, 360)$ and we round with our four decimal digits, the sample variance computed this way is negative. For this particular problem, Exercise 5.11 contains a one-pass algorithm that will compute the sample variance easily. A simpler improvement can be made by subtracting any number in the vicinity, leading to the following simple one-pass algorithm:

$$\sum_{i=1}^{n}(x_i - \bar{x})^2 = \sum_{i=2}^{n}(x_i - x_1)^2 - n(x_1 - \bar{x})^2. \tag{2.5.1}$$

Although this method still faces some cancellation, the Samuelson (1968) inequality limits the effect (see Exercise 2.19).

Example 2.4: *Catastrophic Cancellation – Sample Variance*

$$fl(X_1^2) = 356^2 = (+, 6, .1267)$$

$$fl(X_2^2) = 357^2 = (+, 6, .1274), \quad fl(X_1^2 + X_2^2) = (+, 6, .2541)$$

$$fl(X_3^2) = 358^2 = (+, 6, .1282), \quad fl(X_1^2 + X_2^2 + X_3^2) = (+, 6, .3823)$$

$$fl(X_4^2) = 359^2 = (+, 6, .1289), \quad fl(X_1^2 + \ldots + X_4^2) = (+, 6, .5112)$$

$$fl(X_5^2) = 360^2 = (+, 6, .1296), \quad fl(X_1^2 + \ldots + X_5^2) = (+, 6, .6408)$$

$$fl(n\bar{X}^2) = (+, 6, .1282) \times (+, 1, .5000) = (+, 6, 6410)$$

$$fl(\sum_{i=1}^{n} X_i^2 - n\bar{X}^2) = (+, 6, .6408) - (+, 6, .6410) = negative!$$

Many (if not most) serious cancellation problems can be anticipated and avoided using simple work-arounds. If cancellation cannot be avoided, then avoid amplifying the effect. The use of "pivoting" in solving linear equations in Chapter 3 is simply to avoid amplifying the effect of cancellation error. For problems as simple as adding a list of numbers, pair up positives with negatives so that the pairs all have the same sign. Otherwise, following the principles just mentioned will work: add the small numbers together first and then the larger ones, so that the cancellations at the end have the least effect. However, the biggest payoff lies in reworking the expressions analytically to avoid cancellations. A common source of cancellation problems arises in computing tail probabilities. As discussed in Chapter 7, most distribution functions are written to evaluate the tail to avoid the cancellation in $1 - F(t)$.

Example 2.5: *Tail Probability of the Logistic*

For the logistic distribution, computing the probability in the tail beyond 6 using $1 - F(t) = 1 - (1 + e^{-t})^{-1}$ has the intermediate step of the reciprocal of $(+, 1, .1002)$ giving $(+, 0, .9980)$; then $(+, 1, .1000) - (+, 0, .9980) = (+, -2, .2000)$, which appears acceptable. But compare this result with subtracting analytically, where we have the expressions $1 - F(t) = e^{-t}/(1 + e^{-t}) = 1/(1 + e^{t})$. Using the middle one with $t = 6$ leads to the division $(+, -2, .2479)/(+, 1, .1002) = (+, -2, .2474)$; using the last gives the reciprocal of $(+, 3, .4044)$ or $(+, -2, .2473)$, which is the correctly rounded form of the exact $.002472623$.

In this last example, the simplicity and small evaluation cost strongly suggest reworking the expressions. Certain expressions cannot be reworked and the use of series expansions is recommended. For example, in evaluating both $\log(1 + x)$ and $e^{x} - 1$ for extremely small x, the intermediate result can lose all accuracy. For our $B = 10$ and $d = 4$, if $x = (+, -5, .1000)$ or smaller then $(1 + x)$ will give $(+, 1, .1000)$, as will e^{x}. Consequently, both $\log(1 + x)$ and $e^{x} - 1$ will be zero when the result (to first order) should actually be x for both. Unavoidable expressions such as this demand coding of series expansions for the extreme cases:

$$\log(1 + x) \approx x - x^2/2 + x^3/3 - \cdots, \tag{2.5.2}$$

$$e^{x} - 1 \approx x + x^2/2! + x^3/3! + x^4/4! + \cdots. \tag{2.5.3}$$

Thankfully, when such rescues are required the series will usually converge very quickly.

The careful reader may have noticed that expression (2.5.2) also includes some cancellation. For most computations, a certain level of cancellation is quite acceptable. Here, for small x, any cancellation would be in a smaller order of magnitude. In Example 2.5, two decimal digits were lost in cancellation, magnifying the relative importance of the rounding error in the intermediate expressions into the second significant digit. If $d = 6$ then the smaller rounding error would still be magnified two places, but only to the fourth significant digit. Such an error may be problematic in optimization (e.g., maximum likelihood estimation), but this level of error may be insignificant in other applications. The decision to rework expressions depends for the most part on how much accuracy will be lost on a relative basis and how much work is required to avoid it. For this tail probability calculation, $t = 6$ may be too rare to be worth the effort.

Another quirk of computer arithmetic is that things rarely add up exactly, unless the numbers can be written exactly in the machine. When we add up $1/3$ three times, $((.3333 + .3333) + .3333)$, the result is $.9999$ and not 1. As a consequence, any iterative algorithm that stops only when the condition is satisfied exactly may be in an infinite loop. The solution is to change any exact test to a "close enough" test – say,

```
IF( ABS( XNEW-XOLD ) .LE. 5.* ABS( XOLD ) * UNIT ) EXIT
```

Squeezing UNIT too small disables this improvement. Another manifestation of the lack of exactness is the sudden discontinuous behavior of a continuous function when changes in the ordinate drop to the order of U. A function that is increasing at x may have a smaller value when computed at $x(1 + U)$ owing to roundoff error. This noisy behavior of an apparently smooth function at these small changes in x can cause problems in numerical differentiation (see Section 8.6).

Many computers offer the option of doing computations in double precision (using $2d$ or more digits in the fraction). As discussed in Section 2.4, the decision to use this option should not be automatic. First of all, many problems do not require a great deal of accuracy; sometimes three decimal digits solves the real problem. Secondly, the single precision is sometimes more than adequate, especially for those machines with 48-bit fractions in base 2. However, the IBM mainframe 6-hex-digit fraction is often inadequate. Another discouraging word is that some numerical problems are not aided at all by double precision, especially problems whose accuracy is limited by the accuracy of the input. Finally, additions usually take twice as long, and multiplications are three to four times slower.

On some machines, the computation of inner products can be improved cheaply with an intermediate step. Sometimes the product of two single precision numbers produces a double precision product automatically. If this is accessible, then adding those products in double precision is a cheap way to improve the accuracy, making the error nearly independent of n. The code in Fortran 90/95 for the inner product of two single precision arrays A and B, writing the result in a double precision variable S, is simply

```
S = 0.D0
DO I = 1,N
S = S + DPROD( A(I), B(I) )
ENDDO
```

Some implementations use the conversion DBLE(A(I)*B(I)). This trick is called "accumulating inner products in double precision."

Finally, there is the problem of accumulated roundoff error, encountered when adding (or multiplying) many, many numbers. This is particularly the case in the next chapter, when the typical task is the computation of the inner product of two vectors of length n. Coarsely summarizing, the error analysis follows the route

$$\mathrm{fl}(x_1 + x_2) = (x_1 + x_2)(1 + u_1),$$

$$\mathrm{fl}((x_1 + x_2) + x_3) = (x_1 + x_2)(1 + u_1)(1 + u_2) + x_3(1 + u_2),$$

$$\mathrm{fl}(\cdots((x_1 + x_2) + x_3)\cdots + x_n) = (x_1 + x_2)\prod_{i=1}^{n-1}(1 + u_i) + x_3\prod_{i=2}^{n-1}(1 + u_i)$$

$$+ \cdots + x_n(1 + u_{n-1}), \qquad (2.5.4)$$

with each $|u_i| \le U$. This last expression can explain the mechanism. First, if U is small, then these products look like sums to the first order. The error part of the right side of (2.5.4) then behaves like

$$\sum_{j=1}^{n} u_j \left(\sum_{i=1}^{j} x_i \right).$$

Since the index j orders the summation, it is clear that adding smallest to largest would minimize the effect. More rigorous analysis can follow one of two lines. For statisticians, the natural route would be to treat u_j as an independent random variable with each uniform$(-U, +U)$, which would lead to a relative standard error of approximately $n^{1/2}U$. The more pessimistic numerical analysis route would try to bound the error, and that would lead to the more pessimistic nU approximate relative error. The second implication of (2.5.4) is that the error grows with the sample size; being a pessimistic person, I would begin to worry when nU grows large. For our $B = 10$ and $d = 4$ situation with $U = .0005$ (rounding), adding more than 200 numbers would begin to squeeze the first digit. Note that, as n grows larger, approximating the products with sums begins to fail and everything will collapse, as in our previous example of adding 54,321 numbers all equal to 1.

2.6   The Pale and Beyond

The Pale was the region around Dublin beyond which the protection (or oppression) of the English government did not extend. Going "beyond the Pale" meant venturing out of the ordinary, with both positive and negative connotations. The arithmetic on a computer also has its capabilities and limitations, and one should be well armed before venturing beyond certain guideposts. After a discussion of those warning signs, a number of techniques are introduced that break through some of these limitations.

In beginning work on a new machine, learning its limitations is essential. The first among these limitations are the largest and smallest floating point numbers. Experience has shown the value of controlling overflow and underflow. Overflow arises from attempting to compute a number so large that it cannot be written as a floating point number. Similarly, an underflow is caused by computing a number that is too small; usually the computer sets the number to zero and proceeds without warning. Although apparently harmless, often a subsequent attempt to divide by zero is flagged or, worse still, a division of zero by zero occurs.

Consider the simple problem of computing a binomial probability when n and k are large:

$$f(k \mid n, p) = \binom{n}{k} p^k (1 - p)^{(n-k)}. \tag{2.6.1}$$

For $n = 80$ and $k = 40$ and using IEEE standard arithmetic, the computation of the binomial coefficient will overflow. For a not immoderate $p = .01$, an underflow message will be given – as arising in calling EXP, of all places, since the code P**K will be converted to

```
EXP( REAL( K ) * LOG( P ) )
```

These computations are more naturally computed by taking logarithms (see Chapter 7) and using the log-gamma function $\text{ALGAMA}(X) = \log \Gamma(x) = \log(x - 1)!$:

```
FKGNPL = ALGAMA( N+1. )+( K*LOG( P )-ALGAMA( K+1. )  )  &
&          +( (N-K)*LOG( 1.-P )-ALGAMA( N-K+1. )  )
```

Three points need to be emphasized. First, if the final result (e.g., a log likelihood) can be computed, then interruptions by overflows and underflows are intolerable. Second, one should design underflows to harmlessly flush to zero. Third, use overflows to signal errors or inappropriate use of the algorithm.

These prescriptions merit reiteration. If the result is expressible, then the algorithm should be designed to perform the task. If the binomial probability is not expressible, then perhaps its log is. For maximum likelihood estimation, this alternative result suffices. The intermediate steps, however, should not cause a failure. Since underflows are usually not signaled as errors and are just set to zero, the corresponding overflows that are not errors should be reworked to be underflows. The cumulative distribution function (cdf) $F(t) = e^t/(1 + e^t)$ must be reworked as $1/(1 + e^{-t})$. Overflows can then be used to signal problems. The largest number available can usually be used to set input or design specifications. Instead of testing input for meeting specifications, inappropriate use of an algorithm will then just overflow. This approach is not recommended for commercial software, but it is easy and effective for personal use.

On some machines, especially those using the single precision IEEE standard, the range of available numbers $10^{\pm38}$ can be limiting. Bayesian problems find this limit quickly, since a constant factor cancels out of any inference but remains in the likelihood as an annoyance. Here, self-management of the fraction and exponent can effectively extend the range of the floating point arithmetic when strictly positive numbers are added or multiplied. The number is represented by a floating point variable D and an integer I, and its value given by $D \times 2^I$. The subroutine ADJUST performs a normalization that keeps D between 1 and 16 and uses a large negative integer for I to indicate zero or a negative.

```
      SUBROUTINE ADJUST(D,I)
 ! NORMALIZES D WHILE KEEPING CONSTANT VALUE OF D * (2**I)
      INTEGER, PARAMETER ::  IBIG = -2147483644
      REAL, INTENT (IN OUT) ::  D
      INTEGER, INTENT(IN OUT) ::  I
      IF ( D .GT. 0.0 ) THEN
        DO WHILE ( D .LT. 1.0 )
        D = D*16.
        I = I-4
        ENDDO
        DO WHILE ( D .GT. 16.0 )
        D = D/16.
        I = I+4
        ENDDO
              ELSE
      I = IBIG ! IF D < 0 THEN I= -BIG
              ENDIF
      RETURN
      END SUBROUTINE ADJUST
```

To store the product of a simple floating point number A and a number represented by D and I, the code is

```
D = D*A
CALL ADJUST(D,I)
```

To store the product of the pairs (A, I) and (B, J) back in (C, K), the code is

```
K = I + J
C = A * B
CALL ADJUST(C,K)
```

A more common problem is the sum of two positive numbers:

```
K = MAX( I, J )
C = 0.
IF( I-K .GT. -24 ) C = C + (A * 2 ** (I-K) )
IF( J-K .GT. -24 ) C = C + (B * 2 ** (J-K) )
CALL ADJUST(C,K)
```

The choice of "-24" depends on the machine epsilon, to be discussed shortly. Notice that the two tests avoid controllable underflows, as well as unnecessary computation, while possible overflows have not been checked. Once certain precautions have been taken, any unexpected overflow should be considered a catastrophic error, causing the program to stop. In Fortran 95, three intrinsic functions make these calculations a bit easier, normalizing D to be between $1/2$ and 1. If $X = D * 2^I$ with $1/2 \leq D < 1$, then the intrinsic FRACTION(X) gives D and EXPONENT(X) gives I. The scaling by powers of two can be done easily using SCALE(D,I) to reproduce $X = D * 2^I$.

The second limitation to be learned is the accuracy of the floating point arithmetic. One item discussed previously is the machine unit U, which relates the level of rounding error. The second quantity is the machine epsilon ε_m, defined as the smallest number that – when added to 1 – will change its value. Usually U and ε_m are very close to each other and can almost be used interchangeably. The machine epsilon can be used to save computations: if a number to be added is too small, then often some of its computation can be avoided. The other use of ε_m is in testing for equality, as discussed in Section 2.4. The IEEE standard recommends a function NEXTAFTER to give the neighboring value in the representable numbers $\mathcal{F}$. Usually $x(1 + \varepsilon_m)$ suffices, as will $x(1 + U)$, although a slight overestimation of each is preferred. The machine unit U usually governs the accuracy of the floating point operations. As noted at the end of the previous section, the relative error when adding n numbers is approximately nU, with the approximation failing quickly as nU becomes no longer small.

The guideposts for adding or multiplying many numbers are comparatively clear. When nU is small, the relative error is around nU. For $U \approx 10^{-6}$, $n = 1000$ should still give three decimal digits, with improvements if the smallest numbers are added first. The multiplication guidepost is the same. But as n grows larger, some other routes should be considered to maintain accuracy. The first, and usually the best and the easiest, is to add in double precision. This will usually cost only twice as much, and its biggest drawback is keeping careful track of which variables are single and which are double precision. The second route is a pairing algorithm, and the third is a "best-ever" two-list summation algorithm. Dekker (1971) provided still another alternative.

In adding n numbers, at least $n - 1$ additions are required. From (2.5.4) we see that the order in which they are added can make a difference. Yet not only the order but also the combinations make a difference, since the associative law fails in floating point addition. In the simple addition algorithm, the first number appears with every addition error u_j in (2.5.4), and adding smallest first is an improvement. Suppose, however, that we add the first two numbers together, then the third and fourth et cetera, as $x_{2j-1} + x_{2j}$. Then add the pairs together to get sums of four numbers, and add the fours together to get eights, continuing until completion. Then each item x_j is associated not with $n - j = O(n)$ errors u_i but with only $k = \log_2 n$ errors, when $n = 2^k$. This improvement is substantial, and the algorithm is rather easy to code; see the demonstration code **sum24**.

If we look even more closely at the problem of adding n numbers, the only thing very clear is that we should add the smallest two numbers together. Yet once that is done, the problem is substantially the same but with $n - 1$ numbers, one from the sum and the other $n - 2$ remaining from the original list. At this point, we should either add the smallest two from the original list or the smallest to the sum. In general, we just add the smallest two numbers around. Although this looks like a nightmare to code as an algorithm, if the numbers are initially sorted into a single ordered list $\{x_j\}$ then the algorithm is rather simple. The key is to form a second list $\{s_j\}$ of sums. Each addition then takes two from the front of two lists, two from one list or one from each, and the sum formed goes on the back of the sum list $\{s_j\}$, since it is larger than any previous sum. When the original list $\{x_j\}$ is depleted, the sum list $\{s_j\}$ takes the role of the original list, and the process is repeated until only one element remains. This algorithm can be coded with a couple of pointers and using no extra storage, but it is much more complicated than the pairing algorithm. The comparison algorithm to find the smallest two of the four elements in the first two positions of the two lists is difficult to code and cannot be done very quickly. But this is the best that can be done to add a list of numbers; the effort may not be worth the payoff in most applications. See the demonstration code **sum3**.

The addition algorithms just discussed address adding positive numbers only. The danger of cancellation complicates any sum of mixed-sign numbers. As discussed previously, the best way to deal with cancellation is to take care of differences analytically. But now suppose that we do have a long list of m positive numbers and n negative numbers, how can we add them to get the best result? Following an analogy of the previous algorithm, suppose we have ordered the two lists of numbers in increasing magnitude. The obvious strategy is to add the smallest two numbers of opposite sign together. In contrast to the previous case, the resultant sum will be smaller in magnitude than any other number available. The next step is to add the next number of opposite sign to this sum. If the sum of the two smallest is negative, then we add positives until the sum turns positive, then negatives until the sum turns negative again, until one side runs out, at which point the sum and the list remaining have the same sign. The principle is that all of the cancellation is done early, so that no cancellation is done at the end.

Finally, three methods are strictly beyond the pale and should be considered only when an important result cannot be found any other way. The first method is *interval arithmetic* (see Moore 1979 or Alefeld and Herzberger 1983), which can guarantee the accuracy of its computations. The accuracy of any result computed using floating point arithmetic is often difficult, and sometimes impossible, to assess. We have a single number, but no sense of variation, as if statistically we had a point estimate and no standard error. But recall that computers can perform only the elementary operations of add, subtract, multiply, and divide. In interval arithmetic, instead of a single number x we use an interval that can be labeled as $X = (\underline{x}, \bar{x})$. All of the arithmetic operations can then be applied and defined on these intervals; for example, $X + Y = (\underline{x} + \underline{y}, \bar{x} + \bar{y})$ and $X - Y = (\underline{x} - \bar{y}, \bar{x} - \underline{y})$. As any expression is computed using these arithmetic operations, an interval is produced that is guaranteed to hold the true result. Of course, occasionally this interval can be too wide to be useful, but sometimes the results are impressive (Wang and Kennedy 1994). For the same result, some algorithms will give better (narrower) intervals than others. Software for performing interval arithmetic is available but not widely so, and most problems do not warrant such effort for a rock-solid answer.

A second method for handling problems outside the ordinary is multiple precision arithmetic. Here, several words are chained together to represent a number to extreme accuracy. Addition and subtraction are relatively straightforward, following the same carry and normalization done bit by bit in the machine instructions. The key to the usefulness of multiple precision arithmetic is that multiplication is also not too difficult. Recall the multiplication tables learned in elementary school for base-10 arithmetic. The single precision multiply instruction takes place in base-$2^{d/2}$ arithmetic, and the long multiplication simply requires chaining and addition of the partial products. Brent (1978) and Smith (1991) have produced Fortran-based multiple precision packages. For an interesting application that computes the digits of π, see Bailey (1988).

The third and final approach for unusual problems are methods for doing rational arithmetic. Here, the results are entirely exact and the computations are all performed using integers. Different representations can be used. The simplest one, and the only one recommended for amateurs, is to represent a number using its prime factorization by the list of exponents: $33/34 = 2^{-1}3^1 5^0 7^0 11^1 13^0 17^{-1} = (-1, 1, 0, 0, 1, 0, -1)$. Multiplication or division is very easy, but addition and subtraction can be problematic when the primes become large. One work-around is to keep some prime factors as integers – representing the number by two integers for numerator and denominator involving only large primes – and use the list for the smaller primes. The alternative method uses multiple modulus residue techniques. Two examples of applications are Keller-McNulty and Kennedy (1985) and Alfeld and Eyre (1991). The interested reader should consult these papers and the references therein after reading Knuth (1997b, sec. 4.3.2).

2.7 Conditioned Problems and Stable Algorithms

The jargon word "condition" connotes, in a broad sense, the ease with which a problem can be solved; that is, a badly conditioned problem is hard to solve. Between the handwaving heuristics and the meticulous mathematical drudgery, an important distinction is often lost between the condition of a problem and the stability of an algorithm to solve that problem.

Numerical algorithms are often viewed as producing output as a function of input:

$$\text{output} = f(\text{input}).$$

The *condition* of a problem can be viewed as a general derivative of the output as a function of the input, a measure of the difference of $f(\text{input} + \delta)$ from output. Usually, this difference is measured in relative changes in both the input and output,

$$\frac{|f(\text{input} + \delta) - \text{output}|}{\text{output}} = \text{condition} \frac{|\delta|}{\text{input}}. \tag{2.7.1}$$

The condition of a problem measures the relative change in the output due to a relative change in the input. In terms of derivatives, the condition number C of a problem is conveniently approximated by

$$C = |xf'(x)/f(x)|. \tag{2.7.2}$$

For many problems, derivatives do not make sense and a more precise mathematical specification is necessary. This is particularly the case in Section 3.6, where we discuss the accuracy of the solution of linear equations.

As an example of conditioning, consider the problem of finding the smaller root of the polynomial equation

$$z^2 - x_1 z + x_2 = 0, \tag{2.7.3}$$

where both x_1 and $x_2 > 0$. Consider in particular the case where x_2 is quite small, so that both roots are positive with (say) one large z_1 and the other z_2 near zero. If we write the quadratic formula for the smaller root z_2,

$$z_2(x_1, x_2) = \left(x_1 - \sqrt{x_1^2 - 4x_2}\right)/2, \tag{2.7.4}$$

and then take the partial derivative with respect to x_2, we obtain $(x_1^2 - 4x_2)^{-1/2} = 1/|z_1 - z_2|$. It is not surprising that the roots are difficult to find when they are close together. Following the formula (2.7.2) with x_1 fixed yields $C = |z_1/(z_1 - z_2)|$, which for the particular case of one small and one large root gives a condition number nearly equal to 1.

Now consider solving the equation (2.7.3) using the quadratic formula

$$z = \left(-b \pm \sqrt{b^2 - 4ac}\right)/2 \tag{2.7.5}$$

for the polynomial equation $az^2 + bz + c = 0$, and contrast the performance of the method for solution with the condition of the problem. It is clear that, when the roots are nearly equal, the discriminant $(b^2 - 4ac)$ will be computed with catastrophic cancellation. Yet consider computing the smaller root of the equation

$$z^2 - 8.42z + 0.04 = 0 \tag{2.7.6}$$

using four decimal digits. First the discriminant is 70.74, its square root is 8.411, subtracting from 8.420 gives .009000, and dividing by 2 produces the result .004500, which is not very close to the true smaller root of .0047533. An alternative form of the quadratic formula (reciprocal of largest root of quadratic in negative powers of z) gives

$$2c/\left[-b + \sqrt{b^2 - 4ac}\right]. \qquad (2.7.7)$$

Computing the smaller root this way, the square root is the same 8.411, but the expression in brackets is 16.83 and the computed root is 2(0.04000)/16.83 = .004753, which is on the money. If we change x_2 to .05, then the usual formula yields .006000 while the alternative method gives .005942, accurate to four digits again. Notice that the effect of the relative change of .01/.04 in the input yields a change of .0012/.00475 in the output.

This example illustrates the difference between the condition of the problem and the numerical stability of the method to solve it. Solving the equation is a very well-conditioned problem, for the roots are well separated and the condition number is roughly 1. But one method of computing the root is not stable, whereas the other method gives a very accurate result.

Analyses of the condition of a problem and of the stability of the computational method are sources of confidence in the computed solution. The analysis of stability is usually done in a backwards error analysis fashion – that the computed solution $f^*(x)$ is the exact solution of a problem with different input $f(x^*)$. Starting with expressions such as $\mathrm{fl}(z) = z(1 + u)$, this backwards error analysis states how close x^* is to x. Algorithms where x^* is close to x are stable. A highly satisfactory consequence is the stability on the level of the accuracy of the input. The condition number permits assessment of how the differences between x^* and x are magnified in the output.

In the preceding example, looking only at the $x_2 = .04$ input coefficient, the first computed root of .0045 is the exact solution for the problem where $x_2^* = .03786975$. Now if the difference $|.04 - .03787| \approx .00213$ is at the level of the accuracy of the input, as in the sense of a standard error, then .0045 should be an acceptable solution.

Programs and Demonstrations

fixex *Demonstration of fixed point arithmetic and internal representation*
Ten integers are written out in internal format in half-integers (kind = 2). The most negative number is decreased by one and then negated, resulting in no change.

floatex *Demonstration of floating point arithmetic and its internal representation*
Seven interesting numbers are written in their internal representation and written also as if the internal representations were read as fixed point numbers.

macheps *Algorithm to find the machine epsilon in single precision arithmetic*
A few small numbers are added to 1 and compared to 1. The machine epsilon is defined to be the smallest number added to 1 that yields a sum other than one.

sum24 *Demonstration of two algorithms for summation of positive numbers*
Two subprograms are demonstrated for summing three examples, $S_1 = \sum_{j=1}^{n} j$, $S_2 = \sum_{j=1}^{n} j^2$, and $S_3 = \sum_{j=1}^{n} j^{-1}$. One algorithm, **sum2**, follows the pairing method described in Section 2.5. Another version of this method, **sum4**, can be put in a loop and does not require the entire series to be stored in a list. Both do the same summation.

sum3 *Demonstration of the "best" algorithm for summation*
A third "best" method is implemented in the subroutine **sum3** to add the same series as in **sum24**. Note that **sum3** requires the initial list of numbers to be sorted.

tab21d *Double precision values for Table 2.1.*
Versions in Fortran, R, and SAS provide double precision values for Table 2.1, including extremely large and small values.

Exercises

In the appropriate exercises, use the arithmetic methods (e.g. two's complement) that your computer uses.

2.1 Write the following as fixed point numbers using $M = 16$ bits: (a) -1234; (b) 55; (c) 8191; (d) -10.

2.2 Write the numbers in Exercise 2.1 as floating point numbers, and also: (e) $2/3$; (f) $1/10$.

2.3 (a) Write -10 as a 32-bit fixed point number.
(b) What would its value be if it is read as a floating point number?

2.4 (a) Prove that $n!/k!(n-k)!$ is always an integer.
(b) For your computer, for what value of n will (2.3.2) lead to an overflow?

2.5 Knuth gives some transcendental numbers in octal (base 8) as follows:

$$\pi = 3.11037552421026430215142306_{\text{eight}},$$
$$e = 2.55760521305053551246527734_{\text{eight}},$$
$$\gamma = 0.44742147706766606172232157_{\text{eight}} \quad (\text{Euler's } \gamma).$$

(a) Convert these to six-digit decimal numbers and check your result.
(b) How are they written as floating point numbers?
(c) Write them also as double precision numbers.
(d) What is the value of the first word of (c) when read as a single precision number?

2.6 Suppose all of the bits of a 32-bit word were IID (independent and identically distributed) Bernoulli random variables with $p = 1/2$. What is the distribution of the value when it is read as a floating point number? Describe the general behavior of the distribution function.

2.7 The smallest number that can be added to 1 that gives a sum that is different from 1 is called the machine epsilon, ε_m. Find the machine epsilon and compare it to what you guessed analytically.

2.8 For $n = 30$ and $p = 1/2$, compute the probability that a binomial random variable is greater than 20 and estimate the accuracy of your answer. Compare it to the normal approximation.

2.9 Can the computed average of two floating point numbers $(x + y)/2$ (sum, then divide) be smaller than either one? Give an example (two digits are enough) in base 10 or 16. Is it possible in base 2?

2.10 The transcendental number e can be represented by the series

$$e = 1 + 1 + 1/2 + 1/6 + \cdots + 1/(i!) + \cdots .$$

Compute e by summing this series in order from $i = 0$, which is from largest to smallest. Compare this to the result from summing from smallest (take i large enough) to the largest.

2.11 Compare the evaluation of e^{-x} for $x = 1, 2, 3, 4$ using:
(a) the alternating series $e^{-x} = 1 - x + x^2/2 - x^3/3! + \cdots + (-1)^j x^j/j! + \cdots$;
(b) the reciprocal of the nonalternating series

$$1/(1 + x + x^2/2 + x^3/3! + \cdots + x^j/j! + \cdots).$$

2.12 The harmonic series $H_n = \sum_{j=1}^{n}(1/j)$ is known to diverge, but on a computer it will appear to converge. Compute H_n until the value no longer changes with n. Compare the stopping point with what can be guessed analytically, using ε_m and the approximation

$$H_n = 1 + 1/2 + 1/3 + \cdots + 1/n = .577215664 + \log n + o(n)$$

by equating ε_m and $(n + 1)^{-1}/H_n$ (see Knuth 1997a, p. 160).

2.13 Compare the accuracy of four approaches to the similar convergent alternating series

$$S_n = 1 - 1/2 + 1/3 - 1/4 + 1/5 - 1/6 + 1/7 - 1/8 + \cdots + (-1)^{n+1}/n,$$

where $\lim_{n \to \infty} S_n = \log_e 2$.
(a) Add from largest to smallest (1 to n).
(b) Add from smallest to largest (n to 1).
(c) Add the pairs first: $(1 - 1/2) + (1/3 - 1/4) + \cdots$.
(d) Add the pairs analytically: sum $1/((2k - 1)(2k))$ from $k = 1$.

2.14 Find the values of t where cancellation will be serious in the following expressions, and rework to avoid the cancellation:
(a) $1/t - 1/\sqrt{t^2 + a}$;
(b) $e^{-2t^2} - e^{-8t^2}$;
(c) $\log(e^{t+s} - e^t)$;
(d) $[(1 + e^{-t})^2 - 1]t^2 e^{-t}$.

2.15 On the computer you are using, what is the smallest number X for which EXP(X) does not underflow? What is the largest number X such that EXP(X) does not overflow?

2.16 Following (2.7.2), compute the condition number for each of the following functions $f(x)$, and give the values of x for which the condition number is large:
(a) $f(x) = e^x$;
(b) $f(x) = \log(x)$;
(c) $f(x) = \log(1 + x)$;

(d) $f(x) = \Phi^{-1}(x)$;

(e) $f(x) = x/\sqrt{1+x^2}$.

Are there any surprises?

2.17 Let the real number z lie between $(+, E, F)$ and $(+, E, F+B^{-d})$. Carefully verify (2.2.3).

2.18 Write the Fortran code to add $\exp(A)$ to $D*2^I$, using ADJUST if necessary, and reuse D and I to represent the sum.

2.19 Samuelson's inequality (also attributed to K. R. Nair) gives a bound on the extremes in a sample in terms of the mean and variance:

$$|x_i - \bar{x}| \le s\sqrt{n-1}.$$

Use this to bound the cancellation in (2.5.1) by giving a bound on the ratio

$$n(x_1 - \bar{x})^2 \Big/ \sum (x_i - x_1)^2.$$

2.20 The Lewis–Goodman–Miller algorithm for generating random numbers is given by the integer relation $z_{n+1} = 16807z_n \bmod (2^{31} - 1)$. The portability problem with this method is that the rules for fixed point overflow vary greatly. For a computer using two's complement that allows an integer overflow to go unflagged, the following code was proposed:

```
Z = 16807 * Z
IF ( Z .LT. 0 ) Z = ( Z + 2147483647 ) + 1
```

Check to see if your computer behaves this way by checking this algorithm, beginning with $z_1 = 1$, and see if $z_{10001} = 1043618065$ (Park and Miller 1988).

2.21 Change the coefficient in (2.7.6) to .038 and redo the computations. Comment.

2.22 On your computer, what is the smallest integer that cannot be exactly represented as a floating point number?

2.23 Prove that any positive number z can be written as a base-B number using the digits $\{0, 1, \ldots, B-1\}$ as in (2.2.1).

2.24 In Bayesian analysis, a normalization constant often cancels out of the numerator and denominator of posterior calculations. Since most of the analysis is first done in logs, often a choice is available to compute $\exp(u - v)$ or $\exp(u)/\exp(v)$. Which is better, or does it make a difference at all? Compare the two methods for $u \approx v$ with values such as $\pm 1, \pm 5, \pm 10, \pm 100$. Can you show analytically which one should be better?

2.25 The Cantor function $g(x)$ is a weird function often used as a counterexample in analysis. It takes constant values on the middle third of intervals:

$$g(x) = 1/2 \quad \text{for } x \in (1/3, 2/3),$$
$$g(x) = 1/4 \quad \text{for } x \in (1/9, 2/9),$$
$$g(x) = 3/4 \quad \text{for } x \in (7/9, 8/9),$$

and so on. Royden (1968, p. 47) gave the following precise definition. Begin with the base-3 expansion of $x = \sum_{j=1}^{\infty} a_j 3^{-j}$ and let N be the index of the first-time $a_j = 1$. Now let $b_j = a_j/2$ for $j < N$ (notice that b_j is 0 or 1) and $b_N = 1$, so that $g(x) = \sum_{j=1}^{N} b_j 2^{-j}$. The Cantor function is monotone nondecreasing and continuous almost everywhere, with a derivative existing almost everywhere that is zero, although the function goes from $g(0) = 0$ to $g(1) = 1$. However weird it may be, can you write an algorithm to compute $g(x)$ for all representable numbers $\mathcal{F}$? Plot it on $(0, 1)$. Does it appear as you would expect?

2.26 The budget of the United States government is on the order of 3,500,000,000,000 dollars. The lowest unit of currency, however, is the cent with 100 cents per dollar. Could SAS or R keep track of each cent as an integer?

2.27 Tsao (1974) derived a statistical model for the relative error ϵ in chopped floating point computations as $\epsilon = U/Z$, where U is uniformly distributed on $\left[0, \, B^{-d}\right)$ independently of Z whose density is $1/(\log_e(B)z)$ on $[1/B, 1)$. Is the confidence interval $(0, m)$, where $Pr(U/Z \le m) = .95$, substantially different from the bound B^{1-d} given in Section 2.5?

References

The fascinating (and surprisingly difficult) subject of arithmetic is beautifully explained in Knuth (1997b). The numerical analysis text of Forsythe, Malcolm, and Moler (1977) gives a good exposition of accuracy problems and excellent exercises. Stewart (1973) presents conditioning, stability, and the mathematics of roundoff error. The IBM document (Anonymous 1956) is exemplary of the information available in the manuals that accompany computers. The subroutine ADJUST appears as Algol code for Cholesky decomposition (see Section 3.4) by Martin, Peters, and Wilkinson (1965), reprinted in Wilkinson and Reinsch (1971). W. Kahan was the driving force behind the IEEE standard, but many of his papers are technical reports or conference proceedings (e.g. Kahan, Palmer, and Coonen 1979) and thus are not readily available.

Gotz Alefeld and Jurgen Herzberger (1983), *Introduction to Interval Computations*. New York: Academic Press.

Peter Alfeld and David J. Eyre (1991), "The Exact Analysis of Sparse Rectangular Systems," *ACM Transactions on Mathematical Software* 17: 502–18.

Anonymous (1956), *Number Systems*. Poughkeepsie, NY: IBM Corporation.

David H. Bailey (1988), "The Computation of π to 29,360,000 Decimal Digits Using Borweins' Quartically Convergent Algorithm," *Mathematics of Computation* 50: 283–96.

Richard P. Brent (1978), "A Fortran Multiple-Precision Arithmetic Package," *ACM Transactions on Mathematical Software* 4: 57–70.

W. J. Cody (1988), "Algorithm 665, MACHAR: A Subroutine to Dynamically Determine Machine Parameters," *ACM Transactions on Mathematical Software* 14: 303–11.

Germund Dahlquist and Ake Bjorck (1974), *Numerical Methods* (trans. by N. Anderson). Englewood Cliffs, NJ: Prentice-Hall.

T. J. Dekker (1971), "A Floating-Point Technique for Extending the Available Precision," *Numerische Mathematik* 18: 224–42.

George E. Forsythe, Michael A. Malcolm, and Cleve B. Moler (1977), *Computer Methods for Mathematical Computations*. Englewood Cliffs, NJ: Prentice-Hall.

David Goldberg (1991), "What Every Computer Scientist Should Know about Floating Point Arithmetic," *ACM Computing Surveys* 23: 5–48.

Institute of Electrical and Electronics Engineers (1985), "IEEE Standard for Binary Floating Point Arithmetic," Standard 754-1985, IEEE, New York.

W. Kahan, J. Palmer, and J. Coonen (1979), "A Proposed IEEE-CS Standard for Binary Floating Point Arithmetic," *Proceedings of the Twelfth Interface Symposium on Computer Science and Statistics*, pp. 32–6, University of Waterloo.

Sallie Keller-McNulty and William J. Kennedy (1985), "Error-free Computation of a Reflexive Generalized Inverse," *Linear Algebra and Its Applications* 67: 157–67.

Donald E. Knuth (1997a), *The Art of Computer Programming* (vol. 1: Fundamental Algorithms), 3rd ed. Reading, MA: Addison-Wesley.

Donald E. Knuth (1997b), *The Art of Computer Programming* (vol. 2: Seminumerical Algorithms), 3rd. ed. Reading, MA: Addison-Wesley.

Ulrich W. Kulisch and Willard L. Miranker (1981), *Computer Arithmetic in Theory and Practice.* New York: Academic Press.

R. S. Martin, G. Peters, and J. H. Wilkinson (1965), "Symmetric Decomposition of a Positive Definite Matrix," *Numerische Mathematik* 7: 363–83.

Ramon E. Moore (1979), *Methods and Applications of Interval Analysis.* Philadelphia: SIAM.

Michael L. Overton (2001), *Numerical Computing with IEEE Floating Point Arithmetic;* Philadelphia: SIAM.

Stephen K. Park and Keith W. Miller (1988), "Random Number Generators: Good Ones Are Hard to Find," *Communications of the ACM* 31: 1192–1201.

H. L. Royden (1968), *Real Analysis,* 2nd ed. New York: Macmillan.

Paul A. Samuelson (1968), "How Deviant Can You Be?" *Journal of the American Statistical Association* 63: 1522–5.

David M. Smith (1991), "Algorithm 693: A Fortran Package for Floating-Point Multiple-Precision Arithmetic," *ACM Transactions on Mathematical Software* 17: 273–83.

G. W. Stewart (1973), *Introduction to Matrix Computations.* New York: Academic Press.

Nai-kuan Tsao (1974), "On the Distribution of Significant Digits and Roundoff Errors," *Communications of the ACM* 17: 269–271.

Morgan C. Wang and William J. Kennedy (1994), "Self-Validating Computations of Probabilities for Selected Central and Noncentral Univariate Probability Functions," *Journal of the American Statistical Association* 89: 878–87.

J. H. Wilkinson and C. Reinsch (Eds.) (1971), *Linear Algebra.* New York: Springer-Verlag.

3

Matrices and Linear Equations

3.1 Introduction

In recent years, linear algebra has become as fundamental a mathematical tool as calculus. Since its role in statistics is so prominent, matrix computations and the solution of linear equations are fundamental to the computing of statistics. Hence the treatment in this chapter is rather traditional. The study of one particular statistical problem, regression, is postponed, and some problems arising in time-series analysis are discussed in the next chapter.

Numerical analysts always talk about the solution to a system of equations, $\mathbf{Ax} = \mathbf{b}$, for the thought of computing an inverse is considered (for reasons often unstated) naive and gauche. Although the tone is haughty, the reasoning is sound, and while the mathematics of $\mathbf{A}^{-1}\mathbf{B}$ speaks of inverses, its computation means solving systems of equations with several right-hand sides. To emphasize, although the algebra may be written in terms of inverses, careful analysis to convert the computations to solving systems of equations with many right-hand sides may lead to substantial savings in computing time.

The systems of equations to be treated here will always be square and consistent – that is, they will always have a solution. When this assumption is violated, the problem of solving a system of equations changes its nature, sometimes to a regression problem (discussed in Chapter 5) or to an eigenproblem (Chapter 6).

The first topic to be covered is an introduction to the computational and storage tricks that are so useful in matrix computations. Other acts of computational sleight of hand will be introduced as they arise. Solving linear equations begins with the simplest cases, triangular systems. The most common method of solving general linear equations, Gaussian elimination, is described in detail in Section 3.4. Factoring positive definite matrices, so valuable in statistics, is discussed in Section 3.5. Matrix norms are introduced in Section 3.6 and are used to analyze accuracy and conditioning in Section 3.7. Further topics in numerical linear algebra are discussed in Chapter 4.

Notation is critically important for communicating complicated algorithms clearly and succinctly. All matrices will be denoted by a capital roman letter in boldface (e.g. $\mathbf{A}$). All vectors are column vectors unless otherwise indicated, and are denoted by lowercase roman letters (e.g. $\mathbf{b}$). The notation for an individual element of a vector is a simple subscript b_i; for a matrix, A_{ij} denotes the element in row i and column j. To denote a particular column, $\mathbf{A}_{.j}$ will be used; for a row, $\mathbf{A}_{i.}$ is the notation. A superscript capital T indicates a transpose, $\mathbf{b}^\mathrm{T}$. The ith elementary vector is denoted by $\mathbf{e}_i$, whose elements are zero except for a one in the ith component.

To continue with notation, there are a number of special types of matrices that are commonly encountered:

lower triangular – $A_{ij} = 0$ for $i < j$;
upper triangular – $A_{ij} = 0$ for $i > j$;
diagonal – $A_{ij} = 0$ for $i \neq j$;
tridiagonal – $A_{ij} = 0$ for $|i - j| > 1$;
positive definite – symmetric, with $\mathbf{x}^\mathrm{T}\mathbf{A}\mathbf{x} > 0$ for all $\mathbf{x} \neq 0$;
orthogonal – $\mathbf{A}^\mathrm{T}\mathbf{A} = \mathbf{I}$;
permutation – $A_{ij} = 1$ if $i = \pi(j)$ and $= 0$ otherwise, where π is a permutation;
elementary permutation – $P(i, j)$ is an identity, except rows (or columns) i and j are switched.

Matrix operations can be written symbolically in a much simpler fashion than they can be coded in a language such as Fortran. Consequently, considerable effort has been made in software development to codify and simplify computational linear algebra. Within the Fortran community, most mathematical library developers (IMSL, NAg) have produced subprograms to compute matrix multiplications and solve equations as well as eigenproblems and specialized matrix problems. In the public domain, the BLAS (basic linear algebra subroutine) routines of LAPACK handle the fundamental steps, and LAPACK contains routines for solving equations, computing factorizations and least squares problems, and solving eigenproblems. Other software developers have taken a different route. A generation ago, Iverson invented a specialized language (APL) that handles vector and matrix constructs automatically, but its cryptic symbols have been a major obstacle to its acceptance. However, having used APL years ago with mnemonics in place of the symbols, I can attest to its power and usefulness. Following in the same spirit have been John Sall's development of IML within the SAS statistical system, the mathematical software system GAUSS, and the vector–matrix structures with the Bell Lab's S language. In these systems, underlying the special symbols and routines are the same Gaussian elimination and Cholesky factorization algorithms – though the user may be (blissfully or otherwise) unaware of them.

3.2   Matrix Operations

The craft of matrix computations can be described as skills for survival under deprivation of space and time. These two factors often limit the size of the problem that can be solved; doing without prepares us for making the most of what is available. Conservation of space is often achieved by overwriting the solution on the input. Methods that require fewer arithmetic operations are constantly sought. Since reductions of an order of magnitude are rare, percentage gains in speed are highly valued. Often, the gain is merely avoiding computing a quantity (e.g. 0) whose value is known first-hand. Improvements begin as early as the fundamental problem of matrix multiplication.

Suppose we wish to multiply a matrix $\mathbf{A}$ (with m rows and n columns) and a vector $\mathbf{y}$ (of length n) and then store the product in $\mathbf{z}$. The code may be written as

```
do i=1,m
s=0.
do j=1,n
s=s+a( i,j ) * y( j )
end do  ! loop on j
z( i )=s
end do  ! loop on i
```

where the multiplication can be seen as a stacking of the inner products $z_i = \mathbf{A}_i.\mathbf{y}$. In a different view, $\mathbf{z}$ is a linear combination of the columns of $\mathbf{A}$:

```
z=0.
do j=1,n
do i=1,m
z( i )=z( i )+a( i,j ) * y( j )
end do  ! loop on i
end do  ! loop on j
```

Which method is better? Well, for small to moderate m and n, it hardly matters since both perform mn multiplications and additions (or flops). But for very large matrices, the second one may be much, much faster, because the matrix is accessed in the way that it is stored in Fortran, by columns. The first method may not work at all for very large ($m, n \gg 1000$) matrices, since each fetch of an element could generate a page fault.

More importantly, some matrices have a structure that can be exploited in a particular way to save both time and space. An example is a square matrix $\mathbf{A}$ with the special form $\mathbf{A} = \mathbf{I}_n + \mathbf{u}\mathbf{v}^\mathrm{T}$. Then the product can be written

$$\mathbf{A}\mathbf{y} = (\mathbf{I}_n + \mathbf{u}\mathbf{v}^\mathrm{T})\mathbf{y} = \mathbf{y} + \mathbf{u}(\mathbf{v}^\mathrm{T}\mathbf{y}),$$

which leads to the simple code

```
s=0.
do i=1,n
s=s+v( i ) * y( i )
end do  ! loop on i
do i=1,n
z( i )=y( i )+s * u( i )
end do  ! loop on i
```

Whereas the usual matrix–vector multiplication requires n^2 multiplications, this code uses only $2n$. But notice that I took the liberty of storing the matrix $\mathbf{A}$ with only what is needed to produce it – namely, the vectors $\mathbf{u}$ and $\mathbf{v}$. In addition, if the vector $\mathbf{y}$ happens to be no longer needed, then **z** can be written on top of it, rewriting the penultimate code line as

```
y( i )=y( i )+s * u( i )
```

In spite of the potential danger, this trick is universally practiced to save space and produce crisp and clever code.

The avoidance of computation is best seen with the multiplication of triangular matrices. If **A** is upper triangular, then the product **Ay** can be computed by

```
do i=1,n
s=0.
do j=i,n
s=s+a( i,j ) * y( j )
end do   ! loop on j
z( i )=s
end do   ! loop on i
```

and the number of flops is $n(n + 1)/2$, reduced roughly by half. If the bottom part of **y** is zero (say, for $j > k$), then the upper limit of the do-loops is changed from n to k, further reducing the effort. The savings in multiplying two upper triangular matrices should now be apparent.

Some other tricks for saving space or time are relatively transparent. A matrix that can be produced with just a few numbers, such as a diagonal matrix or our $\mathbf{I}_n + \mathbf{u}\mathbf{v}^{\mathrm{T}}$ matrix, can be stored with substantially fewer than n^2 locations. Moreover, when storage space is at a premium, the elements of a matrix such as $\mathbf{I}_n + \mathbf{u}\mathbf{v}^{\mathrm{T}}$ would be computed only as needed. Symmetric or triangular matrices require only half the usual space; in fact, in Section 3.3, an upper triangular matrix and a unit (i.e., ones on the diagonal) lower triangular matrix are stored together in just n^2 locations. Remember that space is commonly the limiting factor in large problems.

3.3 Solving Triangular Systems

The systems of linear equations $\mathbf{A}\mathbf{x} = \mathbf{b}$ that are simplest to solve are triangular systems, where the matrix **A** is either upper or lower triangular. The case where **A** is diagonal is the simplest of all, and the code is trivial:

```
do i=1,n
x( i )=b( i )/a( i )
end do   ! loop on i
```

Notice that only the useful part of **A** is stored, and that the solution could be written on the input vector **b** with the statement

```
b( i )=b( i )/a( i )
```

Lower triangular systems can be solved in a straightforward fashion from the top down. First x_1 is computed, and this is used to compute x_2, et cetera, yielding the naive code

```
do i=1,n
s=0.
if( i>1 ) then
    im1=i-1
    do j=1,im1
    s=s+a( i,j ) * x( j )
    end do  ! loop on j
end if  ! ( i>1 )
x( i )=(b( i )-s)/a( i,i )
end do  ! loop on i
```

If we want to overwrite the solution vector on top of **b**, then the code is a little cleaner:

```
do i=1,n
if( i>1 ) then
    im1=i-1
    do j=1,im1
    b( i )=b( i )-a( i,j ) * b( j )
    end do  ! loop on j
end if  ! ( i>1 )
b( i )=b( i )/a( i,i )
end do  ! loop on i
```

In contrast, upper triangular systems are solved from the bottom up:

```
do ii=1,n
i=n+1-ii  ! count down from n to 1
if( n>i ) then
    ip1=i+1
    do j=ip1,n
    b( i )=b( i )-a( i,j ) * b( j )
    end do  ! loop on j
end if  ! ( n>i )
b( i )=b( i )/a( i,i )
end do  ! loop on i
```

We are assuming that the matrix **A** is nonsingular and so A_{ii} will never be zero; hence these algorithms will be able to obtain a solution to the equations.

3.4   Gaussian Elimination

The success enjoyed in solving triangular systems must be tempered with the realization that few real problems are triangular. But if a full system of linear equations could be converted to a triangular system, then that full system could be solved. The only legal operation for such a conversion is premultiplication by nonsingular matrix $\mathbf{B}$. That is, the system

$$\mathbf{Ax} = \mathbf{b} \quad \text{is equivalent to} \quad \mathbf{BAx} = \mathbf{Bb}, \tag{3.4.1}$$

so we seek a matrix $\mathbf{B}$ whose product $(\mathbf{BA})$ is triangular. In its simplest form, (3.4.1) is just adding multiples of rows together. Gaussian elimination constructs a sequence of simple matrices, each adding multiples of rows together, producing a triangular system in the end.

The first step in Gaussian elimination is the elimination of the elements in the first column of the matrix (with the exception of the first element) by adding multiples of the first row to the other rows. The multiple $-A_{i1}/A_{11}$ of the first row, when added to the ith row, will yield a zero in the first element of that row. If $\mathbf{M}^{(1)}$ denotes the matrix that adds those multiples of the first rows to the other rows, then the first step can be written with $\mathbf{A}^{(0)} = \mathbf{A}$ as

$$\mathbf{M}^{(1)}\mathbf{A}^{(0)} = \mathbf{A}^{(1)}$$

or

$$\begin{bmatrix} 1 & 0 & 0 & 0 \\ -A_{21}/A_{11} & 1 & 0 & 0 \\ -A_{31}/A_{11} & 0 & 1 & 0 \\ -A_{41}/A_{11} & 0 & 0 & 1 \end{bmatrix} \begin{bmatrix} A_{11}^{(0)} & A_{12}^{(0)} & A_{13}^{(0)} & A_{14}^{(0)} \\ A_{21}^{(0)} & A_{22}^{(0)} & A_{23}^{(0)} & A_{24}^{(0)} \\ A_{31}^{(0)} & A_{32}^{(0)} & A_{33}^{(0)} & A_{34}^{(0)} \\ A_{41}^{(0)} & A_{42}^{(0)} & A_{43}^{(0)} & A_{44}^{(0)} \end{bmatrix}$$

$$= \begin{bmatrix} A_{11}^{(1)} & A_{12}^{(1)} & A_{13}^{(1)} & A_{14}^{(1)} \\ 0 & A_{22}^{(1)} & A_{23}^{(1)} & A_{24}^{(1)} \\ 0 & A_{32}^{(1)} & A_{33}^{(1)} & A_{34}^{(1)} \\ 0 & A_{42}^{(1)} & A_{43}^{(1)} & A_{44}^{(1)} \end{bmatrix}.$$

Notice that the elements in the first row do not change. Next, we want to force zeros (eliminate) in the second column, but without introducing nonzeros in places where we just put zeros. This time, we add multiples of the second row, so that this second step is

$$\mathbf{M}^{(2)}\mathbf{A}^{(1)} = \mathbf{A}^{(2)}$$

or

$$\begin{bmatrix} 1 & 0 & 0 & 0 \\ 0 & 1 & 0 & 0 \\ 0 & -A_{32}^{(1)}/A_{22}^{(1)} & 1 & 0 \\ 0 & -A_{42}^{(1)}/A_{22}^{(1)} & 0 & 1 \end{bmatrix} \begin{bmatrix} A_{11}^{(1)} & A_{12}^{(1)} & A_{13}^{(1)} & A_{14}^{(1)} \\ 0 & A_{22}^{(1)} & A_{23}^{(1)} & A_{24}^{(1)} \\ 0 & A_{32}^{(1)} & A_{33}^{(1)} & A_{34}^{(1)} \\ 0 & A_{42}^{(1)} & A_{43}^{(1)} & A_{44}^{(1)} \end{bmatrix}$$

$$= \begin{bmatrix} A_{11}^{(2)} & A_{12}^{(2)} & A_{13}^{(2)} & A_{14}^{(2)} \\ 0 & A_{22}^{(2)} & A_{23}^{(2)} & A_{24}^{(2)} \\ 0 & 0 & A_{33}^{(2)} & A_{34}^{(2)} \\ 0 & 0 & A_{43}^{(2)} & A_{44}^{(2)} \end{bmatrix}.$$

Again, elements in the first two rows are left unchanged. The continuation of this procedure is the construction of a sequence of matrices $\mathbf{M}^{(k)}$, which are identity matrices except for the kth column below the diagonal, whose elements are the multipliers

$$M_{ik}^{(k)} = -A_{ik}^{(k-1)}/A_{kk}^{(k-1)}, \quad i = k+1, \ldots, n.$$

Each matrix $\mathbf{M}^{(k)}$ is lower triangular and can be written as

$$\mathbf{M}^{(k)} = \mathbf{I} - \mathbf{m}^{(k)}\mathbf{e}_k^{\mathrm{T}}, \tag{3.4.2}$$

where the column vector of multipliers has elements

$$m_i^{(k)} = \begin{cases} 0 & \text{if } i \le k, \\ A_{ik}^{(k-1)}/A_{kk}^{(k-1)} & \text{if } i = k+1, \ldots, n. \end{cases} \tag{3.4.3}$$

Then a sequence of matrices $\mathbf{A}^{(k)} = \mathbf{M}^{(k)}\mathbf{A}^{(k-1)}$ are produced, the last of which ($\mathbf{A}^{(n-1)}$) is upper triangular. This has been the plan: to convert the problem into solving a triangular system. Of course, to solve the original problem, we must not forget to multiply the right-hand side $\mathbf{b}$ by $\mathbf{M}^{(k)}$ at each step and then backsolve the upper triangular system so produced.

Notice that we can solve the triangular system if its diagonal elements, $A_{kk}^{(n-1)}$ ($k = 1, \ldots, n$), are all nonzero. Recall that these are the divisors (also called "pivots") in the $\mathbf{M}$ matrices for each step, so that if one of these were zero then the procedure would have stopped earlier. In fact, the product of the first j of these diagonal elements equals the determinant of the submatrix of $\mathbf{A}$ formed by the first j rows and columns. But can the procedure for Gaussian elimination described so far solve the problem intended for it – namely, a square and consistent set of equations? The answer is simply that it cannot, for a trivial counterexample is

$$\begin{bmatrix} 0 & 1 \\ 1 & 0 \end{bmatrix} \begin{bmatrix} x_1 \\ x_2 \end{bmatrix} = \begin{bmatrix} b_1 \\ b_2 \end{bmatrix}.$$

However, the simple permutation of the two rows in this expression yields an upper triangular system. So when faced with a pivot that is zero, an alternative is to permute two rows of the current $\mathbf{A}^{(k)}$ (and the right-hand side also) and so avoid this trap. Initially, any nonzero element in the kth column on or below the diagonal (switching a row above the diagonal will mess up the pattern of zeros) appears to be a candidate. Yet we know that, with floating point numbers, exact zeros are rare; for this problem, near zeros might occur from a real zero through roundoff error. But before accepting just any candidate that is "not too close" to zero, why not take the one that is actually the farthest from zero? That is exactly what ought to be done, to switch row k with the row (say, row j) with the largest (in absolute value) element in the kth column on or below the diagonal. Premultiplication by an elementary permutation matrix, $\mathbf{P}(k, j)$, switches rows k and j. The sequence of matrices can now be written

$$\mathbf{A}^{(k)} = \mathbf{M}^{(k)}\mathbf{P}(k, j_k)\mathbf{A}^{(k-1)}, \tag{3.4.4}$$

and the computations for the right-hand side are

$$\mathbf{M}^{(n-1)}\mathbf{P}(n-1, j_{n-1}) \cdots \mathbf{M}^{(2)}\mathbf{P}(2, j_2)\mathbf{M}^{(1)}\mathbf{P}(1, j_1)\mathbf{b}. \tag{3.4.5}$$

These permutations, known as *partial pivoting,* must be done in order to solve the problem that was posed – a system of consistent equations. The additional effort of searching for the largest of $(n - k)$ elements is easy and only $O(n^2)$ in magnitude.

When implementing Gaussian elimination with partial pivoting, the original matrix is usually destroyed and overwritten at each step by $\mathbf{A}^{(k)}$, as is the right-hand side. If $\mathbf{A}$ or $\mathbf{b}$ must be saved, then make a copy. The computations that produce the zeros in the lower triangular part are not done. Moreover, each column $\mathbf{m}^{(k)}$ can be stored in the column of zeros that are created at each step, so that the matrices $\mathbf{M}^{(k)}$ can be saved without using any more space. Remarkably, storing the matrices in this way leads to a useful factorization of the matrix $\mathbf{A}$:

$$\mathbf{PA} = \mathbf{LU}, \tag{3.4.6}$$

where $\mathbf{U} = \mathbf{A}^{(n-1)}$ is upper triangular and the matrix $\mathbf{P}$ is the permutation matrix composed of the product of the elementary ones

$$\mathbf{P} = \mathbf{P}(n - 1, j_{n-1}) \cdots \mathbf{P}(2, j_2)\mathbf{P}(1, j_1). \tag{3.4.7}$$

The matrix $\mathbf{L}$ is a unit (ones on the diagonal) lower triangular matrix whose elements below the diagonal are those stored in the zero part of $\mathbf{U} = \mathbf{A}^{(n-1)}$, permuted as the rows of $\mathbf{A}^{(k)}$ are

$$\mathbf{L} = \mathbf{I}_n + \mathbf{m}_*^{(1)}\mathbf{e}_1^{\mathrm{T}} + \cdots + \mathbf{m}_*^{(n-1)}\mathbf{e}_{n-1}^{\mathrm{T}}, \tag{3.4.8}$$

where

$$\mathbf{m}_*^{(k)} = \mathbf{P}(n - 1, j_{n-1}) \cdots \mathbf{P}(k + 1, j_{k+1})\mathbf{m}^{(k)}. \tag{3.4.9}$$

The details are examined in Exercises 3.6–3.9.

Example 3.1: *Gaussian Elimination to Produce the LU Factorization*

$$\mathbf{A} = \begin{bmatrix} 1 & 2 & -1 & 0 \\ 1/2 & 1 & 0 & 1 \\ 0 & 2 & -1/2 & 3/2 \\ 1 & -1 & 3/2 & 0 \end{bmatrix}$$

and the final result is

$$\mathbf{PA} = \mathbf{LU} = \begin{bmatrix} 1 & 2 & -1 & 0 \\ 1 & -1 & 3/2 & 0 \\ 0 & 2 & -1/2 & 3/2 \\ 1/2 & 1 & 0 & 1 \end{bmatrix}.$$

The maximum elements of column 1 are in rows 1 and 4, with no gain in switching, so $\mathbf{P}(1, 1) = \mathbf{I}_n$ is the first permutation matrix.

$$\mathbf{A} = \mathbf{A}^{(0)} = \begin{bmatrix} 1 & 2 & -1 & 0 \\ 1/2 & 1 & 0 & 1 \\ 0 & 2 & -1/2 & 3/2 \\ 1 & -1 & 3/2 & 0 \end{bmatrix},$$

$$\mathbf{m}^{(1)} = \begin{bmatrix} 0 \\ 1/2 \\ 0 \\ 1 \end{bmatrix}, \qquad \mathbf{M}^{(1)}\mathbf{P}(1,1)\mathbf{A}^{(0)} = \mathbf{A}^{(1)}.$$

The maximum eligible element of column 2 is in row 4; switch rows 2 and 4, so $\mathbf{P}(2,4)$ is the second permutation matrix.

$$\mathbf{A}^{(1)} = \begin{bmatrix} 1 & 2 & -1 & 0 \\ 0 & 0 & 1/2 & 1 \\ 0 & 2 & -1/2 & 3/2 \\ 0 & -3 & 5/2 & 0 \end{bmatrix}, \qquad \mathbf{P}(2,4)\mathbf{A}^{(1)} = \begin{bmatrix} 1 & 2 & -1 & 0 \\ 0 & -3 & 5/2 & 0 \\ 0 & 2 & -1/2 & 3/2 \\ 0 & 0 & 1/2 & 1 \end{bmatrix},$$

$$\mathbf{m}^{(2)} = \begin{bmatrix} 0 \\ 0 \\ -2/3 \\ 0 \end{bmatrix}, \qquad \mathbf{M}^{(2)}\mathbf{P}(2,4)\mathbf{A}^{(1)} = \mathbf{A}^{(2)}.$$

The maximum element of column 3 is in row 3; no switching, so $\mathbf{P}(3,3) = \mathbf{I}_n$.

$$A^{(2)} = \begin{bmatrix} 1 & 2 & -1 & 0 \\ 0 & -3 & 5/2 & 0 \\ 0 & 0 & 7/6 & 3/2 \\ 0 & 0 & 1/2 & 1 \end{bmatrix}, \qquad \mathbf{P}(3,3)\mathbf{A}^{(2)} = \begin{bmatrix} 1 & 2 & -1 & 0 \\ 0 & -3 & 5/2 & 0 \\ 0 & 0 & 7/6 & 3/2 \\ 0 & 0 & 1/2 & 1 \end{bmatrix},$$

$$\mathbf{m}^{(3)} = \begin{bmatrix} 0 \\ 0 \\ 0 \\ 3/7 \end{bmatrix}, \qquad \mathbf{M}^{(3)}\mathbf{P}(3,3)\mathbf{A}^{(2)} = \mathbf{A}^{(3)} = \mathbf{U} = \begin{bmatrix} 1 & 2 & -1 & 0 \\ 0 & -3 & 5/2 & 0 \\ 0 & 0 & 7/6 & 3/2 \\ 0 & 0 & 0 & 5/14 \end{bmatrix},$$

$$\mathbf{P}(3,3)\mathbf{P}(2,4)\mathbf{m}^{(1)} = \begin{bmatrix} 0 \\ 1 \\ 0 \\ 1/2 \end{bmatrix}.$$

Continuing with $\mathbf{P}(3,3)\mathbf{m}^{(2)}$, we can construct the lower factor $\mathbf{L}$ from (3.4.8):

$$\mathbf{L} = \mathbf{I} + \begin{bmatrix} 0 \\ 1 \\ 0 \\ 1/2 \end{bmatrix}\mathbf{e}_1^{\mathrm{T}} + \begin{bmatrix} 0 \\ 0 \\ -2/3 \\ 0 \end{bmatrix}\mathbf{e}_2^{\mathrm{T}} + \begin{bmatrix} 0 \\ 0 \\ 0 \\ 3/7 \end{bmatrix}\mathbf{e}_3^{\mathrm{T}} = \begin{bmatrix} 1 & 0 & 0 & 0 \\ 1 & 1 & 0 & 0 \\ 0 & -2/3 & 1 & 0 \\ 1/2 & 0 & 3/7 & 1 \end{bmatrix}.$$

As originally posed, the problem required that the right-hand side **b** be known in advance; however, once the factorization of **A** is computed, the solution of a new system of equations **Ax** = **b** can be done easily:

(1) permute the right-hand side **Pb**;
(2) solve the triangular system **Ly** = (**Pb**) for **y**;
(3) solve the triangular system **Ux** = **y** for **x**.

The advantage of this approach (i.e., computing the factorization and solving two triangular systems) over computing the inverse $\mathbf{A}^{-1}$ and multiplying $(\mathbf{A}^{-1})\mathbf{b}$ can be seen after the accounting of the work.

Example 3.2: *Solving a System of Equations with Gaussian Elimination*

$$\begin{bmatrix} 1 & 2 & -1 & 0 \\ 1/2 & 1 & 0 & 1 \\ 0 & 2 & -1/2 & 3/2 \\ 1 & -1 & 3/2 & 0 \end{bmatrix} \begin{bmatrix} x_1 \\ x_2 \\ x_3 \\ x_4 \end{bmatrix} = \begin{bmatrix} 1/2 \\ 1 \\ 3/2 \\ 2 \end{bmatrix}.$$

In the form **Ax** = **b**, the matrix **A** is the same as in Example 3.1, so let's use the factorization obtained there using Gaussian elimination: **PA** = **LU**. First solve **Ly** = (**Pb**) for **y**:

$$\mathbf{Ly} = \begin{bmatrix} 1 & 0 & 0 & 0 \\ 1 & 1 & 0 & 0 \\ 0 & -2/3 & 1 & 0 \\ 1/2 & 0 & 3/7 & 1 \end{bmatrix} \begin{bmatrix} y_1 \\ y_2 \\ y_3 \\ y_4 \end{bmatrix} = \mathbf{P}(3,3)\mathbf{P}(2,4)\mathbf{P}(1,1)\mathbf{b} = \begin{bmatrix} 1/2 \\ 2 \\ 3/2 \\ 1 \end{bmatrix},$$

$$\text{so } \mathbf{y} = \begin{bmatrix} 1/2 \\ 3/2 \\ 5/2 \\ -9/28 \end{bmatrix}.$$

Having **y**, now solve **Ux** = **y** for **x**:

$$\mathbf{Ux} = \begin{bmatrix} 1 & 2 & -1 & 0 \\ 0 & -3 & 5/2 & 0 \\ 0 & 0 & 7/6 & 3/2 \\ 0 & 0 & 0 & 5/14 \end{bmatrix} \begin{bmatrix} x_1 \\ x_2 \\ x_3 \\ x_4 \end{bmatrix} = \mathbf{y} = \begin{bmatrix} 1/2 \\ 3/2 \\ 5/2 \\ -9/28 \end{bmatrix}, \quad \text{so } \mathbf{x} = \begin{bmatrix} -7/10 \\ 9/4 \\ 33/10 \\ -9/10 \end{bmatrix}.$$

Computing the factorization requires $(2n - 3)(n - 1)(n - 2)/6$ multiplys and $(n - 1)(n - 2)/2$ divides as well as an equal number of additions and subtractions, or $n^3/3 + O(n^2)$ floating point operations or "flops." Solving the two triangular systems requires n^2 flops for each right-hand side. To compute the inverse from the factorization requires an additional $\frac{2}{3}n^3 + O(n^2)$ flops (see Exercise 3.2). To compute the inverse by full elimination (as in Section 4.2) also requires n^3 flops, so that the extra setup cost in computing the inverse is $\frac{2}{3}n^3$ flops. Multiplying the inverse and the right-hand side vector takes the same n^2 as solving the two triangular systems. In other words, the marginal cost for each additional right-hand side is the same under both schemes. Computing the inverse requires at least twice as much additional work as the factorization. We conclude that the inverse of a matrix should *never* be computed, unless:

(1) it is absolutely necessary to compute standard errors;
(2) the number of right-hand sides is so much larger than n that the extra cost is insignificant; or
(3) the size of n is so small that the costs are irrelevant.

Finally, one computation that is important in statistics is the determinant of a matrix. Some formulations of the determinant require an inordinate number of computations for a numerically suspect result. However, Gaussian elimination enables an efficient evaluation of the determinant, merely by multiplying the diagonal elements of $\mathbf{U}$ together and then adjusting by the odd or even number of permutations $\mathbf{P}(k, j_k)$, since

$$\det(\mathbf{P})\det(\mathbf{A}) = \det(\mathbf{PA}) = \det(\mathbf{LU}) = \det(\mathbf{U}).$$

The determinant of $\mathbf{P}(k, j_k)$ is -1 unless $k = j_k$, and the determinant of $\mathbf{L}$ is just 1.

3.5   Cholesky Decomposition

In statistics, the matrix $\mathbf{A}$ in the solution of linear equations $\mathbf{Ax} = \mathbf{b}$ is more often positive definite than not. The covariance matrix of a multivariate random variable $\mathbf{Y}$ is always nonnegative definite. The variance of a linear combination of the components $\text{var}(\mathbf{c}^T\mathbf{Y})$ can be expressed as a quadratic form in the covariance matrix $\mathbf{c}^T\text{cov}(\mathbf{Y})\mathbf{c}$. Because variances are nonnegative, so will be the quadratic form. If the covariance matrix is nonsingular then no nonzero linear combination $\mathbf{c}$ can give a zero variance or quadratic form, and the matrix is then called positive definite. Positive definite matrices arise in other areas wherever the matrix can be viewed as some form of covariance or as a sum of squares and cross-products matrix.

Gaussian elimination can be used to solve a system of equations with a positive definite matrix, but it cannot exploit the positive definiteness property. Positive definiteness is common enough and useful enough to warrant special treatment. Instead of an LU factorization, a positive definite matrix $\mathbf{A}$ can be factored into $\mathbf{LL}^T$, which exploits the symmetry of the matrix. Construction of this lower triangular matrix $\mathbf{L}$ also demonstrates that the original matrix $\mathbf{A}$ is positive definite.

The Cholesky decomposition (or square root algorithm) is inductive – assuming first that the matrix formed by the first $(k-1)$ rows and columns $\mathbf{A}^{[k-1]}$ has been factored,

$$\mathbf{A}^{[k-1]} = \mathbf{L}^{[k-1]}(\mathbf{L}^{[k-1]})^T,$$

to produce the factors for $\mathbf{A}^{[k]}$. Starting the induction is easy, just $A_{11} = L_{11}^2$. So now look at the kth step, factoring a $k \times k$ matrix, to find the new row of $\mathbf{L}^{[k]}$:

$$\begin{bmatrix} \mathbf{A}^{[k-1]} & \mathbf{a}^{[k]} \\ \mathbf{a}^{[k]T} & A_{kk} \end{bmatrix} = \begin{bmatrix} \mathbf{L}^{[k-1]} & \mathbf{0} \\ \boldsymbol{\ell}^{[k]T} & L_{kk} \end{bmatrix} \mathbf{L}^{[k]}$$

$$= \begin{bmatrix} \mathbf{L}^{[k-1]} & \mathbf{0} \\ \boldsymbol{\ell}^{[k]T} & L_{kk} \end{bmatrix} \begin{bmatrix} \mathbf{L}^{[k-1]T} & \boldsymbol{\ell}^{[k]} \\ \mathbf{0} & L_{kk} \end{bmatrix} \begin{matrix} k-1 \\ 1 \end{matrix}.$$

Because the factorization of $\mathbf{A}^{[k-1]}$ is assumed, this step presents two equations to be solved for the unknown $\boldsymbol{\ell}^{[k]}$ and L_{kk}, which comprise the kth row of $\mathbf{L}^{[k]}$:

$$\mathbf{L}^{[k-1]}\boldsymbol{\ell}^{[k]} = \mathbf{a}^{[k]} \tag{3.5.1}$$

and

$$L_{kk}^2 = A_{kk} - \boldsymbol{\ell}^{[k]\mathrm{T}}\boldsymbol{\ell}^{[k]}. \tag{3.5.2}$$

The first part of step k consists of solving the triangular system of equations (3.5.1) for $\boldsymbol{\ell}^{[k]}$ using the known $\mathbf{a}^{[k]}$ and previously computed $(k-1) \times (k-1)$ matrix $\mathbf{L}^{[k-1]}$. The second part of step k is computing the sum of squares of the solution vector $\boldsymbol{\ell}^{[k]}$, subtracting from the diagonal A_{kk}, and computing a square root for L_{kk}. Whether the right-hand side of (3.5.2) is positive serves as a test of the positive definiteness of $\mathbf{A}^{[k]}$, since a quadratic form in $\mathbf{A}$ with the vector

$$\begin{bmatrix} -(\mathbf{A}^{[k]})^{-1}\mathbf{a}^{[k]} \\ 1 \\ \mathbf{0} \end{bmatrix} \begin{matrix} k-1 \\ 1 \\ n-k \end{matrix}$$

will yield the right-hand side of (3.5.2). Thus, if the matrix $\mathbf{A}$ is positive definite then square roots can be computed at every step and the algorithm will run to completion, since each $\mathbf{L}^{[k]}$ will be nonsingular. If the factorization can be computed, then any quadratic form will be nonnegative because

$$\mathbf{x}^{\mathrm{T}}\mathbf{A}\mathbf{x} = \mathbf{x}^{\mathrm{T}}\mathbf{L}\mathbf{L}^{\mathrm{T}}\mathbf{x} = (\mathbf{L}^{\mathrm{T}}\mathbf{x})^{\mathrm{T}}(\mathbf{L}^{\mathrm{T}}\mathbf{x}) = \mathbf{y}^{\mathrm{T}}\mathbf{y} \geq 0$$

for $\mathbf{L}^{\mathrm{T}}\mathbf{x} = \mathbf{y}$. Since $\mathbf{L}$ is nonsingular, a zero $\mathbf{y}$ will occur only with a zero $\mathbf{x}$.

The Cholesky decomposition algorithm does require the computation of n square roots. Although a square root is a comparatively easy nonarithmetic operation, a variation of the Cholesky method, known as the "Cholesky decomposition without square roots," lives up to its name. The difference is that two matrices, one unit lower triangular $\mathbf{M}$ and one diagonal $\mathbf{D}$, are computed to yield $\mathbf{A} = \mathbf{M}\mathbf{D}\mathbf{M}^{\mathrm{T}}$. Again the algorithm is inductive; the beginning is just as simple, $D_{11} = A_{11}$, and the kth step is

$$\begin{bmatrix} \mathbf{A}^{[k-1]} & \mathbf{a}^{[k]} \\ \mathbf{a}^{[k]\mathrm{T}} & A_{kk} \end{bmatrix} = \begin{bmatrix} \mathbf{M}^{[k-1]} & \mathbf{0} \\ \mathbf{m}^{[k]\mathrm{T}} & 1 \end{bmatrix} \begin{bmatrix} \mathbf{D}^{[k-1]} & \mathbf{0} \\ \mathbf{0} & D_{kk} \end{bmatrix} \mathbf{M}^{[k]\mathrm{T}}.$$

The two equations to solve are the triangular system for $\mathbf{m}^{[k]}$,

$$\mathbf{M}^{[k-1]}\mathbf{D}^{[k-1]}\mathbf{m}^{[k]} = \mathbf{a}^{[k]} \tag{3.5.3}$$

and

$$D_{kk} = A_{kk} - \mathbf{m}^{[k]\mathrm{T}}\mathbf{D}^{[k-1]}\mathbf{m}^{[k]}. \tag{3.5.4}$$

Positive definite matrices are symmetric, so it should not be surprising that a matrix could be reproduced with only the $n(n+1)/2$ elements of $\mathbf{L}$. Since actually only about half of the n^2 storage locations for $\mathbf{A}$ or $\mathbf{L}$ are needed, can these matrices be stored in a compressed fashion? The answer is, of course, Yes, and the most convenient method is commonly called *symmetric storage mode,* although it is also useful for triangular matrices. Here, only the lower triangular part is stored; it is stored in a linear list, counting the elements along a row until the diagonal, as follows:

$$
\begin{array}{llllll}
1 & & & & \\
2 & 3 & & & \\
4 & 5 & 6 & & \\
7 & 8 & 9 & 10 & \\
11 & 12 & 13 & 14 & 15 \\
16 & \ldots,
\end{array}
$$

so that the i, j element is stored in location $(I * (I - 1))/2 + J$. If the matrix $\mathbf{A}$ is stored in this fashion, then $\mathbf{L}$ can be overwritten in the same space.

An accounting of the work in Cholesky factorization provides a valuable comparison. The factoring of an $n \times n$ matrix $\mathbf{A}$ into $\mathbf{LL}^\mathrm{T}$ requires a solution of a triangular system of length $(k - 1)$ at step k, requiring $k(k - 1)/2$ flops plus $(k - 1)$ more multiplys for the diagonal element. The total is then $n^3/6 + O(n^2)$ flops and n square roots. The effect of avoiding the square roots is only $O(n)$. Since the LU factorization from Gaussian elimination is $n^3/3 + O(n^2)$, the reduction by half in Cholesky's exploitation of symmetry should be expected. Although symmetry seems to be the only property exploited, note that the positive definite property is essential. Symmetric but not positive definite matrices are difficult to factor in a similar way.

Example 3.3: *Cholesky Factorization*

$$
\mathbf{A} = \begin{bmatrix} 4 & 2 & 2 & 4 \\ 2 & 5 & 7 & 0 \\ 2 & 7 & 19 & 11 \\ 4 & 0 & 11 & 25 \end{bmatrix} = \mathbf{LL}^\mathrm{T}, \quad \text{where } \mathbf{L} = \begin{bmatrix} 2 & 0 & 0 & 0 \\ 1 & 2 & 0 & 0 \\ 1 & 3 & 3 & 0 \\ 2 & -1 & 4 & 2 \end{bmatrix}.
$$

$k = 1$: $L_{11} = \sqrt{A_{11}} = \sqrt{4} = 2$.

$k = 2$: Solve $L_{11}L_{21} = A_{21}$ for the unknown L_{21}: $2L_{21} = 2$ gives $L_{21} = 1$; $L_{21}^2 + L_{22}^2 = A_{22}$, so that $1 + L_{22}^2 = 5$, leaving $L_{22} = 2$.

$k = 3$: Solve $\mathbf{L}^{[2]}\boldsymbol{\ell}^{[3]} = \mathbf{a}^{[3]}$, which is $\begin{bmatrix} 2 & 0 \\ 1 & 2 \end{bmatrix}\begin{bmatrix} L_{31} \\ L_{32} \end{bmatrix} = \begin{bmatrix} 2 \\ 7 \end{bmatrix}$, so $L_{31} = 1$ and $L_{32} = 3$; $L_{31}^2 + L_{32}^2 + L_{33}^2 = A_{33}$, so that $1 + 9 + L_{33}^2 = 19$, leaving $L_{33} = 3$.

$k = 4$: Solve $\mathbf{L}^{[3]}\boldsymbol{\ell}^{[4]} = \mathbf{a}^{[4]}$, which is $\begin{bmatrix} 2 & 0 & 0 \\ 1 & 2 & 0 \\ 1 & 3 & 3 \end{bmatrix}\begin{bmatrix} L_{41} \\ L_{42} \\ L_{43} \end{bmatrix} = \begin{bmatrix} 4 \\ 0 \\ 11 \end{bmatrix}$, so $L_{41} = 2$, $L_{42} = -1$, and $L_{43} = 4$; $L_{41}^2 + L_{42}^2 + L_{43}^2 + L_{44}^2 = A_{44}$, so that $4 + 1 + 16 + L_{44}^2 = 25$, leaving $L_{44} = 2$.

For the determinant, $|\mathbf{A}| = |\mathbf{L}|^2 = (2 \times 2 \times 3 \times 4)^2 = 24^2 = 2^8 \times (9/4)$ with $1 \le 9/4 \le 16$.

The advantages of avoiding computing the inverse of a matrix (discussed at the end of Section 3.4) are more easily seen when the matrix is positive definite. For computing a quadratic form in the inverse, say $\mathbf{x}^T\mathbf{A}^{-1}\mathbf{x}$, the Cholesky method leads to the following steps:

(1) factor $\mathbf{A} = \mathbf{L}\mathbf{L}^T$ ($n^3/6$ flops);
(2) solve the lower triangular system $\mathbf{L}\mathbf{y} = \mathbf{x}$ ($n^2/2$ flops);
(3) multiply $\mathbf{y}^T\mathbf{y} = \mathbf{x}^T\mathbf{L}^{-T}\mathbf{L}^{-1}\mathbf{x} = \mathbf{x}^T\mathbf{A}^{-1}\mathbf{x}$ (n flops).

Computing a common expression like $\mathbf{B}^T\mathbf{A}^{-1}\mathbf{B}$, where $\mathbf{B}$ is $n \times m$, can be done similarly as follows:

(1) factor $\mathbf{A} = \mathbf{L}\mathbf{L}^T$ ($n^3/6$ flops);
(2) solve the m lower triangular systems $\mathbf{L}\mathbf{C} = \mathbf{B}$ ($mn^2/2$ flops);
(3) multiply $\mathbf{C}^T\mathbf{C} = \mathbf{B}^T\mathbf{L}^{-T}\mathbf{L}^{-1}\mathbf{B} = \mathbf{B}^T\mathbf{A}^{-1}\mathbf{B}$ ($m^2n/2$ flops).

The $\mathbf{M}\mathbf{D}\mathbf{M}^T$ algorithm without square roots leads to a similar solution.

Example 3.4: *Solving a System of Equations Using Cholesky Factorization*

$$\mathbf{A}\mathbf{x} = \begin{bmatrix} 4 & 2 & 2 & 4 \\ 2 & 5 & 7 & 0 \\ 2 & 7 & 19 & 11 \\ 4 & 0 & 11 & 25 \end{bmatrix} \begin{bmatrix} x_1 \\ x_2 \\ x_3 \\ x_4 \end{bmatrix} = \mathbf{b} = \begin{bmatrix} -1 \\ 1 \\ 5/2 \\ 1/4 \end{bmatrix}.$$

First solve $\mathbf{L}\mathbf{y} = \mathbf{b}$ for the unknown vector $\mathbf{y}$:

$$\mathbf{L}\mathbf{y} = \begin{bmatrix} 2 & 0 & 0 & 0 \\ 1 & 2 & 0 & 0 \\ 1 & 3 & 3 & 0 \\ 2 & -1 & 4 & 2 \end{bmatrix} \begin{bmatrix} y_1 \\ y_2 \\ y_3 \\ y_4 \end{bmatrix} = \mathbf{b} = \begin{bmatrix} -1 \\ 1 \\ 5/2 \\ 1/4 \end{bmatrix}, \quad \text{so } \mathbf{y} = \begin{bmatrix} -1/2 \\ 3/4 \\ 1/4 \\ 1/2 \end{bmatrix}.$$

Then solve $\mathbf{L}^T\mathbf{x} = \mathbf{y}$ for the unknown vector $\mathbf{x}$:

$$\mathbf{L}^T\mathbf{x} = \begin{bmatrix} 2 & 1 & 1 & 2 \\ 0 & 2 & 3 & -1 \\ 0 & 0 & 3 & 4 \\ 0 & 0 & 0 & 2 \end{bmatrix} \begin{bmatrix} x_1 \\ x_2 \\ x_3 \\ x_4 \end{bmatrix} = \mathbf{y} = \begin{bmatrix} -1/2 \\ 3/4 \\ 1/4 \\ 1/2 \end{bmatrix}, \quad \text{so } \mathbf{x} = \begin{bmatrix} -13/16 \\ 7/8 \\ -1/4 \\ 1/4 \end{bmatrix}.$$

Finally, one of the most useful applications of the Cholesky factorization is as a parameterization for a positive definite matrix. This form of factorization is unique, so that the correspondence between $\mathbf{A}$ and $\mathbf{L}$ is one-to-one. Moreover, some ugly calculus can (a) show that the transformation is continuous and (b) find its Jacobian. Parameterization by $\mathbf{L}$, with just positive diagonals, imposes the positive definite constraint implicitly and avoids the complicated quadratic nonnegativity constraints, which are difficult to impose explicitly.

3.6 Matrix Norms

Before analyzing the condition of the problem of solving a system of linear equations, we need to examine ways of measuring the size of matrices. These techniques have statistical applications other than in this narrow problem, but they are rarely discussed elsewhere. As a result, this discussion will appear more mathematical than the reader might expect.

Norms are used to measure the sizes of things because rescaling just rescales the norm, and the triangle inequality is satisfied. Before looking at measuring the size of matrices, consider first the norms of vectors. The length of a vector can be measured by the p-norms,

$$\|\mathbf{a}\|_p = \left(\sum_{i=1}^n |a_i|^p \right)^{1/p},$$

with the provision that, for $p = \infty$, $\|\mathbf{a}\|_\infty = \max_i |a_i|$. The other two important choices for p give familiar results: $p = 2$ gives the traditional Euclidean norm, and for $p = 1$ we have $\|\mathbf{a}\|_1 = \sum |a_i|$. Rescaling a vector $c\mathbf{a}$ with $c > 0$ just rescales the norm $\|c\mathbf{a}\| = c\|\mathbf{a}\|$, and the triangle inequality is satisfied: $\|\mathbf{a} + \mathbf{b}\| \le \|\mathbf{a}\| + \|\mathbf{b}\|$. These well-known vector norms are then used to derive norms for general $m \times n$ matrices. The p-norm of a matrix $\mathbf{A}$ is the supremum over all vectors $\mathbf{x}$ of the ratio

$$\frac{\sup_\mathbf{x} \|\mathbf{A}\mathbf{x}\|_p}{\|\mathbf{x}\|_p} = \|\mathbf{A}\|_p.$$

Here, all of the norms are taken using the same value of p. Three values of p give simple and intuitive values for these norms as follows:

(1) for $p = 1$, $\|\mathbf{A}\| = \max_j \sum_i |A_{ij}|$ (column sum norm);
(2) for $p = 2$, $\|\mathbf{A}\| = $ (largest eigenvalue of $\mathbf{A}^T\mathbf{A}$)$^{1/2}$ (Euclidean norm);
(3) for $p = \infty$, $\|\mathbf{A}\| = \max_i \sum_j |A_{ij}|$ (row sum norm).

The simplicity of the 1 and ∞ norms make these two the most common for use in numerical analysis, while the Euclidean norm is the natural one for least squares and eigenproblems as well as most problems in statistics. A fourth easily computed norm, the Frobenius norm, can be used with $p = 2$:

$$\|\mathbf{A}\|_F = \left[\sum_{i=1}^m \sum_{j=1}^n A_{ij}^2 \right]^{1/2} \quad \text{(Frobenius norm)}.$$

The simplicity of the Frobenius norm over the usual 2-norm can be exploited through the inequality $\|\mathbf{A}\|_2 \le \|\mathbf{A}\|_F$. All of these matrix norms are designed to satisfy the inequality

$$\|\mathbf{A}\mathbf{x}\|_p \le \|\mathbf{A}\|_p \|\mathbf{x}\|_p \tag{3.6.1}$$

in order to bound the effect of multiplication; the Frobenius norm satisfies (3.6.1) with $p = 2$. This simple relation can be extended to handle products and powers of matrices in the following way:

$$\|\mathbf{A}\mathbf{B}\mathbf{x}\|_p \le \|\mathbf{A}\|_p \|\mathbf{B}\mathbf{x}\|_p \le \|\mathbf{A}\|_p \|\mathbf{B}\|_p \|\mathbf{x}\|_p, \tag{3.6.2}$$

so that $\|\mathbf{AB}\|_p \le \|\mathbf{A}\|_p \|\mathbf{B}\|_p$. For $\mathbf{A} = \mathbf{B}$, this relation becomes $\|\mathbf{A}^2\|_p \le \|\mathbf{A}\|_p^2$, and extending to powers gives $\|\mathbf{A}^k\|_p \le \|\mathbf{A}\|_p^k$.

For applications of these norms, consider first the von Neumann series

$$(\mathbf{I} - \mathbf{B})^{-1} = \mathbf{I} + \mathbf{B} + \mathbf{B}^2 + \mathbf{B}^3 + \cdots . \tag{3.6.3}$$

In what sense is this infinite series in matrices the inverse of a matrix? More fundamentally, what is the meaning of such an infinite series? The natural route is to define the infinite series as the limit of the partial sum

$$\sum_{k=0}^{\infty} \mathbf{B}^k \equiv \lim_{m \to \infty} \mathbf{S}_m, \quad \text{where } \mathbf{S}_m \equiv \mathbf{I} + \mathbf{B} + \mathbf{B}^2 + \cdots + \mathbf{B}^m.$$

The meaning of the limit (and whether the limit exists) depends on the norm $\|\mathbf{B}\| = b$, for simplicity. In this case, $\|S_m\| \le 1 + b + b^2 + \cdots + b^m = (1 - b^{m+1})/(1 - b)$, and the series converges in an absolute sense only if b is strictly less than 1. If $b = 1$, then the bound is infinite and the result is inconclusive. Examining the inverse, notice that

$$(\mathbf{I} - \mathbf{B})\mathbf{S}_m = \mathbf{I} - \mathbf{B}^{m+1};$$

the difference from the identity converges to zero if $\|\mathbf{B}\| = b < 1$, since

$$\|\mathbf{I} - (\mathbf{I} - \mathbf{B})\mathbf{S}_m\| = \|\mathbf{I} - (\mathbf{I} - \mathbf{B}^{m+1})\| = \|\mathbf{B}^{m+1}\| \le b^{m+1} \to 0.$$

Consequently, if $\|\mathbf{B}\| < 1$ then the infinite series makes sense, and it does express the inverse of a matrix.

3.7 Accuracy and Conditioning

In Section 2.7, a distinction was made between the conditioning of a problem and the stability of an algorithm to compute a solution to that problem. *Conditioning,* remember, measured the effect of small changes of the input, here $\mathbf{A}$ and $\mathbf{b}$, on the solution vector $\mathbf{x}$. *Stability* measured the closeness of the given problem to the problem whose exact solution is the computed solution $\mathbf{x}^*$. Analysis of stability focuses on the algorithms and the arithmetic. This section begins with conditioning, using the mathematical tools of matrix norms begun in the previous section.

For the analysis of the conditioning of the solution of the linear equations $\mathbf{Ax} = \mathbf{b}$, the first main result is

$$\|\mathbf{A}^{-1} - (\mathbf{A} + \mathbf{E})^{-1}\|_p \le \frac{\|\mathbf{A}^{-1}\|_p \|\mathbf{A}^{-1}\mathbf{E}\|_p}{1 - \|\mathbf{A}^{-1}\mathbf{E}\|_p}. \tag{3.7.1}$$

(Stewart 1973, thm. 3.3.6). Using (3.7.1), defining the quantity $\kappa = \|\mathbf{A}\|_p \|\mathbf{A}^{-1}\|_p$, and dividing both numerator and denominator on the right by $\|\mathbf{A}^{-1}\|$ yields the inequality

$$\frac{\|\mathbf{A}^{-1} - (\mathbf{A} + \mathbf{E})^{-1}\|_p}{\|\mathbf{A}^{-1}\|_p} \le \frac{\kappa \|\mathbf{E}\|_p / \|\mathbf{A}\|_p}{1 - \kappa \|\mathbf{E}\|_p / \|\mathbf{A}\|_p}. \tag{3.7.2}$$

The left-hand side of (3.7.2) shows the relative change in the magnitude of the inverse of the matrix $\mathbf{A}$. As $\|\mathbf{E}\|_p$ gets small, the denominator of the right-hand side approaches unity; then

$$\kappa = \|\mathbf{A}\|_p \|\mathbf{A}^{-1}\|_p \qquad\qquad (3.7.3)$$

can be appropriately called the *condition number* of the matrix $\mathbf{A}$, since it is the factor that magnifies the relative change in the matrix $\mathbf{A}$. Mathematically, the solution of a system of equations is only the inverse of the transformation $\mathbf{A}$, so the right-hand side $\mathbf{b}$ does not affect the conditioning of the problem. If the elements of the inverse are much larger in magnitude than just the reciprocals of any typical element of the original matrix, then this serves as a warning that the condition number will likely be large. Recall that when we have multicollinearity in regression the variances, reflecting $(\mathbf{X}^T\mathbf{X})^{-1}$, are unusually large and thus reflect the poor conditioning of the problem (for the problem of estimation).

Example 3.5: *Condition of the Hilbert Matrix and the Condition Estimate*
The Hilbert matrix is a notoriously badly conditioned matrix arising from a rather simple form: $A_{ij} = 1/(i + j - 1)$. This matrix arises in many situations; one of the simplest is as the inner product matrix of the polynomial basis functions $\{1, x, x^2, \dots\}$ with respect to the integral on the unit interval. That is, let $f_j(x) \equiv x^{j-1}$, and define $\langle f, g \rangle = \int_0^1 f(x)g(x)\,dx = A_{ij}$. These matrices have been used for years to push matrix routines to the limit. Whereas the elements of the matrix are reciprocals of integers and thus cannot be accurately expressed in floating point arithmetic, the elements of the inverse *are* integers – and large ones at that.

To compute the condition number of a Hilbert matrix of order n, begin with the norm of the matrix, which is rather easy: $\|\mathbf{A}\|_\infty = H_n = 1 + 1/2 + \cdots + 1/n$, the harmonic sum, since the max row sum occurs in the first row. Knuth (1997, pp. 38, 474–5) gave a formula for the elements of the inverse matrix $\mathbf{B}$:

$$(\mathbf{A}^{-1})_{ij} = B_{ij} = (-1)^{i+j}j\binom{i+j-2}{i-1}\binom{i+n-1}{i-1}\binom{j+n-1}{n-i}\binom{n}{j},$$

so $\|\mathbf{A}^{-1}\|_\infty$ can also be computed. The elements of the inverse hit the fixed point overflow rather quickly, for values as small as $n = 8$. The routine **gaucpp** also computes the Golub–van Loan version of the Cline, Moler, Stewart, and Wilkinson (1979) method for computing an estimate $1/\hat{\kappa}$ of the reciprocal of the condition number $1/\kappa$. These Hilbert matrices can then be used to evaluate the performance of this estimator, using the inverse matrix $\mathbf{B} = \mathbf{A}^{-1}$ as the input matrix since the roundoff error in entry can be avoided by using $\mathbf{B}$ (the elements of $\mathbf{A}$ cannot be entered exactly). The following table shows how badly conditioned the Hilbert matrix is:

n	$1/\kappa$	$1/\hat{\kappa}$
2	4×10^{-2}	7×10^{-2}
3	1×10^{-3}	2×10^{-3}
4	4×10^{-5}	5×10^{-5}
5	1×10^{-6}	2×10^{-6}
6	3×10^{-8}	5×10^{-8}
7	1×10^{-9}	1×10^{-9}

The estimate $1/\hat{\kappa}$ does a very good job of keeping close to the true with these matrices. When the reciprocal of the condition drops below the machine unit, then one cannot expect a method such as Gaussian elimination to work. See the demonstration program **chex35**.

A second result gives us an inequality on the computed solution $\mathbf{x}^*$ to the problem $\mathbf{A}\mathbf{x} = \mathbf{b}$:

$$\frac{\|\mathbf{x} - \mathbf{x}^*\|_p}{\|\mathbf{x}\|_p} \leq \frac{\kappa \|\mathbf{b} - \mathbf{b}^*\|_p}{\|\mathbf{b}\|_p}, \tag{3.7.4}$$

where $\mathbf{b}^* = \mathbf{A}\mathbf{x}^*$ so that $\mathbf{b} - \mathbf{b}^*$ is the computed residual. More directly, (3.7.4) shows how relative changes in the input – here, the right-hand side $\mathbf{b}$ – are amplified by κ to bound the relative error changes in the solution. The bad news revealed in (3.7.4) is that, when the condition number κ is large, a small residual $\mathbf{b} - \mathbf{b}^*$ may belie a large error in the computed solution $\mathbf{x}^*$. In practice, this result should be used in the following way: since the right-hand side $\mathbf{b}$ must be rounded with an error $O(U)$, it follows that the relative error in the computed solution could be as large as $O(\kappa U)$.

Example 3.6: Condition of Interpolation
In Chapter 7, the numerical instability of interpolation with high-degree polynomials will be discussed in more detail. Here, the interpolation problem merely presents two easy cases of a badly conditioned system of equations and one that is not so severe. Interpolation of a function $f(x)$ at n points $\{x_i, i = 1, \ldots, n\}$ with a polynomial of degree $n - 1$ leads to the problem of solving a system of equations for each point i $(i = 1, \ldots, n)$:

$$c_1 + c_2 x_i + c_3 x_i^2 + \cdots + c_n x_i^{n-1} = y_i = f(x_i).$$

Writing these in matrix form as $\mathbf{A}\mathbf{c} = \mathbf{y}$ produces a *Vandermonde matrix,* with entries $A_{ij} = x_i^{j-1}$. Various properties of Vandermonde matrices are known in closed form, usually following its connection with interpolation. Here we are interested in solving a system of equations and watching how the solution changes with small changes in the right-hand side $\mathbf{y}$. Two choices of abscissas $\{x_i\}$ are available in the demonstration program **chex36**:

(1) equally spaced abscissas, $x_i = (2i - 1 - n)/2n$;
(2) Chebyshev abscissas, $x_i = \cos\big((2i - 1)\pi)/2n\big)$.

The interpolated function has less effect, in this case $f(x) = 1/(1 + x^2)$. The condition numbers for these two choices vary tremendously, even for small values of n. For $n = 4$, which gives cubic interpolation, the equally spaced Vandermonde matrix has an estimated reciprocal condition number $1/\hat{\kappa}$ of .01 (computed using **gaucpp**). Also for $n = 4$, the matrix formed by using the Chebyshev abscissas has $1/\hat{\kappa} = .37$, which is rather well conditioned. The effects of these different abscissas can be seen as the right-hand sides are perturbed by $\pm\varepsilon$ in mimicking (3.7.4). For ε at 10^{-5}, the relative change in the solution $\mathbf{c}$ is magnified by a factor of 85 for the equally spaced case but by a factor of only 5 for the Chebyshev case. See the program **chex36** for further details; see also Exercise 3.24.

The analysis of the stability of Gaussian elimination leads to a great deal of detailed mathematics (see e.g. Stewart 1973, sec. 3.5). Exact error analysis, for all of the hard work, turns out to give predictions that are unrealistically pessimistic in practice. Conflicting with this experience is that the matrices that provide the worst cases *can* be constructed, so that the theory cannot be improved to give less pessimistic error bounds. For most practical problems, however, Gaussian elimination with partial pivoting should be considered a stable algorithm. That is, the computed solution $\mathbf{x}^*$ is the exact solution to the problem $(\mathbf{A} + \mathbf{E})\mathbf{x} = \mathbf{b}$, where $\|\mathbf{E}\|$ is $O(\|\mathbf{A}\|U)$. The warning signals for the exceptional cases are computed solutions that are inordinately large in value and pivots that are threateningly small. Cholesky decomposition is stable, unconditionally so if the inner products are accumulated in double precision. A generation ago, the common prediction was that roundoff error would limit the size of matrices for which linear equations could be solved to around $n = 100$. That prediction has not been realized and now appears foolish.

If these comforting words are not sufficient, there are tools for improving the condition of the problem and the accuracy of the solution. For the latter, iterative improvement is discussed in the next chapter. The condition of the problem can be improved by judicious scaling of the problem – that is, multiplying all of the rows of $\mathbf{A}$ and also $\mathbf{b}$ by the same constant. Similarly, the columns of $\mathbf{A}$ can be adjusted if reciprocal adjustments are made on the solution vector $\mathbf{x}$. When all of the elements of the matrix are nearly the same magnitude, then the condition number can be reduced dramatically and many difficulties avoided. Even without a conscious effort to equalize the magnitudes of the elements, the common sense of avoiding any great disparities will prevent most problems. However, no automatic method of rescaling rows and columns has been found that can cure all ills.

Finally, although the condition number κ of a matrix holds the key to the accuracy of the solution, computing the condition number faces real obstacles. In particular, the inverse matrix $\mathbf{A}^{-1}$ needs to be computed, despite the contrary admonition at the beginning of this chapter. Computing the inverse entails $\frac{2}{3}n^3 + O(n^2)$ flops in additional work, but it is difficult to compute in cases where the condition number is large. Another route would be to compute the Euclidean norm, but this eigenproblem would be even more costly. We seek a method of computing the condition number κ (or a reliable estimate) in $O(n^2)$ additional work. Such an estimate should remain reliable even as κ grows large. Cline et al. (1979) proposed an estimator satisfying these requirements; Golub and van Loan (1996, pp. 76–8) presented a version based on the ∞-norm. This method is used by **gaucpp** and exploited in **chex36**. The accuracy of this estimate is assessed by **cdnxpmt**; see the following example.

Example 3.7: *Performance of the Condition Estimator* $1/\hat{\kappa}$
Stewart (1980) discussed the generation of random orthogonal matrices, but the goal of his paper is a Monte Carlo study of the performance of the condition estimator of Cline et al. (1979). Stewart's approach is to compute matrices with

approximately the same 2-norm yet with the ability to accurately and simply compute the matrix and its inverse. This part of his methodology is beyond the level of this chapter, but the reader would be well equipped after reading Chapter 5. In the file **cdnxpmt.out** are the results of a Monte Carlo study of my implementation of the Golub–van Loan ∞-norm version of this method (described previously). The study is a three-factor $\{n,$ condition number (2-norm), construction$\}$ factorial with two replications. Since the condition number under the 2-norm is the square root of the ratio of the largest and smallest eigenvalues of $\mathbf{A}^T\mathbf{A}$, two simple methods of construction were used by Stewart to arrange the intermediate eigenvalues: all but the smallest equal (sharp break), and exponentially decaying from the largest to the smallest. Four levels of n (5, 10, 25, 50) and four levels of κ_2 (10, 100, 10^3, 10^4) were used, and the median of the ratio $\kappa_\infty/\hat{\kappa}_\infty$ from 25 sample matrices was reported as the statistic. Over this wide range, the condition estimator $\hat{\kappa}$ tends to underestimate, with the worst cases at $n = 50$, and slightly worse for larger condition numbers. Although the underestimate may appear grievous with ratios as big as 20, from a practical point of view the performance of $\hat{\kappa}$ makes it a useful tool because it involves comparatively little additional computation over the required Gaussian elimination LU factorization. See Exercise 3.26 and **cdnxpmt**.

For positive definite systems of equations, that is, when $\mathbf{A}$ is positive definite, a different type of evidence on the condition of the problem may be available when an algorithm to compute the Cholesky factorization fails. An instinctive response to the failure of Cholesky is to ignore the theoretical positive definiteness and use another method, such as Gaussian elimination, to compute a solution to these equations. The question to ask, however, is whether a solution computed using Gaussian elimination (or any other method) has any real value. Because of rounding error, we are computing the exact solution to a nearby problem – with $\mathbf{A} + \mathbf{E}$ as the matrix – but this matrix is singular. The failure of Cholesky brings us back to the original problem to find another route, but it should also trigger a question whether a solution computed some other way would have any value.

Finally, this discussion about the condition number would be incomplete without the following caveat. The condition number is a useful summary of the ease or difficulty in solving a linear system of equations, reflected in how changes in the matrix $\mathbf{A}$ or the right-hand side $\mathbf{b}$ affects the solution. The particular application will suggest the *magnitude* and *pattern* of the changes. Some elements of the matrix are always exactly one; some elements may have been already rounded to four decimal digits. Take, for example, the following simple 3×3 matrix

$$\mathbf{A} = \begin{bmatrix} 100 & 0 & -200 \\ 1 & -1 & 0 \\ 0 & .01 & -.01 \end{bmatrix}$$

whose condition number according to the $p = 1$ norm is approximately 10^5. Indeed, if we add 10^{-6} to each element of $\mathbf{A}$, we will see changes in the inverse of approximately .2.

But the scaling of the rows of the problem may suggest that certain patterns of the changes are unlikely. Depending on the application, it may be that possible changes in the first rows of **A** are 100 times as big as what one might expect in the second row, and the changes in the third row may be $1/100$ of changes in the second row. And so, the change matrix $\mathbf{E}_1$ below may be quite unlikely, but $\mathbf{E}_2$ more realistic

$$\mathbf{E}_1 = \begin{bmatrix} 10^{-6} & 10^{-6} & 10^{-6} \\ 10^{-6} & 10^{-6} & 10^{-6} \\ 10^{-6} & 10^{-6} & 10^{-6} \end{bmatrix}, \mathbf{E}_2 = \begin{bmatrix} .0001 & .0001 & .0001 \\ 10^{-6} & 1^{-6} & 10^{-6} \\ 10^{-8} & 10^{-8} & 10^{-8} \end{bmatrix}.$$

In such a case, the matrix **A** is *artificially ill-conditioned* (Stewart and Sun, 1990, p. 122ff); we should scale the rows of **A** appropriately, leading to a matrix whose condition number is just 15. If we are looking at changes in the right hand side, again, *depending on the application*, if we expect changes something like $\mathbf{e}_1 = (10^{-6}, 10^{-6}, 10^{-6})^T$, then, again, 10^5 is the appropriate condition number. But if the pattern may be more like $\mathbf{e}_2 = (.0001, 10^{-6}, 10^{-8})^T$, then the problem is artificially ill-conditioned and the rows of **A** should be rescaled.

More generally, if by appropriate rescaling we change an ill-conditioned problem to a well-conditioned one, then we can say that the original problem was artificially ill-conditioned. The particular application dictates what scaling might be appropriate. For solving linear equations, if changes in any component of the right-hand side **b** are equivalent, based on the application, then rescaling rows would not be appropriate. If changes in any component of the solution vector are viewed equally, then rescaling rows should be similarly proscribed.

3.8   Matrix Computations in R

Even though vector and matrix computation is a natural part of R, the user must be mindful of its eccentricities. Vectors are just vectors, not necessarily row nor column. Hence careful programming means using *inner*() and *outer*() for clarity. The transpose operator $t()$ coerces a vector into a matrix with a single row. Similarly, the matrix multiplication operator $\% * \%$ will coerce its operands into matrices and check for conformity. The non matrix multiplication operator $*$ presents potential dangers that the naive user may not be able to imagine. Suppose X is a matrix and z is a scalar – oops, a vector of length 1. While $z * X$ looks like scaling a matrix, in reality z is coerced into a matrix conformable with X by recycling the single value in z, and then the constructed matrix and X are multiplied element-by-element. Now if z is a vector, again z will be coerced into a matrix by recycling. If $length(z)$ matches $dim(X)[1]$ (number of rows of X), then $z * X$ will rescale the rows of X and give the same result as $diag(z)\% * \%X$. If $length(z)$ is not the same as $dim(X)[1]$, then all sorts of garbage may be computed. And if $prod(dim(X))\%\%length(z) == 0$, that is, integer division gave a zero remainder – or – the recycling of z went through a full cycle, then no warning would be issued. If used properly, however, this coercion and recycing can be powerful.

Suppose the matrix **A** is $m \times n$, **z** has length m, and **w** has length n. Then $z * A$ rescales the rows of **A** and $A * w$ rescales the columns. Say, we had a weighted regression problem, like $\mathbf{X}$ is $N \times p$, for which we wanted to compute $\mathbf{X}^T\mathbf{W}^{-1}\mathbf{X}$ where $\mathbf{W}$ is diagonal with its elements stored in the vector $\mathbf{w}$. Here are three ways to compute $\mathbf{X}^T\mathbf{W}^{-1}\mathbf{X}$

1. t(X)%*% solve(diag(w),X)
2. t(X)%*% diag(1/w) %*% X
3. t(X/w)%*% X or t(X) %*% (X/w)

The first method solves a system of equations with multiple right-hand sides to get $\mathbf{W}^{-1}\mathbf{X}$ and does not exploit the diagonal structure of $\mathbf{W}$. (Using *forwardsolve* or *backsolve* would at least exploit triangularity and cut the cost/time in half.) The second method does exploit the diagonal structure, but constructs an $N \times N$ matrix. The third method is fast, efficient, and dangerous without prominent comments about its use of coercion and recycling. For large values of N, the first method takes $O(N^3)$ time and $O(N^2)$ space, and usually space will limit the size of the problem. The second method takes $O(N^2)$ time but still $O(N^2)$ space, whereas the third method takes but $O(Np^2)$ time and just p^2 space. The savings in time and space are dramatic here, but that advantage must be tempered with the acknowledgment of the dangers of cryptic code that exploits peculiarities of the software.

Some people may argue that the savings in time or space that involve only a factor of two are not worth the human effort to exploit. In some ways, R follows this way of thinking. Using the LU factorization from Gaussian elimination instead of computing the inverse of a matrix only cuts the computation by a factor of two. In R, although we cannot get the LU factorization from the function *solve*, we can have a matrix as a right hand side. Similarly, the triangular matrices that arise from Cholesky or QR (Chapter 5) are usually stored as full matrices, taking twice the space as necessary. Nonetheless, triangular solvers *forwardsolve* and *backsolve* are available to save computation.

The reader should also note that R's function for Cholesky factorization *chol* produces the upper triangular factor $\mathbf{R} = \mathbf{L}^T$ or the factorization $\mathbf{A} = \mathbf{R}^T\mathbf{R} = \mathbf{L}\mathbf{L}^T$. The reasoning behind this choice will not be clear until Chapter 5. Notice that this is a different factorization that would be computed from Exercise 3.25.

Programs and Demonstrations

gauspp *Test/demonstration program for Gaussian elimination*
The matrix given in Example 3.1 is factored using the LU factorization of Gaussian elimination. The system of equations given in Example 3.2 is then solved. The subprograms:

gauspp – computes the LU factorization, storing $\mathbf{L}$ and $\mathbf{U}$ on top of the original matrix $\mathbf{L}$. The permutation matrix is given by a list $\pi(j)$. The last (nth) element of this list gives an indicator of the computed rank of the matrix: $\pi(n) = n$ if the routine proceeded to completion, $\pi(n) = j$ if the last successful pivot was on step j.

gausse – solves the system of linear equations using the LU factorization computed by **gauspp**.

gaucpp   *Demonstration program for Gaussian elimination with a condition estimate*
As in **gauspp**, the LU factorization of Gaussian elimination is computed, with a call
to **gauspp**. Additionally, **gaucpp** also computes the reciprocal of the estimate of
the condition number κ using the ∞-norm and the Golub–van Loan version of the
Cline et al. method. The subprograms:
gaucpp – computes LU factorization and $1/\hat{\kappa}$.
gauspp – called by **gaucpp** to compute LU factorization.
gausse – solves the system of equations.

chlsky   *Demonstration program for Cholesky factorization*
The matrix given in Example 3.3 is factored using Cholesky factorization. Next, the
system of equations of Example 3.4 is solved. The subprograms:
chlsky – computes Cholesky factorization and the determinant in $D \times 2^I$ fashion.
chlshi – solves the system of equations in the matrix $\mathbf{L}$.
chlsih – solves the system of equations in the matrix $\mathbf{L}^T$.
adjust – normalizes a number by using the $D \times 2^I$ form so that $1 \leq D \leq 16$.

chlzky   *Demonstration program for Cholesky factorization using symmetric storage*
mode
The matrix given in Example 3.3 is factored using Cholesky factorization. Next,
the system of equations of Example 3.4 is solved. Symmetric storage is used here
to save space and allow for easier passing of subprogram arguments. The subprograms:
chlzky – computes Cholesky factorization and the determinant in $D \times 2^I$ fashion.
chlzhi – solves the system of equations in the matrix $\mathbf{L}$.
chlzih – solves the system of equations in the matrix $\mathbf{L}^T$.
adjust – normalizes a number by using the $D \times 2^I$ form so that $1 \leq D \leq 16$.

chlsoi   *Demonstration program for computing the inverse of a matrix from the*
Cholesky factor
The matrix given in Example 3.3 is factored using Cholesky factorization. Then the
inverse is computed, overwriting the Cholesky factor. The upper triangular part of
the original matrix is left unchanged. The subprograms include **chlsky** and **adjust**,
as well as:
chlsoi – overwrites the Cholesky factor $\mathbf{L}$ with the inverse matrix $\mathbf{L}^{-T}\mathbf{L}^{-1} = (\mathbf{L}\mathbf{L}^T)^{-1}$.
In the R version, the inverse is computed using the R function **chol2inv**.

chlzoi   *Demonstration program for computing the inverse of a matrix from the*
Cholesky factor using symmetric storage mode
The matrix given in Example 3.3 is factored using Cholesky factorization, then the
inverse is computed and overwritten on the Cholesky factor. Symmetric storage is
used here to save space and allow for easier passing of subprogram arguments. The
subprograms include **chlzky** and **adjust**, as well as:
chlzoi – overwrites the Cholesky factor $\mathbf{L}$ with the inverse matrix $\mathbf{L}^{-T}\mathbf{L}^{-1} = (\mathbf{L}\mathbf{L}^T)^{-1}$.

chex35 *Demonstration of condition of Hilbert matrices*
For $n = 1, \ldots, 7$, the norm and the inverse of Hilbert matrices of order n are computed, and the condition estimate is computed via **gaucpp** to compare with the exact value. For $n = 8$, fixed point overflow would be encountered in computing the inverse exactly using fixed point arithmetic. The subprograms are as in **gaucpp**, with the addition of:
ibicof – fixed point computation of binomial coefficients; uses many tabled values.

chex36 *Demonstration program for the condition number of a matrix for solving equations*
As described in Example 3.6, a system of equations arising from an interpolation problem are solved; then the right-hand sides are perturbed and the effect on the computed solution analyzed, following the inequality (3.6.4). Both types of interpolation (equally spaced and Chebyshev) are demonstrated. Subprograms are the same as in **gaucpp**.
In the R version, the condition number is computed directly with inverse computed using the R function **solve**.

cdnxpmt *Monte Carlo study of the performance of the condition estimate*
As described in Example 3.7, a study by Stewart (1980) was emulated using the Golub–van Loan ∞-norm version of the Cline et al. (1979) condition estimate. The results of the three-factor (with ten replications) factorial experiment are in **cdnxpmt.out**.
In the R version, a different reciprocal condition estimate is computed from the R function **rcond**. Another R function **kappa** computes the exact condition for $p = 2$ from the SVD (Chapter 6).

Exercises

3.1 In Gaussian elimination with partial pivoting, show that if we cannot find a nonzero pivot then the matrix is singular.

3.2 Let $\mathbf{L}$ be lower triangular and let $\mathbf{e}_k^{\mathrm{T}} = (0 \ldots 1 \ldots 0)$.
    (a) Write an algorithm to solve $\mathbf{L}\mathbf{x} = \mathbf{e}_k$.
    (b) Where are the known zeros in the solution vector?
    (c) What columns of $\mathbf{L}$ are not needed?
    (d) Write an algorithm to overwrite $\mathbf{L}$ with $\mathbf{L}^{-1}$.

3.3 Repeat Exercise 3.2(a)–(d) with an upper triangular matrix $\mathbf{U}$.

3.4 Let $\mathbf{A}$ be positive definite, and let $\mathbf{A}^{(k)}$ be the result of k steps of Gaussian elimination (without pivoting). Partition both $\mathbf{A}$ and $\mathbf{A}^{(k)}$ at k rows and columns to form

$$\mathbf{A} = \begin{bmatrix} \mathbf{B} & \mathbf{C} \\ \mathbf{C}^{\mathrm{T}} & \mathbf{D} \end{bmatrix} \quad \text{and} \quad \mathbf{A}^{(k)} = \begin{bmatrix} \mathbf{B}^* & \mathbf{C}^* \\ \mathbf{0} & \mathbf{D}^* \end{bmatrix}.$$

Show that $\mathbf{D}^* = \mathbf{D} - \mathbf{C}^{\mathrm{T}}\mathbf{B}^{-1}\mathbf{C}$. Where is this matrix found in statistics? If $\mathbf{A}$ is positive definite, is pivoting necessary?

3.5 Describe a procedure for computing a bilinear form in the inverse of a positive definite matrix $\mathbf{A}$, $\mathbf{x}^{\mathrm{T}}\mathbf{A}^{-1}\mathbf{y}$.

The next four exercises concern the missing steps in Gaussian elimination, (3.4.6) through (3.4.9).

3.6 Show that $\mathbf{P}(k, j)\mathbf{M}^{(i)} = [\mathbf{I}_n - \mathbf{P}(k, j)\mathbf{m}^{(i)}\mathbf{e}_i^T]\mathbf{P}(k, j)$ for matrices $\mathbf{M}^{(i)}$ in (3.4.2) and (3.4.3) when both k and j exceed i.

3.7 For $\mathbf{M}_*^{(k)} = \mathbf{I}_n - \mathbf{m}_*^{(k)}\mathbf{e}_k^T$ (recall (3.4.9)), show that

$$\mathbf{M}^{(n-1)}\mathbf{P}(n-1, j_{n-1}) \cdots \mathbf{M}^{(2)}\mathbf{P}(2, j_2)\mathbf{M}^{(1)}\mathbf{P}(1, j_1)$$
$$= \mathbf{M}_*^{(n-1)} \cdots \mathbf{M}_*^{(1)}\mathbf{P}(n-1, j_{n-1}) \cdots \mathbf{P}(1, j_1).$$

3.8 Show that $(\mathbf{M}_*^{(k+1)}\mathbf{M}_*^{(k)})^{-1} = \mathbf{I} + \mathbf{m}_*^{(k)}\mathbf{e}_k^T + \mathbf{m}_*^{(k+1)}\mathbf{e}_{k+1}^T$.

3.9 Show that $\mathbf{PA} = \mathbf{LU}$ where $\mathbf{L}$ is given by (3.4.8).

3.10 A matrix $\mathbf{A}$ is positive definite if and only if the determinants of all of its leading minors are positive. Use the formula of the determinant of a partitioned matrix to show that

$$\det(\mathbf{A}^{[k]}) = \mathbf{L}_{kk}^2 \det(\mathbf{A}^{[k-1]}),$$

so that Cholesky factorization will work if and only if the matrix is positive definite.

3.11 Show mathematically that the Hilbert matrix (Example 3.5) is positive definite.

3.12 Compute the Cholesky decomposition of the Hilbert matrix for $n = 4$.

3.13 Suppose the matrix $\mathbf{A}$ is positive semidefinite and singular, with rank $n-1$. Will Cholesky factorization run to completion?

3.14 Verify your conclusions from Exercise 3.13 by factoring the multinomial covariance matrix $\text{diag}(p_1, \ldots, p_n) - \mathbf{pp}^T$, where $\mathbf{p}^T = (p_1, \ldots, p_n)$ with $n = 4$ and probabilities $(.4, .3, .2, .1)$.

3.15 Using Cholesky and Exercise 3.2, write a subroutine to compute the inverse of a positive definite matrix. Can it be done using only the $n(n+1)/2$ storage locations in symmetric storage mode?

3.16 Prove that $\|\mathbf{A}\|_\infty = \max_i \sum_j |A_{ij}|$.

3.17 Prove that $\|\mathbf{A}\|_2 = $ (largest eigenvalue of $\mathbf{A}^T\mathbf{A}$)$^{1/2}$. Also show that the condition number of the matrix $\mathbf{A}$ based on the $p = 2$ norm $\kappa_2(\mathbf{A})$ is the square root of the ratio of the largest and smallest eigenvalues of $\mathbf{A}^T\mathbf{A}$.

3.18 Show that $\|\mathbf{A}\|_F = (\text{trace }\mathbf{A}^T\mathbf{A})^{1/2}$ and $\|\mathbf{A}\|_2 \le \|\mathbf{A}\|_F$.

3.19 Show that, if $\lim_{k\to\infty}\|\mathbf{A}^{(k)}\|_p = 0$ for some p, then the sequence of matrices $\mathbf{A}^{(k)}$ converges for all p-norms for $p \ge 1$.

3.20 Consider the matrix $\mathbf{B} = (1/\sqrt{50})\begin{bmatrix} 4 & 2 \\ 1/2 & 13/2 \end{bmatrix}$. Show that $\|\mathbf{B}\|_\infty < \|\mathbf{B}\|_2 = 1 < \|\mathbf{B}\|_1$.

3.21 Consider $\mathbf{B}$ given in Exercise 3.20. What happens with the von Neumann series (3.6.3), and does this conflict with Exercise 3.19? (You do not need to prove Exercise 3.19.)

3.22 Using (3.7.1), show that the inverse of a matrix is a continuous function of its elements.

3.23 Use the Sherman–Morrison–Woodbury formula for a rank-1 update of the inverse

$$(\mathbf{A} + \mathbf{uv}^T)^{-1} = \mathbf{A}^{-1} - \frac{1}{1 + \mathbf{v}^T\mathbf{A}^{-1}\mathbf{u}}\mathbf{A}^{-1}\mathbf{uv}^T\mathbf{A}^{-1} \qquad (3.9.1)$$

to find the derivative of the inverse of a matrix with respect to one of its elements. (*Hint:* Use $\mathbf{u} = \delta\mathbf{e}_i$ and $\mathbf{v} = \mathbf{e}_j$.)

3.24 Using similar tools and $det\,(\mathbf{I} + \mathbf{ab}^T) = 1 + \mathbf{b}^T\mathbf{a}$, find the derivative of the determinant of a matrix with respect to its elements. (It will be a matrix.)

3.25 Another variation on Cholesky starts at the lower right-hand corner and constructs an upper triangular matrix $\mathbf{R}$ such that a positive definite matrix $\mathbf{A}$ can be factored as $\mathbf{A} = \mathbf{RR}^T$. Show the algebra for the induction step and apply this method to the 3×3 matrix

$$\begin{bmatrix} 9 & 2 & -2 \\ 2 & 1 & 0 \\ -2 & 0 & 4 \end{bmatrix}$$

3.26 Some stochastic processes X_t bring some challenges to Cholesky. Consider the stochastic process X_t with the covariance kernel of the form $Cov(X_t, X_s) = \exp\{-|t - s|\}$. Let $t_i = i/n$ for $i = 1, \ldots, n$ be points of evaluation of X_t for $t \in [0, 1]$, and let $\mathbf{A}^{(n)}$ be the covariance matrix, so $(\mathbf{A}^{(n)})_{ij} = \exp\{-|i - j|/n\}$. For various values of n, say $10, 20, 30, \ldots$, compute the Cholesky factors of $\mathbf{A}^{(n)}$ and also the condition numbers $\kappa = \|\mathbf{A}^{(n)}\|\,\|(\mathbf{A}^{(n)})^{-1}\|$ using the $p = 1$ or $p = \infty$ norms. Does scaling with a parameter α in $(\mathbf{A}^{(n)})_{ij} = \exp\{-\alpha|i - j|/n\}$ make much of a difference?

3.27 Consider a different covariance kernel of the form $Cov(X_t, X_s) = \exp\{-\alpha(t - s)^2\}$, leading to the covariance matrix $(\mathbf{B}^{(n)})_{ij} = \exp\{-\alpha((i - j)/n)^2\}$. Analyze $\mathbf{B}^{(n)}$ similarly and determine the value of the dimension n where Cholesky fails numerically.

3.28 Can you improve the condition number of the Vandermonde matrix used in the interpolation problem in Example 3.6 (**chex36**) by rescaling rows and columns?

3.29 By rescaling the rows and/or columns of the inverse of the Hilbert matrix used in Example 3.5 and **chex35**, can you improve the condition number?

3.30 Analyze the data in **cdnxpmt.out** as the factorial experiment described in Example 3.7.

3.31 If $\mathbf{A} = \text{diag}(10^{-3}, 1, 10^3)$ then $\kappa(\mathbf{A}) = 10^6$, and someone might say that this appears to be a large condition number for such a simple matrix. Comment.

References

The Stewart (1973) and Golub and van Loan (1996) books are outstanding: clearly written with attention to both mathematical interest and practicalities. The course I took from Stewart as a graduate student (following publication of his book) has been a major influence in my understanding of linear algebra and regression. Papers with Algol code are collected in the Wilkinson–Reinsch (1971) volume; the LINPACK (Dongarra et al. 1979) and LAPACK (Anderson et al. 1995) guides have more code and less mathematics. Jennings (1977) discusses computational efficiencies in detail. The Demmel (1988) article should be interesting to statisticians.

E. Anderson, Z. Bai, C. Bishof, J. Demmel, J. Dongarra, J. Du Croz, A. Greenbaum, S. Hammarling, A. McKenney, S. Ostrouchov, and D. Sorenson (1995), *LAPACK Users' Guide*. Philadelphia: SIAM.

A. K. Cline, C. B. Moler, G. W. Stewart, and J. H. Wilkinson (1979), "An Estimate for the Condition Number of a Matrix," *SIAM Journal of Numerical Analysis* 16: 368–75.

James W. Demmel (1988), "The Probability That a Numerical Analysis Problem Is Difficult," *Mathematics of Computation* 50: 449–80.

J. J. Dongarra, J. R. Bunch, C. B. Moler, and G. W. Stewart (1979), *LINPACK Users' Guide.* Philadelphia: SIAM.

Gene H. Golub and Charles van Loan (1996), *Matrix Computations,* 3rd. ed. Baltimore: Johns Hopkins University Press.

Alton S. Householder (1975), *The Theory of Matrices in Numerical Analysis.* New York: Dover.

Ilse C. F. Ipsen (2009), *Numerical Matrix Analysis.* Philadelphia: SIAM.

Alan Jennings (1977), *Matrix Computation for Engineers and Scientists.* New York: Wiley.

Donald E. Knuth (1997), *The Art of Computer Programming* (vol. 1: Fundamental Algorithms), 3rd ed. Reading, MA: Addison-Wesley.

Peter Lancaster and Miron Tismenetsky (1985), *The Theory of Matrices,* 2nd ed. Orlando, FL: Academic Press.

G. W. Stewart (1973), *Introduction to Matrix Computations.* New York: Academic Press.

G. W. Stewart (1980), "The Efficient Generation of Random Orthogonal Matrices with an Application to Condition Estimators," *SIAM Journal of Numerical Analysis* 17: 403–9.

G. W. Stewart and Ji-guang Sun (1990), *Matrix Perturbation Theory.* Boston: Academic Press.

J. H. Wilkinson and C. Reinsch (Eds.) (1971), *Linear Algebra.* New York: Springer-Verlag.

4

More Methods for Solving Linear Equations

4.1 Introduction

The previous chapter dwelled on the fundamental methods of matrix computations. In this chapter, more specialized methods are considered. The first topic is an alternative approach to solving general systems of equations – full elimination (often the method taught in beginning linear algebra courses), which has some advantages whenever the inverse is required. Next, our goal is reducing the effort in solving equations by exploiting the structure of a matrix. One such structure is bandedness, and the Cholesky factorization of a banded positive definite matrix is then applied to time-series computations, cutting the work from $O(n^3)$ to $O(n)$. Next is the Toeplitz structure, also arising in time-series analysis, where the work can be reduced to $O(n^2)$ in a more general setting. Sparse matrix methods are designed to exploit unstructured patterns of zeros and so avoid unneeded work. Finally, iterative methods are discussed, beginning with iterative improvement.

4.2 Full Elimination with Complete Pivoting

Gaussian elimination creates an upper triangular matrix, column by column, by adding multiples of a row to the rows below it and placing zeros below the diagonal of each column. An alternative is to place zeros throughout that column – with the exception of the pivot position, which could be made equal to one. The matrix that changes a column $\mathbf{a}$ to an elementary vector $\mathbf{e}_q$, pivoting on the qth element, has a similar form to that used in Gaussian elimination:

$$\mathbf{M} = \mathbf{I} - \mathbf{me}_q^\mathsf{T},$$

where $\mathbf{m} = (1/a_q)(\mathbf{a} - \mathbf{e}_q)$. This matrix is called a Gauss–Jordan transformation, and the method is sometimes known as Gauss–Jordan elimination. When such a matrix is constructed from the rth column of a matrix, pivoting on the qth element of that column, then premultiplying by this Gauss–Jordan transformation adds multiples of the qth row to the other rows and changes the rth column to $\mathbf{e}_q$. The strategy of full elimination is to multiply by a sequence of these transformations $\mathbf{M}^{(k)}$ and so change the original matrix to a permutation matrix. Permuting the rows of the product of these matrices will then produce the inverse.

Notice that, if column r has been pivoted in (i.e., once it is made into an elementary vector $\mathbf{e}_q$), then a second pivot in that column changes nothing because (a) the only nonzero element in that column is in the qth position and (b) the $\mathbf{M}$ matrix is just the identity. Also, pivoting subsequently in row q will add multiples of the one in column r to the zeros in column r, thus destroying the structure of zeros just constructed. Consequently, pivoting should be done only once in each row and column, requiring index vectors to keep track of what has been done. In Gaussian elimination with partial pivoting, the pivot candidates are just the elements on or below the diagonal in the current column; but for full elimination no such restriction exists, and any element in a not previously pivoted row or column is a candidate. Pivoting on the largest (in absolute value) element of the submatrix is called *complete* pivoting, and it has its merits when accuracy is considered.

Summarizing, our strategy is thus to multiply by a sequence of matrices $\mathbf{M}^{(k)} = \mathbf{I} - \mathbf{m}^{(k)}\mathbf{e}_{q(k)}^{\mathrm{T}}$ so that the product is a permutation matrix

$$\mathbf{P} = \mathbf{M}^{(n)} \cdots \mathbf{M}^{(2)}\mathbf{M}^{(1)}\mathbf{A}. \tag{4.2.1}$$

If, at step k, the pivot element is in row $q(k)$ and column $r(k)$ of the matrix

$$\mathbf{A}^{(k-1)} = \mathbf{M}^{(k-1)} \cdots \mathbf{M}^{(1)}\mathbf{A},$$

then the permutation matrix $\mathbf{P}$ can be written as

$$\mathbf{P} = \sum \mathbf{e}_{r(k)}\mathbf{e}_{q(k)}^{\mathrm{T}}.$$

When this method is implemented as a textbook procedure and the computation done by pencil and paper, an identity matrix is commonly augmented to the right and the matrices $\mathbf{M}^{(k)}$ multiplied together there. But on the computer, the additional n^2 storage required may not be available. Moreover, additional storage is not actually required, since every nontrivial column added at a step to the augmented matrix is accompanied by the trivializing of a column in the original matrix. So the clever strategy is to store the new columns $q(k)$ on top of the old ones $r(k)$ to be discarded. The problem with that procedure is that $\mathbf{m}^{(k)}$ slightly modified (the modification is $\mathbf{M}^{(k)}\mathbf{e}_q = \mathbf{e}_q - \mathbf{m}^{(k)}$) should be placed in column q of the augmented matrix, when the only space available is in column r. The consequence of placing the real column $q(k)$ in column $r(k)$ is that the matrix at the end is now

$$\mathbf{B} = \mathbf{M}^{(n)} \cdots \mathbf{M}^{(2)}\mathbf{M}^{(1)}\mathbf{P}^{\mathrm{T}}. \tag{4.2.2}$$

Combining (4.2.1) and (4.2.2), the inverse of the original matrix $\mathbf{A}$ can be computed from

$$\mathbf{A}^{-1} = \mathbf{P}^{\mathrm{T}}\mathbf{B}\mathbf{P},$$

so that both the rows and columns of $\mathbf{B}$ must be permuted. The best way to do the permutation is: begin with the inverse permutation, switching columns or rows as the case may be; correspondingly switch the elements of the permutation; and then run through the cycles until the result of the permutation inversions (switches) is the identity permutation.

As with other methods of computing the inverse, full elimination with full pivoting requires n^3 flops. The extra search brought on by the full pivoting is not the insignificant overhead as in the case of partial pivoting, but it also is $O(n^3)$ work. Although this method has fallen out of favor because it is slightly slower for solving equations (see Exercise 4.2), it has survived as an effective method for matrix updating in linear programming. In recent years, full elimination has been used to advantage in the vectorizations of supercomputers and array processors.

Example 4.1: *Full Elimination with Complete Pivoting*
The biggest elements are in $(1, 2)$ and $(4, 2)$; let's use the first one, $(p, q) = (1, 2)$.

$$\mathbf{A} = \mathbf{A}^{(0)} = \begin{bmatrix} 1 & 2 & -1 & 0 \\ 1/2 & 1 & 0 & 1 \\ 0 & 2 & -1/2 & 3/2 \\ 1 & -1 & 3/2 & 0 \end{bmatrix}, \quad \mathbf{m}^{(1)} = (1/2) \begin{bmatrix} 2-1 \\ 1 \\ 2 \\ -1 \end{bmatrix} = \begin{bmatrix} 1/2 \\ 1/2 \\ 1 \\ -1/2 \end{bmatrix}.$$

Then $\mathbf{M}^{(1)} = \mathbf{I} - \mathbf{m}^{(1)}\mathbf{e}_2$. Augmenting $\mathbf{A} = \mathbf{A}^{(0)}$ with $\mathbf{I}$, mimicking the usual hand calculations, the first step is $\mathbf{M}^{(1)}(\mathbf{A}^{(0)} \mid \mathbf{I}) = (\mathbf{A}^{(1)} \mid \mathbf{M}^{(1)})$:

$$\begin{bmatrix} 1/2 & 0 & 0 & 0 \\ -1/2 & 1 & 0 & 0 \\ -1 & 0 & 1 & 0 \\ 1/2 & 0 & 0 & 1 \end{bmatrix} \begin{bmatrix} 1 & 2 & -1 & 0 & 1 & 0 & 0 & 0 \\ 1/2 & 1 & 0 & 1 & 0 & 1 & 0 & 0 \\ 0 & 2 & -1/2 & 3/2 & 0 & 0 & 1 & 0 \\ 1 & -1 & 3/2 & 0 & 0 & 0 & 0 & 1 \end{bmatrix} = .$$

Ignoring the first row and second column, the largest element of $\mathbf{A}^{(1)}$ is at $(q, r) = (3, 4)$:

$$\begin{bmatrix} 1/2 & 1 & -1/2 & 0 & 1/2 & 0 & 0 & 0 \\ 0 & 0 & 1/2 & 1 & -1/2 & 1 & 0 & 0 \\ -1 & 0 & 1/2 & 3/2 & -1 & 0 & 1 & 0 \\ 3/2 & 0 & 1 & 0 & 1/2 & 0 & 0 & 1 \end{bmatrix},$$

$$\text{so } \mathbf{m}^{(2)} = (2/3) \begin{bmatrix} 0 \\ 1 \\ 3/2-1 \\ 0 \end{bmatrix} = \begin{bmatrix} 0 \\ 2/3 \\ 1/3 \\ 0 \end{bmatrix}.$$

Then $\mathbf{M}^{(2)} = \mathbf{I} - \mathbf{m}^{(2)}\mathbf{e}_3$, and the next step is $\mathbf{M}^{(2)}(\mathbf{A}^{(1)} \mid \mathbf{M}^{(1)}) = (\mathbf{A}^{(2)} \mid \mathbf{M}^{(2)}\mathbf{M}^{(1)})$:

$$\begin{bmatrix} 1 & 0 & 0 & 0 \\ 0 & 1 & -2/3 & 0 \\ 0 & 0 & 2/3 & 0 \\ 0 & 0 & 0 & 1 \end{bmatrix} \begin{bmatrix} 1/2 & 1 & -1/2 & 0 & 1/2 & 0 & 0 & 0 \\ 0 & 0 & 1/2 & 1 & -1/2 & 1 & 0 & 0 \\ -1 & 0 & 1/2 & 3/2 & -1 & 0 & 1 & 0 \\ 3/2 & 0 & 1 & 0 & 1/2 & 0 & 0 & 1 \end{bmatrix} = .$$

Now ignoring the first and third rows and the second and fourth columns, the largest element of $\mathbf{A}^{(2)}$ is at $(q, r) = (4, 1)$:

$$\begin{bmatrix} 1/2 & 1 & -1/2 & 0 & 1/2 & 0 & 0 & 0 \\ 2/3 & 0 & 1/6 & 0 & 1/6 & 1 & -2/3 & 0 \\ -2/3 & 0 & 1/3 & 1 & -2/3 & 0 & 2/3 & 0 \\ 3/2 & 0 & 1 & 0 & 1/2 & 0 & 0 & 1 \end{bmatrix},$$

$$\text{so } \mathbf{m}^{(3)} = (2/3) \begin{bmatrix} 1/2 \\ 2/3 \\ -2/3 \\ 3/2 - 1 \end{bmatrix} = \begin{bmatrix} 1/3 \\ 4/9 \\ -4/9 \\ 1/3 \end{bmatrix};$$

$\mathbf{M}^{(3)} = \mathbf{I} - \mathbf{m}^{(3)}\mathbf{e}_4$, and the third step gives $\mathbf{M}^{(3)}(\mathbf{A}^{(2)} \mid \mathbf{M}^{(2)}\mathbf{M}^{(1)}) = (\mathbf{A}^{(3)} \mid \mathbf{M}^{(3)}\mathbf{M}^{(2)}\mathbf{M}^{(1)})$:

$$\begin{bmatrix} 1 & 0 & 0 & -1/3 \\ 0 & 1 & 0 & -4/9 \\ 0 & 0 & 1 & 4/9 \\ 0 & 0 & 0 & 2/3 \end{bmatrix} \begin{bmatrix} 1/2 & 1 & -1/2 & 0 & 1/2 & 0 & 0 & 0 \\ 2/3 & 0 & 1/6 & 0 & 1/6 & 1 & -2/3 & 0 \\ -2/3 & 0 & 1/3 & 1 & -2/3 & 0 & 2/3 & 0 \\ 3/2 & 0 & 1 & 0 & 1/2 & 0 & 0 & 1 \end{bmatrix} = .$$

The only eligible element of $\mathbf{A}^{(3)}$ is in row 2, column 3, so $(q, r) = (3, 4)$:

$$\begin{bmatrix} 0 & 1 & -5/6 & 0 & 1/3 & 0 & 0 & -1/3 \\ 0 & 0 & -5/18 & 0 & -1/18 & 1 & -2/3 & -4/9 \\ 0 & 0 & 7/9 & 1 & -4/9 & 0 & 2/3 & 4/9 \\ 1 & 0 & 2/3 & 0 & 1/3 & 0 & 0 & 2/3 \end{bmatrix},$$

$$\text{so } \mathbf{m}^{(4)} = (-18/5) \begin{bmatrix} -5/6 \\ -5/18 - 1 \\ 7/9 \\ 2/3 \end{bmatrix} = \begin{bmatrix} 3 \\ 23/5 \\ -14/5 \\ -12/5 \end{bmatrix}.$$

Finally, $\mathbf{M}^{(4)} = \mathbf{I} - \mathbf{m}^{(4)}\mathbf{e}_3$. The last step completes the effort,

$$\mathbf{M}^{(4)}(\mathbf{A}^{(3)} \mid \mathbf{M}^{(3)}\mathbf{M}^{(2)}\mathbf{M}^{(1)}) = (\mathbf{A}^{(4)} \mid \mathbf{M}^{(4)}\mathbf{M}^{(3)}\mathbf{M}^{(2)}\mathbf{M}^{(1)}) = (\mathbf{P} \mid \mathbf{PA}^{-1}):$$

$$\begin{bmatrix} 1 & -3 & 0 & 0 \\ 0 & -18/5 & 0 & 0 \\ 0 & 14/5 & 1 & 0 \\ 0 & 12/5 & 0 & 1 \end{bmatrix} \begin{bmatrix} 0 & 1 & -5/6 & 0 & 1/3 & 0 & 0 & -1/3 \\ 0 & 0 & -5/18 & 0 & -1/18 & 1 & -2/3 & -4/9 \\ 0 & 0 & 7/9 & 1 & -4/9 & 0 & 2/3 & 4/9 \\ 1 & 0 & 2/3 & 0 & 1/3 & 0 & 0 & 2/3 \end{bmatrix}$$

$$= \begin{bmatrix} 0 & 1 & 0 & 0 & 1/2 & -3 & 2 & 1 \\ 0 & 0 & 1 & 0 & 1/5 & -18/5 & 12/5 & 8/5 \\ 0 & 0 & 0 & 1 & -3/5 & 14/5 & -6/5 & -4/5 \\ 1 & 0 & 0 & 0 & 1/5 & 12/5 & -8/5 & -2/5 \end{bmatrix},$$

$$\text{so } \mathbf{A}^{-1} = \begin{bmatrix} 1/5 & 12/5 & -8/5 & -2/5 \\ 1/2 & -3 & 2 & 1 \\ 1/5 & -18/5 & 12/5 & 8/5 \\ -3/5 & 14/5 & -6/5 & -4/5 \end{bmatrix}.$$

4.3 Banded Matrices

Great savings in space and time are available in solving systems of linear equations when the matrix has a structure that can be exploited. Banded matrices are relatively common, and the savings require little effort. A matrix $\mathbf{A}$ is said to have

lower bandwidth p if $A_{ij} = 0$ for all $i > j + p$;
upper bandwidth q if $A_{ij} = 0$ for all $j > i + q$.

A matrix with upper bandwidth q and lower bandwidth p has no more than $p + q + 1$ nonzero elements in each row (or column). Storing only the not-known-to-be-zero elements, by rows or by columns, requires no more than $n(p + q + 1)$ locations, which is a substantial savings whenever $p + q + 1 \ll n$. Storing by rows suggests renaming the column index to $j - i + p + 1$, so that A_{ij} is in $A(i, j - i + p + 1)$.

Exploiting the banded structure does face an obstacle in that the problem must be reasonably well conditioned. With Gaussian elimination, for example, pivoting could destroy much of the pattern of zeros on which the savings is based. Consequently, none of the methods considered here permit pivoting or even (in the case of Cholesky decomposition) need it at all.

First of all, consider the LU factorization that is computed by Gaussian elimination. If the matrix $\mathbf{A}$ has bandwidths p and q, then the factored matrices are also banded, that is, $\mathbf{L}$ is lower triangular with bandwidth p and $\mathbf{U}$ is upper triangular with bandwidth q. Simple modifications to the usual Gaussian elimination algorithm are used to achieve the savings; see Golub and van Loan (1996, sec. 5.3) and Exercise 4.5. More importantly, the savings in time is substantial. The work to compute the LU factorization is merely $O(npq)$, much less than the $O(n^3/3)$ that the usual full matrix requires. Solving the two triangular systems is then only $O(np + nq)$, also much smaller. When p and q are small, these systems of equations require only $O(n)$ computations to solve – a dramatic improvement.

Example 4.2: Tridiagonal Matrix
Consider the tridiagonal system where $p = q = 1$. Then the matrix can be stored using just three vectors, and the LU factorization from Gaussian elimination requires just n simple steps, modifying only two of the vectors. Indexing the matrix by rows – with d_i denoting the diagonal entries, e_i the elements above the main diagonal, and c_i those below – we obtain

$$
\begin{bmatrix} d_1 & e_1 & 0 & 0 \\ c_2 & d_2 & e_2 & 0 \\ 0 & c_3 & d_3 & e_3 \\ 0 & 0 & c_4 & d_4 \end{bmatrix} = \begin{bmatrix} 1 & 0 & 0 & 0 \\ L_2 & 1 & 0 & 0 \\ 0 & L_3 & 1 & 0 \\ 0 & 0 & L_4 & 1 \end{bmatrix} \begin{bmatrix} d_1^* & e_1 & 0 & 0 \\ 0 & d_2^* & e_2 & 0 \\ 0 & 0 & d_3^* & e_3 \\ 0 & 0 & 0 & d_4^* \end{bmatrix}
$$

for the $n = 4$ case. The algorithm overwrites L_k on c_k and d_k^* on d_k, and it can be coded as

```
do i=2,n
c( i )=c( i )/d( i-1 )
d( i )=d( i )-e( i-1 ) * c( i )
end do  ! loop on i
```

Coding the solution of the two triangular systems, first $\mathbf{Ly} = \mathbf{b}$ and then $\mathbf{Ux} = \mathbf{y}$, is also easy:

```
!            solve lower triangular system Ly=b
do i=2,n
b( i )=b( i )-c( i-1 ) * b( i-1 )
end do  ! loop on i
!            solve upper triangular system Ux=y
b( n )=b( n )/d( n )
do ii=2,n
i=n+1-ii      ! count backwards from n-1 to 1
b( i )=( b( i )-e( i ) * b( i+1 ) )/d( i )
end do  ! loop on ii
```

Altogether, only $5n - 4$ flops are required to both factor and solve the system of equations for a tridiagonal matrix. This efficiency will be exploited in spline approximations in Chapter 7.

A similar scheme can be used for banded matrices that can be viewed with a block tridiagonal structure, where each position is now occupied by a $k \times k$ submatrix. Then the block LU factorization looks like

$$
\begin{bmatrix}
\mathbf{D}_1 & \mathbf{E}_1 & \mathbf{0} & \mathbf{0} \\
\mathbf{C}_2 & \mathbf{D}_2 & \mathbf{E}_2 & \mathbf{0} \\
\mathbf{0} & \mathbf{C}_3 & \mathbf{D}_3 & \mathbf{E}_3 \\
\mathbf{0} & \mathbf{0} & \mathbf{C}_4 & \mathbf{D}_4
\end{bmatrix}
=
\begin{bmatrix}
\mathbf{I} & \mathbf{0} & \mathbf{0} & \mathbf{0} \\
\mathbf{L}_2 & \mathbf{I} & \mathbf{0} & \mathbf{0} \\
\mathbf{0} & \mathbf{L}_3 & \mathbf{I} & \mathbf{0} \\
\mathbf{0} & \mathbf{0} & \mathbf{L}_4 & \mathbf{I}
\end{bmatrix}
\begin{bmatrix}
\mathbf{D}_1^* & \mathbf{E}_1 & \mathbf{0} & \mathbf{0} \\
\mathbf{0} & \mathbf{D}_2^* & \mathbf{E}_2 & \mathbf{0} \\
\mathbf{0} & \mathbf{0} & \mathbf{D}_3^* & \mathbf{E}_3 \\
\mathbf{0} & \mathbf{0} & \mathbf{0} & \mathbf{D}_4^*
\end{bmatrix},
$$

and the algorithm for the factorization is

$\mathbf{D}_1^* = \mathbf{D}_1$
for $i = 2, \ldots, n$
  solve $\mathbf{L}_i \mathbf{D}_{i-1}^* = \mathbf{C}_i$ for $\mathbf{L}_i$ and store in $\mathbf{C}_i$
  overwrite $\mathbf{D}_i$ with $\mathbf{D}_i^* = \mathbf{D}_i - \mathbf{L}_i \mathbf{E}_{i-1}$.

The advantages are that structure in the submatrices $\mathbf{C}_i$ and $\mathbf{E}_i$ can be exploited. When they are full, then stay with the banded elimination scheme. Again, the condition of the method depends upon the condition of the matrices $\mathbf{D}_i^*$. In some differential equations problems, these matrices can be proven to be well conditioned. If this is not possible then extreme care should be exercised, since this method could collapse when any $\mathbf{D}_i^*$ is near singular.

Cholesky decomposition of a banded positive definite matrix offers similar savings. If the upper (and, by symmetry, lower) bandwidth is q, then the total bandwidth is

$2q + 1$ and the Cholesky factor $\mathbf{L}$ also has a lower bandwidth of q. To see this, consider the step-k system of equations (3.4.1) to be solved,

$$\mathbf{L}^{(k-1)}\boldsymbol{\ell}^{(k)} = \mathbf{a}^{(k)}.$$

Now, since the matrix $\mathbf{A}$ has upper bandwidth q, at step $k = q + j$, the first j elements of $\mathbf{a}^{(k)}$ are zero. And since lower triangular systems are solved from the top down, the first j elements of $\boldsymbol{\ell}^{(k)}$ will also be zero. The result is a lower triangular matrix $\mathbf{L}$ with lower bandwidth q and with fewer than $n(q + 1)$ elements. The required effort for factoring the matrix and computing the determinant and any bilinear forms is $O(n(q+1))$, substantially smaller than $n^3/6$.

4.4 Applications to ARMA Time-Series Models

The autoregressive moving average (ARMA) process $\{z_t\}$ of order (p, q), centered about zero, is defined by the stochastic difference equation

$$\phi(B)z_t = \theta(B)e_t, \tag{4.4.1}$$

where B is the backshift operator $Bz_t = z_{t-1}$ and ϕ and θ are polynomials of degrees p and q, respectively,

$$\phi(w) = 1 - \phi_1 w - \cdots - \phi_p w^p. \tag{4.4.2}$$

Under the assumption of normally distributed errors, a finite segment of this process $z = (z_1, \ldots, z_n)^{\mathsf{T}}$ is observed, which has a multivariate normal distribution with zero mean and covariance matrix proportional to $\mathbf{A}_n$. Since this ARMA process is stationary, the covariance matrix satisfies

$$(\mathbf{A}_n)_{ij} = \text{cov}(z_i, z_j) = \gamma(i - j) = \gamma(|i - j|), \tag{4.4.3}$$

where the covariance function $\gamma(k)$ depends on the parameters of the model, $\phi_1, \ldots, \phi_p$, $\theta_1, \ldots, \theta_q$. Such a matrix satisfying (4.4.3) is called *Toeplitz,* and algorithms for solving equations with the general Toeplitz structure will be treated in Section 4.5. The ARMA model enforces additional structure that can be exploited to reduce the computations to $O(n)$.

The computations required for a likelihood or Bayesian analysis are the determinant of $\mathbf{A}_n$ and bilinear forms in the inverse, $\mathbf{x}^{\mathsf{T}}\mathbf{A}_n^{-1}\mathbf{y}$; more specifically, $\hat{\mu} = \mathbf{1}^{\mathsf{T}}\mathbf{A}_n^{-1}\mathbf{z}/\mathbf{1}^{\mathsf{T}}\mathbf{A}_n^{-1}\mathbf{1}$ and the quadratic form $Q = \mathbf{z}^{\mathsf{T}}\mathbf{A}_n^{-1}\mathbf{z} - (\mathbf{1}^{\mathsf{T}}\mathbf{A}_n^{-1}\mathbf{z})^2/\mathbf{1}^{\mathsf{T}}\mathbf{A}_n^{-1}\mathbf{1}$ are required. Note that if $p = 0$, the pure MA(q) process, then the covariance matrix is banded and $\gamma(k) = 0$ for $k > q$. As discussed in Section 4.3, the Cholesky factor $\mathbf{L}$ of a positive definite matrix with total bandwidth $(2q + 1)$ can be computed in only $O(n(q + 1))$ time. The determinant can be computed on the way, and any bilinear form in the inverse requires just $O(nq)$ flops. Careful examination shows that only the $q + 1$ values of $\gamma(k)$ are needed to create $\mathbf{A}_n$ and that $\mathbf{L}\mathbf{v} = \mathbf{y}$ can be solved using only $O(q^2)$ space. Since lower triangular systems are solved from the top down, from the bandedness of $\mathbf{L}$ it follows that, once v_k is obtained, row k of $\mathbf{L}$ is no longer needed. Consequently, exact likelihood analysis of a pure moving average process requires only $O(nq)$ time and $O(q^2)$ space, which makes the analysis of long (large n, moderate q) time series feasible.

Example 4.3: *Cholesky Factorization of a Moving Average Covariance Matrix*
The moving average time-series model follows the stochastic difference equation

$$z_t = e_t - \theta e_{t-1} \quad (t = 1, \ldots, n),$$

where the $\{z_t\}$ are observed and $\{e_t\}$ are unobserved errors. Taking $\sigma_e^2 = 1$, the covariance function $\gamma(k)$ for the process $\{z_t\}$ takes the form $\gamma(0) = 1 + \theta^2$, $\gamma(1) = -\theta$, and $\gamma(j) = 0$ for $j > 1$, so that the covariance matrix is banded with bandwidth 1:

$$\mathbf{A} = \begin{bmatrix} 1+\theta^2 & -\theta & 0 & 0 \\ -\theta & 1+\theta^2 & -\theta & 0 \\ 0 & -\theta & 1+\theta^2 & -\theta \\ 0 & 0 & -\theta & 1+\theta^2 \end{bmatrix}.$$

Computing the Cholesky factor is straightforward: $L_{11} = \sqrt{1 + \theta^2}$, $L_{12} = -\theta/L_{11}$, and then $L_{22} = \sqrt{L_{12}^2 + 1 + \theta^2}$ gives the first two rows of the factor $\mathbf{L}$. The next step is to solve

$$\begin{bmatrix} L_{11} & 0 \\ L_{12} & L_{22} \end{bmatrix} \begin{bmatrix} L_{31} \\ L_{32} \end{bmatrix} = \begin{bmatrix} 0 \\ -\theta \end{bmatrix}, \quad \text{so } L_{31} = 0 \text{ and } L_{32} = -\theta/L_{22};$$

completing row 3 yields $L_{33} = \sqrt{L_{32}^2 + 1 + \theta^2}$. The pattern of zeros should now be evident, and the series of diagonal and subdiagonal elements are convergent: $L_{kk} \to 1$ and $L_{k,k-1} \to -\theta$ (see Exercise 4.7).

Achieving the same savings for the more general ARMA model hinges on converting the series $\{z_t\}$ to a moving average series. Notice that, if the operator $\phi(B)$ is applied to z_t, then the series $\{w_t\}$ constructed from $\{z_t\}$ by

$$w_t = z_t - \phi_1 z_{t-1} - \cdots - \phi_p z_{t-p} \tag{4.4.4}$$

has the same covariance structure as an MA(q) process. However, because z_{-1} and others are unknown, w_t can be constructed by (4.4.4) only for $t = p+1, \ldots, n$. But if the first few z_t are left alone, $w_t = z_t$, then the series $\{w_t\}$ has a covariance matrix whose bandwidth is $m = \max(p, q)$. More specifically, define w_t by

$$w_t = \begin{cases} z_t & \text{if } t = 1, \ldots, m, \\ z_t - \phi_1 z_{t-1} - \cdots - \phi_p z_{t-p} & \text{if } t = m+1, \ldots, n, \end{cases} \tag{4.4.5}$$

and correspondingly define the matrix $\mathbf{B}$ by

$$\mathbf{B} = \begin{bmatrix} \mathbf{I}_m & \mathbf{0} \\ \mathbf{B}_1 & \mathbf{B}_2 \end{bmatrix}, \quad \begin{array}{l} m = \max(p, q) \\ n - m \end{array}$$

where the submatrix $(\mathbf{B}_1 \ \mathbf{B}_2)$ has rows of the form

$$0 \ \ldots \ 0 \ 0 \ -\phi_p \ -\phi_{p-1} \ \ldots \ -\phi_1 \ 1 \ 0 \ 0 \ \ldots$$

and where the ones are lined up on the diagonal of **B**. Hence **B** is unit lower triangular with bandwidth p. The covariance matrix of $\{w_t\}$ is then

$$\mathrm{cov}(\mathbf{w}) = \mathrm{cov}(\mathbf{Bz}) = \begin{bmatrix} \mathbf{A}_m & \mathbf{D}^\mathsf{T} \\ \mathbf{D} & \mathbf{C} \end{bmatrix} = \mathbf{BA}_n\mathbf{B}^\mathsf{T}, \qquad (4.4.6)$$

where $\mathbf{A}_m$ has the same shape as before and $\mathbf{C}$ is the covariance matrix of an MA(q) process. The matrix $\mathbf{D}$ is zero except for its upper right corner; its entries are covariances of z_t and e_s for $t > s$. Consequently, $\mathbf{BA}_n\mathbf{B}^\mathsf{T}$ is a positive definite covariance matrix with total bandwidth $(2m+1)$, so that the Cholesky factorization

$$\mathbf{BA}_n\mathbf{B}^\mathsf{T} = \mathbf{LL}^\mathsf{T} \qquad (4.4.7)$$

yields a lower triangular factor $\mathbf{L}$ with bandwidth m. Then a bilinear form in the inverse of $\mathbf{A}_n$ can be computed using

$$\mathbf{x}^\mathsf{T}\mathbf{A}_n^{-1}\mathbf{y} = \mathbf{x}^\mathsf{T}(\mathbf{B}^{-1}\mathbf{LL}^\mathsf{T}\mathbf{B}^{-\mathsf{T}})^{-1}\mathbf{y} = (\mathbf{L}^{-1}\mathbf{Bx})^\mathsf{T}(\mathbf{L}^{-1}\mathbf{By}). \qquad (4.4.8)$$

The factorization requires $O(nm)$ flops and the storage needed is $O(m^2)$. The total work for computing the bilinear form in the inverse is $O(n(p+q+1))$, which is such a substantial savings that exact analysis of long time series is feasible.

Example 4.4: *Computing the Likelihood of an* ARMA$(1, 1)$ *Model*
Consider now the covariance matrix of an ARMA$(1, 1)$ process defined by the equation

$$z_t - \phi z_{t-1} = e_t - e_{t-1}.$$

The covariance function $\gamma(k)$ takes on the following values:

$$\gamma(0) = \frac{1+\theta^2-2\phi\theta}{1-\phi^2}\sigma_e^2, \qquad \gamma(1) = \frac{(1-\phi\theta)(\phi-\theta)}{1-\phi^2}\sigma_e^2,$$

$$\gamma(j) = \phi\gamma(j-1) \quad \text{for } j \geq 2.$$

To show how this approach works, consider just $n = 4$ and construct the series $\{w_t\}$:

$$w_1 = z_1,$$
$$w_2 = z_2 - \phi z_1,$$
$$w_3 = z_3 - \phi z_2,$$
$$w_4 = z_4 - \phi z_3.$$

Beginning with $\mathbf{z} \sim N_n(\mu\mathbf{1}, \sigma_e^2\mathbf{A}_n)$, we have $\mathbf{w} = \mathbf{z} \sim N_n(\mu\mathbf{B1}, \sigma_e^2\mathbf{BAB}^\mathsf{T})$, where

$$\mathbf{B} = \begin{bmatrix} 1 & 0 & 0 & 0 \\ -\phi & 1 & 0 & 0 \\ 0 & -\phi & 1 & 0 \\ 0 & 0 & -\phi & 1 \end{bmatrix} \quad \text{and}$$

$$(\mathbf{BAB}^\mathsf{T}) = \begin{bmatrix} * & -\theta & 0 & 0 \\ -\theta & 1+\theta^2 & -\theta & 0 \\ 0 & -\theta & 1+\theta^2 & -\theta \\ 0 & 0 & -\theta & 1+\theta^2 \end{bmatrix} \sigma_e^2;$$

the missing element $(*)$ is $\gamma(0)/\sigma_e^2$, since $w_1 = z_1$. Notice that, except for the 1,1 element, the covariance matrix for $\mathbf{w}$ is that of an MA(1) process. For the case $\phi = .9$ and $\theta = .5$, we have

$$
\mathbf{z} = \begin{bmatrix} -2 \\ 1 \\ 0 \\ 1 \end{bmatrix}, \quad
\mathbf{Bz} = \begin{bmatrix} -2 \\ 2.8 \\ -0.9 \\ 1 \end{bmatrix}, \quad
\mathbf{B1} = \begin{bmatrix} 1 \\ .1 \\ .1 \\ .1 \end{bmatrix},
$$

$$
\mathbf{BAB}^\mathrm{T} = \begin{bmatrix}
1.84 & -.5 & 0 & 0 \\
-.5 & 1.25 & -.5 & 0 \\
0 & -.5 & 1.25 & -.5 \\
0 & 0 & -.5 & 1.25
\end{bmatrix}, \quad \text{so}
$$

$$
\mathbf{L} = \begin{bmatrix}
1.36 & 0 & 0 & 0 \\
-.37 & 1.06 & 0 & 0 \\
0 & -.47 & 1.01 & 0 \\
0 & 0 & -.49 & 1.00
\end{bmatrix} \quad \text{and then}
$$

$$
\mathbf{L}^{-1}\mathbf{Bz} = \begin{bmatrix} -1.47 \\ 2.14 \\ .11 \\ 1.05 \end{bmatrix} \quad \text{and} \quad
\mathbf{L}^{-1}\mathbf{B1} = \begin{bmatrix} .74 \\ .35 \\ .26 \\ .23 \end{bmatrix}.
$$

The MLE (maximum likelihood estimator) for μ is then $\hat{\mu} = \mathbf{1}^\mathrm{T}\mathbf{A}^{-1}\mathbf{z}/\mathbf{1}^\mathrm{T}\mathbf{A}^{-1}\mathbf{1} = -.063/.79 = -.080$ with $|\mathbf{A}| = 2.12$, and the quadratic form for the likelihood is $\mathbf{z}^\mathrm{T}\mathbf{A}^{-1}\mathbf{z} - (\mathbf{1}^\mathrm{T}\mathbf{A}^{-1}\mathbf{z})^2/\mathbf{1}^\mathrm{T}\mathbf{A}^{-1}\mathbf{1} = 7.86$. See the demonstration **chex44**.

4.5   Toeplitz Systems

The covariance matrix of every stationary time series process $\{z_t\}$, observed at regularly spaced intervals, has the Toeplitz structure given by (4.4.3). But since most applications use ARMA models, or models that can be put into ARMA form, the savings outlined in the previous section are much more important. When a stationary process can *not* be put in the ARMA form – as happens, for example, with fractionally differenced processes (see Hosking 1981 or Haslett and Raftery 1989) – then the savings are not so great but still are an improvement over the $O(n^3)$ flops required by the usual Cholesky route.

Let $\mathbf{A}_n$ be a Toeplitz matrix as in (4.4.3) and let $\mathbf{P}_n$ be the permutation matrix that reverses order, $1 \leftrightarrow n, \ldots, i \leftrightarrow n+1-i$; then note that $\mathbf{P}_n$ is symmetric and

$$
\mathbf{P}_n\mathbf{A}_n\mathbf{P}_n = \mathbf{A}_n. \tag{4.5.1}
$$

Normalize the covariance function $\gamma(k)$ into correlations $r(k) = \gamma(k)/\gamma(0)$, so that $r(0) = 1$ and the diagonal elements of $\mathbf{A}_n$ are all one. For a likelihood-based analysis, there are two systems of equations to be solved in addition to computing the determinant. The first system consists of the more specific Yule–Walker equations

$$\mathbf{A}_n \mathbf{b}^{(n)} = -\mathbf{r}^{(n)}, \tag{4.5.2}$$

where $\mathbf{r}$ is the vector $\mathbf{r} = (r(1), \ldots, r(n))^\mathsf{T}$ of length n; similarly, $\mathbf{b}^{(n)}$ has length n. When these equations arise in estimating autoregressive parameters, an improved algorithm is really not needed because n is seldom very large. However, a faster solution to (4.5.2), attributed to Durbin (1960), is an integral part of the fast solution of the more general problem,

$$\mathbf{A}_n \mathbf{x}^{(n)} = \mathbf{y}^{(n)}, \tag{4.5.3}$$

which is due to Levinson (1947). The improved algorithms utilize recursion, using the solution to the problem of size k to solve the problem of size $k + 1$.

Let us begin by partitioning the determinant into the first n rows and columns as

$$|\mathbf{A}_{n+1}| = \begin{vmatrix} \mathbf{A}_n & \mathbf{P}_n \mathbf{r}^{(n)} \\ \mathbf{r}^{(n)\mathsf{T}} \mathbf{P}_n & 1 \end{vmatrix} = |\mathbf{A}_n|(1 - \mathbf{r}^{(n)\mathsf{T}} \mathbf{P}_n \mathbf{A}_n^{-1} \mathbf{P}_n \mathbf{r}^{(n)}),$$

following the expression for partitioned matrices and using the solution to (4.5.2),

$$\mathbf{P}_n \mathbf{b}^{(n)} = -\mathbf{P}_n \mathbf{A}_n^{-1} \mathbf{r}^{(n)} = -\mathbf{A}_n^{-1} \mathbf{P}_n \mathbf{r}^{(n)}. \tag{4.5.4}$$

Then, defining $d_{n+1} = 1 + \mathbf{r}^{(n)\mathsf{T}} \mathbf{b}^{(n)}$, the determinant can be computed recursively by

$$|\mathbf{A}_{n+1}| = |\mathbf{A}_n| d_{n+1}. \tag{4.5.5}$$

Now the Yule–Walker equations (4.5.2) for $n + 1$ variables are written as

$$\begin{bmatrix} \mathbf{A}_n & \mathbf{P}_n \mathbf{r}^{(n)} \\ \mathbf{r}^{(n)\mathsf{T}} \mathbf{P}_n & 1 \end{bmatrix} \begin{bmatrix} \mathbf{b}_*^{(n+1)} \\ b_{n+1}^{(n+1)} \end{bmatrix} = -\begin{bmatrix} \mathbf{r}^{(n)} \\ r_{n+1} \end{bmatrix},$$

where $\mathbf{b}_*^{(n+1)}$ denotes the vector of the first n elements of the $(n + 1)$ vector $\mathbf{b}^{(n+1)}$. Adding $\mathbf{b}^{(n)\mathsf{T}} \mathbf{P}_n = -\mathbf{r}^{(n)\mathsf{T}} \mathbf{P}_n \mathbf{A}_n^{-1}$ times the first block of equations to the last equations eliminates $\mathbf{b}_*^{(n+1)}$ and leads to

$$[1 + \mathbf{b}^{(n)\mathsf{T}} \mathbf{r}^{(n)}] b_{n+1}^{(n+1)} = -r_{n+1} - \mathbf{b}^{(n)\mathsf{T}} \mathbf{P}_n \mathbf{r}^{(n)}. \tag{4.5.6}$$

Defining the negative of the right-hand side of (4.5.6) as $e_{n+1} = r_{n+1} + \mathbf{b}^{(n)\mathsf{T}} \mathbf{P}_n \mathbf{r}^{(n)}$ gives the last element of the new vector as

$$b_{n+1}^{(n+1)} = -e_{n+1}/d_{n+1}. \tag{4.5.7a}$$

Plugging this back into the first set of equations, the remaining elements $\mathbf{b}_*^{(n+1)}$ can be computed from $\mathbf{b}^{(n)}$:

$$\mathbf{b}_*^{(n+1)} = \mathbf{A}_n^{-1} \left[(e_{n+1}/d_{n+1}) \mathbf{P}_n \mathbf{r}^{(n)} - \mathbf{r}^{(n)} \right] = \mathbf{b}^{(n)} + b_{n+1}^{(n+1)} \mathbf{P}_n \mathbf{b}^{(n)}. \tag{4.5.7b}$$

The result is that $\mathbf{b}^{(k)}$ can be computed recursively from $\mathbf{b}^{(k-1)}$, and so on, taking $O(k)$ at each step; the total is $O(n^2)$. Solving the more general system (4.5.3) follows similar steps, since now adding $\mathbf{b}^{(n)\mathsf{T}} \mathbf{P}_n$ times the first block of equations to the last leaves

$$d_{n+1} x_{n+1}^{(n+1)} = y_{n+1} + \mathbf{b}^{(n)T} \mathbf{P}_n \mathbf{y}^{(n)} = y_{n+1} - \mathbf{r}^{(n)\mathsf{T}} \mathbf{P}_n \mathbf{x}^{(n)} = f_{n+1}, \tag{4.5.8a}$$

so that the new element is $x_{n+1}^{(n+1)} = f_{n+1}/d_{n+1}$. Substitution for the other elements $\mathbf{x}_*^{(n+1)}$ produces

$$\mathbf{A}_n\mathbf{x}_*^{(n+1)} = \mathbf{y}^{(n)} - x_{n+1}^{(n+1)}\mathbf{P}_n\mathbf{r}^{(n)},$$

so that the update step is

$$\mathbf{x}_*^{(n+1)} = \mathbf{A}_n^{-1}\mathbf{y}^{(n)} - x_{n+1}^{(n+1)}\mathbf{A}_n^{-1}\mathbf{P}_n\mathbf{r}^{(n)} = \mathbf{x}^{(n)} + x_{n+1}^{(n+1)}\mathbf{P}_n\mathbf{b}^{(n)}. \qquad (4.5.8b)$$

Note that the solutions (4.5.8) require solving the Yule–Walker equations and that the work is $O(n^2)$. The Levinson–Durbin method can be expressed algorithmically as follows.

(1) Let $d_1 = 1$, $b_1^{(1)} = -r_1$, and $x_1^{(1)} = y_1$.
(2) Then, for $k = 2, \ldots, n$:
   (i) compute the scalars

$$d_k = 1 + \mathbf{r}^{(k-1)\mathrm{T}}\mathbf{b}^{(k-1)},$$
$$e_k = r_k + \mathbf{b}^{(k-1)\mathrm{T}}\mathbf{P}_{k-1}\mathbf{r}^{(k-1)},$$
$$f_k = y_k - \mathbf{r}^{(k-1)\mathrm{T}}\mathbf{P}_{k-1}\mathbf{x}^{(k-1)};$$

   and then
   (ii) update the vectors – first the new elements $b_k^{(k)} = -e_k/d_k$ and $x_k^{(k)} = f_k/d_k$; then

$$\mathbf{b}_*^{(k)} = \mathbf{b}^{(k-1)} + b_k^{(k)}\mathbf{P}_{k-1}\mathbf{b}^{(k-1)},$$
$$\mathbf{x}_*^{(k)} = \mathbf{x}^{(k-1)} + x_k^{(k)}\mathbf{P}_{k-1}\mathbf{b}^{(k-1)}.$$

The reader is warned to be careful in updating $\mathbf{b}$ as shown here; updating elements i and $k - i$ at the same time will avoid an overwrite error. In likelihood analysis, the quadratic form $s_n = \mathbf{1}^{\mathrm{T}}\mathbf{A}_n^{-1}\mathbf{1}$ is usually needed. The update step for this quantity is

$$s_k = s_{k-1} + (1 + \mathbf{1}^{\mathrm{T}}\mathbf{b}^{(k-1)})^2/d_k; \qquad (4.5.9)$$

the details are outlined in Exercise 4.14. An alternative computation for $d_{k+1} = d_k(1 - b_k^{(k)2})$ is presented in Exercise 4.15.

Some authors do not recommend solving these systems by the Levinson–Durbin algorithm, but Cybenko (1980) stated that the algorithm is as stable as the corresponding Cholesky method. He contends that the condition of the equations causes the erratic behavior, especially when the Yule–Walker equations correspond to processes that are nearly nonstationary, with roots of the characteristic polynomial near unity. An approach for evaluating this contention is outlined in Exercise 4.16. The Levinson–Durbin algorithm is related to tests for stationarity (Monahan 1984; Pagano 1973). An inversion algorithm for a Toeplitz matrix by Trench (1964) is notable for its novelty, taking only $O(n^2)$; however, the inverse is rarely needed. Nonetheless, a Cholesky factorization would be quite useful. With a few reinventions of the wheel came the discovery that the Levinson-Durbin algorithm does produce a Cholesky factorization, not for $\mathbf{A}_n$, but for $\mathbf{A}_n^{-1}$.

Consider the following calculation for $0 \le k < n$ based on a different partitioning

$$\mathbf{A}_n \begin{bmatrix} \mathbf{0}_{n-k-1} \\ 1 \\ \mathbf{b}^{(k)} \end{bmatrix} = \begin{bmatrix} \mathbf{A}_{n-k-1} & * & * \\ * & 1 & \mathbf{r}^{(k)T} \\ * & \mathbf{r}^{(k)} & \mathbf{A}_k \end{bmatrix} \begin{bmatrix} \mathbf{0}_{n-k-1} \\ 1 \\ \mathbf{b}^{(k)} \end{bmatrix} = \begin{bmatrix} * \\ d_{k+1} \\ \mathbf{0}_k \end{bmatrix}$$

where $*$ represents not-known-to-be-zero elements. Now construct the lower triangular matrix $\mathbf{C}_n$ based on similarly stacked columns:

$$\mathbf{C}_n = \begin{bmatrix} 1 & 0 & 0 & \cdots & 0 & 0 \\ b_1^{(n-1)} & 1 & 0 & \cdots & 0 & 0 \\ b_2^{(n-1)} & b_1^{(n-2)} & 1 & \cdots & 0 & 0 \\ \cdots & & & \cdots & & \\ b_{n-2}^{(n-1)} & b_{n-3}^{(n-2)} & b_{n-2}^{(n-3)} & \cdots & 1 & 0 \\ b_{n-1}^{(n-1)} & b_{n-2}^{(n-2)} & b_{n-3}^{(n-3)} & \cdots & b_1^{(1)} & 1 \end{bmatrix}.$$

Then we see that $\mathbf{A}_n\mathbf{C}_n$ is upper triangular with diagonal elements d_{n-k+1}. Then premultiply by the upper triangular $\mathbf{C}_n^T$ to form the upper triangular product $\mathbf{D}_n = \mathbf{C}_n^T\mathbf{A}_n\mathbf{C}_n$. But since $\mathbf{D}_n$ is also symmetric, then $\mathbf{D}_n$ must be diagonal, and its diagonal elements are $(\mathbf{D}_n)_{jj} = d_{n-j+1}$. Some algebra gives $\mathbf{A}_n^{-1} = (\mathbf{C}_n\mathbf{D}_n^{-1/2})(\mathbf{C}_n\mathbf{D}_n^{-1/2})^T$, so that a Cholesky factorization for the inverse merely requires rescaling the columns of $\mathbf{C}_n$.

Example 4.5: *Levinson–Durbin Algorithm for* ARMA$(1, 1)$ *problem*
Consider the ARMA$(1, 1)$ problem with $n = 4$, $\phi = .9$, and $\theta = .5$ as described in Example 4.4. Since the covariance matrix for such a process is Toeplitz, let us recompute the MLE for μ and the quadratic form using the Levinson–Durbin algorithm. Here the correlations are $r(0) = 1$, $r(1) = .6286$, $r(2) = .5657$, $r(3) = .5091$, and $r(4) = .4582$. The data are $z_1 = -2$, $z_2 = 1$, $z_3 = 0$, and $z_4 = 1$ and supply the values for $\mathbf{y}$ here.

$k = 1$: $d_1 = 1$, $s_1 = 1$, $b_1 = -.6286$, and $x_1 = -2$.

$k = 2$: $d_2 = 1 + r_1b_1 = 1 - b_1^2 = .6049$ and $s_2 = s_1 + (1 + b_1)^2/d_2 = 1.2280$; also, $e_2 = r_2 + b_1r_1 = .1706$ and $f_2 = y_2 - r_1x_1 = 2.2572$, so that $b_2 = -e_2/d_2 = -.2820$ and $x_2 = f_2/d_2 = 3.7314$; then, updating yields $b_1 = b_1 + b_2b_1 = -.4513$ and $x_1 = x_1 + x_2b_1 = -4.3456$.

$k = 3$: $d_3 = d_2(1 - b_2^2) = .5568$ and $s_3 = s_2 + (1 + b_1 + b_2)^2/d_3 = 1.3557$; also, $e_3 = r_3 + r_1b_2 + r_2b_1 = .0765$ and $f_3 = y_3 - r_1x_2 - r_2x_1 = .1127$, so that the new vectors are $b_3 = -e_3/d_3 = -.1375$ and $x_3 = f_3/d_3 = .2026$; then, updating yields $b_1 = b_1 + b_3b_2 = -.4126$, $b_2 = b_2 + b_3b_1 = -.2200$ and $x_1 = x_1 + x_3b_2 = -4.4026$, $x_2 = x_2 + x_3b_1 = 3.6400$.

$k = 4$: $d_4 = d_3(1 - b_3^2) = .5463$ and $s_4 = s_3 + (1 + b_1 + b_2 + b_3)^2/d_4 = 1.4526$; also, $e_4 = r_4 + r_1b_3 + r_2b_2 + r_3b_1 = .0373$ and $f_4 = y_4 - r_1x_3 - r_2x_2 - r_3x_1 = .7014$, so that the new vectors are $b_4 = -e_4/d_4 = -.0683$ and $x_4 = f_4/d_4 = 1.9314$; then, updating yields $b_1 = b_1 + b_4b_3 = -.4031$, $b_2 = b_2 + b_4b_2 = -.2050$, $b_3 = b_3 + b_4b_1 = -.1093$ and $x_1 = x_1 + x_4b_3 = -4.6682$, $x_2 = x_2 + x_4b_2 = 3.2151$, $x_3 = x_3 + x_4b_1 = -.5941$.

The MLE for μ is then

$$\hat{\mu} = \mathbf{1}^T \mathbf{A}^{-1} \mathbf{z} / \mathbf{1}^T \mathbf{A}^{-1} \mathbf{1} = (x_1 + \cdots + x_4)/s_4 = -.1158/1.4526 = -.0797,$$

as before in Example 4.4. The quadratic form $\mathbf{z}^T \mathbf{A}^{-1} \mathbf{z} - (\mathbf{1}^T \mathbf{A}^{-1} \mathbf{z})^2 / \mathbf{1}^T \mathbf{A}^{-1} \mathbf{1}$ has been rescaled by $\gamma(0) = 1.8421$, so $(y_1 x_1 + \cdots + y_4 x_4) - (x_1 + \cdots + x_4)^2 / s_4 = (14.4829) - (-.1158)^2 / 1.4526 = 14.4737$ should be divided by 1.8421 to yield 7.8572, agreeing with Example 4.4. Also, the determinant of the covariance matrix can be computed as $\gamma(0)^4 d_1 d_2 d_3 d_4 = 2.1187$ as before. The reader should note that the results given here are rounded from IEEE arithmetic and that recomputing with four decimal digits will give surprisingly different results. The nearness of the AR coefficient $\phi = .9$ to the stationary limit of 1 suggests that this problem may not be well conditioned. See the demonstration **chex45**.

4.6   Sparse Matrices

In this chapter, the structure of a matrix has been exploited to reduce the effort required to solve a system of equations. In the case of Toeplitz matrices, the effort for solving a system of equations can be reduced from the usual $O(n^3)$ to $O(n^2)$. For banded matrices, the effort can be dropped another factor of n, down to $O(n)$, although the constant depends on the bandwidth $p + q$. Attributing this reduction in effort to the $O(n)$ not-known-to-be-zero ("nonzero") elements would be a misleading oversimplification, even though multiplying a vector by a matrix with $O(n)$ nonzero elements does take $O(n)$ flops. If completely exploitable, the number of flops required by multiplication can match the number of nonzeros. However, the banded structure is exploited in solving a system of equations. Recall from Section 4.3 that the LU factorization requires $O(npq)$ flops; if p or q were near (say) $n/2$, then the savings would be but a fraction and not an order of n. If the banded structure were lost, then the savings in solving a system of linear equations would be lost.

Sparse matrices are those whose nonzero elements do not have an exploitable pattern. As such, the distribution of their nonzero elements is assumed to be somewhat random but with a fraction k of nonzeros in each row or column, making $kn + O(1)$ nonzero elements in all. Nonetheless, many techniques have been devised that take particular advantage of the sparsity, although this discussion will focus only on some simple methods for storage and matrix–vector multiplication.

In statistics, there are two major sources of sparse matrices. In a queuing model, a Markov chain is commonly used to model the changes from one state to another. As the model becomes complicated, the transition matrix $\mathbf{Q}$ grows rapidly in size to hundreds or thousands of states, although most states may permit transition to only a few k others. These problems usually require the stationary probability vectors, which involve solving an eigenproblem in $\mathbf{Q}^T$. Occasionally, the probability vector that is m time steps ahead is needed, $\mathbf{p}^T \mathbf{Q}^m$. Matrix–vector multiplication is the key here, as well as for the eigenproblem discussed in Chapter 6.

The second statistical application of sparse matrices is constructing the design matrix $\mathbf{X}$ of complicated experimental designs. Here both the rows (observations) and columns (parameters) may be large while most entries are zeros, with typically only one nonzero appearing in a set of columns corresponding to a particular treatment or interaction. Missing cells destroy patterns that could otherwise be exploited. Conjugate gradient methods (Section 5.10) are designed to exploit just the computation of **Xb** for candidate estimate vectors **b**.

The key to sparse matrix techniques is storage of the nonzeros. Recall that storage is usually the limiting factor in the size of problem that can be solved. Storing just the nonzeros would reduce space requirements substantially, from n^2 down to kn. However, in order to keep track of the location of the nonzeros, another kn space is needed to store the addresses. Methods for storage are designed with the application in mind: matrix multiplication or solving equations; whether elements will be added, deleted, or changed; whether the matrix needs to be traversed by row or column or both. Since this discussion concerns only matrix–vector multiplication **Ax**, we need only consider the following two rather simple-minded approaches.

In the first scheme, assume that **x** and the product **y** will both fit in memory. Construct three lists $A(k), r(k), c(k)$ from the nonzero elements of **A**; hence, if the kth nonzero element is A_{ij} then $A(k) = A_{ij}$, $r(k) = i$, and $c(k) = j$. If the elements of **A** could be stored in main memory, then the update step could look like the Fortran code:

```
do k=1, many
i=r( k )
j=c( k )
y( i )=y( i )+A( k ) * x( j )
end do   ! loop on k
```

The elements of **A** could also be read in as a linear list, even from a mass storage device, along with the corresponding row and column. In Fortran, this version of the update step could be

```
do k=1, many
read( unit, frmt ) i, j, a
y( i )=y( i )+a * x( j )
end do   ! loop on k
```

If stored in main memory, this scheme would allow the elements to be changed or deleted, or added at the end (or replacing a deletion).

For the second simple scheme, assume that both **A** and **x** will fit into main memory, together with the product **y**. For matrix multiplication, we will be traversing the matrix by rows. Construct first the list of nonzero elements of **A**, in order from the first row to the last. Then construct two other lists, one of length n giving the number of nonzeros in each row LGTHRW(I). The second list, COLLIST(K), gives the column index for each corresponding element of **A**. The code for the product **Ax** may look like this:

```
!     multiply A*x=y
k=0   ! count nonzero entries
do i=1,n
jmx=lgthrw(i)   ! how many in this row?
y(i)=0.
```

```
do jj=1,jmx
k=k+1   ! next nonzero pointer
j=collist(k)  ! column index
y(i)=y(i)+A(k)*x(j)  ! A(i,j)*x(j)
end do  ! loop on jj
end do  ! loop on i
```

These are but two simple schemes, yet either one is sufficient to exploit sparseness for matrix multiplication.

Example 4.6: *Sparse Matrix Multiplication*

Harrod and Plemmons (1984) gave the following 10×10 matrix **A** as the transpose of a transition matrix for a Markov chain. We have just listed the heart of the Fortran code for multiplying $\mathbf{Ax} = \mathbf{y}$; after the matrix we list the declarations.

$$
\begin{bmatrix}
.2 & & & & & & .1 & & & \\
 & .1 & .1 & & .5 & .5 & & & .1 & .4 \\
 & & & .6 & & & .9 & & & \\
.6 & & & & & & & & & \\
 & .6 & & .3 & .5 & .2 & .7 & & & \\
 & & & & & & & & .8 & .4 \\
 & .3 & & & & & .2 & & & \\
 & & .8 & & & & & & & \\
 & & & & & .3 & & & & \\
.2 & & .1 & .1 & & & .1 & & .1 & .2
\end{bmatrix}
$$

```
!    demo of sparse matrix multiplication
!    see Example 4.6
implicit none
integer, parameter :: n=10  ! dimension
integer, parameter :: nnz=28  ! number of nonzeroes
integer, DIMENSION(n) ::  lgthrw  ! # nonzeroes by row
integer, DIMENSION(nnz) ::  collist  ! column indices
integer k,i,jmx,jj,j
real, DIMENSION(nnz) ::  A  ! transition probs
real, DIMENSION(n) ::  x,y  ! vectors
!
21 FORMAT(10f8.4)
!
data lgthrw/ 2, 6, 2, 1, 5, 2, 2, 1, 1, 6 /
DATA collist/ 1,8, 2,3,5,6,9,10, 4,8, 1, 2,4,5,6,7, 9,10, 2,7, &
&       3, 6, 1,3,4,7,9,10 /
DATA A/ .2, 3*.1, 2*.5, .1, .4, .6, .9, 2*.6, .3, .5, .2, .7, &
&   .8, .4, .3, .2, .8, .3, .2, 4*.1, .2 /
DATA x/ 10*.1 /
```

4.7   Iterative Methods

The first iterative scheme to be treated is iterative improvement. Suppose the system $\mathbf{Ax} = \mathbf{b}$ is large (n large) and full (or not otherwise structured), and suppose that it is sufficiently ill conditioned that the computed solution $\mathbf{x}^*$ is not very accurate. If $\kappa(\mathbf{A})$ is the condition number and U is the machine unit, then $U\kappa$ is larger than required. The common response is to recompute the solution in double precision. A single precision solution requires $n^3/3 + O(n^2)$ flops and so it follows that, if a double precision floating point operation takes comparatively 3 flops (or it could be 4), then the double precision route will take n^3 flops – three times as much work. The presumed relative accuracy is κU^2 for the double precision solution.

As an alternative, suppose the residual

$$\mathbf{r}^* = \mathbf{b} - \mathbf{A}\mathbf{x}^* \qquad (4.7.1)$$

is computed and that the solution $\mathbf{d}^*$ for the system $\mathbf{A}\mathbf{d} = \mathbf{r}^*$ is computed and added to $\mathbf{x}^*$,

$$\mathbf{x}^{**} = \mathbf{x}^* + \mathbf{d}^*, \qquad (4.7.2)$$

to improve accuracy. Cancellation occurs in computing the residual $\mathbf{r}^*$, so $\mathbf{x}^{**}$ is not likely to be an improvement. But if the residual computations (4.7.1) are done in double precision, then $\mathbf{x}^{**}$ will be more accurate. If these steps are repeated k times, then the relative accuracy of the improved solution is roughly $\max(U, (\kappa U)^k)$ as long as $\kappa U < 1$.

The computation required for iterative improvement is substantially less than that for completely double precision calculations. Since the residual $\mathbf{r}^*$ must be done in double precision, this step takes roughly $3n^2$ flops. But once $\mathbf{PA} = \mathbf{LU}$ has been computed, solving the system $\mathbf{A}\mathbf{d} = \mathbf{r}^*$ requires only n^2 flops. For k steps the cost is merely $4kn^2$ flops, so that the break-even point on work is $k = n/6$. Although iterative improvement can enlarge the size of problems that are feasible, the drawbacks are that it is dependent on both hardware and software and is also cumbersome to code.

Other iterative methods exploit the difference in the orders of magnitude between multiplying a vector $O(n^2)$ and solving a system of equations $O(n^3)$. If the matrix is sparse (i.e., if the number of nonzero elements is $O(n)$) and not banded, then this advantage is accentuated because the number of multiplications is only the number of nonzero elements of the matrix. These methods begin with an approximate solution $\mathbf{x}^{(0)}$ and iterate by solving a related equation, so that (at convergence) the fixed point $\mathbf{x}^{(\text{last})}$ gives the solution of the equation $\mathbf{A}\mathbf{x} = \mathbf{b}$.

For solving the system of equations $\mathbf{A}\mathbf{x} = \mathbf{b}$, decompose into $\mathbf{A} = \mathbf{L} + \mathbf{D} + \mathbf{U}$, where $\mathbf{D}$ is a diagonal matrix composed of the diagonal elements of $\mathbf{A}$, $\mathbf{L}$ is strictly lower triangular, and $\mathbf{U}$ is strictly upper triangular. The *Jacobi* method can be viewed as solving equation i for x_i using the other components of $\mathbf{x}$ as known, coming from the previous iteration, so that the steps for $i = 1, \ldots, n$,

$$x_i^{(k+1)} = \frac{b_i - \sum_{j \neq i} A_{ij} x_j^{(k)}}{A_{ii}} \qquad (4.7.3)$$

can be rewritten algebraically as

$$\mathbf{x}^{(k+1)} = \mathbf{D}^{-1}[\mathbf{b} - (\mathbf{L} + \mathbf{U})\mathbf{x}^{(k)}]. \qquad (4.7.4)$$

Note that, at convergence, (4.7.4) can be rewritten as

$$\mathbf{D}\mathbf{x} = \mathbf{b} - \mathbf{L}\mathbf{x} - \mathbf{U}\mathbf{x} \iff (\mathbf{L} + \mathbf{D} + \mathbf{U})\mathbf{x} = \mathbf{b}.$$

The error can be found from the iteration step (4.7.4) to be

$$(\mathbf{x}^{(k+1)} - \mathbf{x}) = -\mathbf{D}^{-1}(\mathbf{L} + \mathbf{U})(\mathbf{x}^{(k)} - \mathbf{x}) = \mathbf{C}^{k+1}(\mathbf{x}^{(0)} - \mathbf{x}), \qquad (4.7.5)$$

where $\mathbf{C} = -\mathbf{D}^{-1}(\mathbf{L} + \mathbf{U})$. It should then be clear that the convergence of the Jacobi iteration depends on $\|\mathbf{C}\| < 1$, since

$$\|\mathbf{x}^{(k+1)} - \mathbf{x}\| \leq \|\mathbf{C}\|^{k+1}\|\mathbf{x}^{(0)} - \mathbf{x}\|. \qquad (4.7.6)$$

Whereas Jacobi updates $\mathbf{x}^{(k+1)}$ all at once, the *Gauss–Seidel* iterative scheme updates each element of the solution (one at a time) and uses it for the next. The update step takes the form

$$x_i^{(k+1)} = \frac{b_i - \sum_{j<i} A_{ij} x_j^{(k+1)} - \sum_{j>i} A_{ij} x_j^{(k)}}{A_{ii}};$$

rewriting in vector form looks like solving the system of equations

$$(\mathbf{L} + \mathbf{D})\mathbf{x}^{(k+1)} = \mathbf{b} - \mathbf{U}\mathbf{x}^{(k)}, \qquad (4.7.7)$$

which can be written algebraically as

$$\mathbf{x}^{(k+1)} = (\mathbf{L} + \mathbf{D})^{-1}(\mathbf{b} - \mathbf{U}\mathbf{x}^{(k)}). \qquad (4.7.8)$$

Similarly to the Jacobi technique, the rate of convergence for the Gauss–Seidel method depends on the norm

$$\|(\mathbf{L} + \mathbf{D})^{-1}\mathbf{U}\|.$$

For some problems, it is possible to obtain the norm of the matrix analytically. Modifications of the Gauss–Seidel scheme, called successive over-relaxation (SOR), produce faster or surer convergence by adjusting w in

$$\mathbf{x}^{(k+1)} = (w\mathbf{L} + \mathbf{D})^{-1}[w\mathbf{b} - ((1-w)\mathbf{D} - w\mathbf{U})\mathbf{x}^{(k)}],$$

but this requires a great deal of preparation or knowledge of the problem.

4.8   Linear Programming

Many practical problems, as well as some important statistical ones, can be expressed as a *linear programming problem*: maximize or minimize a linear combination of variables subject to linear constraints. To begin, write the objective function as minimize $\mathbf{c}^T\mathbf{x}$, where $\mathbf{x}$ is the vector of variables and $\mathbf{c}$ the coefficients or *costs* to be minimized. The linear constraints can be written as $\mathbf{A}\mathbf{x} \leq \mathbf{b}$ and $\mathbf{x} \geq \mathbf{0}$, where the inequalities are applied to each component. To view the geometry of the problem, recall that $\mathbf{a}^T\mathbf{x} = b$ defines a hyperplane and the inequality $\mathbf{a}^T\mathbf{x} \leq b$ the half-space bounded by that hyperplane. Since each row of the constraint matrix $\mathbf{A}$ defines one of those hyperplanes, the system of inequality constraints $\mathbf{A}\mathbf{x} \leq \mathbf{b}$ expresses the intersection of these half-spaces. The nonnegativity constraint $\mathbf{x} \geq \mathbf{0}$ restricts $\mathbf{x}$ to the positive orthant. This means that the set of *feasible solutions* is a solid in $d-$dimensional space with boundaries formed by the hyperplanes. Optimizing a linear function means pushing in a direction of improvement until a boundary is reached. In this situation, it means that the minimum of the objective function must occur at a corner (vertex) of this solid.

Backing up for a moment, notice that the inequality constraints of the form $\mathbf{a}^T\mathbf{x} \leq b$ can be rewritten as an equality constraint $\mathbf{a}^T\mathbf{x} + x_s = b$ with the introduction of a non-negative ($x_s \geq 0$) slack variable $\mathbf{x}_s$ with zero cost coefficient (and vice versa). So we could also view the problem as

$$\text{minimize } \mathbf{c}^T\mathbf{x} \text{ subject to } \mathbf{Ax} = \mathbf{b}, \mathbf{x} \geq \mathbf{0}.$$

At this point, the vertices of this solid are points where the boundaries are all encountered, which means that components of $\mathbf{x}$ are involved either with solving $\mathbf{Ax} = \mathbf{b}$ or hitting the boundary of $\mathbf{x} \geq \mathbf{0}$. Since the latter restriction means that these components are zero, the corners or vertices are points where some of the components of $\mathbf{x}$ are zero, and the others are solving $\mathbf{Ax} = \mathbf{b}$, also known as a *basic feasible solution*. Denote the former (nonbasic) components as $\mathbf{x}_\mathcal{N} = \mathbf{0}$ and the latter (basic) as $\mathbf{x}_B$ and partition accordingly

$$\mathbf{Ax} = [\mathbf{B} \quad \mathbf{N}] \begin{bmatrix} \mathbf{x}_B \\ \mathbf{x}_\mathcal{N} \end{bmatrix} = \mathbf{b}$$

and $\mathbf{c}^T = (\mathbf{x}_B, \mathbf{x}_\mathcal{N})$. If we have a basic feasible solution $\overline{\mathbf{x}}^T = (\overline{\mathbf{x}}_B^T, \overline{\mathbf{x}}_\mathcal{N}^T)$, then $\overline{\mathbf{x}}_\mathcal{N} = \mathbf{0}$ and $\mathbf{B}\overline{\mathbf{x}}_B = \mathbf{b}$ or $\overline{\mathbf{x}}_B = \mathbf{B}^{-1}\mathbf{b}$.

The simplex algorithm begins with a basic, feasible solution (a corner) and searches along its edges for a direction that gives an improvement (reduction) in the cost function to move to another basic, feasible solution or vertex. All solutions to $\mathbf{Ax} = \mathbf{b}$ can be written as

$$\mathbf{x} = \begin{bmatrix} \mathbf{x}_B \\ \mathbf{x}_\mathcal{N} \end{bmatrix} = \overline{\mathbf{x}} + (\mathbf{I} - \mathbf{A}^g\mathbf{A})\mathbf{y} = \begin{bmatrix} \overline{\mathbf{x}}_B \\ \mathbf{0} \end{bmatrix} + \begin{bmatrix} -\mathbf{B}^{-1}\mathbf{N} \\ \mathbf{I} \end{bmatrix} \mathbf{y}_\mathcal{N} \qquad (4.8.1)$$

using the generalized inverse $\mathbf{A}^g = \begin{bmatrix} \mathbf{B}^{-1} \\ \mathbf{0} \end{bmatrix}$. Let's look carefully at this equation.

Even though the vector $\mathbf{y}_\mathcal{N}$ includes all free variables, because of the nonnegativity constraint, we can only consider positive values. For an incremental increase in component j of $\mathbf{y}_\mathcal{N}$, the cost changes by $c_j - \mathbf{c}_B^T\mathbf{B}^{-1}\mathbf{N}_{.j} = d_j$. If these are all positive, then all departures from that vertex increase the cost and we have found the minimum. If for some j, we have $d_j < 0$, the cost will decrease by increasing component j, we have found a feasible direction. But notice that increasing component j by y_j also means changing the basic variables by $-\mathbf{B}\mathbf{N}_{.j}y_j$ to satisfy $\mathbf{Ax} = \mathbf{b}$ reaching the limit when one of these basic variables hits zero (when we reach the next vertex). If for some feasible direction, we find $-\mathbf{B}\mathbf{N}_{.j}$ to be all positive, then all basic variables will continue to increase and the problem has an unbounded solution. So the simplex algorithm follows:

1. start with a basic feasible solution
2. for all columns j not in basis, compute d_j
3. if all d_j are positive, we have the solution

4. for some column j where $d_j < 0$ (why not biggest?) find the smallest value of y_j that makes a basic variable zero (and now non-basic) (if none, stop due to unbounded solution)

5. move to new vertex where j now is among basic variables.

The simplex algorithm requires a basic feasible solution to get started. Sometimes in converting inequality constraints to equality constraints, a basic feasible solution may be easy to find. But if that is not available, a two-phase method can be used. In the first phase, set the cost vector to zero and augment with nonnegative auxiliary variables $\mathbf{x}^a$ with cost vector $c_a = \mathbf{1}$. Now recast problem as minimize $c_a^T \mathbf{x}^a$ subject to $\mathbf{Ax} + \mathbf{Ex}^a = \mathbf{b}$ with an easy to find basic feasible solution. If the components of $\mathbf{b}$ are all nonnegative, take $\mathbf{E} = \mathbf{I}$ and $\mathbf{x}^a = \mathbf{b}$. If a component of $\mathbf{b}$ is negative, then change the signs of everything in that equation, including RHS $\mathbf{b}$, so that $\mathbf{E}$ remains diagonal with ± 1's there. Now use the simplex algorithm to solve this linear program. If the costs are driven to zero, then all of the auxiliary variables should have been driven to zero and we should now have a basic feasible solution using only the original variables. In the second phase, drop the auxiliary variables, reestablish the original cost vector, and solve the original problem.

Other tricks abound. A maximization problem can be changed to a minimization problem simply by negating the cost vector $\mathbf{c}$. A variable that is not restricted to be nonnegative can be rewritten as the difference of two nonnegative variables $x = x^+ - x^-$; one will be nonbasic and its absolute value is $x = x^+ + x^-$. Duality says that the *primal* problem: minimize $\mathbf{c}^T \mathbf{x}$ subject to $\mathbf{Ax} \le \mathbf{b}, \mathbf{x} \ge \mathbf{0}$ is related to the *dual* problem: maximize $\mathbf{b}^T \mathbf{u}$ subject to $\mathbf{A}^T \mathbf{u} \ge \mathbf{c}, \mathbf{u} \ge \mathbf{0}$. Although the two problems differ in size and shape, they have the same Lagrangian. The solution to one can be used to find a solution to the other.

The main computational task in the simplex algorithm is the repeated solving of linear equations $\mathbf{Bx}_{\mathcal{B}} = \mathbf{b}$. From one step to the next, only one column of $\mathbf{B}$ is changed. For small or modest problems that easily fit in memory, the easiest way to do the computation is to use full elimination as described in Section 4.2. Begin with the full matrix $\mathbf{A}$ and index set $\mathcal{B}$ of basic variables. The using row pivoting, select column $j \in \mathcal{B}$ of initially $\mathbf{A}$, then $\mathbf{M}^{(1)}\mathbf{A}$, $\mathbf{M}^{(2)}\mathbf{M}^{(1)}\mathbf{A}$, etc. to form $\mathbf{a}$, and then $\mathbf{M} = \mathbf{I} - \frac{1}{a_q}(\mathbf{a} - \mathbf{e}_q)\mathbf{e}_q^T$ until $\mathcal{B}$ is exhausted and $\mathbf{B}^{-1}\mathbf{A}$ computed. Then to bring column j into the basis and drop q, use column j of $\mathbf{B}^{-1}\mathbf{A}$ as the new vector $\mathbf{a}$ to compute a new full column elimination matrix $\mathbf{M}$. Multiplying through produces $\mathbf{MB}^{-1}\mathbf{A}$ corresponding to $\mathbf{B}_{new}^{-1}\mathbf{A}$ with a different index set.

For large problems or just a large number of iterations, the rounding error can accumulate in $\mathbf{B}^{-1}\mathbf{A}$, suggesting periodic restarts at the current basic feasible solution. Secondly, in many applications, the matrix $\mathbf{A}$ may be very large and very sparse. In these cases, the computational scheme described above is quite inadequate as both space and cost preclude computation and storage of $\mathbf{B}^{-1}\mathbf{N}$.

The first step is to store the current $\mathbf{B}^{-1}$ as a product of matrices $\mathbf{M}^{(i)}$ by storing just the vectors $\mathbf{a}$ from each step. By computing once $\pi = \mathbf{B}^{-T}\mathbf{c}_{\mathcal{B}}$, we can compute d_j from the original matrix $\mathbf{A}$ as $c_j - \pi^T \mathbf{N}_{.j}$. Only in Step 4 are the elements of $\mathbf{B}^{-1}\mathbf{N}$ needed and only for one column: to check for an unbounded solution, to update the solution, and to find the new $\mathbf{a}^{(i)}$ to form $\mathbf{M}^{(i)}$. As a result, the main computational tasks are (algebraically) multiplying vectors by $\mathbf{B}^{-1}$ and $\mathbf{B}^{-T}$, where $\mathbf{B}^{-1} = \prod_i \mathbf{M}^{(i)}$. The former is easy, as we can write

$$\mathbf{B}^{-1}\mathbf{N}_{.j} = \prod_{i=1} \mathbf{M}^{(i)}\mathbf{N}_{.j} = \left(\prod_{i=2} \mathbf{M}^{(i)}\right) \mathbf{M}^{(1)}\mathbf{N}_{.j}$$

$$= \left(\prod_{i=2} \mathbf{M}^{(i)}\right) \left[\mathbf{I} - \frac{1}{a_q^{(1)}}(\mathbf{a}^{(1)} - \mathbf{e}_q)\mathbf{e}_q^T\right] \mathbf{N}_{.j}$$

$$= \left(\prod_{i=2} \mathbf{M}^{(i)}\right) \left[\mathbf{N}_{.j} - \frac{1}{a_q^{(1)}}(\mathbf{a}^{(1)} - \mathbf{e}_q)N_{qj}\right].$$

The latter is a little more complicated

$$\mathbf{B}^{-T}\mathbf{c}_\mathcal{B} = \left(\prod_{i=1}^{k} \mathbf{M}^{(i)}\right)^T \mathbf{c}_\mathcal{B} = \left(\prod_{i=1}^{k-1} \mathbf{M}^{(i)}\right)^T \mathbf{M}^{(k)T}\mathbf{c}_\mathcal{B}$$

$$= \left(\prod_{i=1}^{k-1} \mathbf{M}^{(i)}\right)^T \left[\mathbf{I} - \frac{1}{a_q^{(k)}}\mathbf{e}_q(\mathbf{a}^{(k)} - \mathbf{e}_q)^T\right] \mathbf{c}_\mathcal{B}$$

$$= \left(\prod_{i=1}^{k-1} \mathbf{M}^{(i)}\right) \left[\mathbf{c}_\mathcal{B} - \mathbf{e}_q \frac{(\mathbf{a}^{(k)} - \mathbf{e}_q)^T\mathbf{c}_\mathcal{B}}{a_q^{(k)}}\right].$$

where a single element of $\mathbf{c}_\mathcal{B}$ is updated at each step.

For even a very sparse matrix $\mathbf{A}$, $\mathbf{B}^{-1}\mathbf{N}_{.j}$ becomes less sparse with each step, hence $\mathbf{a}^{(i)}$ becomes less sparse and the storage for $\mathbf{B}^{-1}$ increases. Restarts will restore some sparseness as well as clean off some rounding error. However, full elimination with pivoting only at the beginning (or at restart) lacks the stability of factored forms such as the LU decomposition from Gaussian elimination. Bartels and Golub (1969) propose a method for storing $\mathbf{B}^{-1}$ in a sparse, factored form that maintains stability. Its discussion is beyond the scope of this book.

Programs and Demonstrations

mirse *Test/demonstration program for full elimination with complete pivoting*
The matrix given in Example 4.1 is inverted in place, a system of equations in that matrix is solved, and the solution is overwritten on the right-hand side. Code for output has been included in **mirse** in lower case for demonstration purposes and can be deleted.
mirse – computes the inverse, solution, and determinant of a system of equations.

chex44 *Demonstration of methods for likelihood computations for ARMA models*
The methods outlined in Section 4.4 are demonstrated using the ARMA(1, 1) process of Example 4.4; banded Cholesky factorization is used to solve the equations. In the

R version, the results are computed directly as banded factorization is not native nor easily coded in R.

chex45 *Test/demonstration of the Levinson–Durbin algorithm*
The data and parameters of Examples 4.4 and 4.5 are taken for the computation of the likelihood quantities using the Levinson–Durbin algorithm for Toeplitz matrices. These results are compared with the straightforward computation using Cholesky in **chex44**. The new subprogram is:
levdrb – computes the solution of the Yule–Walker equations, and another with the same Toeplitz structure and correlation function; also computes a quadratic form in the inverse with the vector **1**.

chex46 *Sparse matrix demonstration*
A simple vector is premultiplied by the sparse matrix **Q** in Example 4.6 as a demonstration of sparse matrix multiplication.

smplx *Simplex algorithm for Linear Programming*
The simplex algorithm described in Section 4.8 is tested using four problems. The R version is simple as $\mathbf{B}^{-1}\mathbf{A}$ is stored and updated. In the Fortran version, $\mathbf{B}^{-1}$ is stored in product form and sparse matrix tools are used to represent the matrix **A** as well as $\mathbf{a}^{(i)}$ for $\mathbf{B}^{-1}$.

Exercises

4.1 Recompute the solution to the interpolation problem in Example 3.6 (code in **chex36**) using full elimination with complete pivoting (**mirse**). Compare its accuracy.

4.2 Determine the work (in flops) for computing just the solution to a system of linear equations using full elimination with complete pivoting. How much additional work is needed to compute the inverse?

4.3 Does full elimination with partial pivoting make any sense?

4.4 Can Gaussian elimination be modified to do complete pivoting?

4.5 Modify the code for Gaussian elimination to exploit the structure of a banded matrix. Store the matrix taking $n(p + q + 1)$ locations.

4.6 Jennings (1977, p. 244) gave the following (transpose of) transition matrix ($n = 7$) for a Markov chain:
diagonals (A_{ii}) are .9, .6, .7, .6, .7, .7, .8;
superdiagonals ($A_{i,i+1}$) are .3, .2, .3, .2, .3, .2;
second subdiagonal ($A_{i+2,i}$) are all .1.
Write code to multiply any vector **x** by this transition matrix **A**, exploiting its banded structure.

4.7 As described in Example 4.4, the covariance matrix of an MA(1) process is tridiagonal, with main diagonal $1 + \theta^2$ and sub/superdiagonals $-\theta$. For the Cholesky factorization of **A** without square roots, $\mathbf{MDM}^{\mathrm{T}}$, what are D_{nn} and $M_{n,n-1}$? Find their limits as n approaches infinity.

4.8 For the covariance matrix $\mathbf{A}_{N+n}$ of an ARMA(p, q) process, partitioned as

$$\mathbf{A}_{N+n} = \begin{bmatrix} \mathbf{A}_N & \mathbf{A}_{12} \\ \mathbf{A}_{21} & \mathbf{A}_n \end{bmatrix}, \quad \begin{matrix} N \\ n \end{matrix}$$

give an algorithm for computing the forecast covariance matrix, $\mathbf{A}_n - \mathbf{A}_{21}\mathbf{A}_N^{-1}\mathbf{A}_{12}$.

4.9 Can the methods outlined in Section 4.4 for ARMA models adjust to missing values?

4.10 Suppose the matrix $\mathbf{A}$ is $n \times n$, positive definite, and banded with bandwidth $q = 5$. Suppose the vector $\mathbf{b}$ is zero except for nonzero entries in three consecutive locations, say b_k, b_{k+1}, and b_{k+2}. How much work does it take to compute $\mathbf{b}^{\mathrm{T}}\mathbf{A}^{-1}\mathbf{b}$? Can you do it in less than $O(n^3)$ flops?

4.11 For $n = 7$ and $r(k)$ given below, compare the solutions to the Yule–Walker equations computed by (a) Cholesky and (b) Levinson–Durbin methods. Compute the condition number of the correlation matrix, or an estimate using **gaucpp**.

$$\begin{aligned} r(0) &= 1, & r(5) &= 0.477, \\ r(1) &= 0.726, & r(6) &= 0.429, \\ r(2) &= 0.654, & r(7) &= 0.386, \\ r(3) &= 0.588, & r(8) &= 0.347. \end{aligned}$$

4.12 Repeat Exercise 4.11 with the correlation sequence for a fractionally differenced process of order d with $|d| < 1/2$, using $r(0) = 1, r(1) = d/(1-d), r(j) = (j-1+d)r(j-1)/(j-d)$, and different values of d.

4.13 Compute some iterative improvements to Example 3.5 or Example 3.6.

4.14 For a Toeplitz matrix $\mathbf{A}$, prove the update for $s_n = \mathbf{1}^{\mathrm{T}}\mathbf{A}_n^{-1}\mathbf{1}$ described in (4.5.9) as

$$s_{n+1} = s_n + (1 + \mathbf{1}^{\mathrm{T}}\mathbf{b}^{(n)})^2/d_{n+1}.$$

(*Hint:* Two routes are available; either follow the Levinson–Durbin algorithm with right-hand side vector $\mathbf{1}$, or show directly using the formula for the inverse of a partitioned matrix.)

4.15 Prove the alternative update formula for d_n in the Levinson–Durbin algorithm $d_{n+1} = d_n(1 - (b_n^{(n)})^2)$. (*Hint:* One route is to rewrite the formula for $1 + \mathbf{r}^{(n+1)\mathrm{T}}\mathbf{b}^{(n+1)}$ in terms of $\mathbf{r}^{(n)}$ and $\mathbf{b}^{(n)}$ and then substitute.)

4.16 Cybenko (1980) contended that the instability attributed to the Levinson–Durbin algorithm really stems from the condition of the problems presented for it to solve. Design a Monte Carlo experiment to address this issue. Examine the effect on the condition as the largest root of the autoregressive operator approaches unity. Compare Levinson–Durbin, Cholesky, and the methods outlined in Section 4.4.

4.17 Use sparse matrix tools to store the following 6×6 matrix (Jennings 1977, p. 246):

$$\begin{bmatrix} .8 & .6 & .1 & & & \\ & & .4 & & & \\ & & & & & \\ .2 & .3 & & 1 & & \\ & & .4 & & .4 & 1 \\ & .1 & .1 & & .6 & \end{bmatrix}.$$

4.18   Repeat Exercise 4.11 with $r(k) = \exp(-k^2/s)$, beginning with $s = 1$ and the same $n = 7$. Compute the condition number and increase the sample size n until Cholesky fails. Modify s and determine whether the condition improves or worsens with larger or smaller s.

4.19   The Cholesky factorization can fail for nearly singular matrices in trying to take the square root of something that became negative due to rounding error. Can the Cholesky factorization from the Levinson-Durbin algorithm fail in the same manner or is it different? What is the point of failure?

4.20   Maximize $x_1 + 2x_2 + 3x_3$ subject to $\sum_i x_i = 1$ and $1 \geq x_1 \geq x_2 \geq x_3 \geq 0$ as a linear programming problem.

References

Golub and van Loan (1996) discuss banded matrices in detail, as well as Toeplitz and iterative methods. Banded Cholesky factorization goes back to Martin and Wilkinson (1965); extending it from the MA to the general ARMA case is due to Ansley (1979). For more on the Toeplitz case, see Cybenko's (1980) article. The literature of sparse matrices is continually changing, but the applicability to statistical applications is quite limited; Jennings (1977) extensively discusses applications of iterative methods.

Craig F. Ansley (1979), "An Algorithm for the Exact Likelihood of a Mixed Autoregressive-Moving Average Process," *Biometrika* 66: 59–65.

Richard H. Bartels and Gene H. Golub (1969), "The Simplex Method of Linear Programming Using LU Decomposition," *Communications of the ACM*, 12: 266–68.

G. E. P. Box and G. M. Jenkins (1972), *Time Series Analysis: Forecasting and Control.* San Francisco: Holden-Day.

George Cybenko (1980), "The Numerical Stability of the Levinson–Durbin Algorithm for Toeplitz Systems of Equations," *SIAM Journal of Scientific and Statistical Computing* 1: 303–19.

J. Durbin (1960), "The Fitting of Time Series Models," *Revue Internationale Institut de Statistique* 28: 233–43.

Gene H. Golub and Charles van Loan (1996), *Matrix Computations,* 3rd ed. Baltimore: Johns Hopkins University Press.

W. J. Harrod and R. J. Plemmons (1984), "Comparison of Some Direct Methods for Computing Stationary Distributions of Markov Chains," *SIAM Journal of Scientific and Statistical Computing* 5: 453–69.

John Haslett and Adrian Raftery (1989), "Space-Time Modelling with Long-Memory Dependence: Assessing Ireland's Wind Power Resource," *Applied Statistics* 38: 1–50.

J. R. M. Hosking (1981), "Fractional Differencing," *Biometrika* 68: 165–76.

Alan Jennings (1977), *Matrix Computation for Engineers and Scientists.* New York: Wiley.

C. T. Kelley (1995), *Iterative Methods for Linear and Nonlinear Equations.* Philadelphia: SIAM.

Norman Levinson (1947), "The Weiner RMS Error Criterion in Filter Design and Prediction," *Journal of Mathematics and Physics* 26: 261–78.

R. S. Martin and J. H. Wilkinson (1965), "Symmetric Decomposition of Positive Definite Band Matrices," *Numerische Mathematik* 7: 355–61.

John F. Monahan (1984), "A Note on Enforcing Stationarity in Autoregressive-Moving Average Models," *Biometrika* 71: 403–4.

Bruce A. Murtagh (1981), *Advanced Linear Programming* New York: McGraw-Hill.

Marcello Pagano (1973), "When is an Autoregressive Scheme Stationary?" *Communications in Statistics* 1: 533–44.

William F. Trench (1964), "An Algorithm for the Inversion of Finite Toeplitz Matrices," *Journal of SIAM* 12: 515–22.

5

Regression Computations

5.1 Introduction

Fitting models by minimizing the sum of squares is the most commonly used and most powerful statistical tool. There are many computational methods for the solution of the linear least-squares problem, as it is known in numerical analysis. After the statistical background of the problem is discussed, the condition of the problem will be analyzed. Then the many computational methods for solving this problem will be discussed in turn, with comparisons of strengths and weaknesses. The first method is the simplest: solving the normal equations using Cholesky factorization, which is fast and requires little storage but has its drawbacks in accuracy. Next are the three orthogonalization methods – Gram–Schmidt (and its modified form), Householder transformations, and Givens transformations – all of which are computationally stable. A discussion of regression diagnostics and hypothesis tests follows. These are then followed by the conjugate gradient method, which is well suited for the very large and sparse problems arising in experimental designs. Applications of elimination methods, the abbreviated Doolittle method and the Sweep operator, are discussed next. Some personal comments conclude the chapter.

The statistical motivation for least squares is the estimation of the coefficients of a linear regression model,

$$y_i = x_{i1}b_1 + \cdots + x_{ip}b_p + e_i = \mathbf{x}_i.\mathbf{b} + e_i, \tag{5.1.1}$$

where y_i is the observed dependent variable. The independent or explanatory variables are the x_{ij}, and their unknown coefficients $\mathbf{b}$ are the objects of interest. The errors or disturbances e_i are random variables that are usually assumed to be uncorrelated with constant variance. Stacking the equations for the ith observation, $i = 1, \ldots, n$, yields the vector model

$$\mathbf{y} = \mathbf{Xb} + \mathbf{e}, \quad \mathrm{cov}(\mathbf{e}) = \sigma^2 \mathbf{I}_n,$$

where the $n \times p$ matrix $\mathbf{X}$ is called the *design matrix*. Setting the gradient of the sum-of-squares function

$$S(\mathbf{b}) = (\mathbf{y} - \mathbf{Xb})^{\mathrm{T}}(\mathbf{y} - \mathbf{Xb}) \tag{5.1.2}$$

with respect to the vector $\mathbf{b}$ to zero, the necessary condition for the minimizing vector $\hat{\mathbf{b}}$, dictates that $\hat{\mathbf{b}}$ must be a solution to the normal equations

$$\mathbf{X}^{\mathrm{T}}\mathbf{Xb} = \mathbf{X}^{\mathrm{T}}\mathbf{y}, \tag{5.1.3}$$

91

which can be rewritten as

$$\mathbf{X}^T(\mathbf{y} - \mathbf{X}\hat{\mathbf{b}}) = \mathbf{X}^T\hat{\mathbf{e}} = \mathbf{0}, \tag{5.1.4}$$

which defines the residual vector $\hat{\mathbf{e}}$. Another useful notation is the projection matrix $\mathbf{P_X}$, which enables the (orthogonal) projection of $\mathbf{y}$ onto the column space of $\mathbf{X}$, the fitted values, to be written as

$$\hat{\mathbf{y}} = \mathbf{P_X}\mathbf{y} = \mathbf{X}\hat{\mathbf{b}}$$

and the residual vector to be written as the difference $\hat{\mathbf{e}} = \mathbf{y} - \hat{\mathbf{y}} = (\mathbf{I} - \mathbf{P_X})\mathbf{y}$. These two components of $\mathbf{y}$ are orthogonal.

If the design matrix $\mathbf{X}$ has full column rank (i.e., if rank($\mathbf{X}$) $= p$) then the matrix $\mathbf{X}^T\mathbf{X}$ is nonsingular and positive definite, and the solution to the normal equations (5.1.3) is unique and minimizes $S(\mathbf{b})$. Handling the case where $\mathbf{X}$ may not have full column rank presents some options in strategy. Since overparameterized models make the expression of the design matrix so convenient, especially for analysis of variance and covariance, requiring a full-rank $\mathbf{X}$ would be restrictive and inconvenient for these problems. Any solution $\hat{\mathbf{b}}$ will suffice for statistical purposes (Searle 1973, chap. 6), so the easiest route is to solve the full-rank subset of the normal equations and make the coefficients zero for the other, redundant variables. Heuristic methods work best for finding the rank degeneracies. The key is to detect explanatory variables, or columns of $\mathbf{X}$, whose error sums of squares are near zero when regressed on other explanatory variables. This heuristic approach can be followed for most of the methods included in this exposition. Finally, the non–full-rank case, where the cause is not overparameterization, presents a quite different problem. Mathematically, the unique Moore–Penrose inverse $\mathbf{X}^+$ leads to a unique least-squares solution $\mathbf{X}^+\mathbf{y}$. Computationally, however, finding $\mathbf{X}^+$ requires the singular value decomposition of the matrix $\mathbf{X}$, which is best described as an eigenproblem (discussed in Chapter 6) and differs in spirit from the least-squares problem, usually going under the name of "principal components regression."

Though the quantities that must be computed in the solution of a linear least-squares problem may vary, two quantities, the solution vector $\hat{\mathbf{b}}$ and the error sum of squares

$$\text{SSE} = S(\hat{\mathbf{b}}) = (\mathbf{y} - \mathbf{X}\hat{\mathbf{b}})^T(\mathbf{y} - \mathbf{X}\hat{\mathbf{b}}) = \hat{\mathbf{e}}^T\hat{\mathbf{e}}, \tag{5.1.5}$$

are nearly always needed. At the next level of importance are the residuals $\hat{\mathbf{e}}$ and $(\mathbf{X}^T\mathbf{X})^{-1}$, the (unscaled) covariance matrix of $\hat{\mathbf{b}}$,

$$\text{cov}(\hat{\mathbf{b}}) = \sigma^2(\mathbf{X}^T\mathbf{X})^{-1}.$$

Other ancillary statistics are constrained solutions, hypothesis test statistics, and confidence intervals for predictions or forecasts. In addition, orthonormal bases for the column space of $\mathbf{X}$ or its orthogonal complement may replace the projection matrices $\mathbf{P_X}$ and $\mathbf{I} - \mathbf{P_X}$ for computational purposes. These matrices also play an important role in regression diagnostics. Multivariate regression (i.e., several responses for each observation) presents no real difficulties, since the coefficients for each dependent variable can be computed in a repetitive fashion.

Weighted observations, or occasions where the covariance matrix of the disturbances **e** is not a scaled identity matrix, present different problems. If the covariance matrix of the disturbances is known up to a constant scale factor,

$$\text{cov}(\mathbf{e}) = \sigma^2 \mathbf{G},$$

then the generalized least squares (GLS) normal equations are

$$\mathbf{X}^{\mathsf{T}}\mathbf{G}^{-1}\mathbf{X}\mathbf{b} = \mathbf{X}^{\mathsf{T}}\mathbf{G}^{-1}\mathbf{y}, \tag{5.1.6}$$

for which the methods given here must be modified, either explicitly – by constructing (via Cholesky decomposition of **G**) new values $\mathbf{X}^* = \mathbf{G}^{-1/2}\mathbf{X}$ and $\mathbf{y}^* = \mathbf{G}^{-1/2}\mathbf{y}$ – or implicitly.

5.2   Condition of the Regression Problem

The condition of a problem measures the magnitude of the change in the solution to a problem to small perturbations in the input. The input quantities here are **X** and **y**, and both affect the solution, albeit in different ways. The condition of the problem will be analyzed for the case where **X** has full column rank in order to keep the results simple. Also, all norms here are Euclidean ($p = 2$) norms, which are natural for this problem.

In contrast to the solution of linear equations, changes in the dependent variable **y** do affect the condition of the least-squares problem. First consider $\mathbf{y}^*$ as an observed vector close to **y** and $\hat{\mathbf{b}}^*$ as the least-squares vector for it, and similarly for $\hat{\mathbf{e}}^*$. Then the following inequality (Stewart 1973, thm. 5.2.4) presents $\kappa^*(\mathbf{X})$ as the condition number for regression:

$$\frac{\|\hat{\mathbf{b}} - \hat{\mathbf{b}}^*\|}{\|\hat{\mathbf{b}}\|} \leq \kappa^*(\mathbf{X})\frac{\|\hat{\mathbf{y}} - \hat{\mathbf{y}}^*\|}{\|\hat{\mathbf{y}}\|}, \tag{5.2.1}$$

where $\kappa^*(\mathbf{X})$ is related to the condition number computed in the solution of linear equations

$$\kappa^*(\mathbf{X})^2 = \|\mathbf{X}^{\mathsf{T}}\mathbf{X}\|\|(\mathbf{X}^{\mathsf{T}}\mathbf{X})^{-1}\| = \kappa(\mathbf{X}^{\mathsf{T}}\mathbf{X}). \tag{5.2.2}$$

Notice that κ^* is the ratio of the largest to the smallest singular values of **X**, the square root of the ratio of the largest and smallest eigenvalues of $\mathbf{X}^{\mathsf{T}}\mathbf{X}$. The notable conclusion from this result is that only those perturbations that result in changes in the fitted values $\hat{\mathbf{y}}$ will affect the solution. The inequality (5.2.1) and the condition number κ^* are useful in regression diagnostics, which examine sensitivity from a strictly statistical viewpoint.

Example 5.1: *Condition of Regression for* **y**

Let $\mathbf{X} = \begin{bmatrix} 1 & 1 \\ 1 & 1 \\ 1 & 1.1 \\ 1 & 1.1 \end{bmatrix}$, so $\mathbf{X}^{\mathsf{T}}\mathbf{X} = \begin{bmatrix} 4.00 & 4.20 \\ 4.20 & 4.42 \end{bmatrix}$; then $\mathbf{y} = \begin{bmatrix} .9 \\ 1.0 \\ 1.0 \\ 1.1 \end{bmatrix}$ gives $\hat{\mathbf{y}} = \begin{bmatrix} .95 \\ .95 \\ 1.05 \\ 1.05 \end{bmatrix}$

and $\hat{\mathbf{b}} = \begin{bmatrix} -0.05 \\ 1.00 \end{bmatrix}$. Now change to $\mathbf{y}^* = \begin{bmatrix} .9 \\ 0.99 \\ 1.01 \\ 1.1 \end{bmatrix}$ to get $\hat{\mathbf{y}}^* = \begin{bmatrix} .945 \\ .945 \\ 1.055 \\ 1.055 \end{bmatrix}$ and $\hat{\mathbf{b}}^* = $

$\begin{bmatrix} -0.155 \\ 1.1 \end{bmatrix}$. The norms are $\|\hat{\mathbf{b}}\| = 1.00125$, $\|\hat{\mathbf{b}} - \hat{\mathbf{b}}^*\| = 0.145$, $\|\hat{\mathbf{y}}\| = 2.00$, and $\|\hat{\mathbf{y}} - \hat{\mathbf{y}}^*\| = 0.01$, and the condition number is a large $\kappa^*(\mathbf{X}) = 42.076$. The inequality (5.2.2) gives $.145 = \frac{.145}{1.00125} \leq 42.076 \frac{.01}{2.00} = .210$.

The second inequality (Stewart 1973, thm. 5.2.7) measures the effect of perturbations in the design matrix $\mathbf{X}$, so that the solution $\hat{\mathbf{b}}^*$ solves the least-squares problem with $\mathbf{X} + \mathbf{E}$ and also satisfies

$$\frac{\|\hat{\mathbf{b}} - \hat{\mathbf{b}}^*\|}{\|\hat{\mathbf{b}}\|} \leq 2\kappa^* \frac{\|\mathbf{P_X E}\|}{\|\mathbf{X}\|} + 4\kappa^{*2} \frac{\|(\mathbf{I} - \mathbf{P_X})\mathbf{E}\| \|\hat{\mathbf{e}}\|}{\|\mathbf{X}\| \|\hat{\mathbf{y}}\|} + 8\kappa^{*3} \frac{\|(\mathbf{I} - \mathbf{P_X})\mathbf{E}\|^2}{\|\mathbf{X}\|^2}; \quad (5.2.3)$$

the third term can be ignored if the perturbation $\mathbf{E}$ is much smaller than $\kappa^*(\mathbf{X})$ is large.

This second inequality is complicated yet quite revealing, for it indicates that the sensitivity to changes in $\mathbf{X}$ depend on how well the data fit the model. If the model fits very well, then $\hat{\mathbf{e}}$ is much smaller than $\hat{\mathbf{y}}$ in norm and the second term on the right-hand side of (5.2.3) disappears. However, if $\hat{\mathbf{e}}$ is not small, then the condition number of the least-squares problem is essentially squared, $\kappa^*(\mathbf{X})^2$. In most cases, $\mathbf{P_X E}$ and $(\mathbf{I} - \mathbf{P_X})\mathbf{E}$ will be about the same size.

Example 5.2: *Condition of Regression for* $\mathbf{X}$

As before, let $\mathbf{X} = \begin{bmatrix} 1 & 1 \\ 1 & 1 \\ 1 & 1.1 \\ 1 & 1.1 \end{bmatrix}$; then $\mathbf{y} = \begin{bmatrix} .97 \\ .98 \\ 1.02 \\ 1.03 \end{bmatrix}$ gives $\hat{\mathbf{y}} = \begin{bmatrix} .975 \\ .975 \\ 1.025 \\ 1.025 \end{bmatrix}$ and $\hat{\mathbf{b}} = $

$\begin{bmatrix} 0.475 \\ 0.500 \end{bmatrix}$. Now change $\mathbf{X}$ by $\mathbf{E}$ as $\mathbf{E} = \begin{bmatrix} 0 & -.001 \\ 0 & 0 \\ 0 & 0 \\ 0 & .001 \end{bmatrix}$, giving $\mathbf{X} + \mathbf{E} = \begin{bmatrix} 1 & 0.999 \\ 1 & 1.000 \\ 1 & 1.100 \\ 1 & 1.101 \end{bmatrix}$

with residual $\hat{\mathbf{e}} = \begin{bmatrix} -.005 \\ .005 \\ -.005 \\ .005 \end{bmatrix}$ and new $\hat{\mathbf{b}}^* = \begin{bmatrix} 0.4792 \\ 0.4960 \end{bmatrix}$, so that the inequality gives

$$.008405 = \frac{.0058}{.689656}$$

$$\leq 2(42.076)\frac{.001}{2.9} + 4(42.076)^2 \frac{(.001)(.01)}{(2.9)(2)} + 8(42.076)^3 \frac{(.001)^2}{(2.9)^2}$$

$$= .0290 + .0122 + .0709 = .1121,$$

which is not close, with $\|\mathbf{P_X E}\| = \|(\mathbf{I} - \mathbf{P_X})\mathbf{E}\| = \|\hat{\mathbf{e}}\| = .001$. But now change $\mathbf{y}$ for the same $\hat{\mathbf{b}}$: $\mathbf{y} = \begin{bmatrix} 1.55 \\ 0.40 \\ 1.55 \\ 0.50 \end{bmatrix}$ and still $\hat{\mathbf{b}} = \begin{bmatrix} 0.475 \\ 0.500 \end{bmatrix}$, but now $\hat{\mathbf{e}} = \begin{bmatrix} .575 \\ -.575 \\ .475 \\ -.475 \end{bmatrix}$ with $\hat{\mathbf{b}}^* = \begin{bmatrix} 0.5935 \\ 0.3872 \end{bmatrix}$, so the inequality becomes

$$.2372 = \frac{.1636}{.689656}$$

$$\leq 2(42.076)\frac{.001}{2.9} + 4(42.076)^2\frac{(.001)(1.05)}{(2.9)(2)} + 8(42.076)^3\frac{(.001)^2}{(2.9)^2}$$

$$= .0290 + 1.2820 + .0705 = 1.3815.$$

These results, though not surprising from a statistical viewpoint, are fundamental to the analysis of the accuracy of the methods examined here. The condition number is the square root of the ratio of the largest and smallest eigenvalues of $\mathbf{X}^T\mathbf{X}$. If the data fit the model well, then the regression coefficients are not as sensitive to small perturbations as when the residuals are large. From the computational viewpoint, the backwards error analysis relates the computed solution to the exact solution of a nearby problem – that is, slightly perturbed $\mathbf{X}$ and $\mathbf{y}$. From backward error analysis and the condition of the regression problem previously analyzed, the accuracy of the computed solution can be determined.

Once the accuracy of the computed solution is determined, it should be evaluated in two ways. First, it should be compared to the statistical accuracy (i.e., the standard errors) of the coefficients. A computed coefficient that is inaccurate in the third significant digit presents no difficulties when a confidence interval spans an order of magnitude, but severe problems can arise if the standard error affects only the fifth significant digit. Notice that the condition number reflects the magnitude of the standard errors in the norm of the unscaled covariance matrix $(\mathbf{X}^T\mathbf{X})^{-1}$. Consequently, if the condition number is large, suggesting a sizable computational error, then the statistical error will usually be large also and reflected in a large covariance matrix.

A second way to view the accuracy of a least-squares solution is to consider how accurately the input variables $\mathbf{X}$ as well as $\mathbf{y}$ are measured. If the presumed errors here are as large as those imputed from the backwards error analysis, then the regression model with fixed $\mathbf{X}$ may be questioned, as well as the sources of error for $\mathbf{y}$. The analyses of the accuracy of the least-squares methods may lead one to infer that the least-squares problem is quite difficult computationally, but in fact the occasions of difficulty are usually those where the solution has limited usefulness. Great efforts to compute an accurate solution to the numerical problem may be wasted when the solution has little statistical accuracy.

The test problem of Longley exemplifies wasted effort. Longley (1967) constructed an econometric model using some published economic variables. The explanatory variables were nearly collinear, and although the model made no real sense it did present a difficult test problem – so difficult that only a sound program could produce "accurate" results. However, since the explanatory variables were rounded off for publication, the true problem has not been solved; only a problem close to it (using rounded data) has been solved. Beaton, Rubin, and Barone (1976) argued that the true problem was one that could be rounded to the published data, so they added uniform (relative) noise $\mathbf{E}$ at the level of rounding to produce data from the distribution of possible true problems $(\mathbf{X} + \mathbf{E})$. They found that (a) the computed coefficients were widely distributed and (b) the regression solution from the published data was far from the center of this distribution. Such a lack of precision in the problem made computing an accurate solution unwarranted. Further comments on accuracy of methods are postponed to Section 5.12.

5.3   Solving the Normal Equations

When $\mathbf{X}$ has full column rank, the easiest method for finding the least-squares vector $\hat{\mathbf{b}}$ is to solve the positive definite system of normal equations. The obvious approach is to use Cholesky factorization on the positive definite matrix $\mathbf{X}^T\mathbf{X}$ and solve two triangular systems. The accompanying error sum of squares and covariance matrix are easily computed. The plan is:

(1) compute $\mathbf{X}^T\mathbf{X}$ and $\mathbf{X}^T\mathbf{y}$;
(2) factor $\mathbf{X}^T\mathbf{X} = \mathbf{L}\mathbf{L}^T$;
(3) solve $\mathbf{L}\mathbf{w} = \mathbf{X}^T\mathbf{y}$ for $\mathbf{w}$;
(4) compute SSE by subtraction, SSE $= \mathbf{y}^T\mathbf{y} - \mathbf{w}^T\mathbf{w}$;
(5) solve $\mathbf{L}^T\mathbf{b} = \mathbf{w}$ for $\mathbf{b}$ to obtain $\hat{\mathbf{b}}$;
(6) invert $\mathbf{L}$ in place;
(7) multiply $\mathbf{L}^{-T}\mathbf{L}^{-1} = (\mathbf{X}^T\mathbf{X})^{-1}$.

Computing the solution to the least-squares problem in this way requires $np^2/2 + p^3/6$ flops. More importantly, only $p(p+3)/2$ storage locations are required. These advantages of speed and low storage requirements make this method the first choice for regression computations. However, the drawback of this method is that severe loss of accuracy can occur.

The most straightforward problem is that the condition of this method is at best that of solving the normal equations, $\kappa(\mathbf{X}^T\mathbf{X})$. Since the condition of the least-squares problem can be $\kappa^*(\mathbf{X}) = \sqrt{\kappa(\mathbf{X}^T\mathbf{X})}$, there are problems for which this method is certainly inferior. Another pitfall is that the computed $\mathbf{X}^T\mathbf{X}$ can easily fail to be positive definite and the Cholesky factorization impossible, as will be shown in Example 5.3. The trick of accumulating inner products in double precision for $\mathbf{X}^T\mathbf{X}$ and $\mathbf{X}^T\mathbf{y}$ will cure neither of these two problems, but it does shed light on the path to a successful solution. Once the inner product matrix $\mathbf{X}^T\mathbf{X}$ is computed in double precision, solving the small ($p \times p$) normal equations in double precision is then relatively inexpensive and will yield an accurate solution as long as $U\kappa(\mathbf{X}^T\mathbf{X})$ is less than unity.

The method just described – accumulating the inner products in double precision to obtain $\mathbf{X}^T\mathbf{X}$ and $\mathbf{X}^T\mathbf{y}$ in double precision and then solving the normal equations in double precision – is highly recommended for computing the coefficient vector. Other ancillary statistics (e.g. residuals) may not be computed as accurately, however.

Example 5.3: *Computationally Singular Matrix*

For $\mathbf{X} = \begin{bmatrix} 1 & 1 \\ 1 & 1 \\ 1 & 1.01 \\ 1 & 1.01 \end{bmatrix}$, $\mathbf{X}^T\mathbf{X} = \begin{bmatrix} 4 & 4.02 \\ 4.02 & 4.0402 \end{bmatrix}$, but rounded to four decimal digits is

$\begin{bmatrix} 4.000 & 4.020 \\ 4.020 & 4.040 \end{bmatrix}$. Cholesky says L_{11} is 2 and $L_{21} = 2.010$, but $4.040 - 2.010^2 = 0.000$ (when computed to four decimal digits) so that, for this method, $\mathbf{X}^T\mathbf{X}$ is computationally singular.

Finally, Example 5.3 suggests a rule of thumb for the use of this method. First of all, the number of digits to represent the needed numbers is doubled in forming $\mathbf{X}^T\mathbf{X}$. Second, the condition number will magnify any roundoff error, so extra digits will be needed to represent $\mathbf{X}^T\mathbf{X}$. Thus, for Example 5.1, we might figure two digits for $\mathbf{X}$ becomes four for holding $\mathbf{X}^T\mathbf{X}$, and squaring the condition number gives 1764 so four more digits are needed, totaling eight for solving the normal equations. As the number of observations grows, more digits will be required.

5.4 Gram–Schmidt Orthogonalization

The classical Gram–Schmidt algorithm is a method for producing a sequence of orthonormal vectors from a set of linearly independent vectors. For the regression problem, the linearly independent vectors will be columns of the $\mathbf{X}$ matrix, denoted by $\mathbf{X}_{\cdot 1}, \mathbf{X}_{\cdot 2}, \ldots, \mathbf{X}_{\cdot p}$. The orthonormal vectors are then used to solve the least-squares problem.

The immediate objective is to perform a factorization on $\mathbf{X}$ as follows:

$$\mathbf{X} = \mathbf{QR}, \quad \text{where } \mathbf{Q}^T\mathbf{Q} = \mathbf{I}_p, \tag{5.4.1}$$

so that $\mathbf{Q}$ has orthonormal columns $\mathbf{Q}_{\cdot 1}, \mathbf{Q}_{\cdot 2}, \ldots, \mathbf{Q}_{\cdot p}$ and $\mathbf{R}$ is upper triangular. The classical or regular Gram–Schmidt (RGS) method can be described as a sequence of regressions. At step i, column i of X, $\mathbf{X}_{\cdot i}$ is regressed on the orthonormal columns $\mathbf{Q}_{\cdot j}$, $j = 1, \ldots, i - 1$. Since the explanatory variables are orthonormal, the regression coefficients R_{ji} are easily computed:

$$R_{ji} = \mathbf{Q}_{\cdot j}^T\mathbf{X}_{\cdot i}, \quad j = 1, \ldots, i - 1. \tag{5.4.2}$$

The length of the residual vector is then computed for normalization,

$$R_{ii} = \left\| \mathbf{X}_{\cdot i} - \sum_{j=1}^{i-1} R_{ji}\mathbf{Q}_{\cdot j} \right\|, \tag{5.4.3}$$

and the new orthonormal vector is the normalized residual vector

$$\mathbf{Q}_{\cdot i} = \frac{\mathbf{X}_{\cdot i} - \sum R_{ji}\mathbf{Q}_{\cdot j}}{R_{ii}}. \tag{5.4.4}$$

This QR factorization, as it is called, is related to the Cholesky factorization of $\mathbf{X}^T\mathbf{X}$; that is, $\mathbf{R}$ is merely the transpose of $\mathbf{L}$. The matrix with orthonormal columns $\mathbf{Q}$ can then be written as $\mathbf{XL}^{-T}$. These relationships can be used to solve the least-squares problem: since

$$\mathbf{X}^T\mathbf{Xb} = \mathbf{X}^T\mathbf{y} \iff \mathbf{LL}^T\mathbf{b} = \mathbf{LQ}^T\mathbf{y},$$

taking an $\mathbf{L}$ from both sides produces

$$\mathbf{Rb} = \mathbf{Q}^T \mathbf{y}, \tag{5.4.5}$$

which is a simple triangular system to be solved. Although multiplying the problem of minimizing $\mathbf{y} - \mathbf{Xb}$ by an orthogonal matrix leads to a stable method of solving the least-squares problem, the pitfall in using RGS is that the columns $\mathbf{Q}$ so computed may not be very orthogonal and hence $\mathbf{Q}^T \mathbf{y}$ may not be computed very accurately. As a result, although solving (5.4.5) appears to have the condition of $\kappa^*(\mathbf{X})$, in actuality the condition is still $\kappa(\mathbf{X}^T \mathbf{X})$ – as it is with solving the normal equations. A well-conditioned problem may have been transformed to a poorly conditioned one. Nonetheless, solving (5.4.5) is really what should be solved; a better orthonormalization method is all that is needed.

The better way to orthonormalize the columns of $\mathbf{X}$ is merely a modification of the regular Gram–Schmidt method, appropriately called "modified Gram–Schmidt" (MGS). The main difference is that every time a new orthonormal column $\mathbf{Q}_{\cdot j}$ is found, each subsequent column of $\mathbf{X}$ is replaced by the residuals from a regression on $\mathbf{Q}_{\cdot j}$. Denote column i of $\mathbf{X}$ at step j by $\mathbf{X}_{\cdot i}^{(j)}$. Then the first part of step j is just normalization:

$$R_{jj} = \|\mathbf{X}_{\cdot j}^{(j)}\| \quad \text{and} \quad \mathbf{Q}_{\cdot j} = \mathbf{X}_{\cdot j}^{(j)}/R_{jj}.$$

Then update the columns of $\mathbf{X}$ ($\mathbf{X} = \mathbf{X}^{(1)}$) with the coefficients

$$R_{ji} = \mathbf{Q}_{\cdot j}^T \mathbf{X}_{\cdot i}^{(j)}$$

and the residuals for $i = j + 1, \dots, p$,

$$\mathbf{X}_{\cdot i}^{(j+1)} = \mathbf{X}_{\cdot i}^{(j)} - R_{ji} \mathbf{Q}_{\cdot j}.$$

Although these two methods are mathematically equivalent, only MGS is recommended, for it produces accurate vectors $\hat{\mathbf{b}}$ and reasonably orthogonal residuals. One disadvantage is that $\mathbf{X}$ must be stored and overwritten with $\mathbf{Q}$; another is that about np^2 flops are needed, about twice that for solving the normal equations by Cholesky. Also, the computed matrix $\mathbf{Q}$ may not have orthonormal columns even from the modified version.

The method of iterative improvement described in (4.10) can be applied to the regression problem by constructing the system of equations

$$\begin{bmatrix} \mathbf{I}_n & \mathbf{X} \\ \mathbf{X}^T & \mathbf{0} \end{bmatrix} \begin{bmatrix} \mathbf{e} \\ \mathbf{b} \end{bmatrix} = \begin{bmatrix} \mathbf{y} \\ \mathbf{0} \end{bmatrix}. \tag{5.4.6}$$

Dahlquist and Bjorck (1974, p. 205) gave a detailed description of using MGS with iterative improvement.

Finally, since R_{jj} can be viewed as a residual sum of squares of the regression of column j of $\mathbf{X}$ on the previous columns, this quantity can be used as both a pivoting technique and a test for collinearity in MGS. If column j is linearly dependent on the previous ones, then R_{jj} is zero and can be tested for it. Moreover, the best order for taking regressors are the ones with the most variation, which are the ones whose sum of squares will be largest. Hence a preferential order can be based upon the sums of squares of the remaining columns of $\mathbf{X}^{(j)}$.

Example 5.4: *Regular and Modified Gram–Schmidt*
For a simple quadratic regression problem with $n = 6$ observations, let's do both
RGS and MGS using four-digit decimal arithmetic. We will follow RGS first and
then back up for MGS, since the two methods differ only in the last two steps.

$$\mathbf{X} = \mathbf{X}^{(1)} = \begin{bmatrix} 1 & 1 & 1 \\ 1 & 2 & 4 \\ 1 & 3 & 9 \\ 1 & 4 & 16 \\ 1 & 5 & 25 \\ 1 & 6 & 36 \end{bmatrix}, \quad \text{so } R_{11} = 2.449 \text{ and } \mathbf{Q}_{\cdot 1} = \begin{bmatrix} .4082 \\ .4082 \\ .4082 \\ .4082 \\ .4082 \\ .4082 \end{bmatrix}.$$

Next, $R_{12} = 8.573$, and

$$\mathbf{X}_{\cdot 2} - R_{12}\mathbf{Q}_{\cdot 1} = \begin{bmatrix} 1 - 3.499 \\ 2 - 3.499 \\ 3 - 3.499 \\ 4 - 3.499 \\ 5 - 3.499 \\ 6 - 3.499 \end{bmatrix} = \begin{bmatrix} -2.499 \\ -1.499 \\ -.4990 \\ .5010 \\ 1.501 \\ 2.501 \end{bmatrix},$$

$$R_{22} = 4.183, \quad \text{and} \quad \mathbf{Q}_{\cdot 2} = \begin{bmatrix} -.5974 \\ -.3584 \\ -.1193 \\ .1198 \\ .3588 \\ .5979 \end{bmatrix}.$$

At this point the two methods depart, with RGS computing the next vector in one
step: $R_{13} = 37.15$ and $R_{23} = 29.31$, so

$$\mathbf{X}_{\cdot 3} - R_{13}\mathbf{Q}_{\cdot 1} - R_{23}\mathbf{Q}_{\cdot 2} = \begin{bmatrix} 1 - 15.16 + 17.51 \\ 4 - 15.16 + 10.51 \\ 9 - 15.16 + 3.497 \\ 16 - 15.16 - 3.511 \\ 25 - 15.16 - 10.52 \\ 36 - 15.16 - 17.52 \end{bmatrix} = \begin{bmatrix} 3.350 \\ -.6600 \\ -2.663 \\ -2.671 \\ -.6800 \\ 3.320 \end{bmatrix}.$$

Instead, MGS computes $R_{13} = 37.15$,

$$\mathbf{X}_{\cdot 3}^{(2)} = \mathbf{X}_{\cdot 3} - R_{13}\mathbf{Q}_{\cdot 1} = \begin{bmatrix} 1 - 15.16 \\ 4 - 15.16 \\ 9 - 15.16 \\ 16 - 15.16 \\ 25 - 15.16 \\ 36 - 15.16 \end{bmatrix} = \begin{bmatrix} -14.16 \\ -11.16 \\ -6.16 \\ .84 \\ 9.84 \\ 20.84 \end{bmatrix}, \quad \text{and}$$

$$\mathbf{X}_{\cdot 3}^{(3)} - R_{23}\mathbf{Q}_{\cdot 2} = \begin{bmatrix} -14.16 + 17.49 \\ -11.16 + 10.49 \\ -6.16 + 3.493 \\ .84 - 3.508 \\ 9.84 - 10.51 \\ 20.84 - 17.51 \end{bmatrix} = \begin{bmatrix} 3.330 \\ -.6700 \\ -2.667 \\ -2.668 \\ -.6700 \\ 3.330 \end{bmatrix},$$

with $R_{23} = 29.28$ instead of 29.31 from RGS. Notice that the two residual vectors differ before normalization to $\mathbf{Q}_{\cdot 3}$, with MGS much closer to the exact $[10/3, -2/3, -8/3, -8/3, -2/3, 10/3]$.

5.5   Householder Transformations

Householder transformations are simple but powerful matrices that are used to introduce zeros into a matrix. For the least-squares problem, they are used to triangularize $\mathbf{X}$, forming the same QR factorization as in Gram–Schmidt. In eigenproblems they are used to change a symmetric matrix into a tridiagonal one. Householder transformations are simple rank-1 updates of identity matrices that are orthogonal and can be used to annihilate a vector. Because they are orthogonal, a great number can be used without the accumulation of roundoff errors affecting the sums of squares.

The matrix $\mathbf{U} = \mathbf{I} - d\mathbf{u}\mathbf{u}^\mathsf{T}$ can be shown to be symmetric and orthogonal ($\mathbf{U}^\mathsf{T}\mathbf{U} = \mathbf{U}\mathbf{U}^\mathsf{T} = \mathbf{I}$) when $d = 2/\mathbf{u}^\mathsf{T}\mathbf{u}$. For any vector $\mathbf{x}$, a vector $\mathbf{u}$ (which defines a matrix $\mathbf{U}$) can be found such that $\mathbf{U}\mathbf{x} = s\mathbf{e}_1$ for a scalar s. To show this, consider $\mathbf{u} = \mathbf{x} + s\mathbf{e}_1$ where $s^2 = \mathbf{x}^\mathsf{T}\mathbf{x}$. Notice that the scalar

$$d = \frac{2}{\mathbf{u}^\mathsf{T}\mathbf{u}} = \frac{2}{\mathbf{x}^\mathsf{T}\mathbf{x} + 2sx_1 + s^2} = \frac{1}{s^2 + sx_1},$$

so that the computations yield

$$\mathbf{U}\mathbf{x} = (\mathbf{I} - d\mathbf{u}\mathbf{u}^\mathsf{T})\mathbf{x} = \mathbf{x} - \mathbf{u}(d\mathbf{u}^\mathsf{T}\mathbf{x})$$
$$= \mathbf{x} - (\mathbf{x} + s\mathbf{e}_1)(\mathbf{x} + s\mathbf{e}_1)^\mathsf{T}\mathbf{x}/(s^2 + sx_1)$$
$$= \mathbf{x} - (\mathbf{x} + s\mathbf{e}_1) = -s\mathbf{e}_1.$$

Although the choice of the sign of s is somewhat arbitrary, it is prudent to choose it to be the same as x_1 so that the algorithm will avoid the case where $\mathbf{u}$ is the zero vector and attempt to divide by zero. Also, the possible overflow due to the squaring of the elements is avoidable if the largest element of **x** is found and used to divide **u** and multiply d accordingly.

Example 5.5: *Householder Transformation*

We have $\mathbf{x} = \begin{bmatrix} -1 \\ 2 \\ -2 \\ 4 \end{bmatrix}$, $\mathbf{x}^\mathsf{T}\mathbf{x} = s^2 = 25$, $d = 1/20$, and $\mathbf{u} = \begin{bmatrix} 4 \\ 2 \\ -2 \\ 4 \end{bmatrix}$, so

$$\mathbf{U} = \mathbf{I}_4 - \frac{1}{20}\mathbf{u}\mathbf{u}^\mathsf{T} = \begin{bmatrix} 1/5 & -2/5 & 2/5 & -4/5 \\ -2/5 & 4/5 & 1/5 & -2/5 \\ 2/5 & 1/5 & 4/5 & 2/5 \\ -4/5 & -2/5 & 2/5 & 1/5 \end{bmatrix}.$$

Now multiply:

$$\mathbf{U}\mathbf{x} = \mathbf{x} - \frac{\mathbf{u}^\mathsf{T}\mathbf{x}}{d}\mathbf{u} = \begin{bmatrix} -1 \\ 2 \\ -2 \\ 4 \end{bmatrix} - \frac{20}{20}\begin{bmatrix} 4 \\ 2 \\ -2 \\ 4 \end{bmatrix}$$

$$= \begin{bmatrix} 1/5 & -2/5 & 2/5 & -4/5 \\ -2/5 & 4/5 & 1/5 & -2/5 \\ 2/5 & 1/5 & 4/5 & 2/5 \\ -4/5 & -2/5 & 2/5 & 1/5 \end{bmatrix}\begin{bmatrix} -1 \\ 2 \\ -2 \\ 4 \end{bmatrix} = \begin{bmatrix} -5 \\ 0 \\ 0 \\ 0 \end{bmatrix}.$$

Notice that s was taken to be positive (see Exercise 5.6).

5.6 Householder Transformations for Least Squares

The method of solving the least-squares problem using Householder transformation can be viewed in two ways. The annihilation property can be seen as converting the problem to a triangular one, as in Gaussian elimination; the method can also be seen as computing a QR factorization. The orthogonal property can be seen as rotating n-dimensional space into the column space of **X** and its orthogonal complement. In reality, of course, all of these are at work.

The problem of minimizing the square of the distance between the observed **y** and linear combinations of columns of **X** is unaffected by a rotation (a multiplication by an orthogonal matrix), since the norm remains the same:

$$S(\mathbf{b}) = \|\mathbf{y} - \mathbf{X}\mathbf{b}\|^2 = \|\mathbf{U}\mathbf{y} - \mathbf{U}\mathbf{X}\mathbf{b}\|^2. \tag{5.6.1}$$

Now the new problem is no easier to solve unless **UX** has a simpler structure. Using the annihilation property discussed in Section 5.5, a Householder transformation $\mathbf{U}_1$ can be constructed to place zeros throughout the first column of **X**, with the exception of the first element. Introducing zeros in more columns – without disturbing the zeros already introduced – requires a bit of care. For the second column, construct the

$(n - 1)$-dimensional annihilator to operate on the last $(n - 1)$ elements (leaving the first one alone) to zero out the last $(n - 2)$ elements of the second column. Then the zeros in the first column will be left unaffected. These steps are repeated to produce a sequence of orthogonal matrices $\mathbf{U}_1, \mathbf{U}_2, \ldots, \mathbf{U}_p$ such that their product with $\mathbf{X}$ will be triangular.

Let

$$\mathbf{U}_i = \begin{bmatrix} \mathbf{I}_{i-1} & \mathbf{0} \\ \mathbf{0} & \mathbf{U}^{(i)} \end{bmatrix}, \quad \text{where } \mathbf{U}^{(i)} = \mathbf{I}_{n-i+1} - d_i \mathbf{u}^{(i)} \mathbf{u}^{(i)\mathrm{T}};$$

after $i - 1$ steps, $\mathbf{U}_{i-1}\mathbf{U}_{i-2} \cdots \mathbf{U}_1 \mathbf{X}$ is computed to yield

$$\begin{array}{ccc} i-1 & 1 & p-i \end{array}$$

$$\begin{bmatrix} \mathbf{R}^{(i-1)} & \mathbf{r}^{(i-1)} & \mathbf{B}^{(i-1)} \\ \mathbf{0} & \mathbf{c}^{(i-1)} & \mathbf{D}^{(i-1)} \end{bmatrix} \cdot \begin{array}{c} i-1 \\ n-i+1 \end{array}$$

At step i, choose $\mathbf{u}^{(i)} = \mathbf{c}^{(i-1)} + s_i \mathbf{e}_1$ (with $s_i = \|\mathbf{c}^{(i-1)}\|$) to form $\mathbf{U}^{(i)}$ and $\mathbf{U}_i$, so

$$\mathbf{U}_i \mathbf{U}_{i-1} \cdots \mathbf{U}_1 \mathbf{X} = \begin{bmatrix} \mathbf{R}^{(i-1)} & \mathbf{r}^{(i)} & \mathbf{B}^{(i)} \\ \mathbf{0} & r_{ii}\mathbf{e}_1 & \mathbf{U}^{(i)}\mathbf{D}^{(i-1)} \end{bmatrix} = \begin{bmatrix} \mathbf{R}^{(i)} & \mathbf{B}^{(i)} \\ \mathbf{0} & \mathbf{D}^{(i)} \end{bmatrix} \cdot \begin{array}{c} i \\ n-i \end{array}$$

After p steps (each column of $\mathbf{X}$), both $\mathbf{B}$ and $\mathbf{D}$ disappear to leave $\mathbf{R}^{(p)} = \mathbf{R}$, which is an upper triangular matrix. After partitioning $\mathbf{U}_p \cdots \mathbf{U}_1 \mathbf{y}$ into its first p and last $n - p$ elements, denoted by $\mathbf{z}^{(1)}$ and the remainder $\mathbf{z}^{(2)}$, the least-squares problem has been transformed to

$$\|\mathbf{y} - \mathbf{Xb}\|^2 = \|\mathbf{U}_p \cdots \mathbf{U}_1(\mathbf{y} - \mathbf{Xb})\|^2 = \left\| \begin{bmatrix} \mathbf{z}^{(1)} \\ \mathbf{z}^{(2)} \end{bmatrix} - \begin{bmatrix} \mathbf{Rb} \\ \mathbf{0} \end{bmatrix} \right\|^2 = \|\mathbf{z}^{(1)} - \mathbf{Rb}\|^2 + \|\mathbf{z}^{(2)}\|^2,$$

so that the sum of squares is easily minimized by solving $\mathbf{Rb} = \mathbf{z}^{(1)}$ to make the first piece zero. The second piece that does not include $\mathbf{b}$ cannot be reduced and is the residual sum of squares, SSE. Notice also that $\mathbf{X}^\mathrm{T}\mathbf{X} = \mathbf{R}^\mathrm{T}\mathbf{R}$, so that $\mathbf{R}$ is the same matrix obtained by Cholesky decomposition (except, perhaps, for a sign). The plan can then be given for computing all of the needed quantities as follows:

(1) create and multiply $\mathbf{U}_1, \ldots, \mathbf{U}_p$ on $\mathbf{X}$ and $\mathbf{y}$;
(2) solve $\mathbf{Rb} = \mathbf{z}^{(1)}$ to obtain $\hat{\mathbf{b}}$;
(3) SSR $= \|\mathbf{z}^{(1)}\|^2$ and SSE $= \|\mathbf{z}^{(2)}\|^2$;
(4) invert $\mathbf{R}$ and multiply to get $(\mathbf{X}^\mathrm{T}\mathbf{X})^{-1} = \mathbf{R}^{-1}\mathbf{R}^{-\mathrm{T}}$;
(5) multiply $\mathbf{U}_p$ through $\mathbf{U}_1$ on $\mathbf{z}^{(2)}$ (augmented with p zeros) for the residuals.

Although the design matrix $\mathbf{X}$ must be stored for this method, the transformations $\mathbf{U}_i$ can be stored by overwriting $\mathbf{X}$ in the bottom part with the vectors $\mathbf{u}^{(i)}$, $i = 1, \ldots, p$. These transformations are needed to compute the residuals, or to compute orthonormal basis vectors for the column space of $\mathbf{X}$ or its orthogonal complement. The matrix $\mathbf{Q}$ of the QR factorization can be computed by

$$\mathbf{Q} = \mathbf{U}_1 \mathbf{U}_2 \cdots \mathbf{U}_p \begin{bmatrix} \mathbf{I}_p \\ \mathbf{0} \end{bmatrix}; \qquad (5.6.2)$$

the basis vectors for the orthogonal complement can be computed by reversing the identity matrix and the zero matrix and expanding the dimension to $n - p$. Saving the scalars s_i speeds these calculations.

This method is somewhat slower than the other methods discussed, requiring roughly np^2 flops for computing $\hat{\mathbf{b}}$. More flops are required for the ancillary statistics. A sequence of regression problems, where one column is added to the design matrix at a time, can be easily solved by stopping at each step to solve $\mathbf{R}^{(i)}\mathbf{b} = \mathbf{z}^{(1)(i)}$. Using the Householder transformation to solve the least-squares problem is among the most accurate methods, producing good residuals and orthogonal basis vectors close to orthogonal. Stability for virtually any sample size can be ensured by accumulating inner products in double precision.

The Householder transformation approach for least squares is perhaps the best designed for a method of pivoting that can test for rank and improve stability. If column i of $\mathbf{X}$ is linearly dependent on the previous $i - 1$ columns, then $\mathbf{c}^{(i-1)}$ and hence its norm s_i will be zero. Because a small value of s_i hints at collinearity, the norms of other columns in $\mathbf{D}^{(i-1)}$ should be compared and column i of the current matrix (composed of $\mathbf{r}^{(i-1)}$ and $\mathbf{c}^{(i-1)}$) should be switched with the column with the largest norm of its bottom part. These norms can be updated at each step to reduce the computations. This strategy will also ensure that the most varying (and potentially most significant) columns are used first. Although testing on s_i to check rank has its risks, it is a sound strategy that will be successful for many problems.

Example 5.6: *Simple Linear Regression with Householder Transformations*

We have $\mathbf{X} = \begin{bmatrix} 1 & 1 \\ 1 & 2 \\ 1 & 3 \\ 1 & 4 \end{bmatrix}$, so $\mathbf{c}^{(1)} = \begin{bmatrix} 1 \\ 1 \\ 1 \\ 1 \end{bmatrix}$, $s_1 = 2$, $\mathbf{u}^{(1)} = \begin{bmatrix} 3 \\ 1 \\ 1 \\ 1 \end{bmatrix}$, $d_1 = 1/6$, and

$$\mathbf{U}^{(1)} = \mathbf{I}_4 - d_1 \mathbf{u}^{(1)} \mathbf{u}^{(1)\mathrm{T}} = \mathbf{U}_1,\ \text{so}$$

$$\mathbf{U}_1 \mathbf{X} = \begin{bmatrix} -1/2 & -1/2 & -1/2 & -1/2 \\ -1/2 & 5/6 & -1/6 & -1/6 \\ -1/2 & -1/6 & 5/6 & -1/6 \\ -1/2 & -1/6 & -1/6 & 5/6 \end{bmatrix} \begin{bmatrix} 1 & 1 \\ 1 & 2 \\ 1 & 3 \\ 1 & 4 \end{bmatrix} = \begin{bmatrix} -2 & -5 \\ 0 & 0 \\ 0 & 1 \\ 0 & 2 \end{bmatrix}.$$

Now $\mathbf{c}^{(2)} = \begin{bmatrix} 0 \\ 1 \\ 2 \end{bmatrix}$, $s_2 = \sqrt{5}$, $\mathbf{u}^{(2)} = \begin{bmatrix} \sqrt{5} \\ 1 \\ 2 \end{bmatrix}$, $d_2 = 2/10 = 1/5$, and $\mathbf{U}^{(2)} = \mathbf{I}_3 - d_2 \mathbf{u}^{(2)} \mathbf{u}^{(2)\mathrm{T}}$, so

$$\mathbf{U}_2 \mathbf{U}_1 \mathbf{X} = \begin{bmatrix} 1 & 0 & 0 & 0 \\ 0 & 0 & -1/\sqrt{5} & -2/\sqrt{5} \\ 0 & -1/\sqrt{5} & 4/5 & -2/5 \\ 0 & -2/\sqrt{5} & -2/5 & 1/5 \end{bmatrix} \begin{bmatrix} -2 & -5 \\ 0 & 0 \\ 0 & 1 \\ 0 & 2 \end{bmatrix} = \begin{bmatrix} -2 & -5 \\ 0 & -\sqrt{5} \\ 0 & 0 \\ 0 & 0 \end{bmatrix}.$$

For $\mathbf{z}$, notice that the first row of $\mathbf{U}_2\mathbf{U}_1$ is $[-1/2, -1/2, -1/2, -1/2]$ and that the second row of $\mathbf{U}_2\mathbf{U}_1$ can be written as $(1/(6\sqrt{5}))[9, 3, -3, -9]$, so that

$$\mathbf{z}^{(1)} - \mathbf{Rb} = \begin{bmatrix} -(y_1 + y_2 + y_3 + y_4)/2 \\ (3y_1 + y_2 - y_3 - 3y_4)/(2\sqrt{5}) \end{bmatrix} - \begin{bmatrix} -2 & -5 \\ 0 & -\sqrt{5} \end{bmatrix} \begin{bmatrix} b_1 \\ b_2 \end{bmatrix}.$$

In R, the function *qr* computes the QR factorization via Householder transformations. This function returns a list of (qr) a matrix the same size as $\mathbf{X}$, ($rank$) the computed rank of the matrix, (aux) an auxiliary vector, and ($pivot$) the list of pivots. What is needed, of course, is the information to reconstruct the matrices $\mathbf{U}_1, \ldots, \mathbf{U}_p$. The upper triangular matrix $\mathbf{R}$ is stored in the upper triangular part of (qr). To construct the matrices $\mathbf{U}_i, i = 1, \ldots, p$, we need the vectors $\mathbf{u}^{(i)}$ and those vectors, scaled by s_i, are stored in the remainder of (qr), with one exception. Each vector $\mathbf{u}^{(i)}$ has $n - i + 1$ elements, but there are only $n - i$ elements below the diagonal. Those homeless first elements of $\mathbf{u}^{(i)}$ are stored in (aux), again scaled by s_i, so that they are also equal to $\|(1/s_i)\mathbf{u}^{(i)}\|^2$. Two useful tools are *qr.qy* and *qr.qty*, which premultiply a vector/matrix with $\mathbf{U}_1 \cdots \mathbf{U}_p$ and $\mathbf{U}_p \cdots \mathbf{U}_1$, respectively.

5.7 Givens Transformations

Givens transformations are similar in properties and purposes to Householder transformations, but they have a different structure. They are orthogonal and can be used as an annihilator in least-squares problems. They are also used in computing the QR factorization that drives the QR algorithm for computing eigenvalues. Givens transformations are based on an obvious extension of the simplest orthogonal matrix.

Consider the 2×2 orthogonal matrix, which can be written in two ways:

$$\begin{bmatrix} \sin t & \cos t \\ -\cos t & \sin t \end{bmatrix} = \begin{bmatrix} a & b \\ -b & a \end{bmatrix}, \quad \text{where } a^2 + b^2 = 1.$$

A 2×2 matrix $\mathbf{U}$ can be constructed so that the product $\mathbf{Ux}$ is zero in its second element simply by taking $a = x_1/\sqrt{x_1^2 + x_2^2}$ and also $b = x_2/\sqrt{x_1^2 + x_2^2}$, so

$$\mathbf{Ux} = \frac{1}{\sqrt{x_1^2 + x_2^2}} \begin{bmatrix} x_1 & x_2 \\ -x_2 & x_1 \end{bmatrix} \begin{bmatrix} x_1 \\ x_2 \end{bmatrix} = \begin{bmatrix} \sqrt{x_1^2 + x_2^2} \\ 0 \end{bmatrix}.$$

The Givens transformation is merely a generalization of this, placing a zero in one element of a vector and changing only one other:

$$\mathbf{U}_{ij}\mathbf{x} = \begin{bmatrix} \mathbf{I}_{i-1} & 0 & 0 & 0 & 0 \\ 0 & x_i/s & 0 & x_j/s & 0 \\ 0 & 0 & \mathbf{I}_{j-i-1} & 0 & 0 \\ 0 & -x_j/s & 0 & x_i/s & 0 \\ 0 & 0 & 0 & 0 & \mathbf{I}_{n-j} \end{bmatrix} \begin{bmatrix} \cdots \\ x_i \\ \cdots \\ x_j \\ \cdots \end{bmatrix} = \begin{bmatrix} \cdots \\ s \\ \cdots \\ 0 \\ \cdots \end{bmatrix},$$

where $s = \sqrt{x_i^2 + x_j^2}$. Notice that only elements i and j of $\mathbf{x}$ are changed; the others remain the same. For any vector $\mathbf{y}$, then, only the i and j elements are changed in computing the product $\mathbf{U}_{ij}\mathbf{y}$. And if both $\mathbf{y}_i$ and $\mathbf{y}_j$ are zero then the product is just $\mathbf{y}$, and nothing happens. Finally, since these matrices are really just a function of an angle, only one number is needed to represent the matrix (in addition to the indices i and j). Stewart (1976) proposed the following rule for using the single number ρ to represent the 2×2 matrix:

if $a = 0$, then $\rho = 1$;
if $|b| < |a|$, then $\rho = \text{sign}(a)b/2$; $\qquad\qquad\qquad$ (5.7.1)
if $|a| \le |b|$, then $\rho = 2\,\text{sign}(b)/a$.

5.8 Givens Transformations for Least Squares

Solving the least-squares problem using Givens transformations follows the same strategy as employed with Householder transformations. Orthogonal matrices are constructed to introduce zeros in $\mathbf{UX}$ until the resultant product is upper triangular. Again, care must be exercised to preserve zeros produced by the previous steps.

Let $\mathbf{U}_{ij}$ be the Givens transformation that changes only the i and j elements of a vector. Then the effect of $\mathbf{U}_{ij}$ on a matrix such as $\mathbf{X}$ is to change rows i and j. For solving the least-squares problem, $\mathbf{U}_{ij}$ is constructed so that a zero is produced in column i and row j of the current matrix, $\mathbf{UU}\cdots\mathbf{UX}$, using elements ii and ji. The sequence of matrices can be ordered in two ways.

(1) *Go down each column*:
do $i = 1, p$
do $j = i + 1, n$
$\quad$ compute $\mathbf{U}_{ij}\mathbf{U}\cdots\mathbf{U}_{12}(\mathbf{X} \mid \mathbf{y})$
end do ! loop on j
end do ! loop on i
(2) *Go across each row*:
do $j = 2, n$
do $i = 1, \min(j - 1, p)$
$\quad$ compute $\mathbf{U}_{ij}\mathbf{UU}_{12}(\mathbf{X} \mid \mathbf{y})$
end do ! loop on i
end do ! loop on j

The first method is similar to the pattern used with Householder transformations. The second method is ideal when intermediate results are needed and more observations are added. The remainder of the analysis, including the accuracy of the method, follows that of the Householder procedure. That is, represent the product of the orthogonal matrices by $\mathbf{Q} = \prod_i \prod_j \mathbf{U}_{ij}$, then

$$\mathbf{U}_{pn}\cdots\mathbf{U}_{12}(\mathbf{X} \mid \mathbf{y}) = \mathbf{Q}(\mathbf{X} \mid \mathbf{y}) = \begin{pmatrix} \mathbf{R} & \mathbf{z}^{(1)} \\ \mathbf{0} & \mathbf{z}^{(2)} \end{pmatrix}. \qquad (5.8.1)$$

The regression coefficients are then computed by solving $\mathbf{Rb} = \mathbf{z}^{(1)}$.

When compared to Householder, this method takes more work: roughly $2np^2$, with np square roots to be computed. A square root is a relatively easy nonarithmetic function, yet $O(np)$ is substantial and so "fast" methods have been devised (Gentleman 1973) to avoid them, but not without a loss of simplicity.

The great advantage of this method can be exploited by using the second scheme. Once j exceeds p, each new observation – with a row in $\mathbf{X}$ and an element in $\mathbf{y}$ – is "processed" into an updated $\mathbf{R}$ and $\mathbf{z}$. But since $\mathbf{z}^{(2)}$ is sometimes used only for its sum of squares, only the error sum of squares is updated, not all $\mathbf{z}^{(2)}$. The storage needed is merely $p(p+1)/2+1$, and observations can easily be added and the regression results updated. An update of a Cholesky decomposition can be computed in the same way. That is, to compute the decomposition $\mathbf{MM}^T$ of the matrix with a rank-1 update $\mathbf{A} = \mathbf{LL}^T + \mathbf{ww}^T$, write the matrix $\mathbf{A}$ as an inner product,

$$(\mathbf{L} \mid \mathbf{w})\begin{pmatrix} \mathbf{L}^T \\ \mathbf{w}^T \end{pmatrix} = \mathbf{B}^T\mathbf{B}; \tag{5.8.2}$$

then the Givens update of the matrix $\mathbf{B}$, zeroing out its last row and updating the upper triangular part $\mathbf{L}^T$ on top, produces the Cholesky factor $\mathbf{M}^T$:

$$\mathbf{U}_p \cdots \mathbf{U}_1 \begin{pmatrix} \mathbf{L}^T \\ \mathbf{w}^T \end{pmatrix} = \begin{pmatrix} \mathbf{M}^T \\ \mathbf{0} \end{pmatrix}.$$

Note that the work is $O(p^2)$.

Example 5.7: *Simple Linear Regression with Givens Transformations*

We have $\mathbf{X} = \begin{bmatrix} 1 & 1 \\ 1 & 2 \\ 1 & 3 \\ 1 & 4 \end{bmatrix}$, so use $\begin{bmatrix} 1 \\ 1 \end{bmatrix}$; then

$$\mathbf{U}_{12}\mathbf{X} = \begin{bmatrix} 1/\sqrt{2} & 1/\sqrt{2} & 0 & 0 \\ -1/\sqrt{2} & 1/\sqrt{2} & 0 & 0 \\ 0 & 0 & 1 & 0 \\ 0 & 0 & 0 & 1 \end{bmatrix}\begin{bmatrix} 1 & 1 \\ 1 & 2 \\ 1 & 3 \\ 1 & 4 \end{bmatrix} = \begin{bmatrix} \sqrt{2} & 3/\sqrt{2} \\ 0 & +1/\sqrt{2} \\ 1 & 3 \\ 1 & 4 \end{bmatrix}.$$

Use $\begin{bmatrix} \sqrt{2} \\ 1 \end{bmatrix}$ to get $\mathbf{U}_{13}$, so

$$\mathbf{U}_{13}\mathbf{U}_{12}\mathbf{X} = \begin{bmatrix} \sqrt{2/3} & 0 & 1/\sqrt{3} & 0 \\ 0 & 1 & 0 & 0 \\ -1/\sqrt{3} & 0 & \sqrt{2/3} & 0 \\ 0 & 0 & 0 & 1 \end{bmatrix}\begin{bmatrix} \sqrt{2} & 3/\sqrt{2} \\ 0 & +1/\sqrt{2} \\ 1 & 3 \\ 1 & 4 \end{bmatrix}$$

$$= \begin{bmatrix} \sqrt{3} & 2\sqrt{3} \\ 0 & +1/\sqrt{2} \\ 0 & \sqrt{3/2} \\ 1 & 4 \end{bmatrix};$$

use $\begin{bmatrix} +1/\sqrt{2} \\ \sqrt{3/2} \end{bmatrix}$ to get $\mathbf{U}_{23}$, so

$$\mathbf{U}_{23}\mathbf{U}_{13}\mathbf{U}_{12}\mathbf{X} = \begin{bmatrix} 1 & 0 & 0 & 0 \\ 0 & +1/2 & \sqrt{3}/2 & 0 \\ 0 & -\sqrt{3}/2 & +1/2 & 0 \\ 0 & 0 & 0 & 1 \end{bmatrix} \begin{bmatrix} \sqrt{3} & 2\sqrt{3} \\ 0 & +1/\sqrt{2} \\ 0 & \sqrt{3/2} \\ 1 & 4 \end{bmatrix}$$

$$= \begin{bmatrix} \sqrt{3} & 2\sqrt{3} \\ 0 & \sqrt{2} \\ 0 & 0 \\ 1 & 4 \end{bmatrix};$$

use $\begin{bmatrix} \sqrt{3} \\ 1 \end{bmatrix}$ to get $\mathbf{U}_{14}$, so

$$\mathbf{U}_{14}\mathbf{U}_{23}\mathbf{U}_{13}\mathbf{U}_{12}\mathbf{X} = \begin{bmatrix} \sqrt{3}/2 & 0 & 0 & 1/2 \\ 0 & 1 & 0 & 0 \\ 0 & 0 & 1 & 0 \\ -1/2 & 0 & 0 & \sqrt{3}/2 \end{bmatrix} \begin{bmatrix} \sqrt{3} & 2\sqrt{3} \\ 0 & \sqrt{2} \\ 0 & 0 \\ 1 & 4 \end{bmatrix} = \begin{bmatrix} 2 & 5 \\ 0 & \sqrt{2} \\ 0 & 0 \\ 0 & \sqrt{3} \end{bmatrix};$$

use $\begin{bmatrix} \sqrt{2} \\ \sqrt{3} \end{bmatrix}$ to get $\mathbf{U}_{24}$, so

$$\mathbf{U}_{24}\mathbf{U}_{14}\mathbf{U}_{23}\mathbf{U}_{13}\mathbf{U}_{12}\mathbf{X} = \begin{bmatrix} 1 & 0 & 0 & 0 \\ 0 & \sqrt{2/5} & 0 & \sqrt{3/5} \\ 0 & 0 & 1 & 0 \\ 0 & -\sqrt{3/5} & 0 & \sqrt{2/5} \end{bmatrix} \begin{bmatrix} 2 & 5 \\ 0 & \sqrt{2} \\ 0 & 0 \\ 0 & \sqrt{3} \end{bmatrix} = \begin{bmatrix} 2 & 5 \\ 0 & \sqrt{5} \\ 0 & 0 \\ 0 & 0 \end{bmatrix}.$$

5.9 Regression Diagnostics

Now that the main methods for regression have been discussed, our attention can turn to the computation of ancillary information, beginning with some statistics that have been suggested for diagnosing problems arising in regression. For the statistical background, the reader is advised to consult a textbook on regression (e.g. Myers 1989). For the more statistically adept, further details about these diagnostics can be found in Belsley, Kuh, and Welsch (1980) or Cook and Weisberg (1982). The viewpoint taken in this section is purely computational.

Prominent in the analysis of both residuals and influence is the so-called hat matrix $\mathbf{H} = \mathbf{X}(\mathbf{X}^{\mathsf{T}}\mathbf{X})^{-1}\mathbf{X}^{\mathsf{T}}$, also known as the regression projection matrix $\mathbf{P}_{\mathbf{X}}$. Nonetheless, usually only the diagonal elements $H_{ii} = h_i$ are needed – which is a relief, since $\mathbf{H}$ is $n \times n$. Different methods are available for computing h_i depending on which computational route is taken from those discussed here: Cholesky solution of the normal equations, modified Gram–Schmidt, Householder, or Givens.

The computation of the diagonal elements of $\mathbf{H}$ (or of the entire matrix, for that matter) is easy whenever the matrix $\mathbf{Q}$ of the QR factorization is available, since

$\mathbf{H} = \mathbf{Q}\mathbf{Q}^T$. This result easily follows from the factorization $\mathbf{X} = \mathbf{Q}\mathbf{R}$, so $\mathbf{X}\mathbf{R}^{-1} = \mathbf{Q}$ and $\mathbf{X}^T\mathbf{X} = \mathbf{R}^T\mathbf{R}$. Deriving the diagonal elements h_i requires only the sum of squares of the rows of $\mathbf{Q}$. Since MGS produces the matrix $\mathbf{Q}$, this one is easy. For the other orthogonalization methods, a special effort must be made to obtain $\mathbf{Q}$. For Householder transformations, this has been discussed and led to (5.6.2). For Givens, construct a matrix with the first p columns of an $n \times n$ identity matrix and then apply the orthogonal transformations in reverse order; that is (for Example 5.7),

$$\mathbf{Q} = \mathbf{U}_{12}\mathbf{U}_{13}\mathbf{U}_{23}\mathbf{U}_{14}\mathbf{U}_{24}\begin{bmatrix} \mathbf{I}_p \\ \mathbf{0} \end{bmatrix}. \tag{5.9.1}$$

Remaining among the methods is solving the normal equations by Cholesky in double precision, and the approach for obtaining $\mathbf{H}$ is simple. Let $\mathbf{X}_{i\cdot}$ be the ith row of the design matrix; then, following

$$\mathbf{H} = \mathbf{X}(\mathbf{X}^T\mathbf{X})^{-1}\mathbf{X}^T = \mathbf{X}\mathbf{R}^{-1}\mathbf{R}^{-T}\mathbf{X}^T,$$

merely solve $\mathbf{R}^T\mathbf{w} = \mathbf{X}_{i\cdot}^T$ to get $\mathbf{X}_{i\cdot}\mathbf{R}^{-1} = \mathbf{w}^T$ and compute the sum of squares of $\mathbf{w}$ to get h_i.

From this point, things actually get easier, although some of the expressions at first appear cryptic. One residual diagnostic is the predicted sum of squares for residuals (PRESS), which arises from a comparison of each observation to the prediction computed without that observation and follows specifically the spirit of the jackknife. Notationally,

$$\text{PRESS} = \sum_{i=1}^n (y_i - \hat{y}_{i,-i})^2 = \sum_{i=1}^n \hat{e}_{i,-i}^2, \tag{5.9.2}$$

where $\hat{y}_{i,-i}$ denotes the fitted value for the ith observation computed from the $n-1$ observations, excluding the ith. The PRESS residual $\hat{e}_{i,-i}$ can be found from a simple formula:

$$\hat{e}_{i,-i} = \frac{y_i - \hat{y}_i}{1 - h_i} = \frac{\hat{e}_i}{1 - h_i}. \tag{5.9.3}$$

Hidden within this is the Sherman–Morrison–Woodbury formula for the inverse of an updated matrix:

$$(\mathbf{A} + \mathbf{u}\mathbf{v}^T)^{-1} = \mathbf{A}^{-1} - \frac{\mathbf{A}^{-1}\mathbf{u}\mathbf{v}^T\mathbf{A}^{-1}}{1 + \mathbf{v}^T\mathbf{A}^{-1}\mathbf{u}}. \tag{5.9.4}$$

Now let $\mathbf{x}_i$ be the ith row of $\mathbf{X}$ made into a column vector; then the algebra begins with

$$\hat{y}_{i,-i} = \mathbf{x}_i^T[\mathbf{X}^T\mathbf{X} - \mathbf{x}_i\mathbf{x}_i^T]^{-1}(\mathbf{X}^T\mathbf{y} - \mathbf{x}_i y_i)$$

$$= \mathbf{x}_i^T\left[(\mathbf{X}^T\mathbf{X})^{-1} + \frac{(\mathbf{X}^T\mathbf{X})^{-1}\mathbf{x}_i\mathbf{x}_i^T(\mathbf{X}^T\mathbf{X})^{-1}}{1 - h_i}\right](\mathbf{X}^T\mathbf{y} - \mathbf{x}_i y_i) \tag{5.9.5}$$

and finishes with (5.9.3) (see Exercise 5.16). As a result, although the PRESS residuals appear to require n different regressions, with some clever manipulations they require only h_i.

Also used in the analysis of residuals is an estimate of the variance parameter deleting the ith observation, s^2_{-i}, found by

$$s^2_{-i} = \frac{\text{SSE} - \hat{e}_i^2/(1 - h_i)}{n - p - 1}. \tag{5.9.6}$$

This estimate is then used in an externally Studentized residual (sometimes called "R-Student"),

$$t_i = \frac{\hat{e}_i}{s_{-i}\sqrt{1 - h_i}}, \tag{5.9.7}$$

giving a view of a residual with a known Student's t distribution with $n - p - 2$ degrees of freedom. The measure of influence of an observation DFFITS$_i$ has a similar form, and the estimate of scale σ can be either the usual one or s_{-i}, as in the latter expression;

$$\text{DFFITS}_i = \frac{\hat{e}_i}{\sigma\sqrt{1 - h_i}}\sqrt{\frac{h_i}{1 - h_i}} = t_i\sqrt{\frac{h_i}{1 - h_i}}.$$

Notice that no new computations appear to be required by these diagnostic statistics. A measure of influence of observation i on the jth regression coefficient is

$$\text{DFBETAS}_{j,i} = \frac{\hat{b}_j - \hat{b}_{j,-i}}{s_{-i}\sqrt{[(\mathbf{X}^{\mathsf{T}}\mathbf{X})^{-1}]_{jj}}}, \tag{5.9.8}$$

where $\hat{b}_{j,-i}$ denotes the estimate of the jth regression coefficient computed omitting the ith observation. Again, this looks bad; but again, analysis similar to that just described (see e.g. Myers 1989, apx. B.7) leads to the simplified expression

$$\text{DFBETAS}_{j,i} = t_i \frac{Z_{ji}}{\sqrt{1 - h_i}\sqrt{[(\mathbf{X}^{\mathsf{T}}\mathbf{X})^{-1}]_{jj}}}, \tag{5.9.9}$$

where t_i is the Studentized residual given in (5.9.7) and Z_{ji} is the (j, i)th element of $\mathbf{Z}$, where

$$\mathbf{Z} = (\mathbf{X}^{\mathsf{T}}\mathbf{X})^{-1}\mathbf{X}^{\mathsf{T}} = \mathbf{R}^{-1}\mathbf{Q}^{\mathsf{T}}.$$

Since all of the methods discussed so far create $\mathbf{R}$ (or its negative, in the case of Householder), the matrix $\mathbf{Z}$ can be found by following the same route as for $\mathbf{Q}$.

Finally, Cook's D (for distance) measures the entire change (similar to Hotelling's T^2) in the coefficient vector following the omission of the ith observation,

$$D_i = (\hat{\mathbf{b}} - \hat{\mathbf{b}}_{-i})^{\mathsf{T}}(\mathbf{X}^{\mathsf{T}}\mathbf{X})(\hat{\mathbf{b}} - \hat{\mathbf{b}}_{-i})/ps^2, \tag{5.9.10}$$

where $\hat{\mathbf{b}}_{-i}$ is the coefficient vector computed without the ith observation. Again, this expression can be simplified to

$$D_i = \frac{\hat{e}_i^2 h_i}{(1 - h_i)^2 s^2 p}, \tag{5.9.11}$$

which requires no special computations.

5.10   Hypothesis Tests

The main tool of statistical inference in regression is the test of a hypothesis H that is expressed as a set of linear equality constraints on the parameters,

$$H : \mathbf{K}^T \mathbf{b} = \mathbf{m}, \tag{5.10.1}$$

where $\mathbf{K}$ is a full column rank matrix of size $p \times s$. If the coefficient estimate that minimizes $S(\mathbf{b})$ (subject to the constraints H) is denoted by $\tilde{\mathbf{b}}$, then the statistic for testing this hypothesis is

$$F = \frac{[S(\tilde{\mathbf{b}}) - S(\hat{\mathbf{b}})]/s}{S(\hat{\mathbf{b}})/(n - p)}. \tag{5.10.2}$$

The numerator in (5.10.2) can be found algebraically from $\mathbf{K}$, $\hat{\mathbf{b}}$, and the computations from the unrestricted regression

$$S(\tilde{\mathbf{b}}) - S(\hat{\mathbf{b}}) = (\mathbf{K}^T \hat{\mathbf{b}} - \mathbf{m})^T [\mathbf{K}^T (\mathbf{X}^T \mathbf{X})^{-1} \mathbf{K}]^{-1} (\mathbf{K}^T \hat{\mathbf{b}} - \mathbf{m}),$$

but the potential for catastrophic cancellation is large. There are better ways of computing the test statistic and the constrained estimate $\tilde{\mathbf{b}}$. Both approaches to be presented here are reparameterization methods, designed to produce the usual statistics from the unconstrained problem as well as $\tilde{\mathbf{b}}$ and $S(\tilde{\mathbf{b}})$ from the constrained one. Both are designed to work with any of the orthogonalization methods – MGS, Householder, or Givens.

Before addressing either of these methods, consider that the most important hypotheses to be tested is whether or not to include a variable (or set of variables) in the regression equation. Here, the sequential and partial sums of squares are required. The sequential sums of squares are the regression sum of squares for each variable as it is introduced into the model and reduces the error sum of squares. For this, the orthogonalization methods work best. The partial sums of squares for a variable is the difference in error sum of squares when the variable is deleted from the model, essentially the numerator sum of squares for the F-test for that variable's significance. For the case of a single variable, the easiest approach is just to use the t-test. For a set of variables arising in an experimental design problem with many levels for each factor, running separate regressions for the subset models may be easiest. A comparison of the two following approaches for obtaining partial sums of squares is the object of Exercise 5.23.

The first method for general hypothesis tests uses an orthogonal reparameterization. The first step is to find a matrix $\mathbf{G}$ that performs an upside-down and backwards QR factorization of $\mathbf{K}$, that is,

$$\mathbf{GK} = \begin{bmatrix} \mathbf{0} \\ \mathbf{K}_2^* \end{bmatrix}, \quad \begin{matrix} p - s \\ s \end{matrix}$$

where $\mathbf{K}_2^*$ is lower triangular and nonsingular. This can be done using either Householder or Givens methods but in an upside-down and backwards form. That is, for the Householder method, annihilate the last column of $\mathbf{K}$ (except for the last element), then the next-to-last column (except for the last two elements), and so on (see Exercise 5.8). The reparameterized model is then

$$\mathbf{y} = \mathbf{Xb} + \mathbf{e} = (\mathbf{XG})(\mathbf{G}^T\mathbf{b}) + \mathbf{e} = \mathbf{Wc} + \mathbf{e}, \qquad (5.10.3)$$

so that the new parameter vector is $\mathbf{c} = \mathbf{G}^T\mathbf{b}$ and the hypothesis is restated as a square nonsingular system

$$H : \mathbf{K}_2^{*T}\mathbf{c}_2 = \mathbf{m}, \qquad (5.10.4)$$

where $\mathbf{c}_2$ is the lower part of $\mathbf{c}$. Now use any of the orthogonalization methods for regression (MGS, Householder, or Givens) on the new design matrix $\mathbf{W} = (\mathbf{W}_1 \ \mathbf{W}_2) = \mathbf{XG}$ to obtain

$$\mathbf{Q}^T(\mathbf{y} - \mathbf{Wc}) = \begin{bmatrix} \mathbf{z}_1 \\ \mathbf{z}_2 \\ \mathbf{z}_3 \end{bmatrix} - \begin{bmatrix} \mathbf{R}_{11} & \mathbf{R}_{12} \\ \mathbf{0} & \mathbf{R}_{22} \\ \mathbf{0} & \mathbf{0} \end{bmatrix} \begin{bmatrix} \mathbf{c}_1 \\ \mathbf{c}_2 \end{bmatrix}, \qquad \begin{matrix} p-s \\ s \\ n-p \end{matrix} \qquad (5.10.5)$$

which is the vector whose norm is to be minimized. To perform the unconstrained minimization, simply solve the system of equations

$$\begin{bmatrix} \mathbf{R}_{11} & \mathbf{R}_{12} \\ \mathbf{0} & \mathbf{R}_{22} \end{bmatrix} \begin{bmatrix} \mathbf{c}_1 \\ \mathbf{c}_2 \end{bmatrix} = \begin{bmatrix} \mathbf{z}_1 \\ \mathbf{z}_2 \end{bmatrix}$$

to obtain the vector $\hat{\mathbf{c}}$. Then the unconstrained vector is $\hat{\mathbf{b}} = \mathbf{G}^T\hat{\mathbf{c}}$, and the other values can be found by undoing the reparameterization – for example, $(\mathbf{X}^T\mathbf{X})^{-1} = (\mathbf{GR}^{-1})(\mathbf{GR}^{-1})^T$.

To perform the constrained minimization, first solve for $\tilde{\mathbf{c}}_2$ by solving (5.10.4). Then solve

$$\mathbf{R}_{11}\mathbf{c}_1 = \mathbf{z}_1 - \mathbf{R}_{12}\tilde{\mathbf{c}}_2 \qquad (5.10.6)$$

to obtain $\tilde{\mathbf{c}}_1$, so that the constrained estimator is $\tilde{\mathbf{b}} = \mathbf{G}\tilde{\mathbf{c}}$. The difference in the error sum of squares can then be computed directly, from (5.10.5), as the square of the length of the subvector $\mathbf{z}_2 - \mathbf{R}_{22}\tilde{\mathbf{c}}_2$.

The alternative method uses elimination as the basis for the reparameterization. Perform full column elimination with full row and column pivoting on the system of equations described by the hypothesis H, again in a backwards fashion, to obtain an equivalent form

$$H : \mathbf{K}^T\mathbf{b} = \mathbf{m} \iff (\mathbf{K}^{*T} \ \mathbf{I}_s)(\mathbf{Pb}) = \mathbf{m}^*, \qquad (5.10.7)$$

with the reparameterized vector $\mathbf{c} = \mathbf{Pb}$ simply a permuted order. Similarly, permute the columns of $\mathbf{X}$ to obtain $\mathbf{W} = (\mathbf{W}_1 \ \mathbf{W}_2) = \mathbf{XP}^T$. Then perform the steps of MGS (or Householder or Givens) to reach (5.10.5). The unconstrained results follow from solving (5.10.6) and permuting back to obtain $\tilde{\mathbf{b}}$.

The constrained results are much more difficult in this alternative method. The hypothesis in (5.10.7) can be seen as giving $\mathbf{c}_2$ in terms of $\mathbf{c}_1$ (i.e., $\mathbf{c}_2 = \mathbf{m}^* - \mathbf{K}^{*T}\mathbf{c}_1$) so that, upon reaching (5.10.5), the vector whose length is to be minimized is

$$\mathbf{X}^*\mathbf{c}_1 - \mathbf{z}^* = \begin{bmatrix} \mathbf{R}_{11} - \mathbf{R}_{12}\mathbf{K}^{*T} \\ -\mathbf{R}_{22}\mathbf{K}^{*T} \end{bmatrix} \mathbf{c}_1 - \begin{bmatrix} \mathbf{z}_1 - \mathbf{R}_{12}\mathbf{m}^* \\ \mathbf{z}_2 - \mathbf{R}_{22}\mathbf{m}^* \end{bmatrix} \qquad \begin{matrix} p-s \\ s \end{matrix} \qquad (5.10.8)$$

as a function of c_1 only, which is a regression problem still to be solved. This much smaller least-squares problem can be solved by triangularizing the matrix $\mathbf{X}$ via Householder or Givens to obtain

$$Q(\mathbf{X}^*\mathbf{c}_1 - \mathbf{z}^*) = \begin{bmatrix} \mathbf{R}^{**} \\ \mathbf{0} \end{bmatrix} \mathbf{c}_1 - \begin{bmatrix} \mathbf{z}_1^{**} \\ \mathbf{z}_2^{**} \end{bmatrix},$$

whose length is minimized by solving $\mathbf{R}^{**}\mathbf{c}_1 = \mathbf{z}_1^{**}$ for the constrained estimate $\tilde{\mathbf{c}}_1$. The remainder of the coefficient estimates are found from $\tilde{\mathbf{c}}_2 = \mathbf{m}^* - \mathbf{K}^{*T}\tilde{\mathbf{c}}_1$. The difference in the error sum of squares, $S(\tilde{\mathbf{b}}) - S(\hat{\mathbf{b}})$, will appear as the sum of squares of $\mathbf{z}_2^{**}$.

Another textbook method (Searle 1973, chap. 3) follows the reparameterization just given in a more direct manner, using the regression model under the hypothesis as

$$\mathbf{y} - \mathbf{W}_2\mathbf{m}^* = (\mathbf{W}_1 - \mathbf{W}_2\mathbf{K}^{*T})\mathbf{c}_1 + \mathbf{e}.$$

The constrained problem is then a regression with a design matrix $\mathbf{W}_1 - \mathbf{W}_2\mathbf{K}^{*T}$ and dependent variable $\mathbf{y} - \mathbf{W}_2\mathbf{m}^*$. This least-squares problem must be solved at some point; the previous method suggests waiting until the end so that the unconstrained results are also available.

Still another textbook method is to solve directly the Lagrangian equation that arises from the constrained optimization formulation,

$$\begin{bmatrix} \mathbf{X}^T\mathbf{X} & \mathbf{K} \\ \mathbf{K}^T & \mathbf{0} \end{bmatrix} \begin{bmatrix} \mathbf{b} \\ \theta \end{bmatrix} = \begin{bmatrix} \mathbf{X}^T\mathbf{y} \\ \mathbf{m} \end{bmatrix}. \tag{5.10.9}$$

Although simply stated, this is not a positive definite system and so the stable Cholesky method cannot be used. The condition should be about $\kappa(\mathbf{X}^T\mathbf{X})$, so this approach can be much more difficult.

5.11   Conjugate Gradient Methods

Storage requirements have been emphasized in our discussion of the various methods for least-squares problems. A method that requires $O(p^2)$ storage has a distinct advantage over one (e.g. Householder) that requires $O(np)$, the advantage being that its set of computationally feasible problems is considerably larger. But in the case of large factorial models (or small computers), this set may not be large enough to contain important problems. Conjugate gradient methods require only $O(p)$ storage; hence they can solve much larger problems on smaller computers than the other methods. While the advantage of a conjugate gradient (CG) approach is its small storage requirements, its biggest disadvantage is that only $\hat{\mathbf{b}}$ and SSE are produced. Its obstacles to numerical stability are such that a solution cannot be expected to be found in a finite number of steps, so the method should be viewed in practice as an iterative method. Often special efforts are needed to bring slow convergence to a tolerable rate. This method should only be considered when storage requirements preclude other approaches.

The conjugate gradient method can be viewed as a sequence of line searches to find the minimum of the sum-of-squares function $S(\mathbf{b})$. That is, consider minimizing along the line $\mathbf{b} + a\mathbf{q}$, constructing $S^*(a) = S(\mathbf{b} + a\mathbf{q})$. Then the optimal a is given by

$$a^* = \frac{\mathbf{q}^T\mathbf{X}^T(\mathbf{y} - \mathbf{Xb})}{\mathbf{q}^T\mathbf{X}^T\mathbf{Xq}} = -\frac{\mathbf{q}^T(\nabla S(\mathbf{b}))}{2\mathbf{q}^T\mathbf{X}^T\mathbf{Xq}}. \tag{5.11.1}$$

However, pursuing the best direction – the gradient – leads to the steepest descent method, which suffers from zig-zagging that can be crippling. Instead, a sequence of directions $\{\mathbf{q}_k\}$ is sought such that, at each step, searching along the new direction $\mathbf{q}_k$ yields the optimum $\mathbf{b}^{(k)}$ found by the updating formula

$$\mathbf{b}^{(k)} = \mathbf{b}^{(k-1)} - a_k\mathbf{q}_k, \tag{5.11.2}$$

which minimizes $S(\mathbf{b})$ over the manifold span$\{\mathbf{q}_1, \ldots, \mathbf{q}_k\}$. If this can be achieved, then the line search will actually make progress toward the global optimum and not merely marginal gains, as in steepest descent.

To see that this is possible, impose on the directions the requirement that they must be mutually conjugate with respect to $\mathbf{X}^T\mathbf{X}$,

$$\mathbf{q}_i^T\mathbf{X}^T\mathbf{Xq}_j = 0 \quad \text{for } i \neq j. \tag{5.11.3}$$

By stacking the directions $\mathbf{q}_j$ as columns in a $p \times k$ matrix $\mathbf{Q}_k$, the step-k optimization problem can be written as finding the vector $\mathbf{z}$ and scalar a to minimize

$$S(\mathbf{Q}_{k-1}\mathbf{z} + a\mathbf{q}_k) = S(\mathbf{Q}_{k-1}\mathbf{z}) - 2a\mathbf{q}_k^T\mathbf{X}^T\mathbf{y} + a^2\mathbf{q}_k^T\mathbf{X}^T\mathbf{Xq}_k, \tag{5.11.4}$$

since the missing term is $2a\mathbf{q}_k^T\mathbf{X}^T\mathbf{XQz}$, which is zero owing to (5.11.3). This step-k problem obviously decouples into the first part, finding the best $\mathbf{z}$, which was the step-$(k-1)$ problem that led to $S(\mathbf{b}^{(k-1)})$, and the second part, for which the optimal a_k is given by

$$a_k = \mathbf{q}_k^T\mathbf{X}^T\mathbf{y}/\mathbf{q}_k^T\mathbf{X}^T\mathbf{Xq}_k. \tag{5.11.5}$$

This appears to differ from the optimal given by (5.11.1); however, since $\mathbf{b}^{(k-1)} = \mathbf{Q}_{k-1}\mathbf{z}$ for some $\mathbf{z}$, it follows that $q_k \perp \mathbf{b}^{(k-1)}$ and the missing piece is zero.

The problem of finding a new $\mathbf{q}_k$ that satisfies (5.11.3) is solvable by a form of Gram–Schmidt, but this would cost so much in time and space that it would defeat the purpose of the method. Moreover, the best direction at any step is to go opposite the gradient. So the best choice for $\mathbf{q}_k$ is the vector whose direction is close to the gradient while retaining the orthogonality relationship (5.11.3); this is a least-squares problem. Fortunately, this best $\mathbf{q}_k$ can be shown to be a linear combination of two vectors $\mathbf{q}_{k-1}$ and $\nabla S(\mathbf{b}^{(k-1)})/2 = \mathbf{g}_{k-1}$. The relationship is

$$\mathbf{q}_k = \mathbf{g}_{k-1} + c_k\mathbf{q}_{k-1}, \tag{5.11.6}$$

where

$$c_k = -\mathbf{q}_{k-1}^T\mathbf{X}^T\mathbf{Xg}_{k-1}/\mathbf{q}_{k-1}^T\mathbf{X}^T\mathbf{Xq}_{k-1}. \tag{5.11.7}$$

The conjugate gradient iteration can then be written as follows:

$$c_k = -\mathbf{q}_{k-1}^T\mathbf{X}^T\mathbf{Xg}_{k-1}/\mathbf{q}_{k-1}^T\mathbf{X}^T\mathbf{Xq}_{k-1},$$

$$\mathbf{q}_k = \mathbf{g}_{k-1} + c_k\mathbf{q}_{k-1},$$

$$a_k = -\mathbf{q}_k^T\mathbf{g}_{k-1}/\mathbf{q}_k^T\mathbf{X}^T\mathbf{Xq}_k,$$

$$\mathbf{b}^{(k)} = \mathbf{b}^{(k-1)} + a_k\mathbf{q}_k,$$

$$\mathbf{g}_k = \mathbf{X}^T(\mathbf{Xb}^{(k)} - \mathbf{y}) \text{ or } \mathbf{g}_{k-1} + a_k\mathbf{X}^T\mathbf{Xq}_k.$$

Although this CG iteration appears to require two multiplications of the matrix $\mathbf{X}^T\mathbf{X}$ and a vector, through the use of one of several recursive relationships (as in the last step) we can reduce the multiplications to only one. One such technique is to compute the vector $\mathbf{h}_k = \mathbf{X}^T\mathbf{X}\mathbf{q}_k$. The algorithm can then be written informally, using just $4p$ (and a constant number more) storage locations:

(0) $\mathbf{b} = \mathbf{0}$, $\mathbf{q} = \mathbf{g} = -\mathbf{X}^T\mathbf{y}$, $c = 0$
(1) for $k = 1, 2, 3, \ldots$ until convergence
(2)   if $(k \neq 1)$ then $c = -\mathbf{h}^T\mathbf{g}/u$ and $\mathbf{q} = \mathbf{g} + c\mathbf{q}$
(3)   compute $\mathbf{h} = \mathbf{X}^T\mathbf{X}\mathbf{q}$ and $u = \mathbf{q}^T\mathbf{X}^T\mathbf{X}\mathbf{q} = \mathbf{q}^T\mathbf{h}$
(4) $a = -\mathbf{q}^T\mathbf{g}/u$
(5) $\mathbf{b} = \mathbf{b} + a\mathbf{q}$
(6) $\mathbf{g} = \mathbf{g} + a\mathbf{h}$

Because the orthogonality and conjugate relationships are quickly lost owing to roundoff error, a restart by setting $c = 0$ is recommended every p iterations. Notice that the least-squares problem should be solved in just p iterations, according to the mathematics; the conjugate gradient method should be considered as an iterative method that could require more or fewer iterations. Moreover, the conjugate gradient method can be used for more general problems, where the function to be minimized is successively approximated by a quadratic. In this case, it is necessary to compute the gradient directly at each step.

The convergence of the CG algorithm can be improved greatly by preconditioning the matrix $\mathbf{X}^T\mathbf{X}$ – usually by something easily computable, like the inverse of the matrix composed only of its diagonal elements. Some aspects of the preconditioning, as well as the applicability of CG to solving any positive definite system of equations, behave similarly to successive over-relaxation in the modification of Gauss–Seidel and Jacobi methods (see Section 4.7). Many advances in preconditioning, especially for least-squares problems, are due to Hemmerle. Preconditioning and balancing are critical for the convergence of CG. Since the search direction often follows the steepest descent direction, the performance of CG can suffer from the same zig-zagging that slows steepest descent searches to a walk. Because the zig-zagging results from contours of the sum-of-squares function that are highly eccentric, the preconditioning and balancing are aimed at reducing this eccentricity so that the direction of steepest descent points directly at the minimum.

Although the product matrix $\mathbf{X}^T\mathbf{X}$ appears in the formulation of the conjugate gradient algorithm, the matrix is never to be stored; doing so would require $O(p^2)$ storage, for which Cholesky or Givens methods could be used for the least-squares problem. The applications for which CG will prove its worth are large, unbalanced design problems with many factors and levels. The information within any observation consists only of (a) the value of the dependent variable and (b) the values of the levels of the various factors. To illustrate, consider the following example.

Example 5.8: *Update Code for Conjugate Gradients*
Consider a two-factor cross-classified model with no interaction, following

$$y_{ijk} = \mu + \alpha_i + \beta_j + e_{ijk} \quad (1, \ldots, I, \ j = 1, \ldots, J, \ k = 1, \ldots, n_{ij}).$$

Then the data can be stored with just y, i, j given for each observation. The following full-rank parameterization preserves simplicity but not balance:

$$b(1) = \mu,$$
$$b(i + 1) = \alpha_i \quad \text{for } i = 1, \dots, I - 1, \qquad (5.11.8)$$
$$b(I + j) = \beta_j \quad \text{for } j = 1, \dots, J - 1,$$

using the identifying restrictions $\alpha_I = \beta_J = 0$. Other parameterizations that might affect centering, such as $b(i + 1) = \alpha_i - \alpha_I$ and $b(I + j) = \beta_j - \beta_J$, may do better but lead to more complicated code. Changing the character of the index k – from counting replicates to counting observations – leads to the following code for computing $\mathbf{h} = \mathbf{X}^T\mathbf{X}\mathbf{q}$ in step (3):

```
do k=1,N
i=factor1(k)
j=factor2(k)
s=q(1)
if( i .ne. I ) s=s+q(i+1)
if( j .ne. J ) s=s+q(I+j)
h(1)=h(1)+s
if( i .ne. I ) h(i+1)=h(i+1)+s
if( j .ne. J ) h(I+j)=h(I+j)+s
end do  ! loop on k
```

The approach given here on conjugate gradients is basically the original Hestenes–Stiefel algorithm. Modifications by Beale and others, and by Hemmerle for the least-squares problem specifically, are discussed in Golub and van Loan (1984) and in McIntosh (1982). Preconditioning and balance (see McIntosh 1982, pp. 70ff) are difficult tools that govern the performance of CG.

5.12   Doolittle, the Sweep, and All Possible Regressions

Two techniques – elimination methods both – have not yet been applied to the least squares problem. One is Gaussian elimination, which leads to the abbreviated Doolittle method that was popular among statisticians in the age of desk calculators. The other technique is full (Gauss-Jordan) elimination, which leads to the sweep operator.

The Doolittle (1878) method is a direct computation of an LU factorization of a symmetric matrix without the intermediate results that are computed in Gaussian elimination. Applying Doolittle to the normal equations leads to a compact scheme with no wasted effort. Consider the result of Gaussian elimination on the augmented matrix

$$(\mathbf{X}^T\mathbf{X} \quad \mathbf{X}^T\mathbf{y} \quad \mathbf{I}_p) \to (\mathbf{U} \quad \mathbf{L}^{-1}\mathbf{X}^T\mathbf{y} \quad \mathbf{L}^{-1}) \qquad (5.12.1)$$

Completion of the effort requires simply the solution of the triangular system $\mathbf{U}\mathbf{b} = \mathbf{L}^{-1}\mathbf{X}^T\mathbf{y}$ to find $\hat{\mathbf{b}}$, and the inverse matrix can be found by solving similar systems with columns of $\mathbf{L}^{-1}$. The great savings comes from symmetry – both in the elimination, which is done one row at a time, and also in the partial solutions of the calculations of the inverse.

The sweep operator can be viewed as a compact form of full (Gauss-Jordan) elimination of an $n \times n$ symmetric matrix $\mathbf{A}$. Consider full elimination on the augmented matrix below, partitioned with a single row/column and the remainder

$$(\mathbf{A} \quad \mathbf{B} \quad \mathbf{I}) = \begin{pmatrix} A_{11} & \mathbf{a}^{(1)T} & \mathbf{B}_{1.} & 1 & \mathbf{0} \\ \mathbf{a}^{(1)} & \mathbf{A}^{(1)} & \mathbf{B}^{(1)} & \mathbf{0} & \mathbf{I}_{n-1} \end{pmatrix} \qquad (5.12.2)$$

where the matrix $\mathbf{B}$ may be included whose columns are RHS of equations $\mathbf{Ax} = \mathbf{b}$ to be solved. Elimination (without pivoting) is equivalent to multiplying by a sequence of matrices $\mathbf{M}_1, \mathbf{M}_2, \ldots, \mathbf{M}_n$, where the first step is

$$\mathbf{M}_1(\mathbf{A} \quad \mathbf{B} \quad \mathbf{I}) = \begin{pmatrix} 1/A_{11} & \mathbf{0} \\ -\mathbf{a}^{(1)}/A_{11} & \mathbf{I} \end{pmatrix} \times \begin{pmatrix} A_{11} & \mathbf{a}^{(1)T} & \mathbf{B}_{1.} & 1 & \mathbf{0} \\ \mathbf{a}^{(1)} & \mathbf{A}^{(1)} & \mathbf{B}^{(1)} & \mathbf{0} & \mathbf{I}_{n-1} \end{pmatrix}$$

$$= \begin{pmatrix} 1 & \mathbf{a}^{(1)T}/A_{11} & \mathbf{B}_{1.}/A_{11} & 1/A_{11} & \mathbf{0} \\ \mathbf{0} & \mathbf{A}^{(1)} - \mathbf{a}^{(1)}\mathbf{a}^{(1)T}/A_{11} & \mathbf{B}^{(1)} - \mathbf{B}_{1.}\mathbf{a}^{(1)}/A_{11} & -\mathbf{a}^{(1)}/A_{11} & \mathbf{I}_{n-1} \end{pmatrix}.$$

Now if we continued and eliminated each column, we would have the inverse and solutions to equations:

$$\mathbf{M}_n \ldots \mathbf{M}_2\mathbf{M}_1(\mathbf{A} \quad \mathbf{B} \quad \mathbf{I}) = (\mathbf{I} \quad \mathbf{A}^{-1}\mathbf{B} \quad \mathbf{A}^{-1}). \qquad (5.12.3)$$

But if we stopped partway, after eliminating p rows/columns, or *sweeping* the first p rows/columns, we would have

$$\mathbf{M}_p \ldots \mathbf{M}_1(\mathbf{A} \quad \mathbf{B} \quad \mathbf{I}) = \begin{pmatrix} \mathbf{A}_{11}^{-1} & \mathbf{0} \\ -\mathbf{A}_{21}\mathbf{A}_{11}^{-1} & \mathbf{I} \end{pmatrix} \times \begin{pmatrix} \mathbf{A}_{11} & \mathbf{A}_{12} & \mathbf{B}_1 & \mathbf{I}_p & \mathbf{0} \\ \mathbf{A}_{21} & \mathbf{A}_{22} & \mathbf{B}_2 & \mathbf{0} & \mathbf{I}_{n-p} \end{pmatrix}$$

$$= \begin{pmatrix} \mathbf{I}_p & \mathbf{A}_{11}^{-1}\mathbf{A}_{12} & \mathbf{A}_{11}^{-1}\mathbf{B}_1 & \mathbf{A}_{11}^{-1} & \mathbf{0} \\ \mathbf{0} & \mathbf{A}_{22} - \mathbf{A}_{21}\mathbf{A}_{11}^{-1}\mathbf{A}_{12} & \mathbf{B}_2 - \mathbf{A}_{21}\mathbf{A}_{11}^{-1}\mathbf{B}_1 & -\mathbf{A}_{21}\mathbf{A}_{11}^{-1} & \mathbf{I}_{n-p} \end{pmatrix}.$$

partitioning now as p and $n - p$ rows/columns.

Notice that as columns of the appended identity matrix are changed, similar columns are created in the first columns. If we store those changed columns where the new ones were created to save space (and never store the identity), we can define the sweep operator, either as sweeping a single row/column, as

$$\begin{pmatrix} A_{11} & \mathbf{a}^{(1)T} & \mathbf{B}_{1.} \\ \mathbf{a}^{(1)} & \mathbf{A}^{(1)} & \mathbf{B}^{(1)} \end{pmatrix} \rightarrow sweep(1)$$

$$\rightarrow \begin{pmatrix} 1/A_{11} & \mathbf{a}^{(1)T}/A_{11} & \mathbf{B}_{1.}/A_{11} \\ -\mathbf{a}^{(1)}/A_{11} & \mathbf{A}^{(1)} - \mathbf{a}^{(1)}\mathbf{a}^{(1)T}/A_{11} & \mathbf{B}^{(1)} - \mathbf{B}_{1.}\mathbf{a}^{(1)}/A_{11} \end{pmatrix}$$

$$(5.12.4)$$

or in block form

$$\begin{pmatrix} \mathbf{A}_{11} & \mathbf{A}_{12} & \mathbf{B}_1 \\ \mathbf{A}_{21} & \mathbf{A}_{22} & \mathbf{B}_2 \end{pmatrix} \rightarrow sweep(1:p)$$

$$\rightarrow \begin{pmatrix} \mathbf{A}_{11}^{-1} & \mathbf{A}_{11}^{-1}\mathbf{A}_{12} & \mathbf{A}_{11}^{-1}\mathbf{B}_1 \\ -\mathbf{A}_{21}\mathbf{A}_{11}^{-1} & \mathbf{A}_{22} - \mathbf{A}_{21}\mathbf{A}_{11}^{-1}\mathbf{A}_{12} & \mathbf{B}_2 - \mathbf{A}_{21}\mathbf{A}_{11}^{-1}\mathbf{B}_1 \end{pmatrix}.$$

$$(5.12.5)$$

The effectiveness of the sweep operator for regression can now be seen when applied to the cross products matrix:

$$\begin{pmatrix} \mathbf{X}^T\mathbf{X} & \mathbf{X}^T\mathbf{y} \\ \mathbf{X}^T\mathbf{y} & \mathbf{y}^T\mathbf{y} \end{pmatrix} \rightarrow sweep(1:p) \rightarrow \begin{pmatrix} (\mathbf{X}^T\mathbf{X})^{-1} & \hat{\mathbf{b}} \\ -\hat{\mathbf{b}} & \mathbf{y}^T(\mathbf{I} - \mathbf{P}_X)\mathbf{y} \end{pmatrix}. \qquad (5.12.6)$$

The full power of the sweep can best be seen when a subset of the potential regressors are swept, say, the first p_1 corresponding to $\mathbf{X}$, with p_2 columns corresponding to $\mathbf{Z}$ remaining, and generalizing to multivariate regression:

$$\begin{pmatrix} \mathbf{X}^T\mathbf{X} & \mathbf{X}^T\mathbf{Z} & \mathbf{X}^T\mathbf{Y} \\ \mathbf{Z}^T\mathbf{X} & \mathbf{Z}^T\mathbf{Z} & \mathbf{Z}^T\mathbf{Y} \\ \mathbf{Y}^T\mathbf{X} & \mathbf{Y}^T\mathbf{Z} & \mathbf{Y}^T\mathbf{Y} \end{pmatrix} \rightarrow sweep(1:p_1)$$

$$\rightarrow \begin{pmatrix} (\mathbf{X}^T\mathbf{X})^{-1} & (\mathbf{X}^T\mathbf{X})^{-1}\mathbf{X}^T\mathbf{Z} & (\mathbf{X}^T\mathbf{X})^{-1}\mathbf{X}^T\mathbf{Y} \\ -\mathbf{Z}^T\mathbf{X}(\mathbf{X}^T\mathbf{X})^{-1} & \mathbf{Z}^T(\mathbf{I} - \mathbf{P}_X)\mathbf{Z} & \mathbf{Z}^T(\mathbf{I} - \mathbf{P}_X)\mathbf{Y} \\ -\mathbf{Y}^T\mathbf{X}(\mathbf{X}^T\mathbf{X})^{-1} & \mathbf{Y}^T(\mathbf{I} - \mathbf{P}_X)\mathbf{Z} & \mathbf{Y}^T(\mathbf{I} - \mathbf{P}_X)\mathbf{Y} \end{pmatrix}.$$

$$(5.12.7)$$

First of all, the capitalization $\mathbf{Y}$ indicates the ease of adding multiple dependent variables. Next, coefficients for models including only subsets of the explanatory variables can be found along the way, as well as their error sums of squares. But notice also the middle term in (5.12.4). If the columns of $\mathbf{Z}$ are linearly dependent on $\mathbf{X}$, then this "error" sum of squares is zero (theoretically). Computationally, this quantity can be compared to a tolerance as a test for singularity. Because of the definiteness of the matrices on the diagonal of the tableau, there is no need at all to pivot, except for these dependencies; even in that case, sweeping row k also means column k, so that the pivots are all on the diagonal.

The sweep operator has two other useful properties: (1) *reversibility* – sweeping row/column k twice is the same as not sweeping at all; and (2) *commutativity* – the order in which the sweeps are done has no effect (mathematically). But the most important property of the sweep operator is its simplicity. If we denote the current tableau by the $m \times m$ matrix $\mathbf{A}$, then sweeping row/column k (which is equivalent to adding/deleting the variable k in the regression) and overwriting the new tableau takes the following code:

```
d=A(k,k)
do j=1,m
A(k,j)=A(k,j)/d
end do  ! loop on j
do i=1,m
if( i .ne. k ) then
  b=A(i,k)
  do j=1,m
  A(i,j)=A(i,j)-b*A(k,j)
  end do  ! loop on j
  A(i,k)=-b/d
  end if  ! if( i .ne. k )
end do  ! loop on i
A(k,k)=1/d
```

```
regsweep <- function(A,k) {
        d <- A[k,k]                    # sweep out row k, col k
        A[k,] <- A[k,]/d
        b <- A[,k]
        b[k] <- 0                      # don't change row k here
        A <- A - outer(b,A[k,])        # main operation
        A[,k] <- -b/d                  # fix col k
        A[k,k] <- 1/d                  # diagonal element & done
        regsweep <- A        }
```

These properties make the sweep operator perfect for variable selection algorithms, since adding or deleting a variable merely means doing a sweep operation. The only drawback is that a system of normal equations is being solved and so the sweep should only be done in double precision – unless the native arithmetic has a lot of precision to spare.

The most demanding variable selection procedure is one requiring that *all* subsets of a given set of explanatory variables be considered, that is, the problem of computing all possible regressions. Given p variables, this means 2^p regressions (if we include the null regression with no explanatory variables). Schatzoff, Tsao, and Feinberg (1968) described a procedure to compute the results of all possible regressions using the sweep operator, with no wasted effort. The one drawback of sweep becomes even more prominent in this case, since the errors accumulate through a large number of steps. Furnival (1971) offered a modification that requires more storage but avoids backtracking; he also advocated the use of Gaussian elimination over sweep. Furnival and Wilson (1974) proposed further improvements, which include avoiding some of the subset regressions that can be shown (through the use of bounds) not to be promising. Clarke (1981) provided an alternative scheme using Givens transformations.

5.13   Alternatives to Least Squares

Many alternatives to least squares have been proposed over the years in response a variety of issues, for example, multicollinearity, robustness, and model selection. While these alternatives lead to different objective criteria, their computational methods often rely on the tools outlined earlier in this chapter.

Often an indication of multicollinearity is the presence of large estimated coefficients, but not necessarily significantly different from zero (small t statistics). So a simple modification might be to restrict the coefficients, say, to $\|\mathbf{b}\| < c$ or the more general $(\mathbf{b} - \mathbf{b}^*)^T \mathbf{A} (\mathbf{b} - \mathbf{b}^*) \le c^2$. If $\|\mathbf{b}\| < c$, then the least squares estimates solve the problem; if not, then the restriction will hold at the elliptical boundary $\mathbf{b}^T \mathbf{b} = c^2$ or the general $(\mathbf{b} - \mathbf{b}^*)^T \mathbf{A} (\mathbf{b} - \mathbf{b}^*) = c^2$. Since the least squares contours in $\mathbf{b}$ are also elliptical, the solution to this modified least squares problem will occur when the gradient vector of the least squares is orthogonal to the tangent plane of the bounding ellipsoid – which is orthogonal to its gradient vector. In other words, the solution will occur when these two gradient vectors are pointing in opposite directions: there is some scalar λ such that

$$\mathbf{X}^T (\mathbf{y} - \mathbf{X}b) = \lambda \mathbf{A}(\mathbf{b} - \mathbf{b}^*),$$

which also gives the solution to the penalized least squares problem

$$\min (\mathbf{y} - \mathbf{X}b)^T (\mathbf{y} - \mathbf{X}b) + \lambda (\mathbf{b} - \mathbf{b}^*)^T \mathbf{A}(\mathbf{b} - \mathbf{b}^*).$$

See also Exercise 5.31 (Ridge Regression).

While Euclidean geometry is based on the $p = 2$ norm, statisticians have also considered the $p = 1$ norm (see Exercise 5.36 for the $p = \infty$ norm). Here the objective function to be minimized involves absolute values instead of squares

$$g(\mathbf{b}) = \sum_{i=1}^N |y_i - \mathbf{x}_i^T \mathbf{b}|.$$

This *median regression* or L_1 regression problem can be formulated as a linear programming problem (Section 4.8) by separating the positive and negative residuals, $\mathbf{e}^+$ and $\mathbf{e}^-$, respectively, as well as the positive and negative parts of the coefficients $\mathbf{b}^+$ and $\mathbf{b}^-$

$$\min \mathbf{1}^T \mathbf{e}^+ + \mathbf{1}^T \mathbf{e}^- \text{ subject to } \mathbf{y} = \mathbf{X}(\mathbf{b}^+ - \mathbf{b}^-) + \mathbf{e}^+ - \mathbf{e}^-$$

with $\mathbf{b}^+, \mathbf{b}^-, \mathbf{e}^+, \mathbf{e}^-$ each $\geq \mathbf{0}$. Portnoy and Koenker (1997) discuss this approach as well as alternatives, including the dual problem and interior point methods – modifying non-smooth problems with smooth penalty functions – for problems where the sample size N is very large. Only a small step to the function

$$\rho_\tau(u) = \begin{cases} \tau & \text{if } u \leq 0 \\ 1 - \tau & \text{if } u > 0 \end{cases}$$

leads to quantile regression, where the objective function is

$$g(\mathbf{b}) = \sum_{i=1}^N \rho_\tau(y_i - \mathbf{x}_i^T \mathbf{b}).$$

For each value of the quantile value τ ($0 < \tau < 1$), we can find the optimal $\hat{\mathbf{b}}$, where the special case $\tau = 1/2$ corresponds to the median, absolute values and the *median regression* mentioned above. In another direction, the function $\rho(u)$ can be modified from $\rho(u) = u^2$ (least squares) or $\rho(u) = |u|$ (median regression) to other forms of *robust regression*. One common form is due to Huber (1964):

$$\rho_{Huber}(u) = \begin{cases} u^2/2 & \text{if } |u| \leq c \\ cu - c^2/2 & \text{if } |u| > c \end{cases}$$

which behaves like least squares for small residuals and like median regression for large residuals. In this way, the coefficient estimates are less sensitive or *robust* to extreme observations (*outliers*). Computational methods for these objective functions are similar to those of maximum likelihood; these methods are called *M-estimators* for this reason. See Chapter 9 for the discussion of maximum likelihood methods.

A different combination of quadratic fit and linear or absolute value constraints lead to the *lasso* (Tibshirani, 1996). Here the goal is to minimize the error sum of squares subject to the constraint that the L_1 norm of the coefficient vector is below a bound:

$$\min_{\mathbf{b}} (\mathbf{y} - \mathbf{Xb})^T (\mathbf{y} - \mathbf{Xb}) \text{ subject to } \sum_j |b_j| \leq t.$$

As before, if the least squares solution $\hat{\mathbf{b}}$ satisfies the constraint, we're done. Otherwise, the solution will occur when the least squares elliptical contours hit the planar faces of the constraint. This problem can be viewed as a *quadratic programming* problem (e.g., Gill and Murray, 1978; Lawson and Hansen, 1974) of the general form

$$\min_{\mathbf{b}} \frac{1}{2} \mathbf{x}^T \mathbf{G} \mathbf{x} + \mathbf{c}^T \mathbf{x} \text{ subject to } \mathbf{A}^T \mathbf{x} \geq \mathbf{b}$$

whose algorithms traverse the points where those planar faces – corresponding to equality constraints – intersect the elliptical contours. A sure-fire approach to finding a solution is to solve least squares problems at all subsets of those equality constraints. But performing a similar step to the L_1 problem earlier, let $\mathbf{b} = \mathbf{b}^+ + \mathbf{b}^-$ where $\mathbf{b}^+$ and $\mathbf{b}^-$ are constrained to be nonnegative. Then the lasso problem can be viewed as a least squares problem in $2p$ variables subject to $2p + 1$ simple linear constraints, and quadratic programming tools that exploit the simple, sparse structure can be very effective. Osborne et al. (2000) propose an effective algorithm exploiting the dual problem, and Kim et al. (2008) propose another that can be extended to generalized regression problems (Chapter 9). Other variations on the lasso (e.g., elastic net, OSCAR, etc.) lead to similar quadratic programming problems with simple and sparse constraints. If the constraint bound t is not considered given, but found, say, by minimizing cross validation, then the solutions must be found for many values of t. A modification of the LARS algorithm (Efron et al. 2004), can be used to find lasso solutions for all values of t.

5.14 Comments

After so many methods have been presented, an inevitable question is: Which one is best? Because each method was developed for a set of circumstances in which the others were considered inferior, it follows that, depending on the situation, there may be a "best" method. The different methods have certain advantages and disadvantages: storage requirements, speed, flexibility, ease of adding or deleting variables and/or observations, ease of testing hypotheses, ease of testing for rank deficiencies, and numerical stability. The best method, should there be one, will depend on the characteristics of the problem and the purposes to which the results will be put.

When considering a general method, say a workhorse routine, the difficulties mount. The computing environment must be considered: storage available, accuracy of the arithmetic, speed of I/O and disk access. But the demands of the consumer direct the decisions of what quantities are computed, regardless of whether overparameterized models are permitted and regardless of what options are offered and of limitations that may exist on problem size. From my own point of view, designing and implementing a general method is a burdensome task worth avoiding. Hence only two, special-purpose codes are given in this chapter for regression. Since there is not a "best" method and since the workhorse routines in available statistical software systems are so good, the only call for most statisticians to write their own regression routine is a special-purpose problem. In such a case, the features of the special problem dictate which method to use.

The reader may conclude that the least-squares problem is a computational nightmare. That is not true. First, the methods that have advantages in accuracy are trying to make the most out of arithmetic with limited accuracy. Using some of the other methods, such as Cholesky or sweep, can produce results just as accurate (if not more so) by using the brute strength technique of performing the calculations in double precision; this is inelegant but successful. Second, determining the rank of a matrix is quite a difficult problem, one that is best avoided. The preferred procedure would be to quit once an explanatory variable is found to be linearly dependent on the others, but that would require a full-rank parameterization for design models. Since forming a full-rank parameterization for a complicated design model is such a tedious task, and since the tests for linear dependence work so well in practice (especially for design problems whose entries are integers), the risk is worth the great savings in effort. Finally, the source of the computational difficulties is that the problem of cancellation – which is so fundamental to arithmetic – becomes magnified when taking the difference of sums of squares. That main principle underlies all of the methods here, and it carries over to the use of all statistical software for regression. However, centering and rescaling can always improve the condition of the problem.

Example 5.9: *Centering and scaling for quadratic regression*
Consider fitting a quadratic regression model to an annual response y_i, say, for the 21 years 1990–2010

$$E(y_i) = \beta_0 + \beta_1 x_i + \beta_2 x_i^2$$

where $x_i = 1989 + i, i = 1, \ldots, 21$. The table below gives the condition number κ_* for the design matrix with rows $(1, x_i, x_i^2)$, along with some other parameterizations. Scaling the columns leads to the design matrix $\mathbf{W}$ and improves the condition. Centering x_i with its mean leads to $\mathbf{U}$; centering the columns of $\mathbf{X}$ leads to $\mathbf{Z}$.

design matrix	rows	κ_*
$\mathbf{X}$	$1, x_i, x_i^2$	5×10^{11}
$\mathbf{W}$	$1, x_i/\overline{x}, (x_i/\overline{x})^2$	5×10^5
$\mathbf{U}$	$1, x_i - \overline{x}, (x_i - \overline{x})^2$	74
$\mathbf{Z}$	$1, x_i - \overline{x}, x_i^2 - \overline{x^2}$	74

The reader may be quite surprised at the enormous condition number κ_* of $\mathbf{X}$ for so simple a problem. Rescaling the covariate columns of $\mathbf{X}$ drops the condition substantially, but see Exercise 5.33 to examine whether the ill conditioning of **X** is artificial or not. Centering the covariate has a dramatic effect on the condition. The parameterization **U** has additional appeal because its two reparameterized coefficients are easily interpreted as the mean response and slope at the center.

Programs and Demonstrations

chex57   *Check of Example 5.7, simple linear regression with Givens transformations*
The operations of Example 5.7 are repeated, with creation of the Givens transformation and premultiplying on **X**. Also, the product matrix $\mathbf{Q} = \mathbf{U}_{mn} \cdots \mathbf{U}_{21}$ is computed by starting with an identity and premultiplying the Givens transformations in succession.
rot734 – subroutine to compute a Givens transformation beginning with two elements, following a careful routine given by Stewart (1973) as Algorithm 7.3.4.

flyreg   *Demonstration of regression using Givens transformations "on the fly"*
One advantage of doing regression via Givens transformation follows the second looping scheme on page 96, where new observations (rows of **X**) are added as available, or "on the fly." Since the crucial intermediate values are the matrix **R**, $\mathbf{z}^{(1)}$, and SSE, only these quantities are kept; neither **y** nor **X** are stored, and **R** is kept in symmetric/triangular fashion. Once all of the observations are available (or at any intermediate point), regression coefficients can be found by solving $\mathbf{Rb} = \mathbf{z}^{(1)}$ using **chlzih** from Chapter 3; for computing $(\mathbf{X}^T\mathbf{X})^{-1}$ at the end, the routine **chlzoi** is employed. The problem solved is Exercise 13.1 from Brownlee (1965, pp. 462–4).
flyreg – computes updates for regression by Givens transformations.

sweep   *Demonstration of the sweep operator for regression*
Using the same problem from Brownlee as **flyreg**, the sweep operator is used to compute regression coefficients. Each variable, beginning with the intercept, is swept in succession, and then swept out to end up with the original augmented sums of squares and cross-products matrix, as in (5.12.4). The code is remarkably short. The computations are done in single precision; the interested reader should try this in double precision.
sweep – subroutine that performs the sweep operator on a particular row/column of a matrix.

Exercises

5.1   In Example 5.1, the same fit is obtained using the matrix

$$\mathbf{Z} = \begin{bmatrix} 1 & 0 \\ 1 & 0 \\ 1 & 1 \\ 1 & 1 \end{bmatrix}.$$

Find $\kappa^*(\mathbf{Z})$.

5.2 Steel and Torrie (1980, tab. 19.1) listed the following growth data on cabbages:

$$\text{Week } (X): \quad 1 \quad 2 \quad 3 \quad 4 \quad 5 \quad 6$$
$$\text{Height } (Y): \quad 4.5 \quad 5.5 \quad 6.5 \quad 8.0 \quad 10.0 \quad 12.0 \text{ cm}$$

Compute simple linear regression estimates by solving the normal equations via Cholesky for the model

$$y_i = b_1 + b_2 x_i + e_i,$$

using only four decimal digits.

5.3 Redo Exercise 5.2 with six or eight decimal digits and compare the results.

5.4 For small values of n and p and $X_{ij} = i^{j-1}$, perform the Gram–Schmidt orthonormalization analytically and find $\mathbf{R}^{-1}\mathbf{Q}^T = (\mathbf{X}^T\mathbf{X})^{-1}\mathbf{X}^T$. You should be reminded of orthogonal polynomials.

5.5 With the data from Exercise 5.2 and using the results of Example 5.4, estimate the coefficients of the model $y_i = b_1 + b_2 x_i + b_3 x_i^2 + e_i$ via regular and modified Gram–Schmidt, using only four decimal digits.

5.6 How do things change in Example 5.5 when s is taken to be negative (as would be recommended)?

5.7 Construct the Householder transformation $\mathbf{U}$ so that $\mathbf{U}\mathbf{x} = -s\mathbf{e}_n$.

5.8 Modify the regression method using Householder transformations to produce the following factorization with the lower triangular matrix $\mathbf{L}$:

$$\mathbf{U}_p \cdots \mathbf{U}_1 \mathbf{X} = \begin{bmatrix} \mathbf{0} \\ \mathbf{L} \end{bmatrix}. \quad \begin{array}{c} n-p \\ p \end{array}$$

5.9 Verify the method given in step (5) for computation of residuals using Householder transformations (see Section 5.6).

5.10 For

$$\mathbf{X} = \begin{bmatrix} 1 & 0 & 0 \\ 1 & 1 & 0 \\ 1 & 0 & 1 \\ 1 & 1 & 1 \end{bmatrix} \quad \text{and} \quad \mathbf{y} = \begin{bmatrix} 0 \\ 1 \\ 2 \\ 3 \end{bmatrix},$$

solve the least-squares problem with Householder.

5.11 (See Chan et al. 1983.) Show that the following updating algorithm for computing the sample mean and variance is really just the Givens method for the simplest regression problem (just a common mean):

$$T_i = T_{i-1} + y_i \quad \text{and} \quad S_i = S_{i-1} + (iy_i - T_i)^2/[i(i-1)].$$

Show that it is equivalent to the following code:

```
s=0.
ss=0.
do i=1,n
d=(y(i)-s)/i
ss=ss+(i-1)*(y(i)-s)*d
s=s+d
end do  ! loop on i
```

5.12 How would the Householder method work for the same problem of estimating a mean?

5.13 Compare the formulas given in Exercise 5.11 with the usual ones for computing a mean and variance for the sample $y_i = 2^{12} + i$ for $i = 1, \ldots, 16$.

5.14 Update your solution to Exercise 5.5 with the additional observation $y_7 = 15.5$, using Givens transformations.

5.15 Stewart (1976) proposed a single number ρ to represent a Givens transformation in (5.7.1). Show how to reproduce a and b from ρ.

5.16 Using the Sherman–Morrison–Woodbury formula (5.9.4), fill in the details of the proof of (5.9.3), including the details of (5.9.5).

5.17 Prove the Sherman–Morrison–Woodbury formula (5.9.4).

5.18 Verify (5.9.6).

5.19 Prove the equivalence of (5.9.8) and (5.9.9).

5.20 Prove the simplification of the expressions for Cook's D from (5.9.10) and (5.9.11).

5.21 Compute all of the regression diagnostics using your solution to Exercise 5.5.

5.22 Using your solution to Exercise 5.5 (or Exercise 5.14, for that matter), test the hypothesis $H : b_2 = 2b_3$; follow both routes considered in Section 5.10 as well as the straightforward expression

$$(\mathbf{K}^T\hat{\mathbf{b}} - \mathbf{m})^T[\mathbf{K}^T(\mathbf{X}^T\mathbf{X})^{-1}\mathbf{K}]^{-1}(\mathbf{K}^T\hat{\mathbf{b}} - \mathbf{m}).$$

Discuss how a comparison could be made among the methods.

5.23 Consider a two-way crossed classified model with no interaction and with (say) four levels on the first factor and two on the second. How would you compute partial sums of squares for the factors using the results from any of the orthogonalization methods?

5.24 For testing the hypothesis in Exercise 5.22, find a condition number for solving the system of equations (5.10.9).

5.25 Let $\mathbf{x}_*^T$ be a row of $\mathbf{X}$. What is the condition of the problem of finding $\mathbf{x}_*^T\hat{\mathbf{b}}$?

5.26 Compute κ^* for $\mathbf{X}$ in Example 5.3.

5.27 Recommend a method for computing $\mathbf{P_X}\mathbf{v}$ and $\mathbf{v}^T\mathbf{P_X}\mathbf{v}$. Compare its operation count to its possible competitors. Does the same method work well for $(\mathbf{I} - \mathbf{P_X})\mathbf{v}$ and $\mathbf{v}^T(\mathbf{I} - \mathbf{P_X})\mathbf{v}$?

5.28 Compute your solution to Exercise 5.5 (Exercise 5.2 with a quadratic model) using the sweep operator. Compute all of the partial and sequential sums of squares as well.

5.29 Write a program to do regression using Householder transformations in single precision and try it out (a trial by fire, indeed) on the Longley (1967) data. (Debug using something else, of course!)

5.30 Write a program to do regression using the sweep operator in double precision, and try it out on the Longley (1967) data.

5.31 *Ridge regression* is an alternative method to gain stability in cases of multicollinearity; it uses the modified coefficient estimator

$$\hat{\mathbf{b}}_\lambda = (\mathbf{X}^T\mathbf{X} + \lambda\mathbf{I}_p)^{-1}\mathbf{X}^T\mathbf{y}.$$

Show that $\hat{\mathbf{b}}_\lambda$ is continuous in λ. Suggest methods for computing $\hat{\mathbf{b}}_\lambda$.

5.32 Are the Householder and Givens transformations for annihilating the second element of a 2-dimensional vector the same?

5.33 In Example 5.9, the design matrix $\mathbf{X}$ has an intercept column, and covariate columns x_i, and x_i^2. Rescaling the covariate columns to $x_i/\overline{x}$ and $(x_i/\overline{x})^2$ drops the condition substantially, suggesting the condition number for $\mathbf{X}$ may be artificially large. Consider the situation where the change in the design matrix arose from changes in the recording date, say, moved one day because of a holiday (1/365.25), or due to a leap year effect (.25/365.25). What would be the effect on the solution to this least squares problem for changes such as these on the four design matrices given in Example 5.9?

5.34 Consider the multiple regression problem including an intercept with the following list of explanatory variables:

$$
\begin{aligned}
&c1 = cos(2\pi i/7) & &s1 = sin(2\pi i/7) \\
&c2 = cos(2\pi 2i/7) & &s2 = sin(2\pi 2i/7) \\
&c3 = cos(2\pi 3i/7) & &s3 = sin(2\pi 3i/7) \\
&c4 = cos(2\pi 4i/7) & &s4 = sin(2\pi 4i/7) \\
&c5 = cos(2\pi 5i/7) & &s5 = sin(2\pi 5i/7) \\
&c6 = cos(2\pi 6i/7) & &s6 = sin(2\pi 6i/7)
\end{aligned}
$$

for $i = 1, \ldots, N$.

a) Show that the last six variables (c4, s4, ..., s6) are linearly dependent on the first six (c1, s1, ..., s3) and an intercept.

b) Test whether the regression software that you commonly use can detect dependencies among the explanatory variables, using 3.1416 as your approximation for π, and various values of N.

c) Repeat this exercise with a cruder approximation 3.14 for π or a more precise one.

d) Repeat this exercise with 4 in place of 7 (that is, $2\pi i/4$, $4\pi i/4$, etc.).

5.35 Suggest effective methods for solving the penalized least squares problem

$$\min(\mathbf{y} - \mathbf{X}\mathbf{b})^T (\mathbf{y} - \mathbf{X}\mathbf{b}) + \lambda(\mathbf{b} - \mathbf{b}^*)^T \mathbf{A}(\mathbf{b} - \mathbf{b}^*)$$

for several values of λ at once.

5.36 Formulate the $p = \infty$ norm regression $min_{\mathbf{b}} \, max_i \, |y_i - \mathbf{x}_i^T\mathbf{b}|$ as a linear programming problem. Demonstrate the sensitivity of the resulting estimators to outliers.

5.37 Show that if the random variable U has df F, then the value of s that minimizes $E[\rho_\tau(U - s)]$ is s^* such that $F(s^*) = \tau$.

5.38 Using the heart disease data in *brown463.dat* used by **flyreg**, compute the median regression coefficients using the linear programming code from Chapter 4.

5.39 Formulate the quantile regression problem $min \sum_{i=1}^{N} \rho_\tau(y_i - \mathbf{x}_i^T\mathbf{b})$ as a linear programming problem.

References

The main reference works on least squares are the books by Stewart (1973), Golub and van Loan (1984), and Lawson and Hanson (1974). The Golub, Klema, and Peters (1980) article gives some useful practical guidance. The Bjorck (1967) paper is the original on MGS. The Doolittle method, which is remarkably efficient for hand calculation, can be found in Snedecor and Cochran (1967) or in any traditional (i.e. old) book on statistical methods. Goodnight's (1979) insightful tutorial explains sweep and a little of how it is used in the SAS package. Freund's (1979) article includes two nice regression problems. Velleman and Welsch (1981) discuss computations for regression diagnostics.

There are many more articles on the problems (or lack thereof) of computing least-squares solutions in the literature – stretching back more than a generation. There is also a lot of controversy. The Beaton (1977; Beaton et al. 1976) articles, and those of Wampler (1980), Goodnight (1979), and Longley (1967), include references to most of the remaining literature on the subject.

Albert E. Beaton (1977), "Comment on 'More on Computational Accuracy in Regression'," *Journal of the American Statistical Association* 72: 600.

Albert E. Beaton, Donald B. Rubin, and John L. Barone (1976), "The Acceptability of Regression Solutions: Another Look at Computational Accuracy," *Journal of the American Statistical Association* 71: 158–68.

D. A. Belsley, E. Kuh, and R. E. Welsch (1980), *Regression Diagnostics: Identifying Influential Data and Sources of Collinearity.* New York: Wiley.

Ake Bjorck (1967), "Solving Least Squares Problems by Gram–Schmidt Orthogonalization," *BIT* 7: 1–21.

K. A. Brownlee (1965), *Statistical Theory and Methodology in Science and Engineering,* 2nd ed. New York: Wiley.

Tony F. Chan, Gene H. Golub, and Randall J. LeVeque (1983), "Algorithms for Computing the Sample Variance," *American Statistician* 37: 242–7.

M. R. B. Clarke (1981), "AS 163: A Givens Algorithm for Moving from One Linear Model to Another without Going Back to the Data," *Applied Statistics* 30: 198–203.

R. D. Cook and S. Weisberg (1982), *Residuals and Influence in Regression.* New York: Chapman & Hall.

Germund Dahlquist and Ake Bjorck (1974), *Numerical Methods* (trans. by N. Anderson). Englewood Cliffs, NJ: Prentice-Hall.

M. H. Doolittle (1878), *United States Coast Guard and Geodetic Survey Report,* vol. 115.

Bradley Efron, Trevor Hastie, Iain Johnstone, and Robert Tibshirani (2004), "Least Angle Regression," *Annals of Statistics* 32: 407–499.

R. J. Freund (1979), "Multicollinearity etc., Some 'New' Examples," in *Proceedings of the Statistical Computing Section,* pp. 111–12. Washington, DC: American Statistical Association.

George M. Furnival (1971), "All Possible Regressions with Less Computation," *Technometrics* 13: 403–8.

George M. Furnival and Robert W. Wilson, Jr. (1974), "Regressions by Leaps and Bounds," *Technometrics* 16: 499–511.

W. Morven Gentleman (1973), "Least Squares Computations by Givens Transformations without Square Roots," *Journal of the Institute of Mathematics and Its Applications* 12: 329–36.

Philip E. Gill and Walter Murray (1978), "Numerically Stable Methods for Quadratic Programming," *Mathematical Programming* 14: 349–372.

Gene Golub, Virginia Klema, and Stephen C. Peters (1980), "Rules and Software for Detecting Rank Degeneracy," *Journal of Econometrics* 12: 41–8.

Gene H. Golub and Charles van Loan (1984), *Matrix Computations.* Baltimore: Johns Hopkins University Press.

James H. Goodnight (1979), "A Tutorial on the SWEEP Operator," *American Statistician* 33: 149–58.

Peter J. Huber (1964), "Robust Estimation of a Location Parameter", *Annals of Mathematical Statistics* 35: 73–101.

Jinseog Kim, Yuwon Kim, and Yongdai Kim (2008), "A Gradient-Based Optimization Algorithm for LASSO," *Journal of Computational and Graphical Statistics* 17: 994–1009.

Charles L. Lawson and Richard J. Hanson (1974), *Solving Least Squares Problems.* Englewood Cliffs, NJ: Prentice-Hall.

James W. Longley (1967), "An Appraisal of Least Squares Programs for the Electronic Computer for the Point of View of the User," *Journal of the American Statistical Association* 62: 819–41.

Allen McIntosh (1982), *Fitting Linear Models: An Application of Conjugate Gradient Algorithms.* New York: Springer-Verlag.

Raymond H. Myers (1989), *Classical and Modern Regression with Applications,* 2nd ed. Boston: PWS-Kent.

Michael R. Osborne, Brett Presnell, and Berwin A. Turlach (2000), "On the LASSO and Its Dual," *Journal of Computational and Graphical Statistics* 9: 319–337.

Stephen Portnoy and Roger Koenker (1997), "The Gaussian Hare and the Laplacian Tortoise: Computability of Square-Error versus Absolute-error Estimators," *Statistical Science,* 12: 279–300.

M. Schatzoff, R. Tsao, and S. Feinberg (1968), "Efficient Calculation of All Possible Regressions," *Technometrics* 10: 769–79.

Shayle R. Searle (1973), *Linear Models.* New York: Wiley.

George W. Snedecor and William G. Cochran (1967), *Statistical Methods,* 6th ed. Ames: Iowa State University Press.

R. G. D. Steel and J. H. Torrie (1980), *Principles and Procedures of Statistics,* 2nd ed. New York: McGraw-Hill.

G. W. Stewart (1973), *Introduction to Matrix Computations.* New York: Academic Press.

G. W. Stewart (1976), "The Economic Storage of Plane Rotations," *Numerische Mathematik* 25: 137–8.

Robert Tibshirani (1996), "Regression Shrinkage and Selection via the Lasso," *Journal of the Royal Statistical Society* 58: 267–288.

Paul F. Velleman and Roy E. Welsch (1981), "Efficient Computing of Regression Diagnostics," *American Statistician* 35: 234–42.

Roy H. Wampler (1980), "Test Procedures and Test Problems for Least Squares Algorithms," *Journal of Econometrics* 12: 3–22.

6

Eigenproblems

6.1 Introduction

Statistical problems requiring the computation of eigenvalues and eigenvectors fall into two distinct categories. In the first category, the matrix of interest is symmetric and positive definite, a covariance matrix arising in a multivariate statistical analysis. Often all of the eigenvalues and vectors need to be computed. But when the eigenproblem for a general matrix is faced, such as a transition matrix for a Markov chain or a coefficient matrix for a multivariate autoregressive process, often only the largest eigenvalue (or some of the largest) is required, along with its associated eigenvector. In this second category, the demands are more limited, compensating for a more difficult problem, and some knowledge of the eigenvalues is usually available. This chapter begins with the matrix theory in Section 6.2 and proceeds to the simple and general power methods, which are designed for problems in that second category. The next two sections attack the symmetric problem, which is followed by the related problem of computing the singular value decomposition in Section 6.6. The relationships of the many statistical problems with these algorithms will be discussed in Section 6.7. Although complex analysis will be avoided whenever possible, the problem of complex principal components analysis (CPCA) using a complex version of singular value decomposition requires full use of complex analysis.

6.2 Theory

An eigenvalue of a square matrix $\mathbf{A}$ of size n is a solution to the polynomial equation of degree n in the variable s,

$$c(s) = |\mathbf{A} - s\mathbf{I}_n| = 0, \tag{6.2.1}$$

where $\mathbf{A}$ is the $n \times n$ matrix and the polynomial $c(s)$ is called the *characteristic polynomial*. Although for the moment this discussion is confined to real matrices, the roots may well occur in complex pairs. The eigenvector associated with an eigenvalue s is the (nonnull) vector $\mathbf{x}$ that satisfies

$$\mathbf{A}\mathbf{x} = s\mathbf{x}, \tag{6.2.2}$$

or, in another light, a vector in the null space of $\mathbf{A} - s\mathbf{I}_n$. Since the determinant of a transpose is the same as that of the matrix itself, an eigenvalue of $\mathbf{A}$ is also an eigenvalue of $\mathbf{A}^T$. However, a vector that is a (right) eigenvector of $\mathbf{A}^T$ also satisfies

$$y^T A = s y^T \tag{6.2.3}$$

and is called a left eigenvector of the matrix A.

If the null space is 1-dimensional then the vector is determined only to a scale factor. Eigenvectors are commonly normalized to have unit Euclidean length (which is still undetermined as to sign), although alternatives of the 1 and ∞ p-norms have their advantages. For higher-dimensional null spaces, an orthonormal basis is sought, making the Euclidean norm natural. For the spectral decomposition, the Euclidean normalization is required.

Note that the polynomial equation (6.2.1) may have multiple roots. If the dimension of the null space (geometric multiplicity) is smaller than the (algebraic) multiplicity of a root, then the matrix is called "defective" and is much more difficult to work with. But since this is rare in the real world, the only requirement is to be careful in stating the mathematical results. Since polynomial equations cannot be solved directly for polynomials of degree more than 4, eigenproblems must be solved by iterative methods. The following list of results begins with the most general case.

Result 1 (Similarity Transformations): *If s and x are an eigenvalue–eigenvector pair for a matrix A, then s and Bx are a pair for the matrix BAB^{-1}.*

Result 2 (Shift): *If s and x are an eigenvalue–eigenvector pair for a matrix A, then $s - r$ and x are a pair for $A - rI$.*

Result 3: *The eigenvectors of distinct eigenvalues are linearly independent.*

The first two results follow from algebraic manipulations and lead to powerful computational tools; the third result leads to some useful mathematical consequences. If the eigenvectors are stacked side by side as columns in a matrix X, then the definition (6.2.2) can be written as $AX = XS$, where $S = \text{diag}(s_1, s_2, \ldots, s_n)$. If the matrix A is nondefective then the matrix X has n linearly independent columns and so is nonsingular. Postmultiplying and premultiplying by the inverse of X then yields the equivalence of the left eigenvectors and the rows of X^{-1} as well as the biorthogonality of the left and right eigenvectors. Stacking the left eigenvectors as columns in Y yields $Y = X^{-1}$ and (rather subtly) $Y^T X = I_n$.

Result 4 (Spectral Decomposition): $A = \sum_i s_i x_i y_i^T$, *where x_i are the right eigenvectors and y_i are the left eigenvectors.*

The difficulty of solving an eigenproblem should naturally be compared to that of finding the roots of the characteristic polynomial $c(s)$, although this approach is seldom taken. Both problems are not too difficult when the roots are real and well separated. But when multiple roots are encountered (this is rare in practice), the polynomial becomes difficult to solve whereas the eigenvalue problem itself encounters no real difficulty. Mathematically, multiple roots require finding any one set of orthonormal basis vectors for the null space, if possible. In practice, when roots become close together, the eigenvalues can be found without great difficulty while the respective eigenvectors become less well-defined.

The sensitivity of the eigenvalue problem is succinctly stated in the following application of the Gershgorin theorem.

Result 5: *The eigenvalues of* **A** *lie in the union of the disks*

$$D_i = \left\{ s : |s - A_{ii}| \le \sum_{j \ne i} |A_{ij}| \right\}.$$

Result 6: *Let* **A** *be nondefective, and let* $\mathbf{X}^{-1}\mathbf{A}\mathbf{X} = \mathbf{S} = \operatorname{diag}(s_i)$. *Then the eigenvalues of* $\mathbf{A} + \mathbf{E}$ *lie in the union of the disks*

$$D_i = \{ s : |s - s_i| \le \kappa(\mathbf{X}) \| E \|_p \},$$

where the condition number κ *is computed with the same norm.*

One consequence of these results is simply that the eigenvalues are continuous functions of the elements of the matrix. Note that Result 6 gives a condition number for the eigenvalue problem. No such stability result exists for the eigenvector problem, except for the heuristic that eigenvectors of well-separated eigenvalues are less sensitive. For the statistical results for eigenvalues and eigenvectors of sample covariance matrices, see Mardia, Kent, and Bibby (1979, chap. 8).

6.3   Power Methods

Consider the analogy to the matrix eigenproblem of forced oscillation. An operator **A** acts on a state **x** repeatedly until a steady state is reached, where the result is just an increase in amplitude $s\mathbf{x}$. Similarly, in Markov chains, the stationary probability vector can be obtained by successively multiplying an initial vector by the transition matrix. As a method for finding an eigenvalue and its associated eigenvector, the procedure is to multiply successively a vector by the matrix of interest and then normalize. The vector, under suitable conditions, will converge to the eigenvector associated with the largest eigenvalue.

The power method and its variants are designed to find the largest eigenvalue and its vector, or a set of eigenvalues and their vectors. In the case of the probability transition matrix of a Markov chain, the largest eigenvalue is unity and the stationary probability vector is the associated left eigenvector. Also of interest may be the next largest eigenvalues (and their vectors), which give an indication of intermediate-term performance. In the case of the coefficient matrix of an autoregressive process, the primary goal is to check the stationarity of the process – whether all of the eigenvalues are less than unity in absolute value.

The algorithm for the power method begins with an initial vector $\mathbf{z}^{(0)}$ and computes

$$\mathbf{v}^{(k)} = \mathbf{A}\mathbf{z}^{(k-1)} \quad \text{for } k = 1, 2, \dots \tag{6.3.1}$$

and then normalizes, dividing by the length $\|\mathbf{v}^{(k)}\|$, to produce the next vector

$$\mathbf{z}^{(k)} = \frac{\mathbf{v}^{(k)}}{\|\mathbf{v}^{(k)}\|}. \tag{6.3.2}$$

In practice, the norm chosen is either $p = 2$ (Euclidean) or $p = \infty$, although occasionally the length of the first element is used. The convergence of the power method depends largely on the properties of the matrix $\mathbf{A}$.

If the matrix $\mathbf{A}$ is nondefective, then write the initial vector in terms of the right eigenvectors $\mathbf{x}^{(i)}$ of $\mathbf{A}$:

$$\mathbf{z}^{(0)} = \sum_i a_i \mathbf{x}^{(i)}. \tag{6.3.3}$$

If we write the spectral decomposition $\mathbf{A} = \sum s_i \mathbf{x}^{(i)} \mathbf{y}^{(i)\mathrm{T}}$, then $\mathbf{A}^k$ becomes $\sum s_i^k \mathbf{x}^{(i)} \mathbf{y}^{(i)\mathrm{T}}$ and the unnormalized vector $\mathbf{v}^{(k)}$ becomes

$$\mathbf{v}^{(k)} = \frac{\sum a_i s_i^k \mathbf{x}^{(i)}}{\|\mathbf{v}^{(k-1)}\|}. \tag{6.3.4}$$

If the eigenvalues are ordered as $|s_1| > |s_2| \geq \cdots \geq |s_n|$ (with the first inequality strict) and if a_1 is nonzero, then $\mathbf{z}^{(k)}$ converges to $\mathbf{x}^{(1)}$ and $\|\mathbf{v}^{(k)}\|$ converges to $|s_1|$.

Example 6.1: *Simple Power Method*
Consider the $n = 3$ problem; let $\mathbf{A}$ and simple $\mathbf{z}^{(0)}$ be as follows and avoid normalization for simplicity. $\mathbf{A} = \begin{bmatrix} 5 & 4 & 2 \\ 0 & 1 & 0 \\ 1 & 1 & 4 \end{bmatrix}$ and $\mathbf{z}^{(0)} = \begin{bmatrix} 1 \\ 1 \\ 1 \end{bmatrix}$, so $\mathbf{A}\mathbf{z}^{(0)} = \begin{bmatrix} 11 \\ 1 \\ 6 \end{bmatrix}$,

$\mathbf{A}^2\mathbf{z}^{(0)} = \begin{bmatrix} 71 \\ 1 \\ 36 \end{bmatrix}$, and $\mathbf{A}^3\mathbf{z}^{(0)} = \begin{bmatrix} 431 \\ 1 \\ 216 \end{bmatrix}$; hence, let's guess that $\mathbf{x}^{(1)} = \begin{bmatrix} 2 \\ 0 \\ 1 \end{bmatrix}$, so

$$\begin{bmatrix} 5 & 4 & 2 \\ 0 & 1 & 0 \\ 1 & 1 & 4 \end{bmatrix} \begin{bmatrix} 2 \\ 0 \\ 1 \end{bmatrix} = \begin{bmatrix} 12 \\ 0 \\ 6 \end{bmatrix} = 6 \begin{bmatrix} 2 \\ 0 \\ 1 \end{bmatrix}$$

and thus $s_1 = 6$.

The exhaustive analysis of the convergence requires considerable attention to detail. First of all, if a_1 is zero, then $\mathbf{z}^{(k)}$ may converge to the eigenvector corresponding to the second largest eigenvalue. However, roundoff error may turn the vector around to converge to $\mathbf{x}^{(1)}$. Some implementations begin with a random initial vector $\mathbf{z}^{(0)}$ to overcome this possibility. If s_1 is a single root, then its sign can be found by tracking the change in sign of the largest element of $\mathbf{v}^{(k)}$. If s_1 is a multiple root, then $\mathbf{z}^{(k)}$ could converge but instead may simply float in the eigenspace of the root s_1 owing to roundoff error; however, $\|\mathbf{v}^{(k)}\|$ will still converge to $|s_1|$. Similarly, if the largest (in modulus) eigenvalues form a complex pair, then $\|\mathbf{v}^{(k)}\|$ will still converge to $|s_1|$ while the vector $\mathbf{z}^{(k)}$ wanders. Finally, the rate of convergence of the power method depends entirely upon the convergence of the ratio $|s_2/s_1|^k$ to zero. If the second largest root is not far from the largest, then convergence may indeed be slow.

The straightforward power method has the great advantages of simplicity and that its specialty – finding the largest eigenvalue and its associated vector – is often all that is called for. For large sparse matrices, this method is particularly useful because a matrix multiplication can be computed using only the nonzero elements and only one vector need be stored. For the analysis of large queuing systems modeled by a Markov chain, the probability transition matrix is very large and often very sparse (Example 4.6 is comparatively small). For these problems, both the storage required and the effort for each iteration depends only on the number of nonnull transitions. However, a few of the largest eigenvalues (say, the largest p) are also commonly desired.

When the largest few eigenvalues are real, the power method can be extended by orthonormalizing a set of vectors; this is known as *orthogonal iteration*. Begin with a matrix $\mathbf{Z}^{(0)}$ with p orthonormal columns and multiply by $\mathbf{A}$ to obtain $\mathbf{V}^{(k)} = \mathbf{A}\mathbf{Z}^{(k-1)}$. Then perform a QR factorization (by Householder or modified Gram–Schmidt) to obtain a new $\mathbf{Z}^{(k)}$ with orthonormal columns and an upper triangular $\mathbf{R}^{(k)}$. The result is that $\mathbf{Z}^{(k)}$ converges (save for sign flips) to the matrix whose columns form an orthonormal basis for the eigenspace of the largest eigenvalues (technically, the dominant invariant subspace). If sequences $\mathbf{Z}^{(k)}$ and $\mathbf{R}^{(k)}$ converge then they produce part of the real Schur decomposition of the matrix $\mathbf{A}$. The real Schur decomposition consists of orthogonal $\mathbf{Q}$ and block triangular $\mathbf{T}$, with diagonal blocks of sizes 1 (real) and 2 (complex pair) so that $\mathbf{Q}^T\mathbf{A}\mathbf{Q} = \mathbf{T}$; hence, if the largest eigenvalues are real, then $\mathbf{R}^{(k)}$ converges to $\mathbf{T}$ with the largest eigenvalues on the diagonal. The first column of $\mathbf{Z}$ will be the first eigenvector, and the other eigenvectors can be found from the other columns (see Exercise 6.3). Multiple roots are no problem, since the orthonormalization will produce an orthonormal basis. The demonstration program **orthit** computes the largest eigenvalues and their vectors for a simple transition matrix from Jennings (1977, p. 244). However, if there is a complex pair among the largest eigenvalues then the power method – or its extension, orthogonal iteration – cannot really make the transition from a purely real problem to a complex one.

Although the power method appears to have an advantage in solving large sparse Markov chain problems, the reader is cautioned that the size and difficulty of these problems can grow quickly. The simple problem demonstrated with **orthit** has its second eigenvalue around .93, which leads to very slow convergence. In a comparison of approaches to these problems as applied to computer networks, W. J. Stewart's (1978) smallest problem used $n = 20$ and the seventh largest eigenvalue at .90, for which the power method is painfully slow. (Direct methods have been proposed for finding the stationary vectors for a Markov chain; see Harrod and Plemmons 1984 for a comparison.) One variant of the power method that is effective for eigenproblems is called *lopsided simultaneous iteration*. At each step where a matrix $\mathbf{Z}^{(k)}$ is formed, a smaller (order-p) full-matrix eigenvalue problem is solved to accelerate and reorient the problem. Since the convergence can be very fast, solving a relatively small problem using a special method turns out to be quite effective in the long run. Jennings (1977, chap. 10) discussed the method, and an implementation was presented by Stewart and Jennings (1981).

Before continuing with more useful material, the reason for the power method and the lopsided iteration shortcut is that a general eigenproblem is relatively difficult to compute. None of the advantages of the symmetric problem are available, and though the matrix may be real, the resulting eigenvalues and vectors can well be complex. Golub and van Loan (1989) discussed the problem in detail, but (thankfully) a complete solution to the nonsymmetric eigenproblem is rarely needed in statistics.

There are two variants of the power method whose combination is quite effective. The first extension uses the trick of *shifting*. Instead of multiplying by $\mathbf{A}$, it is just as easy to multiply by $(\mathbf{A} - r\mathbf{I})$, so that the eigenvalues are now $s_i - r$. This can be used to change the domain of convergence to a different eigenvalue, or to accelerate convergence. A second variant of the power method is to use the matrix $\mathbf{A}^{-1}$. Multiplying by this matrix will cause the power method to head toward the largest eigenvalue of the inverse, which is the reciprocal of the smallest eigenvalue of the matrix $\mathbf{A}$. This technique is called the *inverse power method* and can be more effective than one might expect. Moreover, computation of the inverse can be avoided by first computing the LU decomposition of $(\mathbf{A} - r\mathbf{I})$ and then performing the multiplication by solving a pair of triangular systems. The inverse power method can be used directly to find the smallest eigenvalue and its associated eigenvector.

The combination of the inverse power method with shifting produces dramatic improvements. Apply the power method to the matrix $(\mathbf{A} - r\mathbf{I})^{-1}$, and the eigenvalue closest to r is found with its eigenvector. The convergence rate depends on the ratio of the largest eigenvalue to the next and so, for the inverse power method with shift, the rate depends on the ratio $|s^* - r|/\min_i |s_i - r|$, which indicates that the best shift heads straight for a singular matrix and trouble. However, although the LU decomposition of such a nearly singular matrix is badly conditioned, the inverse power method overcomes this and is stable in practice. For the two problems outlined here, a particular eigenvalue equal to (or near) unity is of particular interest, making the choice of shift obvious. For other problems, two sources of good approximations are the power method (with orthogonal iteration) and the Rayleigh quotient $\mathbf{x}^{\mathrm{T}}\mathbf{A}\mathbf{x}/\mathbf{x}^{\mathrm{T}}\mathbf{x}$ from a starting vector $\mathbf{x}$ (see Exercise 6.15). For Markov chain problems, the direct methods previously mentioned can be viewed as inverse power methods with a shift toward the eigenvalue $s = 1$ with just a single iteration.

6.4 The Symmetric Eigenproblem and Tridiagonalization

When the matrix is symmetric, the eigenproblem becomes much simpler to solve. The left eigenvectors are the same as the right ones, and the worries are few.

Result 7: *A symmetric matrix is nondefective and has all real eigenvalues.*

Result 8: *If $\mathbf{A}$ is symmetric then there exists an orthogonal matrix $\mathbf{X}$ such that $\mathbf{X}^{\mathrm{T}}\mathbf{A}\mathbf{X} = \mathbf{S} = \mathrm{diag}(s_1, \ldots, s_n)$, so that the columns of $\mathbf{X}$ are eigenvectors.*

When generalizing symmetry for the complex domain, the transpose is replaced with a conjugate transpose, and a matrix whose conjugate transpose is the same as the original matrix is called *Hermitian*; notationally, $\mathbf{A}^{\mathrm{H}} = \mathbf{A}$. A complex Hermitian eigenproblem with matrix $\mathbf{A}_{\mathrm{real}} + i\mathbf{A}_{\mathrm{imaginary}}$ can be rewritten as

$$\begin{bmatrix} \mathbf{A}_{\text{real}} & -\mathbf{A}_{\text{imaginary}} \\ \mathbf{A}_{\text{imaginary}} & \mathbf{A}_{\text{real}} \end{bmatrix} \begin{bmatrix} \mathbf{x}_{\text{real}} \\ \mathbf{x}_{\text{imaginary}} \end{bmatrix} = s \begin{bmatrix} \mathbf{x}_{\text{real}} \\ \mathbf{x}_{\text{imaginary}} \end{bmatrix}, \qquad (6.4.1)$$

where the eigenvalue s is real.

Perhaps the first consequence worth noting is that the power method and orthogonal iteration will always work for symmetric matrices. The disadvantage is that these methods are not particularly well suited for computing all of the eigenvalues and eigenvectors. A method is sought that can converge as fast as the inverse power method incorporating a shift, with close approximations to roots easily available and faster ways of doing the multiplication. This may sound like too much to ask, but it is not beyond reach.

The first step is taking advantage of similarity transformations to change the original eigenproblem into a similar one where the matrix multiplication is much easier. Notice that, when $p = n$, a full matrix multiplication in an orthogonal iteration $\mathbf{AZ}$ takes $O(n^3)$ work, which is costly for a single iteration even if rapid convergence is achievable. Even for a single vector, the power method requires $O(n^2)$.

The similarity transformation is from $\mathbf{A}$ to $\mathbf{BAB}^{-1}$. The goal is to make the new matrix as sparse as possible. If $\mathbf{BAB}^{-1}$ were diagonal then the eigenproblem would be solved – which, of course, cannot be done without iterations. The next best thing is to make $\mathbf{A}$ into a tridiagonal $\mathbf{BAB}^{-1}$, which is an achievable result. Then the work for each iteration step will be $O(n)$ for a single vector and at worst $O(n^2)$ for orthogonal iteration. The technique is a modification of the Householder method last used in the regression problem.

Tridiagonalization begins with a partitioning of the matrix $\mathbf{A}$:

$$\mathbf{A} = \begin{bmatrix} a_{11} & a_{21} & \mathbf{a}_{\#1}^{\mathsf{T}} \\ a_{21} & a_{22} & \mathbf{a}_{\#2}^{\mathsf{T}} \\ \mathbf{a}_{\#1} & \mathbf{a}_{\#2} & \mathbf{A}_{22} \end{bmatrix}. \quad \begin{matrix} 1 \\ 1 \\ n-2 \end{matrix}$$

Now find a Householder transformation that can zero out the last $n - 2$ entries in the first column. The transformation matrix U_1 is nested as a submatrix in the form

$$\mathbf{U}_1 = \begin{bmatrix} 1 & \mathbf{0} \\ \mathbf{0} & \mathbf{U}^{(1)} \end{bmatrix}, \quad \text{so that } \mathbf{U}^{(1)} \begin{bmatrix} a_{21} \\ \mathbf{a}_{\#1} \end{bmatrix} = \begin{bmatrix} b_2 \\ \mathbf{0} \end{bmatrix}. \quad \begin{matrix} 1 \\ n-2 \end{matrix}$$

Multiplying $\mathbf{U}_1$ in front and then behind $\mathbf{A}$ produces

$$\mathbf{U}_1 \mathbf{A} \mathbf{U}_1 = \begin{bmatrix} a_{11} & a_{21} & \mathbf{a}_{\#1}^{\mathsf{T}} \\ b_2 & * & * \\ \mathbf{0} & * & * \end{bmatrix} \mathbf{U}_1 = \begin{bmatrix} a_{11} & b_2 & \mathbf{0} \\ b_2 & * & * \\ \mathbf{0} & * & * \end{bmatrix},$$

where asterisks denote elements changed in these computations. It should now be apparent that the next step is to eliminate the last $n - 3$ elements in the second column and row with an appropriate $\mathbf{U}_2$, continuing on with this until we get $\mathbf{U}_{n-2}$. The full similarity sequence gives the matrix $\mathbf{U}_{n-2} \cdots \mathbf{U}_1 \mathbf{A} \mathbf{U}_1 \cdots \mathbf{U}_{n-2}$, which will be a symmetric tridiagonal matrix. The transformation $\mathbf{B}$ is then $\mathbf{U}_{n-2} \cdots \mathbf{U}_1$. See Example 6.2 and the demonstration program **tridig**.

Example 6.2: *Householder Transformations for Tridiagonalization*

$$A = \begin{bmatrix} 3 & 2 & -1 & 2 \\ 2 & 3 & 2 & 1 \\ -1 & 2 & 3 & 4 \\ 2 & 1 & 4 & 7 \end{bmatrix} \quad \text{and} \quad x^{(1)} = \begin{bmatrix} 2 \\ -1 \\ 2 \end{bmatrix}, \quad \text{so}$$

$$s_1 = 3 \quad \text{and} \quad u^{(1)} = \begin{bmatrix} 5 \\ -1 \\ 2 \end{bmatrix}; \quad \text{hence} \quad U_1 A = \begin{bmatrix} 3 & 2 & -1 & 2 \\ -3 & -2 & -3 & -4 \\ 0 & 3 & 4 & 5 \\ 0 & -1 & 2 & 5 \end{bmatrix}.$$

Then form

$$U_1 A U_1 = \begin{bmatrix} 3 & -3 & 0 & 0 \\ -3 & 3 & -4 & -2 \\ 0 & -4 & 5.4 & 2.2 \\ 0 & -2 & 2.2 & 4.6 \end{bmatrix}.$$

The next step uses $x^{(2)} = \begin{bmatrix} -4 \\ -2 \end{bmatrix}$ and gets messier.

6.5 The QR Algorithm

The QR algorithm is a superlative method of computing all the eigenvalues (and eigen-vectors, if necessary) of a real symmetric tridiagonal matrix. It is fast, efficient, and stable. The convergence rate in practice is roughly an eigenvalue every two or three it-erations. The algorithm's performance is remarkable, considering the apparent futility of the iteration. Denote the original matrix (already made tridiagonal) by A_0 and the result of k similarity transforms by A_k. The algorithm is the sequential application of two apparently harmless steps, using an origin shift t.

First step: Do a QR factorization of $A_k - t_k I$ using the Givens method, where Q is orthogonal and R is upper triangular:

$$A_k - t_k I = Q_k R_k. \tag{6.5.1}$$

Second step: Retridiagonalize by multiplying R by Q on the right and then adding back the shift:

$$A_{k+1} = R_k Q_k + t_k I = Q_k^T (A_k - t_k I) Q_k + t_k I = Q_k^T A_k Q_k. \tag{6.5.2}$$

Thus, all that happens is a simple similarity transformation at each iteration. The result is that A_k converges to a diagonal matrix, so the eigenvalues are the diagonal entries of A_{last} and the eigenvectors are the columns of $Q_1 Q_2 \cdots Q_{\text{last}}$.

To understand the success of this computation, disregard momentarily the origin shift and consider the product of the orthogonal similarity matrices $P_k = Q_1 \cdots Q_k$. According to Parlett and Poole (1973), the QR iteration can be viewed as a simultane-ous iteration of the power method and the inverse power method. Consequently, the first columns of P_k are converging (relatively slowly) to a set of basis vectors of the dominant invariant subspace, as in orthogonal iteration. At the same time, the last row of P_k is converging to a vector orthogonal – which will be the eigenvector of the smallest eigenvalue – as if the inverse power method were employed.

Now consider the origin shift, and recall that the inverse power method with an origin shift is much more effective than the power method with a shift. So the best way to incorporate a shift into the QR algorithm is to find the smallest eigenvalues first. The most common one is the Wilkinson shift, the eigenvalue of the last 2×2 diagonal submatrix closest to the (n, n) element of A_k. The result of these iterations with the shift recomputed each time is that the $(n, n-1)$ element converges to zero at a cubic rate. In practice, usually only two or three iterations are needed to produce another eigenvalue. At convergence, one eigenvalue has been found, but the problem is now one smaller in size. This process is then repeated, finding one eigenvalue after another until the final problem is trivial.

Eigenvectors should not be computed if they are not required, since they are much more costly to compute. When needed, then: if the Householder transformations U_j arose in the tridiagonalization to form the matrix A_0, then the matrix X of eigenvectors is computed from

$$X = U_1 U_2 \cdots U_{n-2} Q_1 Q_2 \cdots Q_{\text{last}}.$$

Although the details of the algorithm differ with each implementation, the combination of the tridiagonal structure, symmetry, and the Givens transformations produces a beautiful algorithm. The shift can be incorporated implicitly without forming the matrix $A_k - rI$; all that is required is the first Givens transformation, which would zero out the first subdiagonal element of $A_k - rI$. Once applied to A_k, the remaining computations – premultiplying by the other $n-2$ Givens rotations and then postmultiplying – amount to a "zero chasing" to reproduce the tridiagonal form.

This first rotation produces a nonzero outside the tridiagonal band in positions marked 1 in the $(1, 3)$ and $(3, 1)$ elements:

$$A_k = \begin{bmatrix} x & x & 0 & 0 & 0 \\ x & x & x & 0 & 0 \\ 0 & x & x & x & 0 \\ 0 & 0 & x & x & x \\ 0 & 0 & 0 & x & x \end{bmatrix}, \qquad A_{k+1} = Q_k^T A_k Q_k = \begin{bmatrix} x & x & 1 & 0 & 0 \\ x & x & x & 2 & 0 \\ 1 & x & x & x & 3 \\ 0 & 2 & x & x & x \\ 0 & 0 & 3 & x & x \end{bmatrix}.$$

A second Givens rotation is sought to remove this nonzero by moving it further down in the matrix, to the position marked 2. This new one is moved further down until no new nonzero entries are created, essentially eliminating the one created by the first rotation. Each step can be done on the fly, requiring little storage, and symmetry cuts the work in half. The details of the implementation become rather tedious, and the demonstration programs **qreig0** and **qreig1** compute the eigenvalues without and with (respectively) the eigenvectors.

6.6 Singular Value Decomposition

The singular value decomposition (SVD) of a matrix has many more applications than one might expect. Computationally, it provides (a) the soundest way to determine the rank of a matrix, (b) the construction of the Moore–Penrose pseudoinverse, and (c) the smallest norm solution to an undetermined least-squares problem. In statistics, it is often used for regression diagnostics, data reduction, and graphical clustering. It also provides the solution to some multivariate statistical problems. First of all, definitions and constructions are in order.

Theorem: *Let* A *be an* $m \times n$ *matrix* ($m \geq n$ *for definiteness*) *with real elements. Then there exist orthogonal matrices* U *and* V *such that* $V^TAU = D$, *where* D ($m \times n$) *is diagonal with entries* d_i *in decreasing order.*

The columns of U are the right singular vectors of A, and the columns of V are the left singular vectors. The elements d_i are known as the *singular values* of the matrix A. These singular values are not the eigenvalues of A, but they are related to (and constructed from) an eigenproblem.

Recall that the positive eigenvalues of A^TA and AA^T are the same. Moreover, the eigenvectors are related. Let $u^{(i)}$ be an eigenvector of A^TA with eigenvalue s_i; then

$$A^TAu^{(i)} = s_iu^{(i)}. \tag{6.6.1}$$

Premultiplying by A yields $AA^TAu^{(i)} = s_iAu^{(i)}$, so that $Au^{(i)}$ is also an unnormalized eigenvector of AA^T with the same eigenvalue. The squared length of $Au^{(i)}$ is s_i, so premultiplying by an eigenvector $v^{(j)}$ of AA^T results in the equation

$$v^{(j)T}Au^{(i)} = \sqrt{s_i}\delta(i, j), \tag{6.6.2}$$

where the δ is a Kronecker delta. Stacking the eigenvectors of the matrices A^TA into U and AA^T into V produces exactly the SVD definition. The singular values d_i are the square roots of the positive eigenvalues, and the decomposition form of the result is written as

$$A = VDU^T = \sum d_iv^{(i)}u^{(i)T}. \tag{6.6.3}$$

Unless A is square, either A^TA or AA^T (or both) have zero eigenvalues, and often multiple ones, so both U and V may not be definite. But the decomposition for distinct positive singular values will be unique (up to sign), since the arbitrariness occurs where the d_i are zero.

An obvious approach to computing the singular value decomposition is solving the smaller of the two eigenproblems. The drawback of this approach is the squaring of the elements, which is never a good idea and can be avoided. The best method is first to convert the problem to a manageable one, as was done in the tridiagonalization. The iteration, then, is that of solving the eigenproblem by QR but without computing the inner product. Since this sounds like making an omelet without cracking eggs, on to the details.

The goal of the tridiagonalization step, as a prelude to the QR algorithm, was to reduce a matrix (by similarity transformations) to the smallest number of nonzeros – without solving the whole problem. Using orthogonal matrices gave stability as well as ease, since the result (being symmetric) cut the work in half. In this case, symmetry is not available, but the matrix can be premultiplied and postmultiplied to reduce it to upper bidiagonal form. That is, the diagonal (as far as it goes) is nonzero, as is the first superdiagonal. If the matrix is tall and skinny, $m \geq n$, then the bidiagonal matrix has only $2n - 1$ nonzero elements. The method for this is to use Householder transformations for producing zeros. Premultiplying by one on the left can zero out all but the first element in the first column, changing the entire matrix. Then postmultiplying by a Householder transformation that zeros out the last $n - 2$ elements on the first row, changing the last $n - 1$ columns, can leave the first column alone, with the $m - 1$ zeros in the first column intact. The second Householder transform on the left zeros out the last $n - 2$ elements in the second column, changing all of the elements in the last $m - 2$ rows, but leaves the zeros in the first row and column intact. The second Householder transform on the right puts zeros in the last $n - 3$ elements in the second column, changing all of the elements in the last $n - 2$ columns, but will leave intact the zeros introduced in the first row and first two columns. The result of the transformations on the left, n unless the matrix is square $(n - 1)$, makes the matrix upper triangular in the same way as the QR factorization in Chapter 5. The transformations on the right $(n - 2)$ act in the same way as in the tridiagonalization in Section 6.4, just producing more zeros. If the right and left ones do not alternate, then zeros will be overwritten. After these steps, the result is an upper bidiagonal matrix **B** such that $\mathbf{H}_L^T \mathbf{A} \mathbf{H}_R = \mathbf{B}$.

Example 6.3: *Bidiagonalization*

Begin with $\mathbf{A} = \begin{bmatrix} 2 & 1 & 2 \\ 0 & -2.8 & 0.4 \\ -1 & -2 & 1 \\ 2 & 4 & 3 \end{bmatrix}$; then $s^2 = 9$ and $\mathbf{u} = \begin{bmatrix} 5 \\ 0 \\ -1 \\ 2 \end{bmatrix}$ with $d = 1/15$. The

new matrix is $\mathbf{H}_L^{(1)} \mathbf{A} = \begin{bmatrix} -3 & -4 & -3 \\ 0 & -2.8 & 0.4 \\ 0 & -1 & 2 \\ 0 & 2 & 1 \end{bmatrix}$. Then, on the right, $s^2 = 25$ and so $\mathbf{u} =$

$\begin{bmatrix} -9 \\ -3 \end{bmatrix}$ with $d = 1/45$, yielding the next matrix $\mathbf{H}_L^{(1)} \mathbf{A} \mathbf{H}_R^{(1)} = \begin{bmatrix} -3 & 5 & 0 \\ 0 & 2 & 2 \\ 0 & -0.4 & 2.2 \\ 0 & -2.2 & -0.4 \end{bmatrix}$.

Then, on the left, $s^2 = 9$ and so $\mathbf{u} = \begin{bmatrix} 5 \\ -0.4 \\ -2.2 \end{bmatrix}$ with $d = 1/15$, yielding the

next matrix $\mathbf{H}_L^{(2)} \mathbf{H}_L^{(1)} \mathbf{A} \mathbf{H}_R^{(1)} = \begin{bmatrix} -3 & 5 & 0 \\ 0 & -3 & -4/3 \\ 0 & 0 & 37/15 \\ 0 & 0 & 16/15 \end{bmatrix}$. The last ugly step gives $\mathbf{B} =$

$\begin{bmatrix} -3 & 5 & 0 \\ 0 & -3 & -4/3 \\ 0 & 0 & -\sqrt{65}/3 \\ 0 & 0 & 0 \end{bmatrix}$.

Lawson and Hanson (1974) mentioned an alternative method that becomes effective when $m \gg 2n$. Chan (1982) analyzed this approach completely and also provided Fortran code. The idea is to first compute the QR factorization by Householder methods. Then the left and right Householder transformations on the smaller $(n \times n)$ matrix **R** will run much faster, taking about half the work when $m \gg n$. Golub and van Loan (1989) have recommended this approach whenever $m > 5n/3$.

Now, if the inner product $\mathbf{B}^T\mathbf{B}$ is formed then the matrix is tridiagonal and set up to do QR iterations. However, the trick is not to form the inner product. But the QR iteration wants a rotation in a particular direction, based on the leading submatrix and the shift based on the last submatrix. Computing this Givens transformation based on the inner product, though, is no problem, since any accumulation of errors affects merely the accuracy of the shift and rotation and hence just the speed of convergence. So the shift is found by forming the last submatrix from the last columns of **B**. Then the first Givens transformation is found from the shift and the first two columns of **B**. Applied on the right of **B**, and not to the left of $\mathbf{B}^T\mathbf{B}$, this first transformation changes elements in the first two columns, and its application to the second row will introduce a nonzero in the $(2, 1)$ element. The rest of the work in the iteration, like in the implicit QR algorithm, involves Givens transformations on the left and right, chasing the nonzero element introduced in the first step in the $(2, 1)$ location out of the matrix and placing **B** back into its upper bidiagonal form. The chasing goes $(2, 1)$ to $(1, 3)$ to $(3, 2)$ to $(2, 4), \ldots, (k+1, k)$ to $(k, k-1), \ldots,$ to $(n, n-1)$ and out. The sequence is given by the following matrix:

$$\begin{bmatrix} x & x & 2 & 0 & 0 \\ 1 & x & x & 4 & 0 \\ 0 & 3 & x & x & 6 \\ 0 & 0 & 5 & x & x \\ 0 & 0 & 0 & 7 & x \end{bmatrix}. \tag{6.6.4}$$

Since the procedure is essentially a QR step, the iterations produce a sequence of upper bidiagonal matrices that converge to a diagonal matrix of singular values. Accumulating the Givens rotations on the left (**P**s) and right (**Q**s) will yield the singular vectors. If the computations produced the diagonal matrix **D**,

$$\mathbf{D} = \mathbf{P}_{\text{last}}^T \cdots \mathbf{P}_1^T \mathbf{B} \mathbf{Q}_1 \cdots \mathbf{Q}_{\text{last}} = \mathbf{P}_{\text{last}}^T \cdots \mathbf{P}_1^T \mathbf{H}_L^T \mathbf{A} \mathbf{H}_R \mathbf{Q}_1 \cdots \mathbf{Q}_{\text{last}}, \tag{6.6.5}$$

then the singular vector matrices can be found as

$$\mathbf{U} = \mathbf{H}_R \mathbf{Q}_1 \cdots \mathbf{Q}_{\text{last}} \quad \text{and} \quad \mathbf{V} = \mathbf{H}_L \mathbf{P}_1 \cdots \mathbf{P}_{\text{last}}. \tag{6.6.6}$$

A subtle problem arises when the leading superdiagonal element has converged prematurely. In the symmetric QR algorithm, while the last off-diagonal elements converge most quickly, the first few off-diagonal elements are converging slowly to zero. If the $(1, 2)$ element of **B** has already reached zero, then the first Givens transformation (with or without shift) is just the identity, and no nonzeros are introduced nor need to be chased out. As a result, the algorithm stops dead without a check for convergence at the beginning as well as the end of the superdiagonal.

6.7   Applications

The needs for eigenproblem solutions vary throughout the many areas of statistics. Two areas have already been thoroughly discussed: computing stationary probability vectors in Markov chains; and finding the largest eigenvalue of a coefficient matrix in a multivariate autoregressive time-series model. Whereas some of the statistics that require an eigenproblem solution are straightforward, others require considerable effort to turn them into a solvable eigenproblem.

(A)   *Roy's Test*

The most frequent call for the solution of an eigenproblem arises in the testing of multivariate hypotheses. The techniques of Chapter 5 can be used to compute the sum-of-squares matrices $\mathbf{E}$ for error and $\mathbf{H}$ for the hypothesis. Roy's test, a union–intersection test, requires the largest eigenvalue of the matrix $\mathbf{E}^{-1}\mathbf{H}$ as well as its eigenvector. Since this matrix is not symmetric and the problem is really a symmetric one, it is best posed as the generalized eigenproblem

$$\mathbf{Ax} = s\mathbf{Bx}, \tag{6.7.1}$$

where $\mathbf{A} = \mathbf{H}$ and $\mathbf{B} = \mathbf{E}$. In most circumstances, the matrix $\mathbf{B}$ is known to be positive definite. The best approach is to factor the matrix $\mathbf{B}$ using Cholesky, $\mathbf{B} = \mathbf{LL}^{T}$; then premultiplying $\mathbf{Hx} = s\mathbf{Ex}$ by $\mathbf{L}^{-1}$ yields the equivalent problem

$$(\mathbf{L}^{-1}\mathbf{HL}^{-T})(\mathbf{L}^{T}\mathbf{x}) = s\mathbf{L}^{T}\mathbf{x}. \tag{6.7.2}$$

Because the new problem is a symmetric one, the QR algorithm can be used to compute all of the eigenvalues and vectors. Note that only symmetry is required for the QR algorithm; the positive definiteness merely ensures nonsingularity. Commonly, $\mathbf{E}$ is semidefinite when the components add to a constant. Since this also applies to $\mathbf{H}$, the problem can be overcome statistically by simply dropping one dimension; without this fix, the problem is very difficult.

(B)   *Principal Components*

Principal components is a data reduction technique designed to determine the modes of variation of a multivariate random variable in high dimensions. The goal is to squeeze a high-dimensional distribution into a smaller-dimensional space that has most of the variation. Although principal components operates as if the dimensionality of an undisturbed signal is smaller and the remaining dimensions are noise, the noise is not modeled as an additive noise or measurement error (as in factor analysis). Rather, the high dimensionality is seen to be unwieldy; moving to fewer dimensions is necessary for any useful data analysis.

This method is used to find the linear combinations of vectors that maximize the variation. Obviously, the single linear combination that maximizes the variance will be the first eigenvector of the covariance matrix. Finding the k linear combinations (and orthonormalizing them) amounts to finding the k largest eigenvalues and their eigenvectors; the solution is again the QR algorithm. Although the number k that is sought may be small, seldom is the dimension of the covariance matrix so large that an orthogonal iteration would be a significant or necessary improvement.

(C) Moore–Penrose Pseudoinverse

In most problems involving generalized inverses, any one will do. Many such problems, such as a non–full-rank least-squares problem, can be solved by adapting techniques – such as QR factorization with Householder or Givens methods – to the possibility of rank deficiencies. However, the singular value decomposition is the necessary tool for some special problems.

The first problem is construction of the Moore–Penrose (MP) pseudoinverse, which is the unique generalized inverse $\mathbf{A}^+$ that satisfies the conditions:

(1) $\mathbf{AA}^+\mathbf{A} = \mathbf{A}$;
(2) $\mathbf{A}^+\mathbf{AA}^+ = \mathbf{A}^+$;
(3) $(\mathbf{AA}^+)^{\mathrm{T}} = \mathbf{AA}^+$;
(4) $(\mathbf{A}^+\mathbf{A})^{\mathrm{T}} = \mathbf{A}^+\mathbf{A}$.

Because of its uniqueness, it is necessary only to show that the proposed solution satisfies the four conditions. The solution is constructed from the SVD of $\mathbf{A} = \mathbf{VDU}^{\mathrm{T}}$. Since $\mathbf{D}$ is diagonal, form the MP inverse ($\mathbf{D}^+$) of it by taking the reciprocals of the positive diagonal elements, leaving the remaining elements zero. Then form the matrix

$$\mathbf{A}^+ = \mathbf{UD}^+\mathbf{V}^{\mathrm{T}}, \tag{6.7.3}$$

which can be shown (Exercise 6.22) to satisfy the four conditions.

A tough problem is glossed over in the proposed solution for the MP inverse. The computed singular values are unlikely to be all positive when the matrix $\mathbf{A}$ is not full column (or row) rank, because of rounding error. Moreover, this ought to be expected because almost all matrices have no linear dependencies (in the measure theoretic sense). The best we can compute is the exact solution to a nearby problem, and almost all of the nearby problems have all positive singular values. The decision must be made regarding how small is small – that is, to decide the rank of $\mathbf{A}$. This decision was faced previously, in Gaussian elimination as well as in Householder QR factorization. But with the SVD, the decision is much easier owing to the following condition result:

$$|d_k(\mathbf{A} + \mathbf{E}) - d_k(\mathbf{A})| \le \|\mathbf{E}\|_2, \tag{6.7.4}$$

where $d_k(\cdot)$ denotes the kth singular value of the matrix argument. Essentially, the condition of the SVD is 1. For real problems, the matrix $\mathbf{E}$ reflects the accuracy of the input and can be used to "test" against zero, meaning a linear dependency.

The statistical value of the MP inverse follows from its use in constructing the minimum norm least-squares solution. That is, when there exist multiple solutions to the normal equations

$$\mathbf{X}^{\mathrm{T}}\mathbf{Xb} = \mathbf{X}^{\mathrm{T}}\mathbf{y},$$

the solution $\mathbf{b}^* = \mathbf{X}^+\mathbf{y}$ has the smallest Euclidean length (Exercise 6.23).

(D) *PC Scores and Regression*

The relationship between the SVD, rank degeneracy, multicollinearity, and biased regression can be viewed as a part of principal components regression. Suppose that rows $\mathbf{x}^{(k)\mathrm{T}}$ form a design matrix $\mathbf{X}$ $(n \times m)$ and that the dependent observations are stored in a vector $\mathbf{y}$. An SVD of the design matrix $\mathbf{X} = \mathbf{VDU}^{\mathrm{T}}$ facilitates the computation of the regression coefficients

$$\hat{\mathbf{b}} = \sum \left(\frac{\mathbf{v}^{(i)\mathrm{T}}\mathbf{y}}{d_i} \right) \mathbf{u}^{(i)}, \tag{6.7.5}$$

where $\mathbf{v}^{(i)}$ and $\mathbf{u}^{(i)}$ are columns of $\mathbf{V}$ and $\mathbf{U}$, respectively.

Now if both $\mathbf{y}$ and $\mathbf{X}$ are centered (mean subtracted), then d_i^2 are the eigenvalues of the (rescaled) covariance matrix $\mathbf{X}^{\mathrm{T}}\mathbf{X}$ whose eigenvectors are $\mathbf{u}^{(i)}$. Hence principal components on the observations $\mathbf{x}^{(k)}$ would produce the components $\mathbf{u}^{(i)}$ and the component score vectors

$$\mathbf{z}^{(i)} = \mathbf{X}\mathbf{u}^{(i)} = d_i\mathbf{v}^{(i)}. \tag{6.7.6}$$

Retaining p components means putting the m-dimensional distribution of $\mathbf{X}$ into the p-dimensional distribution of $\mathbf{Z}$. The $\mathbf{Z}$ space has most of the variation, so that the regression could be done in the transformed space – where the $\mathbf{z}^{(i)}$ are orthogonal and with sum of squares d_i^2 – so that transforming back to the $\mathbf{X}$ space yields the same expression as (6.7.5), except that the summation is stopped at p. This is principal components regression.

Another viewpoint, purely computational, sees the p components as the result of deciding $d_{p+1} = \cdots = d_m = 0$, as if the problem were one of rank deficiency. Then computing the principal components regression coefficients is the same as a minimum norm solution to the least-squares problem. See Mardia et al. (1979, chap. 8) for the statistical view of rank deficiency.

Returning to the statistics, the motivation for principal components regression is the behavior of regression coefficients under multicollinearity. By retaining many explanatory variables, the risk of misspecification is lessened but with the cost of less precise estimates; the variances are large because $\mathbf{X}^{\mathrm{T}}\mathbf{X}$ is nearly deficient in rank. By moving to principal components regression, some bias must be faced but with great improvements in accuracy. The goal is to determine which subset of the variables may have the greatest effect on the dependent variable, with the hope of discarding the others.

Computationally, the SVD allows for a sound decision as to the multicollinearity and the true rank of the design matrix $\mathbf{X}$. The computation of the coefficient estimate is simplified and flexible regarding the number of components to be retained.

(E) *Canonical Correlation*

The objective in canonical correlation is to find the two linear combinations $\mathbf{a}^{\mathrm{T}}\mathbf{x}$ and $\mathbf{b}^{\mathrm{T}}\mathbf{y}$ that have the largest correlation. Both the correlations and the combinations themselves (which lead to canonical variables) are of interest and need to be calculated. Two possible problems are faced: one where the covariance matrices only are given; a second where the multivariate observations are available.

For the first case, let the joint covariance matrix of $\mathbf{x}$ and $\mathbf{y}$ be given by

$$\begin{bmatrix} \mathbf{S}_{xx} & \mathbf{S}_{xy} \\ \mathbf{S}_{yx} & \mathbf{S}_{yy} \end{bmatrix} ; \quad \begin{matrix} p \\ q \end{matrix}$$

then the problem is to maximize $\mathbf{a}^T\mathbf{S}_{xy}\mathbf{b}$ subject to $\mathbf{a}^T\mathbf{S}_{xx}\mathbf{a} = \mathbf{b}^T\mathbf{S}_{yy}\mathbf{b} = 1$, which includes the normalizations. Now factor the two covariance matrices by Cholesky,

$$\mathbf{S}_{xx} = \mathbf{LL}^T \quad \text{and} \quad \mathbf{S}_{yy} = \mathbf{MM}^T,$$

so that the new problem is maximizing $\mathbf{v}^T\mathbf{Cu}$ subject to $\mathbf{u}^T\mathbf{u} = \mathbf{v}^T\mathbf{v} = 1$, where the new matrix is $\mathbf{C} = \mathbf{L}^{-1}\mathbf{S}_{xy}\mathbf{M}^{-T}$ $(p \times q)$. Now, to maximize $\mathbf{v}$ for a fixed $\mathbf{u}$ means taking $\mathbf{v}$ to be proportional to $\mathbf{Cu}$. The problem then becomes maximizing $(\mathbf{Cu})^T\mathbf{Cu} = \mathbf{u}^T\mathbf{C}^T\mathbf{Cu}$, so that maximizing over $\mathbf{u}$ yields $\mathbf{u}$ as the eigenvector of largest eigenvalue of $\mathbf{C}^T\mathbf{C}$. This should suddenly start to look like singular value decomposition, since the best value for $\mathbf{v}$ is proportional to $\mathbf{Cu}$, which yields the eigenvector of $\mathbf{CC}^T$. The consequence is that the best linear combinations $\mathbf{u}$ and $\mathbf{v}$ are the right and left singular vectors corresponding to the largest singular value of $\mathbf{C}$ that is the correlation. Returning to the original space by $\mathbf{a} = \mathbf{L}^{-T}\mathbf{v}$ and $\mathbf{b} = \mathbf{M}^{-1}\mathbf{u}$ yields the canonical vectors, and the canonical variables are $\mathbf{a}^T\mathbf{x}$ and $\mathbf{b}^T\mathbf{y}$.

The computations required for this side of the problem are the two Cholesky factorizations and the solving of two sets of triangular systems of equations to produce $\mathbf{C}$. Then the SVD of $\mathbf{C}$ is computed and two triangular systems are solved to get back to $\mathbf{a}$ and $\mathbf{b}$.

When the centered variables are stacked in matrices $\mathbf{X}$ and $\mathbf{Y}$, the computations take a slightly different route. The first step is to move to orthonormalized variables, using Householder to form the QR factorizations

$$\mathbf{X} = \mathbf{Q}_x\mathbf{R}_x \quad \text{and} \quad \mathbf{Y} = \mathbf{Q}_y\mathbf{R}_y.$$

Then the matrix $\mathbf{C}$ is formed by

$$\mathbf{C} = \mathbf{Q}_x^T\mathbf{Q}_y,$$

which again is $p \times q$. Then the singular value decomposition is computed for $\mathbf{C} = \mathbf{VDU}^T$. The linear combinations are found from $\mathbf{a} = \mathbf{Q}_x\mathbf{v}^{(1)}$ and $\mathbf{b} = \mathbf{Q}_y\mathbf{u}^{(1)}$. Notice that other canonical variables can be formed from the other singular values, up to $\min(p, q)$. Also note that the matrix $\mathbf{C}$ appearing in the two cases is not the same matrix. Even changing $\mathbf{S}_{xx}$ and the others to be sample covariance matrices, $\mathbf{C}$ needs to be normalized by the number of observations n (or $n-1$) to be identical.

(F) *Procrustes Rotation*

The problem here is to find an orthogonal matrix that rotates one set of data closest to another. More specifically, let $\mathbf{X}$ and $\mathbf{Y}$ (both $n \times p$) be centered data matrices. We seek an orthogonal matrix $\mathbf{Q}$ that minimizes $\|\mathbf{Y} - \mathbf{XQ}\|_F$, where the subscript F denotes the Frobenius norm of a matrix – the square root of the sum of squares of all of its elements. This problem also arises in multidimensional scaling. Alternatively, the criterion can be written as

$$\|\mathbf{Y} - \mathbf{XQ}\|^2 = \text{tr}(\mathbf{Y}^T\mathbf{Y}) - 2\,\text{tr}(\mathbf{Y}^T\mathbf{XQ}) + \text{tr}(\mathbf{X}^T\mathbf{X}).$$

Again, the solution involves the singular value decomposition. Compute $C = Y^T X$ and its SVD $C = VDU^T$. Then the optimal orthogonal matrix is $Q = VU^T$. Golub and van Loan (1989, p. 582) presented a clear, short proof of this result.

6.8 Complex Singular Value Decomposition

I have avoided the complex eigenproblems so far for three reasons: they are very different and difficult, and they are encountered rarely in statistics. The complex version of SVD, however, has an important statistical application in the analysis of spatiotemporal series that may have signals that are traveling waves.

The complex singular value decomposition (CSVD) of a complex-valued matrix A takes the same form as the real version, with

$$A = VDU^H = \sum d_i v^{(i)} u^{(i)H}, \tag{6.8.1}$$

where the superscript H denotes conjugate transpose. Here, the matrices U and V are unitary, satisfying $U^H U = UU^H = I_n$ and $V^H V = VV^H = I_m$. The CSVD is also related to the eigenproblems in the Hermitian matrices $A^H A$ and AA^H as

$$A^H A u^{(i)} = d_i^2 u^{(i)} \quad \text{and} \quad AA^H v^{(i)} = d_i^2 v^{(i)}. \tag{6.8.2}$$

These matrices are Hermitian and so their eigenvalues are real, although the eigenvectors will be complex. The inner product form of both $A^H A$ and AA^H ensure that both are nonnegative definite; hence the eigenvalues will be nonnegative, allowing d_i^2 to be written as in (6.8.2).

The computational approach for CSVD is the same as for the real case: bidiagonalize A and solve the symmetric, oops, Hermitian eigenproblem with $A^H A$ without computing the inner products. The two obstacles are that the tools we have relied upon, Householder and Givens transformations, need to be adjusted for working on complex matrices.

The complex version of the Householder transformation looks very similar to the real version, $U = I - d u u^H$, with $d = 2/\|u\|^2$. Its use for annihilating a vector requires some attention to detail. As in Section 5.5, consider constructing the Householder transform U to make $Ux = -se_1$. Similar to the previous construction, compute $s^2 = x^H x = \|x\|^2$ and form $u = x + se_1$. Then the product Ux needs two smaller steps, $u^H u = x^H x + \tilde{x}_1 s + \tilde{s} x_1 + s^2$ and $u^H x = s^2 + \tilde{s} x_1$ (where the symbol $\tilde{\ }$ denotes conjugate), giving

$$Ux = (I - d u u^H)x = x - \frac{2u^H x}{u^H u} u = x - \frac{2s^2 + 2\tilde{s} x_1}{2s^2 + 2\,\text{Re}(\tilde{s} x_1)}(x + se_1). \tag{6.8.3}$$

The right-hand side of (6.8.3) will be equal to $-se_1$ only if $\tilde{s} x_1 = \text{Re}(\tilde{s} x_1)$. Note, however, that in going to complex numbers only the magnitude of s has been determined (unlike the real case, where two choices for s arising from $s^2 = \|x\|^2$ led to a choice of signs). The argument for s should be chosen so that $\tilde{s} x_1 = \text{Re}(\tilde{s} x_1)$, which is satisfied by

$$s = \frac{x_1}{|x_1|}\|x\|. \tag{6.8.4}$$

Example 6.4: *Complex Householder Transformation*

Let $\mathbf{x} = \begin{bmatrix} 1+i \\ 1-i \\ 2 \\ 1 \end{bmatrix}$; then $\mathbf{x}^H \mathbf{x} = 9$ and $s = (1+i)\frac{3}{\sqrt{2}}$ and so

$$\mathbf{u} = \begin{bmatrix} (1+i)\left(\frac{3}{\sqrt{2}}+1\right) \\ 1-i \\ 2 \\ 1 \end{bmatrix}.$$

Then $\mathbf{u}^H \mathbf{u} = 18 + 6\sqrt{2} = 2\mathbf{u}^H \mathbf{x}$, so

$$\mathbf{Ux} = (\mathbf{I} - d\mathbf{u}\mathbf{u}^H)\mathbf{x} = \mathbf{x} - \frac{2\mathbf{u}^H \mathbf{x}}{\mathbf{u}^H \mathbf{u}}\mathbf{u}$$

$$= \begin{bmatrix} 1+i \\ 1-i \\ 2 \\ 1 \end{bmatrix} - \frac{2(9+3\sqrt{2})}{18+6\sqrt{2}} \begin{bmatrix} (1+i)\left(\frac{3}{\sqrt{2}}+1\right) \\ 1-i \\ 2 \\ 1 \end{bmatrix} = \begin{bmatrix} -(1+i)\frac{3}{\sqrt{2}} \\ 0 \\ 0 \\ 0 \end{bmatrix}.$$

To construct the complex version of the Givens transformation, all that is required is the solution to the simple 2×2 case, for which the solution is

$$\mathbf{U} = \frac{1}{\sqrt{\tilde{x}_1 x_1 + \tilde{x}_2 x_2}} \begin{bmatrix} \tilde{x}_1 & \tilde{x}_2 \\ -x_2 & x_1 \end{bmatrix}. \tag{6.8.5}$$

Although the conjugates in the first row look a little out of place, this is the matrix for annihilation, since

$$\mathbf{Ux} = \frac{1}{\sqrt{\tilde{x}_1 x_1 + \tilde{x}_2 x_2}} \begin{bmatrix} \tilde{x}_1 & \tilde{x}_2 \\ -x_2 & x_1 \end{bmatrix} \begin{bmatrix} x_1 \\ x_2 \end{bmatrix} = \begin{bmatrix} \sqrt{\tilde{x}_1 x_1 + \tilde{x}_2 x_2} \\ 0 \end{bmatrix}. \tag{6.8.6}$$

The computational route for CSVD follows the real SVD approach. The first step is to pre- and postmultiply $\mathbf{A}$ by complex Householder transformations to form the bidiagonal matrix $\mathbf{B} = \mathbf{H}_L^H \mathbf{A} \mathbf{H}_R$. Next come the sequence of iterations, beginning by finding the Wilkinson shift t for the matrix $\mathbf{B}^H \mathbf{B}$ by forming the last 2×2 submatrix. The first complex Givens transformation of the QR step (as in 6.5.1) for $\mathbf{B}^H \mathbf{B} - t\mathbf{I}_n$ is then found and applied to the right of $\mathbf{B}$. This introduces a nonzero in the $(2,1)$ position of $\mathbf{B}$, whereafter a sequence of Givens transformations chases the nonzero around and out of $\mathbf{B}$ in the same order as (6.6.4). These iterations lead to a diagonal matrix $\mathbf{D}$ of singular values at convergence. Accumulating the Givens rotations on the left ($\mathbf{P}$s) and right ($\mathbf{Q}$s) will yield the singular vectors. If the computations produced the diagonal matrix

$$\mathbf{D} = \mathbf{P}_{\text{last}}^H \cdots \mathbf{P}_1^H \mathbf{B} \mathbf{Q}_1 \cdots \mathbf{Q}_{\text{last}} = \mathbf{P}_{\text{last}}^H \cdots \mathbf{P}_1^H \mathbf{H}_L^H \mathbf{A} \mathbf{H}_R \mathbf{Q}_1 \cdots \mathbf{Q}_{\text{last}}, \tag{6.8.7}$$

then the singular vector matrices can be found as

$$\mathbf{U} = \mathbf{H}_R \mathbf{Q}_1 \cdots \mathbf{Q}_{\text{last}} \quad \text{and} \quad \mathbf{V} = \mathbf{H}_L \mathbf{P}_1 \cdots \mathbf{P}_{\text{last}}. \tag{6.8.8}$$

Programs and Demonstrations

orthit *Test/demonstration program for orthogonal iteration*
The largest four eigenvalues are found, along with the eigenvectors, for four test matrices. The first case is the matrix given by Jennings (1977, p. 244), and the convergence is unsurprisingly slow. Modified Gram–Schmidt (see Section 5.4) is used for the QR factorization.
mgsqr – a simple-minded version of modified Gram–Schmidt.
orthit.dat – file holding test matrices.

tridig *Test/demonstration program of tridiagonalization of a symmetric matrix*
Four sample symmetric matrices of order $n = 3, 4, 5, 6$ are tridiagonalized using Householder transformations, as described in Section 6.4.
tridig – does the tridiagonalization and stores the Householder matrices in compact form.
expndh – computes the orthogonal matrix that does the tridiagonalization.

qreig0 *Demonstration program of the QR eigenproblem algorithm*
The eigenvalues of four sample symmetric matrices are found, but no eigenvectors.
qreig0 – subroutine that takes a tridiagonal matrix from **tridig** and computes the eigenvalues.
rot734 – computes the annihilating Givens transformation, following G. W. Stewart's (1973) Algorithm 7.3.4.

qreig1 *Test/demonstration program of the QR eigenproblem algorithms,*
but with vectors
Eigenvalues and vectors for the same four sample symmetric matrices are found. The routine **tridig** is used to do the tridiagonalization, and the orthogonal matrix of the tridiagonalization, which is an input for **qreig1**, found from **expndh**. Vectors returned in an orthogonal matrix. (Also uses routine **rot734**.)
qreig1 – computes the eigenvalues and vectors from the symmetric tridiagonal matrix.

bidiag *Test/demonstration program for the Householder bidiagonalization algorithm*
The matrix from Example 6.3 is bidiagonalized, along with two others, and the orthogonal matrices are also formed from compact storage. The bidiagonalization is checked, as well as the orthogonal matrices.
bidiag – bidiagonalizes matrix as in Section 6.6 and stores transformations in compact form.
expndb – expands Householder transformations from compact form to make orthogonal matrices.

rsvd0 *Demonstration program for SVD using Golub–Reinsch*
Singular values for three examples are computed. The routine **bidiag** does the bidiagonalization. (Also uses **rot734**.)
rsvd0 – computes the singular values only of a bidiagonal matrix.

rsvd1 *Test/demonstration program for singular value decomposition*
The singular values and vectors for three examples are computed. The routine **bidiag** does the initial bidiagonalization, storing the matrices in compact form, expanded to full form by **expndb**. The decomposition is checked, as well as the matrices of left and right singular vectors for orthogonality. (Uses **rot734**.)
rsvd1 – computes singular values and vectors of a bidiagonal matrix.

bidiac *Test/demonstration program for complex bidiagonalization*
Three complex matrices are bidiagonalized using complex Householder transformations as described in Section 6.8, and the transformations are stored in compact form. The unitary matrices are formed by **expndc** and the bidiagonalization is checked, as well as the unitary matrices.
bidiac – bidiagonalizes matrix using complex Householder transformations.
expndc – expands transformations from **bidiac** into unitary matrices.

csvd0 *Demonstration program for complex singular value decomposition*
The singular values only for three complex matrices are computed. The routine **bidiac** computes the complex bidiagonalization. (Uses **rot734**.)
csvd0 – computes singular values only for a complex bidiagonal matrix.

csvd1 *Test/demonstration program for computing the complex singular value decomposition*
Singular values and vectors for three complex matrices are computed. The routine **bidiac** does the initial bidiagonalization, storing the matrices in compact form, expanded to full form by **expndc**. The decomposition is checked, and the matrices of left and right singular vectors are checked to be unitary. (Uses **rot734**.)
csvd1 – computes singular values and vectors of a complex bidiagonal matrix.

Exercises

6.1 For the matrix below, compute the largest eigenvalue and its vector using the power method:

$$\begin{bmatrix} 1 & -3 & -2 & 1 \\ -3 & 10 & -3 & 6 \\ -2 & -3 & 3 & -2 \\ 1 & 6 & -2 & 1 \end{bmatrix}.$$

6.2 Apply the orthogonal iteration method to the matrix above, using all four columns ($p = 4$). Describe the behavior of $\mathbf{Z}^{(k)}$ and $\mathbf{R}^{(k)}$.

6.3 Let $\mathbf{Z}$ have p orthonormal columns and let $\mathbf{AZ} = \mathbf{ZR}$, where $\mathbf{R}$ is upper triangular. For $p = 2$, show that R_{22} is an eigenvalue and find its eigenvector in terms of the first two columns of $\mathbf{Z}$. For general p, find the eigenvectors corresponding to the diagonal elements of $\mathbf{R}$ that are eigenvalues of $\mathbf{A}$.

6.4 Apply the orthogonal iteration method to the matrix below for $q = 2$:

$$\begin{bmatrix} 8 & -3 & -2 & 0 & 6 & 5 \\ -3 & 6 & 1 & -6 & 0 & -2 \\ -2 & 1 & 5 & -5 & 2 & 0 \\ 0 & -6 & -5 & 8 & -3 & -2 \\ 6 & 0 & 2 & -3 & 6 & 1 \\ 5 & -2 & 0 & -2 & 1 & 5 \end{bmatrix}.$$

6.5 Find the left eigenvector corresponding to the largest eigenvalue of the matrix below using the power method:

$$\begin{bmatrix} .6561 & .2916 & .0486 & .0036 & .0001 \\ .2401 & .4116 & .2646 & .0756 & .0081 \\ .0625 & .2500 & .3750 & .2500 & .0625 \\ .0081 & .0756 & .2646 & .4116 & .2401 \\ .0001 & .0036 & .0486 & .2916 & .6561 \end{bmatrix}.$$

6.6 For the matrix of Exercise 6.5, apply the power method using shifts of $1/2$ and $-1/2$. How effective are they? Are there other shifts that may work better? Try them.

6.7 For the matrix of Exercise 6.5, find the eigenvalue closest to one using the inverse power method. Compare the convergence with results from the two previous exercises. Are any problems encountered with singularity?

6.8 For the matrix of Exercise 6.5, apply the orthogonal iteration method and find the three largest eigenvalues and their vectors.

6.9 Apply the orthogonal iteration method to the following matrix:

$$\begin{bmatrix} 1 & -1 & 3 \\ 0 & 2 & 0 \\ -1 & 3 & 4 \end{bmatrix}.$$

6.10 Find all of the eigenvalues and vectors of the matrix in Example 6.1.

6.11 Suppose we exchange the values in the $(1, 1)$ and $(1, 2)$ entries in the matrix in Example 6.1 and then recompute the eigenvalues. Apply the Gershgorin Result 6 first. This may be a good time to try the inverse power method with a shift.

6.12 Apply the technique of Lagrange multipliers to the problem of maximizing $\mathbf{x}^T\mathbf{A}\mathbf{x}$ subject to $\mathbf{x}^T\mathbf{x} = 1$. Show how it relates to the matrix eigenproblem.

6.13 For a symmetric matrix of order n, how much work is required to reduce it to tridiagonal form through the use of similarity transformations?

6.14 Find the two eigenvalues of a 2×2 symmetric matrix. Which one is closest to the $(2, 2)$ element?

6.15 Let $\mathbf{A}$ be the matrix in Example 6.1. For some continuous distribution in $\mathcal{R}^3$, generate random vectors $\mathbf{x}^{(i)}$ ($i = 1, \ldots, n$) for n of at least 100, and compute $u_i = \mathbf{x}^{(i)T}\mathbf{A}\mathbf{x}^{(i)}/\mathbf{x}^{(i)T}\mathbf{x}^{(i)}$. What are the maximum and minimum values of u_i?

6.16 Show that solving the real eigenproblem of (6.4.1) really solves the eigenproblem of a Hermitian matrix.

6.17 Finish Example 6.2.

6.18 Show that the choice of s in (6.8.4) does the job for the complex Householder transformation. Do you still have a choice for the sign?

6.19 Compute the eigenvalues and eigenvectors of the Hermitian matrix

$$\begin{bmatrix} 1 & -3+6i & -2+5i \\ -3-6i & 10 & -3-2i \\ -2-5i & -3+2i & 3 \end{bmatrix}.$$

6.20 Compute the eigenvalues and eigenvectors of the symmetric tridiagonal matrix with diagonal entries all zero and off diagonals $k/\sqrt{4k^2-1}$ (cf. the Gauss–Legendre quadrature (10.2.12)).

6.21 Compute the Roy largest root statistic and the eigenvector of the generalized eigenproblem $\mathbf{Ax} = s\mathbf{Bx}$, where

$$\mathbf{A} = \mathbf{H} = \begin{bmatrix} 63.21 & -19.95 & 165.25 & 71.28 \\ -19.95 & 11.35 & -57.24 & -22.93 \\ 165.25 & -57.24 & 437.11 & 186.78 \\ 71.28 & -22.93 & 186.78 & 80.41 \end{bmatrix},$$

$$\mathbf{B} = \mathbf{E} = \begin{bmatrix} 38.60 & 13.63 & 24.62 & 5.64 \\ 13.63 & 16.96 & 8.12 & 4.81 \\ 24.62 & 8.12 & 27.22 & 6.27 \\ 5.64 & 4.81 & 6.27 & 6.16 \end{bmatrix}.$$

(Fisher's iris data; Mardia et al. 1979, pp. 344ff).

6.22 Show that $\mathbf{A}^+ = \mathbf{UD}^+\mathbf{V}^\mathrm{T}$ satisfies the four Moore–Penrose conditions.

6.23 Show that $\mathbf{X}^+\mathbf{y}$ has the shortest length of all solutions to the normal equations $\mathbf{X}^\mathrm{T}\mathbf{Xb} = \mathbf{X}^\mathrm{T}\mathbf{y}$.

6.24 The Frobenius norm $\|\mathbf{A}\|_F$ of a matrix is the square root of the sum of the squares of the elements. Show that $\|\mathbf{A}\|_F^2 = \mathrm{tr}(\mathbf{A}^\mathrm{T}\mathbf{A})$.

6.25 Compute the SVD of the matrices $\mathbf{X}$ and $\mathbf{X}+\mathbf{E}$ in Examples 5.1 and 5.2, and compare the results with (6.7.4).

6.26 Suppose the joint covariance matrix of $\mathbf{x}$ and $\mathbf{y}$ (both $p = q = 3$) is given by the matrix in Exercise 6.4. Find the canonical correlations.

6.27 Analyze the following matrix (given by Jennings 1977, p. 246), which is more problematic – this chain is not irreducible:

$$\begin{bmatrix} .8 & .6 & .1 & 0 & 0 & 0 \\ 0 & 0 & .4 & 0 & 0 & 0 \\ 0 & 0 & 0 & 0 & 0 & 0 \\ .2 & .3 & 0 & 1 & 0 & 0 \\ 0 & 0 & .4 & 0 & .4 & 1 \\ 0 & .1 & .1 & 0 & .6 & 0 \end{bmatrix}.$$

6.28 Combine sparse matrix multiplication techniques with the power method to find the stationary probability vector for the transition matrix given in Example 4.6.

6.29 Recall that eigenvectors, once normalized, are only unique up to a sign, that is, if $\mathbf{Ax} = s\mathbf{x}$, then $\mathbf{A}(-\mathbf{x}) = s(-\mathbf{x})$. In the SVD where $\mathbf{A} = \mathbf{UDV}^T$, if we insist that the diagonal elements of $\mathbf{D}$ are nonnegative, can we still choose some arbitrary signs for the left and right vectors? For the complex SVD, show that the singular vectors can be scaled using an imaginary number while still ensuring that the diagonal elements of $\mathbf{D}$ are nonnegative. Suppose we computed two equivalent complex decompositions, $\mathbf{A} = \mathbf{U}_1\mathbf{DV}_1^H = \mathbf{U}_2\mathbf{DV}_2^H$; what are the relationships among $\mathbf{U}_1$, $\mathbf{U}_2$, $\mathbf{V}_1$, and $\mathbf{V}_2$?

References

I have leaned heavily on the books by G. W. Stewart (1973) and Golub and van Loan (1989) for this chapter. Each have their strengths: Stewart better for the details of the algorithms; Golub and van Loan for completeness. The old monograph *Linear Algebra* (Wilkinson and Reinsch 1971) has many algorithms, although they are in Algol. For a modern Fortran library, LAPACK is most notable (Anderson et al. 1995), though the needs of most statisticians are rather simple. Lawson and Hanson (1974) include the proof of convergence of the QR algorithm in an appendix. Mardia et al. (1979) is quite comprehensive and always discusses the computation of statistics. The volume edited by W. J. Stewart (1991) presents the state of the art for Markov chain problems.

E. Anderson, Z. Bai, C. Bishof, J. Demmel, J. Dongarra, J. Du Croz, A. Greenbaum, S. Hammarling, A. McKenney, S. Ostrouchov, and D. Sorenson (1995), *LAPACK Users' Guide*. Philadelphia: SIAM.

T. F. Chan (1982), "An Improved Algorithm for Computing the Singular Value Decomposition," *ACM Transactions on Mathematical Software* 8: 72–88.

Gene H. Golub and Charles van Loan (1989), *Matrix Computations,* 2nd ed. Baltimore: Johns Hopkins University Press.

W. J. Harrod and R. J. Plemmons (1984), "Comparison of Some Direct Methods for Computing Stationary Distributions of Markov Chains," *SIAM Journal of Scientific and Statistical Computing* 5: 453–68.

Alan Jennings (1977), *Matrix Computation for Engineers and Scientists*. New York: Wiley.

Charles L. Lawson and Richard J. Hanson (1974), *Solving Least Squares Problems*. Englewood Cliffs, NJ: Prentice-Hall.

K. V. Mardia, J. T. Kent, and J. M. Bibby (1979), *Multivariate Analysis*. London: Academic Press.

B. N. Parlett and W. G. Poole (1973), "A Geometric Theory for the QR, LU and Power Iterations," *SIAM Journal of Numerical Analysis* 10: 389–412.

G. W. Stewart (1973), *Introduction to Matrix Computations*. New York: Academic Press.

William J. Stewart (1978), "A Comparison of Numerical Techniques in Markov Modeling," *Communications of the ACM* 21: 144–52.

William J. Stewart (Ed.) (1991), *Numerical Solution of Markov Chains*. New York: Marcel Dekker.

William J. Stewart and Alan Jennings (1981), "A Simultaneous Iteration Method for Real Matrices," *ACM Transactions on Mathematical Software* 7: 184–98.

J. H. Wilkinson (1965), *The Algebraic Eigenvalue Problem*. London: Oxford University Press.

J. H. Wilkinson and C. Reinsch (Eds.) (1971), *Linear Algebra*. New York: Springer-Verlag.

7

Functions: Interpolation, Smoothing, and Approximation

7.1 Introduction

As discussed in Chapter 2, the computer can perform only a few arithmetic operations: addition, subtraction, multiplication, and division. Hence, the evaluation of any function must be expressed in terms of these operations only. We have already mentioned the square root function, but nothing has been said regarding its computation. In this chapter, the evaluation of nonarithmetic functions will be addressed, as well as other aspects of the problem: interpolation, smoothing, and approximation.

In *interpolation*, a function f is sought that connects a set of points (x_i, z_i), $i = 1, \ldots, n$; that is,

$$z_i = f(x_i) \quad \text{for } i = 1, \ldots, n.$$

Usually, the interpolating function f is used to approximate a function, say $z(x)$, whose values are known only at specified abscissas x_i, as in a table. In the past, this has been the most important topic in numerical analysis. At present, most interpolations are done on a calculator or by hand.

The problem of *smoothing* is essentially the statistical problem of regression, or least-squares curve fitting. Here the objective is to find a function f within a class of functions, usually some form of polynomial, that fits data points (x_i, y_i):

$$\text{minimize} \sum_{i=1}^{n} [y_i - f(x_i)]^2.$$

Smoothing differs from interpolation by permitting a less than perfect fit with the potential of a more appealing (smoother) function f. The change in notation from z_i to y_i is intended to distinguish the exactness of z_i in contrast to y_i.

The *approximation* problem also permits a less than perfect fit, but the fit is evaluated over the full range of a function g. The class of functions considered for fitting are arithmetic functions – those that can be evaluated on the computer. Usually only particular subsets are considered, such as polynomials or rational functions, and often the optimum fitting function is less important than being sufficiently close to the target g. Here distance is measured using an L_p-norm,

$$\left[\int |f(x) - g(x)|^p w(x)\, dx \right]^{1/p},$$

where $w(x)$ is a nonnegative weight function. The usual values of p are 1, 2, and ∞, the last of which acts as a sup norm.

The most common class of functions used in all three applications are polynomials,

$$p(x) = a_0 + a_1 x + a_2 x^2 + \cdots + a_m x^m,$$

which are easy to evaluate. Horner's method, an efficient way of evaluating polynomials, can be coded as

```
PX=A0+X*( A1+X*( A2+X*( A3+A4*X )))
```

for the case $m = 4$. In general, Horner's method requires only m multiplications and m additions for a polynomial of degree m. The mathematical usefulness of polynomials is expressed in Weierstrass's theorem, which says that any function over a finite range can be approximated arbitrarily well by a polynomial. However, this result must be taken with some caution because, outside of that finite range, the polynomial will grow unboundedly.

An alternative (which also has a similar Weierstrass result) is the class of rational functions, which can be expressed as the ratio of two polynomials, p and q:

$$r(x) = \frac{p(x)}{q(x)} = \frac{a_0 + a_1 x + \cdots + a_m x^m}{b_0 + b_1 x + \cdots + b_n x^n}.$$

Note that rational functions are also easy to evaluate; they are widely used to approximate functions, since their behavior outside a finite range can be made more stable. Mathematically, they are not as easy to work with as polynomials.

A third class of functions are *splines,* which are piecewise polynomials with additional smoothness properties (such as continuity) and, in the most commonly used cubic spline, continuous first and second derivatives. Splines are relatively new, but they are particularly effective in applications because of their implicit smoothness and stable behavior.

Another class of functions (which will not be discussed here) is the class of trigonometric polynomials,

$$t(x) = a_0 + a_1 \cos(x) + b_1 \sin(x) + \cdots + a_k \cos(kx) + b_k \sin(kx)$$
$$+ \cdots + a_m \cos(mx) + b_m \sin(mx).$$

In interpolation, these functions are directly related to the discrete Fourier transform, which will be discussed in Chapter 14. In smoothing, they are used in trigonometric regression in time-series analysis for estimating periodic trends. In approximation, they are used in Fourier series, where the mathematics leads to powerful and useful results. However, for most of the problems addressed in this chapter, trigonometric polynomials are not appropriate because their direct evaluation is not so simple.

In the next section, the interpolation problem will be discussed using polynomials and rational functions. Interpolatory cubic splines are introduced in Section 7.3, followed by their application to regression and smoothing in Section 7.4. In Section 7.5, the approximation problem is faced from a mathematical viewpoint, and the practical side of approximating functions is addressed in Section 7.6. Approximations for probability functions are discussed in Section 7.7.

7.2 Interpolation

The most common application is the linear interpolation of the tabled values of a function $z(x)$. With just two points, (x_0, z_0) and (x_1, z_1), the interpolant is the linear function

$$f(x) = z_0 + (z_1 - z_0)[(x - x_0)/(x_1 - x_0)]. \tag{7.2.1}$$

Viewing the expression in brackets as the proportion p of the interval, f can be rewritten as $(1 - p)z_0 + pz_1$. Written this way, clearly the approximant f passes through the two points.

Quadratic approximation is equally straightforward when the abscissas are equally spaced. Let z_{-1}, z_0, z_1 be three ordinates from equally spaced abscissas. Then for a proportion p of the interval, $p = 2(x - x_0)/(x_1 - x_{-1})$, the quadratic interpolant is

$$f(p) = [(z_{-1} - 2z_0 + z_1)/2]p^2 + [(z_{-1} - z_1)/2]p + z_0, \tag{7.2.2}$$

where p is in the interval $[-1, 1]$. Notice that the values z_{-1}, z_0, z_1 are attained at $p = -1, 0, 1$ (or x_{-1}, x_0, x_1), respectively. If the abscissas are not equally spaced then the following general approach must be followed.

In the general interpolation problem, we seek a function f to pass through a set of points (x_i, z_i), $i = 1, \ldots, n$; that is, $z_i = f(x_i)$. The solution can be formed by construction. First define

$$g(x) = (x - x_1)(x - x_2) \cdots (x - x_n) \tag{7.2.3}$$

and let $d_i(x) = g(x)/[(x - x_i)g'(x_i)]$, so that $d_i(x)$ is a polynomial of degree $(n - 1)$ whose values at the abscissas resemble the Kronecker delta function: $d_i(x_i) = 1$ and $d_i(x_j) = 0$ if $i \neq j$. Another way of writing $d_i(x)$ is

$$d_i(x) = \frac{\prod_{j \neq i}(x - x_j)}{\prod_{j \neq i}(x_i - x_j)}.$$

Then the interpolant f is a polynomial of degree $(n - 1)$, which can be written as

$$f(x) = \sum_{i=1}^{n} z_i d_i(x). \tag{7.2.4}$$

An alternative method for solving the general interpolation problem is to set up a system of linear equations of the form $\sum a_{j-1} x_i^{j-1} = z_i$. Starting the column index at 1, construct the $n \times n$ matrix $\mathbf{A}$ with entries $A_{ij} = (x_i)^{j-1}$; then the right-hand sides are $b_i = z_i$ for $i = 1, \ldots, n$, and the solution vector holds the coefficients of the interpolating polynomial $(a_0, a_1, \ldots, a_{n-1})$.

Example 7.1: General Interpolation Problem
Let's do a quadratic interpolation of the square root function $z(x) = \sqrt{x}$ at $x = 1/16, 1/4$, and 1. Following (7.2.4), we have the formula for the interpolant $f(x)$,

$$f(x) = \frac{1}{4}\frac{(x-1/4)(x-1)}{(1/16-1/4)(1/16-1)}$$

$$+ \frac{1}{2}\frac{(x-1/16)(x-1)}{(1/4-1/16)(1/4-1)} + 1\frac{(x-1/16)(x-1/4)}{(1-1/16)(1-1/4)}$$

$$= (7 + 70x - 32x^2)/45 = a_0 + a_1 x + a_2 x^2.$$

Setting up the system of linear equations leads to

$$\begin{bmatrix} 1 & 1/16 & 1/256 \\ 1 & 1/4 & 1/16 \\ 1 & 1 & 1 \end{bmatrix}\begin{bmatrix} a_0 \\ a_1 \\ a_2 \end{bmatrix} = \begin{bmatrix} 1/4 \\ 1/2 \\ 1 \end{bmatrix}.$$

The accuracy of interpolation of (x_i, z_i) for a function $z(x)$ can be found using Newton's formulas, which extend the mean value theorem.

Theorem: *If $z^{(n)}(x)$ exists, then for every x in $[x_1, x_n]$ there is a w in $[x_1, x_n]$ such that, for the interpolant $f(x)$,*

$$z(x) - f(x) = \frac{g(x)z^{(n)}(w)}{n!}, \tag{7.2.5}$$

where $g(x)$ is given by (7.2.3).

For a proof, see Davis (1975, p. 56).

A solution to the general interpolation problem should be considered a mathematical solution, with some limitations on its applicability. As n grows, the interpolant often wiggles frantically to reach all of the data points. When the number of points (and hence the degree of the polynomial) grows large, this wiggling can get out of hand, leading to what is known as Runge's phenomenon (see Figures 7.1 and 7.2, and codes **runge1** and **runge2**). In this example, a smooth function is being approximated by a high-degree polynomial that is constructed by interpolating points of the function. At the center of the range of the abscissas the approximation is very good, but the interpolant wiggles so badly that the approximation is terrible at the ends. Extrapolation outside the range of the abscissas is hopeless.

Examining the right side of (7.2.5) reveals that some control can be exercised over $g(x)$ by choosing the interpolation abscissas. The optimum values of the abscissas for the interval $(-1, 1)$ are the zeros of the Chebyshev polynomial $T_n(x)$, $x_i = \cos\left(\frac{2i-1}{2n}\pi\right)$. Figure 7.2 shows the difference in performance by this alternative to equally spaced abscissas.

For inverse interpolation, the roles of function and argument are reversed. The interpolant $f(x)$ is still used as an approximation for the function $z(x)$, but a value of z^* is given and the value of x is sought that satisfies $z(x) = z^*$. In the linear case, the formula is rather simple; solving $(1 - p)y_0 + py_1 = y^*$ yields

$$p = (z^* - z_0)/(z_1 - z_0)$$

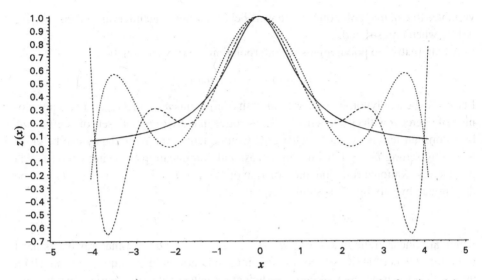

Figure 7.1. Runge phenomenon with equal spacing. The solid line shows the function $z(x) = 1/(1 + x^2)$; the dashed lines are 7- and 9-point interpolants.

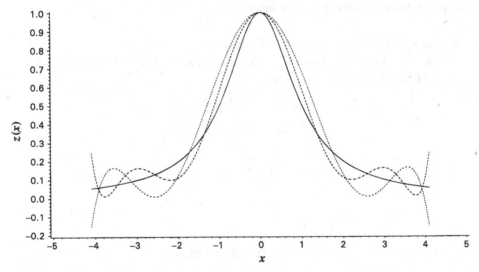

Figure 7.2. Runge phenomenon with Chebyshev spacing. The solid line shows the function $z(x) = 1/(1 + x^2)$; the dashed lines are 7- and 9-point interpolants.

and $x = (1 - p)x_0 + px_1$. In the quadratic case, the right-hand side of (7.2.4) is set equal to z^* and the resulting quadratic equation is solved for p.

The mean value theorem implies that a smooth function can be approximated by a linear or quadratic function on an interval. The quality of the approximation depends on the smoothness of the function $z(x)$ and the size of the interval. In some statistical problems, the original variable does not work so well. As seen in Exercises 7.4 and 7.6, changing the variable (say, to $1/x$) can improve matters, especially for an unbounded variable. Recall that polynomials are well-behaved only in an interval, and can behave wildly when unrestricted.

An alternative to polynomials for interpolation are rational functions,

$$r_{m,n}(x) = p_m(x)/q_n(x).$$

Let $p_m(x)$ be a polynomial of degree m with coefficients a_i, and let $q_n(x)$ be a polynomial of degree n with coefficients b_i. Then notice that dividing both sets of coefficients by a constant leaves $r_{m,n}(x)$ unchanged. Consequently, the redundancy can be eliminated by setting $b_0 = 1$, with only occasional complications, leaving $(m + n + 1)$ parameters. Rational function interpolation of (x_i, z_i), $i = 1, \ldots, (m + n + 1)$, can be determined by solving the system of equations

$$p_m(x_i) = z_i q_n(x_i), \quad i = 1, \ldots, (m + n + 1), \tag{7.2.6}$$

which are linear in the unknowns $(a_0, a_1, \ldots, a_m, b_1, \ldots, b_n)$. Some drawbacks need to be faced, since (i) the system of equations may not yield a unique solution, (ii) a unique solution is necessary but not sufficient for determining the rational function interpolant, and (iii) the system of equations is often badly conditioned. Overcoming these obstacles may be worth the effort since rational functions are often more flexible than polynomials for approximating functions.

Example 7.2: *Rational Function Interpolation*
Applying the formula (7.2.6) with $m = n = 1$ to the quadratic interpolation problem of Example 7.1 leads to the equations

$$a_0 + a_1/16 = (1/4)(1 + b_1/16),$$
$$a_0 + a_1/4 = (1/2)(1 + b_1/4),$$
$$a_0 + a_1 = (1)(1 + b_1).$$

Solving for the unknowns a_0, a_1, b_1 gives $a_0 = 1/7$, $a_1 = 2$, $b_1 = 8/7$, and $r(x) = (1/7 + 2x)/(1 + 8x/7)$.

7.3 Interpolating Splines

Although linear and quadratic methods are simple and easy to use, a more appealing solution to the interpolation problem can be found using cubic splines. These are piecewise cubic polynomials with a continuous first derivative (piecewise quadratic) and second derivative (piecewise linear). These functions are not very difficult to use (evaluating either the spline function or its derivative or indefinite integral), nor are they difficult to determine for the interpolation problem discussed here or for the smoothing problem (see Section 7.4).

The derivation of the interpolatory cubic spline is straightforward, but it is complicated by many details. The mathematical objective is to determine the function $S(x)$ that interpolates a set of points (z_i, x_i) for $i = 1, \ldots, n$ while minimizing a "lack of smoothness" criterion,

$$\int |S''(x)|^2 \, dx. \tag{7.3.1}$$

The solution is a cubic spline. The abscissas x_j are known as the *knots*, which delimit the intervals $I_j = [x_{j-1}, x_j]$ of length $h_j = x_j - x_{j-1}$ for $j = 2, \ldots, n$. Since we know that the cubic spline $S(x)$ is piecewise cubic, we can obtain a simple expression for the piecewise linear $S''(x)$ on the interval I_j:

$$S''(x) = \frac{M_{j-1}(x_j - x)}{h_j} + \frac{M_j(x - x_{j-1})}{h_j}, \tag{7.3.2}$$

where $S''(x_j) = M_j$ ($j = 1, \ldots, n$), the second derivatives at the knots. These M_j appear to be unknown parameters at the moment, but they can be determined using the constraints on $S(x)$. By integrating $S''(x)$ twice and enforcing the interpolation constraints $S(x_j) = z_j$ we can obtain, for x in I_j,

$$S(x) = \frac{M_{j-1}(x_j - x)^3 + M_j(x - x_{j-1})^3}{6h_j} + \frac{(z_{j-1} - M_{j-1}h_j^2/6)(x_j - x)}{h_j}$$

$$+ \frac{(z_j - M_j h_j^2/6)(x - x_{j-1})}{h_j}. \tag{7.3.3}$$

Then, by differentiating, the enforcement of the derivative constraint $S'(x_j^-) = S'(x_j^+)$ yields a system of $n - 2$ linear equations in M_j, $j = 1, \ldots, n$:

$$S'(x_j^-) = (h_j/6)M_{j-1} + (h_j/3)M_j + (z_j - z_{j-1})/h_j,$$
$$S'(x_j^+) = (-h_{j+1}/3)M_j + (-h_{j+1}/6)M_{j+1} + (z_{j+1} - z_j)/h_{j+1}. \tag{7.3.4}$$

Setting these two equal, $S'(x_j^-) = S'(x_j^+)$, yields the equations

$$M_{j-1}(h_j/6) + M_j(h_j + h_{j+1})/3 + M_{j+1}(h_{j+1}/6) = s_{j+1} - s_j, \tag{7.3.5}$$

where $s_j = (z_j - z_{j-1})/h_j$. Dividing each of these equations by $(h_j + h_{j+1})/6$ yields $n - 2$ equations involving only M_{j-1}, M_j, and M_{j+1} and whose coefficients are $h_j/(h_j + h_{j+1})$, 2, and $h_{j+1}/(h_j + h_{j+1})$, respectively. Note that the right-hand sides

$$d_j = \frac{6(s_{j+1} - s_j)}{h_j + h_{j+1}} \quad \text{for } j = 2, \ldots, n-1 \tag{7.3.6}$$

are linear combinations of the interpolated ordinates z_j. To uniquely determine M_j, two additional constraints are needed, which can be written as

$$2M_1 + p_1 M_2 = d_1,$$
$$p_n M_{n-1} + 2M_n = d_n. \tag{7.3.7}$$

Then form the set of linear equations $\mathbf{Dm} = \mathbf{d}$, where the elements of $\mathbf{m}$ are M_j, the elements of $\mathbf{d}$ are d_j from (7.3.6) and (7.3.7), and the matrix $\mathbf{D}$ is tridiagonal with diagonal elements all equal to 2. For $j = 2, \ldots, n-1$, the superdiagonal elements $D_{j,j+1}$ are $h_j/(h_j + h_{j+1})$ and the subdiagonal elements $D_{j,j-1}$ are their complements $h_{j+1}/(h_j + h_{j+1})$. The remaining elements of $\mathbf{D}$ are $D_{1,2} = p_1$ and $D_{n,n-1} = p_n$. The equations take the form

$$
\begin{bmatrix}
2 & p_1 & 0 & 0 & \cdots & & & \\
h_2/(h_2+h_3) & 2 & h_3/(h_2+h_3) & 0 & \cdots & & & \\
0 & \cdots & \cdots & \cdots & 0 & & & \\
0 & 0 & h_j/(h_j+h_{j+1}) & 2 & h_{j+1}/(h_j+h_{j+1}) & 0 & & 0 \\
0 & 0 & \cdots & \cdots & \cdots & & & \\
& & 0 & h_{n-1}/(h_{n-1}+h_n) & 2 & h_n/(h_{n-1}+h_n) & \\
& & & 0 & p_n & 2 &
\end{bmatrix}
\begin{bmatrix}
M_1 \\ M_2 \\ \cdots \\ M_j \\ \cdots \\ M_{n-1} \\ M_n
\end{bmatrix}
$$

$$
=
\begin{bmatrix}
d_1 \\ d_2 \\ \cdots \\ d_j \\ \cdots \\ d_{n-1} \\ d_n
\end{bmatrix}.
\tag{7.3.8}
$$

The additional constraints (7.3.7) arise as a priori information and usually take one of three forms as follows.

(1) Force the first derivatives at the endpoints, $S'(x_1) = z_1'$ and $S'(x_n) = z_n'$, requiring z_1' and z_n'. These constraints are implemented by setting $D_{1,2} = p_1 = D_{n,n-1} = p_n = 1$ and, for the right-hand side,

$$
d_1 = 6(s_2 - z_1')/h_2 \quad \text{and} \quad d_n = 6(z_n' - s_n)/h_n.
\tag{7.3.9}
$$

(2) Force the second derivatives at the endpoints, $S''(x_1) = z_1''$ and $S''(x_n) = z_n''$, given z_1'' and z_n''. These constraints are implemented by setting $d_1 = 2z_1''$ and $d_n = 2z_n''$ and also $p_1 = p_n = 0$. An important special case is the *natural spline*, where $M_1 = M_n = 0$.

(3) Force the ratio of second derivatives at the endpoints to take given values r_1 and r_n. These constraints are effected by $p_1 = -2r_1$ and $p_n = -2r_n$, with $d_1 = d_n = 0$.

Backing away from the computational details, the result is a piecewise cubic function with continuous first and second derivatives. In order to construct it, first some constants (s_j and d_j) must be computed and a tridiagonal system of equations solved as a setup. The matrix **D** is tridiagonal and can be solved in $O(n)$ time and space. Then, to evaluate the cubic spline interpolant at some argument, the appropriate interval must be determined and then just a simple cubic function evaluated.

In practice, the spline is both flexible and stable. It can fit nonpolynomial functions well because it fits differently over each interval. The effect of a difficult fit on one interval dissipates quickly and does not affect the fit in remote intervals. The time and space complexity impose no real obstacles to the possible size of the problem. Compare the polynomial interpolation with the performance of the spline in Figure 7.3 (see also **splint**).

The spline can be used for more than just approximating a function $z(x)$. In the next section, the spline function will be used for curve fitting. The interpolant can be

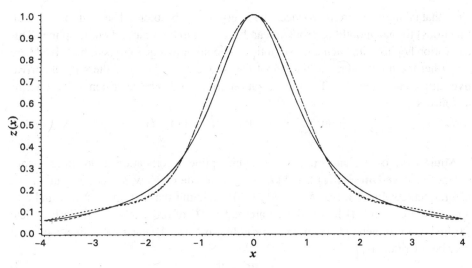

Figure 7.3. Spline interpolation. The solid line shows the function $z(x) = 1/(1 + x^2)$; the dashed lines are the natural spline and spline fit with endpoint derivative conditions.

integrated to estimate the integral of the function $z(x)$, leading to a numerical integration formula that is similar to the trapezoid rule. More importantly, the derivatives of the spline interpolant make very good estimators of the derivatives of the function $z(x)$. The following bound expresses just how well the derivatives $S^{(k)}$ ($k = 0, 1, 2, 3$) perform as estimates. When $z_i = z(x_i)$ – that is, when the interpolant $S(x)$ is approximating a function $z(x)$ – one can show that

$$|z^{(k)}(x) - S^{(k)}(x)| \leq C_k M h^{4-k} \tag{7.3.10}$$

for $k = 0, 1, 2, 3$ when $|z^{(4)}(x)| \leq M$. Hall and Meyer (1976) gave the constants as $C_0 = 5/384$, $C_1 = 1/24$, $C_2 = 3/8$, and $C_3 = (b + 1/b)/2$, where $h = \max h_j$ and $b = (\max h_j)/(\min h_j)$. These results will be useful in Chapter 12, where the derivative of the spline interpolant of an empirical distribution function is used as a density estimator.

7.4   Curve Fitting with Splines: Smoothing and Regression

As soon as the interpolation constraint is relaxed and the ordinates are no longer considered to be exact, the problem becomes a statistical one and much more complicated. Two approaches are considered. In one case, examined later this section, the family of spline functions is used as a regression function and least-squares coefficients are estimated to determine the best fit. In the other case, the usual least-squares objective changes to seeking both smoothness and a good fit to the data (x_i, y_i), $i = 1, \ldots, n$. More specifically, a function $S(x)$ is sought to minimize a combination of the two:

$$\sum_{i=1}^{n} [y_i - S(x_i)]^2 + t \int |S''(x)|^2 \, dx. \tag{7.4.1}$$

Note that taking t to zero reproduces the interpolation problem. The solution (over all functions) to the smoothing problem can be shown to be a natural cubic spline. This derivation begins with such an assumption. The unknown quantities to be solved here are either the fitted values of the smoothing spline $z_j = S(x_j)$ or the second derivatives at the endpoints M_j. The minimization criterion can be rewritten in these terms as follows:

$$\min \sum_j [y_j - z_j]^2 + t \int |S''(x)|^2 \, dx. \tag{7.4.2}$$

Minimizing over $\mathbf{z}$ and $\mathbf{m}$, with the cubic spline specification included as a constraint, we have $\mathbf{Dm} = \mathbf{d(z)}$ using (7.3.6) to compute $\mathbf{d}$. Now, since the solution is a natural cubic spline (so that $M_1 = M_n = 0$), deleting the first and last row and column from the matrix $\mathbf{D}$ leaves the square matrix $\mathbf{D}^*$ of order $n - 2$. Similarly, delete the first and last elements of $\mathbf{m}$ and $\mathbf{d}$, yielding $\mathbf{m}^*$ and $\mathbf{d}^*$; then the spline constraint may be rewritten as

$$\mathbf{D}^* \mathbf{m}^* = \mathbf{d}^*. \tag{7.4.3}$$

For this discussion only, the indexing of these starred matrices and vectors of order $n - 2$ will be from 2 to $n - 1$. The smoothness part can be simplified by computing

$$\int_{I_j} [S''(x)]^2 \, dx = \frac{h_j}{3} [M_{j-1}^2 + M_j M_{j-1} + M_j^2]. \tag{7.4.4}$$

Because $M_1 = M_n = 0$, the sum of these pieces can now be written as a quadratic form in the slopes M_j, $\frac{1}{6}\mathbf{m}^{*\mathrm{T}} \mathbf{E}^* \mathbf{m}^*$, with the $n - 2$ square matrix

$$\mathbf{E}^* = \begin{bmatrix} 2(h_2 + h_3) & h_3 & 0 & 0 & \cdots \\ h_3 & 2(h_3 + h_4) & h_4 & 0 & \cdots \\ 0 & h_4 & 2(h_4 + h_5) & h_5 & 0 \\ 0 & 0 & h_5 & 2(h_5 + h_6) & \cdots \\ 0 & 0 & & \cdots & \end{bmatrix}. \tag{7.4.5}$$

Note that $\mathbf{E}^*$ is positive definite and tridiagonal; it is also related to $\mathbf{D}^*$ by $\mathbf{D}^* = (\mathbf{H}^*)^{-1}\mathbf{E}^*$, where $\mathbf{H}^*$ is the diagonal matrix with elements $(h_j + h_{j+1})$, $j = 2, \ldots, n - 1$. The spline constraint can be rewritten, with the right-hand side simplifying (recall (7.3.5)) to

$$\mathbf{E}^* \mathbf{m}^* = \mathbf{H}^* \mathbf{d}^* = 6\mathbf{Cz}. \tag{7.4.6}$$

Here the matrix $\mathbf{C}$ is $(n - 2) \times n$ and banded, with rows of the form

$$0 \; \cdots \; 0 \; 1/h_j \; -(1/h_j + 1/h_{j+1}) \; 1/h_{j+1} \; 0 \; \cdots \; 0$$

(three nonzero elements) for $j = 2, \ldots, n - 1$.

Now the minimization problem can be rewritten in matrix terms as

$$\min (\mathbf{y} - \mathbf{z})^{\mathrm{T}}(\mathbf{y} - \mathbf{z}) + (t/6)\mathbf{m}^{*\mathrm{T}} \mathbf{E}^* \mathbf{m}^* \quad \text{subject to } \mathbf{E}^* \mathbf{m}^* = 6\mathbf{Cz}. \tag{7.4.7}$$

The use of Lagrange multipliers suggests computing the stationary point of the Lagrangian L,

$$L(\mathbf{z}, \mathbf{m}^*, \mathbf{s}) = (\mathbf{y} - \mathbf{z})^{\mathrm{T}}(\mathbf{y} - \mathbf{z}) + (t/6)\mathbf{m}^{*\mathrm{T}} \mathbf{E}^* \mathbf{m}^* - \mathbf{s}^{\mathrm{T}}(\mathbf{E}^* \mathbf{m}^* - 6\mathbf{Cz}),$$

which leads to the following system of equations for $\mathbf{m}^*$:

$$(\mathbf{E}^* + 6t\mathbf{CC}^T)\mathbf{m}^* = 6\mathbf{Cy}. \tag{7.4.8}$$

To solve for the fitted values $\mathbf{z}$, merely compute

$$\mathbf{z} = \mathbf{y} - t\mathbf{C}^T\mathbf{m}^* = \mathbf{A}(t)\mathbf{y}. \tag{7.4.9}$$

Note that (a) the introduction of the matrix $\mathbf{A}(t)$ suggests that the fitted values $\mathbf{z}$ are linear combinations of the observations $\mathbf{y}$ and (b) given t, $\mathbf{A}(t)$ takes the role of a hat matrix $\mathbf{H}$ in regression (see Section 5.9).

The smoothing problem has now been expressed mathematically in terms of a system of linear equations in (7.4.8), with another expression for the fitted values $\mathbf{z}$. Addressing the computations, notice that the matrix in (7.4.8) is both positive definite (symmetric) and banded with bandwidth 5 ($p = q = 2$). The Cholesky factorization then requires roughly $3n$ in space and $O(n)$ time, so the vector of second derivatives $\mathbf{m}^*$ can be computed in $O(n)$ time and space; computing the fitted values $\mathbf{z}$ requires another set of $O(n)$ computations but no additional space. See **splsmu** for the computation.

This discussion has treated the smoothing parameter t as given a priori. In some circles, however, this has been viewed as a unknown parameter $\lambda = t/n$, to be found from the data as the value that performs best in terms of goodness of fit. The recommended method, *generalized cross-validation* (GCV), is computationally very demanding (Hutchinson 1986; Bates et al. 1987), since it aims to minimize

$$\text{GCV}(\lambda) = \frac{n^{-1}\|(\mathbf{I}_n - \mathbf{A}(n\lambda))\mathbf{y}\|^2}{(n^{-1}\operatorname{tr}(\mathbf{I} - \mathbf{A}(n\lambda)))^2}. \tag{7.4.10}$$

Generalized cross-validation requires repeated computation of the estimation matrix

$$\mathbf{A}(t) = [\mathbf{I} - 6t\mathbf{C}^T(\mathbf{E}^* + 6t\mathbf{CC}^T)^{-1}\mathbf{C}] = [\mathbf{I} + 6t\mathbf{C}^T\mathbf{E}^{*-1}\mathbf{C}]^{-1}, \tag{7.4.11}$$

as well as its trace, while searching for the best value for t. The most effective approach is a spectral decomposition of the matrix

$$\mathbf{C}^T\mathbf{E}^{*-1}\mathbf{C} = \mathbf{UGU}^T,$$

where $\mathbf{G}$ is diagonal (eigenvalues) and $\mathbf{U}$ is orthogonal (eigenvectors). Once this $O(n^3)$ investment is made, $\sum(z_i - y_i)^2$ and $\operatorname{tr}\mathbf{A}(t) = \sum(1 + 6tg_i)^{-1}$ can be computed directly. Note that the trace cannot be computed without $O(n^3)$ work (Exercise 7.20) for a given value of t.

The alternative use of cubic splines as a regression function arises from viewing the knots k_j as points of change of the function. Poirier (1973) viewed the knots as points of structural change or changes in regime. Splines fit well into this scenario, where the underlying regression function is smooth and changes only subtly. This differs from the smoothing splines in that the knots are fixed and known (and not very many), rather than occurring at every abscissa x_i as with the smoothing splines. The form of the regression function is then the cubic spline $S(x)$ given by (7.3.3), interpolating (k_j, z_j), where the z_j are unknown and serve as parameters of the problem. For any given x, $S(x)$ is a linear function of the fitted values z_j and the second derivatives M_j; this is written as

$$S(x) = \mathbf{p}(x)^T\mathbf{m} + \mathbf{q}(x)^T\mathbf{z}. \qquad (7.4.12)$$

However, the other parameters M_j are linearly related to the fitted values by the spline equation $\mathbf{Dm} = \mathbf{d}$, where the right-hand side values $\mathbf{d}$ are linear functions of $\mathbf{z}$. Recall that the right-hand side values of (7.3.5) can be written as $\mathbf{Cz}$, where $\mathbf{C}$ has rows

$$0 \ \ldots \ 0 \ 1/h_j \ -(1/h_j + 1/h_{j+1}) \ 1/h_{j+1} \ 0 \ \ldots \ 0.$$

So, for any given value of x, the value of the regression function $S(x)$ is a linear function of the unknown parameters z_j; this is expressed mathematically as

$$S(x) = \mathbf{w}(x)^T\mathbf{z} = [6\mathbf{p}(x)^T\mathbf{E}^{-1}\mathbf{C} + \mathbf{q}(x)^T]\mathbf{z}. \qquad (7.4.13)$$

The statistical model for the observations (x_i, y_i), $i = 1, \ldots, N$, can then be written in the familiar form

$$y_i = S(x_i) + e_i = \mathbf{w}_i^T\mathbf{z} + e_i, \qquad (7.4.14)$$

where the errors e_i are IID with variance σ^2. The remainder of the analysis is straightforward regression, once the row $\mathbf{w}_i$ of the design matrix $\mathbf{W}$ is formed. The important computations are the estimates of the regression coefficients, which are the fitted values of the regression function at the knots k_j, the estimate of the variance of the errors $\hat{\sigma}^2$, and the matrix $(\mathbf{W}^T\mathbf{W})^{-1}$ for the covariances of the coefficient estimates. Poirier (1973) gave the details for computing standard errors of fitted values and predictions as well as hypothesis tests regarding structural change. The second derivatives of the estimated regression function can be computed using the fitted values at the knots. See the demonstration program **splrgm**.

These two methods should be viewed as two extremes of a spectrum of regression and smoothing methods using piecewise polynomials. As a more flexible alternative to simple polynomial regression, *regression splines* offer changes in a higher derivative at the knots while maintaining continuity at lower levels. In both cases, we have knots $(x_i, i = 1, \ldots, n)$ that include both endpoints of the domain $[x_1, x_n]$ and change points $(x_2, \ldots, x_{n-2})$ where a higher derivative changes. Now we also have for design points u_j, $j = 1, \ldots, N$ where the response y_j is observed. For polynomial regression of degree p, we can write the fitting function as $S(u) = \mathbf{r}(u)^T\beta$ where $\mathbf{r}(u) = (1, u, u^2, \ldots, u^p)^T$, and so a $N \times (p + 1)$ design matrix $\mathbf{X}$ can be constructed with rows $\mathbf{r}(u_j)^T$, $j = 1, \ldots, N$ with the goal of minimizing $\|\mathbf{y} - \mathbf{X}\beta\|^2$. Extending to piecewise polynomials with knots, we add $(n - 1)$ columns to the design matrix $\mathbf{X}$ corresponding to the knots to form $\mathbf{X}_T$, so now

$$\mathbf{r}(u) = (1, u, u^2, \ldots, u^p, (u - x_2)_+^p, \ldots, (u - x_{n-1})_+^p)^T$$

where $(u)_+ = \max(0, u)$. The functions in $\mathbf{r}(u)$ above are sometimes referred to as the *truncated power basis* for the linear space of continuous piecewise polynomial functions whose $(p - 1)$ derivatives are also continuous. The design matrix $\mathbf{X}_T$ with rows $\mathbf{r}(u_j)^T$ will be $N \times (n + p - 1)$.

Basis splines, or *B-splines*, provide an equivalent basis for the same linear space of functions. B-spline functions are much more complicated to compute, but they lead to a much better-conditioned design matrix $\mathbf{X}$. B-splines can be constructed beginning with $n - 1$ functions of degree $p = 0$, which are step functions $B_{i1}(u) = 1$ if $x_i \leq u <$

x_{i+1} and zero otherwise. B-splines of higher degree can be found from the recursion formula

$$B_{ik}(u) = \frac{(u - x_i)}{(x_{i+k-1} - x_i)} B_{i,k-1}(u) + \frac{(x_{i+k} - u)}{(x_{i+k} - x_{i+1})} B_{i+1,k-1}(u)$$

and by padding with extra knots on the ends: $x_m = x_1$ for $m < 1$ and $x_m = x_n$ for $m > n$. There are n linear B-splines, $n + 1$ quadratic B-splines, and $n + p - 1$ B-splines $B_{i,p+1}(u), i = 1, \ldots, n + p - 1$ of degree p. As with the truncated power basis, these can be used to fill a $N \times (n + p - 1)$ design matrix $\mathbf{X}_B$.

The tradeoff between fit and smoothness expressed in (7.4.2) can be generalized to

$$\|\mathbf{y} - \mathbf{X}\beta\|^2 + \lambda^{2p}\beta^T\mathbf{D}\beta. \tag{7.4.15}$$

Ruppert et al. (2003) follows the truncated power basis parameterization with $\mathbf{X}_T$ and suggests $diag(\mathbf{D}) = (\mathbf{0}_{p+1}, \mathbf{1}_{n-2})$. Other choices and parameterizations lead to more complicated nonnegative definite matrices $\mathbf{D}$. In this context, the natural cubic smoothing splines have $p = 3$, knots at all of the design points, a more complicated $\mathbf{D}$, and the natural constraint of $S''(x_1) = S''(x_n) = 0$ leads to linear constraints on β. The natural cubic regression splines also have $p = 3$, the same linear constraints on β, but $\mathbf{D} = 0$. As before with smoothing splines, the solutions to (7.4.15) or its normal equations equivalent

$$(\mathbf{X}^T\mathbf{X} + \lambda^{2p}\mathbf{D})\beta = \mathbf{X}^T\mathbf{y}$$

or for its fitted values

$$\hat{\mathbf{y}} = \mathbf{A}(\lambda)\mathbf{y} = \mathbf{X}(\mathbf{X}^T\mathbf{X} + \lambda^{2p}\mathbf{D})^{-1}\mathbf{X}^T\mathbf{y}$$

may be sought for several values of λ, which suggests similar computation to (7.4.11) previously for smoothing splines. Construct the Cholesky decomposition $\mathbf{X}^T\mathbf{X} = \mathbf{L}\mathbf{L}^T$, and then compute the spectral decomposition of $\mathbf{L}^{-1}\mathbf{D}\mathbf{L}^{-T} = \mathbf{U}\mathbf{G}\mathbf{U}^T$ where $\mathbf{G}$ is the diagonal matrix of eigenvalues, and $\mathbf{U}$ the orthogonal matrix of eigenvectors. If we compute the QR decomposition of $\mathbf{X}$ (via MGS, Householder, or Givens) as $\mathbf{X} = \mathbf{Q}\mathbf{L}^T$, then we can write

$$\hat{\mathbf{y}} = \mathbf{A}(\lambda)\mathbf{y} = \mathbf{Q}\mathbf{U}(\mathbf{I} + \lambda^{2p}\mathbf{G})^{-1}\mathbf{U}^T\mathbf{Q}^T\mathbf{y}$$

and $\mathbf{I} + \lambda^{2p}\mathbf{G}$ is diagonal. As previously with GCV, other measures of fit require the computation of the traces of $\mathbf{A}$ and $\mathbf{A}\mathbf{A}^T$; both $tr\mathbf{A}(\lambda) = \sum_k(1 + \lambda^{2p}G_{kk})^{-1}$ and $tr\mathbf{A}(\lambda)\mathbf{A}(\lambda)^T = \sum_k(1 + \lambda^{2p}G_{kk})^{-2}$ can be easily computed for varying values of λ.

7.5 Mathematical Approximation

Before facing the practical problem of evaluating a nonarithmetic function on a computer, consider first the best approximation of a function in a mathematical sense. The distance between two functions is measured by the L_p-norm

$$\|f - g\|_p = \left[\int |f(x) - g(x)|^p w(x)\, dx\right]^{1/p}.$$

In this discussion, only two values of p are considered. For $p = 2$, the distance is given by

$$d(f, g) = \left[\int |f(x) - g(x)|^2 w(x) \, dx \right]^{1/2}.$$

For $p = \infty$, the distance is sup norm, sometimes called the Chebyshev norm,

$$E(f, g) = \sup_x |f(x) - g(x)|.$$

The former ($p = 2$) lends itself more readily to analytic solutions, whereas solutions to the latter ($p = \infty$) problem are more applicable to computer approximations.

The problem of best L_2 approximation can be simplified by introducing an inner product between two functions,

$$\langle f, g \rangle = \int f(x) g(x) w(x) \, dx.$$

Generalizing the idea of the Euclidean norm to functions and using $\| f \|^2 = \langle f, f \rangle$, the distance can be written as a squared length,

$$d(f, g) = \| f - g \| = [\langle f - g, f - g \rangle]^{1/2}.$$

Many of the concepts of linear algebra and Euclidean geometry can now be extended by replacing vectors with functions and replacing the inner product $\mathbf{a}^T \mathbf{b}$ with $\langle f, g \rangle$. The best approximation in L_2 can then be solved by least squares.

Translating a few more concepts of linear algebra clears the path to the solution. *Linear independence* of a set of functions $\{y^{(i)}\}$ means that no linear combination gives a function of zero norm,

$$\left\| \sum a_i y^{(i)}(x) \right\| \neq 0.$$

Two functions are *orthogonal* if their inner product is zero, $\langle f, g \rangle = 0$. Completeness of a set of orthonormal functions means that a function orthogonal to every member is a function with zero norm.

An orthogonal basis, a set of vectors (functions) that are mutually orthogonal, is fundamental. The difference here is that the number of dimensions can be countably infinite. For the most important cases, the linearly independent set of functions are the polynomials $\{1, x, x^2, \ldots, x^i, \ldots\}$. For different domains and weight functions, the resulting orthogonal polynomials can be determined. For the most common choices of domains and weights, the polynomials and interrelationships are well known. A short summary of useful results is given in Tables 7.1 and 7.2. Abramowitz and Stegun (1970) included most of the well-known results; further information can be found in Szego (1959).

These families of orthogonal polynomials also have the important property of *closure*: any function with finite L_2-norm can be written as an infinite linear combination of orthogonal polynomials $\{q^{(i)}\}$. More specifically, this is expressed as a limit

$$\lim_{n \to \infty} \left\| f - \sum_{i=0}^{n} a_i q^{(i)} \right\| = 0.$$

Table 7.1. *Domains and weights of common*
orthogonal polynomials

Domain	Weight	Polynomials	Notation
$[-1, 1]$	1	Legendre	$P_n(x)$
$[-1, 1]$	$(1 - x^2)^{-1/2}$	Chebyshev (1st kind)	$T_n(x)$
$[-1, 1]$	$(1 - x^2)^{1/2}$	Chebyshev (2nd kind)	$U_n(x)$
$[0, \infty)$	$\exp(-x)$	Laguerre	$L_n(x)$
$(-\infty, \infty)$	$\exp(-x^2)$	Hermite	$H_n(x)$
$(-\infty, \infty)$	$\exp(-x^2/2)$	Modified Hermite	$He_n(x)$

The coefficients a_i of this approximation are called the *Fourier coefficients* of the function f and arise as a solution to the least-squares problem

$$\min_{a_i} \left\| f - \sum_{i=0}^{n} a_i q^{(i)} \right\|.$$

Following the usual result of least squares with orthogonal variables, the coefficients are found by the inner product $a_i = \langle f, q^{(i)} \rangle$. Computing these Fourier coefficients will produce the best L_2 approximation of a function f on a particular domain and with a particular weight.

Before undertaking the L_∞ problem, consider an interesting property of the Chebyshev polynomials (first kind) $T_n(x)$. Namely, $|T_n(x)| \leq 2^{1-n}$, where the maximum is attained at $n + 1$ points: the endpoints and $n - 1$ places in between the zeros. Of all polynomials with leading coefficient 1, $T_n(x)$ has the smallest sup norm. It achieves this by taking its extrema to the same value as often as possible. In this way, it optimizes the sup norm of the function $g(x) = (x - x_1)(x - x_2) \cdots (x - x_n)$, which was posed in the Section 7.2 discussion of avoiding Runge's phenomenon with interpolation. This "equal wiggle" property leads to optimal Chebyshev approximation of functions.

The solution to the least maximum (L_∞) approximation problem for polynomials can be expressed in the following theorem.

Theorem: *Let $f(x)$ be continuous on $[a, b]$ and let $p(x)$ be the polynomial of degree n that minimizes*

$$E(f, p) = \max_{a \leq x \leq b} |f(x) - p(x)|,$$

so that $E(f, p) = E_n$. Let $e(x) = f(x) - p(x)$. Then there are $n + 2$ points $a \leq x_1 < x_2 < \cdots < x_{n+2} \leq b$, where $e(x)$ takes the values E_n or $-E_n$ with alternating signs, $e(x_k) = -e(x_{k-1})$.

For a proof, see Davis (1975, sec 7.6).

This result characterizes the solution to the L_∞ problem, but it does not provide an algorithm for its construction. The following example shows the mathematical difficulty of even a very simple problem.

Table 7.2. *Other information on common*
orthogonal polynomials

Legendre Polynomials
The first few: $P_0(x) = 1$
$\qquad\qquad\quad P_1(x) = x$
$\qquad\qquad\quad P_2(x) = [3x^2 - 1]/2$ $\qquad$ Norm $\|P_n\|^2 = 2/(2n + 1)$
$\qquad\qquad\quad P_3(x) = [5x^3 - 3x]/2$
$\qquad\qquad\quad P_4(x) = [35x^4 - 30x^2 + 3]/8$
Recurrence formula: $(n + 1)P_{n+1}(x) = (2n + 1)xP_n(x) - nP_{n-1}(x)$

Chebyshev Polynomials (1st kind)
The first few: $T_0(x) = 1$
$\qquad\qquad\quad T_1(x) = x$
$\qquad\qquad\quad T_2(x) = 2x^2 - 1$ $\qquad$ Norm $\|T_n\|^2 = \begin{cases} \pi/2 & \text{for } n \neq 0 \\ \pi & \text{for } n = 0 \end{cases}$
$\qquad\qquad\quad T_3(x) = 4x^3 - 3x$
$\qquad\qquad\quad T_4(x) = 8x^4 - 8x^2 + 1$
Recurrence formula: $T_{n+1}(x) = 2xT_n(x) - T_{n-1}(x)$

Chebyshev Polynomials (2nd kind)
The first few: $U_0(x) = 1$
$\qquad\qquad\quad U_1(x) = 2x$
$\qquad\qquad\quad U_2(x) = 4x^2 - 1$ $\qquad$ Norm $\|U_n\|^2 = \pi/2$
$\qquad\qquad\quad U_3(x) = 8x^3 - 4x$
$\qquad\qquad\quad U_4(x) = 16x^4 - 12x^2 + 1$
Recurrence formula: $U_{n+1}(x) = 2xU_n(x) - U_{n-1}(x)$

Laguerre Polynomials
The first few: $L_0(x) = 1$
$\qquad\qquad\quad L_1(x) = 1 - x$
$\qquad\qquad\quad L_2(x) = [2 - 4x + x^2]/2$ $\qquad$ Norm $\|L_n\|^2 = 1$
$\qquad\qquad\quad L_3(x) = [6 - 18x + 9x^2 - x^3]/6$
$\qquad\qquad\quad L_4(x) = [24 - 96x + 72x^2 - 16x^3 + x^4]/24$
Recurrence formula: $(n + 1)L_{n+1}(x) = (2n + 1 - x)L_n(x) - nL_{n-1}(x)$

Hermite Polynomials
The first few: $H_0(x) = 1$
$\qquad\qquad\quad H_1(x) = 2x$
$\qquad\qquad\quad H_2(x) = 4x^2 - 2$ $\qquad$ Norm $\|H_n\|^2 = 2^n n! \pi^{1/2}$
$\qquad\qquad\quad H_3(x) = 8x^3 - 12x$
$\qquad\qquad\quad H_4(x) = 16x^4 - 48x^2 + 12$
Recurrence formula: $H_{n+1}(x) = 2xH_n(x) - 2nH_{n-1}(x)$

Modified Hermite Polynomials
The first few: $He_0(x) = 1$
$\qquad\qquad\quad He_1(x) = x$
$\qquad\qquad\quad He_2(x) = x^2 - 1$ $\qquad$ Norm $\|He_n\|^2 = n! \sqrt{2\pi}$
$\qquad\qquad\quad He_3(x) = x^3 - 3x$
$\qquad\qquad\quad He_4(x) = x^4 - 6x^2 + 3$
Recurrence formula: $He_{n+1}(x) = xHe_n(x) - nHe_{n-1}(x)$

Example 7.3: *Chebyshev or Least Maximum Approximation*

Let's find the best linear function $a_0 + a_1 x$ to approximate $f(x) = \sqrt{x}$ on the interval $(1/16, 1)$. Taking the two endpoints to have the same difference, since we will have three extrema we have two equations for $x = 1/16$ and $x = 1$,

$$a_0 + a_1/16 - 1/4 = E,$$
$$a_0 + a_1 - 1 = E.$$

Subtracting these two yields $a_1 = 4/5$, and the merged equation is $a_0 - 1/5 = E$. Next, find the extreme point in the middle by finding the extreme point of $a_0 + (4/5)x - \sqrt{x}$, which has a zero derivative at $x = 25/64$. This leads to a new equation with this extreme point taking the value $-E$,

$$a_0 + (4/5)(25/64) - 5/8 = -E.$$

Combined with the former result, this leads to the solution $a_0 = 41/160$ and $E = 9/160$.

The methods used to find least maximum approximations for either polynomials or rational functions are variations on what is called "the second algorithm of Remes." To generalize further, weights should be included for the solution to the more general problem,

$$\min_{p,q} \max_x |f(x) - p(x)/q(x)|/w(x),$$

to allow for absolute error with $w(x) = 1$ and for relative error with $w(x) = f(x)$. These methods are all heuristic, iteratively trying to force the "equal wiggle" property of the error. Cody, Fraser, and Hart (1968) proposed the following iterative solution to the equations

$$p(x_i) - q(x_i)f(x_i) = (-1)^i E w(x_i) q(x_i) \tag{7.5.1}$$

for estimated extreme points $\{x_i, i = 1, \ldots, r\}$. If p and q are polynomials of degree m and n, then $r = m + n + 2$. The Cody et al. approach involves writing the denominator polynomial as $q(x) = 1 + q^*(x)$ in order to isolate the nonlinearity in these equations:

$$p(x_i) - q(x_i)f(x_i) - (-1)^i E w(x_i) q^*(x_i) = (-1)^i E w(x_i). \tag{7.5.2}$$

Now, given $\{x_i, i = 1, \ldots, r\}$, both $w(x_i) = w_i$ and $f(x_i) = f_i$ are fixed. Replacing E on the left-hand side of (7.5.2) with the value E_{old} from the previous iteration leads to a system of linear – yes, linear – equations ($r = m + n + 2$ of them) in the $m + n + 1$ coefficients and one more for E (from the right):

$$p(x_i) - q^*(x_i)f_i - (-1)^i E_{old} w_i q^*(x_i) - (-1)^i E w_i = f_i. \tag{7.5.3}$$

Once these values are found, the roots of $f(x) = p(x)/q(x)$ are then found and used to find the extrema $\{x_i, i = 1, \ldots, r\}$ for the next round. The modified equations (7.5.3) are then solved again to find new coefficients and a new value of E. In practice, this heuristic method either converges quickly to the least maximum solution or fails quickly when no solution exists. Their algorithm is named "Chebyshev" and was used to compute many approximations in the landmark volume by Hart et al. (1968). Other heuristic approaches aim to solve the nonlinear equations (7.5.1), which can also apply to other, nonlinear, approximations (see Monahan and Stefanski 1992).

7.6   Practical Approximation Techniques

As mentioned previously, the computer can perform only the simple arithmetic operations. How then, one might ask, can we compute $\tanh^{-1}(r)$? Within every black box for the square root or logarithm resides a body of instructions that employ only addition, subtraction, multiplication, and division. Most of the time, library routines are available to compute the trigonometric functions, logs, exponentials, and square and cube roots. Occasionally, the gamma and error functions are not available and so the task of constructing approximation routines must be faced. In some software systems (e.g., SAS, GAUSS, S), most of the probability functions, such as the incomplete gamma and beta functions, will also be included. Even so, whenever we strain our available computational tools we must know how they work in order to know their limits. This discussion will focus on two important functions – the square root $s(x) = \sqrt{x}$ and the gamma $\Gamma(x)$ functions – examining how these approximations are done and where their limits may be.

The mathematical definition of a function, a computing formula, and a practical algorithm for its evaluation on a computer are all very different. Defining the gamma function as an integral, or as the limit of an infinite product, does not express a practical method of evaluation when the only tools available are arithmetic ones. A computing formula, such as a power series expansion, may express mathematically a method of evaluation using arithmetic operations. But because of the realities of finiteness and roundoff error, computing formulas should still be considered mathematical abstractions. For the construction of a practical algorithm, these computing formulas often serve a vital role of a starting point from which "exact values" can be computed – values that can be made as accurate as desired. From a mathematical viewpoint, all computational methods are approximations.

The practical evaluation of a function on a computer requires constant attention to efficiencies and specifications. We seek an algorithm to compute a given function that is fast, requires little storage and code, but still achieves a given level of accuracy. The specifications for a library function are that it should produce a logical result (which may include an overflow) for every argument for which it is defined. Moreover, the result produced should be completely accurate – or as accurate as could be expected. For the square root function, there may be many numbers whose square gives the argument when rounded. Any one of them should be considered completely accurate, and anything less than these specifications should be referred to as only an approximation. Constructing a routine to meet this library standard is a burdensome task. Moreover, for some difficult problems, even constructing a good approximation can be quite difficult, and the resulting code can vary in speed by a factor of 10, depending on the argument.

In the practical design of algorithms for computing nonarithmetic functions, *range reduction* is the most effective tool for saving work. If an algorithm were available to compute $s(x) = \sqrt{x}$ only on the interval $(1/2, 1)$, then applying the simple relation $s(4x) = 2s(x)$ extends the range to include $(2, 4)$. Then the relation $s(2x) = s(2)s(x)$ can be applied to fill in $(1, 2)$, once $s(2)$ is computed; this approach can be extended to cover the whole positive axis. Range reduction can be easily exploited, especially for binary floating point arithmetic. Since x can be expressed as $a2^k$ with $1 \leq a < 2$, the range is already reduced to that of the fraction. The exponent is then halved, and the remainder when k is odd included with the fraction producing $s(2)s(a)$.

Having reduced the range of the argument to the interval $(1/2, 1)$ an effective computing formula can be obtained from Taylor's expansion of $s(x)$ around 1,

$$s(x) = 1 + (1/2)(x-1) - (1/8)(x-1)^2 + (1/16)(x-1)^3 - (5/128)(x-1)^4 \cdots . \quad (7.6.1)$$

Denote the expansion including terms to $(x-1)^n$ as $s_n(x)$, and notice that $s_n(x)$ converges uniformly in x to $s(x)$. Finding the value of n such that $E(s_n, s) < U$, the machine unit, appears to have solved the problem of approximating the square root function $s(x)$. However, two important items have not yet been considered. One possible problem is that roundoff error, especially from cancellation in the alternating series, may prevent computational achievement of such a small approximation error. The second consideration is the possibility of doing better for the same effort – the same number of multiplications and additions. Toward this end, consider the following simple alternatives to $s_2(x)$ that can be considered, each taking two multiplications and two additions.

(1) Interpolate $s(x)$ at three points chosen according to Chebyshev interpolation.
(2) Find the least maximum approximation among quadratic polynomials using the methods of Section 7.5.
(3) Find the best rational function approximation with degrees 1 and 1, again using the methods of Section 7.5. (A division costs nearly the same as a multiplication.)

There are certainly other alternatives that could be entertained (see e.g. Fike 1968, p. 25). Some will be more accurate computationally; others will be very easy or very hard to find. But considering the requirements of a library function – small storage and high speed with impeccable accuracy – the techniques of approximation by polynomials and rational functions with range reduction can rarely be improved upon. Considering the nearly limitless number of times the square root function will be called, an extensive initial investment is justified in determining the best computational algorithm.

Hastings (1955) found a number of rational function approximations to the common functions; according to legend, these were found by eyeball and trial and error. Many of these remarkably effective approximations were listed in Abramowitz and Stegun (1970). Fike (1968) described the various mathematical techniques for constructing approximations, compiling a great variety of work to that point in time. Following a single approach, Hart led a systematic effort of computing and publishing a long list of best uniform rational function approximations for many common functions (Hart et al.

1968). Their method was the "Chebyshev" algorithm mentioned in Section 7.5. These coefficients have been tabled – along with the maximum relative or absolute error – for square and cube roots, exponential and hyperbolic functions, trigonometric functions, and gamma and error functions. To show how this work can be applied, consider the implementation for the gamma function.

Range reduction for the gamma function $\Gamma(x)$ follows the formula $\Gamma(x + 1) = x\Gamma(x)$, but it cannot be exploited as easily as the square root. For large values of x, Stirling's approximation can be used more effectively than the range reduction. Following Hart et al. (1968), for 41 choices of m and n, the coefficients for rational function approximations and their errors are tabled for the interval $[2, 3]$. For the infinite intervals $[8, \infty)$ and $[12, \infty)$, rational function approximations are given for the correction $\theta(x)$ to Stirling's approximation to $\ln \Gamma(x)$,

$$\theta(x) = \ln \Gamma(x) - \left[(x - 1/2) \ln x - x + \ln\left(\sqrt{2\pi}\right) \right]. \tag{7.6.2}$$

Now some planning is necessary. The gamma function grows very fast, exceeding the range for real numbers for modest values of the argument; hence flags for both overflow and negative integers are required. One may decide not to permit negative arguments at all. The log of the gamma function, however, is rather stable, although Stirling's approximation will not work well for small values. Two modules are then required: one for $\Gamma(x)$, usually called GAMMA; another for $\ln \Gamma(x)$, usually called ALGAMA. For small and modest values of the argument, range reduction reduces the problem to computing $\Gamma(x)$ for the interval $[2, 3]$. For ALGAMA, this result is then logged. For large values of the argument x, the correction $\theta(x)$ is computed and then Stirling's approximation is used to compute $\ln \Gamma(x)$. For GAMMA, this result is then exponentiated, except for when it will overflow. This last step is precarious, since a small relative error can be severely amplified (recall Exercise 2.16). See the demonstration of **gamma** for an updated version of an implementation written by the author when he was a graduate student.

One of the essential lessons to be learned here is that writing such library routines is difficult and tedious – a problem that should not be sought out. (Necessity has forced such efforts upon the author; usually the need is subsequently questioned.) Other lessons involve understanding that (a) these library routines are nothing magical, (b) the routines have their limitations and shortcomings, and (c) these problems must be kept in mind in everyday use.

7.7 Computing Probability Functions

Whereas many computers and calculators provide approximations for the common (nonarithmetic) mathematical functions – square root, trigonometric functions, and log and exponential functions – such facilities are not regularly supplied for the distribution functions used in statistics, such as normal, t, F, chi-square, Poisson, and binomial. However, most commercial software libraries for scientific computation include routines for computing these functions: the NAG library, IMSL's SFUN/LIB, as well as collections such as FUNPACK and the ACM algorithms. Other software systems – such as SAS, R, and GAUSS – have most of the probability functions. Maintained libraries are generally quite reliable, but one should still check the results of these routines whenever their accuracy is being severely challenged. Keep in mind also that, for the more difficult problems, an accurate approximation (of, say, an incomplete gamma function) may require orders of magnitude more computation than for the evaluation of a trigonometric function.

Because the accuracy specifications for library routines often grossly exceed what may be needed for statistical applications, approximations of varying quality have considerable appeal. For the common statistical distributions (Student's t, chi-square, and F), the usual computational approach is to devise corrections to the asymptotic normal approximation. Since these functions now have two or three arguments, the accuracy that was available with rational function approximation can no longer be achieved without completely exploiting the behavior of the function. Ling (1978) compared the accuracy of a number of methods for computing tail probabilities for t, chi-square, and F distributions.

The mathematical definitions of the functions to be discussed here are well known from a statistical viewpoint: distribution functions with well-known density functions. As previously noted, the mathematical definition is often not very valuable in computation. Computational formulas are needed – usually taking the form of power series, asymptotic approximations, or continued fractions. For the common functions, the best source for such formulas is Abramowitz and Stegun (1970), whose numbers will be cited without further reference. For the less common functions, such formulas are part of the study of the topic (e.g., the Smirnov distribution in nonparametrics).

Note that, in nearly all cases, the focus is on the tail of the distribution. The reasoning is that (a) the values of statistical interest are in the tails, not the center, and (b) evaluating in terms of the cumulative distribution function cannot give great accuracy, because the numbers are all near unity and blindly subtracting from 1 risks serious cancellation error.

(A) *Normal Distribution*

The central distribution to all statistics is the normal distribution, whose density function is denoted by ϕ and distribution function by $\Phi(x)$. The function Φ is related to the more common error function "erf" as follows:

$$\Phi(x) = \left[\operatorname{erf}\left(x/\sqrt{2}\right) + 1\right]/2 = \operatorname{erfc}\left(-x/\sqrt{2}\right)/2. \tag{7.7.1}$$

Recall that $\Phi(-x) = 1 - \Phi(x)$ and $\operatorname{erfc}(u) = 1 - \operatorname{erf}(u)$. Abramowitz and Stegun gave power series expansions (their 26.2.1 and 26.2.11) as computing formulas for $\Phi(x)$, but they are not as effective as the continued fractions (their 26.2.14 and 26.2.15):

$$1 - \Phi(x) = \phi(x)/(xg(x^2)), \tag{7.7.2}$$

$$\Phi(x) = 1/2 + \phi(x)h(x), \tag{7.7.3}$$

where

$$g(w) = 1 + \cfrac{w^{-1}}{1 + \cfrac{2/w}{1 + \cfrac{3/w}{1 + \cdots}}} \quad \text{and} \quad h(x) = \cfrac{x}{1 - \cfrac{x^2}{3 + \cfrac{2x^2}{5 - \cfrac{3x^2}{7 + \cfrac{4x^2}{9 + \cdots}}}}}.$$

The first expression (7.7.2) is best for larger values of x (say, $x > 1.3$); (7.7.3) is better for x near zero.

The error function and its complement are commonly part of the Fortran libraries, appearing as often as the gamma function. Both functions are needed, since using (7.7.1) for large negative x will yield substantial cancellation. The error function and its complement are usually computed using rational function approximations for intervals, and corrections are provided to asymptotic formulas for the tails. Recall that a similar strategy was followed for the gamma function in Section 7.6. When high accuracy is not required and if erf and erfc are not available, the Hastings (1955) approximations are recommended; Abramowitz and Stegun listed several (26.2.16–23). A number of simple approximations have been proposed and are often suggested for hand calculators. A more recent one by Vedder (1993), following the spirit of the logistic distribution, gives

$$\Phi(x) \approx [1 + \exp(-ax - bx^3)]^{-1}, \tag{7.7.4}$$

where $a = 2\sqrt{2/\pi}$ and $b = \sqrt{2/\pi}(4 - \pi)/(3\pi)$. See the demonstration **normals** for some comparisons.

(B) *Logarithm of the Normal Distribution Function*

Although erf and erfc can be used to compute $\Phi(x)$ for most applications, the accuracy (for large $|x|$) when computing $\ln \Phi(x)$ is lost. For large values of x, $\ln \Phi(x) \sim x^{-1}\phi(x)$ whereas using erf would entail the log of a quantity near 1 and a consequent loss of significant digits. For large negative values, $\ln \Phi(x) \sim -x^2/2$ yet erfc would encounter underflow very quickly. In these cases, the accuracy is lost in storing the intermediate quantities. One route is to recode: in the former case, express the intermediate quantity as $1 - d$ and then compute $\ln(1 - d)$ as a power series that converges quickly. However, the latter case requires a correction for the asymptotic formula that is not readily available. For these reasons – and for improved speed – the author (Monahan 1981) devised a direct approximation for $\ln \Phi(x)$, called ALNPHI, which is included in the demonstration **normals**.

(C) *Student's t Distribution*

For the Student's t distribution, let $Q(t \mid k)$ denote the tail probability for k degrees of freedom,

$$Q(t \mid k) = \Pr(X > t \mid X \sim \text{Student's } t \text{ with } k \text{ df}).$$

Note that, for integer values, $Q(t \mid k)$ can be evaluated analytically using the formulas (26.7.3 and 26.7.4) given by Abramowitz and Stegun, whose evaluation effort is proportional to k:

$$Q(t \mid k)$$
$$= \begin{cases} \frac{1}{2} - \frac{\theta}{\pi}, & k = 1, \\ \frac{1}{2} - \frac{1}{\pi}\left\{\theta + \sin\theta\left[\cos\theta + \frac{2}{3}\cos^3\theta + \cdots + \frac{2\times4\times\cdots\times(k-3)}{1\times3\times\cdots\times(k-2)}\cos^{k-2}\theta\right]\right\} & k \text{ odd}, \\ \frac{1}{2} - \sin\theta\left\{1 + \frac{1}{2}\cos^2\theta + \frac{1\times3}{2\times4}\cos^4\theta + \cdots + \frac{1\times3\times\cdots\times(k-3)}{2\times4\times\cdots\times(k-2)}\cos^{k-2}\theta\right\} & k \text{ even}, \end{cases}$$
$$(7.7.5)$$

where $\tan\theta = t/\sqrt{k}$ or $\theta = \arctan\left(t/\sqrt{k}\right)$. Note the potential for cancellation for large values of $t/\sqrt{k}$; particular care needs to be taken, which may include reworking the arctan calculation. For exact evaluation with large values of k, an alternative representation that uses the incomplete beta function,

$$Q(t \mid k) = \tfrac{1}{2}I_x(k/2, 1/2) \quad \text{for } x = k/(k + t^2), \tag{7.7.6}$$

would be preferred. The incomplete beta function $I_x(\cdot, \cdot)$ will be discussed further in the context of the F distribution.

For more accurate results, in particular for large values of t, the first step is avoiding some of the trigonometric evaluations. Notice that if $\theta = \arctan\left(t/\sqrt{k}\right)$ then

$$\sin(\theta) = 1/\sqrt{1 + k/t^2} \quad \text{and} \quad \cos(\theta) = \left(\sqrt{k}/t\right)/\sqrt{1 + k/t^2},$$

so $Q(t \mid k)$ can be computed for k even without sine and cosine. Write $w = k/t^2$; then, for even k we have

$$Q(t \mid k) = \frac{\sqrt{1 + w} - B}{2\sqrt{1 + w}}, \quad \text{where } B = \sum_{j=1}^{n/2-1} c_j \left(\frac{w}{1 + w}\right)^j \tag{7.7.7}$$

with $c_j = (2j - 1)c_{j-1}/(2j)$ and $c_0 = 1$. A similar expression obtains for k odd:

$$Q(t \mid k) = \frac{1}{\pi}\left[\frac{\pi}{2} - \arctan\left(\frac{t}{\sqrt{k}}\right) - \frac{\sqrt{w}}{1 + w}\sum_{j=1}^{(n-3)/2} d_j w^j\right], \tag{7.7.8}$$

where $d_j = 2jd_{j-1}/(2j + 1)$ and $d_0 = 1$. Now, for very large t and small w, serious cancellation occurs in both cases. For even k, however, expand $\sqrt{1 + w}$ in a power series as in (7.6.1),

$$\sqrt{1 + w} = 1 + \tfrac{1}{2}w - \tfrac{1}{8}w^2 + \tfrac{1}{16}w^3 - \tfrac{5}{128}w^4 + \tfrac{7}{256}w^5 - \cdots;$$

then the subtraction in the numerator $\sqrt{1 + w} - B$ of (7.7.7) is done matching powers of w. (Notice that analytic cancellation is not possible.) For (7.7.8) (k odd), expand in another power series,

$$\frac{\pi}{2} - \arctan\left(\frac{t}{\sqrt{k}}\right) = \frac{1}{\sqrt{w}}\left[1 - \frac{w}{3} + \frac{w^2}{5} - \frac{w^3}{7} + \frac{w^4}{9} - \cdots\right],$$

but then multiply by $(1 + w)$ and cancel analytically the coefficients of like powers of w. See the demonstration program **ttail**, as well as Exercises 7.36 and 7.37.

(D) *Chi-Square, Poisson, and Incomplete Gamma*

For the chi-square distribution, let $Q(x \mid m)$ denote the tail probability for m degrees of freedom,

$$Q(x \mid m) = \Pr(X > x \mid X \sim \text{chi-square with } m \text{ df}).$$

For integer values of m, $Q(x \mid m)$ can be found analytically; however, since the number of terms increases with m, this route is seldom practical. This result follows from its relationship with the Poisson,

$$\Pr(Y < j \mid Y \sim \text{Poisson}(\lambda)) = Q(\lambda/2 \mid j).$$

Abramowitz and Stegun gave two power series expansions, neither of which can be used blindly. For high accuracy, Gautschi (1979) gave algorithms for computing the incomplete gamma function $\Gamma(m, x)$, which is related to the chi-square tail by the identity $Q(x \mid m) = 1 - \Gamma(m/2, x/2)/\Gamma(m/2)$. For computing the incomplete gamma function,

$$\Gamma(a, x) = \int_0^x t^{a-1} e^{-t} \, dt, \tag{7.7.9}$$

Gautschi broke the problem down into three parts. For small x $(x < 1.5)$ and smaller a, he suggested using an alternating power series:

$$\Gamma(a, x) = \Gamma(a) - \frac{x^a}{a} - x^a \sum_{j=1}^{\infty} \frac{(-x)^j}{(a+j)j!}.$$

For $a < x$, he suggested a rewritten form of the continued fraction due to Legendre:

$$\Gamma(a, x) = \cfrac{(x+1-a)^{-1} x^a e^{-x}}{1 + \cfrac{\alpha_1}{1 + \cfrac{\alpha_2}{1 + \cfrac{\alpha_3}{1 + \cdots}}}}, \quad \text{where } \alpha_j = \frac{j(a-j)}{(x+2j-1-a)(x+2j+1+a)}.$$

For $a > x$, Gautschi suggested the power series for the tail:

$$1 - \frac{\Gamma(a, x)}{\Gamma(a)} = x^a e^{-x} \sum_0^{\infty} \frac{x^j}{\Gamma(a+j+1)}.$$

These methods are implemented in two forms, **pgamma** for $\Gamma(a, x)/\Gamma(a)$ and the complementary **qgamma** for $1 - \Gamma(a, x)/\Gamma(a)$.

For approximations, the most common is the Wilson–Hilferty,

$$Q(x \mid m) \approx 1 - \Phi\left\{ \frac{(x/m)^{1/2} - (1 - 2/(9m))}{2/(9m)} \right\}, \tag{7.7.10}$$

which is accurate for large values of m.

(E) *F and Beta Distributions*

Before relating these two distributions, first define

$$Q(x \mid m_1, m_2) = \Pr(X > x \mid X \sim F \text{ with } m_1 \text{ and } m_2 \text{ df}).$$

Then the tail probability is related to the incomplete beta function by

$$Q(x \mid m_1, m_2) = I_y(m_2/2, m_1/2) \quad \text{for } y = m_2/(m_2 + xm_1), \qquad (7.7.11)$$

where $\Pr(Y \le y \mid Y \sim \text{beta}(a, b)) = I_y(a, b)$ is the incomplete beta integral

$$I_y(a, b) = \frac{\Gamma(a+b)}{\Gamma(a)\Gamma(b)} \int_0^y t^{a-1}(1-t)^{b-1} \, dt \quad (0 < a, \ 0 < b, \ 0 \le x \le 1). \quad (7.7.12)$$

Exact formulas are available for integer a and b (or even m_1 and m_2), but the effort will be proportional to the smaller of the pair of arguments. Accurate evaluation of the incomplete beta function is a difficult task. For values of b below 1, the following power series is effective:

$$I_y(a, b) = \frac{\Gamma(a+b)}{\Gamma(a+1)\Gamma(b)} y^a \left[1 + a \sum_{j=1}^{\infty} \frac{(1-b)(2-b)\cdots(j-b)y^j}{j! \, (a+j)} \right]. \quad (7.7.13)$$

A reduction–duplication formula can be used to reduce b below 1 while increasing a:

$$I_y(a, b) = \frac{\Gamma(a+b)}{\Gamma(a+1)\Gamma(b)} y^a (1-y)^{b-1} + I_y(a+1, b-1). \quad (7.7.14)$$

DiDonato and Morris (1992) gave an improved version of a continued fraction expression for large values of a and b:

$$I_y(a, b) = \frac{\Gamma(a+b)}{\Gamma(a)\Gamma(b)} \cfrac{y^a(1-y)^b}{\beta_0 + \cfrac{\alpha_1}{\beta_1 + \cfrac{\alpha_2}{\beta_2 + \cfrac{\alpha_3}{\beta_3 + \cdots}}}},$$

where

$$\beta_1 = \frac{a}{a+b}(\lambda + 1), \qquad \lambda = a - (a+b)y,$$

$$\alpha_j = \frac{(a+j-1)(a+b+j-1)}{(a+2j-1)^2} j(b-j)y^2,$$

$$\beta_j = j + \frac{j(b-j)y}{a+2j-1} + \frac{a+j}{a+2j+1}[\lambda + 1 + n(2-y)].$$

The power series method works best for small values of y, and the continued fraction works best for $y < a/(a + b)$. For other situations, a reflection–symmetry relation is employed:

$$I_y(a, b) = 1 - I_{1-y}(b, a). \qquad (7.7.15)$$

Thus, the grand strategy is to (i) use the continued fraction when both a and b are large (> 20) and (ii) use (7.7.14) to reduce **b** below 1 and then use the power series method. With one caveat, this approach works reasonably well and is implemented in **bratio**. That caveat regards the difficult situation with large values of a, small b, and large y (or the complement: small a, large b, and small y). Slow convergence of the power series can be avoided using reflection (7.7.15), but only to face major loss in accuracy due to cancellation. This situation is so bad that DiDonato and Morris return both pieces, $I_y(a, b)$ and $1 - I_y(a, b)$, as well as constructing a special method for this case. The code in **bratio** does not achieve the precision of other codes in this chapter, since that pursuit would merely lead to reproducing the algorithm of DiDonato and Morris (1992). Bosten and Battiste (1973) gave an effective algorithm for computing the incomplete beta function that also employs the power series method and a reduction formula, but it can be slow for large values of a and b. Majumder and Bhattacharjee (1973) coded a method of Soper (1921), employing the reduction formula (7.7.14) but using a slower method based on the relation

$$I_y(a, b) = \frac{\Gamma(a + b)}{\Gamma(a + 1)\Gamma(b)} y^a (1 - y)^b + I_y(a + 1, b), \qquad (7.7.16)$$

essentially increasing a until $I_y(a + k, b)$ vanishes.

(F) *Inverse Normal*

For most cases, the percentile points of a distribution are usually found by computing the root to the equation $P(x) = u$; these problems will be faced in Chapter 8. For the normal distribution, however, there is considerable call for computing $\Phi^{-1}(u)$. Odeh and Evans (1974) found a rational function approximation in the transformed variable $y = \sqrt{-2 \log u}$ of the form

$$\Phi^{-1}(u) \approx y + p(y)/q(y).$$

Bailey (1981, in the same journal but without reference to Odeh and Evans) proposed a two-piece approximation based on the same transformation. One advantage of Vedder's (1993) simple approximation normal distribution function (7.7.4) is that the inverse is not terribly complicated:

$$\Phi^{-1}(u) \approx -2\sqrt{A} \sinh\left\{ \sinh^{-1}\left(\frac{B}{A\sqrt{A}} \right) \Big/ 3 \right\}, \qquad (7.7.17)$$

where $A = a/(3b)$ and $B = (1 - u)/(2ub)$.

(G) *Bivariate Normal*

Among the many functions encountered in statistics, the last to be discussed here is the bivariate normal distribution function:

$$P(x, y, r) = \Pr(X \leq x, Y \leq y \mid X, Y \sim N(0, 1), \text{cov}(X, Y) = r).$$

A simple power series expansion in the correlation r exists (Abramowitz and Stegun, 26.3.29), but it is notoriously slow in converging for large values of r. Dresner (1978) gave a clever method that can be used at any level of accuracy. Using three different identities, Dresner converted all cases to a double integral over the whole first quadrant of a function that can be shown to be bounded between 0 and 1. Integration by a product Gauss–Laguerre quadrature formula (see Chapter 10) gives higher accuracy for additional evaluations. A product 5-point rule (25 evaluations) gives more than six digits; four times as much effort (10-point rule) yields nearly twelve digits. Dresner and Wesolowsky (1990) made some marginal improvements. Divgi (1979) took a completely different direction, expressing the probability in terms of triangular sector (following a route of Ruben 1961) and then finding an accurate approximation for an integral therein. See the demonstration **bvnrml** for a comparison of the two methods.

Programs and Demonstrations

runge1 *Demonstration of the Runge phenomenon from interpolation at equally spaced points*
Using equally spaced points on $(-4, +4)$, a polynomial interpolating the function $z(x) = 1/(1+x^2)$ is found by solving a system of linear equations using **gauspp** and **gausse**. The routine **gaucpp** also gives a condition estimate described in Chapter 3.

runge2 *Contrasting performance of polynomial interpolation*
In contrast to **runge1**, the interpolant is determined by the roots of the Chebyshev polynomials $T_n(x)$, $x_i = \cos\left(\frac{2i-1}{2n}\pi\right)$. The same function is used and the same computation route is followed.

splint *Contrasting performance of spline interpolation*
In contrast to **runge1** and **runge2**, the cubic spline interpolation is used on the same function $z(x)$ on equally spaced points in the interval $(-4, +4)$ following the methods described in Section 7.3.
splstn – subroutine to solve (7.3.8) for the second derivatives M_j with natural spline conditions.
splstd – subroutine to solve (7.3.8) for the second derivatives M_j with derivative conditions.
strids – solves a tridiagonal system of equations using banded Gaussian elimination.
splev – evaluates the interpolatory cubic spline function $S(x)$.
jfind – given x, finds the appropriate interval I_j; used by **splev**.

splsmu *Test/demonstration of smoothing splines*
Eubank (1988, pp. 271–2) gave an example of smoothing splines with $n = 72$ observations, stating that the value $\lambda = 1.38$ minimizes the GCV criterion (7.4.10)

(but uses $\lambda = .699163$). In this problem, the observations are equally spaced in x (time) with $h_j = 1$, making the problem relatively easy. The smoothing spline is found by two computational routes. The first route is a demonstration of the routine **splsmu**. The second route takes advantage of the simple structure arising from the equal spacing, leading to constant bands on the matrix ($\mathbf{E}^* + 6t\mathbf{CC}^\mathrm{T}$) of (7.4.8) with the diagonal $4 + 36t$: first, super/sub $1 - 24t$; second, super/sub diagonal $6t$. This matrix is then Toeplitz and so the methods of Section 3.5 can be employed; thus, the second route is to use the Levinson–Durbin algorithm. These two quite different methods agree on this rather large problem in single precision, but they disagree somewhat with Eubank's results. (I shall resist the temptation to speculate on the reasons, stating only that I would tend to rely on my own results.)

splsmu – subroutine to compute fitted values **z** and second derivatives **m** for smoothing splines.

levdrb – Levinson–Durbin algorithm described in Chapter 3.

eppright.dat – data used in Eubank's example, from Eppright et al. (1972).

splrgm   *Test/demonstration program of interpolatory cubic spline regression*
Poirier (1973) gave an example of the average speed of the winners of the Indianapolis 500 races for the years 1911–71 (excepting the war years 1917–18 and 1942–45). These interruptions also may be points of technological change, and so four knots are used in his analysis – at years 11, 17.5, 43.5, and 72. The estimates of fitted values at the knots are computed, along with their estimated covariance matrix and the estimates of the second derivatives there. Also computed is the error sum of squares from two routes.

splrgm – computes estimates of fitted values and second derivatives for regression splines. (Uses **chlzoi** and **rot734**, Givens rotations.)

indy500.dat – winning speeds for the Indianapolis 500 for 1911–71.

gamma   *Test/demonstration of gamma and log of the gamma function*
The gamma function routine GAMMA and the natural log routine ALGAMA are tested by computing values that appear in Tables 6.1, 6.3, and 6.4 of Abramowitz and Stegun (1970). See the file **dgamma** for a double precision version (**dgamma** and **dlgama**).

gamma – computes gamma function for positive arguments.

algama – computes the natural logarithm of the gamma function for positive arguments.

normals   *Comparison of methods to compute the normal distribution function*
Several routines are evaluated in three different comparisons. Two routines for the $\Phi(x)$ and $1 - \Phi(x)$ are given: one pair (of library quality) uses rational function approximations from Hart et al. (1968); the other pair uses the simple approximation of Vedder (1993). The algorithm for $\log(\Phi(x))$ (Monahan 1981) is also tested and compared. The first test is to produce a simple table. Next the tail probabilities from **alnphi** are checked against Table 26.2 in Abramowitz and Stegun. Finally, some random arguments are generated so that the various routines can be compared.

cdfn – computes the normal distribution function to library quality.

cdcn – computes the complement of the normal distribution function, $1 - \Phi(x)$; companion to **cdfn**.

cdfved – computes the normal distribution function using Vedder's approximation.

cdcved – computes the complement of the normal distribution function, $1 - \Phi(x)$; companion to **cdfved**.

alnphi – computes the natural logarithm of the normal distribution function.

ttail *Test/demonstration program for Student's t tail probabilities*
Reproduces Abramowitz and Stegun's table of t critical values using secant search. Implemented in double precision only.

ttail – computes complementary distribution function $(1 - F)$ of Student's t distribution.

secant – secant root-finding code; see Section 8.3.

pgama *Test/demonstration for incomplete gamma function*
Compares results for integer values of a to analytic results, and computes gamma ratio and complement for several values of a and x for comparison. The file **pdgama** has a double precision version of the code (**pdgama** and **qdgama**), as well as **dlgama**.

pgama – computes incomplete gamma ratio $\Gamma(a, x)/\Gamma(a)$ using methods of Section 7.7(E).

qgama – computes complementary incomplete gamma ratio, $1 - \Gamma(a, x)/\Gamma(a)$.

algama – computes log of gamma function.

bratio *Test/demonstration of incomplete beta function*
Uses methods as described in Section 7.7(E) for computing the incomplete beta function. Also uses **algama** for computing log of the gamma function.

bratio – computes incomplete beta function.

bvnrml *Computes bivariate normal probabilities*
Two algorithms are compared here, one by Dresner (1978) and one by Divgi (1979), that employ quite different methods; but the results compare well. Both methods use **cdfn** for $\Phi(x)$.

p2norm – controlling routine for Dresner's method; employs reproduction formulas.

q2norm – part of Dresner group of routines; called by **p2norm**; calls **phihkr**.

phihkr – core routine of Dresner's method that does the numerical integration.

pdivgi – controlling routine for Divgi's method; calls **rubenw**.

rubenw – computes Divgi's approximation to Ruben's W function.

Exercises

7.1 Given F_1, F_2, F_3 and $F_0 = 0$, find the derivative at the origin of the cubic interpolant of the points (i, F_i) for $i = 0, 1, 2, 3$.

7.2 Interpolate the square root function at $x = 1/4$, $1/2$, and 1 with a quadratic function.

7.3 Interpolate the square root function at $x = 1/4$, $1/2$, and 1 with a rational function that is linear in both numerator and denominator.

7.4   From a table of F critical values for $\nu_1 = 3$ degrees of freedom and for three values of $\nu_2 = 60$, 120, and ∞ df, we have (respectively) 2.76, 2.68, and 2.61. Find the critical value for $\nu_2 = 75$ df by three methods: (a) linear interpolation on ν_2; (b) linear interpolation on $1/\nu_2$; (c) quadratic interpolation on $1/\nu_2$.

7.5   Given the following table values, find x_p such that $\Phi(x_p) = .99$ by linear and quadratic inverse interpolation.

x	$\Phi(x)$
2.3	.98927589
2.4	.99180246
2.5	.99379033

7.6   The following table gives t critical values for .01, .005, and .0005 for certain values of degrees of freedom. Interpolate the following t table for 40 df in two ways, once with df as the variable and once for 1/df. Which method gets closer to the correct values of 2.423, 2.704, and 3.551?

df	Level		
	.01	.005	.0005
30	2.457	2.750	3.646
60	2.390	2.660	3.460
120	2.358	2.617	3.373
∞	2.326	2.526	3.291

7.7   Fuller (1996, p. 363) gave tables for the critical values of Fisher's periodogram test statistic Y, which is the maximum of m χ_2^2 random variables divided by their average. For one test level, interpolate this table to obtain critical values for $m = 25$. Which method gets closer to the correct values of 5.130, 5.701, and 6.955?

m	Level		
	.10	.05	.01
20	4.862	5.408	6.594
30	5.346	5.935	7.237
40	5.681	6.295	7.663

7.8   Fuller (1996, p. 364) also gave the exact distribution function for Fisher's periodogram test statistic cited in Exercise 7.7:

$$1 - F(y) = \sum_{j=1}^{k} (-1)^{j-1} \binom{m}{j} \left(1 - \frac{jy}{m}\right)^{m-1}, \quad \text{where } k = \left[\frac{m}{y}\right] \text{ and } y \in [1, m].$$

Discuss the difficulties in its computation; then write an algorithm to compute them and check your results from that exercise.

7.9   Compare your code in Exercise 7.8 to the approximation given by Bloomfield (1976, p. 112):

$$\hat{F}(y + \log m) = \exp(-e^{-y}).$$

7.10 Interpolate the logarithmic function at the integers 1 through n; use the general formulas or solve a system of equations. Does this problem display the Runge phenomenon?

7.11 Following Examples 7.1 and 7.2, find the rational function interpolant at equally spaced points on $(-4, +4)$ using (7.2.6). Does this interpolant exhibit the Runge behavior?

7.12 Verify equation (7.3.2) by showing that S'' is linear and $S''(x_j) = M_j$.

7.13 Obtain (7.3.3) from (7.3.2), and show that $S(x_j) = z_j$.

7.14 Find the derivative of the cubic spline given by (7.3.3). Write a routine for its evaluation following the form of **splev**.

7.15 Using your solution to Exercise 7.14, compare the derivative of the spline found in **splint** with the derivative of the function interpolated, $z'(x) = -2x(1 + x^2)^{-2}$.

7.16 Using the solution to Exercise 7.14, check the accuracy of spline derivatives given by (7.3.10) for $k = 0, 1, 2$.

7.17 Show that $\int |S''(x)|^2 \, dx = (1/6) \mathbf{m}^{*\mathrm{T}} \mathbf{E}^* \mathbf{m}^*$.

7.18 Suppose we integrate a cubic spline interpolant from x_1 to x_n. What is the value in terms of zs and xs?

7.19 Taking the smoothing parameter $\mathbf{t}$ to zero in (7.4.1) forces interpolation of the smoothing spline. What happens as $t \to \infty$? Describe the resultant regression problem, taking the easy case of equally spaced points.

7.20 Let $\mathbf{A}$ be a banded positive definite matrix with bandwidth p, and let $\mathbf{b}$ be a vector with all elements zero excepting just one nonzero element. How much work does it take to compute $\mathbf{b}^{\mathrm{T}} \mathbf{A}^{-1} \mathbf{b}$?

7.21 Compute the 5×5 matrix $\mathbf{V}$ whose elements are $V_{ij} = \langle x^{i-1}, x^{j-1} \rangle = \int_{-1}^{1} x^{i+j-2} \, dx$. Have you seen this matrix before?

7.22 Compute the Cholesky factor of the matrix $\mathbf{V}$ found in Exercise 7.21. Relate this to the Legendre polynomials in Table 7.2.

7.23 Expand e^x in terms of Legendre polynomials to at least $P_3(x)$.

7.24 Write code to compute the Wallis function

$$\frac{\Gamma\left(\frac{1}{2}(k+1)\right)}{\Gamma\left(\frac{1}{2}\right)\Gamma\left(\frac{1}{2}(k+2)\right)}$$

for integer k. What is the behavior as $k \to \infty$?

7.25 Compute the best L_2 approximation by a polynomial of degree 2 to the square root function on the interval $[1/2, 1]$.

7.26 Compute the best L_∞ approximation by a polynomial of degree 2 to the square root function on the interval $[1/2, 1]$.

7.27 Why should sqrt(x) be preferred to x**0.5 as a way to compute a square root?

7.28 Write an algorithm to compute the approximation in Exercise 7.23 using the recursive formula given in Dahlquist and Bjorck (1974, sec. 4.4.3). This formula makes an orthogonal series expansion as fast as Horner's method for any polynomial.

7.29 *Economizing Power Series.* Define $s_4(x)$ as the fourth-degree polynomial approximation from the power series expansion (7.6.1). Approximate $s_4(x)$ further by a quadratic by substituting $(3/4)(x-1)$ for $(x-1)^3$ and $(x-1)^2 - 1/8$ for $(x-1)^4$; compare the quadratic approximation that follows from these substitutions to the Chebyshev approximation from Exercise 7.3. (These substitutions arise from the minimum norm property of $T_n(x)$: $T_3(u) = u^3 - (3/4)u$ and $T_4(u) = u^4 - u^2 + 1/8$.)

7.30 For a fixed level of accuracy – say, 10^{-6} – how many steps are needed in the continued fractions g and h of (7.7.2) and (7.7.3) for various values of the arguments?

7.31 The correction $\theta(x)$ in (7.6.2) for Stirling's formula has the series expansion

$$\theta(x) = \frac{1}{12x} - \frac{1}{360x^3} + \frac{1}{1260x^5} - \frac{1}{1680x^7} + \cdots + \frac{B_{2m}}{2m(2m-1)x^{2m-1}} + \cdots,$$

where the higher terms (not needed for this exercise) involve Bernoulli numbers B_k. Computing a least maximum approximation on an infinite interval such as $[8, \infty]$ seems forbidding until you consider changing variables to $u = 1/x$. Find a least maximum approximation for $\theta(x)$ using just two constants.

7.32 Draw a graph of the error, both absolute and relative, in Vedder's approximation (7.7.4).

7.33 Lew (1981) gave another simple approximation to $\Phi(x)$:

$$1 - \Phi(x) \approx \begin{cases} 1/2 - (x - x^3/7)/\sqrt{2\pi} & \text{for } 0 \le x \le 1, \\ (1+x)\phi(x)/(1+x+x^2) & \text{for } x > 1. \end{cases}$$

Compare this approximation with Vedder's. Which do you prefer?

7.34 Verify the inverse of Vedder's approximation (7.7.17).

7.35 Compare Odeh and Evan's (1974) formula for $\Phi^{-1}(u)$ to Vedder's method.

7.36 Prove the following power series representation for the tail probabilities for Student's t distribution:

$$Q(t \mid k) = \frac{\Gamma((k+1)/2)}{\Gamma(k/2)\sqrt{\pi}} u^{-k/2} \sum_{j=0}^{\infty} \frac{c_j}{(k+2j)u^j},$$

where

$$c_0 = 1, \quad c_j = \frac{2j-1}{2j} c_{j-1}, \quad \text{and} \quad u = 1 + \frac{t^2}{k}.$$

(*Hint:* Change variables $y = 1/\sqrt{1 + t^2/k}$ and then expand $1/\sqrt{1-v}$ in a power series, as in (7.6.1).)

7.37 Implement the power series in Exercise 7.36 as a computational formula and compare its performance to that of **ttail**. Which is better?

7.38 The density of the correlation coefficient r of a sample of size $N = n+1$ from a bivariate normal distribution with correlation ρ is given by

$$f(r \mid \rho) = \frac{(n-1)\Gamma(n)}{\sqrt{2\pi}} (1-\rho^2)^{n/2}(1-\rho r)^{-n+1/2}(1-r^2)^{(n-3)/2}$$

$$\times \sum_{j=0}^{\infty} \frac{\Gamma\left(j + \frac{1}{2}\right)^2}{\Gamma\left(\frac{1}{2}\right)^2 \Gamma\left(n + j + \frac{1}{2}\right)} \frac{(1+\rho r)^j}{2^j j!}.$$

(a) Simplify the gamma functions to facilitate computation.
(b) Write code to compute this function for any value of r and ρ.
(c) Plot the density for $\rho = \pm 1/3$ and 0 and check symmetry.

7.39 Consider the knots $x_i = \frac{i-1}{n-1}, i = 1, \ldots, n$, and design points $u_j = \frac{j}{N}, j = 1, \ldots, N$. a) For $n = 10$ and $N = 50$ and degree $p = 3$, construct the design matrices $\mathbf{X}_T$ using the truncated power basis and $\mathbf{X}_B$ using B-splines. b) Find the linear transformation $\mathbf{C}$ such that $\mathbf{X}_B = \mathbf{X}_T \mathbf{C}$. c) Compute the condition numbers for $\mathbf{X}_T$ and $\mathbf{X}_B$. d) Repeat with varying values of n, N, and p.

7.40 An alternative method for computing the solution to (7.4.15) is to augment the design matrix $\mathbf{X}$ with rows $\lambda^p \mathbf{L}$ where $\mathbf{L}\mathbf{L}^T$ is the Cholesky decomposition of $\mathbf{D}$, and zeros as the corresponding responses to $\mathbf{y}$ and then solve the least squares problem. a) Verify the algebra behind this approach. b) Can this be modified easily for varying values of λ? (Hint: Givens 'on the fly')

7.41 Show that for the B-spline functions $B_{ik}(u)$, $\sum_i B_{ik}(u) = 1$.

7.42 Using B-splines, the rows of $\mathbf{X}_B$ have only $p - 1$ nonzero entries. Show that the inner product matrix $\mathbf{X}_B^T \mathbf{X}_B$ is banded and find its bandwidth. Can this structure be exploited in the computation of

$$\mathbf{A}(\lambda)\mathbf{y} = \mathbf{X}(\mathbf{X}^T \mathbf{X} + \lambda^{2p}\mathbf{D})^{-1}\mathbf{X}^T$$

when the number of knots n is large?

References

The *Handbook of Mathematical Functions* (Abramowitz and Stegun 1970) includes a great wealth of practical information. Identities, series expansions, asymptotic formulas, and approximations are given for many of the functions mentioned in this chapter, as well as relationships with other functions and the best tables extant. In addition, there are chapters on numerical methods and probability functions. In the abstract direction, the book by Davis (1975) is well written and contains much of the mathematical background for all of numerical analysis. Further information on interpolation can be found in many good numerical analysis texts. Ahlberg, Nilsson, and Walsh (1967) is still a good reference on splines; the original Reinsch (1967, 1971) papers on smoothing splines are clearly presented. The book by Hart et al. (1968) includes a practical guide in addition to tables of approximating functions.

Milton Abramowitz and Irene A. Stegun (Eds.) (1970), *Handbook of Mathematical Functions.* New York: Dover.

J. H. Ahlberg, E. N. Nilsson, and J. L. Walsh (1967), *The Theory of Splines and Their Applications.* New York: Academic Press.

B. J. R. Bailey (1981), "Alternatives to Hastings' Approximation to the Inverse of the Normal Cumulative Distribution Function," *Applied Statistics* 30: 275–6.

Douglas M. Bates, Mary J. Lindstrom, Grace Wahba, and Brian S. Yandell (1987), "GCVPACK: Routines for Generalized Cross Validation," *Communications in Statistics B* 16: 263–97.

Peter Bloomfield (1976), *Fourier Analysis of Time Series: An Introduction.* New York: Wiley.

N. E. Bosten and E. L. Battiste (1973), "Remark on Algorithm 179, Incomplete Beta Ratio," *Communications of the ACM* 17: 156–7.

W. J. Cody, W. Fraser, and J. F. Hart (1968), "Rational Chebyshev Approximation Using Linear Equations," *Numerische Mathematik* 12: 242–51.

William J. Cody and William Waite (1980), *Software Manual for the Elementary Functions.* Englewood Cliffs, NJ: Prentice-Hall.

P. Craven and G. Wahba (1979), "Smoothing Noisy Data with Spline Functions," *Numerische Mathematik* 31: 377–403.

Germund Dahlquist and Ake Bjorck (1974), *Numerical Methods* (trans. by N. Anderson). Englewood Cliffs, NJ: Prentice-Hall.

Philip J. Davis (1975), *Interpolation and Approximation*. New York: Dover.

Carl De Boor (1978), *A Practical Guide to Splines*. New York: Springer-Verlag.

Armido R. DiDonato and Alfred H. Morris, Jr. (1992), "Algorithm 708: Significant Digit Computation of the Incomplete Beta Ratio," *ACM Transactions on Mathematical Software* 18: 360–73.

D. R. Divgi (1979), "Calculation of Univariate and Bivariate Normal Probability Functions," *Annals of Statistics* 7: 903–10.

Zvi Dresner (1978), "Computation of the Bivariate Normal Integral," *Mathematics of Computation* 32: 277–9.

Zvi Dresner and G. O. Wesolowsky (1990), "On the Computation of the Bivariate Normal Integral," *Journal of Statistical Computation and Simulation* 35: 101–7.

E. S. Eppright, H. M. Fox, B. A. Fryer, G. H. Lamkin, V. M. Vivian, and E. S. Fuller (1972), "Nutrition of Infants and Preschool Children in the North Central Region of the United States of America," *World Review of Nutrition and Dietetics* 14: 269–332.

R. L. Eubank (1988), *Spline Smoothing and Nonparametric Regression*. New York: Marcel Dekker.

C. T. Fike (1968), *Computer Evaluation of Mathematical Functions*. Englewood Cliffs, NJ: Prentice-Hall.

Wayne A. Fuller (1996), *Introduction to Statistical Time Series*, 2nd ed. New York: Wiley.

W. Gautschi (1979), "A Computational Procedure for Incomplete Gamma Functions," *ACM Transactions on Mathematical Software* 5: 466–81.

C. A. Hall and W. W. Meyer (1976), "Optimal Error Bounds for Cubic Spline Interpolation," *Journal of Approximation Theory* 16: 105–22.

John F. Hart, E. W. Cheney, Charles L. Lawson, Hans J. Maehly, Charles K. Mesztenyi, John R. Rice, Henry G. Thatcher, Jr., and Christoph Witzgall (1968), *Computer Approximations*. New York: Wiley; reprinted 1978 by Krieger (Malabar, FL).

C. Hastings (1955), *Approximations for Digital Computers*. Princeton, NJ: Princeton University Press.

M. F. Hutchinson (1986), "Algorithm 642: A Fast Procedure for Calculating Minimum Cross-Validation Cubic Smoothing Splines," *ACM Transactions on Mathematical Software* 12: 150–3.

Robert A. Lew (1981), "An Approximation to the Cumulative Normal Distribution with Simple Coefficients," *Applied Statistics* 30: 299–301.

Robert F. Ling (1978), "A Study of the Accuracy of Some Approximation for t, chi-square, and F Tail Probabilities," *Journal of the American Statistical Association* 73: 274–83.

K. L. Majumder and G. P. Bhattacharjee (1973), "Algorithm AS63: The Incomplete Beta Integral," *Applied Statistics* 22: 409–11.

John F. Monahan (1981), "Approximating the Log of the Normal Cumulative," in W. F. Eddy (Ed.), *Computer Science and Statistics: Proceedings of the Thirteenth Annual Symposium on the Interface*, pp. 304–7. New York: Springer-Verlag.

John F. Monahan and Leonard A. Stefanski (1992), "Normal Scale Mixture Approximations to $F^*(z)$ and Computation of the Logistic–Normal Integral," in N. Balakrishnan (Ed.), *Handbook of the Logistic Distribution*, pp. 529–40. New York: Marcel Dekker.

R. E. Odeh and J. O. Evans (1974), "Algorithm AS70: The Percentile Points of the Normal Distribution," *Applied Statistics* 23: 96–7.

Dale J. Poirier (1973), "Piecewise Regression Using Cubic Splines," *Journal of the American Statistical Association* 68: 515–24.

Christian H. Reinsch (1967), "Smoothing by Spline Functions," *Numerische Mathematik* 10: 177–83.

Christian H. Reinsch (1971), "Smoothing by Spline Functions II," *Numerische Mathematik* 16: 451–4.

Harold Ruben (1961), "Probability Contents of Regions under Spherical Normal Distributions III: The Bivariate Normal Integral," *Annals of Mathematical Statistics* 32: 171–86.

David Ruppert, M. P. Wand, and R. J. Carroll (2003), *Semiparametric Regression*. New York: Cambridge University Press.

B. W. Silverman (1985), "Some Aspects of the Spline Smoothing Approach to Nonparametric Regression Curve Fitting," *Journal of the Royal Statistical Society B* 47: 1–52.

H. E. Soper (1921), "The Numerical Evaluation of the Incomplete Beta-Function," in *Tracts for Computers* (no. 7). Cambridge University Press.

G. Szego (1959), *Orthogonal Polynomials*. Providence, RI: American Mathematical Society.

John D. Vedder (1993), "An Invertible Approximation to the Normal Distribution Function," *Computational Statistics and Data Analysis* 16: 119–23.

8

Introduction to Optimization and Nonlinear Equations

8.1 Introduction

This chapter serves as an appetizer to the main course, maximum likelihood and non-linear least squares. This is stated so boldly because many statistical problems of this type originate in estimation problems with maximum likelihood (or a similar criterion) as the goal. Our discussion begins with some of the background calculus and definitions. Next, the discussion turns to the safe and slow methods for optimization in a single variable, for which the statistical term "nonparametric" has the correct connotations. Next, the root-finding problem is addressed with the standard techniques, Newton and secant methods, followed by a brief presentation of convergence rates. After a short digression on stopping and condition, the multivariate problem is first approached with Newton's methods. After a second digression on numerical differentiation, quasi-Newton methods are discussed for optimization and nonlinear equations. Discussions of condition, scaling, and implementation conclude the chapter.

Some topics are *not* addressed in this discussion. One problem is the solution of polynomial equations, which arise rarely in an isolated form in statistics. Constrained optimization can often be avoided through reparameterization. The specialized problem of nonlinear regression is postponed until the next chapter, to be treated as a special topic in maximum likelihood.

Before attacking the problems at hand, it is wise to review some foundations to gain a clearer perspective of the situation. The cornerstone for everything are the first results of calculus, the primary tools in applied mathematics. These results will first be stated in their univariate form. Before this, let us begin with some definitions.

A function f on an interval $[a, b]$ is (strictly) *monotone increasing* if and only if $f(x) < f(y)$ for every $a \leq x < y \leq b$. A *monotone nondecreasing* function satisfies the weak inequality $f(x) \leq f(y)$, and similar adjustments can be made for (strictly) decreasing and nonincreasing.

A function f is (strictly) *unimodal* with *mode* (maximum) at x if and only if f is strictly monotone increasing for $y < x$ and strictly monotone decreasing for $y > x$.

A function f has a *local maximum* at x if and only if there exists a $\delta > 0$ such that $f(y) < f(x)$ for all y with $|y - x| < \delta$.

Theorem 8.1: *If f has a local maximum (minimum) at x and if the derivative $f'(x)$ exists, then $f'(x) = 0$.*

Corollary 8.2: *If f is differentiable on [a, b], then the zeros of f are separated by the zeros of f'.*

Theorem 8.3 (Mean Value Theorem): *If f is continuous in [a, b] and differentiable in (a, b), then there exists c in (a, b) such that $f(b) - f(a) = (b - a)f'(c)$. In other words: There is a tangent parallel to the secant.*

At the risk of overstating the obvious, the first theorem tells where extreme points can occur. Its contraposition – if the derivative at an interior point is *not* zero then the point is not a local optimum – rules out all but a few points (all but one, it is hoped) from consideration. The corollary gives some warning about the ability of function to wiggle. The mean value theorem can be interpreted as stating that all smooth functions are locally linear.

Instead of proceeding to further results along this line, the results need to be restated for the multivariate case, since many of the problems to be faced involve several variables. Now **x** represents a vector of dimension p while the function f is still real-valued, so $f : \mathcal{R}^p \to \mathcal{R}$. The (column) vector of partial derivatives of f evaluated at **x**, also known as the *gradient,* will be denoted by $\nabla f(\mathbf{x})$. The matrix of second partial derivatives evaluated at **x** will be denoted by $\nabla^2 f(\mathbf{x})$, sometimes called the Hessian matrix and denoted by $\mathbf{H}(\mathbf{x})$.

A function f has a *local maximum* (minimum) at **x** if and only if there exists $\delta > 0$ such that $f(\mathbf{y}) \leq f(\mathbf{x})$ for all **y** such that $\|\mathbf{y} - \mathbf{x}\| \leq \delta$. Note that the Euclidean norm is used as the metric.

Theorem 8.4: *If f is continuous and if ∇f exists for all **x** in a region S and has a local maximum (minimum) at **x** in the interior of S, then $\nabla f(\mathbf{x}) = \mathbf{0}$.*

Mean Value Theorems

Theorem 8.5 (Linear): *If f and ∇f are continuous in a region S, then there exists a point **t** on a line segment between **x** and **y** such that*

$$f(\mathbf{x}) = f(\mathbf{y}) + (\mathbf{x} - \mathbf{y})^{\mathsf{T}} \nabla f(\mathbf{t}). \tag{8.1.1}$$

Theorem 8.6 (Quadratic): *If, in addition, $\nabla^2 f(\mathbf{x})$ is continuous on S, then there exists a point **t** in S such that*

$$f(\mathbf{x}) = f(\mathbf{y}) + (\mathbf{x} - \mathbf{y})^{\mathsf{T}} \nabla f(\mathbf{y}) + \tfrac{1}{2}(\mathbf{x} - \mathbf{y})^{\mathsf{T}} \nabla^2 f(\mathbf{t})(\mathbf{x} - \mathbf{y}). \tag{8.1.2}$$

Theorem 8.7: *If $\nabla f(x) = 0$ and $\mathbf{H}(\mathbf{x})$ is continuous and positive (resp., negative) definite for a point **x** in an open convex set, then **x** is a local minimum (resp., maximum).*

For a multivariate function **g** of a vector **x** mapping from $\mathcal{R}^m$ to $\mathcal{R}^n$, the matrix of partial derivatives will be denoted by $\mathbf{J_g}(\mathbf{x})$, so that the (i, j) element is the partial derivative of the ith component of **g** with respect to x_j. Hence, for an affine (generalization of linear) function $\mathbf{g}(\mathbf{x}) = \mathbf{Gx} + \mathbf{h}$, it follows that $\mathbf{J_g} = \mathbf{G}$. The big difference here is that the sought mean value theorem does not exist. However, the best available result has the same basic conclusion: all smooth functions are locally affine.

Theorem 8.8: *If* **g** *is continuous and differentiable in an open convex set S and if* **J** *is Lipschitz continuous in a neighborhood of* **x** *in S, then for* **y** *in that neighborhood of* **x** *we have*

$$\|\mathbf{g}(\mathbf{y}) - \mathbf{g}(\mathbf{x}) - \mathbf{J_g}(\mathbf{x})(\mathbf{y} - \mathbf{x})\| \le (\delta/2)\|\mathbf{y} - \mathbf{x}\|^2, \qquad (8.1.3)$$

where δ *is the Lipschitz constant for* $\mathbf{J_g}$. *Hence* **y** *in an open neighborhood of* **x** *satisfies*

$$\|\mathbf{J_g}(\mathbf{y}) - \mathbf{J_g}(\mathbf{x})\| \le \delta\|\mathbf{y} - \mathbf{x}\|.$$

8.2 Safe Univariate Methods: Lattice Search, Golden Section, and Bisection

The first method to be presented in this chapter is designed to solve one of the simpler problems: finding the maximum of a unimodal function f on a discrete set of points $\{1, 2, \ldots, m\}$ – a lattice – hence the name *lattice search.* Although it has limited applicability, it serves as a springboard to the other problems and methods of this chapter.

The strategy of the lattice search can be described as (i) finding good end strategies for finding the mode on a small set of points and then (ii) employing backwards induction to start with the right strategy to match the optimal ending. Optimal strategy here means the fewest evaluations of the function f that will solve all problems that meet the specifications – that is, any strictly unimodal function.

Begin with $m = 2$, which obviously will require two evaluations of f to determine the maximum. For $m = 3$, there are strategies that can solve it in two evaluations for some functions, but it can easily be shown that three evaluations will be required if we are to solve for *all* functions f. For $m = 4$, there is room for improvement. Notice that a single evaluation at the beginning of the search is really valueless, since we have no idea of what "large" is. It therefore makes sense to begin by evaluating f at a pair of points before deciding what to do next. Symmetry says that these points should be placed so that a reversal of indices yields the same configuration. So for the $m = 4$ problem, the choice is whether to begin with evaluations at the pair 1 and 4 or at 2 and 3. It should be apparent that evaluating at 2 and 3 will disqualify 1 from consideration as a possible mode if $f(3) > f(2)$ (for if the mode were at 1 then the function f would not be unimodal) and will disqualify 4 if $f(2) > f(3)$; notice that no such disqualification will occur for evaluating at 1 and 4. So if f is evaluated at 2 and 3 to start, then the mode can be identified with only three evaluations of f. The advantage is the disqualification of a point.

Although the goal is to disqualify as many points as possible, overzealousness is not rewarded. For a very large problem, the most points can be disqualified by taking two evaluations at the middle. While this eliminates half of the points, it requires two evaluations. The remaining subproblem has one point evaluated but, being at the end, it cannot be effectively exploited; the strategy of cutting the problem size in half requires two evaluations. The optimal strategy, tempering disqualifications and

Table 8.1. *Fibonacci numbers*

n	1	2	3	4	5	6	7	8	9	10
F_n	1	2	3	5	8	13	21	34	55	89

placement of points, becomes apparent only by examining some special cases: $m = 7, 12, 20, 33, \ldots$.

First consider $m = 7$. If the opening evaluations are at 3 and 5, then three points will be initially eliminated, leaving a 4-point problem with one evaluation already taken for the best 4-point problem. A 7-point problem can be done in four evaluations.

Next consider $m = 12$. Taking opening evaluations at 5 and 8 will disqualify five points and so leave either $\{1, 2, 3, 4, \underline{5}, 6, 7\}$ or $\{6, 7, \underline{8}, 9, 10, 11, 12\}$, which are 7-point problems. In the first case, the function f has already been evaluated at 5, so that with another evaluation at 3, the 7-point subproblem can be solved with only three additional evaluations for a total of five. The other subproblem has 8 already available, so the additional one for this is at 10 and so again the subproblem requires only three additional evaluations. Notice that if the first two were taken at 5 and 6, then a 6-point problem would remain that would require four more evaluations for a total of six.

Example 8.1: *Examples of Lattice Search*
Consider how the lattice search strategy solves the following two problems, first with $m = 7$.

m	1	2	3	4	5	6	7
f	.0623	.2804	.5454	.5990	.3726	.1307	.0197

Here we first evaluate at $k = 3$ and 5 and find that $f(3) > f(5)$, so the set $\{1, 2, 3, 4\}$ remains. Now evaluate at $k = 2$, finding $f(2) < f(3)$, leaving $\{3, 4\}$; then the final evaluation at $k = 4$ shows that $f(3) < f(4)$, leaving the singleton set $\{4\}$ as the solution.

m	1	2	3	4	5	6	7	8	9	10	11	12
f	.0040	.0321	.1156	.2580	.3976	.4463	.3727	.2312	.1040	.0321	.0061	.0005

In this second problem, evaluate first at 5 and 8 and find that $f(5) > f(8)$, leaving the set $\{1, 2, 3, 4, 5, 6, 7\}$. Next evaluate at $k = 3$ and find $f(3) < f(5)$, leaving $\{4, 5, 6, 7\}$. The next step finds $f(5) < f(6)$, and we finish at $k = 7$, finding $f(7) < f(6)$. The mode is $k = 6$.

The mystery of the optimal strategy of the lattice search is unveiled with the introduction of the Fibonacci numbers,

$$F_0 = F_1 = 1, \ F_2 = 2, \ F_3 = 3, \ F_4 = 5, \ F_5 = 8, \ \ldots, \ F_{n+1} = F_{n-1} + F_n, \ \ldots$$

(see Table 8.1). The special cases have been one fewer than a Fibonacci number, and the required evaluations have been one fewer than the index.

The optimal strategy for searching for the maximum of a unimodal function on a lattice of points $\{1, 2, \ldots, m = F_n - 1\}$ is to begin by evaluating at the points F_{n-2} and F_{n-1}. If $f(F_{n-2}) > f(F_{n-1})$ (i.e., if the left point is higher), then the points $\{F_{n-1}, \ldots, m\}$ are disqualified, leaving the subproblem with the set $\{1, \ldots, F_{n-1} - 1\}$ and with the evaluation at F_{n-2} perfectly placed. Conversely, if $f(F_{n-2}) < f(F_{n-1})$ then the subproblem has the set $\{F_{n-2} + 1, \ldots, F_n - 1\}$, which also has $F_{n-1} - 1$ elements and with the evaluation at F_{n-1} perfectly placed. A problem with $F_n - 1$ points requires $n - 1$ evaluations to solve. Two details remain to be resolved. First, if the values of the function are the same at F_{n-2} and F_{n-1} then, since the function is strictly unimodal, the mode must be between the two points – in which case it doesn't matter which part is discarded. Second, if the number of points m for the problem at hand is not one fewer than a Fibonacci number, then pad the lattice with points on either end to get to one fewer than a Fibonacci number, where the value of the function at any of these additional points is $-\infty$.

Now the more common problem is searching for the maximum of a unimodal function on a continuum, such as the unit interval $(0, 1)$. One solution approach is to imbed a lattice in the unit interval by placing m points (located at $0, 1/(m - 1)$, $2/(m - 1), \ldots, j/(m - 1), \ldots, 1)$ and then take the limit of the lattice search as $m = F_n - 1$ goes to infinity. The lattice search is defined by the first two evaluations on the set, so consider the limit of those first two points,

$$\lim[(F_{n-2} - 1)/(F_n - 1)] \quad \text{and} \quad \lim[(F_{n-1} - 1)/(F_n - 1)].$$

Let the limit of the ratio F_{n-1}/F_n as $n \to \infty$ be denoted by ϕ; then dividing $F_n = F_{n-2} + F_{n-1}$ by F_{n-1} shows that ϕ satisfies the equation $1/\phi = \phi + 1$ (or $\phi^2 + \phi - 1 = 0$). The positive root of this quadratic equation gives $\phi = (\sqrt{5} - 1)/2 = .618\ldots$, also known as the *golden ratio*. Then the limit of the left starting point of the lattice search is $\phi^2 = .382$, which is symmetrically placed opposite the right starting point ϕ.

This limit of the lattice search is called the *golden section search*. The opening two points are taken at locations ϕ^2 and ϕ. If, without loss of generality, $f(\phi^2) > f(\phi)$, then the remaining interval – the interval of uncertainty – is $(0, \phi)$, for which the evaluation at ϕ^2 is perfectly placed as the right opening point for the remaining subproblem. Notice that the golden section search reduces the interval of uncertainty by $\phi = .618$ with each evaluation.

This golden section search is not the optimal search procedure, but it is a method in common use. The optimal procedure, known as the Fibonacci search, strives to reduce the interval of uncertainty as much as possible by taking its two evaluations as close to the middle as is feasible. Since this is practically impossible on a continuum, a minimum separation d is required so that the two evaluations will give different values. The Fibonacci search also requires that the number of evaluations be known in advance. Because of these requirements, and since the loss in efficiency in using the golden section search is at most the cost of one evaluation, the Fibonacci search is rarely used.

Before closing this section, consider the goal of the Fibonacci search: placing the points of evaluation as close to the middle as possible in order to cut the interval of uncertainty in half. It is the practical obstacle of a continuous unimodal function that prevents this goal from being reached. But suppose that the derivative of the function f

were available, or that some differencing technique could be employed that would convert the problem from one of finding the maximum of a unimodal function f to one of finding the root of a monotone function g on the same interval. The result is the search technique known as *bisection* or *Bolzano's method*. Without loss of generality, let the interval be (a, b) and let $g(a) < 0 < g(b)$. Then, with a single evaluation at the midpoint $(a + b)/2$, the interval of uncertainty can be halved. If $g((a + b)/2)) < 0$ then the root is in the interval $((a + b)/2, b)$; otherwise the new interval is $(a, (a + b)/2)$.

Comparison of these two techniques, golden section and bisection searches, reveals the value of additional information or restrictions. The golden section search solves a less restrictive problem, requiring only a strictly unimodal function. The bisection method, if used to solve the same problem, requires that the derivative of the function exist and be available. Whereas the golden section search reduces the length of the interval of uncertainty by $\phi = .618$ with each additional evaluation, bisection reduces the length of the interval by $1/2$ with each additional evaluation. The similarity of the two methods (both require weak assumptions on the problem) will contrast markedly with the methods introduced in the next section.

Example 8.2: *Example of Golden Section and Bisection Searches*
Let's find the maximum of the simple function $f(x) = \frac{4}{3}\log(1+x) - x$ on $(0, 1)$. For golden section, begin with evaluations at $x = .382$ and $x = .618$ and find $f(.382) = .0494$ and $f(.618) = .0236$, so the interval of uncertainty is $(0, .618)$. Next evaluate at $\phi^3 = .23607$; this yields $f(.236) = .0465 < f(.382)$ as the right endpoint, so drop the left side to make the interval $(.236, .618)$. Next, at the right point of the new interval we have $f(.472) = .0435 < f(.382)$ (the left one), so the interval becomes $(.236, .472)$ with length ϕ^3.

For bisection, we want to find the root of $f'(x) = g(x) = (4/3)/(1+x) - 1$, with a priori knowledge that the function is decreasing (actually, $g(0) = 1/3$ and $g(1) = -1/3$). Evaluate first at $x = 1/2$ and find $g(1/2) = -1/9$, so the new interval is $(0, 1/2)$. Next, $g(1/4) = 1/15 > 0$, so drop the left half to make the new interval $(1/4, 1/2)$. The third evaluation gives $g(3/8) = -1/33 < 0$; drop the right side, leaving the interval $(1/4, 3/8)$. The fourth one gives $g(5/16) = -1/63 < 0$, and the new interval of uncertainty is $(1/4, 5/16)$ with length $1/16 = .0625$ versus $\phi^3 = .236$ for golden section.

8.3 Root Finding

The more common problem is solving a single nonlinear equation, $g(x) = 0$, using evaluations of the function g at specified points and, on occasion, evaluations of the derivative. Often the original problem is one of optimization, where the restatement as a root-finding problem is no major obstacle and the motivation is to take advantage of the improved convergence. All the methods presented here have rather simple motivations, approximating $g(x)$ by a linear function and solving the linear approximation to $g(x) = 0$. Moreover, the reader would be correct to infer from the inclusion of several methods that each one exhibits a unique trade-off among speed, safety, and simplicity.

The premier method in many ways is *Newton's method,* whose linear approximation is the tangent line to the function g at a point x_{old}. In terms of the function g and its derivative g', the point–slope formula gives

$$g_t(x) = g(x_{\text{old}}) + g'(x_{\text{old}})(x - x_{\text{old}}). \qquad (8.3.1)$$

The root of the equation $g_t(x) = 0$ is at

$$x_{\text{new}} = x_{\text{old}} - g(x_{\text{old}})/g'(x_{\text{old}}). \qquad (8.3.2)$$

Newton's method is then a sequential application of this formula; the new point for one step becomes the old point for the next iteration:

$$x_{n+1} = x_n - g(x_n)/g'(x_n). \qquad (8.3.3)$$

Notice that the form of the iteration, $x_{n+1} = T(x_n)$, brings to mind the mathematics of contraction mappings. The success of Newton's method relies upon the starting value x_0 lying in the domain of attraction of the root.

However, analysis of the rate of convergence for practical problems will require more stringent (yet simple and reliable) assumptions. To analyze the convergence of Newton's method for the root-finding problem, denote the root by c and the error at iteration n by $e_n = x_n - c$. Then the relative error will be denoted by $d_n = e_n/c = (x_n - c)/c$. The revealing equation is a Taylor expansion of the function g at the root about the value x_n at iteration n:

$$g(c) = 0 = g(x_n) + (c - x_n)g'(x_n) + (c - x_n)^2 g''(t)/2, \qquad (8.3.4)$$

where t lies between x_n and the root c. Moving the first two terms on the rightmost side of (8.3.4) to the left and then dividing through by $g'(x_n)$ yields

$$x_n - c - g(x_n)/g'(x_n) = (x_n - c)^2 [g''(t)/2g'(x_n)].$$

Recognizing the iteration formula (8.3.3) on the left and substituting for the error e_n and e_{n+1}, we have the following result:

$$e_{n+1} = e_n^2 [g''(t)/2g'(x_n)]. \qquad (8.3.5)$$

This expression reveals the *quadratic convergence* of Newton's method – in contrast to the linear convergence of golden section or bisection, where the interval of uncertainty was reduced by a constant factor at each step. To elucidate, suppose the bracketed expression in (8.3.5) approximately equalled unity; then the error would be squared at each step, so that if k digits of accuracy were achieved at one step then the next iteration would achieve $2k$ digits. In practice, the expression in brackets moderates the rate of convergence. Notice that this quantity is small whenever g' is large, so steeply sloped functions are easier. Conversely, if a flat spot of the function is approached then a nearly horizontal linear approximation will be attempted, and the subsequent point may leap far away from the true root. A bounded second derivative is required both to ensure a good rate of convergence and to keep the iteration formula from throwing the new point out of the domain of convergence.

The domain of attraction just mentioned for Newton's method depends on three things. One is a bound on the second derivative in the region $\max|g''(t)|$, and another is a minimum for the slope $g'(x)$. Notice that letting the derivative g' approach zero allows the function to become nearly flat. In such a case, an iteration step could throw the next point far from the original starting point, beyond where the assumption of local linearity of g would apply. The third item that determines the domain of attraction is the starting point. A function with several roots may have several domains of attraction for different roots. The root that is reached by a sequence of Newton iterations may depend on the domain in which the iteration starts. It is also possible to have a domain of divergence, where the iteration sequence diverges (see Exercise 8.8). Since the domains depend on the root(s) and on the bounds on the first and second derivatives, it is rare in practice for anything to be known about the domains (since that information is not available at the outset).

If the original problem to be solved was really the optimization of a function f, then Newton's method can be rewritten to apply to the optimization problem by relating the derivative f' to the function g whose root is sought; that is, $g = f'$. As a consequence, (8.3.3) can be rewritten as

$$x_{n+1} = x_n - f'(x_n)/f''(x_n), \tag{8.3.3*}$$

and the constant part of the convergence expression (8.3.5) is $[f'''(t)/2f''(x_n)]$. Remember, however, that this merely translates the problem into a root-finding problem with the derivative, and the iteration sequence (8.3.3*) could minimize the function f when the intention was to maximize (or vice versa).

Although Newton's method achieves the fastest rate of convergence, its main drawback is that the derivative function must be available, and finding it can be tedious and sometimes nearly impossible. As a result, a method that only requires evaluations of the function g would be preferred in these cases. The approach for this also uses a linear approximation to the function g, but this time based on the 2-point formula for the points $(x_{n-1}, g(x_{n-1}))$ and $(x_n, g(x_n))$:

$$g_s(x) = g(x_n) + \{[g(x_n) - g(x_{n-1})]/[x_n - x_{n-1}]\}(x - x_n). \tag{8.3.6}$$

Notice that this line is the secant line, whereas Newton's method used the tangent line. The root of the linear equation $g_s(x) = 0$ can be found to have a form similar to (8.3.2). When the root of $g_s(x) = 0$ is used as part of an iteration sequence, the formula can be written as

$$x_{n+1} = x_n - \{[x_n - x_{n-1}]/[g(x_n) - g(x_{n-1})]\}g(x_n). \tag{8.3.7}$$

Note that this formula is the same as (8.3.3) but with the reciprocal of the derivative $1/f'(x_n)$, which is considered unavailable, replaced by its approximation – a first difference, the term in braces in (8.3.7). This iteration formula defines what is known as the *secant method,* taking its name from the use of the secant line as its linear approximation.

Analysis of the convergence of the secant method is not as clean as with Newton's method, although a similar expression can be obtained:

$$e_{n+1} \approx Ce_{n-1}e_n,$$

where the constant C is the same as the bracketed expression in (8.3.5). Taking logs of absolute values yields a difference expression similar to that of the Fibonacci numbers, with the surprising and useful result that

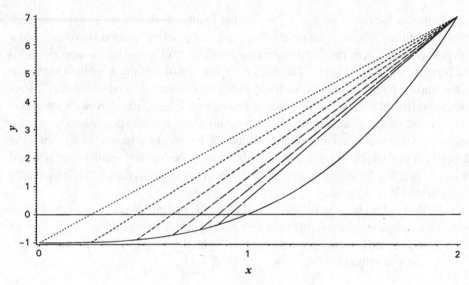

Figure 8.1. Slow convergence of false position method. Solid line shows the function $y(x) = x^3 - 1$; dashed lines are successive interpolants.

$$|e_{n+1}| = O(|e_n|^{1+\phi}),$$

where the exponent $1 + \phi = 1.618$ (owing to its relationship to Fibonacci). Since the exponent $1 + \phi$ lies between the value 1 for linear convergence and the exponent 2 for quadratic convergence, the convergence rate of the secant method is called *superlinear*. Moreover, since Newton's method required evaluation of both g and g', it follows that if the derivative were available but costly (i.e., more than about half the cost of an evaluation of g) then the secant method would actually be faster than Newton's.

While the secant method shares some of the same assets (e.g. fast convergence) as Newton's, it also shares some of the same liabilities. In particular, when a flat portion of the function g is encountered, the secant method can also be thrown far away from the root. The "safe" method of bisection avoided this by ensuring that the root remained in the interval (by keeping one endpoint with the value of g negative and the other with g positive there). Retention of endpoints where g has differing signs is also possible with the secant method. Begin with two points that straddle the root and then, instead of discarding the older of the two points, x_{n-1}, discard the point with the same sign as $g(x_{n+1})$. This method, known as *false position* or *regula falsi,* follows the secant formula but acquires the same safety as bisection by retaining an interval in which the root is sure to lie. The goal of combining rapid convergence and safety is a noble one, but it is not achieved in practice with false position. The problem is that often one endpoint is retained for several iterations and so the analysis of the convergence leads to $e_{n+1} \approx C e_n e_0$. Consequently, although false position has the potential of the superlinear convergence of the secant method, in practice the convergence is essentially linear, with the constant adjusting whenever a true secant step is taken. Figure 8.1 shows the

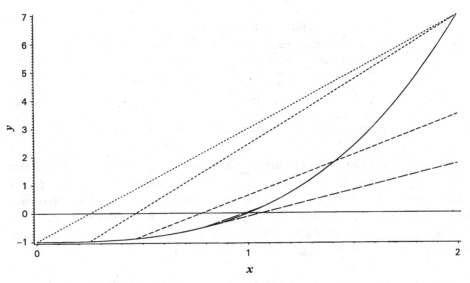

Figure 8.2. Better convergence of Illinois method. Solid line shows the function $y(x) = x^3 - 1$; dashed lines are successive interpolants.

slow convergence of regula falsi on the simple function $g(x) = x^3 - 1$ on the interval $(0, 2)$. Shown are the secant lines for the first six iterations; the next several move slowly closer to right, actually stopping only by finding that $g(x)$ is too close to zero to continue.

The disappointing performance of false position can be corrected with a method known as modified regula falsi or the *Illinois method*. Again the secant formula is used and, as with false position, the pair of points are retained to keep the root bracketed. The difference is that, whenever one endpoint is retained more than once, the value of g there is halved. The result is a shallower secant line and an inclination to move and perform a secant step. If the endpoint remains, the value of g there will be continually halved until a secant step is performed. Although this appears to be a completely artificial modification, experience has shown it to be extraordinarily effective. The mathematics supports this, since the convergence rate is also superlinear (though it is slower than the secant method), $|e_{n+1}| = O(|e_n|^{1.44})$. The Illinois method is highly recommended for any problem where the root can be bracketed and safety is desired. Figure 8.2 shows the performance of the Illinois method on the same problem as before, $g(x) = x^3 - 1$. After keeping the right endpoint twice, the secant line is made shallower by halving the value of g at the right endpoint. After the second halving, the secant line is shallow enough to make a secant step and move the right endpoint. The full course of the iterations for both false position and Illinois is shown in the code **false** (see also Exercise 8.14). Brent (1973) proposed a more complicated (and safe yet effective) method that combines bisection and false position.

Finally, since root-finding problems are often motivated by an optimization problem, one might consider an optimization algorithm analogous to the secant method. That is, for the root-finding problem, two points are used to construct a linear approximation

Table 8.2. *Convergence rates*

Convergence	Root finding	Optimization
Linear	Bisection	Golden section
Superlinear	Secant, Illinois	Quadratic interpolation
Quadratic	Newton	Newton

to the function $g(x)$ and the approximating linear problem is solved. For maximizing a function $f(x)$, say, a quadratic approximation can be constructed using three points. The iteration then concludes by moving to the maximum of the quadratic approxima-tion. The error analysis of such a method is quite interesting, with $e_{n+1} \propto e_{n-1}e_{n-2}$. The convergence is superlinear, but with rate roughly 1.3 (see Exercise 8.6). However, the implementation of such a method faces two obstacles:

(1) finding an apparent local minimum instead of maximum; and
(2) jumping outside an interval known to contain the maximum.

This section concludes with a review of the problems solved and the trade-offs avail-able. In general, speed must be sacrificed in order to gain safety. For the root-finding problem, bisection is the safest algorithm around; its only requirement is that the func-tion g cross the axis only once. False position and Illinois methods require only a form of Lipschitz continuity, whereas secant and Newton methods need well-behaved sec-ond derivatives. Also, there is an obvious advantage to solving the root-finding problem instead of an optimization problem. Table 8.2 illustrates the relationships.

Example 8.3: *A Simple Likelihood to Be Maximized*
In statistics, the most common problems in this area are likelihoods to be maxi-mized or likelihood equations to be solved. Here is a relatively simple one, to be used from time to time in this book. Suppose we have observations $\{1, 1, 1, 1, 1, 1, 2, 2, 2, 3\}$ from the (discrete) logarithmic series distribution with density

$$p(x \mid \theta) = \theta^x/(x(-\log(1-\theta))) \quad \text{for } x = 1, 2, 3, \dots, \ 0 < \theta < 1.$$

Then, neglecting a constant, the log likelihood can be the function to be maxi-mized:

$$f(x) = \left(\sum x_i\right) \log \theta - n \log(-\log(1-\theta)).$$

Solving the likelihood equations means finding the root of the derivative of $f(x)$:

$$f'(x) = g(x) = \frac{\left(\sum x_i\right)}{\theta} + \frac{n}{(1-\theta)\log(1-\theta)} = 0.$$

Figure 8.3 shows the two functions $f(x)$ and $g(x)$ on the interval $(0, 1)$. For this example, $\sum x_i = 15$ and $n = 10$. The code **finder** demonstrates the various methods discussed here on this problem.

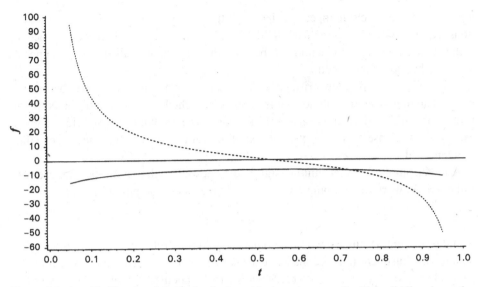

Figure 8.3. Log likelihood and derivative for logarithmic series example. The solid line shows the log likelihood; the dashed line is its derivative.

8.4 First Digression: Stopping and Condition

A well-written algorithm for root-finding or optimization should have three options for termination: too many steps; no change in x; no change in the function. Which one(s) to choose depends upon the particular application. All iterative algorithms should have a maximum number of iterations. Because of the peculiarities of finite-precision arithmetic, no proof of convergence can guarantee a solution found and termination in a finite number of steps. Usually termination due to exceeding the maximum number of iterations indicates a serious error in problem specification. Often this is easily rectified, since most of the time the cause is an error as silly as trying to find (often to the great surprise of the user) the root of a function that is always positive.

Algorithms are designed to terminate when either the change in x is less than ε_x or when g is within ε_g of zero, whichever occurs first. Usually both ε_x and ε_g must be specified; if not, any left unspecified is set to a machine epsilon. To disable one entirely, one trick is to set $\varepsilon = 0$, but this is sometimes not permitted and so is overridden (and often this ε is set to the machine epsilon by design). Several competing issues are involved. The user would like a black box that gives the roots or optima, but such a black box is not achievable. Attempts by the user to get the impossible are then thwarted by the algorithm's designer. In some root-finding applications, no value of x will produce a value of g within ε_g of zero. In such a case, the best value that can be given as the root is one of two points between which the function changes sign. Note that this is exactly what some algorithms (bisection, regula falsi) are designed to do. As far as the computer is concerned, there is no zero of the function but only a point at which the function jumps from one sign to another. On the other side of the coin, the error in evaluating the function may be substantial and so, at the precision of the argument x, the function appears to have multiple roots. In such a case the assumptions required of the function do not hold. Then, as far as the algorithm is concerned, it is the ε_x that has become meaningless because there are many values of x that appear to act as the root of the function.

The most serious problem arises when an algorithm's iteration is stopped because x is not changing, even though no root is being approached. The source of the problem is that some required assumptions on the function do not hold; Exercise 8.13 is a good example of this case. Only by examination of the value of g at "convergence" can this problem be discovered.

Another problem in algorithm design is the choice of relative or absolute change. Either would work for stopping on x, but a relative change stopping rule

$$|x_{n+1} - x_n| < |x_n|\varepsilon_x$$

would be preferable, since it would automatically adjust to changes in magnitude (even though an adjustment must be made for x near zero). In contrast, changes relative to the goal of zero for g are unworkable, so only a user-specified ε_g would make sense for a stopping rule on absolute change, $|g(x_n)| < \varepsilon_g$, based on knowledge of the behavior of the function. Without such knowledge, stopping on g should not be considered. Yet for the optimization problem, if relative changes in the function are small then this may appropriately signal that the goal has been reached. As a result, a relative change stopping rule, $|f(x_{n+1}) - f(x_n)| < |f(x_n)|\varepsilon_f$, makes sense.

The problem of specifying ε_x or ε_f is best viewed as an examination of the *condition* of the problem: as the problem is slightly perturbed, how will the solution change? If perturbations are made in the function g or f, then the solution will change a great deal for a badly conditioned problem but only a little if the problem is well conditioned. This view then takes ε_f and ε_g to the accuracy of the evaluation of the function, which directly limits the accuracy of any possible solution. For the root-finding problem, a simple mean value expression illustrates many of these points:

$$x - c = [g(x) - g(c)]/g'(t). \tag{8.4.1}$$

Suppose the function g can be computed only to a level of accuracy ε_g. Then, manipulating (8.4.1) we find that $|x - c| \le \varepsilon_g/|g'(c)|$, so the imprecision of g is amplified by the condition number $1/|g'(c)|$. This should not be surprising, since steeply sloped functions should be easier to solve than flat ones. Knowledge of the possible accuracy of the function evaluation can determine the achievable accuracy of the solution, but only in extreme cases will the magnitudes of the two εs differ greatly.

For the related optimization problem, the calculus gives

$$(x - c)^2 = 2[f(x) - f(c)]/f''(t), \tag{8.4.2}$$

indicating an apparent condition number of $2/|f''|$ – but only if the square on the left-hand side of (8.4.2) is overlooked. Although $2/f''$ is a good indicator of behavior, the important consequence is that if the function f can only be known to a precision ε_f, then the optimum c can only be known to a precision

$$e_x = \sqrt{2\varepsilon_f/f''(c)}. \tag{8.4.3}$$

Another way to view this result is that if the function can only be known to k digits of accuracy, then the optimum can only be known to $k/2$ digits (taking $f'' = 2$).

8.5   Multivariate Newton's Methods

A simplistic view of multivariate methods for optimizing a real-valued function f of p variables $\mathbf{x}$, or solving $\mathbf{g}(\mathbf{x}) = \mathbf{0}$, is that they are simple extensions of the univariate methods. In many ways, this view is quite insightful; in other ways, it is just simplistic and wrong, since there are subtleties in the multivariate problem that are absent in the univariate case. Note that the multivariate extensions of the methods in Section 8.2 – lattice search, golden section, and bisection – are absent, since in large part such extensions do not exist (but see Vrahatis 1988). Our discussion of the multivariate problem begins with Newton's methods and follows the simplistic view as far as possible. In the next section we digress to examine the problem of numerical differentiation before facing the multivariate problem directly in Section 8.7.

For the univariate root-finding problem of a single nonlinear equation, Newton's method arose from finding the root of a tangent approximation to the function. In the multivariate case, solving $\mathbf{g}(\mathbf{x}) = \mathbf{0}$, the tangent approximation $\mathbf{g}_t(\mathbf{x})$ relies on the multivariate version expressed in Theorem 8.8,

$$\mathbf{g}_t(\mathbf{x}) = \mathbf{g}(\mathbf{x}_{\text{old}}) + \mathbf{J}_\mathbf{g}(\mathbf{x}_{\text{old}})(\mathbf{x} - \mathbf{x}_{\text{old}}). \tag{8.5.1}$$

The solution $\mathbf{x}_{\text{new}}$ to the system of linear equations $\mathbf{g}_t(\mathbf{x}) = \mathbf{0}$, as an approximation to the nonlinear equations, can then be written as

$$\mathbf{x}_{\text{new}} = \mathbf{x}_{\text{old}} - \mathbf{J}_\mathbf{g}(\mathbf{x}_{\text{old}})^{-1}\mathbf{g}(\mathbf{x}_{\text{old}}). \tag{8.5.2}$$

This multivariate version of Newton's method has the same form as the univariate case, and its convergence rate is also quadratic (although the mathematics is much more complicated).

For optimizing a function f of p variables $\mathbf{x}$, begin analogously with the quadratic approximation given by Theorem 8.6,

$$f_q(\mathbf{x}) = f(\mathbf{x}_{\text{old}}) + (\mathbf{x} - \mathbf{x}_{\text{old}})^{\mathrm{T}}\nabla f(\mathbf{x}_{\text{old}}) + \tfrac{1}{2}(\mathbf{x} - \mathbf{x}_{\text{old}})^{\mathrm{T}}\nabla^2 f(\mathbf{t}_{\text{old}})(\mathbf{x} - \mathbf{x}_{\text{old}}). \tag{8.5.3}$$

The stationary point $\mathbf{x}_{\text{new}}$ of $f_q(\mathbf{x})$ is then given by

$$\mathbf{x}_{\text{new}} = \mathbf{x}_{\text{old}} - \mathbf{H}(\mathbf{x}_{\text{old}})^{-1}\nabla f(\mathbf{x}_{\text{old}}), \tag{8.5.4}$$

where $\mathbf{H}(\mathbf{x}) = \nabla^2 f(\mathbf{x})$ is the Hessian matrix. If $\mathbf{H}(\mathbf{x})$ is positive (resp., negative) definite at the stationary point, then a local minimum (resp., maximum) is found; if the Hessian is indefinite then a saddle point is found.

The expression of the Newton iterations (8.5.2) and (8.5.4) with a matrix inverse may spark some concern, but the propriety of that concern depends on the motivation. Computationally, of course, these are linear equations to be solved; an inverse is never computed. In light of the nonlinear equations to be solved, these linear equations are comparatively the easiest problem to be faced. The main concern is that a

p-dimensional system is to be solved at each step. What may be overlooked is the computation of just the $p \times p$ matrix, either $\mathbf{J_g}$ or $\mathbf{H}$. Compared to an evaluation of the p-valued function $\mathbf{g}$, evaluating $\mathbf{J_g}$ costs p times as much work. Compared to an evaluation of f, evaluating $\mathbf{H}$ costs p^2 times as much – and this cost must be paid at every step. Moreover, since the expressions for partial derivatives often become complicated rather quickly, the human effort in coding should not be overlooked.

Facing these costs, alternatives to Newton's methods are sought for both the optimization problem and the solution to systems of nonlinear equations. Anticipated savings in these alternatives are based on two hopes: that (1) the matrix ($\mathbf{H}$ or $\mathbf{J_g}$) may not change much with changes in $\mathbf{x}$ and (2) approximations to the matrix constructed from evaluations may work just as well. Before analyzing these alternative routes, we must investigate the performance of numerical approximations to derivatives.

8.6   Second Digression: Numerical Differentiation

The secant method can be viewed as substituting a difference for a derivative in Newton's method. Recall that, in the point–slope formula in (8.3.6) the expression in braces gives the slope of the secant line: $\{[g(x_n) - g(x_{n-1})]/[x_n - x_{n-1}]\}$. The performance of the secant method depends on the local linearity of the function g, the ability of the secant line to approximate the function, and the quality of the ratio of differences (i.e., $\{\cdot\}$) in estimating the derivative. For other algorithms for both optimization and nonlinear equations, the performance of various numerical differentiation schemes is central to the performance of the method.

The study of calculus begins with the definition of a derivative,

$$f'(x) = \lim_{h \to 0} \frac{f(x+h) - f(x)}{h} = \lim_{h \to 0} \frac{f(x+h) - f(x-h)}{2h};$$

the first expression is that of a forward difference, and the second ratio is called a central difference. In the limit, either will produce the derivative at $\mathbf{x}$; but for finite values of the difference h, the performance can be viewed as a trade-off between speed and accuracy and between bias and variance. If we have the value of a function at a point x, then estimating the derivative at x using forward difference,

$$\hat{f}_1'(x) = [f(x+h) - f(x)]/h, \tag{8.6.1}$$

requires only one additional evaluation of f at $x + h$, whereas the central difference

$$\hat{f}_2'(x) = [f(x+h) - f(x-h)]/(2h) \tag{8.6.2}$$

requires two additional evaluations of f, at $x + h$ and $x - h$. Doubling the cost yields substantial benefits, since the accuracies of the two methods differ dramatically,

$$\hat{f}_1'(x) = f'(x) + O(h) \quad \text{versus} \quad \hat{f}_2'(x) = f'(x) + O(h^2). \tag{8.6.3}$$

Before the reader gets the wise idea that "h versus h^2 doesn't really matter, just take h very small," consider the effect of roundoff error in the evaluation of the function f. Suppose evaluating f involves a roundoff error ε, so that $\mathrm{fl}(f(x)) = f(x) + \varepsilon_x$. Then

$\hat{f}_1'$ will behave like $f' + (\varepsilon_{x+h} - \varepsilon_x)/h$ for small values of h (and the central difference will behave similarly). Since the roundoff error isn't going away, it follows that $\hat{f}_1'$ will behave wildly as h becomes smaller – until $\mathrm{fl}(x+h) = \mathrm{fl}(x)$.

The problem of numerical differentiation can be summarized as trade-offs between cost and accuracy and between bias and variance. The central difference would be preferred if it came for free, which sometimes it does (later for this). It may seem that the size of the difference h should be chosen as small as possible without encountering roundoff error, but this procedure cannot be followed in practice because that threshold is not known. Moreover, because of the alarming behavior when h is too small, experience has shown that it is preferable to live with some bias in the estimate of the derivative rather than to risk a wild result in taking h too small. Practice shows that a good rule of thumb is to take h to be the size of the square root of the machine unit, $\eta = U^{1/2}$ on a relative basis. That is, take $h = \eta x$ so that the relative change is $[(x + \eta x) - x]/(x) = \eta$. In many software codes, the user supplies a typical value for x in case the given x (a starting value) should be zero. A very useful trick addresses the vagaries of floating point arithmetic, alluded to earlier as questioning whether $\mathrm{fl}(x+h) = \mathrm{fl}(x)$. Dennis and Schnabel (1983) suggested dividing not by h but by $\mathrm{fl}(x+h) - \mathrm{fl}(x)$, which would better approximate the real change in the argument of the function. Gill, Murray, and Wright (1981) suggested $\eta = U^{1/3}$, rather than $U^{1/2}$, for central differences.

Second derivatives can be approximated in a similar fashion using second differences,

$$\hat{f}''(x) = \{[f(x+h) - f(x)] - [f(x) - f(x-h)]\}/h^2. \tag{8.6.4}$$

Note that this formula was intentionally written as the difference of two differences, instead of as $f(x+h) - 2f(x) + f(x-h)$, in order to avoid unnecessary cancellation. In this case, the accuracy can be expressed as $\hat{f}''(x) = f''(x) + O(h)$, as for a forward difference. However, the roundoff problem becomes somewhat more severe here, leading to the recommendation that $h = U^{1/3}x$ be taken for the step size, following the same logic as before. Finally, observe that evaluating this second difference requires two additional evaluations, at $x+h$ and $x-h$. If the second derivative is to be approximated, a more accurate central difference comes for free. After some heuristic mathematics, Gill et al. (1981, pp. 340–1) recommended $\eta = U^{1/4}$ for second differences but without fussing over taking differences of differences.

The demonstration code **numdif** shows the performance of numerical differentiation for the function $\log \Gamma(x)$ for various values of $h = 2^{-k}$. The code ALGAMA is used for computing, and $x = 1/2$ was chosen by way of example. Given $\psi(x) \equiv \Gamma'(x)/\Gamma(x)$, we have $\psi(1/2) = 1.96351$ and $\psi'(1/2) = 4.9348022$. For the first derivative, both forward and central differences are compared, labeled f_1' and f_2' (respectively). For the second derivative, f_1'' uses the simple $[f(x+h) - 2f(x) + f(x-h)]/h^2$ whereas f_2'' follows the mathematically equivalent (8.6.4), hoping to save a bit from cancellation. As can be seen from the output, the central difference performs much better than the forward difference, providing three good digits for a range of values of $h = 2^{-k}$ in IEEE single precision arithmetic. For the second derivative, the two expressions rarely differ. The punishment for taking h too small becomes quite obvious, resulting in very large values.

Since this digression comes amid an examination of methods for optimization and nonlinear equations, the multivariate case – namely, partial derivatives – must be addressed. First consider the gradient vector, $\nabla f(\mathbf{x})$. Using $\mathbf{e}_i$ to denote the ith elementary vector, the estimate of the partial derivative with respect to x_i is given by the forward difference $d_i = [f(\mathbf{x} + h\mathbf{e}_i) - f(\mathbf{x})]/h$, and the error is $\|\mathbf{d} - \nabla f\| = O(h)$. For the central difference formula, $d_i = [f(\mathbf{x} + h\mathbf{e}_i) - f(\mathbf{x} - h\mathbf{e}_i)]/h$ and the error is not surprisingly $O(h^2)$. For the Hessian matrix, more evaluations are needed, and the scheme is

$$\hat{H}_{ij} = \{[f(\mathbf{x} + h_i\mathbf{e}_i + h_j\mathbf{e}_j) - f(\mathbf{x} + h_i\mathbf{e}_i)] - [f(\mathbf{x} + h_j\mathbf{e}_j) - f(\mathbf{x})]\}/(h_ih_j), \quad (8.6.5)$$

again computed as the difference of two differences. As with the univariate second difference formula, the error $\|\hat{\mathbf{H}} - \nabla^2 f\|$ is $O(h)$. Sometimes the symmetrized form $\mathbf{H}^* = (\hat{\mathbf{H}} + \hat{\mathbf{H}}^T)/2$ is computed to enforce symmetry in the Hessian matrix (perhaps lost by roundoff). In order to evaluate the estimate $\mathbf{d}$ of the p-dimensional vector of partial derivatives, p evaluations of the function f are needed in addition to the evaluation at $\mathbf{x}$. To compute the Hessian by differences, $\hat{\mathbf{H}}$ or $\mathbf{H}^*$ requires $p(p + 3)/2$ additional evaluations.

The performance of central differences suggests that a little more effort may give much better answers. If we view the central difference as an average of forward differences taken in opposite directions, then a multivariate generalization of central differences follows from taking the average of two versions of (8.6.5) using another pair of elementary vectors in the opposite directions:

$$\begin{aligned}
\tilde{H}_{ij} = (&\{[f(\mathbf{x} + h_i\mathbf{e}_i + h_j\mathbf{e}_j) - f(\mathbf{x} + h_i\mathbf{e}_i)] - [f(\mathbf{x} + h_j\mathbf{e}_j) - f(\mathbf{x})]\} \\
&+ \{[f(\mathbf{x} - h_i\mathbf{e}_i - h_j\mathbf{e}_j) - f(\mathbf{x} - h_i\mathbf{e}_i)] - [f(\mathbf{x} - h_j\mathbf{e}_j) - f(\mathbf{x})]\})/(2h_ih_j).
\end{aligned}$$
$$(8.6.6)$$

That additional effort nearly doubles the work, requiring $p(p + 1)$ evaluations in addition to the center point. Whether the reduction in error to $O(h^2)$ is worth the effort may depend on circumstances. The demonstration **del12f** shows the performance of the algorithm that follows (8.6.6) for computing the Hessian matrix and also central differences by $d_i = [f(\mathbf{x} + h_i\mathbf{e}_i) - f(\mathbf{x} - h_i\mathbf{e}_i)]/h_i$.

An alternative method was suggested by Spendley, Hext, and Himsworth (1962) that also takes $p(p + 3)/2$ evaluations. Their method arose as a simplex experimental design, focusing on the vertices $\mathbf{x} + h_i\mathbf{e}_i$, with the goal of fitting a quadratic response surface. Their design consists of the center point $\mathbf{x}$, midpoints from $\mathbf{x}$ to the simplex vertices $\mathbf{x} + (h_i/2)\mathbf{e}_i$, and midpoints between the simplex vertices $\mathbf{x} + (h_i/2)\mathbf{e}_i + (h_j/2)\mathbf{e}_j$. Going from the responses at these points to the estimates of the gradient and Hessian follows some simple algebra.

The Jacobian matrix $\mathbf{J_g}$ of the nonlinear function $\mathbf{g}(\mathbf{x})$ can be estimated by the difference $\hat{J}_{ij} = [g_i(\mathbf{x} + h_j\mathbf{e}_j) - g_i(\mathbf{x})]/h_j$ for the forward difference case. Since the evaluations of $\mathbf{g}$ yield a vector of values, this can be re-expressed in terms of an entire column,

$$\hat{\mathbf{J}}_{\cdot j} = [\mathbf{g}(\mathbf{x} + h_j\mathbf{e}_j) - \mathbf{g}(\mathbf{x})]/h_j, \quad (8.6.7)$$

with an error $\|\hat{\mathbf{J}}_{\cdot j} - (\mathbf{J_g})_{\cdot j}\|$ of the size of $O(h_j)$. For this case, computing $\hat{\mathbf{J}}$ requires an additional p evaluations of the function $\mathbf{g}$. If this vector-valued function $\mathbf{g}$ is in reality the analytically computed ∇f, then symmetry can be enforced by $\mathbf{H}^* = (\hat{\mathbf{J}} + \hat{\mathbf{J}}^T)/2$.

Before closing this section, two issues should be resolved. By avoiding a too small difference h, numerical derivatives have gained favor in many circles. Confirming the convictions of some is the anecdotal evidence that the major cause of failure in optimization applications is the human error in the coding of analytical derivatives. Before passing judgment on this argument, the reader should attempt coding analytically the gradient and Hessian of the function $[\log(x_1 x_2)/(x_3 x_4)]^2$ used in the demonstration **del12f**. Even though the accuracy from computing numerical derivatives is limited, doing so can prevent major errors as well as embarrassments and a lot of work. In getting back on the fence, however, if the effort is not taxing then you just can't beat the real thing.

The second issue that arises here is the profound effect of the limited precision of the arithmetic. In IEEE single precision with $U \approx 10^{-6}$, taking $h = U^{1/3}$ means $h \approx 10^{-2}$ and so the best that can be expected from forward differences is two good decimal digits, which is unacceptable. At this point, one should entertain moving from single to double precision, even though there are two good reasons for staying with single precision. First, mixing and mismatching single and double precision arithmetic is the most common source of errors, in my experience. The second reason is pedagogical: we reach the limits of floating point arithmetic so much quicker in single precision. Moving to double precision does *not* remove these limits; it only moves them back. In writing this my fear is that, in not seeing these barriers, the reader may forget where they are as the research problem begins to strain the computer. From this point forward, double precision arithmetic is not just permitted, it may be required. But like a parent, I can't hold back the admonition to "be careful!"

8.7 Minimization and Nonlinear Equations

The discussion of the multivariate Newton's method was placed so prominently because it is the main tool for these problems. Only when the full Newton step encounters some problems is it worth employing any line search methods, and even then the Newton direction is followed in the line search. There are certainly side issues – analytic versus numerical derivatives, the use of Newton analogs – but the approach stays pretty simple.

Although the most common problem in statistics is maximizing likelihoods, the ability to talk of positive definite Hessians suggests simplifying the discussion to minimization. In the univariate problem, the gain from moving from a minimization problem to a root-finding problem was embodied in the ratio of ϕ to $\frac{1}{2}$, the rate of decrease in the interval of uncertainty in golden section versus bisection. No such gain applies in the multivariate game, since the minimization problem is really one of solving the nonlinear system of equations $\nabla f(\mathbf{x}) = 0$. In fact, minimization has a few checks for advantage: the function should decrease with each step, and the Hessian matrix should be positive definite. The only advantage for the nonlinear equations is that a solution is found if $\mathbf{g}(\mathbf{x}) = \mathbf{0}$.

In many multivariate problems, the usual route is to convert it to a univariate one. In this case, however, that's not such a good idea. One of the simplest techniques for optimization is the steepest descent or gradient method. The motivation is simple: the direction to move in order to minimize a function is the direction where the slope is steepest. Once the direction is determined, the problem becomes a univariate one, and univariate problems are relatively easy to solve. Mathematically, the steepest descent method can be written as minimizing $f^*(u) = f(\mathbf{x}_{old} - u\mathbf{d})$, where $\mathbf{d} = \nabla f(\mathbf{x}_{old})$. The method stops when there is nowhere to go: either $\mathbf{d} = \mathbf{0}$ or moving to any $u > 0$ leads to an increase in f. One of the advantages of this method is that a constant monitoring of values of f can ensure that a minimum is found (and not a maximum or saddle point). The main disadvantage of the method is that it tends to zig-zag its way to the minimum whenever the problem is badly scaled. Consequently, the steepest descent method is rarely competitive.

Example 8.4: *Steepest Descent Zig-Zag*
Even with a mildly scaled problem, the steepest descent method can do a lot of zig-zagging. Let $f(\mathbf{x}) = x_1^2 + x_2^2/2$ and start at the point $(1, 2)$. Then the first zig in u is

$$f(\mathbf{x} + u\mathbf{d}) = f\begin{pmatrix} 1 - 2u \\ 2 - 2u \end{pmatrix} = (1 - 2u)^2 + (2 - 2u)^2/2,$$

which has a minimum at $u = 2/3$. The pattern of the sequence of points can be quickly found:

$$\begin{pmatrix} 1 \\ 2 \end{pmatrix}, \begin{pmatrix} -1/3 \\ 2/3 \end{pmatrix}, \begin{pmatrix} 1/9 \\ 2/9 \end{pmatrix}, \begin{pmatrix} -1/27 \\ 2/27 \end{pmatrix}, \begin{pmatrix} 1/81 \\ 2/81 \end{pmatrix}, \ldots.$$

Before the reader feels pleased by this geometric rate of convergence, recall that Newton's method would have the answer in one step. Figure 8.4 shows the contours of f and the path of steepest descent.

A line search itself is not a bad idea; a line search in the Newton direction is a great tool for overcoming a troublesome problem encountered often with Newton's method for minimization. Because Newton's method is designed to find the solution to a local quadratic, a step that leaps far beyond "local" can sometimes yield a value for the function f at the new point that is actually larger, say, for a minimization problem. In order not to leap beyond "local," a simple patch is backtracking: search along the Newton's step direction. Suppose the Newton iteration (8.5.2) is $\mathbf{x}_{new} = \mathbf{x}_{old} + \mathbf{s}$; then, when $f(\mathbf{x}_{new}) > f(\mathbf{x}_{old})$, consider the function $f^*(u) = f(\mathbf{x}_{old} - u\mathbf{s})$. Since $f^*(1) > f^*(0)$, the likely reason is that $u = 1$ is much too far from the minimizing value of u. An accurate line search on u is usually wasted computation, so the most common method is to take u that minimizes the quadratic functions of u that fit $f^*(0)$, $f^{*\prime}(0)$, and $f^*(1)$, since all are known (see Exercise 8.19). If this fails to decrease the function, then a cubic can fit the four pieces of information now available. If Newton's method suggests decreases in this direction and yet this backtrack fails (with even very small values of u not yielding any decrease in f), then the usual cause is that the limits

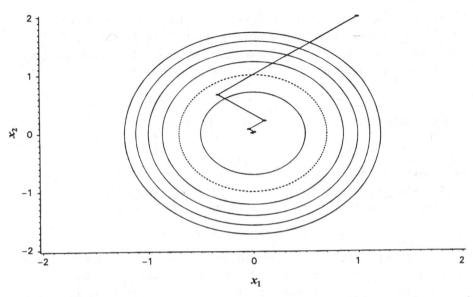

Figure 8.4. Slow convergence of steepest descent. The convergence path zig-zags to the center of the elliptical contours of the objective function $f(x) = x_1^2 + x_2^2/2$.

of accuracy of f have been reached – relative to the tolerances for the gradient being small enough to stop.

Although the overall strategy is to do Newton's method, backtracking if necessary, there are some important side issues that include the choice of analytic versus numerical derivatives or secant versus Newton methods. Many minimizing routines (or nonlinear solvers) offer different versions for these choices, but the criteria are simply these: (i) Are the evaluations cheap or expensive? (ii) Are the analytical derivatives easy or difficult? If the evaluations are cheap then, even if the Hessian must be computed numerically, its evaluation will still be cheap. In such a case, there is no need to employ any secant method – just use Newton and backtracking with either numerical or analytic derivatives; the choice between these two is a matter of convenience. Yes, there is an advantage to having analytical results, but only if they are correct; miscoding is a common mistake even for experienced users, including the author.

If evaluation of the function is expensive, then secant analogs must be entertained. Recall that computing the Hessian takes $O(p^2)$ work; for a statistical problem with n observations, this is often really $O(np^2)$. This cost usually remains the same whether analytic or numerical derivatives are used. Whereas it is important to obtain accurate values of $\mathbf{g}(\mathbf{x})$ or $\nabla f(\mathbf{x})$, especially for determining whether the solution is found, errors in $\mathbf{J_g}$ or $\mathbf{H}$ are more tolerable. Secant analogs use previous observations to approximate these matrices, sacrificing $O(p^2)$ work with a small scale factor to do the linear algebra in order to avoid paying costs like $O(np^2)$. First, Broyden's secant update for nonlinear equations will be discussed, followed by the positive definite secant update for minimization. Readers uninterested in these details should skip to the next section.

A simplistic route to approximate $\mathbf{J_g}$ would be to mimic directly the secant method by finding the linear (affine) function that interpolates the previous p points. Although this would work and give superlinear (barely, as p grows) convergence, it is sensitive to the layout of points and can behave unstably. A better way of doing things is to view the problem as one of updating the current $\mathbf{A}_{old}$ estimate of $\mathbf{J_g}$ to an updated one $\mathbf{A}_{new}$. Now the old matrix is defined by the secant approximation to $\mathbf{g}$,

$$\hat{\mathbf{g}}_{old}(\mathbf{x}) = \mathbf{g}(\mathbf{x}_{old}) + \mathbf{A}_{old}(\mathbf{x} - \mathbf{x}_{old}), \tag{8.7.1}$$

and the secant equation for the new matrix is defined by

$$\mathbf{y}_{new} = \mathbf{g}(\mathbf{x}_{new}) - \mathbf{g}(\mathbf{x}_{old}) = \mathbf{A}_{new}(\mathbf{x}_{new} - \mathbf{x}_{old}) = \mathbf{A}_{new}\mathbf{s}_{new}, \tag{8.7.2}$$

which gives a new affine approximation to $\mathbf{g}$. This approximation is not uniquely determined, requiring only that the change in $\mathbf{g}$ be a linear transformation $\mathbf{A}_{new}$ of the step $\mathbf{s}_{new}$. The difference between these two affine approximations can be expressed by

$$\hat{\mathbf{g}}_{new}(\mathbf{x}) - \hat{\mathbf{g}}_{old}(\mathbf{x}) = (\mathbf{A}_{new} - \mathbf{A}_{old})(\mathbf{x} - \mathbf{x}_{old}) \tag{8.7.3}$$

after combining (8.7.1) and (8.7.2) and some algebra. The goal is to update $\mathbf{A}$ in such a way as to minimize the change in the affine models given in (8.7.3). Reparameterize $\mathbf{x} - \mathbf{x}_{old}$ in terms of a scalar α multiple in the direction $\mathbf{s}_{new}$; then a vector $\mathbf{t}$ orthogonal to that direction gives $\mathbf{x} - \mathbf{x}_{old} = \alpha\mathbf{s}_{new} + \mathbf{t}$, where $\mathbf{t}^T\mathbf{s}_{new} = 0$. The change in the affine model can now be rewritten as

$$\hat{\mathbf{g}}_{new}(\mathbf{x}) - \hat{\mathbf{g}}_{old}(\mathbf{x}) = \alpha(\mathbf{A}_{new} - \mathbf{A}_{old})\mathbf{s}_{new} + (\mathbf{A}_{new} - \mathbf{A}_{old})\mathbf{t}, \tag{8.7.4}$$

and the goal now is expressed as making the last piece in (8.7.4) disappear. That is accomplished by writing $(\mathbf{A}_{new} - \mathbf{A}_{old}) = \mathbf{w}\mathbf{s}_{new}^T$ for some vector $\mathbf{w}$ to be determined. Multiplying this by $\mathbf{s}_{new}$ gives the first equation below; the others are obtained by evaluating (8.7.3) at $\mathbf{x} = \mathbf{x}_{new}$:

$$\begin{aligned}
(\mathbf{A}_{new} - \mathbf{A}_{old})\mathbf{s}_{new} &= \mathbf{w}\mathbf{s}_{new}^T\mathbf{s}_{new} \\
&= \mathbf{g}(\mathbf{x}_{new}) - \mathbf{g}(\mathbf{x}_{old}) - \mathbf{A}_{old}(\mathbf{x}_{new} - \mathbf{x}_{old}) \\
&= \mathbf{y}_{new} - \mathbf{A}_{old}\mathbf{s}_{new},
\end{aligned} \tag{8.7.5}$$

which determines $\mathbf{w} = (\mathbf{y}_{new} - \mathbf{A}_{old}\mathbf{s}_{new})/\mathbf{s}_{new}^T\mathbf{s}_{new}$. All of this work produces a rank-1 update known as *Broyden's secant update*,

$$\mathbf{A}_{new} = \mathbf{A}_{old} + \frac{(\mathbf{y}_{new} - \mathbf{A}_{old}\mathbf{s}_{new})\mathbf{s}_{new}^T}{\mathbf{s}_{new}^T\mathbf{s}_{new}}. \tag{8.7.6}$$

The iteration step for Broyden's method is then given by the Newton-like formula

$$\mathbf{x}_{next} = \mathbf{x}_{new} - \mathbf{A}_{new}^{-1}\mathbf{g}(\mathbf{x}_{new}). \tag{8.7.7}$$

The resulting algorithm, following the iteration step (8.7.7), converges superlinearly to the solution of the nonlinear equations. Broyden's update can be shown to have nice mathematical qualities, and though other updates have qualities at least as nice, none performs as well as (8.7.6) in practice.

The rank-1 nature of Broyden's secant update and the iteration formula written with a matrix inverse may together suggest a Sherman–Morrison–Woodbury (SMW)-type rank-1 matrix inverse updating scheme, $(\mathbf{A} + \mathbf{bc}^T)^{-1} = \mathbf{A}^{-1} - \mathbf{A}^{-1}\mathbf{bc}^T\mathbf{A}^{-1}/(1 + \mathbf{c}^T\mathbf{A}^{-1}\mathbf{b})$. In this form, the inverse of the new matrix is found from the inverse of the old matrix and takes only $O(p^2)$ operations instead of $O(p^3)$. However, when used repeatedly this scheme becomes poorly conditioned and should not be used. A better route is to update the QR factorization of $\mathbf{A}$ in the following way. Let $\mathbf{A}_{\text{old}} = \mathbf{Q}_{\text{old}}\mathbf{R}_{\text{old}}$ be the factorization of the old matrix, where $\mathbf{Q}$ is orthogonal and $\mathbf{R}$ is upper triangular. The new factorization is then written as

$$\mathbf{Q}_{\text{new}}\mathbf{R}_{\text{new}} = \mathbf{Q}_{\text{old}}\mathbf{R}_{\text{old}} + \mathbf{b}\mathbf{c}^{\mathsf{T}} = \mathbf{Q}_{\text{old}}(\mathbf{R}_{\text{old}} + \mathbf{d}\mathbf{c}^{\mathsf{T}}), \qquad (8.7.8)$$

so that the real problem is the factorization $\mathbf{Q}_{\text{upd}}\mathbf{R}_{\text{new}} = \mathbf{R}_{\text{old}} + \mathbf{d}\mathbf{c}^{\mathsf{T}}$.

Consider first the QR factorization of a rank-1 matrix $\mathbf{d}\mathbf{c}^{\mathsf{T}}$ by Givens transformations. Only $(p-1)$ rotations are needed, since the linear combination of rows that puts a zero in the second component of a pair of rows in one column will also put zeros in the second component of each column. Now, for the problem at hand there is a superimposed upper triangular matrix $\mathbf{R}_{\text{old}}$. Because of this, start the rotations at the bottom with rows $(p-1)$ and p, and rotate to put a zero in the pth component of the first column. This rotation, when applied to the whole matrix, will put zeros all along the last row except for the first subdiagonal $(p, p-1)$ element and the diagonal (p, p). Next, move up to rows $(p-2)$ and $(p-1)$, which puts zeros in row $(p-1)$ as far as the first subdiagonal $(p-1, p-2)$. Repeating this for a total of $(p-1)$ rotations produces a matrix that is upper triangular except for the first subdiagonal (this is known as a Hessenberg matrix). An additional $(p-1)$ rotations are needed to put a zero in these places. Since each rotation is applied to every row, costing $O(p)$ operations, it follows that performing $2(p-1)$ rotations (constituting $\mathbf{Q}_{\text{upd}}$) takes a total of $O(p^2)$ operations, which is the same as the unstable SMW update. Hence, solving to compute the step $\mathbf{A}_{\text{new}}^{-1}\mathbf{g}(\mathbf{x}_{\text{new}})$ still takes $O(p^2)$ operations.

Now that the secant analog has been found for the solution to nonlinear equations, our attention turns to finding a similar one for the optimization problem. Obviously, by taking derivatives, the optimization problem can be put into the nonlinear equations format $\nabla f(\mathbf{x}) = \mathbf{0}$. Then the secant equation analogous to (8.7.2) is

$$\mathbf{y}_{\text{new}} = \nabla f(\mathbf{x}_{\text{new}}) - \nabla f(\mathbf{x}_{\text{old}}) = \mathbf{H}_{\text{new}}(\mathbf{x}_{\text{new}} - \mathbf{x}_{\text{old}}) = \mathbf{H}_{\text{new}}\mathbf{s}_{\text{new}}. \qquad (8.7.9)$$

Because $\mathbf{H}$ is here the Hessian matrix of the function f, it must be symmetric – in contrast to the matrix $\mathbf{A}$ of (8.7.2), which has no restrictions. Moreover, if a minimum is sought then a positive definite Hessian matrix would be preferred because, near the solution, the true matrix $\mathbf{H}(\mathbf{x})$ would be positive definite. The objective now is to find an update of a Hessian matrix – from $\mathbf{H}_{\text{old}}$ (which satisfied the secant equation on the previous step) to $\mathbf{H}_{\text{new}}$ at this step – that is simple, fast, and produces a matrix both symmetric and positive definite. Powell (1970) found a symmetrized form of Broyden's secant update (8.7.6), but without a guarantee of positive definiteness. Enforcing positive definiteness is possible only if $\mathbf{s}_{\text{new}}^{\mathsf{T}}\mathbf{y}_{\text{new}} > 0$ (see Dennis and Schnabel 1983, lemma 9.2.1). Using the definition of $\mathbf{y}_{\text{new}}$ in (8.7.9), this condition can be translated to

$$\mathbf{s}_{\text{new}}^{\mathsf{T}}\nabla f(\mathbf{x}_{\text{new}}) > \mathbf{s}_{\text{new}}^{\mathsf{T}}\nabla f(\mathbf{x}_{\text{old}}),$$

which means that the function f is steeper now than before, in the direction of the step $\mathbf{s}_{\text{new}}$. This condition can then be enforced as a part of the search implementation. The resulting symmetric positive definite secant update is commonly known as the BFGS (Broyden–Fletcher–Goldfarb–Shanno) update and takes the form

$$\mathbf{H}_{\text{new}} = \mathbf{H}_{\text{old}} + \frac{\mathbf{y}_{\text{new}}\mathbf{y}_{\text{new}}^{\mathsf{T}}}{\mathbf{y}_{\text{new}}^{\mathsf{T}}\mathbf{s}_{\text{new}}} - \frac{\mathbf{H}_{\text{old}}\mathbf{s}_{\text{new}}\mathbf{s}_{\text{new}}^{\mathsf{T}}\mathbf{H}_{\text{old}}}{\mathbf{s}_{\text{new}}^{\mathsf{T}}\mathbf{H}_{\text{old}}\mathbf{s}_{\text{new}}}. \tag{8.7.10}$$

As with Broyden's secant update, there are other competitors, but the BFGS performs best in practice. The iteration step for this secant analog for optimization takes the familiar form

$$\mathbf{x}_{\text{next}} = \mathbf{x}_{\text{new}} - \mathbf{H}_{\text{new}}^{-1}\nabla f(\mathbf{x}_{\text{new}}). \tag{8.7.11}$$

Again, as with Broyden's secant update, efficient computations with $\mathbf{H}$ and its inverse are a main concern; details for the BFGS update are discussed in Goldfarb (1976). In this case, since $\mathbf{H}$ is positive definite, its Cholesky factor $\mathbf{L}$ can be updated. If we denote the old factor by $\mathbf{L}_{\text{old}}$ (i.e., $\mathbf{H}_{\text{old}} = \mathbf{L}_{\text{old}}\mathbf{L}_{\text{old}}^{\mathsf{T}}$), then the update to the new factor can be written as

$$\mathbf{L}_{\text{new}} = \mathbf{L}_{\text{old}} + \frac{(\mathbf{y}_{\text{new}} - \alpha\mathbf{H}_{\text{old}}\mathbf{s}_{\text{new}})(\alpha\mathbf{L}_{\text{old}}^{\mathsf{T}}\mathbf{s})^{\mathsf{T}}}{\mathbf{y}_{\text{new}}^{\mathsf{T}}\mathbf{s}_{\text{new}}}, \tag{8.7.12}$$

where $\alpha = (\mathbf{y}_{\text{new}}^{\mathsf{T}}\mathbf{s}_{\text{new}}/\mathbf{s}_{\text{new}}^{\mathsf{T}}\mathbf{H}_{\text{old}}\mathbf{s}_{\text{new}})^{1/2}$. This problem is quite similar to the update problem (8.7.8) and with the same QR analog to be pursued, but notice that the orthogonal matrix need not be kept here.

8.8   Condition and Scaling

In Section 8.4, the problem of when to stop an iterative search algorithm led to a discussion of the condition of the problem of root-finding or optimization. In the multivariate case – either solving nonlinear equations or optimizing a function of several variables – the problem of condition becomes more complicated. For the solution to nonlinear equations, the calculus (Theorem 8.8) gives

$$\mathbf{g}(\mathbf{x}) - \mathbf{g}(\mathbf{c}) \approx \mathbf{J}_{\mathbf{g}}(\mathbf{x} - \mathbf{c}); \tag{8.8.1}$$

this reveals that the condition of the problem is essentially that of the local affine approximation, which is merely a system of linear equations. Consequently, the results of Chapter 3 apply, giving a condition number of $\|\mathbf{J}^{-1}\|\|\mathbf{J}\|$. In solving a system of nonlinear equations, the gains from rescaling variables are essentially the same as those for rescaling in the linear case (see Chapter 3).

Stepping back from the mathematics for a moment, consider some of the practical aspects. Mathematically, the condition of the problem as originally posed is usually not subject to any control. Nonetheless, the seriousness of the condition could be exacerbated if we were to repose the problem poorly. To avoid this consequence, consider what can be done to improve the situation. As just mentioned, conditioning for nonlinear equations is essentially the same as for the affine approximant. Keeping all of the variables $\mathbf{x}$ in the same order of magnitude (if possible) is equivalent to column scaling. In the nonlinear equations case, this means reparameterizing the variables to $\mathbf{y} = \mathbf{Dx}$ and redefining the function as $\mathbf{g}(\mathbf{D}^{-1}\mathbf{y})$. Since premultiplication of $\mathbf{g}$ by any nonsingular matrix $\mathbf{A}$ will not change the root of the nonlinear equations, row scaling is available as a linear transformation $\mathbf{Ag}(\mathbf{x})$ to keep each equation at the same magnitude.

This rescaling of variables and equations is best done by the user, since rescaling by algorithm is difficult and often ineffective.

For the optimization problem, the issue of scaling becomes more interesting. Following Gill et al. (1981, pp. 301ff), for a value $\mathbf{x}$ near the optimum $\mathbf{c}$, we have by Theorem 8.6 that

$$f(\mathbf{x}) - f(\mathbf{c}) = (\mathbf{x} - \mathbf{c})^{\mathrm{T}} \mathbf{H} (\mathbf{x} - \mathbf{c})/2.$$

If the function f is accurate only to ε_f, then writing $\mathbf{x} - \mathbf{c} = h\mathbf{d}$ with $\|\mathbf{d}\| = 1$ yields

$$h^2 = \|\mathbf{x} - \mathbf{c}\|^2 \approx 2\varepsilon_f/[\mathbf{d}^{\mathrm{T}} \mathbf{H} \mathbf{d}], \tag{8.8.2}$$

which indicates that the accuracy in the solution depends on the direction. Extreme values of the quadratic form $[\mathbf{d}^{\mathrm{T}} \mathbf{H} \mathbf{d}]$ are, of course, the largest and smallest eigenvalues of the Hessian matrix $\mathbf{H}$. The amplification will then be largest in the direction of the eigenvector of the smallest eigenvalue. If $\mathbf{H}$ is nearly deficient in rank, then the problem will be very badly conditioned and an acceptable solution may stray far in the direction of that eigenvector. Remember that, owing to the nature of the problem, the adjective "acceptable" must be attributed to an apparently inaccurate solution and that no algorithm can be expected to improve upon it. Finally, it is disappointing to find that such a difficulty may not be found by simply examining the gradient. More specifically, the condition of ∇f again depends on the direction and the eigenvalues of $\mathbf{H}$, but now conversely. As a result, in the direction corresponding to small eigenvalues, the gradient could be small and the deviation from the solution large (or vice versa).

Again, the greatest gains in rescaling are from simple applications of common sense. In the optimization problem, however, the only easy tool is reparameterization. The goal is to rescale the variables so that the resultant Hessian matrix is not so badly conditioned. Another point of possible improvement is a rescaling of the function to be optimized, so that the function values themselves are not too large (and convergence never achieved) or too small (and gradients so close to zero that they indicate premature convergence).

Finally, the reader is cautioned to regard apparent convergence from optimization software with a grain of skepticism. For a badly conditioned problem, changing some part of the input to the problem – including stopping criteria – could lead to unacceptable changes in the purported solution. At any hint that assumptions on the function may be violated or the problem is badly conditioned, the reader should take steps to check whether the advertised solution really solved the problem. McCullough and Vinod (2003) suggest commonsense steps that are paraphrased here as questions to be addressed:

1. Is the gradient close enough to zero? If the algorithm stopped because of a small gradient, the solution may change if this stopping condition was tightened or the parameters rescaled. The accuracy of the arithmetic, the computational accuracy of the function, and the condition/scaling affect what might be considered "close enough."

2. Is the apparent convergence rate appropriate? Examine the sequence of iterations or "trace" of the algorithm. Newton-like methods should accelerate to a solution; linearly convergent methods should steadily improve.

3. Is the Hessian negative/positive definite? As just discussed, examining the eigenvalues and eigenvectors of the Hessian can indicate whether a problem is badly conditioned, as well as problematic search directions.
4. Is the function approximately quadratic at the solution? Plotting the function along directions suggested by the eigenvectors of the Hessian can shed light on many potential problems.

8.9   Implementation

The reader has been admonished previously about writing his or her own code where quality maintained software may be available. At this last opportunity, I will list the few situations where the reader might question that admonition. First, for some problems it is easy to code a Newton step – either for optimization or nonlinear equations – and the user has the opportunity to closely monitor its progress. In this case, the reader may enjoy coding his or her own algorithm. Second, in some situations the optimization or root-finding problem is at the core of a larger and longer piece of code, and the problem is sufficiently tractable that the performance of the method can be proven, preferably mathematically but certainly with experience. In other cases, I would urge the reader to use the software that is available. Software for optimization and nonlinear equations that is well-written, documented, and tested can be found in libraries such as NAG, IMSL, and MINPACK. Other algorithms can be found in the ACM algorithms, published in TOMS. The author – with much reluctance, after years of successfully avoiding the temptation and the effort – has taken the plunge to reinvent something as basic as the wheel in some minimizing codes **plum1t** and **plum2t**, following the guidelines of Dennis and Schnabel (1983). Further descriptions of these demonstrations are included in the next section. Although the author has some level of confidence in the quality of this code, it is not maintained professionally and has been included primarily for instructive purposes.

Nearly all of the optimization and nonlinear equation solvers are written as Fortran subroutine subprograms. For reasons cited in Chapter 1, Fortran subprograms can work as black boxes, to be pulled out of a library and put in place to solve whatever problem is at hand. The calling structure is nearly always the same: the user writes function or subroutine subprograms to compute the function or other information ($\mathbf{g}, \nabla f, \mathbf{J_g}, \mathbf{H}$), and the names of these modules are passed as an argument to the solver subroutine. In the driver, which calls the solver, an "external" statement is needed to denote the module names as such (and not as variable names). In order to pass information or data from the driver to the function or gradient modules, the usual method is to use modules. More recent code features the ability to pass vectors through the solver as arguments to both the solver and the function or gradient modules.

In R, a function is an object and can be passed as an argument to another function without a problem. To pass data to a function to be optimized or a root found, most commonly a loglikelihood function or its derivative, R offers three routes. The simplest route is to define the function to be optimized in the global environment with the data that it needs. If the function needs the data variable x, then the user must be careful never to use that variable elsewhere in that workspace. A second route that is similar to Fortran or other "call by name" languages is the "..." argument that is available in most optimizing functions. This allows the optimizing function to be called with more parameters than required, allowing the extra information to be made available to the loglikelihood function. Again, care must be taken in naming and referring to the variables. The third route is to use another function to write the loglikelihood function. We can write a function whose arguments are the data for the problem, whose result is a function to be optimized with just the parameters as arguments. When the writing function is called, it creates the loglikelihood function with the data in its environment. Examine closely the R code in **finder.r** where all three routes are demonstrated.

As discussed previously, Newton methods are usually fastest but they are often cumbersome because they require gradient or Hessian information. Sometimes coding a subprogram to provide this information is difficult; moreover, errors can be made in coding complicated formulas. As a result, many libraries have solvers in pairs: the user can either supply the information or let the solver compute the information using numerical difference methods (discussed in Section 8.6). When the size of the difference is under control, you should use the methods outlined in that section for choosing h. In some routines, h has been chosen much too small and so the solver is virtually useless. Remember, it is better to take h too large and face some bias than get a wild result from taking h too small.

In contrast, recent advances in *automatic differentiation* presage an end of the need for numerical differentiation. By automatic differentiation, we mean methods that can compute the gradient and/or Hessian of a function without the human effort of coding such an auxiliary function. Currently, this has been employed in situations where the software includes a language for models. For example, fitting a nonlinear regression model (Section 9.8) of the form $E(y_i) = \beta_0 + \beta_1 \exp(-\beta_2 x_i)$ may be written in some software in nearly the same set of symbols as the text on this page: $beta0 + beta1 * exp(-beta2 * x)$. As the software parses this text, it recognizes parameters (e.g., $beta1$), vectors (x), addition, multiplications, and the function exp. Automatic differentiation software can then arrange for the computation of both the mean function and the Jacobian matrix using some common pieces to avoid the duplication of effort. Currently, this software can handle most anything except code that involves branching (Griewank and Walther, 2008).

Finally, most solvers require a list of information to solve the problem at hand. Many of these have already been discussed: maximum number of iterations (or function or gradient evaluations), epsilons ($\varepsilon_x, \varepsilon_g, \varepsilon_f$), starting values for **x**, and initial values for a Hessian or Jacobian matrix. A less common but useful technique is to use a (diagonal) rescaling matrix so that the variables can be left in their natural units and automatically rescaled. This can also be used for rescaling to test for convergence on **x** as well as for choosing h for differencing.

8.10 A Non-Newton Method: Nelder-Mead

In a paper previously cited on numerical differentiation, Spendley, Hext, and Himsworth (1962) proposed a search algorithm based on constructing a regular simplex in d

dimensions for the purpose of optimizing the response in a d factor experiment using the responses at $d + 1$ design points. The search process consisted of constructing a new simplex by reflecting through the face opposite of the worst vertex of the simplex. In the case of a regular simplex (i.e., an equilateral triangle in $d = 2$, a regular tetrahedron in $d = 3$), the reflected simplex has only one new point at which the response must be measured. Sequentially updating this minimal set of design points leads to their "simplex" algorithm. Nelder and Mead (1965) modified this idea by relaxing the rigid regular shape of the simplex to just a set of $d + 1$ linearly independent vertices in d-dimensional space and developed an effective search method. The Nelder-Mead algorithm uses only values of the function and does not make the usual assumptions on the smoothness of the function to be minimized. As a result, their algorithm has a reputation for being rather robust, especially with respect to starting values. Using minimal assumptions about the function, however, also means that it will be very slow compared to any Newton-like method – its convergence will not improve greatly as the search approaches the solution. In practice, Nelder-Mead has been often used on difficult problems, or in situations where good starting values (good enough to allow Newton to work well) may not be available.

The algorithm begins with a set of vertices $\{\mathbf{x}^{(i)}, i = 1, \ldots, d+1\}$ forming the simplex in d dimensions. In each step of the algorithm, new points are selected for the simplex, essentially away from bad points, say $\mathbf{x}^{high}$ which has the highest value of the function $f(\mathbf{x})$, and toward good ones, say $\mathbf{x}^{low}$ where the function is smallest. The new point can be written as $\mathbf{x}^{new} = (1 + \alpha)\bar{\mathbf{x}} - \alpha\mathbf{x}^{high}$, where $\mathbf{x}^{high}$ is the largest (worst) vertex and $\bar{\mathbf{x}} = d^{-1}\sum_{j \neq high}\mathbf{x}^{(j)}$, the centroid of the remaining vertices. Comparing the value of the function at this new point f_{new} to $f_{low} = f(\mathbf{x}^{low}) < \ldots < f_{second} = f(\mathbf{x}^{second}) < f_{high} = f(\mathbf{x}^{high})$ leads to variations on this basic step.

If the new point is a definite improvement ($f_{new} < f_{second}$), but not the best ($f_{low} < f_{new}$), then replace the worst $\mathbf{x}^{high}$ with the new point $\mathbf{x}^{new}$ and restart.

If the new point is best, then try to expand the simplex by moving further away from $\mathbf{x}^{high}$ to $\mathbf{x}^{exp} = (1 - \gamma)\bar{\mathbf{x}} + \gamma\mathbf{x}_{new}$, using the expansion coefficient γ. If this newest point $\mathbf{x}^{exp}$ is best, that is, $f(\mathbf{x}^{exp}) < f_{new}$, then replace the worst point $\mathbf{x}^{high}$ in the simplex with this expansion point $\mathbf{x}^{exp}$ and restart; otherwise, replace the worst with the improvement $\mathbf{x}^{new}$ (and restart).

If the new point is only a marginal improvement ($f_{second} < f_{new} < f_{high}$), so that the new point would be the worst point in the new simplex, then the (just reflected) simplex is contracted: $\mathbf{x}^{rcon} = (1 - \beta)\bar{\mathbf{x}} + \beta\mathbf{x}^{high}$. If this new point is better ($f_{rcon} = f(\mathbf{x}^{rcon}) < f_{new}$), then replace the worst with $\mathbf{x}^{rcon}$; otherwise, we must have gone too far and will have to shrink the simplex.

If the new point is now the worst, then going away from the $\mathbf{x}^{high}$ may not have been such a good idea, so we should contract the original simplex back toward $\mathbf{x}^{high}$ and away from $\mathbf{x}^{new}$, and try the point $\mathbf{x}^{icon} = (1 - \beta)\bar{\mathbf{x}} + \beta\mathbf{x}^{new}$. If the new point is an improvement, replace $\mathbf{x}^{high}$ with $\mathbf{x}^{icon}$ in the simplex and restart; otherwise, we'll have to shrink the simplex.

The motivation for shrinking is that if any step away from the current simplex is going up, perhaps the steps are too big and so the simplex is too big. Shrinking brings the other points halfway to the current best $\mathbf{x}^{low}$ following $\mathbf{x}^{(i)}_{shrink} = \mathbf{x}^{low} - \frac{1}{2}(\mathbf{x}^{(i)} - \mathbf{x}^{low})$.

According to Kelley (1999), even under reasonable assumptions, the function value at best point f_{low} is not guaranteed to improve with each step; rather, the average value in the simplex $(d+1)^{-1} \sum_i f(\mathbf{x}^{(i)})$ will be reduced. This is hardly a glowing endorsement, especially compared to Newton-like methods that accelerate as they approach the solution. As a result, Nelder-Mead should not be the first tool to be used on a problem, but one to be utilized when other methods have failed.

Programs and Demonstrations

false   *Convergence of false position and Illinois*
The Illinois method is a powerful hybrid method, combining the safety of bisection or false position (regula falsi) while avoiding the problems of false position in achieving superlinear convergence. As used in Figures 8.1 and 8.2, the function is $g(x) = x^3 - 1$ on the interval $(0, 2)$. Both methods are set up to do 30 iterations (too many). False position stops only when it stumbles onto the root after 25 iterations; Illinois starts slowly, but after its first secant step it quickly finds the root at 1.
regula – performs false position (regula falsi) search.
illini – performs Illinois method search.

finder   *Demonstration of all one-variable root finders and optimizer*
The problem faced here was presented first as Example 8.3; this maximum likelihood problem will be used again later in Chapters 9 and 12.
golden – performs golden section search for a maximum of a given function in an interval.
bisect – performs bisection search for a root of a given function in an interval.
regula – performs regula falsi (false position) search for a root of a given function in an interval.
illini – performs Illinois method search for a root of a given function in an interval.
secant – performs secant search for a root of a given function.
newton – performs Newton search for a root of a given function; also requires its derivative.
In the R version, three ways of passing data to a function to be optimized/root found are demonstrated using the similar R functions **optimize** and **uniroot**.

nelmead   *Demonstration of Nelder-Mead search*
For the same four problems tested in **plum1t/plum2t**, the routine **nelmead** computes the minimum of the functions. In the R version, default method in **optim** is Nelder-Mead.

numdif   *Demonstration of numerical differentiation*
Numerical estimates of the first and second derivatives of the function $f(x) = \log \Gamma(x)$ are computed. The routine ALGAMA is used to compute the function. Forward difference estimates for the first derivative ($\hat{f}_1'(x)$ from (8.6.1)) as well as central differences ($\hat{f}_2'(x)$ from (8.6.2)) are computed. For the second derivative, both expressions f_1'' and f_2'' described on page 185 are employed for comparison.

del12f   *Test/demonstration of numerical differentiation of a multivariate function*
Once maximum likelihood estimates have been computed, the next step is often
to compute the gradient vector and Hessian matrix of the log-likelihood function.
Given the function and differences for each variable, the routine **del12f** computes
the gradient vector (using central differences) and the Hessian (using the generalization given by (8.6.6)). The function used for testing is

$$f(x) = \left\{ \log\left(\frac{x_1 x_2}{x_3 x_4} \right) \right\}^2,$$

which looks pretty simple but can be tricky. The gradient and Hessian were computed at $\mathbf{x} = (1, 2, 3, 4)$.
del12f – computes gradient and Hessian by numerical differentiation.

plum1t   *Test/demonstration of general function minimizer* **plum1t**
For four examples, the routine **plum1t** computes the minimum of a function. Newton's method with backtracking (as recommended by Dennis and Schnabel 1983)
is the approach used. In this version, all derivatives – both gradient and Hessian –
are computed numerically using **del12f**. The first two examples are $p = 4$ and $p = 10$ generalizations of the Rosenbrock (1960) function. The third example is a likelihood from Cox (1970), and the fourth is Example 9.4.1 from Dennis and Schnabel
(1983). The routine **plum1t** requires **del12f** as well as the Cholesky codes **chlzky**,
chlzhi, **chlzih**, and **adjust**.
plum1t – computes the minimum of a function using numerical gradients and Hessians.
In the R version, the similar R function **nlm** is used for the same test problems.

plum2t   *Test/demonstration of general minimizer* **plum2t**
The parallel routine to **plum1t**, but requires a user-supplied routine to compute the
gradient and Hessian analytically. The same four examples as **plum1t** are solved.
The routine **plum2t** also requires the same Cholesky routines **chlzky**, **chlzhi**, **chlzih**,
and **adjust**.
plum2t – computes the minimum of a function using analytic gradients and Hessians.
In the R version, the similar R function **nlm** is used for the same test problems. Gradients and Hessians are attached as attributes to the objective function.

Exercises

8.1   Consider the cubic function $g(x) = x^3 - x - 1$. Show that the three roots of $g(x) = 0$
are separated by $\pm 1/\sqrt{3}$. Find the largest root.

8.2   A simple approximation to the square root of a number x in the interval $[1/16, 1)$ is the
function
$$y_0(x) = 1.681595 - 1.288973/(0.8408065 + x).$$

Find the relative error of y_0 by finding the extreme points of $\left(y_0(x) - \sqrt{x} \right)/\sqrt{x}$ or the
extreme points of $\left(y_0 - \sqrt{x} \right)^2/x$.

8.3 Take the derivative of $f(\mathbf{x} + t\mathbf{p})$ with respect to t to show that the directional derivative of a function $f(\mathbf{x})$ in the direction p is equal to $p^T \nabla f(\mathbf{x})$.

8.4 Prove the linear version of the multivariate mean value theorem (8.1.1).

8.5 Find the constants c_1 and c_2 such that $F_n = c_1\phi^n + c_2\phi^{-n}$ for the nth Fibonacci number.

8.6 Consider the difference equation $y_{n+2} = y_n + y_{n-1}$ with starting values all equal to 1. What is the limit of the ratio y_{n+1}/y_n as $n \to \infty$?

8.7 *Discrete Bisection.* Suppose $Y_1 < Y_2 < \cdots < Y_n$. The problem is to find (quickly) i for a given y such that $Y_i \leq y < Y_{i+1}$. (Let $i = 0$ if $y < Y_1$.)
    (a) Write an algorithm to solve this by applying the bisection algorithm to the function $f(k) = Y_k - y$. Be careful of details.
    (b) Write a Fortran program to compute the empirical distribution function at a given point, given the order statistics.
    (c) For large values of n, how many steps would be required?

8.8 Consider the function $g(x) = x/\sqrt{1 + x^2}$, which has a single root at $x = 0$. For what starting values of x will Newton's method converge to 0? For what values will Newton's method diverge?

8.9 Give the iteration step and the relative error d_{n+1} in terms of d_n for Newton's method applied to the square root problem, that is, finding the root of $f(y) = y^2 - x$. (This algorithm, known as Heron's rule, goes back to ancient times.)

8.10 Suppose we solve Exercise 8.2 and use the estimate y_0 of the square root of x to start two Heron iterations, $y_1 = \frac{1}{2}(y_0 + x/y_0)$ and $y_2 = y_1 - \frac{1}{2}(y_1 - x/y_1)$. What is the relative error of y_2? (This is the single precision algorithm for IBM mainframes; its accuracy is advertised as $2^{-25.9}$.)

8.11 As in Exercise 8.9, analyze the convergence of Newton's method applied to the function $f(y) = y^p - x$ for $p = 3, 4, \ldots$ and also for $p = -1$ (for computers with no floating point division instruction).

8.12 Explain why the secant formula (8.3.7) would be preferred to the following equivalent expression:
$$x_{n+1} = [x_{n-1}g(x_n) - x_n g(x_{n-1})]/[g(x_n) - g(x_{n-1})].$$

8.13 Let us define an estimator of location as the value of μ that minimizes
$$f(\mu) = \sum_{i=1}^{n} |X_i - \mu|^{3/2},$$
giving an estimator part way between the median (exponent 1) and mean (exponent 2).
    (a) Show that the derivative $f'(\mu)$ is monotone increasing.
    (b) Where does the second derivative $f''(\mu)$ *not* exist?
    (c) Find an interval in which the minimum of f must be attained.
    (d) Show that neither Newton's method nor the secant method are guaranteed to work.
    (e) Can regula falsi also fail?
    (f) Of the many methods, what is the best method for computing this estimate?

8.14 A problem similar to that used in Figures 8.1 and 8.2 is finding the root of $g(x) = x^3$ in the interval $(-1, 2)$. How do regula falsi and Illinois perform on this one? Is there something wrong here?

8.15 The Hodges–Lehmann location estimator can be defined as the root of the Wilcoxon statistic

$$W(\mu) = \sum_{i=1}^{n} \operatorname{sign}(X_i - \mu) \operatorname{rank}(|X_i - \mu|).$$

(a) Design an algorithm to compute the estimator that would need to sort only once.
(b) When n modulo 4 is 0 or 3, the estimator is the midpoint of the interval of roots of W. How would you handle that?

8.16 Consider using false position to find the root of the function f on the unit interval

$$f(x) = \begin{cases} -a & \text{for } x < 1 - \varepsilon, \\ b & \text{for } x \geq 1 - \varepsilon, \end{cases}$$

with the starting points $(0, -a)$ and $(1, b)$. Show that the convergence can be made arbitrarily slow by taking $a, b > 0$ to extremes.

8.17 Find the minimum of the gamma function $\Gamma(x)$ in the interval $(1, 2)$.

8.18 Let $f^*(u) = f(\mathbf{x} + u\mathbf{d})$. Find $f^{*\prime}(0)$.

8.19 Suppose we are given $f^*(0)$, $f^*(1)$, and $f^{*\prime}(0)$. Following Exercises 8.18 and 8.3, find the value of u that minimizes a quadratic approximation to $f^*(u)$.

8.20 In the code **numdif**, change x to $x = 3/2$ and then compare the results to both $f'(3/2) = .036489974$ and $f''(3/2) = .9348022005$.

8.21 Compute the percentile points of the normal distribution for $\alpha = .10, .05, .01$ by finding the roots of the equation $\Phi(x) - \alpha = 0$.

8.22 For $t = 1, 2, 3$ and the same values of α as in Exercise 8.21, find the percentile points of the inverse Gaussian distribution with distribution function

$$\Phi\left((x - 1)\sqrt{t/x}\right) + e^{2t}\Phi\left(-(x + 1)\sqrt{t/x}\right).$$

8.23 The Cantor function (see Exercise 2.25) is a continuous and nondecreasing function on $(0, 1)$. Find where the Cantor function crosses $1/3$ numerically.

8.24 Just for fun, using **numdif** and your code for the Cantor function $f(x)$ in Exercise 8.23, what happens when you try to compute numerical derivatives of $f(x)$ at various x?

8.25 In smoothing spline computations, we need to solve nonlinear equations of the form

$$f(t) = \sum_{i} \frac{1}{1 + 6tg_i} = r,$$

for constants $g_i > 0$.
(a) Construct bounds for the root of this equation based on r and the minimum and maximum of g_i.
(b) Recommend a method for solving this nonlinear equation.
(c) Write a function to take r and g_i as input and compute the root.

8.26 (Bodily, 2002) Let $g(x)$ be a stochastic process with zero mean and covariance kernel $Cov(g(x), g(y)) = \gamma(x, y)$. Let $\gamma(x, y)$ have sufficient properties so that we can take derivatives $g'(x)$ such that $Cov(g(x), g'(y)) = \frac{\partial}{\partial y}\gamma(x, y)$ and $Cov(g'(x), g'(y)) =$

$\frac{\partial^2}{\partial x \partial y} \gamma(x, y)$. Consider the computed first difference as having independent random rounding errors e_1 and e_2 with variance ϵ_m^2 as

$$h^{-1}(g(x + h) + e_1) - h^{-1}(g(x) + e_2).$$

(a) Compute the variance as $E\left[h^{-1}(g(x + h) + e_1) - h^{-1}(g(x) + e_2) - g'(x)\right]^2$.

(b) For the covariance kernel $\gamma(x, y) = \sigma^2 e^{-a(x-y)^2}$, find h (to first order) to minimize this variance.

(c) Perform a similar analysis for the central difference $(f(x + h) - f(x - h))/(2h)$.

8.27 Notice that for small values of c, $f_c(u) = \sqrt{c^2 + u^2} \approx |u|$, or in words, $f_c(u)$ is a continuous approximation for the discontinuous function $|u|$. Consider using this approximation to solve the median regression problem as

$$min_\mathbf{b} \sum_i f(y_i - \mathbf{x}_i^T \mathbf{b}).$$

What optimization methods may work here? Will Newton methods work? Why or why not?

References

The two main sources for optimization and nonlinear equations are the books by Dennis and Schnabel (1983) and Gill et al. (1981). They are both well written, and the extent of detail and complexity should deter the reader from writing algorithms while enabling a deeper appreciation of the skill and artistry employed by extant optimizers and nonlinear equation solvers. Of the older references, Wilde (1964) is a favorite. Dowell and Jarratt (1971) derived the convergence rate for the Illinois method.

Christopher H. Bodily (2002), "Numerical Differentiation Using Statistical Design," unpublished Ph.D. thesis, North Carolina State University.

R. P. Brent (1973), *Algorithms for Minimization without Derivatives.* Englewood Cliffs, NJ: Prentice-Hall.

D. R. Cox (1970), *Analysis of Binary Data.* London: Methuen.

J. E. Dennis, Jr. (1984), "A User's Guide to Nonlinear Optimization Algorithms," *Proceedings of the IEEE* 72: 1765–76.

J. E. Dennis, Jr., and R. B. Schnabel (1983), *Numerical Methods for Unconstrained Optimization and Nonlinear Equations.* Englewood Cliffs, NJ: Prentice-Hall.

M. Dowell and P. Jarratt (1971), "A Modified Regula Falsi Method for Computing the Root of an Equation," *BIT* 11: 168–74.

D. M. Gay (1983), "Algorithm 611: Subroutines for Unconstrained Minimization Using a Model/Trust Region Approach," *ACM Transactions on Mathematical Software* 9: 503–24.

P. E. Gill, W. Murray, and M. H. Wright (1981), *Practical Optimization.* London: Academic Press.

D. Goldfarb (1976), "Factorized Variable Metric Methods for Unconstrained Optimization," *Mathematics of Computation* 30: 796–811.

Andreas Griewank and Andrea Walther (2008), *Evaluating Derivatives: Principles and Techniques for Algorithmic Differentiation.* 2nd edition, Philadelphia: SIAM.

C. T. Kelley (1999), *Iterative Methods for Optimization.* Philadelphia: SIAM.

D. G. Luenberger (1984), *Linear and Nonlinear Programming,* 2nd ed. Reading, MA: Addison-Wesley.

B. D. McCullough and H. D. Vinod (2003), "Verifying the Solution from a Nonlinear Solver: A Case Study," *The American Economic Review* 93: 873–91.

J. A. Nelder and R. Mead (1965), "A Simplex Method for Function Minimization," *The Computer Journal* 7: 308–13.

M. J. D. Powell (1970), "A New Algorithm for Unconstrained Optimization," in J. B. Rosen, O. L. Mangasarian, and K. Ritter (Eds.), *Nonlinear Programming,* pp. 31–65. New York: Academic Press.

H. Rosenbrock (1960), "An Automatic Method for Finding the Greatest or Least Value of a Function," *Computer Journal* 3: 175–84.

W. Spendley, G. R. Hext, and F. R. Himsworth (1962), "Sequential Application of Simplex Designs in Optimization and Evolutionary Operation," *Technometrics* 4: 441–61.

Michael N. Vrahatis (1988), "Solving Systems of Nonlinear Equations Using the Nonzero Value of the Topological Degree," *ACM Transactions on Mathematical Software* 14: 312–29.

D. J. Wilde (1964), *Optimum Seeking Methods.* Englewood Cliffs, NJ: Prentice-Hall.

9

Maximum Likelihood and
Nonlinear Regression

9.1 Introduction

Maximum likelihood is generally regarded as the best all-purpose approach for statistical analysis. Outside of the most common statistical procedures, when the "optimal" or "usual" method is unknown, most statisticians follow the principle of maximum likelihood for parameter estimation and statistical hypothesis tests. Bayesian statistical methods also rely heavily on maximum likelihood. The main reason for this reliance is that following the principle of maximum likelihood usually leads to very reasonable and effective estimators and tests. From a theoretical viewpoint, under very mild conditions, maximum likelihood estimators (MLEs) are consistent, asymptotically unbiased, and efficient. Moreover, MLEs are invariant under reparameterizations or transformations: the MLE of a function of the parameter is the function of the MLE. From a practical viewpoint, the estimates and test statistics can be constructed without a great deal of analysis, and large-sample standard errors can be computed. Overall, experience has shown that maximum likelihood works well most of the time.

The biggest computational challenge comes from the naive expectation that any statistical problem can be solved if the maximum of some function is found. Instead of relying solely on the unconstrained optimization methods presented in Chapter 8 to meet this unrealistic expectation, the nature of the likelihood function can be exploited in ways that are more effective for computing MLEs. Since the exploitable properties of likelihood functions follow from the large-sample theory, this chapter will begin with a summary of the consistency and asymptotic normality properties of MLEs. The computational consequences of the theory then follow, with an extended example in Section 9.4 for illustrations. After a discussion of the usual regression problem in this context, the two main extensions that rely on asymptotics – generalized regression and nonlinear regression – will be covered in detail. The final section deals with reparameterizations and constraints.

Our discussion in this chapter of the asymptotic properties of maximum likelihood provides insight into the performance of computational procedures. The attention to rigor may give the appearance of "proving" our results, but the goal is to show how violations of assumptions lead to either (a) failure of MLEs to perform well statistically or (b) the reasons for failure of a computational procedure.

9.2   Notation and Asymptotic Theory of Maximum Likelihood

Let $\mathbf{Y}_1, \mathbf{Y}_2, \ldots, \mathbf{Y}_n$ be independent and identically distributed (IID) observations from one of a family of distributions on $\mathcal{R}^k$ indexed by a p-dimensional parameter $\boldsymbol{\theta}$. Denote the distribution function of the **Y**s by $F(\mathbf{y} \mid \boldsymbol{\theta})$ and the true value of the parameter by $\boldsymbol{\theta}^*$. The likelihood function is the product of the densities $f(\mathbf{y} \mid \boldsymbol{\theta})$ evaluated at the observations, treated as a function of the parameter $\boldsymbol{\theta}$:

$$L_n(\boldsymbol{\theta}) = \prod_{i=1}^{n} f(\mathbf{Y}_i \mid \boldsymbol{\theta});$$

the (natural) logarithm of the likelihood function, called the log-likelihood function, is denoted by

$$\ell_n(\boldsymbol{\theta}) = \log L_n(\boldsymbol{\theta}) = \sum_{i=1}^{n} \log f(\mathbf{Y}_i \mid \boldsymbol{\theta}).$$

Let $E_{\boldsymbol{\theta}}[g(\mathbf{Y})]$ denote the expectation of a function of the random variable with respect to the distribution at the parameter value $\boldsymbol{\theta}$. Then, with only a minor abuse of notation, notice that clearly $E_{\boldsymbol{\theta}}[\ell_n(\boldsymbol{\theta})] = n E_{\boldsymbol{\theta}}[\log f(\mathbf{Y} \mid \boldsymbol{\theta})]$. Pursuing this further, since $n^{-1}\ell_n(\boldsymbol{\theta})$ is an average, the strong law of large numbers dictates that

$$n^{-1}\ell_n(\boldsymbol{\theta}) \to E_{\boldsymbol{\theta}^*}[\log f(\mathbf{Y} \mid \boldsymbol{\theta})] \equiv \ell_*(\boldsymbol{\theta}), \tag{9.2.1}$$

which defines a useful expectation function $\ell_*(\boldsymbol{\theta})$. The maximum likelihood estimate will be denoted by $\hat{\boldsymbol{\theta}}_n$. This is defined to be a value of $\boldsymbol{\theta}$ that attains the maximum; that is,

$$L_n(\hat{\boldsymbol{\theta}}_n) \geq L_n(\boldsymbol{\theta}) \quad \text{for all } \boldsymbol{\theta} \in \Theta.$$

The MLE so defined may not be unique, but that is a problem to be faced later.

Consistency of the maximum likelihood estimate is the foremost result and the one that requires the least in the way of conditions. The heart of the matter is the information inequality, presented here as a lemma. As applied to this discussion, the information inequality leads to $\ell_*(\boldsymbol{\theta}^*) > \ell_*(\boldsymbol{\theta})$; that is, the true parameter value maximizes the mean of this random log-likelihood function.

Lemma 9.1 (Information Inequality): *Let f and g be densities in y. Then*

$$\int (\log g) f(y) \, dy \leq \int (\log f) f(y) \, dy,$$

with equality if and only if $f = g$.

Proof.   See Exercise 9.1 or Wald (1949, lemma 1).   □

The following assumptions, taken mostly from Wald (1949), are essential to proving the consistency of maximum likelihood estimates. Violations of these assumptions are most interesting, since they bear upon some of the computational difficulties. Each assumption will be listed and discussed in turn,

Assumption A1 (Density): *The distribution of the individual* **Y** *observations must have a density $f(\mathbf{y} \mid \boldsymbol{\theta})$ that is either continuous or discrete – not mixed.*

More complicated problems are beyond the level of this discussion.

Assumption A2 (Compactness): *The parameter space $\Theta \subset \mathcal{R}^p$ (set of all possible θ) is closed and bounded and hence is compact with respect to the Euclidean norm.*

Assumption A2 avoids a lot of mathematical headaches, and that avoidance can spark a debate. Given the reality of finite arithmetic on the computer to solve the problem, compactness isn't much of a strain. With respect to applications, the closed and bounded parameter space may not permit some parameterizations where infinity corresponds to a zero. This is also related to the continuity assumption (A5). One pathological failure of ML (Neyman and Scott 1948) occurs with an infinite number of parameters; see Exercise 9.2.

Assumption A3 (Identifiability): *The parameter θ is identified; that is, for any $\theta_1 \neq \theta_2$ there exists a set $A \subset \mathcal{R}^k$ such that $\Pr(\mathbf{Y} \in A \mid \theta = \theta_1) \neq \Pr(\mathbf{Y} \in A \mid \theta = \theta_2)$.*

Violations of A3 usually manifest themselves computationally with an iterative sequence of estimates running around a surface or off to infinity without a change in the value of the likelihood function. Although Assumption A3 requires merely the existence of an informative datum, in finite samples some parameter points on a manifold may be indistinguishable (see Exercise 9.3). Problems where parameter points are nearly unidentified are difficult computationally as well as statistically. The seriousness of the problem can be assessed by computing the mean and variance of the difference $Z = \log(f(\mathbf{Y} \mid \theta_1)) - \log(f(\mathbf{Y} \mid \theta_2))$; see Exercise 9.4.

Assumption A4 (Boundedness): *$E_{\theta^*}[|\log f(\mathbf{Y} \mid \theta^*)|] < \infty$ and, for all θ,*

$$E_{\theta^*}[(\log f(\mathbf{Y} \mid \theta))_+] < \infty,$$

where $(\cdot)_+$ denotes the positive part.

This assumption precludes another pathological case where ML fails; see Exercise 9.5.

Assumption A5 (Continuity): *The density is continuous in θ. That is,*

$$\lim_{\theta_j \to \theta} f(\mathbf{y} \mid \theta_j) = f(\mathbf{y} \mid \theta)$$

for all $\mathbf{y}$ except perhaps on a set of zero probability (with respect to $f(\mathbf{y} \mid \theta^*)$), perhaps depending on θ.

The continuity of the likelihood function $\ell_n(\theta)$ is essential to convergence. However, if the parameter set is discrete (say, a finite number of points) then the proof becomes easier. Nonetheless, finding the MLE without an exhaustive search requires unimodality, which is essential to the lattice search discussed in Section 8.1.

Theorem 9.1 (Consistency): *Under Assumptions A1–A5, the maximum likelihood estimate $\hat{\theta}_n$ converges to θ^*.*

Outline of Proof.   Following the definition in (9.2.1), the information inequality states that $\ell_*(\theta) < \ell_*(\theta^*)$ for all $\theta \neq \theta^*$. The strong law then says that $n^{-1}\{\ell_n(\theta) - \ell_n(\theta^*)\}$ converges to something negative for any θ not in a neighborhood containing the true value of the parameter θ^*. This traps the MLE in a neighborhood of θ^*, since $\ell_n(\hat{\theta}_n) - \ell_n(\theta^*) > 0$. The remainder of the proof consists of the mathematical details. See Wald (1949) for a proof of strong consistency and Wolfowitz (1949) for a weaker version.   □

A problem whose discussion has been postponed is the possibility of the MLE not being unique, with many values of θ attaining the maximum. If no observations Y_i allow for two values of θ to be distinguished (i.e., if there are no realizations in the identifiability set), then the data do not give any information about that region of the parameter space. The more common circumstance is finding the maximum by finding the root of the derivative of the likelihood function, $\nabla\ell_n = \mathbf{0}$, for which there may be multiple roots corresponding to local maxima and minima. Most optimization techniques seek only local optima; multiple starting points and comparison of the likelihood attained at these optima are then required.

It is important to emphasize that the conditions for consistency of the MLE are not very restrictive. However, achieving asymptotic normality requires more restrictive assumptions. The following two examples give some contrasting analysis.

Example 9.1: *Normal Distribution*
Let $Y_1, Y_2, \ldots, Y_n$ be observations IID normal(μ, γ); then

$$\log f(y \mid \theta) = -\frac{1}{2}\log 2\pi - \frac{1}{2}\log\gamma - \frac{(y - \mu)^2}{2\gamma}.$$

Taking expectations at the true value $\theta^* = (\mu^*, \gamma^*)$, we get

$$E_{\theta^*}[\log f(y \mid \theta)] = \ell_*(\mu, \gamma) = -\frac{1}{2}\log 2\pi - \frac{1}{2}\log\gamma - \frac{\gamma^* + (\mu^* - \mu)^2}{2\gamma}.$$

Notice that the maximum of $\ell_*(\mu, \gamma)$ occurs at (μ^*, γ^*).

Example 9.2A: *Uniform Distribution*
Let $Y_1, Y_2, \ldots, Y_n$ be observations IID uniform$(0, \theta)$. Then $\log f(y \mid \theta) = -\log\theta$ for $0 < y < \theta$ and $-\infty$ otherwise. Again taking expectations at the true value θ^*, we get

$$E_{\theta^*}[\log f(y \mid \theta)] = \ell_*(\theta) = \begin{cases} -\log\theta & \text{for } \theta \geq \theta^*, \\ -\infty & \text{for } \theta < \theta^*. \end{cases}$$

Once again, $\ell_*(\theta)$ is maximized at $\theta = \theta^*$.

At this point, three results are fundamental to establish asymptotic normality for MLEs. Central to these is the interchange of limit and integral – or, more specifically, derivative and integral. These conditions are satisfied in many important cases, but the results when they are *not* satisfied are surprising; these cases will be discussed later.

Lemma 9.2: *Under appropriate conditions, $n^{-1/2}\nabla\ell_n(\theta^*) \overset{d}{\to} N_p(0, \mathbf{J}(\theta^*))$, where the covariance matrix is*

$$\mathbf{J}(\theta) = \text{cov}(\nabla \log f(Y \mid \theta) \mid Y \sim f(\mathbf{y} \mid \theta^*)). \tag{9.2.2}$$

Proof.   Let $Z^{(i)} = \nabla \log f(Y_i \mid \theta)$ (evaluated at θ^*). Then, in order to compute $E_{\theta^*}[\mathbf{Z}^{(i)}]$, assumptions are needed to permit pushing the derivative operation inside the integral (expectation):

$$E_{\theta^*}[\mathbf{Z}^{(i)}] = \int \{\nabla \log f(\mathbf{y} \mid \theta)\} f(\mathbf{y} \mid \theta)\, d\mathbf{y}$$

$$= \int \left\{ \frac{\nabla f(\mathbf{y} \mid \theta)}{f(\mathbf{y} \mid \theta)} \right\} f(\mathbf{y} \mid \theta)\, d\mathbf{y} = \int \nabla f(\mathbf{y}|\theta)\, d\mathbf{y}$$

$$= \nabla \int f(\mathbf{y} \mid \theta)\, d\mathbf{y} = \nabla(1) = \mathbf{0}.$$

The interchange of operations occurs at the beginning of the third line. The remainder of the work is just the application of the central limit theorem.   □

Lemma 9.3: *Let $\mathbf{H}_n(\theta) = \nabla^2\ell_n(\theta)$. Then, under the appropriate conditions,*

$$n^{-1}\mathbf{H}_n(\theta) \overset{as}{\longrightarrow} \mathbf{H}(\theta) \quad \text{pointwise in } \theta$$

and $-\mathbf{H}(\theta^*) = \mathbf{J}(\theta^*)$, where $E_{\theta^*}[\nabla^2 \log f(Y \mid \theta)] = \mathbf{H}(\theta)$ is continuous in θ.

Proof.   The first part is merely the strong law; the second part consists of a similar interchange of derivative and expectation.   □

Continuity of $\mathbf{H}(\theta)$ is harder to prove, but quite important.

Theorem 9.2: *Under the appropriate conditions, $\sqrt{n}(\hat{\theta}_n - \theta^*)$ is asymptotically normal, with mean vector $\mathbf{0}$ and covariance matrix $\mathbf{J}(\theta^*)^{-1}$.*

Proof.   The appropriate conditions are needed to permit the Taylor-like expansion of $\nabla\ell_n(\theta)$ similar to Theorem 8.8. Given the appropriate conditions, the linearization gives

$$\|n^{-1/2}[\nabla\ell_n(\hat{\theta}_n) - \nabla\ell_n(\theta^*)] - n^{-1}\nabla^2\ell_n(\theta^*)\{\sqrt{n}(\hat{\theta}_n - \theta^*)\}\| \overset{p}{\to} 0.$$

Now, $\nabla\ell_n(\hat{\theta}_n) = \mathbf{0}$ and Lemma 9.3 give

$$n^{-1}\nabla^2\ell_n(\theta^*) \overset{p}{\to} -\mathbf{J}(\theta^*) \tag{9.2.3}$$

and so, restating with Slutzky (without norms for simplicity), we have

$$n^{-1/2}\nabla\ell_n(\theta^*) - \mathbf{J}(\theta^*)\{\sqrt{n}(\hat{\theta}_n - \theta^*)\} \overset{p}{\to} 0; \tag{9.2.4}$$

hence they both have the same distribution. From Lemma 9.2, the first piece converges in distribution to $N_p(\mathbf{0}, \mathbf{J}(\theta^*))$, so that the result follows by matrix multiplication.   □

This is nice theory, but from a computational point of view, the following result – that asymptotically the log-likelihood function is locally quadratic – is much more powerful. This is a wonderful result, saying that the problem is about as easy as one could have hoped for.

Theorem 9.3: *Asymptotically, for θ in a neighborhood of $\hat{\theta}_n$, the likelihood function is quadratic under the appropriate conditions.*

Proof. Following Theorem 8.6, since $\nabla \ell_n(\hat{\theta}_n)$ is zero we have, for θ near $\hat{\theta}_n$,

$$n^{-1}\ell_n(\theta) = n^{-1}\ell_n(\hat{\theta}_n) + \tfrac{1}{2}(\theta - \hat{\theta}_n)^{\mathsf{T}}[n^{-1}\nabla^2\ell_n(\mathbf{t})](\theta - \hat{\theta}_n)$$

for some value of $\mathbf{t}$ in the same neighborhood. Here the continuity of $\nabla^2\ell_n$ is critical for allowing us to use the approximation $\nabla^2\ell_n(\hat{\theta}_n)$ for the Hessian. $\qquad\square$

The matrix $\mathbf{J}(\theta)$ is called *Fisher's information matrix,* and it measures the information in the likelihood function. Inverting this matrix gives the asymptotic covariance matrix of the MLE $\hat{\theta}_n$. In many theoretical treatments, the estimate $\hat{\theta}_n$ is defined as the root of the likelihood equation $\nabla \ell_n(\theta) = \mathbf{0}$, and consistency is attempted without verifying whether the root attains the maximum or not. This theoretical treatment is noble in that, most often, the optimization problem is restated as a solution to a system of nonlinear equations; yet it would be helpful if local optima could be shown to be asymptotically unimportant. In some cases, all roots of the likelihood equation can be shown to be consistent. However, from this computational perspective, good practice would dictate some verification that at least a maximum was achieved, which can be done by checking the Hessian.

Example 9.3A: *Variance of MLE from Logarithmic Series Distribution*
Example 8.3 gave the likelihood for the logarithmic series distribution with density

$$f(y \mid \theta) = \theta^y/[y(-\log(1-\theta))] \quad \text{for } y = 1, 2, 3, \ldots \text{ and } 0 < \theta < 1.$$

For $n = 10$ and the statistic $\sum y_i = 15$, the log likelihood is

$$\ell_n(\theta) = \text{constant} + \left(\sum y_i\right)\log\theta - n\log(-\log(1-\theta))$$

$$= \text{constant} + 15\log\theta - 10\log(-\log(1-\theta)),$$

and the first and second derivatives are

$$\nabla\ell_n(\theta) = \ell_n'(\theta) = \frac{\left(\sum y_i\right)}{\theta} + \frac{n}{(1-\theta)\log(1-\theta)},$$

$$\nabla^2\ell_n(\theta) = \ell_n''(\theta) = -\frac{\left(\sum y_i\right)}{\theta^2} + \frac{n}{(1-\theta)^2\log(1-\theta)} + \frac{n}{(1-\theta)^2[\log(1-\theta)]^2}.$$

Evaluating at $\hat{\theta}_n = .533589$, we find that $\nabla^2\ell_n(\theta) = -33.9301$ with a variance estimate of 0.02947; the standard error for $\hat{\theta}_n$ is $.1717$. Another estimate is given in the next section.

An annoyance due to maximizing instead of minimizing the likelihood function occurs in the negative definite Hessian $\mathbf{H}_n(\boldsymbol{\theta}) = \nabla^2 \ell_n(\boldsymbol{\theta})$. Since everything previous has dealt with positive definiteness of such matrices, some authors choose to deal instead with an "unlikelihood" function, defined to be either $-\ell_n(\boldsymbol{\theta})$ or $-2\ell_n(\boldsymbol{\theta})$; the latter also goes by the name of "deviance" (McCullagh and Nelder 1992). However, we choose not to do so, and the reader should notice how this sign change propagates throughout the analysis. Computationally, this approach is commonly employed, especially with optimization code designed for minimization rather than maximization.

The most restrictive part of the assumptions is the IID requirement. Relaxing this to independent observations Y_i with density $f_i(y \mid \boldsymbol{\theta})$ would be a great improvement, especially in light of later discussions of nonlinear and generalized regression. The assumptions require only minor notational modifications, since each density f_i must satisfy all of the assumptions. Further technical details are inappropriate for this discussion, though we note a requirement on the information matrices $\mathbf{J}^{(i)}$ from sample i,

$$n^{-1}\{\mathbf{J}^{(1)} + \mathbf{J}^{(2)} + \cdots + \mathbf{J}^{(n)}\} = n^{-1}\{\mathbf{J}_n\} \to \mathbf{J}_\infty \quad \text{(positive definite).} \quad (9.2.5)$$

The notation $\mathbf{J}_n$ corresponds to the sum of information matrices from a non-IID sample of size n.

Before proceeding to the computational consequences, some further remarks on the "appropriate conditions" are necessary. The most common violations of these assumptions occur when the support of the distribution of the observations depends upon the parameter $\boldsymbol{\theta}$. Instead of dire consequences, the situation is in fact improved. Consistency of the MLE is not threatened; close examination reveals that observations occurring outside a region of support for a particular value of $\boldsymbol{\theta}$ lead to a value of $-\infty$ for $\ell_n(\boldsymbol{\theta})$. In such a case, the convergence rate is usually $O_p(n^{-1})$ instead of the usual $O_p(n^{-1/2})$ of Theorem 9.2. A more serious problem arises when differentiability is absent, as (for example) with the Laplace or double exponential distribution, $f(y \mid \theta) = \exp\{-|y - \theta|\}$. The MLE is the sample median, which does converge to the true parameter value θ^* and at the usual $O_p(n^{-1/2})$ rate. In such cases, it is necessary to find other ways of establishing the asymptotics.

Example 9.2B: *Uniform Distribution (cont.)*
As in Example 9.2A, let $Y_1, Y_2, \ldots, Y_n$ be observations IID uniform$(0, \theta)$. Then the MLE of θ is $\hat{\theta}_n = \max\{Y_1, Y_2, \ldots, Y_n\} = X_n$, with $\Pr(X_n \le x) = (x/\theta)^n$. Let $U_n = n(1 - X_n/\theta)$; then $U_n \overset{d}{\to}$ exponential, so that $\hat{\theta}_n - \theta = O_p(n^{-1})$.

Whereas the statistical consequences are not so grave, the computational aspects become perilous. In many of these cases, it is the continuity or smoothness that is absent. As discussed in Chapter 8, Newton's method relies on a quadratic approximation to the function. When this is inappropriate, another computational route must be sought, even though the maximum of $\ell_n(\boldsymbol{\theta})$ may be clear. Often concentrated likelihoods (Section 9.5) can be used to reshape a problem where all of the remaining parameters behave similarly and the function to be maximized is smooth.

9.3 Information, Scoring, and Variance Estimates

The thrust of Theorem 9.3 is that the log-likelihood function is asymptotically locally quadratic. This is a welcome conclusion, since a quadratic optimization problem is the easiest to deal with. Although computing the information matrix $\mathbf{J}(\boldsymbol{\theta})$ is required to find the standard errors for the estimators, the true value $\boldsymbol{\theta}^*$ is not known; this dictates the curvature of the likelihood function, since $\mathbf{J}$ is obviously a function of $\boldsymbol{\theta}$. There are several issues to be resolved and investigated, first among which is the information problem. Several alternatives for optimizing the likelihood function will also be discussed.

A practical view of Theorem 9.3 is that the MLE $\hat{\boldsymbol{\theta}}_n$ is approximately normal with mean vector the true $\boldsymbol{\theta}^*$ and covariance matrix $\mathbf{J}_n(\boldsymbol{\theta}^*)^{-1}$. Since the true $\boldsymbol{\theta}^*$ is unknown, the natural thing to do is putting in the estimate to get $\mathbf{J}_n(\hat{\boldsymbol{\theta}}_n)^{-1}$, basing such a step on continuity of $\mathbf{J}_n(\boldsymbol{\theta})$ and of the inverse of a matrix. This is fitting and proper, but further reflection is required. If we take to heart the conclusion that the likelihood function is approximately quadratic, then the quadratic nature of the observed likelihood $\ell_n(\boldsymbol{\theta})$, and not the expected likelihood $\ell_*(\boldsymbol{\theta})$, dictates the accuracy of the MLE. Consequently, the best measure of the covariance matrix is the inverse of the Hessian $\nabla^2\ell_n$, which is evaluated at the MLE $\hat{\boldsymbol{\theta}}_n$ and commonly referred to as the observed information $\mathbf{H}_n(\hat{\boldsymbol{\theta}}_n)$. The information matrix $\mathbf{J}_n(\boldsymbol{\theta})$, which equals $n\mathbf{J}(\boldsymbol{\theta})$ in the IID case, then represents the average of all samples (of size n) of the Hessian of the likelihood function. Efron and Hinkley (1978) convincingly argued the superiority of the observed information $\nabla^2\ell_n$ over the expected information $\mathbf{J}_n(\boldsymbol{\theta})$.

Another view of the comparison of observed versus expected information is one of effort, human or computer. To obtain the expected information matrix $\mathbf{J}_n(\boldsymbol{\theta})$, the matrix of second partial derivatives must be calculated and then an expectation figured. Sometimes this process is relatively easy; sometimes it is painfully difficult. Rarely is the effort required comparable to writing a routine to compute the observed information, which has a relative constant level of difficulty. However, sometimes both $\nabla^2\ell_n$ and $\mathbf{J}_n$ require too much human effort. In such a case, finite differences can be used to estimate derivatives following the methods in Section 8.6, especially (8.6.6). Alternatively, the BFGS update (8.7.10) produces an estimate of the Hessian following a secant analog method for optimization; commonly the software permits access to this information. These two routes require the least in human effort. Moreover, both are estimating the observed information matrix $\nabla^2\ell_n$, which is preferred to the information matrix even when the latter is easy to obtain.

When the information matrix $\mathbf{J}_n$ can be obtained without a great deal of effort, this knowledge of the quadratic nature of the likelihood function can be exploited to solve any number of problems with the same data. First of all, consider an iteration of Newton's method for computing the MLE:

$$\hat{\boldsymbol{\theta}}^{(j+1)} = \hat{\boldsymbol{\theta}}^{(j)} - [\nabla^2\ell_n]^{-1}\nabla\ell_n. \tag{9.3.1}$$

Replacing this update with $[-\mathbf{J}_n(\hat{\boldsymbol{\theta}}^{(j)})]^{-1}\nabla\ell_n$ saves on the computation of $\nabla^2\ell_n$ and provides a Hessian that is sufficiently accurate to correctly orient the direction to the maximum. This maneuver is called *scoring*, and it can be as effective as Newton's method in finding the MLE. As a statistical procedure, beginning with a consistent estimate $\hat{\boldsymbol{\theta}}^{(1)}$, one scoring step

$$\hat{\boldsymbol{\theta}}^{(2)} = \hat{\boldsymbol{\theta}}^{(1)} - [-\mathbf{J}_n]^{-1}\nabla\ell_n \qquad (9.3.2)$$

produces an efficient estimate (LeCam 1956). Although iterating will lead to an MLE, improvements gained by iterating are only $o_p(n^{-1/2})$ asymptotically.

Another view of the information matrix reveals its evidence on the numerical condition of the problem. Recall that (8.8.2) indicated that the accuracy of the solution to an optimization problem was reflected in the eigenvalues of the Hessian matrix. In this chapter, a large Hessian matrix indicates more accurate estimates in a general sense. Since the covariance matrix is the inverse of the information matrix and since the eigenvalues of the inverse are the reciprocals of those of the information matrix, clearly the condition of the problem and the statistical accuracy are directly related. A small eigenvalue in the information matrix indicates that a certain linear combination of the parameters cannot be estimated well, and this lack of information will contribute to the variances of all of the parameters. In a problem where the parameters are nearly unidentified, there will be little information along a curve or surface; near the MLE, this will manifest itself in a nearly singular information matrix, with the eigenvector indicating the direction of the curve. In contrast, when some parameters are almost completely known (perhaps converging at a faster rate), this will be indicated by a dominant eigenvalue and a vector indicating the parameter or linear combination involved. This domination will destroy any knowledge of the other parameters, which must therefore be handled separately.

Returning to estimating the covariance matrix of $\hat{\boldsymbol{\theta}}_n$, research on misspecification and M-estimation have led to the following "information sandwich" covariance estimator (see Boos 1992 and references therein):

$$\mathbf{V}_n = [\nabla^2\ell_n]^{-1}\left\{ \sum_{i=1}^{n} \mathbf{s}(\mathbf{Y}_i, \hat{\boldsymbol{\theta}}_n)\mathbf{s}(\mathbf{Y}_i, \hat{\boldsymbol{\theta}}_n)^{\mathrm{T}} \right\}[\nabla^2\ell_n]^{-1} \qquad (9.3.3)$$

(which works in spite of misspecification), where $\mathbf{s}(\mathbf{Y}, \boldsymbol{\theta}) = \nabla \log f(\mathbf{Y} \mid \boldsymbol{\theta})$. The reader may note that the expression in braces estimates the covariance matrix of $\nabla\ell_n$; the inverse matrix of the Hessian arises from (9.2.2) and (9.2.3). Although $\mathbf{V}_n$ is rather complicated, it does not present any new computational difficulties.

Example 9.3B: *Variance of MLE from Logarithmic Series Distribution (cont.)*
Applying (9.3.3) to the logarithmic series distribution with data $\{1, 1, 1, 1, 1, 1, 2, 2, 2, 3\}$, we have

$$s(Y, \theta) = \frac{y}{\theta} + \frac{1}{(1 - \theta)\log(1 - \theta)}.$$

At $\hat{\theta}_n = .533589$ we have $s(1, \hat{\theta}_n) = -.93705$, $s(2, \hat{\theta}_n) = 0.93705$, and $s(3, \hat{\theta}_n) = 2.81115$. Hence the expression in braces (in (9.3.3)) becomes $\{6(-0.93705)^2 + 3(0.93705)^2 + (2.81115)^2\} = 15.8050$ and so

$$V_n = (-33.9301)^{-1}\{15.8050\}(-33.9301)^{-1} = .001373.$$

9.4 An Extended Example

In order to illustrate the problems and techniques that have been discussed so far, we devote this section to a single example (Example 9.4) that epitomizes maximum likelihood estimation. The example is a relatively simple one, given by Rao (1973, pp. 370ff). The problem is to estimate gene frequencies of blood antigens A and B by observing the four main blood groups: AB, A, B, and O. Denote the gene frequencies of A and B by θ_1 and θ_2 respectively, and also the probabilities of the four blood groups by π_1, π_2, π_3, and π_4. These probabilities are functions of θ_1 and θ_2:

$$\pi_1(\theta_1, \theta_2) = 2\theta_1\theta_2, \qquad \pi_2(\theta_1, \theta_2) = \theta_1(2 - \theta_1 - 2\theta_2),$$
$$\pi_3(\theta_1, \theta_2) = \theta_2(2 - \theta_2 - 2\theta_1), \qquad \pi_4(\theta_1, \theta_2) = (1 - \theta_1 - \theta_2)^2.$$

The likelihood can be treated in two ways – first, as a multinomial with observed frequencies n_1, n_2, n_3, and n_4. However, to better follow the methodology prescribed here, consider each observation Y_i to be independent and, taking one of four values with the probabilities just given, let

$$f(y \mid \theta_1, \theta_2) = \pi_y \quad \text{for } y = 1, 2, 3, 4.$$

Following either route, the log likelihood can be written as

$$\ell_n(\boldsymbol{\theta}) = n_1 \log \pi_1 + n_2 \log \pi_2 + n_3 \log \pi_3 + n_4 \log \pi_4 + \text{constant}.$$

The likelihood equation then takes a simple form:

$$\nabla \ell_n(\boldsymbol{\theta}) = \sum_{j=1}^{4} \left(\frac{n_j}{\pi_j} \right) \nabla \pi_j(\boldsymbol{\theta}) = \mathbf{0}. \tag{9.4.1}$$

The partial derivatives should be written out for clarity:

$$\nabla \pi_1 = \begin{pmatrix} 2\theta_2 \\ 2\theta_1 \end{pmatrix}, \qquad \nabla \pi_2 = \begin{pmatrix} 2(1 - \theta_1 - \theta_2) \\ -2\theta_1 \end{pmatrix},$$
$$\nabla \pi_3 = \begin{pmatrix} -2\theta_2 \\ 2(1 - \theta_1 - \theta_2) \end{pmatrix}, \qquad \nabla \pi_4 = \begin{pmatrix} 2(1 - \theta_1 - \theta_2) \\ 2(1 - \theta_1 - \theta_2) \end{pmatrix}.$$

The Hessian matrices are much simpler:

$$\nabla^2 \pi_1 = \begin{bmatrix} 0 & 2 \\ 2 & 0 \end{bmatrix}, \qquad \nabla^2 \pi_2 = \begin{bmatrix} -2 & -2 \\ -2 & 0 \end{bmatrix},$$
$$\nabla^2 \pi_3 = \begin{bmatrix} 0 & -2 \\ -2 & -2 \end{bmatrix}, \qquad \nabla^2 \pi_4 = \begin{bmatrix} 2 & 2 \\ 2 & 2 \end{bmatrix}.$$

The Hessian of the likelihood function can then be written in the simple form

$$\mathbf{H}_n(\boldsymbol{\theta}) = \nabla^2 \ell_n(\boldsymbol{\theta}) = \sum_{j=1}^{4} n_j \left[\left(\frac{1}{\pi_j} \right) \nabla^2 \pi_j - \left(\frac{1}{\pi_j^2} \right) \nabla \pi_j (\nabla \pi_j)^{\mathrm{T}} \right], \tag{9.4.2}$$

and the information matrix can be computed in either manner:

Table 9.1. *Convergence of iterative methods for computing MLEs*

Scoring Iteration	θ_1	θ_2	J_{11}	J_{22}	J_{12}	$\ell_n(\theta)$
0	.26300	.07400	8.9815	28.2662	2.4367	−494.6769
1	.26431	.09322	9.0081	22.7634	2.4765	−492.5353
2	.26444	.09317	9.0042	22.7748	2.4766	−492.5353

Newton's Method with Analytical Derivatives Iteration	θ_1	θ_2	$(H_n)_{11}$	$(H_n)_{22}$	$(H_n)_{12}$	$\ell_n(\theta)$
0	.26300	.07400	−3872.33	−15181.08	−1006.17	−494.6769
1	.26556	.08949	−3869.46	−10794.02	−1059.73	−492.6031
2	.26448	.09304	−3899.85	−10083.28	−1067.56	−492.5353
3	.26444	.09317	−3900.90	−10058.49	−1067.86	−492.5353

Newton's Method with Hessian Computed Numerically Iteration	θ_1	θ_2	$(H_n)_{11}$	$(H_n)_{22}$	$(H_n)_{12}$	$\ell_n(\theta)$
0	.26300	.07400	−3875.23	−15232.78	−1015.32	−494.6769
1	.26553	.08943	−3869.50	−10873.76	−1060.18	−492.6051
2	.26449	.09301	−3910.31	−10171.54	−1063.78	−492.5354
3	.26444	.09317	−3891.18	−10078.62	−1065.25	−492.5353

$$E\{-\nabla^2\ell_n(\theta)\} = \text{cov}\{\nabla\ell_n(\theta)\} = N\mathbf{J} = N\left[\sum_{j=1}^{4}\left(\frac{1}{\pi_j}\right)\nabla\pi_j(\nabla\pi_j)^{\mathrm{T}}\right], \qquad (9.4.3)$$

where $N = n_1 + n_2 + n_3 + n_4$.

In his discussion, Rao gives the data as $n_1 = 17$, $n_2 = 182$, $n_3 = 60$, and $n_4 = 176$, so that $N = 435$. The first step is to obtain starting values for computing maximum likelihood estimates of θ_1 and θ_2. In the absence of any better ideas, setting $\pi_j = n_j/N$ for the first two groups and solving for θ_1 and θ_2 gives the starting values $\theta_1^{(0)} = .263$ and $\theta_2^{(0)} = .074$. Three methods are used for computing MLEs: scoring, and Newton's method with analytical derivatives or with numerical derivatives. The results are given in Table 9.1, and contour and surface plots of the log likelihood are given in Figures 9.1 and 9.2. Clearly, all three methods converge to the same value quickly and without hesitation. Also, the Fisher information matrix $N\mathbf{J}$ and the two Hessians all give very similar results for the asymptotic variances. In the contour plot (Figure 9.1), the contour lines mark confidence regions for (θ_1, θ_2) at levels $(1 - 10^{-k}) \times 100\%$ for $k = 1, \ldots, 5$. These are obtained by finding appropriate 10^{-k} tail critical values from the χ_2^2 distribution, dividing by 2, and subtracting them from the maximum likelihood. Consequently, the regions are defined by

$$\{(\theta_1, \theta_2) : -2[\ell_n(\hat{\theta}_1, \hat{\theta}_2) - \ell_n(\theta_1, \theta_2)] \le t_k\}, \qquad (9.4.4)$$

where $\Pr(X > t_k \mid X \sim \chi_2^2) = 10^{-k}$. This approach for constructing confidence regions based on inverting asymptotic χ^2 tests is generally preferred to one that uses intervals for each parameter based on the asymptotic normal distribution.

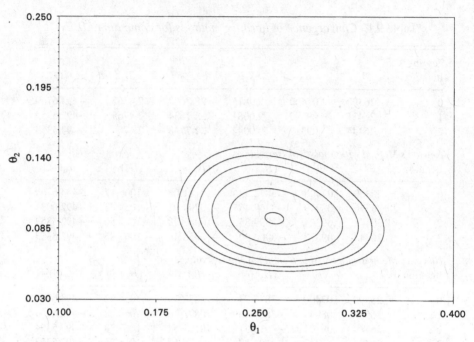

Figure 9.1. Contour plot of log likelihood for Extended Example 9.4. Contour lines mark confidence regions at levels $(1 - 10^{-k}) \times 100\%$ for $k = 1, \ldots, 5$.

The Hessian matrices were computed using a difference of $\theta_j/100$, since the machine unit for the arithmetic was 10^{-6}. As discussed in Section 8.5, precision in numerical differentiation is less important than avoiding anomalies in the computation of the Hessian by finite differences. The estimated covariance matrix of the MLEs for the three methods are, respectively:

$$10^{-6}\begin{bmatrix} 263 & -29 \\ -29 & 104 \end{bmatrix}, \quad 10^{-6}\begin{bmatrix} 264 & -28 \\ -28 & 102 \end{bmatrix}, \quad \text{and} \quad 10^{-6}\begin{bmatrix} 265 & -28 \\ -28 & 102 \end{bmatrix}.$$

The performance of the various methods can depend greatly upon the starting values. In continuing this example, if another point (say, $\theta_1^{(0)} = \theta_2^{(0)} = 0.333$) is chosen for starting values then the scoring algorithm will again converge in three iterations. The first steps are larger, but the algorithm has little trouble in finding the maximum. However, Newton's method gives a step of $(.087, -.337)$, which leaps over the $\theta_2 > 0$ boundary. Enforcing such constraints will be postponed until Section 9.9.

9.5   Concentration, Iteration, and the EM Algorithm

Because the maximum likelihood estimate is defined implicitly – and only occasionally known in an explicit form as a statistic – the maximization process rises in importance. As the previous section attests, the log-likelihood function usually takes on a quadratic shape, and that knowledge can be exploited. Other information about the likelihood

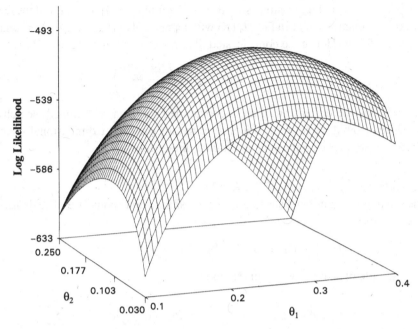

Figure 9.2. Surface plot of log likelihood for Extended Example 9.4.

function can also be exploited in other ways. In cases where the parameters are separable (as variables in an optimization problem), the likelihood function of one subset can be maximized without knowledge of the other subset of variables. More commonly, given one subset of parameters, the MLEs of the other subset can be found explicitly. As a result, a concentrated likelihood function can be used to reduce the dimension of the numerical optimization problem. We will conclude this section by discussing the EM algorithm, which can be used for a variety of problems.

The most commonly used trick in maximum likelihood estimation is the use of a *concentrated* or *profile* likelihood function. Partition the parameter vector into two subsets α and β (of dimensions p_1 and p_2, respectively) and then rewrite the log-likelihood function with two arguments, $\ell_n(\theta) = \ell_n(\alpha, \beta)$. Now suppose that, for a given value of β, the MLEs for the subset α could be found as a function of the others; that is, $\hat{\alpha}_n = \hat{\alpha}(\beta)$. Then construct the concentrated likelihood function as a function only of β,

$$\ell_c(\beta) = \ell_n(\hat{\alpha}(\beta), \beta). \tag{9.5.1}$$

Clearly, maximizing ℓ_c for β will maximize $\ell_n(\alpha, \beta)$ for both α and β (see Exercise 9.11). The main advantage is a reduction in the dimension of the search. The greatest simplifications occur when $\hat{\alpha}$ does not depend on β.

For the first example, consider the basic problem Y_i IID $N(\mu, \sigma^2)$. Then $\hat{\mu} = \bar{Y}$ independently of σ^2 and we have $\ell_c(\sigma) = -(n/2) \log \sigma^2 - \sum (Y_i - \bar{Y})^2/(2\sigma^2)$, which simplifies the problem substantially. For another example, consider a modification of the simple linear regression model

$$y_i = \alpha_1 + \alpha_2 x_i^\beta + e_i, \quad e_i \text{ IID } N(0, \alpha_3). \tag{9.5.2}$$

Given $\beta = b$, the usual regression estimates can be found for $\alpha_1, \alpha_2, \alpha_3$, but these will all be explicit functions of b. In fact, $\ell_c(\beta)$ will depend only on an error sum of squares, since $\hat{\alpha}_3 = \text{SSE}/n$. Hence the concentrated likelihood function becomes simply

$$\ell_c(\beta) = \text{constant} - \frac{n}{2} \log\left(\frac{\text{SSE}(\beta)}{n}\right). \tag{9.5.3}$$

The gain is that the dimension of an unconstrained (or even constrained) search has been reduced from three (or four) dimensions to only one, and 1-dimensional searches are markedly simpler than those in any higher dimension.

Example 9.5: *Concentrated Likelihood*
The 2-parameter gamma distribution offers a simple nontrivial case. The density takes the form

$$f(y \mid \alpha, \beta) = y^{\alpha-1} e^{-y/\beta} / (\beta^\alpha \Gamma(\alpha)) \quad \text{for } y > 0.$$

For a sample of size n, the log likelihood is

$$\ell_n(\alpha, \beta) = -n\alpha \log(\beta) - n \log \Gamma(\alpha) + (\alpha - 1) \sum_{i=1}^{n} \log(Y_i) - \sum_{i=1}^{n} \frac{Y_i}{\beta}.$$

Given α, the likelihood is maximized at $\hat{\beta}(\alpha) = \sum Y_i/(n\alpha)$, so the concentrated likelihood function is

$$\ell_c(\alpha) = -n\alpha \log\left(\sum Y_i/(n\alpha)\right) - n \log \Gamma(\alpha) + (\alpha - 1) \sum_{i=1}^{n} \log(Y_i) - n\alpha.$$

For a demonstration, August rainfall data for $n = 45$ years for Raleigh (North Carolina) were fit to the 2-parameter gamma family. Initial values can be found by the method of moments. A contour plot of the 2-dimensional likelihood surface is given in Figure 9.3, with the curve of $\hat{\beta}(\alpha)$ in Figure 9.4 and the concentrated likelihood function $\ell_c(\alpha)$ plotted in Figure 9.5. See the demonstration **augrain1** for a solution using golden section to maximize the 1-dimensional concentrated likelihood function $\ell_c(\alpha)$. Compare to **augrain2**, which uses **plum1t** from Chapter 8.

Example 9.6: *Concentrated Likelihood*
Bates and Watts (1988, p. 41) gave an example of a rather simple nonlinear regression problem with two parameters:

$$y_i = \theta_1(1 - \exp\{-\theta_2 x_i\}) + e_i.$$

Given θ_2, the problem becomes regression through the origin. The estimator of θ_1 is simply

$$\hat{\theta}_1 = \sum_{i=1}^{n} z_i y_i \bigg/ \sum_{i=1}^{n} z_i^2 \quad \text{where } z_i = 1 - \exp\{-\theta_2 x_i\},$$

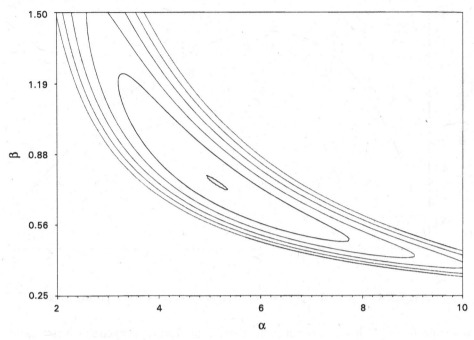

Figure 9.3. Contour plot of log likelihood for August rainfall (Example 9.5). Contour lines mark $(1 - 10)^{-k} \times 100\%$ confidence regions.

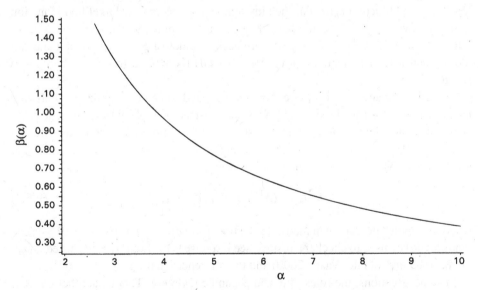

Figure 9.4. Maximum likelihood estimator of β as a function of α for August rainfall.

and the concentrated likelihood function is as in (9.5.3) with

$$\text{SSE}(\theta_2) = \sum_{i=1}^{n}(y_i - \hat{\theta}_1(\theta_2))^2.$$

Compare the demonstration programs **conclk** and **concll**; see also Exercise 9.12.

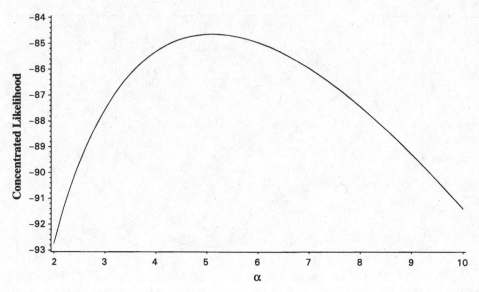

Figure 9.5. Concentrated likelihood function $\ell_c(\alpha) = \ell_n(\alpha, \hat{\beta}(\alpha))$ for August rainfall.

Implementation of this tool is not particularly complicated. Sometimes it is helpful to follow the mathematical specification instead of explicitly coding the concentrated likelihood function. That is, if one has coded a function subprogram to compute the log-likelihood function $\ell_n(\alpha, \beta)$, then implement the concentrated likelihood function in the following way. Code another subprogram to compute $\hat{\alpha}(\beta)$; then, the concentrated likelihood function subprogram will accept values of β as its argument and call the original $\ell_n(\alpha, \beta)$ function with values of $\hat{\alpha}(\beta)$ (computed from its subprogram) and β.

Assessing the accuracy is a little more complicated since the optimization software uses ℓ_c and not ℓ_n. The Hessian $\nabla^2 \ell_n$ is needed instead of $\nabla^2 \ell_c$, whose estimates may be readily available; having written (as just noted) the subprogram to compute $\ell_n(\alpha, \beta)$ then pays off. However, knowing $\nabla^2 \ell_c$ does not help in constructing $\nabla^2 \ell_n$, since at the optimum (where $\nabla \ell_n = \mathbf{0}$) the relationship is

$$\nabla^2 \ell_c = (\mathbf{A}^\mathrm{T} \ \mathbf{I}_{p_2}) \nabla^2 \ell_n \begin{pmatrix} \mathbf{A} \\ \mathbf{I}_{p_2} \end{pmatrix}, \tag{9.5.4}$$

where $\mathbf{A}$ denotes the Jacobian matrix of the transformation $\hat{\alpha}(\beta)$. Even so, (9.5.4) can (and should) be used to check the results; see Exercise 9.10. For inference based on ℓ_c, see Murphy and van der Vaart (2000) and the references therein.

In some situations, the roles of α and β can be reversed. That is, another concentrated likelihood function can be constructed as

$$\ell_c^*(\alpha) = \ell_n(\alpha, \hat{\beta}(\alpha))$$

using an MLE for β for a given $\alpha = \mathbf{a}$. Then an obvious route is to iterate, optimizing each concentrated likelihood function in alternation. This approach can be an effective method for optimizing the joint likelihood $\ell_n(\alpha, \beta)$ when the computation of $\hat{\alpha}(\beta)$ and $\hat{\beta}(\alpha)$ is straightforward and fast. The drawback of this approach is that the convergence can be very slow. When both α and β are univariate, this method optimizes first in one component and then the other. Hence the path of the sequence of steps zig-zags toward the optimum, as steepest descent methods do (see Example 8.4), but taking right-angle turns every time. When α and β are multivariate, the same zig-zagging path is taken with right-angle turns, but now from one hyperplane to another that is orthogonal to it.

Another widely used approach that employs alternating optimization is the EM algorithm of Dempster, Laird, and Rubin (1977; hereafter DLR). This method is best described in terms of its motivation: a way to fill in missing data. Suppose that the model for the process is $f(\mathbf{x} \mid \boldsymbol{\theta})$ but not all of $\mathbf{X}$ is observed – only $\mathbf{Y}(\mathbf{X})$ is available. Then the likelihood for the observed $\mathbf{y}$ is

$$L(\boldsymbol{\theta}) = g(\mathbf{y} \mid \boldsymbol{\theta}) = \int_{\mathbf{Y}^{-1}(\{\mathbf{y}\})} f(\mathbf{x} \mid \boldsymbol{\theta}) \, d\mathbf{x}.$$

Computing L is usually prohibitive, so some other method is needed to maximize the likelihood. The EM algorithm has two steps:

E-step – construct $Q(\boldsymbol{\theta}, \boldsymbol{\phi}) = E\{\log f(\mathbf{x} \mid \boldsymbol{\phi}) \mid \mathbf{y}, \boldsymbol{\theta}\}$;
M-step – maximize $Q(\boldsymbol{\theta}, \boldsymbol{\phi})$ over $\boldsymbol{\theta}$.

Beginning with the starting value $\boldsymbol{\theta}^{(0)}$, the iteration sequence is the formation of $Q(\boldsymbol{\theta}, \boldsymbol{\theta}^{(j)})$ and the maximizing $\boldsymbol{\theta}$ of the M-step becomes $\boldsymbol{\theta}^{(j+1)}$. The E-step is so named because, in many instances (especially in the exponential family), constructing Q is equivalent to finding the *expectation* of the missing data – given the observations and a value of the parameter. The mathematics behind the general nature of the EM algorithm begins with the construction of the function

$$H(\boldsymbol{\theta} \mid \boldsymbol{\phi}) = E\{\log k(\mathbf{x} \mid \mathbf{y}, \boldsymbol{\theta}) \mid \mathbf{y}, \boldsymbol{\theta}\},$$

where $k(\mathbf{x} \mid \mathbf{y}, \boldsymbol{\theta}) = f(\mathbf{x} \mid \boldsymbol{\theta})/g(\mathbf{y} \mid \boldsymbol{\theta})$ can be interpreted as the conditional density of $\mathbf{x}$ given $\mathbf{y}$. Actually, one can view $k(\mathbf{x} \mid \mathbf{y}, \boldsymbol{\theta})$ as an artifact to construct H, whose sole purpose is to write the likelihood in terms of Q:

$$L(\boldsymbol{\theta}) = Q(\boldsymbol{\theta}, \boldsymbol{\phi}) - H(\boldsymbol{\theta} \mid \boldsymbol{\phi}).$$

The hidden key to the algorithm is the application of the information inequality (DLR, lemma 1), which states that $H(\boldsymbol{\theta} \mid \boldsymbol{\phi}) \leq H(\boldsymbol{\phi} \mid \boldsymbol{\phi})$ for all $\boldsymbol{\theta}$. The main result (DLR, thm. 1) is that the likelihood is maximized at convergence. Additionally (DLR, thm. 4), if $\nabla_{11}^2 Q(\boldsymbol{\theta}, \boldsymbol{\phi})$ is strictly negative definite, then $\nabla \ell = \mathbf{0}$ and $\nabla^2 Q(\boldsymbol{\phi}, \boldsymbol{\phi})$ is negative definite at $\boldsymbol{\theta}^{(\infty)}$; the rate of the convergence of the EM algorithm is then given by the largest eigenvalue of

$$\nabla^2 H(\boldsymbol{\phi} \mid \boldsymbol{\phi})[\nabla^2 Q(\boldsymbol{\phi}, \boldsymbol{\phi})]^{-1}$$

evaluated at $\boldsymbol{\theta}^{(\infty)}$.

The advantage of the EM algorithm is that often the steps are straightforward and easy to implement. The missing data motivation often suggests a restatement of a problem in terms of unobservables or latent variables. In this way, sometimes both steps become straightforward. One of the two disadvantages of the EM algorithm is that the convergence can sometimes be slow, owing to the same zig-zag problem as in the other alternation scheme. The other disadvantage, also shared by the alternation scheme, is that the iteration can stop at any stationary point. Thus the process can converge to a saddle point (or to a local maximum), and this unwelcome outcome cannot be discovered without further investigation (see Wu 1983).

9.6 Multiple Regression in the Context of Maximum Likelihood

The intention of this section is to get the reader's feet back on the ground by viewing one of the most common statistical methods as an application of maximum likelihood. In multiple regression we observed the Y_i, which are independent and normally distributed with a mean function $g(\mathbf{x}_i; \boldsymbol{\beta})$ and variance σ^2. The mean function is linear in the p-dimensional parameter vector $\boldsymbol{\beta}$,

$$g(\mathbf{x}_i; \boldsymbol{\beta}) = \boldsymbol{\beta}^T \mathbf{x}_i,$$

and a reparameterization of $\gamma = \sigma^{-2}$ will make some calculations more convenient. Notice that this is the "non-IID" case, and the parameter vector is composed of the linear coefficients $\boldsymbol{\beta}$ and the scale parameter γ. The log-likelihood function can then be written as

$$\ell_n(\boldsymbol{\theta}) = \ell_n(\boldsymbol{\beta}, \gamma) = \text{constant} + (n/2) \log \gamma - \gamma S(\boldsymbol{\beta})/2,$$

where the sum-of-squares function is $S(\boldsymbol{\beta}) = \sum (Y_i - g(\mathbf{x}_i; \boldsymbol{\beta}))^2$. To maximize the likelihood, first take the partial derivative with respect to the scale parameter γ to obtain

$$\frac{\partial \ell_n}{\partial \gamma} = \frac{n/\gamma - S(\boldsymbol{\beta})}{2},$$

which gives the MLE $\hat{\gamma}(\boldsymbol{\beta}) = n/S(\boldsymbol{\beta})$ as a function of the other parameters. Now form the concentrated likelihood function

$$\ell_c(\boldsymbol{\beta}) = \ell_n(\boldsymbol{\beta}, \hat{\gamma}(\boldsymbol{\beta})) = \text{constant} - (n/2) \log S(\boldsymbol{\beta}).$$

Maximizing the concentrated likelihood function is now equivalent to minimizing the sum-of-squares function S, which can be done by $\hat{\boldsymbol{\beta}} = \left(\sum \mathbf{x}_i \mathbf{x}_i^T \right)^{-1} \left(\sum \mathbf{x}_i y_i \right)$. The distribution of the MLEs (exact, finite sample) can be found directly as

$$\hat{\boldsymbol{\beta}} \sim N_p \left(\boldsymbol{\beta}, \left(\gamma \sum \mathbf{x}_i \mathbf{x}_i^T \right)^{-1} \right) \quad \text{and} \quad n\gamma/\hat{\gamma} = \gamma S(\hat{\boldsymbol{\beta}}) \sim \chi^2 \text{ with } n - p \text{ df,}$$

with both distributions independent. Notice that the MLE $\hat{\gamma}$ differs from the unbiased and usual estimate, which uses the degrees of freedom $(n - p)$ as a divisor.

Following the analysis in the preceding sections, the gradient vector of the log likelihood is

$$\nabla \ell_n(\boldsymbol{\beta}, \gamma) = \begin{bmatrix} \gamma \left[\sum \mathbf{x}_i (y_i - \boldsymbol{\beta}^T \mathbf{x}_i) \right] \\ (n/\gamma - S(\boldsymbol{\beta}))/2 \end{bmatrix}; \tag{9.6.1}$$

notice that the first-order conditions $\nabla \ell_n = \mathbf{0}$ are satisfied by the MLE. Now the Hessian matrix of the log-likelihood function takes the form

$$\nabla^2 \ell_n = \begin{bmatrix} -\gamma \left(\sum \mathbf{x}_i \mathbf{x}_i^T \right) & \sum \mathbf{x}_i (y_i - \boldsymbol{\beta}^T \mathbf{x}_i) \\ \sum \mathbf{x}_i^T (y_i - \boldsymbol{\beta}^T \mathbf{x}_i) & -n/(2\gamma^2) \end{bmatrix}, \tag{9.6.2}$$

and the Fisher information matrix can be easily computed as

$$\mathbf{J}_n = E\{-\nabla^2 \ell_n\} = \begin{bmatrix} \gamma\left(\sum \mathbf{x}_i \mathbf{x}_i^{\mathsf{T}}\right) & \mathbf{0} \\ \mathbf{0} & n/(2\gamma^2) \end{bmatrix}. \tag{9.6.3}$$

Notice that the (negative of the) Hessian matrix evaluated at the MLE, which is the observed information matrix $-\mathbf{H}_n$, is the same as the Fisher information matrix $\mathbf{J}_n$, since the off-diagonal pieces correspond to the normal equations. Also, the asymptotic variance of $\hat{\gamma} = \hat{\sigma}^{-2}$ is given appropriately (see Exercise 9.14).

Establishing the consistency and asymptotic normality in multiple regression is easily done directly. Following the previous work, certain conditions must be verified. Most are straightforward, but two are particularly noteworthy. One is Assumption A2, which specifies that the parameter space is closed and bounded. This is not usually a problem, nor is it here, except that it takes on a different form. The reparameterization $\gamma = \sigma^{-2}$ means that bounding γ becomes a bound away from zero for σ^2. Although we have independence and constant variance (homoskedasticity), the fact that Y_i are not IID means that some care needs to be taken. The condition (9.2.5) is equivalent to

$$n^{-1} \sum \mathbf{x}_i \mathbf{x}_i^{\mathsf{T}} \to \mathbf{A} \quad \text{(positive definite)},$$

which should not be surprising. Consider the simple linear regression case $E(Y_i) = \beta_0 + \beta_1 x_i$. Then taking $x_i = 1/i$ fails this condition because the limiting matrix $\mathbf{A}$ has only one nonzero element; the intercept β_0 can be estimated well, but there is only a finite amount of information about the slope. In the general regression situation, this is manifest in a limited amount of information (or none) with respect to certain linear combinations – that is, multicollinearity or nonidentifiability. In contrast, if we take $x_i = i$ then the foregoing limit does not exist; the information on the slope grows too rapidly, and the estimate of the slope $\hat{\beta}_1$ converges at a faster rate $O_p(n^{-1})$ than the usual $O_p(n^{-1/2})$. Although the condition is not satisfied, the situation is better than expected. In this case it is very important to deal with the slope parameter separately from the intercept; see Exercise 9.15.

9.7 Generalized Linear Models

Before reaching the real meat of this chapter – nonlinear regression – two examples of regression in a more general context are to be entertained. Although the term "generalized linear models" is sometimes applied (McCullagh and Nelder 1992), the spirit is simply the application of maximum likelihood. The main thrust is that the observations Y_i are no longer distributed normally but rather according to some other distribution. The mean function is expressed in the same fashion as regression, with unknown coefficients forming a linear combination of explanatory variables.

The first instance to be considered here is logistic regression. Observations in this case consist of the Y_i, which are independent binomial variates from m_i trials, each with probability π_i. The true probabilities π_i are unknown and are modeled as a regression function in $\log(\pi_i/(1 - \pi_i))$:

$$\pi_i = p(\mathbf{x}_i; \boldsymbol{\beta}) = \frac{\exp(\gamma_i)}{1 + \exp(\gamma_i)}, \quad \text{where} \quad \gamma_i = \boldsymbol{\beta}^{\mathsf{T}} \mathbf{x}_i. \tag{9.7.1}$$

Here the explanatory variables may be simply indicators of different groups or covariates, as in the usual normally distributed case. The remainder of the problem is just maximum likelihood analysis. The log-likelihood function can be written as

$$\ell_n(\boldsymbol{\beta}) = \text{constant} + \sum_i [y_i \gamma_i - m_i \log(1 + \exp(\gamma_i))],$$

and the gradient is easily calculated:

$$\nabla \ell_n(\boldsymbol{\beta}) = \sum \left[y_i \mathbf{x}_i - m_i \frac{\exp(\gamma_i)}{1 + \exp(\gamma_i)} \mathbf{x}_i \right] = \sum_{i=1}^{n} \mathbf{x}_i (y_i - m_i \pi_i). \tag{9.7.2}$$

Notice that the form of (9.7.2) is very similar to that found in the usual regression case. Computing next the Hessian matrix, we find

$$\nabla^2 \ell_n(\boldsymbol{\beta}) = - \sum m_i \pi_i (1 - \pi_i) \mathbf{x}_i \mathbf{x}_i^{\mathsf{T}}, \tag{9.7.3}$$

which is nonstochastic and so the information matrices $\nabla^2 \ell_n$ and $\mathbf{J}_n$ are the same. As a result, scoring and Newton's method again coincide and lead to the iterative algorithm

$$\boldsymbol{\beta}^{(j+1)} = \boldsymbol{\beta}^{(j)} + \left[\sum m_i \pi_i (1 - \pi_i) \mathbf{x}_i \mathbf{x}_i^{\mathsf{T}} \right]^{-1} \left[\sum_{i=1}^{n} \mathbf{x}_i (y_i - m_i \pi_i) \right]. \tag{9.7.4}$$

Close examination of this iteration shows the simplicity of the problem's structure. The update resembles the formulation for weighted least squares, where the problem is restated as a heteroskedastic problem (which is true, approximately):

$$Y_i \text{ independent } N(m_i \pi_i, m_i \pi_i (1 - \pi_i)).$$

Notice that the weights $w_i = m_i \pi_i (1 - \pi_i)$ would be updated at each iteration, to be evaluated at the current estimate $\boldsymbol{\beta}^{(j)}$. Consequently, this iteration scheme is an example of iteratively reweighted least squares (IRWLS; Jennrich and Moore 1975), where the observations are reweighted at each iteration and the update follows a weighted regression scheme (not GLS); see Exercise 9.16. The asymptotic normality of the MLE $\hat{\boldsymbol{\beta}}$ follows from Theorem 9.3. The interchange of integral and derivative required by "appropriate conditions" is trivial, since $\nabla^2 \ell_n$ is nonstochastic in this case. For this problem, it will suffice to enforce

$$n^{-1} \sum m_i \pi_i (1 - \pi_i) \mathbf{x}_i \mathbf{x}_i^{\mathsf{T}} \to \mathbf{A} \quad \text{(positive definite)}$$

and bound $\|\mathbf{x}_i\|$.

Some computational difficulties arise with the loglikelihood at infinity. First, the loglikelihood function is linear at infinity, that is, starting at any finite point $\boldsymbol{\beta}^*$ and taking the direction $\mathbf{z}$, we find $\lim_{t \to \infty} \nabla^2 \ell_n(\boldsymbol{\beta}^* + t\mathbf{z}) = 0$ in any direction $\mathbf{z}$, because π_i

goes either to 0 or 1. As a result, the Hessian matrix may approach singularity far away from the MLE. Second, we can determine the slope at infinity in direction $\mathbf{z}$ as

$$lim_{t \to \infty} d\ell_n(\beta^* + t\mathbf{z})/dt = lim_{t \to \infty} \sum_{i=1}^{n} \left[y_i(\mathbf{z}^T \mathbf{x}_i) - \frac{m_i(\mathbf{z}^T \mathbf{x}_i)e^{\mathbf{x}_i^T \beta^* + t(\mathbf{z}^T \mathbf{x}_i)}}{1 + e^{\mathbf{x}_i^T \beta^* + t(\mathbf{z}^T \mathbf{x}_i)}} \right]$$

$$= \sum_{i=1}^{n} \left[(\mathbf{z}^T \mathbf{x}_i)(y_i - m_i s_i(\mathbf{z})) \right] = g(\mathbf{z})$$

where

$$s_i(\mathbf{z}) = \begin{cases} 0 & \text{if } \mathbf{z}^T \mathbf{x}_i < 0, \\ e^{\mathbf{x}_i^T \beta^*}/(1 + e^{\mathbf{x}_i^T \beta^*}) & \text{if } \mathbf{z}^T \mathbf{x}_i = 0, \\ 1 & \text{if } \mathbf{z}^T \mathbf{x}_i > 0 \end{cases}$$

We can see that $g(\mathbf{z})$ will be negative, except if there exists a direction $\mathbf{z}$ that satisfies

- $(\mathbf{z}^T \mathbf{x}_i) < 0$ where $y_i = 0$
- $(\mathbf{z}^T \mathbf{x}_i) > 0$ where $y_i = m_i$
- $(\mathbf{z}^T \mathbf{x}_i) = 0$ where $0 < y_i < m_i$

This situation, where $g(\mathbf{z}) = 0$ and the maximum of the loglikelihood occurs at infinity, is called *complete separation* or *quasi-complete separation* (Albert & Anderson, 1984; Santner & Duffy, 1986), owing to the situation where one group has all or no successes. For example, consider coding the control and treatment dummy variable x_i as 0/1, with $\gamma_i = \beta_0 + \beta_1 x_i$ so that $\mathbf{x}_1^T = (1, 0)$ and $\mathbf{x}_2^T = (1, 1)$. In the complete separation case, $y_1 = 0$ and $y_2 = m_2$, and the loglikelihood is maximized by taking β_0 to $-\infty$ and $\beta_0 + \beta_1$ to $+\infty$. In the quasi-complete separation case with $y_1 < m_1$ and $y_2 = m_2$, the loglikelihood is maximized by taking $\beta_0 = y_1/m_1$ and β_1 infinitely large.

In general, if we construct a matrix $\mathbf{A}$ with rows $\mathbf{x}_i^T$ when $y_i = m_i$ and rows $-\mathbf{x}_i^T$ when $y_i = 0$, then complete separation occurs if there exists a vector $\mathbf{z}$ such that $\mathbf{A}\mathbf{z} > \mathbf{0}$. Using a version of the Minkowski-Farkas lemma, then complete separation is equivalent to finding a solution to $\mathbf{A}^T \mathbf{y} = \mathbf{0}$ for $\mathbf{y} \geq \mathbf{0}$, which in turn is equivalent to finding a feasible solution to a standard linear programming problem (Section 4.8).

For quasi-complete separation, construct a matrix $\mathbf{B}$ with rows $\mathbf{x}_i^T$ when $0 < y_i < m_i$; notice that this cannot occur if $m_i \equiv 1$. The existence of a nonzero vector $\mathbf{z}$ satisfying $\mathbf{A}\mathbf{z} > \mathbf{0}$ and $\mathbf{B}\mathbf{z} = \mathbf{0}$ would indicate quasi-complete separation. To handle this case, construct the matrix $\mathbf{C}$ whose columns form a basis for $\mathcal{N}(\mathbf{B})$ so that $\mathbf{u}$ parameterizes solutions to $\mathbf{B}\mathbf{z} = 0$ through $\mathbf{z} = \mathbf{C}\mathbf{u}$. Now we are looking for a nonzero vector $\mathbf{u}$ that satisfies $\mathbf{A}^*\mathbf{u} > \mathbf{0}$ with $\mathbf{A}^* = \mathbf{A}\mathbf{C}$ which leads to the same linear programming approach with $\mathbf{A}^*$. In practice, if we can show $\mathcal{N}(\mathbf{B}) = \{\mathbf{0}\}$, then separation of either kind is impossible.

Example 9.7: Logistic Regression (Cox)

Cox (1970) gave a very simple example of logistic regression. Here Y_i are the number of ingots not ready for rolling out of m_i after various heating times x_i;

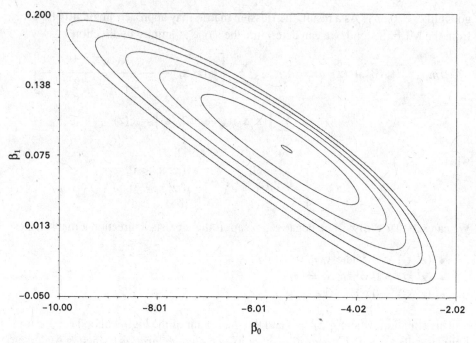

Figure 9.6. Contour plot of log likelihood for Cox logistic regression (Example 9.7). Contour lines mark $(1 - 10^{-k}) \times 100\%$ confidence regions.

the model is relatively simple, with $\gamma_i = \beta_0 + \beta_1 x_i$. The log-likelihood function is shown by Figures 9.6 and 9.7 and the computation by the demonstration program **chex97**. The data ($n = 4$) are as follows.

number m_i	55	157	159	16
not ready y_i	0	2	7	3
heating times x_i	7	14	27	51

The contour lines in Figure 9.6 are constructed according to the method outlined in (9.4.4) for Example 9.4.

Example 9.8: *Logistic Regression (Finney)*
One of the earliest examples of logistic regression is due to Finney (1947), who investigated occurrences of constriction in response to air flow rate (x_{i1}) and volume (x_{i2}) for $n = 39$ individuals ($m_i \equiv 1$). For initial values, take $\beta_1 = \beta_2 = 0$; then $\beta_0 = \text{logit}\left(\sum y_i / \sum m_i\right) = \text{logit}(20/39) = \log(20/19) = 0.0513$. In the demonstration program **chex98**, iteratively reweighted least squares converges in ten iterations.

A similar model uses the Poisson distribution. Let Y_i be independent Poisson variates with mean $\lambda_i = s_i exp(\beta^T \mathbf{x}_i)$, where s_i is a known positive intensity/weight/replicate

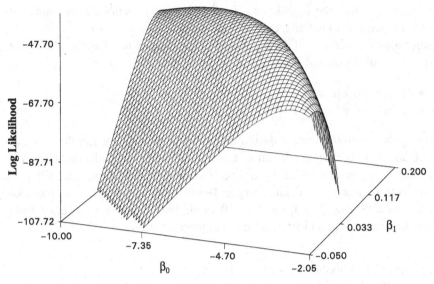

Figure 9.7. Surface plot of log likelihood for Cox logistic regression (Example 9.7).

variable. Then the loglikelihood for $Y_i\, (i = 1, \ldots , n)$ is

$$\ell_n(\beta) = \sum [y_i \log(\lambda_i) - \lambda_i - \log(y_i!)]$$
$$= \sum \left[y_i(\log(s_i) + \beta^T \mathbf{x}_i) - \lambda_i \right] + constant$$

The gradient is then immediately found to be

$$\nabla \ell_n(\boldsymbol{\beta}) = \sum (y_i - \lambda_i)\mathbf{x}_i,$$

and the Hessian is again nonstochastic:

$$\nabla^2 \ell_n(\boldsymbol{\beta}) = -\sum \lambda_i \mathbf{x}_i \mathbf{x}_i^{\mathrm{T}}.$$

Notice that the Newton or scoring iteration takes the same form as (9.7.4). As before, the conditions necessary for asymptotic normality are that $-n^{-1}\nabla^2 \ell_n(\boldsymbol{\beta})$ converge to a positive definite matrix and that $\|\mathbf{x}_i\|$ be bounded. Also, the iteratively weighted least-squares algorithm can likewise be used to find the MLE, using weights $w_i = \lambda_i$.

Quasi-complete separation can also occur in the Poisson case, as the loglikelihood can become linear in the limit, and

$$lim_{t\to\infty}d\ell_n(\beta^* + t\mathbf{z})/dt = lim_{t\to\infty} \sum_{i=1}^{n} \left[y_i(\mathbf{z}^T \mathbf{x}_i) - (\mathbf{z}^T \mathbf{x}_i)s_i e^{\mathbf{x}_i^T \beta^* + t(\mathbf{z}^T \mathbf{x}_i)} \right]$$

$$= \sum_{i=1}^{n} \left[(\mathbf{z}^T \mathbf{x}_i)(y_i - v_i(\mathbf{z})) \right] = g(\mathbf{z})$$

where

$$v_i(\mathbf{z}) = \begin{cases} 0 & \text{if } \mathbf{z}^T \mathbf{x}_i < 0, \\ s_i e^{\mathbf{x}_i^T \beta^*} & \text{if } \mathbf{z}^T \mathbf{x}_i = 0, \\ -\infty & \text{if } \mathbf{z}^T \mathbf{x}_i > 0 \end{cases}$$

One difference from the logistic case is that in some directions $\mathbf{z}$ the slope can go to $-\infty$; in fact, if $g(\mathbf{z})$ is finite, then $g(-\mathbf{z}) = -\infty$.

Separation can occur, and the maximum of the loglikelihood attained at infinity, if there exists a direction $\mathbf{z} \neq \mathbf{0}$ that satisfies

- $(\mathbf{z}^T \mathbf{x}_i) \leq 0$ where $y_i = 0$
- $(\mathbf{z}^T \mathbf{x}_i) = 0$ where $0 < y_i$

Adapting the control/treatment design discussed previously for the Poisson case, if $y_1 > 0$ and $y_2 = 0$, then the direction $\mathbf{z} = (0, -1)^T$ satisfies both conditions and the maximum is attained by taking β_2 to $-\infty$. To discover separation, again fill a matrix $\mathbf{A}$ with rows $\mathbf{x}_i^T$ when $y_i = 0$, and a matrix $\mathbf{B}$ with rows $\mathbf{x}_i^T$ when $y_i > 0$. Existence of a nonzero $\mathbf{z}$ satisfying $\mathbf{A} \geq \mathbf{0}$ and $\mathbf{B}\mathbf{z} = \mathbf{0}$ would indicate separation. For a full rank design, separation is precluded if none of responses y_i are zero.

Example 9.9: *Poisson Regression (Frome)*
Frome (1983) studied cancer death rates by age group and extent of smoking, with nine age groups and seven categories for levels of smoking (so that $n = 63$). Here the responses are Y_{ij}, the number of deaths in category (i, j) out of n_{ij} subjects, and the regression model for the Poisson rate parameter was a two-way analysis of variance parameterized by $\log(\lambda_{ij}/n_{ij}) = \alpha_i + \delta_j$ with $\delta_1 = 0$ for nonsmokers; hence the smoking level parameters δ_j are differences in log death rates. The IRWLS obtains estimates for the 15 parameters in twelve iterations; see **chex99** and Exercise 9.18.

The unifying principles of generalized linear models are (a) a mean function (or its logarithm or logit transform) that is linear in the parameters and (b) a log-likelihood function whose Hessian turns out to be nonstochastic. The distributions that work under this framework extend beyond the binomial (for logistic regression) and Poisson to include gamma, probit, and extreme-value models. Wedderburn (1976) showed that, under common circumstances, the maximum likelihood estimates exist and are unique.

9.8   Nonlinear Regression

In Section 9.6, the linear regression model was described by observations Y_i that were: (a) independent with respect to the normal distribution, with means $g(\mathbf{x}_i, \boldsymbol{\beta}) = \boldsymbol{\beta}^T \mathbf{x}_i$; (b) linear in the unknown parameters $\boldsymbol{\beta}$; and (c) of constant variance $\sigma^2 = 1/\gamma$. In nonlinear regression, however, the mean function may take the notational form of $g(\mathbf{x}_i, \boldsymbol{\beta})$ but without the linearity in the unknown parameters. Usually the application dictates the form of the model $g(\mathbf{x}_i, \boldsymbol{\beta})$, but for our purposes the mean function could just as well be expressed by $g_i(\boldsymbol{\beta})$. If these means were stacked to form a column vector of length equal to the number of observations n, and similarly for the observations Y_i, then the nonlinear regression problem could be rewritten as

$$\mathbf{Y} \sim N_n(\mathbf{g}(\boldsymbol{\beta}), \gamma^{-1}\mathbf{I}_n).$$

The log-likelihood function then follows immediately:

$$\ell_n(\boldsymbol{\beta}, \gamma) = \text{constant} + (n/2) \log \gamma - \gamma S(\boldsymbol{\beta})/2,$$

where the same notation is used for the sum-of-squares function

$$S(\boldsymbol{\beta}) = \|\mathbf{Y} - \mathbf{g}\|^2 = \sum (Y_i - g_i(\boldsymbol{\beta}))^2. \tag{9.8.1}$$

Concentrating on the scale parameter γ, clearly $\hat{\gamma} = n/S(\boldsymbol{\beta})$ and so the concentrated likelihood function for the remaining parameters $\boldsymbol{\beta}$ is

$$\ell_c(\boldsymbol{\beta}) = \text{constant} - (n/2) \log S(\boldsymbol{\beta});$$

hence, maximizing the likelihood for $\boldsymbol{\beta}$ is equivalent to minimizing the error sum of squares. Instead of pursuing this line further, let us return to the likelihood function and compute the gradient

$$\nabla \ell_n(\boldsymbol{\beta}, \gamma) = \begin{bmatrix} \gamma \mathbf{G}^{\mathrm{T}}(\mathbf{Y} - \mathbf{g}) \\ [n/\gamma - S(\boldsymbol{\beta})]/2 \end{bmatrix}, \tag{9.8.2}$$

where $\mathbf{G} = \mathbf{J_g}(\boldsymbol{\beta})$, the Jacobian matrix of the vector-valued function $\mathbf{g}$, so that $G_{ij} = \partial g_i/\partial \beta_j$. (Note the similarity of the matrix $\mathbf{G}$ to the design matrix $\mathbf{X}$ in regression.) Next, the Hessian matrix also resembles its linear regression counterpart,

$$\nabla^2 \ell_n(\boldsymbol{\beta}, \gamma) = \begin{bmatrix} \gamma \left[\sum (Y_i - g_i) \nabla^2 g_i - \mathbf{G}^{\mathrm{T}}\mathbf{G} \right] & \mathbf{G}^{\mathrm{T}}(\mathbf{Y} - \mathbf{g}) \\ (\mathbf{Y} - \mathbf{g})^{\mathrm{T}}\mathbf{G} & -n\gamma^{-2}/2 \end{bmatrix}, \tag{9.8.3}$$

but the Fisher information matrix is even closer:

$$\mathbf{J}_n = E[-\nabla^2 \ell_n(\boldsymbol{\beta}, \gamma)] = \begin{bmatrix} \gamma \mathbf{G}^{\mathrm{T}}\mathbf{G} & 0 \\ 0 & n\gamma^{-2}/2 \end{bmatrix}. \tag{9.8.4}$$

The $\mathbf{J}_n$ of (9.8.4) is equivalent to (9.6.3) for linear regression, with the Jacobian matrix $\mathbf{G}$ taking the place of the design matrix $\mathbf{X}$. An examination of these results suggests several routes for computing nonlinear regression estimates. Each has its strengths and weaknesses, which depend upon the size of the errors or residuals $(Y_i - g_i)$.

The first method, known as Gauss–Newton, can be first viewed as a scoring algorithm with the iteration

$$\boldsymbol{\beta}^{(j+1)} = \boldsymbol{\beta}^{(j)} + (\mathbf{G}^{\mathrm{T}}\mathbf{G})^{-1}\mathbf{G}^{\mathrm{T}}(\mathbf{Y} - \mathbf{g}). \tag{9.8.5}$$

Another view can be formed by taking the affine approximation to the mean function $\mathbf{g}$,

$$\mathbf{g}(\boldsymbol{\beta}) \approx \mathbf{g}(\boldsymbol{\beta}^{(j)}) + \mathbf{G}(\boldsymbol{\beta} - \boldsymbol{\beta}^{(j)}),$$

which now suggests a linear regression locally for $\boldsymbol{\beta}$; the step just given is the least-squares estimate for the difference $\boldsymbol{\beta} - \boldsymbol{\beta}^{(j)}$. Clearly, Gauss–Newton is relatively simple to use, requiring only the computation of $\mathbf{g}$ and $\mathbf{G}$ for a given value of $\boldsymbol{\beta}$. Following this route, the asymptotic covariance matrix for the estimates of $\boldsymbol{\beta}$ would be estimated by $\hat{\gamma}^{-1}(\mathbf{G}^{\mathrm{T}}\mathbf{G})^{-1}$.

Gauss–Newton can be a very effective method for computing nonlinear regression estimates. As the errors $(Y_i - g_i)$ grow small, the Gauss–Newton iteration approaches a Newton step. At its best as such, Gauss–Newton takes steps in the right direction but suffers from the Newton-like problem of taking too large a step. The usual remedy, known as modified or "damped" Gauss–Newton, shortens the step – usually just by successively halving the size of the step until $S(\boldsymbol{\beta})$ decreases. For the alternative suggested in Section 8.7, a line search can be taken along the direction of the step by fitting a quadratic to two points and a derivative (see Exercise 9.20).

Another remedy for shortening the Gauss–Newton step is known as the Levenberg–Marquardt algorithm, which uses a different damped step,

$$\boldsymbol{\beta}^{(j+1)} = \boldsymbol{\beta}^{(j)} + (\mathbf{G}^{\mathrm{T}}\mathbf{G} + \lambda_j \mathbf{I}_p)^{-1}\mathbf{G}^{\mathrm{T}}(\mathbf{Y} - \mathbf{g}). \qquad (9.8.6)$$

This method can be viewed in two ways, one as a damped intermediate between the Newton direction (small λ) and the steepest descent $\mathbf{G}^{\mathrm{T}}(\mathbf{Y} - \mathbf{g})$ for large λ (see Exercise 9.26). Another view is that of a "trust region" algorithm, where λ_j is governed by the size of the trust region $\|\boldsymbol{\beta}^{(j+1)} - \boldsymbol{\beta}^{(j)}\| < \delta$; if the step does not exceed the limit δ, then $\lambda_j = 0$; otherwise, make λ_j large enough to bring the step within range. Moré (1977) explicitly described an effective implementation of the Levenberg–Marquardt algorithm that includes recommendations for rescaling and stopping conditions as well as a modification of an algorithm by Hebden (1973) for seeking λ, so that the step is within upper and lower bounds. The algorithm **nllsq** follows the Moré algorithm closely.

Both Gauss–Newton and Levenberg–Marquardt are computationally more convenient than a full Newton procedure. Although the algebra in iterations (9.8.5) and (9.8.6) display the inverse of a matrix, computationally both methods would use the techniques of Chapter 5 for the calculation of the step (see Exercise 9.26). Gauss–Newton is most effective in small residual problems. As the size of the errors grows to an intermediate level, Gauss–Newton must be modified by adding a line search for continued effectiveness. However, Levenberg–Marquardt works very effectively – for both small and intermediate residual problems – simply by modifying the damping parameter λ_j. For the small residual problems or when close to the minimum, taking λ to zero brings the efficiency of Gauss–Newton. For intermediate or even large residual problems, keeping δ small brings the relative safety of a trust region method.

Obviously, a full Newton step for the nonlinear least-squares problem would involve considerably more computational effort, since the additional piece $\sum(Y_i - g_i)\nabla^2 g_i$ must be calculated. Writing this as requiring $O(np^2)$ additional work may be misleading, since the complexity of g is not being accounted for (regardless of whether $\nabla^2 g_i$ is computed from an analytic formula or by finite differences). In the case of solving systems of nonlinear equations or of unconstrained optimization, secant-style updates have been sought for the Hessian or Jacobian matrices of Newton's method. For the first problem, Broyden found a particularly effective update; for the optimization problem, the BFGS update is used to approximate the Hessian. In the nonlinear regression problem, the matrix to be approximated by secant-style methods is the difference

$$\mathbf{T}(\boldsymbol{\beta}^{(j)}) = \sum (Y_i - g_i)\nabla^2 g_i \text{ evaluated at } \boldsymbol{\beta}^{(j)}.$$

Dennis, Gay, and Welsch (1981) proposed a symmetric update $\mathbf{T}^{(j)}$ that solves a secant equation. Since $\mathbf{T}(\boldsymbol{\beta})$ need not be positive or negative definite, $\mathbf{T}^{(j)}$ is not restricted in this way. Their algorithm NL2SOL begins with $\mathbf{T}^{(0)} = \mathbf{0}$, so that the first step is Gauss–Newton. Thereafter, the iteration is a trust region one, like Levenberg–Marquardt:

$$\boldsymbol{\beta}^{(j+1)} = \boldsymbol{\beta}^{(j)} + (\mathbf{G}^{\mathrm{T}}\mathbf{G} + \mathbf{T}^{(j)} + \lambda_j \mathbf{I}_p)^{-1}\mathbf{G}^{\mathrm{T}}(\mathbf{Y} - \mathbf{g}). \qquad (9.8.7)$$

One view of the method is to perform Gauss–Newton and/or Levenberg–Marquardt early in the process (when both are effective) and then, with better information on $\mathbf{T}$, to take efficient Newton-like steps to close in on the minimum. The implementation of their algorithms allows for the Jacobian matrix $\mathbf{G}$ to be computed either by a user-provided subprogram or by finite differences (NL2SNO).

In discussing the unconstrained optimization problem, the two criteria for stopping were small changes in the function and small changes in the argument. In nonlinear regression, these two should certainly be retained. On rare occasions, a perfect fit is expected and the minimum of $S(\boldsymbol{\beta})$ is zero. Consequently, $S(\boldsymbol{\beta}) \le e_S$ should be the prominent criterion in this situation. Additionally, the nonlinear regression first-order condition $\mathbf{G}^{\mathrm{T}}(\mathbf{Y} - \mathbf{g}) = \mathbf{0}$ corresponds to the least-squares normal equations, indicating the orthogonality of the residuals $(\mathbf{Y} - \mathbf{g})$ and the affine space spanned by the columns of matrix $\mathbf{G}$. This orthogonality can be manipulated into a stopping criterion that focuses on the angle between the residual vector and the affine approximant to the regression function $\mathbf{g}$. Since $\mathbf{G}\boldsymbol{\beta}$ denotes any vector in the affine space, the cosine of the angle between the residual vector and the plane defined by $\mathbf{G}$ is given by

$$\cos\phi(\boldsymbol{\beta}) = \frac{\boldsymbol{\beta}^{\mathrm{T}}\mathbf{G}^{\mathrm{T}}(\mathbf{Y} - \mathbf{g})}{\|\mathbf{G}\boldsymbol{\beta}\|\|\mathbf{Y} - \mathbf{g}\|}.$$

Maximizing this with respect to $\boldsymbol{\beta}$ using the extended Cauchy–Schwarz inequality (see Exercise 9.22) gives

$$\max_{\boldsymbol{\beta}} \cos\phi(\boldsymbol{\beta}) = \cos\phi = \frac{[(\mathbf{Y} - \mathbf{g})^{\mathrm{T}}\mathbf{G}(\mathbf{G}^{\mathrm{T}}\mathbf{G})^{-1}\mathbf{G}^{\mathrm{T}}(\mathbf{Y} - \mathbf{g})]^{1/2}}{\|\mathbf{Y} - \mathbf{g}\|}. \qquad (9.8.8)$$

Squaring this quantity and recognizing the projection matrix

$$\mathbf{P_G} = \mathbf{G}(\mathbf{G}^{\mathrm{T}}\mathbf{G})^{-1}\mathbf{G}^{\mathrm{T}},$$

it follows that the quantity $(\cos\phi)^2 = (\mathbf{Y} - \mathbf{g})^{\mathrm{T}}\mathbf{P_G}(\mathbf{Y} - \mathbf{g})/S(\boldsymbol{\beta})$ gives the fraction of squared length of the residual vector projected into the affine space of $\mathbf{G}$, which should be small at convergence. Hence another stopping criterion is $|\cos\phi| \le \varepsilon_c$; for yet another form, see Bates and Watts (1988, pp. 49ff). See also Exercise 9.23.

Returning to the statistical problem, there are at least three choices for the asymptotic covariance matrix of the nonlinear regression estimates $\hat{\boldsymbol{\beta}}$. The first is $\mathbf{C}_1 = \hat{\sigma}^2(\mathbf{G}^{\mathrm{T}}\mathbf{G})^{-1}$, which follows from Fisher's information or from the Gauss–Newton methodology, where $\hat{\sigma}^2 = S(\hat{\boldsymbol{\beta}})/(n - p)$. Another choice uses the inverse of the observed information, $\mathbf{C}_2 = \hat{\sigma}^2(\mathbf{G}^T\mathbf{G} + \mathbf{T}(\hat{\boldsymbol{\beta}}))^{-1}$, which is more appropriate when the residuals are not negligible. Still another follows from the distribution of the Newton step, $\mathbf{C}_3 = \hat{\sigma}^2(\mathbf{G}^T\mathbf{G} + \mathbf{T}(\hat{\boldsymbol{\beta}}))^{-1}\mathbf{G}^T\mathbf{G}(\mathbf{G}^T\mathbf{G} + \mathbf{T}(\hat{\boldsymbol{\beta}}))^{-1}$, which is certainly the most complicated. Following the sandwich route (9.3.3) leads to a still more complicated

$$\mathbf{C}_4 = (\mathbf{G}^T\mathbf{G} + \mathbf{T}(\hat{\boldsymbol{\beta}}))^{-1}\left\{\sum_{i=1}^{n}(y_i - g_i(\hat{\boldsymbol{\beta}}))^2\mathbf{G}_{i\cdot}^T\mathbf{G}_{i\cdot}\right\}(\mathbf{G}^T\mathbf{G} + \mathbf{T}(\hat{\boldsymbol{\beta}}))^{-1}.$$

The first $\mathbf{C}_1$ is certainly the easiest to compute, since implementing a Gauss–Newton regression program would produce it automatically. The second $\mathbf{C}_2$ points out a problem heretofore ignored: the Hessian may not be positive definite in large residual problems. If a true local minimum is attained then certainly the Hessian must be positive definite, but achieving this at convergence may depend more on the choice of stopping criteria. When the Hessian is involved in the computation, as it is in $\mathbf{C}_2$ and $\mathbf{C}_3$, several routes are available. One is to use the direct formula $(\mathbf{G}^T\mathbf{G} + \mathbf{T}(\hat{\boldsymbol{\beta}}))^{-1}$, which is likely to be the most costly from a computational standpoint. Another route is to use the secant-style update to $\mathbf{T}$ as in NL2SOL. A third route (also used by NL2SOL) computes the Hessian by finite differences.

As in the previous chapter, readers are again advised against writing their own software for nonlinear regression. There are many good resources currently available; moreover, many statistical packages offer a nonlinear regression analysis procedure. For the specific nonlinear least-squares problem, many commercial software packages include either a Gauss–Newton or Levenberg–Marquardt algorithm. The Dennis–Gay–Welsch algorithm NL2SOL is available as part of the ACM collection. This procedure (as do many others) offers many options for convenience. As previously noted, including a routine to compute the Jacobian matrix $\mathbf{G}$ would be preferred to using the option for the routine to approximate $\mathbf{G}$ by finite differences. That preference does not hold when $\mathbf{G}$ is incorrectly coded – a not infrequent problem. As we have noted, computing $\nabla^2 g_i$ does not provide the same advantages and in fact often adds to the computation required for each step. The more important issue regarding options concerns the type of problem encountered: small or zero residual problems, moderate residuals, and large residuals. Gauss–Newton will do the small residual problems easily and probably with less effort than its competitors. Modifications to Gauss–Newton extend what can be considered small. Levenberg–Marquardt techniques are a bit more robust but may not be as fast. The NL2SOL is designed to handle even large residual problems and shines over its competitors when the function evaluations are most costly. The code **nllsq** has proven to be successful at solving many test problems and should suffice in most cases.

9.9 Parameterizations and Constraints

A naive user who has just learned about nonlinear regression may view the mean function $h_i(\alpha) = \log\alpha_1 + x_i\log\alpha_2$ as a nonlinear model. Strictly speaking, that view is completely correct, since the mean function is not linear in the unknown parameters. However, with the simple reparameterization $\beta_1 = \log \alpha_1$ and $\beta_2 = \log \alpha_2$, the mean function can be rewritten as $\beta_1 + \beta_2 x_i$, which is clearly simple linear regression. Computationally, using the formulas for simple linear regression is preferred to the more complicated nonlinear regression techniques. The reparameterization also simplifies statistical matters somewhat, since the asymptotic covariance matrix for the α estimates can be found from the covariance matrix of the β estimates:

$$\text{cov}(\hat{\alpha}) = \mathbf{J}_\alpha \, \text{cov}(\hat{\beta}) \mathbf{J}_\alpha^\mathrm{T},$$

where J_α is the Jacobian matrix of the transformation

$$\alpha_1(\beta) = \exp(\beta_1), \qquad \alpha_2(\beta) = \exp(\beta_2).$$

Another common reparameterization arises in trigonometric regression, where the mean function is written as $\beta_0 + \rho \cos(2\pi f t - \omega)$, where f is the known frequency. The unknown parameters ρ for the amplitude and the phase angle ω can be reparameterized to $\beta_1 = \rho \cos \omega$ and $\alpha_1 = \rho \sin \omega$, producing the mean function $\beta_0 + \beta_1 \cos(2\pi f t) + \alpha_1 \sin(2\pi f t)$, which is linear in the three unknown parameters β_0, β_1, and α_1.

When viewed in terms of the possible mean functions, the reparameterizations do not change anything. In the first case, the fitted mean function will still be a line in the (x, y)-plane. In the second case, the fitted mean function will be a shifted cosine curve with frequency f. Both problems are intrinsically linear regression problems. The reparameterizations are effective in making the problem easier and more stable computationally.

The most convenient form of reparameterization is simply centering and rescaling. Consider the common model $g_i(\beta) = \beta_1 \exp(-\beta_2 x_i)$; this can be rewritten as $g_i(\beta) = \alpha_1[\exp(-\beta_2(x_i - \bar{x}))]$, where $\alpha_1 = [\beta_1 \exp(-\beta_2 \bar{x})]$. Now if the rescaled x-deviations $\beta_2(x_i - \bar{x})$ are small then the response surface is nearly linear, $g_i(\beta) \approx a + bx_i$, and the reparameterization does not mask this fact as the original would. Even if x varies greatly, the centering of the covariate makes the columns of $\mathbf{G}$ nearly orthogonal and so the estimates of the new parameters α_1 and β_2 are closer asymptotically to independence. Bates and Watts (1980) discussed linear and nonlinear models and focused on two measures of curvature, intrinsic and parameter-effects. If the deviations $\beta_2(x_i - \bar{x})$ are small then the model is intrinsically linear. In such a case, much of the parameter-effects curvature can be removed by reparameterization, as it can be removed completely in the two earlier cases. If those deviations are not small then the problem becomes more nonlinear, and the curvature is intrinsic to the model and the design points. Since nonlinear regression techniques work best when the model is closest to linear, parameter-effects curvature should be removed by reparameterization to improve the numerical condition of the problem. Poor conditioning imposed by intrinsic curvature cannot be removed and remains as a computational burden to be overcome.

More specifically, Bates and Watts (1980, 1988) proposed to measure curvature of nonlinear regression models by looking at both the tangent space, spanned by columns of **G**, and the acceleration space, spanned by vectors

$$\ddot{\mathbf{G}}_{jk} = \frac{\partial^2 \mathbf{g}(\boldsymbol{\beta})}{\partial \beta_j \partial \beta_k}. \tag{9.9.1}$$

First form the QR decomposition of $\mathbf{G} = \mathbf{QR}$, where **R** is upper triangular and **Q** has orthogonal columns, using the modified Gram–Schmidt, Householder, or Givens method (see Chapter 5). Then construct matrices $\mathbf{A}^{(j)}$ for each column j of **Q** whose (k, l) element is $\mathbf{A}_{kl}^{(j)} = \mathbf{Q}_{\cdot j}^{\mathrm{T}} \ddot{\mathbf{G}}_{kl}$. The relative parameter-effects curvature matrices are then

$$\mathbf{C}^{(j)} = \mathbf{R}^{-\mathrm{T}} \mathbf{A}^{(j)} \mathbf{R}^{-1} \hat{\sigma}^2 \sqrt{p}. \tag{9.9.2}$$

Continuing the QR factorization by appending columns $\ddot{\mathbf{G}}_{jk}$ to the right of **G** adds additional columns $\mathbf{Q}_{\cdot j}$ indexed by $j > p$, forming additional matrices $\mathbf{A}_{kl}^{(j)} = \mathbf{Q}_{\cdot j}^{\mathrm{T}} \ddot{\mathbf{G}}_{kl}$ and $\mathbf{C}^{(j)}$ from (9.9.2) for $j = p + 1$ to as large as $p(p + 3)/2$. Bates, Hamilton, and Watts (1983) gave code utilizing LINPACK (now LAPACK) routines for QR decomposition with pivoting for columns $j > p$. The ordering of the parameters, or pivoting, greatly affects the matrices $\mathbf{C}^{(j)}$. The code **curve** uses modified Gram–Schmidt without pivoting. The root mean square curvatures – c^θ for the parameter-effects and c^i for intrinsic curvatures, which do not depend on parameter order or pivoting – follow from the expression

$$c^2 = \frac{1}{p(p+2)} \sum_j \left[2 \sum_{k=1}^{p} \sum_{l=1}^{p} (C_{kl}^{(j)})^2 + \left(\sum_{k=1}^{p} C_{kk}^{(j)} \right)^2 \right]. \tag{9.9.3}$$

Taking the sum on j from 1 to p in (9.9.3) gives the expression for the parameter-effects curvature c^θ; summing on j for the remaining nonzero columns gives the intrinsic curvature c^i. See the demonstrations **curve1** and **curve2**.

Reparameterization not only improves the numerical and statistical condition of the problem, it can also be used to enforce constraints. The strategy is to find a transformation **t** from $\mathcal{R}^p$ to the parameter space Θ that is one-to-one, monotone, smooth, and easy to compute. Then, maximizing $\ell_n(\boldsymbol{\theta})$ over constrained Θ can be done by maximizing the function $\ell_n(\mathbf{t}(\boldsymbol{\alpha}))$ over an unconstrained parameter $\boldsymbol{\alpha}$. Fortunately, the inverse of the transformation **t** is rarely needed.

When the parameter space is an interval on the real line, two transformations are commonly used. The function $t(\alpha) = e^\alpha/(1 + e^\alpha)$ is particularly useful for probabilities, since the complement $1 - t$ takes a similar form $(1 + e^\alpha)^{-1}$. A computationally simpler function is $t(\alpha) = \alpha/\sqrt{1 + \alpha^2}$, which transforms the real line to the interval $(-1, +1)$ and is linear at the origin. Either function can be relocated and scaled to cover an arbitrary interval (a, b). For parameters constrained to be positive, the transformation $t(\alpha) = e^\alpha$ is appropriate. Note, however, that a parameter point $\theta = 0$ corresponds to $\alpha \to -\infty$, which may violate the assumption of a compact parameter space.

The problem considered in Section 9.4 provides a good example of the gains from using reparameterization to enforce constraints. Recall first that θ_1 and θ_2 represented gene frequencies, constrained first to the unit interval, and also that $\theta_1 + \theta_2 \leq 1$. Other

Table 9.2. *Convergence of Newton's method with numerical Hessian under reparameterization*

Iteration	α_1	α_2	θ_1	θ_2	$(H_n)_{11}$	$(H_n)_{22}$	$(H_n)_{12}$	$\ell_n(\alpha)$
0	0.0	0.0	.33333	.33333	-152.7913	-179.6468	96.4355	-678.1451
1	-1.32579	-1.78602	.18531	.11696	-112.2743	-85.6885	18.8166	-507.4411
2	-0.82000	-1.90968	.27725	.09325	-147.6034	-69.6789	22.5325	-492.8502
3	-0.88670	-1.93107	.26462	.09312	-144.1447	-69.6716	21.4137	-492.5353
4	-0.88756	-1.93078	.26444	.09317	-142.7205	-69.7197	21.3774	-492.5353

constraints are implied by $0 \leq \pi_2 \leq 1$ and $0 \leq \pi_3 \leq 1$, but they are superfluous. The parameter space Θ is the triangle with vertices $(0, 1)$, $(1, 0)$, and the origin $(0, 0)$. An effective transformation from $\mathcal{R}^2$ is the following:

$$t_1(\alpha_1, \alpha_2) = e^{\alpha_1}/(1 + e^{\alpha_1} + e^{\alpha_2}),$$
$$t_2(\alpha_1, \alpha_2) = e^{\alpha_2}/(1 + e^{\alpha_1} + e^{\alpha_2}). \tag{9.9.4}$$

Now the function $\ell_n(\mathbf{t}(\alpha))$ can be maximized over $\boldsymbol{\alpha}$ without constraints. Recall in the example previously discussed that, when the starting value was changed to $\theta_1 = \theta_2 = .333$, Newton's method wanted to step out of the parameter space. This is not possible with this reparameterization. The analytics are a bit more complicated (providing more incentive to using differences for derivatives), but the first steps are not forbidding:

$$\pi_1 = 2e^{\alpha_1 + \alpha_2}/(1 + e^{\alpha_1} + e^{\alpha_2})^2, \qquad \pi_2 = e^{\alpha_1}(2 + e^{\alpha_1})/(1 + e^{\alpha_1} + e^{\alpha_2})^2,$$
$$\pi_3 = e^{\alpha_2}(2 + e^{\alpha_2})/(1 + e^{\alpha_1} + e^{\alpha_2})^2, \qquad \pi_4 = 1/(1 + e^{\alpha_1} + e^{\alpha_2})^2;$$

$$\nabla \ell_n(\mathbf{t}(\alpha_1, \alpha_2)) = n_1 \begin{pmatrix} 1 \\ 1 \end{pmatrix} + n_2 \begin{pmatrix} 2(1 + e^{\alpha_1})/(2 + e^{\alpha_1}) \\ 0 \end{pmatrix}$$
$$+ n_3 \begin{pmatrix} 0 \\ 2(1 + e^{\alpha_2})/(2 + e^{\alpha_2}) \end{pmatrix} - 2N \begin{pmatrix} e^{\alpha_1}/(1 + e^{\alpha_1} + e^{\alpha_2}) \\ e^{\alpha_2}/(1 + e^{\alpha_1} + e^{\alpha_2}) \end{pmatrix}.$$

The gradient should be computed following this analytic formula, but the remainder of the optimization can be done using Newton's method with the Hessian computed by differences. Table 9.2 gives the iteration sequence for this method (see **chex94rp**). Since the initial conditions correspond to $\alpha_1 = \alpha_2 = 0$, care must be taken not to use the magnitude of the parameters to determine the differences; instead, use either typical values or a minimum value for h. Even the distant starting value led to no difficulties, and this method found the same MLE as before (taking only four iterations). Figures 9.8 and 9.9 give the contour and surface plots (respectively) of the likelihood in this new parameter space. Notice that the plots are smoother than those of the original parameters given in Figures 9.1 and 9.2.

One of the most common nonlinear models is the exponential model $g(\mathbf{x}, \boldsymbol{\beta}) = \beta_1 \exp(-\beta_2 x)$, where occasionally both β_1 and β_2 are constrained to be nonnegative. The transformation $\beta(\alpha) = e^{\alpha}$ is the most common method used to enforce that constraint, even though the derivatives can quickly become complicated. Another common

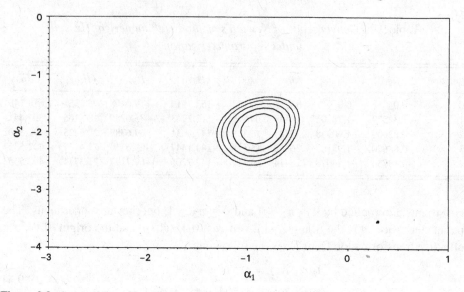

Figure 9.8. Contour plot of log likelihood for Extended Example 9.4 with transformed parameter space. Contour lines mark $(1 - 10^{-k}) \times 100\%$ confidence regions.

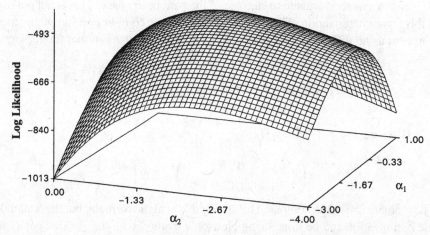

Figure 9.9. Surface plot of log likelihood for Extended Example 9.4 with transformed parameter space.

model obtained by adding another exponential piece $g(\mathbf{x}, \boldsymbol{\beta}) = \beta_1 \exp(-\beta_2 x) + \beta_3 \exp(-\beta_4 x)$ appears to be just as simple, but an identifiability problem arises. Since the parameter value (a, b, c, d) is observationally equivalent to (c, d, a, b), the difficulty can be solved by distinguishing β_2 and β_4. This can be conveniently done by the constraint $\beta_2 < \beta_4$ (with strict inequality, of course). The inequality can be enforced by reparameterization: use either $\beta_2 = \beta_4/(1 + e^{-\alpha})$ or $\beta_4 = \beta_2(1 + e^{\alpha})$. The reader is warned that this problem's simple appearance is deceiving; the problem can actually be so difficult that it has been considered something not to be computed (Acton 1970, p. 253).

Finally, one of the more common constraints is a system of linear equality constraints, $A\beta = c$. Although imposing, this system can be handled by reparameterization. First of all, the sight of m linear constraints suggests that the parameter space should be reduced by the same number of dimensions. Hence the problem is to construct the manifold of solutions to the constraints and then parameterize that manifold; the solution to the maximum likelihood or nonlinear regression problem can then be found by searching the parameters that sweep out the manifold. The dimension of β is p and so the matrix A is $m \times p$, with $m < p$ for the problem to be interesting. The manifold of solutions can be formed by constructing all solutions to the equations $A\beta = c$, which can be written as $\beta = \beta^* + t$, where t is a vector in the null space of A. Recall from Chapter 5 that the null space of A is the orthogonal complement of the range of A^T. So, compute the QR factorization of A^T, using either Householder (preferred) or Givens, to derive

$$A^T = Q\begin{pmatrix} R \\ 0 \end{pmatrix} = (Q_1 \ Q_2)\begin{pmatrix} R \\ 0 \end{pmatrix} = Q_1 R, \quad (9.9.5)$$

where the columns of Q are partitioned with m for Q_1 and with $(m - p)$ for Q_2. Thus the linear equations $A\beta = c$ are rewritten as $R^T Q_1^T \beta = c$, and the manifold of solutions can be written in terms of the $(p - m)$-dimensional parameter vector α as

$$\beta(\alpha) = Q_1 R^{-T} c + Q_2 \alpha, \quad (9.9.6)$$

where the specific solution is $\beta^* = Q_1 R^{-T} c$ and the columns of Q_2 form a basis for the null space of A. The reparameterization changes the parameter space from a constrained one for β in $\mathcal{R}^p$ to an unconstrained one for α in $\mathcal{R}^{p-m}$.

Programs and Demonstrations

chex94 *Analysis of Extended Example 9.4*
Three methods for computing MLEs for Example 9.4 are demonstrated: scoring, and Newton's method with analytical and numerical derivatives. Figures 9.1 and 9.2 show the log-likelihood function.

augrain1 *MLE via concentrated likelihood for 2-parameter gamma (Example 9.5)*
The concentrated likelihood is maximized by golden section to obtain MLEs for the 2-parameter gamma distribution fit to 45 years of August rainfall data from Raleigh, NC. Uses **golden** for golden section search and **del12f** for numerical derivatives to compute asymptotic standard errors. See Figures 9.3 and 9.5 for the log-likelihood contour plot and the concentrated log-likelihood function, respectively.

augrain2 *MLE for 2-parameter gamma (Example 9.5)*
The likelihood for the 2-parameter gamma distribution is fit to 45 years of August rainfall from Raleigh (NC) using the general optimizer **plum1t** from Chapter 8.

conclk, concll *MLE via concentrated likelihood for nonlinear regression*
As described in Example 9.6, this nonlinear regression example can be concentrated to a function of a single variable, which was maximized using **golden**. In **conclk**, the concentrated likelihood was reduced to its simplest form for optimization. In

concll, the log-likelihood function in three parameters $(\theta_1, \theta_2, \sigma^2)$ was left intact and the optimization done using an intermediate routine that supplied MLEs for θ_1 and σ^2 for a given value of θ_2.

chex97 *Logistic regression (Example 9.7)*
MLEs for the logistic regression problem of Cox (1970) are computed via the IRWLS algorithm (9.7.4). See Figures 9.6 and 9.7 for contour and surface plots of the log-likelihood function.

chex98 *Logistic regression (Example 9.8)*
MLEs for the logistic regression problem of Finney (1947) are computed via the IRWLS algorithm (9.7.4).
finney.dat – Finney data.

chex99 *Poisson regression (Example 9.9)*
MLEs for the Poisson regression problem of Frome (1983) are computed via IRWLS.
frome.dat – Frome data.

nllsqu0 *Nonlinear least-squares Test Problem 0*
nllsqu1 *Nonlinear least-squares Test Problem 1*
nllsqu2 *Nonlinear least-squares Test Problem 2*
Three nonlinear least squares problems to test the code **nllsq**. Problem 0 is the linear regression from Exercise 5.5. Problem 1 is from Fuller (1976); Problem 2 is from Gallant (1975). See also the relative curvature demonstrations that follow for further examples. Moré, Garbow, and Hillstrom (1981) presented a battery of challenging test problems. (See also Exercise 9.27.)
nllsq – computes nonlinear least squares estimates following Moré's (1977) algorithm.
fulnls.dat – data for Fuller example.
gallant.dat – data for Gallant example.

chex94rp *Reparameterization of Extended Example 9.4 as discussed in Section 9.9*

rcurv1, **recurv2** *Relative curvature measures*
Two test problems for computing relative curvature matrices $\mathbf{C}^{(j)}$ as discussed in Section 9.9, using the routine **curve**. Both test problems are examples given by Bates and Watts (1980); the first (**rcurv1**) is the puromycin example. The second, the isomerization example, has two parameterizations.
curve – computes relative curvature matrices.
puromy.dat – puromycin data.
isomer.dat – isomerization data.

Exercises

9.1 Prove the information inequality (Lemma 9.1) by applying Jensen's inequality ($-\log x$ is convex) to the function $\log[f(y)/g(y)]$. Recall that equality is reached with Jensen if the function is linear; and these must be densities. Also consider the case when the supports are different.

9.2 As in Neyman and Scott (1948), let $Y_{ij} \sim \text{normal}(\mu_i, \sigma^2)$ (independent) for $i = 1, \ldots, n$ and $j = 1, \ldots, k$. The maximum likelihood estimators are

$$\hat{\mu}_i = \bar{Y}_{i\bullet} \quad \text{and} \quad \hat{\sigma}^2 = \sum_{i=1}^{n} \sum_{j=1}^{k} \frac{(Y_{ij} - \bar{Y}_{i\bullet})^2}{nk}.$$

As $n \to \infty$ with k fixed, show that $\hat{\sigma}^2 \to [(k-1)/k]\sigma^2$ and is not consistent for σ^2.

9.3 Consider the zero-inflated Poisson model, where $\Pr(Y = 0) = p + (1 - p)e^{-\lambda}$ and $\Pr(Y = k) = (1 - p)\lambda^k e^{-\lambda}/k!$ for $k > 0$. For a sample of size n, suppose $Y_1 = \cdots = Y_n = 0$ and describe the contours of the likelihood function of (p, λ).

9.4 In the discussion of Assumption A3 in Section 9.1, computing the mean and variance of the difference in log likelihoods $Z = \log(f(\mathbf{Y} \mid \boldsymbol{\theta}_1)) - \log(f(\mathbf{Y} \mid \boldsymbol{\theta}_2))$ is suggested for assessing near nonidentifiability. For example, let $\boldsymbol{\theta}_1$ represent the distribution of $\mathbf{Y}$, the MA(1) normal time-series model (see Chapter 4) with parameter $\theta = -.3$, and let $\boldsymbol{\theta}_2$ represent the distribution of such a vector from an AR(1) model with parameter $\phi = .3$. Compute the mean and variance of Z (with respect to $\boldsymbol{\theta}_1$ as true) and compute a standardized distance $t = \text{mean}/\sqrt{\text{variance}}$. Although the two models are truly identified, the value of t here is $-0.196/\sqrt{25}$ for $n = 50$ (Monahan 1983). Compute similar values for $n = 100$ using the Levinson–Durbin algorithm.

9.5 Let Y_i be IID with the density of a mixture of two normals,

$$f(y) = p \frac{1}{\sigma\sqrt{2\pi}} \exp\left(-\frac{(y - \mu)^2}{2\sigma^2}\right) + (1 - p)\frac{1}{\sqrt{2\pi}} \exp\left(-\frac{(y - \mu)^2}{2}\right),$$

where p is known but μ and σ are unknown. Show that the log likelihood can be made arbitrarily large by setting $\hat{\mu} = Y_i$ and taking $\sigma \to 0$. Show that Assumption A4 is violated.

9.6 For the Extended Example 9.4, verify Assumptions A1 through A5.

9.7 For the Extended Example 9.4, show that $\text{cov}(\nabla \ell_n) = -E\{\nabla^2 \ell_n\}$.

9.8 For the Extended Example 9.4, compute the eigenvectors and eigenvalues of $\nabla^2 \ell_n$ and relate them to Figure 9.1.

9.9 For the Extended Example 9.4, compute the asymptotic standard errors and correlation.

9.10 Check equation (9.5.4) for the results from Example 9.5, the 2-parameter gamma.

9.11 *Concentrated Likelihood.* Suppose that $\hat{\boldsymbol{\beta}}$ maximizes $\ell_c(\boldsymbol{\beta})$ as defined in (9.5.1). Prove that $(\hat{\boldsymbol{\alpha}}(\hat{\boldsymbol{\beta}}), \hat{\boldsymbol{\beta}})$ maximizes $\ell_n(\boldsymbol{\alpha}, \boldsymbol{\beta})$.

9.12 Compute variance estimates for the nonlinear regression parameters in Example 9.6.

9.13 Recall the slow convergence of steepest descent in Example 8.4. Compare this to the convergence of a Newton step with the incorrect Hessians $\begin{bmatrix} 6 & -2 \\ -2 & 3 \end{bmatrix}$ and $\begin{bmatrix} 4 & -1 \\ -1 & 4 \end{bmatrix}$.

9.14 Show that the variance of $n/S(\hat{\boldsymbol{\beta}})$ in multiple regression is $2\gamma^2/n$ to terms of order n^{-1} (from 9.6.2).

9.15 In simple linear regression, describe the limiting behavior of $n^{-1}\mathbf{X}^{\mathsf{T}}\mathbf{X}$ when: (a) $x_i = 1/i$; (b) $x_i = i$; (c) $x_i = \log i$.

9.16 Show that the iteration step (9.7.4) for logistic (binomial) regression is *not* the same as generalized least squares.

9.17 Compute variance estimates for the logistic regression parameters in Example 9.8.

9.18   Compute variance estimates for the Poisson regression parameters in Example 9.9.

9.19   For the Poisson regression Example 9.9 (Frome), analyze the data with a linear mean function in the two variables and compute variance estimates of the parameters.

9.20   For the sum-of-squares function $S(\beta)$ (from (9.8.1)), compute the derivative in the direction $\mathbf{d}$; that is, take the derivative of $S(\beta + t\mathbf{d})$ with respect to t.

9.21   Modify the least-squares problem $\|\mathbf{Y} - \mathbf{g} - \mathbf{G}(\beta - \beta^{(j)})\|$ so that the Levenberg–Marquardt step (9.8.6) gives the solution. (*Hint:* Add new observations.)

9.22   Prove the extended Cauchy–Schwarz inequality $\max_{\mathbf{x}} \|\mathbf{c}^{\mathsf{T}}\mathbf{x}\|^2/(\mathbf{x}^{\mathsf{T}}\mathbf{B}\mathbf{x}) = \mathbf{c}^{\mathsf{T}}\mathbf{B}^{-1}\mathbf{c}$.

9.23   What is the distribution of the Gauss–Newton step $(\mathbf{G}^{\mathsf{T}}\mathbf{G})^{-1}\mathbf{G}^{\mathsf{T}}[\mathbf{y} - \mathbf{g}(\beta^{(k)})]$ evaluated at the true β^*? Construct an F-test based on this result.

9.24   Compute the nonlinear least-squares estimate for the problem in **nllsqt1** using **plum1t**.

9.25   What is the solution to the trust region constraint on the least-squares problem:

$$\min \|\mathbf{y} - \mathbf{X}\beta\| \quad \text{subject to} \quad \|\beta - \beta^*\| < \delta.$$

9.26   Verify the claims about the limits of the Levenberg–Marquardt step (9.8.6) by taking the limit of λ to both 0 and ∞.

9.27   One of the most challenging ("nasty" may be a better description) nonlinear least-squares problems (Jennrich and Sampson 1968) has $y_i = 2i + 2$ and $g_i(\theta_1, \theta_2) = \exp(i\theta_1) + \exp(i\theta_2)$ for $i = 1, \ldots, n = 10$.
   (a) Draw contour and surface plots of the sum-of-squares function $S(\theta_1, \theta_2)$.
   (b) Try to solve this using **nllsq** (or any other optimizer) starting from (0.3, 0.4).
   (c) Is the sum-of-squares function $S(\theta_1, \theta_2)$ locally quadratic around the optimum at (.2578, .2578)?

9.28   Compute "sandwich" variance estimates from (9.3.3) for the nonlinear least-squares estimate in the problem in **nllsqt1**.

9.29   Compute the relative curvature matrices $\mathbf{C}^{(j)}$ given by (9.9.2) for the problem in **nllsqt1**.

9.30   For the reparameterization of the Extended Example 9.4, use **chex94rp** to compute the analytic Hessian and compare it to the one computed numerically and given in Table 9.2.

9.31   Using the problem in **rcurv1** with regression function $g_i(\theta_1, \theta_2) = \theta_1 x_i/(\theta_2 + x_i)$, plot the sum-of-squares function $S(\theta_1, \theta_2)$. Using the same starting point as in **rcurv1**, plot the trace of the Levenberg–Marquardt step (9.8.6) for values of λ from 0 to 1000.

9.32   Test for complete separation (or quasi-) in the Cox logistic regression problem Example 9.7. What happens if we change the response at the last design point to $y_4 = 16$?

9.33   Find the conditions for complete separation in the probit model, where $Pr(Y_i = 1|\mathbf{x}_i) = \Phi(\mathbf{x}_i^T \beta)$ where Φ is the standard normal cdf. (See Stokes, 2004 for an interesting application.)

9.34   Some badly conditioned problems can be improved dramatically by simply scaling the variables so that the parameters of the problem do not differ by orders of magnitude. For a Gauss-Markov model, $E(\mathbf{y}) = \mathbf{X}\mathbf{b}$, $Cov(\mathbf{y}) = \sigma^2\mathbf{I}$, this may mean using a scaled response $\mathbf{y}^* = c\mathbf{y}$ where c is some scalar, perhaps $c = 1000$ from changing the units of the response from kilograms to grams. We could also scale the covariates and use the design matrix $\mathbf{X}^* = \mathbf{X}\mathbf{D}$ where $\mathbf{D}$ is a diagonal matrix. Now we can rewrite the Gauss-Markov model in terms of the rescaled response and design matrix, $E(\mathbf{y}^*) = \mathbf{X}^*\mathbf{b}^*$, $Cov(\mathbf{y}^*) = \sigma_*^2\mathbf{I}$. a) Write the new parameters in terms of the old, that is, find $S(\mathbf{b})$ and $T(\sigma^2)$ so that $\mathbf{b}^* = S(\mathbf{b})$ and $\sigma_*^2 = T(\sigma^2)$. b) Do the usual least squares estimators give the correct adjustment, that is, are $\hat{\mathbf{b}}^* = S(\hat{\mathbf{b}})$ and $\hat{\sigma}_*^2 = T(\hat{\sigma}_*^2)$? c) For the following problems, examine whether the estimators/algorithm responds properly to changes in scale. Consider whether both c and $\mathbf{D}$ are appropriate, and also (if appropriate) estimating σ^2. i) GLS arising from $Cov(\mathbf{y}) = \sigma^2\mathbf{V}$ with $\mathbf{V}$ known ii) Ridge regression, with $\tilde{\mathbf{b}} = (\mathbf{X}^T\mathbf{X}+k\mathbf{I})^{-1}\mathbf{X}^T\mathbf{y}$ ii) Newton/Scoring for logistic regression

References

The beauty of the maximum likelihood problem is that, in large samples, most problems are approximately quadratic. For further reading on the maximum likelihood theory, Rao (1973) is probably the easiest to read; LeCam (1970) may be more useful. Many of the theory's consequences have appeared only in bits and pieces, and some have never been written down. Jennrich and Moore (1975) is an unusually placed paper that provides some foundation to what had become folklore, including the IRWLS for what McCullagh and Nelder (1992) called "generalized linear models." Dennis and Schnabel (1983) covered nonlinear least-squares computation only briefly; Moré (1977) provided the do-it-yourself details. Bates and Watts (1988) provided the statistical methodology at an applied level; see Gallant (1987) or Wu (1981) for all of the theoretical background.

F. S. Acton (1970), *Numerical Methods That Work*. New York: Harper & Row.

A. Albert and J. A. Anderson (1984), "On the Existence of Maximum Likelihood Estimates in Logistic Regression Models," *Biometrika* 71: 1–10.

Y. Bard (1974), *Nonlinear Parameter Estimation*. New York: Academic Press.

D. M. Bates, D. C. Hamilton, and D. G. Watts (1983), "Calculation of Intrinsic and Parameter-Effects Curvatures for Nonlinear Regression Models," *Communications in Statistics B* 12: 469–77.

D. M. Bates and D. G. Watts (1980), "Relative Curvature Measures of Nonlinearity," *Journal of the Royal Statistical Society B* 42: 1–25.

D. M. Bates and D. G. Watts (1988), *Nonlinear Regression Analysis and Its Applications*. New York: Wiley.

Dennis D. Boos (1992), "On Generalized Score Tests," *American Statistician* 46: 327–33.

D. R. Cox (1970), *Analysis of Binary Data*. London: Methuen.

A. P. Dempster, N. M. Laird, and D. B. Rubin (1977), "Maximum Likelihood from Incomplete Data via the EM Algorithm," *Journal of the Royal Statistical Society B* 39: 1–38.

J. E. Dennis, Jr., D. M. Gay, and Roy E. Welsch (1981), "An Adaptive Nonlinear Least-Squares Algorithm," *ACM Transactions on Mathematical Software* 7: 348–83.

J. E. Dennis, Jr., and R. B. Schnabel (1983), *Numerical Methods for Unconstrained Optimization and Nonlinear Equations*. Englewood Cliffs, NJ: Prentice-Hall.

B. Efron and D. V. Hinkley (1978), "Assessing the Accuracy of the Maximum Likelihood Estimator: Observed versus Expected Fisher Information," *Biometrika* 65: 457–87.

D. J. Finney (1947), "The Estimation from Individual Records of the Relationship Between Dose and Quantal Response," *Biometrika* 34: 320–34.

E. L. Frome (1983), "The Analysis of Rates Using Poisson Regression Models," *Biometrics* 39: 665–74.

W. A. Fuller (1976), *Introduction to Statistical Time Series*. New York: Wiley.

A. R. Gallant (1975), "Nonlinear Regression," *American Statistician* 29: 73–81.

A. R. Gallant (1987), *Nonlinear Statistical Models.* New York: Wiley.

M. D. Hebden (1973), "An Algorithm for Minimization Using Exact Second Derivatives," Report no. TP515, Atomic Energy Research Establishment, Harwell, U.K.

Paul W. Holland and Roy E. Welsch (1977), "Robust Regression Using Iteratively Reweighted Least Squares," *Communications in Statistics* A6: 813–27.

R. I. Jennrich and R. H. Moore (1975), "Maximum Likelihood Estimation by Means of Nonlinear Least Squares," in *Proceedings of the Statistical Computing Section,* pp. 57–65. Washington, DC: American Statistical Association.

R. I. Jennrich and P. F. Sampson (1968), "An Application of Stepwise Regression to Non-Linear Estimation," *Technometrics* 10: 63–72.

L. LeCam (1956), "On the Asymptotic Theory of Estimation and Testing Hypotheses," in *Proceedings of the Third Berkeley Symposium of Mathematical Statistics and Probability,* vol. 1, pp. 129–56. Berkeley: University of California Press.

L. LeCam (1970), "On the Assumptions Used to Prove Asymptotic Normality of Maximum Likelihood Estimators," *Annals of Mathematical Statistics* 41: 802–28.

L. LeCam and G. Yang (1990), *Asymptotics in Statistics: Some Basic Concepts.* New York: Springer-Verlag.

D. Marquardt (1963), "An Algorithm for Least-Squares Estimation of Nonlinear Parameters," *SIAM Journal of Applied Mathematics* 11: 431–41.

P. McCullagh and J. A. Nelder (1992), *Generalized Linear Models,* 2nd ed. New York: Chapman & Hall.

John F. Monahan (1983), "Fully Bayesian Analysis of ARMA Time Series Models," *Journal of Econometrics* 21: 307–31.

Jorge J. Moré (1977), "The Levenberg–Marquardt Algorithm: Implementation and Theory," in G. A. Watson (Ed.), *Numerical Analysis* (Lecture Notes in Mathematics, no. 630), pp. 105–16. Berlin: Springer-Verlag.

Jorge J. Moré, Burton S. Garbow, and Kenneth E. Hillstrom (1981), "Testing Unconstrained Optimization Software," *ACM Transactions on Mathematical Software* 7: 17–41.

S. A. Murphy and A. W. van der Vaart (2000), "On Profile Likelihood," *Journal of the American Statistical Association* 95: 449–65.

J. Neyman and E. Scott (1948), "Consistent Estimates Based on Partially Consistent Observations," *Econometrica* 16: 1–32.

C. R. Rao (1973), *Linear Statistical Inference and Its Applications,* 2nd ed. New York: Wiley.

Thomas J. Santner and Diane E. Duffy (1986), "A Note on A. Albert and J. A. Anderson's Conditions for the Existence of Maximum Likelihood Estimates in Logistic Regression Models," *Biometrika* 73: 755–58.

R. J. Serfling (1980), *Approximation Theorems and Mathematical Statistics.* New York: Wiley.

Houston H. Stokes (2004), "On the Advantage of Using Two or More Econometric Software Systems to Solve the Same Problem," *Journal of Economic and Social Measurement* 29: 307–20.

A. Wald (1949), "Note on the Consistency of the Maximum Likelihood Estimate," *Annals of Mathematical Statistics* 20: 595–601.

R. W. M. Wedderburn (1976), "On the Existence and Uniqueness of the Maximum Likelihood Estimates for Certain Generalized Linear Models," *Biometrika* 63: 27–32.

J. Wolfowitz (1949), "On Wald's Proof of the Consistency of the Maximum Likelihood Estimate," *Annals of Mathematical Statistics* 20: 601–2.

C. F. Jeff Wu (1981), "Asymptotic Theory of Nonlinear Least Squares Estimation," *Annals of Statistics* 9: 501–13.

C. F. Jeff Wu (1983), "On the Convergence Properties of the EM Algorithm," *Annals of Statistics* 11: 95–103.

10

Numerical Integration and
Monte Carlo Methods

10.1 Introduction

The juxtaposition of these two topics may appear strange to many readers. Upon further reflection, the common thread of spreading points in space may become apparent. My point in combining these topics is to emphasize that this thread is not weak. Monte Carlo should be viewed as just another way to compute an integral; numerical integration should be viewed as just another way to sample points in space. Great gains can be made by exploiting the strengths of one approach when the other is floundering. Only with the willingness to adjust one's viewpoint and use these tools in combination can the full array of techniques be brought to bear on a difficult problem.

Tools such as Riemann sums and Simpson's rule characterize the set of tools known as *fixed quadrature* or simply *quadrature*. A viewpoint of these methods as a discretization of the continuous problem of integration is indeed naive. The points are spread in a fixed way in space, with the number of points set in advance. Most of these methods employ a weighting scheme, so that the points (abscissas) where a function is to be evaluated have varying importance. For estimating an integral by evaluating a function at N points in one dimension, the error converges to zero at a rate of $O(N^{-2})$ or better, depending on the smoothness of the function. In higher dimensions, however, this rate slows considerably. Assessing the accuracy of quadrature methods is extremely difficult, and most assessments are quite naive. Quadrature methods for one dimension will be discussed in Section 10.3 and higher-dimensional techniques in Section 10.4.

Generating random variables begins with the generation of independent uniform random variables, to be discussed in Section 10.5. Commonly used techniques employ number theoretic methods and are clearly predictable, but their behavior is sufficiently similar to that of truly random variables as to be preferred to any mechanical means. Here, the number of points to be sampled need not be set in advance, and the vast array of statistical tools can be employed to assess accuracy. The usual statistical convergence rate of $O(N^{-1/2})$ applies in nearly every case, with opportunities to improve the convergence by reducing the variance. Moreover, the dimension of the problem has no effect.

Two practical methods for generating quasirandom sequences occupy a strange intermediate point. As number theoretic methods to place points in space, they are characterized by their filling up space too evenly to appear random. The evenness of filling space is $O(N^{-1})$ and dictates the convergence rate of its integration error, which is affected by dimension in only a minor way. One of these two methods requires the

257

number of points to be set in advance; the other does not. As with quadrature, assessment of accuracy is quite difficult.

Because we seek an accuracy estimate for these quasirandom methods, randomization is introduced in Section 10.7 as one of a number of techniques for improving accuracy. Some of the methods, described as standard techniques in experimental design, are appropriate for simulation experiments. Other methods follow similar statistical tools of conditioning and pairing.

Finally, after some discussion of the differences in these methods, another similarity should be mentioned. Despite the array of methods presented here, the reader should always keep in mind that Monte Carlo and numerical integration problems can often be solved by brute strength alone. Since computing has become cheaper than thinking, the reader should not be afraid to use a simple tool and pound the problem into submission.

10.2   Motivating Problems

Many of the techniques discussed here are specialized within a particular field of statistics and are rarely discussed outside of that realm. In pursuit of the theme of spreading points in space, it is important to discuss these motivating problems, relate the specialized techniques to each other, and explore where combinations of tools might be exploited. In discussing these various fields of statistics, our focus is not their foundation but rather how those foundations motivate the computation problem.

(A)   *Simulation Experiments in Statistics*

Monte Carlo tools in theoretical statistics are mostly used in the evaluation of new techniques. In general terms, data Y are observed arising from a distribution F. Then a researcher may propose an estimator $\hat{\theta}(Y)$ of a characteristic $\theta(F)$ (mean, median, variance, center of symmetry) of this distribution F or, more commonly, a parameter θ of a parametric family F_θ. In many important situations, a researcher can find *analytically* some of the properties of the distribution of this proposed estimator $\hat{\theta}$ (i.e., its mean, variance, etc.). Here, "analytically" means using pencil, paper, brainpower, and probability calculus. For example, if the vector $\mathbf{Y}$ comes from a distribution F that has each of n components independent normal with mean μ and variance σ^2, then a great deal is known about certain estimators of the parameter vector $\theta = (\mu, \sigma^2)$. However, even for this most important case, little may be known about other estimators. For the particular estimator $\hat{\mu} = \text{median}\{Y_i, i = 1, \ldots, n\}$, the mean of its distribution is μ (so it is unbiased) but no simple expression exists for the variance. An expression can be written for the distribution of $\hat{\mu}$, but only in terms of a common (but complicated) function Φ. Changing the underlying distribution F – to, say, independent exponential or logistic random variables – leads to such a different situation that little may be known analytically about the properties of the sample mean and very little about the sample median.

In the 1970s, researchers examined these foundations of statistics and could make very little progress with analytic techniques. Information was largely limited to some useful criteria for constructing estimators, such as maximum likelihood, that led to good estimators (most of the time) as well as knowledge on how these estimators behave in large samples. Expressions for bias may be workable, consistency of the estimator may be easy to prove, and standard errors that work well in large samples may be found. But outside of the normal distribution, very little can be done to analyze the sampling distribution of estimators. The main tool for investigating the performance of alternative estimators of location and scale is the simulation experiment; here, samples Y can be generated from a distribution of interest, the estimates $\hat{\mu}(Y)$ computed, and statistics of the sampling distribution of $\hat{\mu}(Y)$ compiled and analyzed to obtain estimates of the bias, variance, mean squared error (MSE), and so on. The most common question to be addressed by such an experiment is "At what sample size n can the asymptotic results be used?" Other important issues are which estimator performs better, how much better, and for what values of the parameters.

For example, suppose a statistician were encountering severely unbalanced one-way analysis of variance (ANOVA) and wondered whether to use ANOVA or maximum likelihood estimators of the variance components. The model takes the form

$$Y_{ij} = \mu + \alpha_i + e_{ij} \quad \text{for } j = 1, \ldots, n_i \text{ and } i = 1, \ldots, p,$$

with α_i IID $N(0, \sigma_a^2)$ and e_{ij} IID $N(0, \sigma_e^2)$. Two factors may have an effect on the performance of these two estimators: (i) the true ratio of variance components σ_a^2/σ_e^2, and (b) the balance or pattern of the n_i. The experiment now must be designed to address the issues at hand: which method works better, and for what values of the variance ratio σ_a^2/σ_e^2 and what pattern of the n_i. The pattern of the n_i should come from typical experiments that the statistician is concerned about, and the values of the ratio should cover the range of interest. Determining "better" involves the selection of criteria: bias, variance, and MSE as well as the method of comparison. Other design issues such as blocking or pairing arise in use of the same data for both methods and can sometimes be resolved by using the same seeds or starting points for the random number generator. Of course, the sample size of the simulation experiment should be large enough that important differences could be found. With the benefit of more than a dozen years and 20/20 hindsight, improvements on the design for a similar study (Swallow and Monahan 1984) are now embarrassingly obvious.

Finally, although statisticians are more comfortable with the Monte Carlo approach, some salient words in favor of numerical integration are in order. Notice that both estimators are functions of just two sums of squares,

$$B = \sum_{i=1}^{p} n_i(\bar{Y}_{i\cdot} - \bar{Y}_{\cdot\cdot})^2 \quad \text{and} \quad W = \sum_{i=1}^{p}\sum_{j=1}^{n_i}(Y_{ij} - \bar{Y}_{i\cdot})^2,$$

which are scaled independent χ^2 random variables. The MSE of the ANOVA estimator for σ_a^2 could be computed by integrating the function $[S_a(b, w) - \sigma_a^2]^2$, where the estimate is

$$S_a = \left(B - \frac{p-1}{N-p}W \right) \Big/ \left(N - \sum_{i=1}^{p} \frac{n_i^2}{N} \right)$$

with respect to the 2-dimensional joint density of these two random variables (B, W); any other criterion could be computed in a similar manner.

(B) *Hypothesis Tests*

In their abstraction, hypothesis tests appear rather strange. The goal is to determine whether the distribution of the data Y arises from a particular distribution, or has a particular characteristic – a.k.a. the *hypothesis*. The test can be viewed as merely a function of the data $T(Y)$ that takes on values 0 (accept) and 1 (reject). To achieve the goal, the function $T(Y)$ is designed so that it is more likely to reject the hypothesis $T(Y) = 1$ when the hypothesis is not true – a.k.a. the *alternative* – than reject if the hypothesis is true; that is, we hope that

$$E\{T(Y) \mid \text{hypothesis}\} \leq E\{T(Y) \mid \text{alternative}\}.$$

In common practice, the left-hand side is set to be a certain small probability, since it measures an error we wish to avoid; we call this the *level* of the test and denote it by α. The right-hand side is the probability of a correct decision, usually denoted by β and called the *power* of the test. As with estimation, often the distribution of the test function may not be well known outside of a few special situations, and criteria for constructing good tests abound. The most common situation is that enough may be known about the test function under the hypothesis to establish the level, and hopes for power rest on these criteria for good (i.e. powerful) tests.

This situation is by no means universal, for the level may be known only asymptotically or approximately, so that the level can only be referred to as a nominal level or target. Then a simulation experiment would be required to establish whether the test is liberal (level greater than nominal) or conservative (level less than nominal). For example, suppose the data Y were n independent pairs of bivariate normal random variables, and suppose we were interested in a hypothesis about the correlation ρ using the sample correlation r. If the test function were

$$T_0(Y) = 1 \iff t = r\sqrt{\frac{n-2}{1-r^2}} > t_{n-2}(\alpha)$$

then, if the hypothesis were $H : \rho = 0$ and the interesting alternatives $\rho > 0$, the level of the test is well known to be α and the test would have increasing power for positive ρ. However, if we wished to test a different hypothesis – say, $H : \rho = \rho^*$ (where $\rho^* \neq 0$) against the alternative $\rho > \rho^*$ – then the most common test would use Fisher's z transformation, $Z(r) = \tanh^{-1}(r)$; the test function is

$$T_1(Y) = 1 \iff \sqrt{n-3}[Z(r) - Z(\rho^*)] > z(\alpha).$$

The appeal of Fisher's z follows from the complicated distribution of the sample correlation r under this hypothesis; testing requires numerical integration of a difficult function (see Exercise 7.38). The test T_1 raises some interesting new issues. Although the nominal level of this test may be α, a simulation study would be needed to establish whether this approximate test is liberal or conservative, depending on the sample size and hypothesized correlation ρ^*. But there are even more interesting avenues of attack.

As with many hypotheses, generation from the distribution F under the hypothesis is often relatively easy. Suppose that samples $Y^{(i)}$ ($i = 1, \ldots, M$) of n pairs of bivariate normals were generated and that the sample correlations r_i were computed. Then the sampling distribution of r could be estimated and the critical value for r could be determined empirically. That is, find the value r^* such that $\Pr(r(Y) > r^* \mid \text{hypothesis}) = \alpha$. If perhaps $\alpha = 1/k$ and $M = k - 1$ samples were generated, then the test

$$T_2(Y) = 1 \iff r > \max\{r_1, \ldots, r_M\}$$

would also have the appropriate level α. For example, say $\alpha = .10$; if, after 100 samples $Y^{(i)}$ were generated, 50 r_i were larger than the sample correlation r and 50 were smaller, then there would be very little interest in continuing the effort.

Generating from the hypothesis distribution allows considerable freedom in selecting any sort of test statistic. For example, although a simple function of the sample correlation coefficient r is the obvious choice for a test statistic, none of the procedures just mentioned are restricted to such a statistic. Likelihood ratio tests that are too complicated for everyday use can become a practical option when these generation techniques are employed.

Generation from the hypothesis distribution opens a new world for conditional tests. In testing independence in contingency tables, the conditional distribution under the hypothesis is a random table with fixed marginals, which can be generated using the techniques outlined in Section 11.6(C). Given, say, $Y_1, \ldots, Y_{n_1}$ IID $F(y)$ and $Y_{n_1} + 1, \ldots, Y_{n_1+n_2}$ IID $F(y - \Delta)$, conditioning on the sufficient statistic for F under the hypothesis $\Delta = 0$ means that the hypothesis distribution is a random permutation of the indices of the Ys. Generating random permutations – or just random sampling in the two-sample problem – is also covered in Section 11.6(C). These permutation tests, after 50 years in the backwaters of statistics, become practicable with the ability of generating from the permutation distribution. Again, the choice of test statistic is not restricted with permutation tests.

(C) *Bayesian Analysis*

Bayesian statistical methods differ from what may be called sampling theory methods on philosophical grounds that are widely separated. Bayesian philosophy is based on the notion that knowledge, or lack of it, can be expressed in terms of a probability distribution. Whereas a particular parameter θ – say, the mean of a population – may be considered unknown in the sampling theory view, in the Bayesian view *something* will be known about it – and that imperfect information can be expressed in terms of a prior distribution $\pi(t)$ in advance of any experiment or sampling to gain further information. Data Y are obtained to give information about θ, following a model for the data expressed in terms of the density of the data $f(y \mid t)$ conditioned on values of the parameter $\theta = t$. The information from the data Y in the likelihood $f(y \mid t)$ can then be incorporated with the prior information in $\pi(\theta)$ to form the posterior distribution $\pi(t \mid y)$ as the conditional density of the parameter θ given the observed data $Y = y$, following Bayes' theorem: $\pi(t \mid y) \propto \pi(t) f(y \mid t)$. Inference about the parameter will then be based solely on the posterior $\pi(t \mid y)$, which may be a point estimate (e.g., the posterior mean or median), a posterior probability set (an analog to a confidence interval), or a Bayes decision that minimizes expected (with respect to $\pi(t \mid y)$) loss in a more complicated decision problem.

For sampling from certain distributions $f(y \mid \theta)$, there may be a family of prior distributions that lead to posterior distributions in the same family. For example, if Y follows the binomial distribution then we know that, if the prior distribution on the success probability parameter is a member of the beta family of distributions, the posterior will also be in the beta family. The prior–posterior family is called the *conjugate family* for a particular sampling distribution. If the prior information can be expressed well using a conjugate family then Bayesian methodology is simple and convenient to use, since computing the posterior distribution simply means updating the parameters of the prior. Expressing the posterior, however, may still require further numerical tools – for example, computing special functions such as the incomplete gamma or beta integrals. Although conjugate families exist for some of the most important problems, such as normal sampling in regression and ANOVA, these situations are nevertheless as rare as situations in which the sampling distribution of an estimator is known.

In my view, the value of Bayesian methodology in real problems manifests itself when real information is available in the prior and the data are not so informative as to overwhelm the prior. In many of these problems, either no conjugate family is available for the prior or information is lost in forcing its form. Moreover, asymptotic approximations of the likelihood are inappropriate in such small samples. Either the prior or likelihood usually preclude closed-form posteriors, and some form of numerical integration is then required. Consequently, the use of Bayesian methodology requires the numerical expression of the posterior via posterior means and variances, expressing the posterior density, or whatever form is available or necessary.

Hence the numerical work for Bayesian methodology usually requires computing the integral of several functions with respect to the posterior distribution, usually expressed in an unnormalized form:

$$p^*(t) \propto \pi(t \mid y) \propto \pi(t)L(t) = \pi(t)f(y \mid t). \tag{10.2.1}$$

Posterior moments of the parameter are often the easiest way of expressing properties of the posterior distribution. Other characteristics of the posterior distribution, such as posterior probability regions or expected loss, can also be written as the expectation of some function $h(t)$ with respect to the posterior. Since the normalization constant corresponds to the special case of $h(t) \equiv 1$, numerical Bayesian methodology mostly means computing several integrals with the same form $\int h(t)p^*(t)\,dt$ for several different functions h.

In large samples, the differences between Bayesian and sampling theory methods begin to fade. With a lot of data, the prior information $\pi(t)$ becomes dominated by the likelihood $f(y \mid t)$ and so the posterior is essentially the same as the likelihood. The large-sample asymptotics of maximum likelihood (see Chapter 9) now can be used in many cases, leading to a large sample posterior distribution that is approximately normal, with a mean at the maximum likelihood estimate and variance from the inverse of the information quantity. The Bayesian viewpoint reverses roles: the parameter is random with its distribution centered on the estimate. But the conclusions in large samples are essentially identical, and the approximation in Theorem 9.3 now looks like

$$\log p^*(\mathbf{t}) \approx \log p^*(\mathbf{t}_m) - \tfrac{1}{2}(\mathbf{t} - \mathbf{t}_m)^{\mathsf{T}}\mathbf{H}(\mathbf{t} - \mathbf{t}_m), \tag{10.2.2}$$

where $\mathbf{t}_m$ is the mode of the unnormalized posterior p^*.

To illustrate the variety of issues just discussed, consider the variance components problems mentioned previously but with a slightly different characterization and a change in notation:

$$Y_{ij} \sim N(\theta_i, \phi = \sigma_e^2), \quad j = 1, \ldots, n_i;$$
$$\theta_i \sim N(\beta = \mu, \gamma = \sigma_a^2), \quad i = 1, \ldots, p.$$

Then the likelihood for the three fixed parameters (relabeled as $\beta = \mu$, $\phi = \sigma_e^2$, and $\gamma = \sigma_a^2$) can be written as

$$L(b, f, g) = \prod_{i=1}^{p}(n_i g + f)^{-1/2}\exp\left\{-\frac{1}{2}\sum_{i=1}^{p}\frac{(\bar{y}_{i\cdot} - b)^2}{g + f/n_i}\right\} \times f^{-(N-p)/2}\exp\left\{-\frac{\frac{1}{2}W}{f}\right\}.$$

There is no conjugate family for this likelihood and parameterization, but convenience nonetheless suggests a prior of the following form:

$$\beta \sim N(b_0, \phi_0),$$
$$\phi \sim \text{inverse gamma}(a_1, b_1),$$
$$\gamma \sim \text{inverse gamma}(a_2, b_2),$$

with each component independent. The posterior then takes the form

$$p^*(b, f, g) = g^{-(a_2+p/2)-1}e^{-b_2/g} \times f^{-(a_1+N/2)-1}e^{-[b_1+W/2]/f}$$

$$\times \exp\left\{-\frac{\frac{1}{2}(m - b_0)^2}{\phi_0}\right\} \times \prod_{i=1}^{p}\left(\frac{n_i}{f} + \frac{1}{g}\right)^{-1/2}$$

$$\times \exp\left\{-\frac{1}{2}\sum_{i=1}^{p}\frac{(\bar{y}_{i\cdot} - b)^2}{g + f/n_i}\right\}. \tag{10.2.3}$$

From this point, several computational routes are available. First of all, the mean parameter β could be integrated out analytically, since its distribution conditional on the variance components ϕ and γ is univariate normal. The marginal joint distribution of (ϕ, γ) is rather complicated, however, whenever the problem is unbalanced (i.e., unequal n_i), with the reduction in dimension from 3 to 2. Although this drop in dimension certainly makes a great difference in numerical integration, 3-dimensional integrals are not prohibitively expensive. Several other computational routes exploit the large-sample approximate normality of the posterior: importance sampling, randomized integration, and mixed methods (described more fully in Chapter 12). Introduction of θ_i, the unobserved group means, suggests an augmented parameterization that increases the dimension, with the posterior

$$p^*(\mathbf{t}, b, f, g) \propto g^{-(a_2+p/2)-1} \exp\left\{-\frac{b_2 + \frac{1}{2}\sum_i (t_i - b)^2}{g}\right\}$$

$$\times f^{-(a_1+N/2)-1} \exp\left\{-\frac{b_1 + W/2 + \frac{1}{2}\sum_i (\bar{y}_{i\cdot} - t_i)^2}{f}\right\}$$

$$\times \exp\left\{-\frac{\frac{1}{2}(b - b_0)^2}{\phi_0}\right\}.$$

As will be seen in Chapter 13, the marginal distributions of each parameter (given the others) are greatly simplified with the introduction of these unobservables. Markov chain methods – in particular, Gibbs sampling – can be employed to generate vectors from the joint distribution of these $p + 3$ parameters.

10.3   One-Dimensional Quadrature

In calculus, the integral of a function $I(f) = \int f(x)\, dx$ is defined as the limit of upper and lower Riemann sums. For integrating a function $f(x)$ over the interval $[a, b]$, only the most modest assumption – continuity – is required on the function f, so that the limit of left and right Riemann sums,

$$R_n^-(f) = \sum_{i=0}^{n-1} hf(a + ih) \quad \text{and} \quad R_n^+(f) = \sum_{i=1}^{n} hf(a + ih) \tag{10.3.1}$$

(where $h = (b - a)/n$), converge to the integral $I(f)$ as $n \to \infty$. It takes little imagination to see that either a left- or right-handed Riemann sum could be used be used as a method of numerical integration. The modulus of continuity governs the error in this method of approximate integration:

$$|I(f) - R_n(f)| \le (b - a)w(h), \quad \text{where } w(h) = \sup_{|x-y|<h} |f(x) - f(y)|. \tag{10.3.2}$$

Taking the simple average of the left and right Riemann sums leads to one of the more common methods of integration, the *trapezoid* rule,

$$T_n(f) = \frac{h}{2}\left[f(a) + 2\sum_{i=1}^{n-1} f(a + ih) + f(b)\right]. \tag{10.3.3}$$

The name "trapezoid" arises from the linear approximation of f over each subinterval $[a + (i - 1)h, a + ih]$, forming a trapezoid (see Figure 10.1) with the two sides at the endpoints and the interval at the base. The view of the trapezoid rule as an average of the two Riemann sums shows its ability to integrate functions with only the assumption of continuity. Viewing it as a result of a linear approximation to the function f in each subinterval leads to the following error analysis when the function f has a continuous second derivative:

$$I(f) - T_n(f) = -(b - a)^3 f''(\xi)/(12n^2) = -nh^3 f''(\xi)/12 \quad \text{for } \xi \in [a, b]. \tag{10.3.4}$$

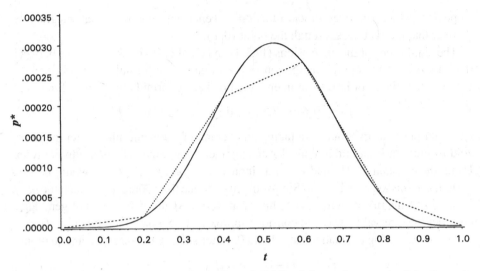

Figure 10.1. Trapezoid rule or linear interpolant. Solid line is log-series posterior from Example 10.1; dashed line is linear interpolant whose integral is the trapezoid rule.

This result shows that the error drops by a factor of 4 when the number of points or evaluations of the function is doubled. Another error result for periodic functions follows from the Euler–Maclaurin formula; when the function has many zero derivatives at the endpoints, dramatic convergence rates can be observed (see Davis and Rabinowitz 1984, sec. 2.9).

These primitive integration rules appear to follow a pattern of smoothness and continuity requirements, approximation, and rates of convergence as the number of function evaluations increases. Riemann sums follow from approximating the function f with step functions in each subinterval. Consequently, only continuity is required for convergence, although that convergence is slow. The trapezoid rule follows from linear approximations and is exact for linear functions. It converges at a quadratic rate, even though it requires only one more evaluation than the Riemann sum. This pattern continues, and the appearance of getting something for nothing is part of the pattern.

A simple alternative to evaluating the function at the endpoints is to evaluate f in the center of each subinterval $[a + (i - 1)h, \ a + ih]$. This leads to the *midpoint* rule,

$$M_n(f) = h \sum_{i=1}^{n} f\left(a + (b - a)\frac{2i - 1}{2n}\right),\tag{10.3.5}$$

whose simplicity belies its effectiveness. The midpoint rule also merely approximates the function f by a step function in each subinterval, yet its convergence rate is competitive with the trapezoid rule:

$$I(f) - M_n(f) = (b - a)^3 f''(\xi)/(24n^2) = nh^3 f''(\xi)/24 \quad \text{for } \xi \in [a, b].\tag{10.3.6}$$

This error result shows that the midpoint rule integrates linear functions exactly while using only one evaluation in each subinterval. After a little examination, this is not so surprising. Without loss of generality, consider integrating the function $f(x) = c + dx$ over the interval $[-1, 1]$. The value of the integral is $I(f) = 2c$, regardless of what the slope d is. Moreover, every linear function – even a step function – that integrates to $2c$ over that interval goes through the point $(0, c)$.

The similarities of the expressions (10.3.4) and (10.3.6) invite comparisons between the trapezoid and midpoint integration rules or quadrature formulas. The differences in the sign of the error lead to an interesting bracketing formula for convex functions,

$$M_n(f) \leq I(f) \leq T_n(f) \quad \text{if} \ \ f''(x) \geq 0 \ \text{on} \ [a, b].$$

After our previous experience in taking an average of Riemann rules to get the trapezoid formula, it is natural to consider an average of the trapezoid and midpoint rules. Using the constants $(1/12$ and $1/24)$ as indicators, $\frac{2}{3}M_n(f) + \frac{1}{3}T_n(f)$ would be suggested, and this average leads to Simpson's rule. Since this route seems much too easy, let us derive the rule by a route only hinted at so far. Again without loss of generality, consider the interval $[-1, 1]$ and consider approximating a quadratic function $f(x) = c + dx + ex^2$ using evaluations at ± 1 and 0. After solving the three linear equations,

$$f(-1) = c - d + e,$$
$$f(0) = c,$$
$$f(1) = c + d + e,$$

we find the coefficients

$$c = f(0), \quad d = (f(1) - f(-1))/2, \quad e = (f(-1) - 2f(0) + f(1))/2,$$

which define the approximant $\hat{f}(x)$. The approximant then has an integral of $I(\hat{f}) = 2c + 2e/3 = (f(-1) + 4f(0) + f(1))/6$, which defines the weighting scheme for Simpson's rule: $1/6, 4/6, 1/6$. Extending this rule to n subintervals covering $[a, b]$, the compound Simpson's rule can be written as

$$S_n(f) = h\left[f(a) + 4\sum_{i=1}^{n} f\left(a + h\frac{2i-1}{2}\right) + 2\sum_{i=1}^{n-1} f(a + ih) + f(b)\right]\Big/6, \quad (10.3.7)$$

where h is the width of the subintervals $(b - a)/n$, as before. The term "compound" has been slipped in here to denote that the rule for a single (sub)interval has been applied to several adjoining (sub)intervals. The midpoint and trapezoid rules were introduced in their compound form.

This compound form makes comparison of the three methods (midpoint, trapezoid, and Simpson) a little tricky. The error analysis for Simpson's rule can be written in both forms: for $\xi \in [a, b]$,

$$I(f) - S_n(f) = -(b - a)^5 f^{(4)}(\xi)/(2880n^4) = -nh^5 f^{(4)}(\xi)/90. \quad (10.3.8)$$

Note that cubic functions are integrated exactly and that convergence is fourth order – that is, doubling the number of evaluations will cut the error by a factor of 16. However, to compare to midpoint and trapezoid rules, remember that Simpson's rule takes two evaluations for each subinterval compared to one for the others.

Example 10.1: *Simple Integration Rules for Bayesian Problem*
Examples 8.3 and 9.3 described data from a sample of size $n = 10$ from the logarithmic series distribution with parameter θ, leading to the (unnormalized) likelihood function

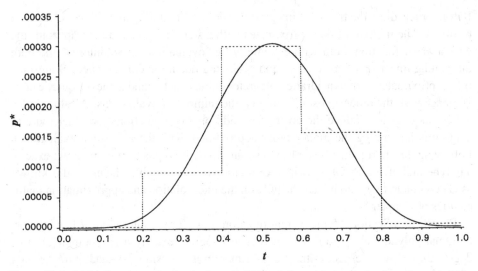

Figure 10.2. Midpoint rule or step interpolant. Solid line is log-series posterior from Example 10.1; dashed line is step function interpolant whose integral is the midpoint rule.

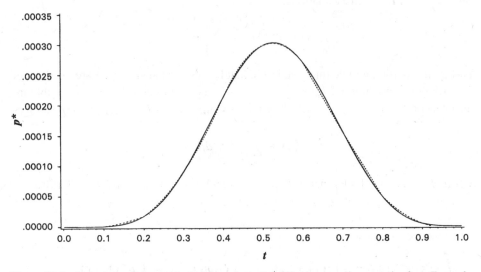

Figure 10.3. Simpson's rule or quadratic interpolant. Solid line is log-series posterior from Example 10.1; dashed line is quadratic interpolant whose integral is Simpson's rule.

$$L(t) = t^{15}/[-\log(1 - t)]^{10}$$

for a prior $\pi(t) = 6t(1 - t)$; the (unnormalized) posterior is then

$$p^*(t) = t^{16}(1 - t)/[-\log(1 - t)]^{10} \quad \text{for } 0 < t < 1.$$

The first function to be integrated is $h_0(t) \equiv 1$ to obtain the normalization constant. Other functions h to be computed are $h_1 = t$ and $h_2(t) = t^2$, yielding (respectively) the posterior mean and variance; see **quad1** for the code. The posterior is plotted in Figures 10.1–10.3, along with the interpolants from trapezoid, midpoint, and Simpson's rules. This is a comparatively easy function to integrate – very smooth, and strongly converging to zero at the endpoints of the interval.

Before proceeding, the thread of integration rules as integrating approximants must be resolved. The midpoint rule approximates with a step function and the trapezoid rule with a linear function, both with essentially one evaluation per subinterval and both integrating linear functions exactly and achieving quadratic convergence. Simpson's rule approximates with a quadratic, integrates cubic exactly, and achieves quartic convergence with the modest cost of doubling the number of evaluations. All three rules are compounded to reduce the error with additional computations. Another route to explore is integrating the higher-order approximant with the additional evaluations. Following the short pattern established so far, could it be possible to integrate exactly a polynomial of degree $2n - 1$ with n evaluations? It is possible; the method is known as Gauss quadrature, and it leans heavily on the interpolation and approximation mathematics of Chapter 7.

Recall from Section 7.5 the weight function $w(x)$ for the interval $[a, b]$ and the orthogonal polynomials $p_n(x)$. The goal is to integrate exactly a polynomial $g(x)$ of degree $2n - 1$ with respect to the weight function $w(x)$ using the quadrature formula of the form $\sum_{i=1}^{n} w_i g(x_i)$. That is, the quadrature formula is defined by the weights w_i and abscissas x_i, which must be constructed to integrate any polynomial of degree $2n - 1$ with n function evaluations:

$$\int_a^b g(x) w(x)\, dx = \sum_{i=1}^{n} w_i g(x_i).$$

Part of the solution will be imposed immediately – that the abscissas x_i are the roots of the orthogonal polynomial $p_n(x)$. Let $q(x)$ be the polynomial of degree $n - 1$ that interpolates $g(x)$ at x_i, $i = 1, \ldots, n$. Then, following Section 7.2, $q(x)$ can be written as

$$q(x) = \sum_{i=1}^{n} g(x_i) d_i(x),$$

where $d_i(x)$ are the delta functions $d_i(x_i) = 1$ and $d_i(x_j) = 0$ when $i \neq j$. The trick is to write $g(x)$ in terms of p_n, q, and a remainder, $g(x) = q(x) + p_n(x) r_{n-1}(x)$, where the remainder $r_{n-1}(x)$ is a polynomial of degree $n - 1$. Then the steps of the integration of g proceed as follows:

$$\int g(x) w(x)\, dx = \int [q(x) + p_n(x) r_{n-1}(x)] w(x)\, dx = \int q(x) w(x)\, dx$$

$$= \int \left[\sum_{i=1}^{n} g(x_i) d_i(x) \right] w(x)\, dx = \sum_{i=1}^{n} g(x_i) \int d_i(x) w(x)\, dx,$$

where the second equality follows since p_n is orthogonal to all polynomials of smaller degree (Exercise 7.28). The last step indicates the solution by defining the weights,

$$w_i = \int_a^b d_i(x) w(x)\, dx. \tag{10.3.9}$$

Exercise 10.5 establishes that the weights w_i are positive (see also Davis 1975, thm. 14.2.1). Proper notation for the abscissas and weights are x_{in} and w_{in} (respectively), since the entire set changes with each value of n. The index n may be added for emphasis or dropped for convenience.

All of this effort in constructing Gauss quadrature formulas pays off in some impressive error analysis,

$$I(f) - \sum_{i=1}^{n} w_i f(x_i) = \frac{f^{(2n)}(\xi)}{(2n)! \, k_n^2} \quad \text{for } \xi \in [a, b]. \tag{10.3.10}$$

Here k_n is the coefficient of the normalized orthogonal polynomials,

$$\frac{p_n(x)}{\|p_n(x)\|} = k_n x^n + c x^{n-1} + \cdots,$$

so that for Gauss–Legendre quadrature with $w(x) \equiv 1$ on $[-1, 1]$, we have $k_4 = (35/8)/\sqrt{2/(2(4)+1)} = \frac{105}{8}\sqrt{2}$. Before the reader takes this result that appears mathematically "best" as the practical best, keep in mind that – unless the function is particularly smooth – the benefit of the large constants in the denominator will be lost in trying to tame the $(2n)$th derivative. Gauss quadrature is predicated on the ability of a single polynomial to approximate the function to be integrated over the entire interval. When that approximation works well, then Gauss quadrature will likewise work well. When a polynomial approximation is quite inappropriate, then Gauss quadrature may perform poorly. At worst, however, the quadrature formula converges in weak* fashion; that is,

$$I(f) - \sum_{i=1}^{n} w_{in} f(x_{in}) \to 0 \quad \text{as } n \to \infty \tag{10.3.11}$$

for any Riemann integrable function on $[a, b]$. In this sense, the abscissas and weights define a sequence of discrete probability distributions that converge to the measure $dW(x)$. For further details, see Davis (1975, sec. 14.4).

The computation of the set of abscissas and weights for each value of the number of evaluations n appears to be a formidable task. Direct evaluation appears to require that all of the roots to a polynomial be determined, and then n integrals for the weights. Some tables have been published for the most popular orthogonal polynomial configurations (Legendre, Hermite, etc.) of intervals and weight functions $w(x)$: see Abramowitz and Stegun (1970), Stroud and Secrest (1966), or Krylov (1962). However, the following general algorithm by Golub and Welsch (1969) is preferred. Recall that the orthogonal polynomials of Section 7.5 follow a three-term recursion relationship. Denote the normalized orthogonal polynomials by $p_n^*(x) = p_n(x)/\|p_n(x)\|$, and write the recursion relationship as follows:

$$x p_{n-1}^*(x) = \alpha_n p_n^*(x) + \beta_n p_{n-1}^*(x) + \alpha_{n-1} p_{n-2}^*(x). \tag{10.3.12}$$

Then construct the symmetric, tridiagonal matrix $\mathbf{A}$ with the coefficients β_n on the diagonal and α_n on the super- and subdiagonals:

$$\mathbf{A} = \begin{bmatrix} \beta_1 & \alpha_1 & 0 & 0 \\ \alpha_1 & \beta_2 & \alpha_2 & 0 \\ 0 & \alpha_2 & \beta_3 & \alpha_3 \\ 0 & 0 & \alpha_3 & \beta_4 \end{bmatrix} \quad \text{for } n = 4.$$

Table 10.1 gives the coefficients for the most commonly used cases.

For example, recall the Legendre polynomials, which have normalization constant $\|P_n(x)\| = \sqrt{2/(2n+1)}$ and recurrence relationship $(n+1)P_{n+1} = (2n+1)xP_n - nP_{n-1}$.

Table 10.1. *Tridiagonal elements for computation of Gauss quadrature abscissas and weights*

Legendre	$\alpha_n = n/\sqrt{4n^2 - 1}$	$\beta_n = 0$
Shifted Legendre	$\alpha_n = (n/2)/\sqrt{4n^2 - 1}$	$\beta_n = 1/2$
Hermite	$\alpha_n = \sqrt{n/2}$	$\beta_n = 0$
Modified Hermite	$\alpha_n = \sqrt{n}$	$\beta_n = 0$
Laguerre	$\alpha_n = \sqrt{n(n + \alpha)}$	$\beta_n = 2n - 1 + \alpha$

Clearly $\beta_n = 0$, and with a little algebra we find $\alpha_n = n/\sqrt{4n^2 - 1}$, which was previously posed in Exercise 6.15. The eigenvalues of **A** are the roots of $p_n^*(x)$, the abscissas x_{in} ($i = 1, \ldots, n$). Denoting the corresponding eigenvectors by $\mathbf{z}^{(i)}$ ($i = 1, \ldots, n$), the weights are found by taking the first components of each $z_1^{(i)}$ and forming $w_{in} = m_0(z_1^{(i)})^2$, where $m_0 = \int_a^b w(x)\,dx$. As a result, this algorithm of Golub and Welsch changes the problem to an easy eigenproblem, already in tridiagonal form, which can be quickly solved using the QR algorithm (Section 6.5).

An important point that I want to make here is that even though the mathematics of Gauss quadrature looks impressive, in practice the convergence rates become evident only in easy problems or special situations. With compounding, Gauss–Legendre 2-point and 3-point rules are competitive with Simpson's rule. Gauss quadrature should be considered for some small problems, especially if they are known to be smooth. But these rules have little to offer for solving difficult problems.

Example 10.1 *(cont.)*

Gauss quadrature can be employed on this posterior in two ways. One method is to use Gauss–Legendre quadrature, shifted from the $[-1, 1]$ interval to the $[0, 1]$ interval; abscissas and weights were computed by **qgaustb** and tabled into **qgauslg.tab**. Another approach is to take advantage of the normal approximation to the posterior. Here the posterior mode is at $t_m = .527167$ and the second derivative there is 42.036, so the posterior is approximately normal centered at the mode and scaled along the θ axis by the variance $s^2 = (1/42.036)$. Then the posterior integrals are rewritten as

$$\int h(t)p^*(t)\,dt = \int h(t)\frac{p^*(t)}{\phi((t - t_m)/s)/s}\phi((t - t_m)/s)/s\,dt$$

$$= \int h(t_m + sz)\frac{p^*(t_m + sz)}{\phi(z)}\phi(z)\,dz. \qquad (10.3.13)$$

As a result, Gauss–Hermite quadrature abscissas and weights can be employed, scaled for statistical problems s with weight function $\exp(-z^2/2)$ instead of $\exp(-z^2)$. These are also tabled by **qgaustb** and stored in **qgaushm.tab**; see the code in **quad2**. Both approaches work well here, owing to the smoothness of the function (in the first case) and the quality of the normal approximation, as shown in Figure 10.4.

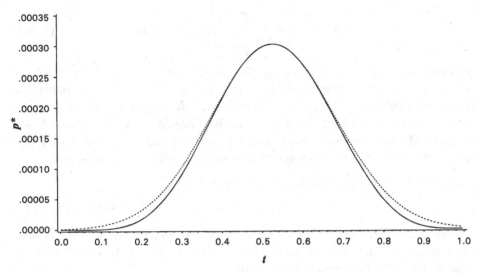

Figure 10.4. Normal approximation of posterior. Solid line is log-series posterior from Example 10.1; dashed line is the normal approximation matching the posterior mode and second derivative.

10.4   Numerical Integration in Two or More Variables

In root-finding and optimization problems, the change from one to two dimensions dramatically changes the nature of the problem and the techniques employed. However, we have seen that, as the number of dimensions increased further, the techniques remained the same and the burden increased only linearly or quadratically – as in the computation of the Jacobian or Hessian matrix of Newton's method. Conversely, in numerical integration the methods do not change so dramatically but the computational burden grows at a faster rate as the number of dimensions grows.

For integrating over a rectangle (the Cartesian product of two intervals), the Cartesian product of integration rules for intervals can be used quite effectively. For example, the product midpoint rule over the unit square is simply

$$M_m \times M_n(f) = \sum_{i=1}^{m} \sum_{j=1}^{n} f\left(\frac{2i-1}{2m}, \frac{2j-1}{2n}\right), \qquad (10.4.1)$$

and it is easy to show (see Exercise 10.8) that the product midpoint rule integrates linear functions of the form $ax + by + c$ exactly. The product Simpson's rule is just the Cartesian product of the interval rule, with a weighting pattern

$$
\begin{array}{ccc}
1 & 4 & 1 \\
4 & 16 & 4 \\
1 & 4 & 1
\end{array}
$$

on the vertices, midpoint, and the midpoints of the sides of the square (or subsquare) for the compound rule. Note that the weights of adjoining squares or rectangles are added, as in the

$$1\ 4\ 2\ 4\ 2\ 4\ 2\ 4\ 1$$

univariate pattern. The Gauss rules can also be used in product form,

$$G_m \times G_n(f) = \sum_{i=1}^{m} \sum_{j=1}^{n} w_{im} w_{jn} f(x_{im}, x_{jn}) \qquad (10.4.2)$$

whether for rectangles, quadrants (Laguerre), or $\mathcal{R}^2$ (Hermite). However, no simple and effective error bounds are available for any of these product rules. The main result (Davis and Rabinowitz 1984, p. 355) is that if a rule R integrates polynomials of degree r in x exactly and integrates S polynomials of degree s in y exactly, then $R \times S$ integrates all linear combinations of terms $x^i y^j$ for $i \leq r$ and $j \leq s$. For example, the product Simpson's rule will integrate exactly a polynomial in (x, y) of the form

$$ax^3 y^3 + bx^3 y^2 + cx^3 y + dx^3 + ex^2 y^3 + fx^2 y^2 + gx^2 y$$
$$+ hx^2 + ixy^3 + jxy^2 + kxy + lx + my^3 + ny^2 + oy + p.$$

However, such a result does not translate easily into an error bound. Take the case of the midpoint rule over the square from the origin to (h_1, h_2). If the entries of the Hessian matrix can be bounded over this square,

$$|(\nabla^2 f)_{ij}| \leq M_{ij},$$

then the error of the midpoint rule can be written as a quadratic form in the matrix $\mathbf{M}$,

$$|I(f) - [M \times M(f)]| \leq (h_1^2 M_{11} + h_2^2 M_{22} + 2h_1 h_2 M_{12})/8. \qquad (10.4.3)$$

If the two variables are measured equally, $h_1 = h_2 = h$, then the error can be written as $O(h^2)$ or quadratic in h. Considerable effort has been put into rules that are exact for various simple functions over a square, cube, or hypercube, but without great success; the reader is referred to Davis and Rabinowitz (1984, p. 361) for further results. One parting note of caution has been reflected in the use of different rules on each coordinate, such as $M_m \times M_n$. Some functions can behave quite differently along a line such as $y = x$, or something similar. Different compounding or formulas will often obviate the need to treat the problem in a special manner; see Exercise 10.9.

Many other regions can be handled by similar means and some simple transformations. For the interior of a circle, changing to polar coordinates (r, θ) allows for the use of a product rule over r and θ, while prudence dictates that the number of points for θ should increase with increasing r. For a region in the plane bounded by a polygon, the natural route is to divide the region into triangles. For integration over a simplex, say

$$\{p_1 + p_2 + p_3 \leq 1, \, 0 \leq p_i \leq 1\},$$

the natural route is to subdivide this polyhedron into others. The methods for handling this problem are similar to the triangle problem, which should be examined in depth.

(A) *Integration over a Triangle*

The midpoint rule analog for the triangle is to evaluate at the centroid of the triangle (where the medians meet) with weight equal to the area of the triangle. Since linear transformations convert any shaped triangle to any other (see Exercise 10.11), let us define the triangle T with vertices $(0,0)$, $(1,0)$, and $(1,1)$ as the fundamental triangle, whose area is $1/2$. The centroid is then the point $(2/3, 1/3)$. To check the midpoint result, the integral of a linear function is

$$\int_0^1 \int_0^x (ax + by + c)\, dy\, dx = a/3 + b/6 + c/2$$
$$= (1/2)(a(2/3) + b(1/3) + c) \qquad (10.4.4)$$

over this triangle T. Similarly, the analog to the trapezoid rule is to evaluate at the endpoints of the triangle with equal weights $(1/6)$, which gives the same result as (10.4.4). The Simpson's rule analog is, of course, to evaluate at the centroid as well as the endpoints, but the weights are $3/8$ at the centroid and $1/24$ at each of the endpoints. Again Simpson's rule is equivalent to the average of midpoint and trapezoid rules, with the midpoint having nine times the weight. The Simpson analog for the triangle can integrate the function $ax^2 + bxy + cy^2 + dx + ey + f$ exactly, but without cubic terms.

Compounding of the triangle rules requires some care. If the fundamental triangle is divided into smaller triangles by adding vertices at $(1/2, 0)$, $(1/2, 1/2)$, and $(0, 1/2)$, then four triangles are formed each with area $1/8$. Each triangle is a right triangle with legs of length $1/2$, with one of them pointing down. In general, if the fundamental triangle is subdivided into right subtriangles with legs $1/k$ long, then k^2 subtriangles are formed with vertices at $(i/k, j/k)$ for i, j satisfying $0 \le j \le i \le k$. Two problems remain: one is to determine the weights of vertices where triangles adjoin, the other is to locate the centroids. For the weights, all of the interior vertices adjoin six triangles, so the weight for interior points is $1/k^2$ for the trapezoid analog. For points on the boundary, where $i = j$ or $j = 0$ or $i = k$, each vertex is shared by three triangles, so their weights are $1/(2k^2)$; finally, weights are $1/(6k^2)$ at the three main vertices. Locating the centroids is another matter, since $k(k-1)/2$ triangles point up and $(k-1)(k-2)/2$ triangles point down. For those subtriangles pointing in the same direction as the fundamental triangle, centroids can be found by simply rescaling and relocating from the original $(2/3, 1/3)$:

$$((i-1)/k + 2/(3k),\ (j-1)/k + 1/(3k)) \quad \text{for } 1 \le j \le i \le k. \qquad (10.4.5)$$

For the subtriangles flipped over, centroids are found at

$$((j-1)/k + 1/(3k),\ (i-1)/k + 2/(3k)) \quad \text{for } 1 < i < j < k. \qquad (10.4.6)$$

Notice that the latter set of indices are the complement of the former, so that both i and j can run from 1 to k, and the decision to switch the order of the coordinates depends on $i < j$.

The result of compounding these triangular rules is an increase in accuracy. Breaking the fundamental triangle into k^2 smaller triangles reduces the error by a factor of roughly $O(k^{-2})$ for the midpoint and trapezoid analogs. For the Simpson analog, the error drops as $O(k^{-3})$. As with the product rules, no simple formula is available.

Example 10.2: *Modification of Extended Example 9.4*
Recall the extended example from Section 9.4, essentially a multinomial with parameterized probabilities whose log likelihood is of the form

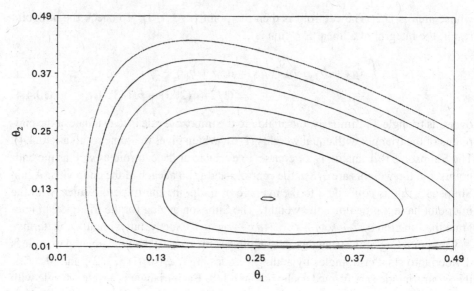

Figure 10.5. Contour plot of log likelihood for Example 10.2. Contour lines mark $(1 - 10^{-k}) \times 100\%$ confidence regions.

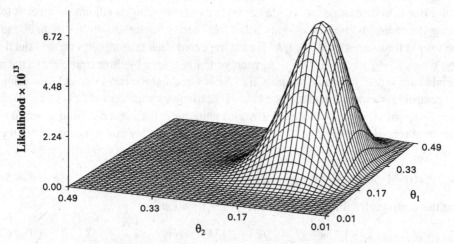

Figure 10.6. Surface plot of log likelihood for Example 10.2.

$$\ell_n(\mathbf{t}) = n_1 \log[2t_1 t_2] + n_2 \log[t_1(2 - t_1 - 2t_2)]$$
$$+ n_3 \log[t_2(2 - t_2 - 2t_1)] + 2n_4 \log[1 - t_1 - t_2];$$

for simplicity, consider the prior to be uniform over the triangular parameter space. The sample size is so large ($N = 435$) in the example that the likelihood dominates, the posterior matches the asymptotic normal approximation, and the problem is not so interesting. Cutting the sample size substantially ($n_1 = 1$, $n_2 = 10$, $n_3 = 4$, $n_4 = 9$) makes the problem more interesting; a contour plot similar to Figure 9.1 is given in Figure 10.5 (Figure 10.6 gives the corresponding surface plot). One simple route for computing the posterior moments is to integrate over the triangular region using the methods just outlined. Both midpoint and Simpson triangular analogs are employed in **chex102t**. Two other methods use the approximate normality of the posterior. Recall that, with the constant prior, the mode $\mathbf{t}_m$ of the posterior $p^*(\mathbf{t})$ is the same as the MLE and the Hessian matrix is the same as before:

$$\mathbf{t}_m = \hat{\boldsymbol{\theta}} = \begin{bmatrix} .265782 \\ .110980 \end{bmatrix}, \qquad \mathbf{H} = -\nabla^2 \log p^* = \begin{bmatrix} 215.1117 & 59.4264 \\ 59.4264 & 472.0310 \end{bmatrix},$$

and $\log p^*(\mathbf{t}_m) = -28.0271$. We may therefore estimate the posterior as a scaled bivariate normal:

$$\log p^*(\mathbf{t}) \approx \log p^*(\mathbf{t}_m) - \tfrac{1}{2}(\mathbf{t} - \mathbf{t}_m)^{\mathsf{T}} \mathbf{H}(\mathbf{t} - \mathbf{t}_m),$$

and $\mathbf{H}^{-1}$ gives the approximate covariance matrix:

$$\mathbf{H}^{-1} = 10^{-6} \begin{bmatrix} 4816 & -606 \\ -606 & 2195 \end{bmatrix}.$$

So the first of two methods that use the normal approximation is to center and scale a product Simpson's rule; the second is to use Gauss–Hermite quadrature. The former (Simpson) is straightforward; the only detail is $p^* = 0$ for values outside the parameter space. Gauss–Hermite quadrature is best explained with a little calculus (extension of (10.3.13)):

$$\iint p^*(\mathbf{t}) \, d\mathbf{t} = \iint p^*(\mathbf{t}_m + \mathbf{L}^{-\mathsf{T}}\mathbf{z})|\mathbf{L}^{-\mathsf{T}}| \, d\mathbf{z}$$

$$= |\mathbf{L}|^{-1} \iint [p^*(\mathbf{t}_m + \mathbf{L}^{-\mathsf{T}}\mathbf{z}) e^{\mathbf{z}^{\mathsf{T}}\mathbf{z}/2}] e^{-\mathbf{z}^{\mathsf{T}}\mathbf{z}/2} \, d\mathbf{z}.$$

Rectangular product Simpson's rule is demonstrated in **chex102s**; Gauss–Hermite integration in **chex102g**.

A few additional comments on Example 10.2 are in order because this problem typifies Bayesian integration problems. First, the sample size for the original problem is so large that integration is·virtually unnecessary. This should be checked, of course, and the methods outlined in Chapter 12 are designed to exploit the large-sample normality. Another important aspect of integrating posterior distributions is that the normalization constant is often enormously large or small, sometimes too big to write in the computer's arithmetic. For Bayesian problems, the normalization constant is often (but not always!) unimportant, so one might be tempted to ignore it altogether. I would caution to the contrary and suggest the route shown in **chex102t/s/g** by integrating $p^*(\mathbf{t})/p^*(\mathbf{t}_m)$, the posterior normalized by the mode. Here, values of the posterior that are alarmingly small can be set to zero in order to avoid underflow and overflow. The actual value of the normalization constant can then be found by reattaching $p^*(\mathbf{t}_m)$. In the demonstration of Example 10.2, some confidence in the computation can be gained by comparing the integration of the normalization constant across methods.

The choice of the three approaches are also typical. Although the triangular methods appear to be the most natural and fit the parameter space, they don't work as well for problems where the posterior mass is so localized – even with the modified (smaller sample size) problem. However, because of the potential for compounding, this problem can be beaten down simply by using a lot of points and ignoring the fact that a third or more – a fraction and not a dimension – are not needed. The product Simpson's rule is another "pound into submission" approach that works well here. Two details are worth worrying about. One worry is whether three or four standard deviations are far enough into the tail to get the whole posterior – this must be checked, usually by comparing the results from different ranges. The second worry is whether the correlations are so large that a substantial effort is wasted. With large correlations, the posterior mass lies entirely along a diagonal, and nearly a dimension of effort is unnecessary. In Example 10.2, however, the correlation is small, the posterior contours are nearly circular, and little effort is wasted. The Gauss–Hermite scheme exploits well the posterior normality, but it is not safe enough to use without exploring the posterior and checking. This method requires much more finesse than the other "pound into submission" methods and can easily give erroneous results in difficult problems, so careful use is required.

(B) *Integration on Surface of a Sphere*

The surface of the sphere in d dimensions (denoted by U_d) is a peculiar space on which to integrate, but it comes up enough times to merit some attention here. More importantly, it arises in some special algorithms in Chapter 12 that exploit the normality of the posterior. The first method is called the *antipodal* rule: just put points at the axes of the sphere and weight them equally. That is, the abscissas are $\pm \mathbf{e}_k$ ($k = 1, \ldots, d$) for each elementary vector and the weights are $|U_d|/2d$, where the area of the surface of the sphere is $|U_d| = 2\pi^{d/2}/\Gamma(d/2)$. Like Simpson's rule, this integration rule will be exact for cubic functions on the surface of the sphere.

The *simplex* rule also uses equally weighted points, but at the vertices of the regular simplex in d dimensions. This produces $d + 1$ points on the surface of the sphere, and this method is exact for quadratic functions. Mysovskikh (1980, p. 232) gives the following formulas for the vertices $\mathbf{a}^{(i)}$, $i = 1, \ldots, d + 1$:

$$a_j^{(i)} = \begin{cases} 0 & \text{for } i < j, \\ v_1 & \text{for } i = j, \\ -v_2 & \text{for } i > j, \end{cases}$$

where

$$v_1 = \sqrt{\frac{(d+1)(d-i+1)}{d(d-i+2)}} \quad \text{and} \quad v_2 = \sqrt{\frac{d+1}{d(d-j+1)(d-j+2)}}.$$

The *symmetric simplex* rule is simply the symmetrization of the simplex rule; the additional points are $\{-\mathbf{a}^{(i)}, i = 1, \ldots, d+1\}$. This rule then uses $2d + 2$ equally weighted points and will be exact for cubic functions, similar to the antipodal rule. The *extended simplex* integration method begins with the same $d+1$ points of the simplex method and then adds their negatives to make $2d + 2$ vertex points. The midpoints of all segments joining all pairs of vertex points are then projected to the surface of U_d. These projected midpoint points are weighted differently than the vertex points (see Mysovskikh 1980, p. 237): $|U_d|[(7-d)d]/[2(d+1)^2(d+2)]$ for the $2d+2$ vertices; for the $d(d+1)$ projected points, the weights are $|U_d|[2(d-1)^2]/[d(d+1)^2(d+2)]$. In the general case there are $(d+1)(d+2)$ points, but we have only six equally weighted points for $d = 2$ and only 14 (not 20) points for $d = 3$ because of duplication. The extended simplex method is exact for all polynomials of degree less than 6. Note that the projected midpoints can also be viewed as abscissas for an equally weighted integration rule using $d(d+1)$ points.

(C) *The Curse and Monte Carlo Integration*

This section ends with a discussion of what is known as "the curse." The reader should have noted that, in the expression (10.4.3), the error bound is roughly $O(h^2)$ for the midpoint rule in two dimensions. Recall that the same was true for one dimension and, following the same mathematics, the error in d dimensions will remain $O(h^2)$, where h is the length of a side. Suppose that making a side of length h requires n points along a dimension; then the number of points to get $O(h^2)$ error is $N = n^d$ total number of function evaluations. Looking at it another way, we can fix the number of evaluations to N; then the error from compounding the midpoint rule is $O(N^{-2/d})$. In $d = 4$ dimensions, $N = 10{,}000$ function evaluations gives only $h \approx .1$, and two digits of accuracy would be the best one could hope for. This enormous effort of N function evaluations achieves little accuracy owing to the number of points needed to fill d-dimensional space. This problem is commonly called "the curse of dimensionality": that the effort needed to achieve a certain level of accuracy grows exponentially with the dimension. The curse may seem disheartening because we have seen (as with bisection in Chapter 8) convergence rates where the error was exponentially decreasing, and that rate is considered slow – to N^{-4} for Simpson's rule in one dimension (Section 10.2). However, whereas previously the usual statistical rate of convergence of $O_p(N^{-1/2})$ was laughably slow, for integrating in four dimensions (or more) that rate no longer looks so slow, especially since it does not depend on the number of dimensions. In practice, the normal approximation to the posterior is usually employed, following the expression

$$\iint p^*(\mathbf{t})\, dt = |\mathbf{L}|^{-1} \iint [p^*(\mathbf{t}_m + \mathbf{L}^{-T}\mathbf{z})e^{\mathbf{z}^T\mathbf{z}/2}]e^{-\mathbf{z}^T\mathbf{z}/2}\, d\mathbf{z}. \tag{10.4.7}$$

Instead of spreading product Simpson's rule (or Gauss–Hermite quadrature) points in $\mathcal{R}^d$, which will not fill it so well, the alternative is generating $\mathbf{z} \sim N_d(\mathbf{0}, \mathbf{I}_d)$; then this function of $\mathbf{z}$,

$$|\mathbf{L}|^{-1}[p^*(\mathbf{t}_m + \mathbf{L}^{-T}\mathbf{z})e^{\mathbf{z}^T\mathbf{z}/2}],$$

has the same expectation as (10.4.7). More importantly, averages will converge at a faster rate, $O(N^{-1/2})$. For modest dimensions (say, $d = 3, 4, 5$), clever integration will compete with Monte Carlo because of the variance – the constant in $O(\cdot)$. However, the key to any Monte Carlo method is the uniform generation, since it is the driving force behind the convergence rate.

10.5   Uniform Pseudorandom Variables

The fundamental distribution in probability theory is the continuous uniform distribution on $(0, 1)$. While mechanical devices are still used to produce random phenomena in gambling situations, such as the balls for state lotteries or shuffling cards for poker, computer applications rely on number theory methods to generate pseudorandom numbers. The term *pseudorandom* connotes the appearance of randomness, even though the outcome may be completely predictable. The quality of an algorithm for generating random, oops, pseudorandom numbers is measured by how closely its performance resembles that of a sequence of independent random variables, in particular, independent uniform deviates on the interval $(0, 1)$. The quality of many algorithms is indeed high, and the conceptual wink of dropping the descriptor "pseudo" is often quite appropriate. While the good properties of these numerical algorithms can often be proven, mechanical devices can never be proven to reliably produce random variables. If a mechanical device did produce an unusual event – say, 100 consecutive heads in coin tosses – then two alternatives remain equally plausible: the device is broken, or an unusual event occurred (as it should every once in a long while). My personal experience of using the mechanical generator at the Institute of Statistical Mathematics in Tokyo in 1982 led to a long conceptual wrestling match that ended only after viewing all of Monte Carlo as just another numerical integration method.

Although the goal is to generate uniform random variables, number theoretic methods actually produce a sequence of integers that appear to have the discrete uniform distribution over the range $\{0, \ldots, m - 1\}$. Dividing by a large value of m will give an excellent approximation of the continuous uniform distribution, but the nature of floating point arithmetic suggests that we generate from the discrete distribution with support on the set of floating point numbers that best approximates the continuous uniform (or any other) distribution. This issue will be postponed until Chapter 11; for now, we will take the straightforward route of dividing the sequence of random integers by m and calling it a sequence of uniform random variables.

(A) *Testing Random Number Generators*

Over the years, researchers have been constantly testing the performance of random number generators in common use. At one time, a common joke was that more random numbers had been generated in testing than in applications. In spite of some needless testing that continues today, the importance of testing generators for new applications remains. The key to testing is that same conceptual wink of dropping the modifier "pseudo." Although the generators in common use are quite predictable and replicable – in fact, that is their big advantage over physical generators – the requirement is that these pseudorandom number generators *resemble a sequence of independent uniform deviates in whatever ways that are important to the application at hand*. Clearly, the most important property for most applications is uniformity over $(0, 1)$. Beyond that, the priorities depend on the application. Some generators with notorious defects may work very well for many applications yet fail on another. Specifically, the generator RANDU will work quite well for integration in one dimension, but the joint

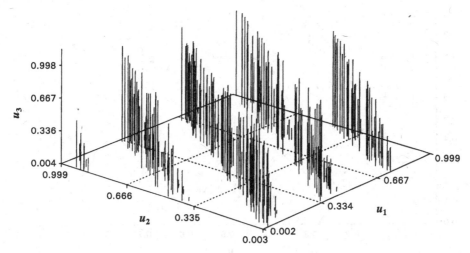

Figure 10.7. Needle plot of successive triples from RANDU in planes 1, 4, 7, 10, and 13.

distribution of successive triples does not look close to the uniform distribution on the unit cube. Theoretical tests have been devised to find certain kinds of defects in generators, and some can help predict poor performance in certain kinds of applications. But neither theoretical tests nor the hodgepodge of goofy tests that have been devised over the years are the final answer. The healthy fear that most researchers have is that the generator they are using has some *unknown* defect. The only way to gain confidence in the results of a simulation experiment is to follow the same practice as with any piece of software: by comparing the performance in a closely related problem where analytical results are available. In theoretical physics, the 2-dimensional Ising model provides a perfect test for related Markov chain Monte Carlo methods (Ferrenberg, Landau, and Wong 1992; Coddington 1994). In these models, analytic results are known for certain quantities, and the performance of different generators used with different simulation algorithms can be compared.

Beyond uniformity, two other departures from the idealized random number generator are cause for immediate concern: the period and the joint distribution in d dimensions. Since all arithmetic methods of generating random numbers are based on simple operators with finite memory on the finite set of integers $\{0, \ldots, m-1\}$, the sequence will eventually repeat. A short period would indicate that many of the integers are never realized and hence dictate some long-term dependence that may also affect short-term dependence. The size of some current simulation experiments is so great that a large segment of the period may be sampled in a simple experiment. In the multidimensional uniform distribution, concern for defects ranges from simple matters such as serial correlation to patterns in high dimensions. This latter concern is also motivated by the fact that most methods for generating random variables place successive pairs on lines in the plane, in planes in 3-dimensional space for successive triples, and so forth. The generator RANDU places successive triples in one of only 15 planes in 3-dimensional space. The planes are nearly vertical in the third dimension, so they show up well in the needle plot of Figure 10.7, which shows planes 1, 4, 7, 10, and 13. Figure 10.8 shows the

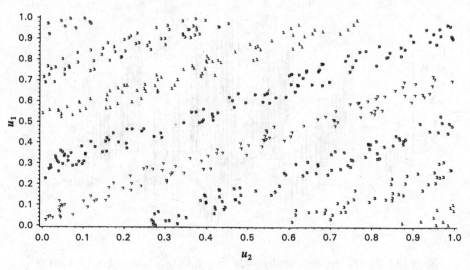

Figure 10.8. Successive pairs from RANDU from odd planes, denoted by $6u_3 + 6u_2 + 9u_1$.

placement of the odd or even planes in two dimensions. Marsaglia (1968, 1972) used the words "fall mainly in the planes" and proposed to measure quality by counting the few number of (hyper)planes onto which all of the k-tuples fell. Another viewpoint measures the maximum distance between the lines ($d = 2$) or planes ($d = 3$), leading to what is called the *spectral test*. Knuth (1997) discussed the spectral test in detail, and Golder (1976) gave a Fortran program for computing the values for multiplicative generators.

(B) *Linear Congruential Generators*

The linear congruential method, the oldest and most popular method for generating pseudorandom sequences, follows the formula

$$X_{n+1} = (aX_n + c) \bmod m, \tag{10.5.1}$$

where "mod m" means the remainder after integer division by m. The constants a, c, and m are integers; a is called the *multiplier, c* the *constant,* and m the *modulus.* The case $c = 0$, which will be slightly faster, is called a *multiplicative* congruential generator. The initial value X_0 used to start the sequence is called the *seed.* We seek a sequence of integers that "look" random, so let us consider the limitations of this approach. Notice that we really have defined a function on the set of integers $\{0, \dots, m - 1\}$, and eventually the sequence must begin to repeat itself. Clearly, m is the longest period possible. In the multiplicative case ($c = 0$), once zero is reached the sequence stays there forever. Naturally, we should want a long sequence before cycling, since noticeable periodicity would not look very random. Taking $a = 1$ and $c = 1$ would certainly give as long a sequence as possible, but the output would still not look random. A second drawback can be seen with the least significant digits. If d is a factor of m, then $Y_n = X_n \bmod d$ will follow the same formula (10.5.1) but with modulus d, so that the sequence $\{Y_n\}$ can have a cycle length of at most d. If m is a power of 2, then mod m or mod d really just selects the rightmost m or d digits, and the rightmost digit will either alternate $0, 1, 0, 1, \ldots$ or be constant.

The goals of long periods and apparent randomness must be tempered with the reality of ease of computation. The linear congruential operations are rather simple and easily performed whenever fixed point multiplication and division are available. Whereas multiplication is usually available, division is more problematic, and the most popular choice of modulus is either a power of 2 or (following some clever programming) one more or less than a power of 2. Moreover, the method becomes quite complicated once the native machine arithmetic cannot do the job. To get a longer period, one route is to use a larger modulus; however, once the modulus exceeds the usual size of fixed point numbers (usually 32 or 48 bits), the step to implement multiple precision for just this problem seems like more work than it's worth. As a result, most generators are machine-dependent, although portable versions have been produced (Schrage 1979).

Number theory can be used to determine the period of linear congruential generators. For the linear ($c \neq 0$) case, the generator has full period m if (i) a and m are relatively prime, (ii) $a - 1$ is a multiple of every prime factor of m, and (iii) $a \bmod 4 = 1$ if m is a multiple of 4. For multiplicative ($c = 0$) generators with m prime, if $a^{(m-1)/q} \neq 1 \bmod m$ for every prime factor q of $m - 1$, then the generator has period $m - 1$. Multiplicative generators with modulus $m = 2^k$ have a period of 2^{k-2} or $m/4$ if $a \equiv 3 \bmod 8$ or $5 \bmod 8$. Often other properties (including serial correlation and distribution of successive pairs) can be established analytically, and the spectral test can be used to establish lattice properties.

The following twelve linear congruential generators have been widely used or recommended, and all have as long a period as possible for the given modulus m. The case of a generator with 2^k not having a full period means not that there are gaps in the numbers produced by the generator but rather that the least significant bits follow a very predictable pattern, as alluded to earlier.

(1) Lewis–Goodman–Miller (1969): $X_{n+1} = 16807 X_n \bmod (2^{31} - 1)$. This generator is one of the oldest and remains in use. Its persistence for over a generation has earned it the name "minimal standard" by Park and Miller (1988), since it has performed well in a great many applications. Its period is $2^{31} - 2$ and its multiplicative nature should limit its usefulness in multidimensional problems, but it still remains competitive. Coded as **ranls** (following Schrage 1979) and as a fast implementation **ranbf** (following Bratley, Fox, and Schrage 1983).

(2) RANDU: $X_{n+1} = 65539 X_n \bmod 2^{31}$. Again one of the oldest (IBM's SSP), RANDU is fast to compute ($65539 = 2^{16} + 3$) but is clearly the most notorious generator owing to its 3-dimensional defects (illustrated in Figures 10.7 and 10.8); its period is 2^{29}. Coded as **randu**.

(3) Park, Miller, and Stockmeyer (1993): $X_{n+1} = 48271 X_n \bmod (2^{31} - 1)$. Offered as an alternative to Lewis–Goodman–Miller, this can be easily implemented and has a similar period of $2^{31} - 2$. Coded as **ranpm** in the same fashion as **ranbf**.

(4) Marsaglia I: $X_{n+1} = 69069 X_n \bmod 2^{32}$;

(5) Marsaglia II: $X_{n+1} = 69069X_n + 1 \bmod 2^{32}$. Marsaglia I and II gained promi-
nence because of the lattice properties of the multiplier. The multiplicative
Marsaglia I generator, coded as **ran69**, has a period of 2^{30}; the linear Marsaglia II, coded as **ran70**, has period 2^{32}.

(6) SAS/IMSL: $X_{n+1} = 397204094X_n \bmod (2^{31} - 1)$. This generator has been
widely used, but was not as portable as others (e.g. Lewis–Goodman–Miller)
until Hormann and Derflinger (1993) suggested a faster implementation, coded
here as **ranhd**. It has a period of $2^{31} - 2$.

(7) Fishman–Moore I: $X_{n+1} = 630360016X_n \bmod (2^{31} - 1)$;

(8) Fishman–Moore II: $X_{n+1} = 742938285X_n \bmod (2^{31} - 1)$;

(9) Fishman–Moore III: $X_{n+1} = 950706376X_n \bmod (2^{31} - 1)$. Fishman and
Moore (1982, 1986) did an exhaustive analysis of multiplicative generators
with modulus $2^{31} - 1$, putting them through a statistically sound battery of
tests. This modulus is particularly noteworthy since it is prime and one less
than a power of 2 for easy computation following methods of Schrage or Hormann and Derflinger. These three choices of multiplier are comparative winners and are coded as **ranf1**, **ranf2**, and **ranf3**, respectively. They all have the
same period of $2^{31} - 2$.

(10) Longer I: $X_{n+1} = aX_n + c \bmod 2^{48}$ with

$$c = B_{\text{hex}} = 11_{\text{ten}} \quad \text{and} \quad a = 5\text{deece66d}_{\text{hex}} = 25,214,903,917;$$

(11) Longer II: $X_{n+1} = aX_n \bmod 2^{48}$ with

$$a = 2875\text{a2e7b175}_{\text{hex}} = 44,485,709,377,909;$$

(12) Longer III: $X_{n+1} = aX_n + c \bmod 2^{48}$ with $c = 1$ and $a = \text{b1a2bc2ec5}_{\text{hex}} = 5^{17}$. These three have been designed for use on machines (e.g. Cray) with 48-bit
fraction arithmetic. A bonus for taking advantage of the native arithmetic is a
longer period than the others. These three have been implemented as **ran48**
(10), **ran49** (11), and **ran50** (12).

(C) *Shift Register Methods*

The strengths of the alternative shift register methods match the weaknesses of the congruential generators. The shift register methods follow a simple recursion relationship:

$$X_n = X_{n-p} \oplus X_{n-p+q}, \quad 1 < q < p, \tag{10.5.2}$$

where the operator $\oplus$ denotes the bit operation of "exclusive or." In its original presentation, X_n represented a single bit. Tausworthe (1965) constructed integers by stringing
consecutive bits together, so that a block from the stream of bits would represent a random integer. Denoting as $\{z_t\}$ a sequence of bits constructed from the recursion (10.5.2),
this approach (called *decimation*) would form

$$Y_n = \sum_{j=1}^{M} 2^{-j} z_{nM+j} \tag{10.5.3}$$

as the random uniform, where M denotes the number of bits in the floating point
fraction. For an alternative route for forming large integers, Lewis and Payne (1973)

suggested the generalized feedback shift register (GFSR) algorithm, which constructs a uniform random variable by taking each bit from a further point upstream in the sequence,

$$Y_n = \sum_{j=1}^{M} 2^{-j} z_{n-s(j)}, \tag{10.5.4}$$

where $s(j)$ denotes the shifts. If we envision the sequence $\{z_t\}$ strung out vertically as a columns of zeros and ones, then copy that column and pull it down by the shift $s(2)$ ($s(1) \equiv 0$) and place it to the right of the first column to form the second. If the sequence $\{z_t\}$ were a long ribbon hanging on a wall with a thumbtack at the top, then at this point we would have two identical ribbons with one hanging lower (the shift) than the other. Hang the third column a little lower (shift $s(3)$) on the wall to the right of the other two, and repeat until we have M identical ribbons hanging on a wall, each hanging a little lower than the one to its left. We have now formed an infinitely long matrix, with each column related by a shift. A row then becomes the bit representation of the integer $X_n = (z_n, z_{n-s(2)}, \ldots, z_{n-s(M)})$, which also follows the recursion (10.5.1) bit by bit, and dividing by 2^{-M} forms the uniform Y_n. If we cut off the top part of the ribbons on the left horizontally, so that the top is even with the top of the last (Mth) ribbon on the right, and then cut off the bottom evenly after p rows, then we have formed the $p \times M$ seed matrix.

The primary advantages of GFSR arise from its lack of dependence on machine arithmetic. First of all, neither multiplication nor division are required, only implementation of the logical exclusive or. Second, the same sequence of uniforms (in reality, its most significant digits) can be produced independent of fraction length M. A third advantage is the possibility of extraordinarily long periods, $2^p - 1$, with appropriately chosen p and q. In contrast with congruential generators, GFSR generators can have outstanding multidimensional properties even in high dimensions. One disadvantage is that the initialization is not nearly as trivial as choosing haphazardly a seed from the phone directory. A minor disadvantage is that the storage is not as simple as the congruential generator: a table of p integers must be stored – either the seed matrix or the most recent p integers.

Lewis and Payne proposed the shifts $s(j) = 100p(j - 1)$ and an initialization run of $5000p$ to dampen out any initial effects from a start-up list of $z_n \equiv 1$. That is, after the seed matrix is formed, the sequence is run through $5000p$ steps and the output discarded. They chose the values $p = 98$ and $q = 27$, yielding a sequence with a period of $2^{98} - 1 \approx 3 \times 10^{29}$, and gave Fortran code for the initialization. Since the initialization procedure is so cumbersome, the suggested route is to initialize only once and store the table of p integers and pointers. Then the analog of the seed in the congruential generators is to read in a table of p integers from a file, either the initialization table or the table stored at the end of the last simulation.

Although one of the advantages of the GFSR generators is its performance in high dimensions, the initialization procedure given by Lewis and Payne does not guarantee that the potential of GFSR will be fully realized. A sequence of M-bit integers with period $2^p - 1$ is called *k-distributed* if every k-tuple of integers appears 2^{p-kM} times during a period – except for zeros, which appear one time fewer. The Lewis and

Payne initialization does not guarantee it, but it leads to a 3-distributed GFSR sequence with $M = 31$ bits. Fushimi and Tezuka (1983) showed that the important condition for 1-distributedness is the nonsingularity of the $p \times M$ seed matrix formed from the initial table. To check for a 2-distributed sequence, Fushimi and Tezuka evaluate the 1-distributedness of the related $2M$-bit sequence formed by consecutive pairs. The relevant seed matrix $\mathbf{W}^{(2)}$ has twice the width, and its left side is just a copy of the original matrix $\mathbf{W}^{(1)}$. The right half of the $\mathbf{W}^{(2)}$ is formed by copying row i from $\mathbf{W}^{(1)}$ into the right half of row $i - 1$ of $\mathbf{W}^{(2)}$, forming a $p \times 2M$ matrix. This procedure can be extended to any k with $kM \leq p$ to investigate the distribution of k-tuples. In addition to the approach of generating a seed matrix and checking, Fushimi and Tezuka also suggested a simple initialization method that can guarantee a k-distributed sequence. Ripley (1987, p. 221) provided code for testing the seed matrix.

Three GFSR generators have been implemented.

(13) Lewis and Payne (1973): $p = 98$ and $q = 27$. This original Lewis and Payne GFSR (with their initialization) is coded as **ranlp**. Note that the initial table is stored in a separate file, and good practice would be to write out the seed matrix at the end to start the next sequence.

(14) Bright and Enison (1979) and Fushimi and Tezuka (1983): $p = 521$ and $q = 32$. This implementation **ranft** was initialized with the help of a linear congruential generator; it has been verified to be 16-distributed for $M = 31$.

(15) Fushimi (pers. comm.): $p = 17$ and $q = 5$. This implementation **ranfu** of a small test sequence has a period that is too short to be practical yet long enough to illustrate the properties of GFSR sequences.

A variation on GFSR generators has gained a great deal of popularity. In the *twisted GFSR*, equation (10.5.2) is modified to

$$X_{n+p} = X_n \oplus (X_{n+q}^u, X_{n+q+1}^l)\mathbf{A}$$

where X_n^u denotes the upper bits, and X_n^l the lower bits, of X_n. With an appropriate choice of the matrix $\mathbf{A}$, this different feedback mechanism leads to extremely long periods and better k-distributedness, with only a modest increase in computation. See Panneton, L'Ecuyer, and Matsumoto (2006) for a discussion of this and further generalizations.

(16) Matsumoto and Nishimura (1998) proposed the *Mersenne twister* that uses $p = 624$ and $q = 397$, and a matrix $\mathbf{A}$ chosen to involve only bit shifts. This popular generator with an advertised period of $2^{19937} - 1$ is implemented in **ranmt**. As with other GFSR generators, a table of length p (seed matrix) and the current pointer need to be stored.

(D) *Recommendations*

My intention in providing the code for so many (sixteen) generators is to permit the reader to embark on any sort of testing scheme that whimsy may conjure. There is no universally accepted generator that works well in all situations. As mentioned previously, testing against similar problems where analytical results are available for comparison should be considered standard scientific computing practice. The Ising model in theoretical physics works well as a test problem for those applications, and poor performance of some common generators has even made the daily newspaper. Both linear congruential generators and GFSR methods have their advocates and detractors, and some techniques of combining generators have been employed to improve some of the old standards.

MacLaren and Marsaglia (1965) suggested the following shuffling scheme for combining two sequences $\{U_k\}$ and $\{V_k\}$.

(0) Fill a table T with $T_j = U_j$ ($j = 1, \ldots, 128$) to initialize.
(1) To generate the sequence X_k, generate new values U_k and V_k.
(2) Use the first seven bits of V_k to get an index J.
(3) Output $X_k = T_J$ as the next random number.
(4) Replace T_J in the table with U_k.

Bays and Durham (1976) suggested an alternative method of (i) using the previous X_{k-1} to get the index J for selecting X_k and then (ii) using only a single sequence. A different way to combine generators is simply to take the sum of the uniforms modulo 1, which still has the uniform distribution. Wichman and Hill (1982) claimed success with three sequences that can be easily computed using only 16-bit arithmetic:

$$U_{n+1} = 171U_n \bmod 30269,$$
$$V_{n+1} = 172V_n \bmod 30307,$$
$$W_{n+1} = 170W_n \bmod 30323;$$

combining yields

$$Y_{n+1} = (U_{n+1}/30269 + V_{n+1}/30307 + W_{n+1}/30323) \bmod 1.$$

A third route is to take a congruential generator and a GFSR generator and then take the bitwise exclusive or. For example, Marsaglia's (1985) Super-Duper used a multiplicative congruential generator and a Tausworthe generator with decimation (10.5.3), but with only limited success. Another approach for combining these two contrasting types looks like GFSR but with multiplication instead of exclusive or,

$$X_n = X_{n-p} * X_{n-p+q} \bmod m, \quad 1 < q < p, \tag{10.5.5}$$

and has shown some promise (Coddington 1994).

Many researchers have worked in the field of generating random numbers, with many of the best mathematical minds of the last 50 years among them. The mathematical analyses have been impressive, especially the works of Knuth (1997) and Neiderreiter (1987, 1992). But in spite of hard work and lots of good ideas, no consensus has been reached on what methods are good and what methods are not. Ripley (1983) put it well: "Protagonists of the Tausworthe and congruential families have been quick to point out deficiencies of the other family, often with ill-advised choices of multiplier of primitive polynomial." I have successfully used congruential generators (Lewis–Goodman–Miller in particular) as well as Lewis and Payne's GFSR.

Because of many years of experience by a large community of users, I have a lot of confidence in them. But if I were to embark on a new area of application that may be a challenge, I would be the first to call myself a fool if I did not begin by comparing the performance of the simulation results to a similar problem for which I had analytical results.

(E) *Multiple Generators*

Some applications, especially simulation studies, may require more than one use of random number generation. In a simulation study, one generator may be needed to generate sample data, another as part of an integration method, and yet another for a random algorithm (e.g., Quicksort, Sec. 14.3). If we are comparing methods that require random sampling, we want to still be able to generate the same data and retain the efficiencies of blocking. Thus we may want to use multiple streams of random numbers without them interfering with each other. In Fortran and similar languages, the simple solution is to make multiple copies of the generating subprogram, and assign them similar names, e.g., RAN, REN, RIN,. . . . However, this can cause problems with blackbox codes that expect the uniform generator to have the same name such as RAN. R has features that make multiple steams easy to implement. We can initialize a generator with the seed 5151917 with "set.seed(5151917)." The function ".Random.seed" retrieves the current state of the generator, either a single number X_n in the case of a simple congruential generator, or as complicated as the seed matrix and pointer for the Mersenne-twister (default). This can be stored and used to restore that state later on. For example,

```
set.seed(5151917)        # set seed for first
                         # (data generating) stream
Y <- rnorm(100)          # generate data
seedGen <- .Random.seed  # save first stream info
set.seed(1917515)        # set seed for second stream
sY <- myQuicksort(Y)     # Quicksort is random algorithm
                         # that uses "runif"
seedQsort <- .Random.seed # save second stream info
.Random.seed <- seedGen  # restore first stream info
Y <- rnorm(100)          # generate data
```

SAS allows the use of multiple seeds for its linear congruential generator, but when the function forms of generators are used, the seed is set at the initial call and not changed. However, the CALL form of RANUNI can be used to save and reestablish seeds.

10.6   Quasi–Monte Carlo Integration

Pseudorandom sequences depend heavily on number theory to determine their properties. Another class of methods, called *number theoretic* or *quasirandom* methods, rely similarly on number theory for their properties. Pseudorandom and quasirandom sequences both attempt to spread points over space, but they do so in quite different ways. Whereas pseudorandom sequences attempt to mimic the properties of truly random sequences, quasirandom sequences attempt to spread points as evenly as possible over space, and they will fill up space more evenly than random or pseudorandom sequences. Two of the three methods for quasirandom sequences are practical, and these two are very different in both spirit and usage. The mathematics may look rather fancy, but either method can be useful – especially when a problem can be pounded into submission by evaluating at a large number of points.

One of the advantages of Monte Carlo integration is its ability to integrate any Lebesgue-integrable function. While the finite precision of the arithmetic limits the integrability to functions with a certain level of smoothness, the spirit remains. In looking at the Riemann sum as an integration rule, we used the modulus of continuity for a bound on the integration error in (10.3.2). Instead of assuming more smoothness – leading to the midpoint, trapezoid, and Simpson's rules – let us go in the opposite direction of assuming less smoothness. If we drop continuity in favor of bounded variation, then the error bound depends on the total variation of the function $V(f)$ and the discrepancy of the set of abscissas D_N:

$$\left| \frac{1}{N} \sum_{i=1}^{N} f(x_i) - \int f(x)\, dx \right| \le V(f) D_N(\{x_i\}). \tag{10.6.1}$$

The *discrepancy* D_N of a sequence of points is the maximum over subintervals of the absolute difference between Lebesgue measure and the measure given by the empirical distribution for those N points (similar to Kolmogorov–Smirnov distance). Clearly, if we can find sequences where the discrepancy decreases quickly, then any function worth integrating can be handled. For sequences of abscissas chosen randomly, the rate of decrease in D_N is $O\left(\sqrt{N^{-1} \log \log N}\right)$, from the law of the iterated logarithm. However, we can construct some sequences where the rate of convergence reaches the much faster rate of $O(N^{-1} \log N)$. If we could fix the number of abscissas, then a set of equally spaced points $x_i = a + i/N$ would give the minimum discrepancy with $D_N = 1/N$ for $0 \le a \le 1/N$. The midpoint rule arises from $a = 1/(2N)$ and the left-handed Riemann sum from $a = 0$ (see Exercise 10.20). One can view the two practical quasirandom methods as trying to generalize this to higher dimensions.

The simplest sequence that gives $O(N^{-1} \log N)$ convergence for the discrepancy is the van der Corput sequence:

$$1/2, 1/4, 3/4, 1/8, 5/8, 3/8, 7/8, 1/16, 9/16, \dots.$$

The van der Corput sequence actually is more general, and the sequence just listed is the base-2 sequence. For the more general case of base b, represent each integer i in base b by the digits $a_j(i)$,

$$a_L(i), a_{L-1}(i), \dots, a_1(i), a_0(i) \quad \text{such that} \quad \sum_{j=0}^{L} a_j(i) b^j = i,$$

where $b^L \leq i < b^{L+1}$. The sequence $\{x_i\}$ is then easily written as

$$x_i = \sum_{j=0}^{L} a_j(i) b^{-j-1} = \phi_b(i), \tag{10.6.2}$$

where the function ϕ_b is called the *radical inverse function*. Note that if $N = 2^L - 1$ then the sequence $\{\phi_2(i), i = 1, \ldots, N\}$ is a permutation of a set of equally spaced points $\{j/N, j = 1, \ldots, N\}$ (see Exercise 10.21). Kuipers and Neiderreiter (1974, p. 127) showed the upper bound on the discrepancy for the van der Corput sequence (though they started with 0) to be

$$ND_N \leq \log(N+1)/\log 2.$$

This gives a faster rate of convergence than Monte Carlo and can handle almost any "computer-integrable" function.

In one dimension, the van der Corput sequence can't do anything that the midpoint rule can't do, but in higher dimensions the product midpoint rule falls under the spell of the curse of dimensionality. Two generalizations of the van der Corput sequence, however, avoid the curse. In d dimensions, the sequence of vectors

$$\mathbf{x}^{(i)} = (\phi_{b_1}(i), \phi_{b_2}(i), \ldots, \phi_{b_d}(i)), \tag{10.6.3}$$

called the *Halton sequence,* forms a sequence of abscissas with discrepancy in d dimensions with convergence rate $D_N^{(d)} = O(N^{-1}(\log N)^d)$ for relatively prime b_j. Here, the generalization of discrepancy to d dimensions is the maximum over hyperrectangles of the distance between Lebesgue measure and the fraction of points in the hyperrectangle. For a fixed number of points N, Hammersley suggested the slick improvement of dropping the rate slightly:

$$\mathbf{x}^{(i)} = (i/N, \phi_{b_1}(i), \ldots, \phi_{b_{d-1}}(i));$$

this reduces the rate to $O(N^{-1}(\log N)^{d-1})$. Figure 10.9 shows the distribution of points from the Halton sequence in two dimensions with bases $b_1 = 2$ and $b_2 = 3$.

In order to translate these discrepancy bounds into useful integration bounds, we need multivariate generalizations of the weak smoothness conditions. If we redefine the modulus of continuity for functions on $\mathcal{R}^d$,

$$w(h) = \sup_{\|\mathbf{u}-\mathbf{v}\| \leq h} |f(\mathbf{u}) - f(\mathbf{v})|,$$

then we can get a bound using multivariate discrepancy for continuous functions on the unit cube:

$$\left| \frac{1}{N} \sum_{i=1}^{N} f(\mathbf{x}^{(i)}) - \int f(\mathbf{x}) \, d\mathbf{x} \right| \leq w(D_N^{(d)}(\{\mathbf{x}^{(i)}\})^{1/d}) \tag{10.6.4}$$

(Proinov 1988). If we abandon continuity for bounded variation (Hardy–Krause style), then for variation $V(f)$ we can use the Koksma–Hlawka inequality

$$\left| \frac{1}{N} \sum_{i=1}^{N} f(\mathbf{x}^{(i)}) - \int f(\mathbf{x}) \, d\mathbf{x} \right| \leq V(f) D_N^{(d)}(\{\mathbf{x}^{(i)}\}). \tag{10.6.5}$$

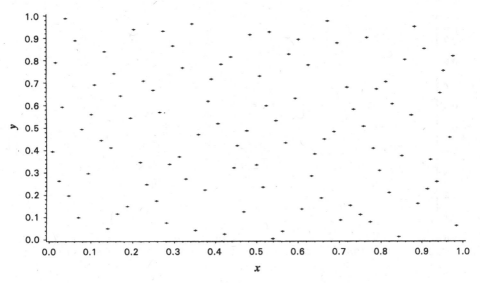

Figure 10.9. First 100 points of Halton sequence with bases 2 (x) and 3 (y).

The consequences of these results are stunning: a convergence rate practically independent of dimension for functions that need not be very smooth, and at a faster rate
than Monte Carlo.

A second method for getting points spread in space, called the *Korobov sequence*
or *good lattice points,* resembles the linear congruential generators. Here, take a vec-
tor **g** whose components $g_1, \ldots, g_d$ are integers, form the sequence $\mathbf{x}^{(i)} = ((i/N)\mathbf{g})$
($i = 1, \ldots, n$) for a fixed number N, and take the remainder for each component. For
component k, the sequence looks like computing ig_k mod N and dividing by N. The
analysis of discrepancy is much more complicated, but Hua and Wang (1981) proved
the existence of good lattice points with a discrepancy $D_N^{(d)} = O(N^{-1}(\log N)^d)$ and
also provided tables of good lattice points for a variety of points N and dimensions d
(see also Fang and Wang 1994, apx. A; Maisonneuve 1972; Kedem and Zaremba 1974).
A set of good lattice points in d dimensions can be projected into fewer dimensions and
still have good properties. Figure 10.10 shows the distribution of good lattice points
with $g_1 = 1$, $g_2 = 89$, and $N = 144$; the figure shows that the points lie on a lattice
that appears to spread evenly over space.

As can be easily seen in Figure 10.9, the Halton sequence looks somewhat random in
two dimensions; it just is "too random" and fills up space too evenly for a truly random
sequence. In contrast, the Korobov point set given in Figure 10.10 looks extremely regular; in fact, all 1-dimensional projections are equally spaced points of the form $x_i =
a + i/N$. These differences suggest the use of Halton sequences when regularity might
be a problem. The other important difference between these two methods affects how
they may be used. Good lattice points require a fixed number of points N to be known
in advance, whereas the Halton sequence does not. These methods share two important
properties with Monte Carlo integration – namely, they can integrate most any function and the convergence is largely unaffected by dimension – but they share with fixed

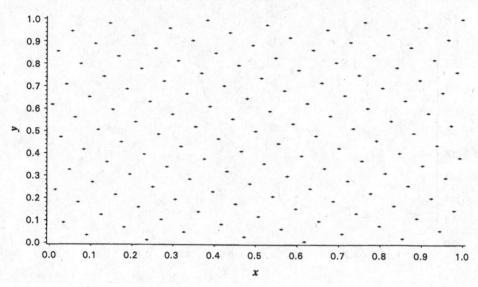

Figure 10.10. Korobov sequence with $N = 144$ points. The constants are $g_1 = 1$ and $g_2 = 89$.

quadrature methods the difficulty in assessing accuracy. Although the theoretical error bounds provided some guidance, rarely are continuity or variation bounds available. The only practical approach is to employ randomization as suggested by Cranley and Patterson (1976), whose approach will be discussed further in Section 10.7.

Example 10.3: *Variance Components Problem – Exchange Rate Data*
Looking over some bills and transactions from a recent trip to England, I noticed the differences in the exchange rates across the variety of dealers: credit-card companies, bank transfers, travelers checks, and so on. In all, there were fifteen transactions across five dealers, with quite unequal sample sizes, recalling the examples cited in earlier sections of this chapter. Consider then the Bayesian variance components model considered in Section 10.2, with priors

$$\beta \sim N(b_0, \phi_0),$$
$$\phi \sim \text{inverse gamma}(a_1, b_1),$$
$$\gamma \sim \text{inverse gamma}(a_2, b_2),$$

with each component independent. The posterior was given in (10.2.3) as

$$p^*(b, f, g) = g^{-(a_2 + p/2) - 1} e^{-b_2/g} \times f^{-(a_1 + N/2) - 1} e^{-[b_1 + W/2]/f}$$

$$\times \exp\left\{ -\frac{\frac{1}{2}(m - b_0)^2}{\phi_0} \right\} \times \prod_{i=1}^{p} \left(\frac{n_i}{f} + \frac{1}{g} \right)^{-1/2}$$

$$\times \exp\left\{ -\frac{1}{2} \sum_{i=1}^{p} \frac{(\bar{y}_{i\cdot} - b)^2}{g + f/n_i} \right\}. \tag{10.6.6}$$

In this situation, $p = 5$, $N = 15$, and the data y_{ij} were $100 \times$ (exchange rate $- 1.6$) to make the data more manageable. The problem, then, was to compute the posterior means and variances. In the demonstration **chex103**, the posterior means and variances were computed with the posterior p^* as before, using these data and some Korobov schemes.

Examination of the demonstration **chex103** shows some of the difficulties in using these quasirandom schemes, especially for Bayesian problems. One big restriction is that the domain of integration is restricted to the unit hypercube or (through transformation) a hyperrectangle. As with Simpson's rule in **chex102s**, the posterior mode and dispersion must be known to a reasonable degree, and some sense of the tail behavior is needed. To align this hyperrectangle in such a way that it captures most of the posterior mass, the best we can do is estimate and hope. In practice, this means computing the posterior mode and using the large-sample normal approximation to estimate the variance. The question of how far into the tail the range must extend – in particular, of whether three or four standard deviations is far enough – can be bedeviling. The only way to know if some posterior mass is unaccounted for is to change the range of some variables and compare. Knowing that the posterior is extremely small at the border of the domain may not be enough. As the dimension rises, the volume increases exponentially, and a lot of mass can be spread very thinly over an exponentially large volume of space.

10.7   Strategy and Tactics

The topics covered so far – fixed quadrature, (pseudo)random sequences, and quasirandom sequences – can be viewed as methods to spread points in space toward the overall goal of computing an integral. Each of these methods has its particular strengths and weaknesses as well as factors that affect its usage. For example, some of the methods require the number of points to be known in advance, whereas others allow complete flexibility. But the most important factors are usually their convergence rates and the availability of accuracy estimates. As mentioned in the introduction to this chapter, great gains can be made in combining these methods, as we shall see in the following excursion through a host of topics that cross these fields.

One problem alluded to several times already is the difficulty in assessing the accuracy with quadrature methods. With quasirandom sequences, Cranley and Patterson (1976) suggested randomizing these fixed methods and then using statistical techniques to analyze the results. For integrating with Korobov sequences, which look like

$$\mathbf{x}^{(k)} = \{(k/N)\mathbf{g}\}, \quad k = 1, \dots, N$$

(the braces indicate taking the fractional part), the change is to compute replicate sequences $i = 1, \dots, M$ of the form

$$\mathbf{x}^{(i,k)} = \{\mathbf{U}^{(i)} + (k/N)\mathbf{g}\}, \quad k = 1, \dots, N,$$

where each component of the vector $\mathbf{U}^{(i)}$ is an independent uniform $(0, 1)$ deviate. Then the integration estimate that has been replicated over i gives independent estimates of the same integral.

The statistical analysis of this approach now becomes blatantly clear if we reduce this to one dimension. Since Korobov rules look like a Riemann sum in one dimension, the integral estimate can be written in several equivalent forms – for example, as

$$T_i = \frac{1}{N} \sum_{k=1}^{N} f\left(\frac{U_i + k - 1}{N}\right).$$

This should be recognized by statisticians as *systematic sampling* with random starting points U_i/N. This estimate of the integral is unbiased, since

$$E[T_i] = \int_0^1 \frac{1}{N} \sum_{k=1}^{N} f\left(\frac{u + k - 1}{N}\right) du = \sum_{k=1}^{N} \int_0^1 f\left(\frac{u + k - 1}{N}\right) \frac{1}{N} du$$

$$= \sum_{k=1}^{N} \int_{(k-1)/N}^{k/N} f(t) \, dt = \int_0^1 f(t) \, dt.$$

The variance $\text{var}(T_i)$ usually decreases at a rate of $O(N^{-2})$, but the rate does depend on the smoothness of the function. Dramatic reduction in variance can be gained if the function is periodic or nearly so.

To summarize, randomization of these quadrature rules allows for the use of the usual statistical methods to analyze these data and provide an estimate of the accuracy. From a statistical viewpoint, randomization of these methods works because the sum T_i itself gives a good estimate of the integral. Overall, the components of T_i are negatively correlated and so the sum has a much smaller variance. As a result, the gain due to systematic sampling will be there as long as the negative correlation is there. As the function f becomes more noisy and less smooth, the values $f((U_i + k - 1)/N)$ become less correlated and the gains from systematic sampling will disappear; then simple random sampling ($N = 1$) will be competitive. Related techniques using randomized quadrature are discussed further in Section 12.7.

One may view this randomization technique as merely a generalization of a commonly used technique in Monte Carlo studies known as *antithetic variates*, which exploits symmetry and negative correlation. Again for $(0, 1)$, often $f(U)$ and $f(1 - U)$ are negatively correlated. As a result, we may compare the variances of two alternatives that each use two function evaluations: first, one average using the same random variable,

$$\text{var}([f(U) + f(1 - U)]/2) = \text{var}(f(U))/2 + \text{cov}(f(U), f(1 - U))/2,$$

and then a second average that uses two independent random variables,

$$\text{var}([f(U) + f(V)]/2) = \text{var}(f(U))/2.$$

Now if the $f(U)$ and $f(1 - U)$ are negatively correlated, then the former will have smaller variance. This technique is not commonly used in statistical simulation experiments; see Geweke (1989) for an illustration of its use in Bayesian problems. For another extension, consider integrating a function $h(z)$ with respect to the standard normal distribution with deviate Z. If $h(Z)$ and $h(-Z)$ are negatively correlated, then we can gain the same sort of antithetic variate improvement. This can be extended (as elaborated in Section 12.7) to more points, gaining – for suitable functions – dramatic reductions in the variance for an estimate of the integral of $h(z)$. These randomized integration rules follow the same principles: unbiased for all functions, reduced variance for many, and dramatic improvement for some.

Example 10.1 *(cont.)*

Recall the logarithmic series data used previously, and recall the use of Gauss–Hermite quadrature in the demonstration **quad2**. It featured the posterior mode t_m as the center of the approximating normal distribution, with variance s^2, using the expression

$$\int h(t)p^*(t)\,dt = \int h(t)\frac{p^*(t)}{\phi((t-t_m)/s)/s}\phi((t-t_m)/s)/s\,dt$$

$$= \int h(t_m+sz)\frac{p^*(t_m+sz)}{\phi(z)}\phi(z)\,dz. \qquad (10.3.13)$$

In demonstration **quad3**, ten trials of 100 samples from the standard normal distribution were used to compute integrals as

$$E\left[\frac{h(t_m+sZ)p^*(t_m+sZ)}{\phi(Z)}\right] = \int h(t_m+sz)\left[\frac{p^*(t_m+sz)}{\phi(z)}\right]\phi(z)\,dz,$$

where $Z \sim N(0,1)$. To exploit antithetic variates, the sample size was cut to 50 while both Z and $-Z$ were used to keep the number of evaluations at 100. Analysis of the output shows that the estimates of the normalization constant and posterior variance had about the same accuracy in both cases, whereas the estimate of the posterior mean from the antithetic variates had a standard error that was $1/100$ of the other. This dramatic improvement occurred only when the variables were strongly negatively correlated. Notice that the sample sizes here are much larger than the previous demonstrations with fixed quadrature. They won't seem so out of place when the dimension increases.

The analysis step (10.3.13) in the foregoing example demonstrates a vital tool known as *importance sampling*. To estimate the posterior mean and variance, the easiest route would be to generate random parameter values from the posterior distribution. This is rarely possible in practice, so random variables are generated from another distribution, say $g(t)$, and the observations weighted to correct:

$$\int h(t)p^*(t)\,dt = \int h(t)\left[\frac{p^*(t)}{g(t)}\right]g(t)\,dt = E_g\{h(T)w(T)\}, \qquad (10.7.1)$$

where T has density $g(t)$ and the *weight function* is

$$w(t) = \frac{p^*(t)}{g(t)}.$$

Essentially, if $g(t)$ samples more frequently than $p^*(t)$ in a particular region, those observations are downweighted. Importance sampling is particularly useful in Bayesian analysis, where the approximate normal distribution serves as a natural approximating distribution $g(t)$ – as employed in the preceding example and in the demonstration **quad3**. The main restriction on the approximating distribution is that the posterior be absolutely continuous with respect to it; that is, if $g(t)$ is zero then $p^*(t)$ must be zero. Problems arise when $g(t)$ gets very small and $p^*(t)$ does not, which can occur if the tail of the posterior behaves more like a Student's t-density than a normal. In such cases, the weight function can become very large and then a few observations will dominate the sample. Methods for detecting this problem are discussed in Section 12.5. The other difficulty with importance sampling is the statistical analysis with weighted observations; the applicable statistical tools are discussed further in Section 12.3. Use of these was avoided in our previous example, where complete replicates were used to assess accuracy.

The principle behind antithetic variates is the same motivation for paired experimental procedures. Here the difference between two highly correlated random variables may have substantially smaller variance. As discussed in Section 10.2, a comparison of two methods of estimation would be enhanced by applying the two methods to the same data. In Monte Carlo experiments, the ability to reproduce random numbers through the use of pseudorandom sequences (discussed in Section 10.5) makes experimental design comparatively easy. Although the need for some constructs (e.g., randomized complete block design) may be absent, the main tools are still blocking or pairing and randomized experimental units.

Examination of location estimates permits some powerful variance reduction tools in the case of sampling from the normal distribution. Suppose the n-dimensional vector $\mathbf{Y}$ has components $Y_i, i = 1, \ldots, n$ which are IID $Normal(\theta, \sigma^2)$. Consider an estimate of location $T(\mathbf{Y})$ satisfying

$$T(\mathbf{y} + \gamma \mathbf{1}) = T(\mathbf{y}) + \gamma, \qquad (10.7.2)$$

where $\mathbf{1}$ is a column vector of ones, so that adding a constant γ to each component shifts the estimate by γ. For example, $T(\mathbf{Y})$ may be the sample mean $\bar{Y}$ or sample median. Suppose that the variance of some statistic $T(\mathbf{Y})$ is sought. Consider first these steps:

$$\mathrm{var}(T(\mathbf{Y})) = \mathrm{var}(T(\mathbf{Y} - \bar{Y}\mathbf{1}) + \bar{Y}) = \mathrm{var}(T(\mathbf{Y} - \bar{Y}\mathbf{1})) + \sigma^2/n, \qquad (10.7.3)$$

since $(\mathbf{Y} - \bar{Y}\mathbf{1})$ and $\bar{Y}$ are independent (see Simon 1976, p. 269). Now estimate the variance of $T(\mathbf{Y} - \bar{Y}\mathbf{1})$ from samples $\mathbf{Y}^{(k)}, k = 1, \ldots, K$, with components generated IID Normal (θ, σ^2) by employing the usual estimator

$$K^{-1} \sum_{k=1}^{K} [T_k - \bar{Y}_k]^2$$

and a simplification from a second use of (10.7.2), since

$$T(\mathbf{Y}^{(k)} - \bar{Y}_k \mathbf{1}) = T(\mathbf{Y}^{(k)}) - \bar{Y}_k = T_k - \bar{Y}_k.$$

Now the estimate of the variance of $T(\mathbf{Y})$ given by

$$\sigma^2/n + K^{-1} \sum_{k=1}^{K} [T_k - \bar{Y}_k]^2$$

will converge much faster than the usual estimator

$$K^{-1} \sum_{k=1}^{K} T_k^2.$$

These steps were widely employed in the important Princeton simulation study (Andrews et al. 1972). This trick (and similar variance reduction techniques) acquired the name "Monte Carlo swindle" because of their surprising effectiveness through a simple algebraic sleight of hand (Relles 1970; Gross 1973; Simon 1976). Similar swindles are available for scale estimates and combinations of location and scale.

A second swindle for comparing the variances of two estimators, say $T(\mathbf{Y})$ and $S(\mathbf{Y})$, that are both unbiased employs the simple antithetic variate advantage of negative correlation. To estimate the difference of the variances, which can be written as

$$\mathrm{var}(T(\mathbf{Y})) - \mathrm{var}(S(\mathbf{Y})) = E(T(\mathbf{Y})^2) - \theta^2 - E(S(\mathbf{Y})^2) + \theta^2,$$

use the average of the difference of the squares $T_k^2 - S_k^2$. A third swindle, again following similar steps, permits estimation of percentiles of the distribution of a estimator based on samples from the normal distribution. Writing $\Pr(T(\mathbf{Y}) < t)$ in terms of an indicator function $E\{I_t(T(\mathbf{Y}))\}$, a series of conditioning steps using $\bar{Y}$ gain the following estimate:

$$
\begin{aligned}
E\{I_t(T(\mathbf{Y}))\} &= E\{I_t(T(\mathbf{Y} - \bar{Y}\mathbf{1}) + \bar{Y})\} \\
&= E\{E[I_t(T(\mathbf{Y} - \bar{Y}\mathbf{1}) + \bar{Y}) \mid \mathbf{Y}^* = \mathbf{Y} - \bar{Y}\mathbf{1}]\} \\
&= E\{\Phi[\sqrt{n}(t - T(\mathbf{Y} - \bar{Y}\mathbf{1}))]\}.
\end{aligned}
\tag{10.7.4}
$$

The last step follows from $\Pr(T(\mathbf{Y} - \bar{Y}\mathbf{1}) + \bar{Y} \le t) = \Phi[\sqrt{n}(t - T(\mathbf{Y} - \bar{Y}\mathbf{1}))]$ and from the distribution function of $\bar{Y}$ as $\Phi(y\sqrt{n})$. This last swindle also provides additional smoothness, since a step function is replaced by a smooth distribution function.

Programs and Demonstrations

quad1 *Primitive quadrature rules for posterior in Example 10.1*
  The 1-dimensional posterior in Example 10.1 is integrated using midpoint, trapezoid, and Simpson's rules to obtain the posterior mean and variance.

qgaustb *Computes abscissas and weights for Gauss rules*
  Abscissas and weights for modified Gauss–Hermite and shifted Gauss–Legendre quadrature rules are (i) computed following the Golub–Welsch approach and the implementation of the QR eigenvalue algorithm **qreig1** from Chapter 6 and then (ii) placed in files **qgaushm.tab** and **qgauslg.tab**.

quad2   *Gauss quadrature rules for posterior in Example 10.1*
The 1-dimensional posterior in Example 10.1 is integrated using modified Gauss–Hermite and shifted Gauss–Legendre quadrature to obtain the posterior mean and variance. The abscissas and weights were read from tables in the files **qgaushm.tab** and **qgauslg.tab**.

chex102t   *Posterior computation for Example 10.2 using triangle quadrature rules*
chex102s   *Posterior computation for Example 10.2 using product Simpson's rule*
chex102g   *Posterior computation for Example 10.2 using product Gauss–Hermite quadrature*
The extended example from Chapter 9 is modified in Example 10.2 by cutting the sample size and making the problem more interesting. Three approaches were used to integrate the posterior; the first approach was to use midpoint and Simpson analogs for integration over the triangular parameter space. The second approach was to ignore the triangular parameter space and use the normal approximation to center and scale a product Simpson's rule. The third also uses the normal approximation, but with product Gauss–Hermite quadrature.

ranls   *Schrage implementation of Lewis–Goodman–Miller uniform random number generator*
ranbf   *Lewis–Goodman–Miller generator implemented using idea of Bratley et al. (1983)*
randu   *Infamous uniform generator*
ranpm   *Multiplicative uniform generator with multiplier recommended by Park et al. (1993)*
ran69   *Multiplicative uniform generator with multiplier recommended by Marsaglia (1972)*
ran70   *Linear congruential generator using multiplier 69069 as in* **ran69**
ranhd   *Multiplicative uniform generator with multiplier 397204094*
ranf1   *Multiplicative uniform generator with multiplier 630360016*
ranf2   *Multiplicative uniform generator with multiplier 742938285*
ranf3   *Multiplicative uniform generator with multiplier 950706376*
ran48   *Linear congruential generator with modulus 2^{48}*
ran49   *Multiplicative uniform generator with modulus 2^{48}*
ran50   *Linear congruential generator with modulus 2^{48}*
ranlp   *Original Lewis and Payne (1973) GFSR uniform generator*
ranft   *GFSR uniform generator with $p = 521$ and $q = 32$*
ranfu   *Fushimi test GFSR uniform generator with $p = 17$ and $q = 5$*
ranmt   *Matsumoto and Nishimura's (1998) Mersenne Twister*
All 17 of these implementations are tested using a simple chi-square test for 1-dimensional uniformity with 64 intervals. Further discussion of appropriate tests is postponed until Chapter 12. All of the implementations are in rather portable Fortran code; none are particularly fast. The three GFSR versions are designed to read in seed matrices as a list of integers.
gfsrlp.tb0 – original seed matrix for Lewis and Payne GFSR.

gfsrft.tb0 – randomly sampled seed matrix for $p = 521$, $q = 32$ GFSR checked for 16-distributedness.
gfsrfu.tb0 – seed matrix for Fushimi test GFSR.

halton   *Demonstration of code to compute van der Corput–Halton sequences*
Code for the radical inverse function is used to compute van der Corput–Halton sequences for several bases. See also Halton and Smith (1964).
ncrmnt – gives list of digits for counting consecutive numbers in base b.
expand – computes a real number from the digits of its base-b expansion.

chex103   *Posterior integration using Korobov rules*
The 3-dimensional variance component problem outlined in Section 10.1 and described further in Example 10.3 is integrated using a Korobov rule to obtain the posterior mean vector and covariance matrix.

quad3   *Randomization of Riemann sum*
The posterior in Example 10.1 is integrated two more times with importance sampling and antithetic variates as described in Section 10.7.

Exercises

10.1   Prove the error bound for the Riemann sum (10.2.2). Obtain a similar result for the midpoint rule.

10.2   Compute the variance of the logistic distribution $\pi^2/3 = 2 \int_0^\infty x^2 e^{-x}(1 + e^{-x})^{-2} dx$ to five decimal digits using a simple quadrature method. The first step is to bound the tail by $2 \int_t^\infty x^2 e^{-x} dx$ by finding an appropriate value of t (and proving the bound). Next find the appropriate value of h so that the integration error from (10.3.6) or Exercise 10.1 is small enough. Finally, integrate over $[0, t]$ using the midpoint rule.

10.3   Suppose we wish to use the midpoint, trapezoid, or Simpson rule for computing normal probabilities, that is, $\int_a^b (2\pi)^{-1/2} \exp\{-u^2/2\} du$ for any values of a and b, where $-3 \leq a < b \leq 3$. To obtain an absolute error of less than .01, how many evaluations would be needed for each method?

10.4   Following Exercise 10.3, implement your scheme and compare the theoretical bounds with practice.

10.5   Use (10.2.9) to show that the weights in Gaussian quadrature are positive by first showing that $[d_i(x)]^2$ is a polynomial of degree $2n - 2$. Now suppose the weights w_j are known, and apply the quadrature formula to the functions $d_i(x)$ and $[d_i(x)]^2$, which both give the result w_i.

10.6   Show that the shifted Gauss–Legendre rule computed in **qgaustb** actually will integrate polynomials of degree 5 exactly by trying $p(x) = 30x^5 + 20x^4 + 12x^3 + 6x^2 + 2x + 1$.

10.7   The 2-point shifted Gauss–Legendre rule has abscissas at $(1 \pm 1/\sqrt{3})/2$ and equal weights. Compare the performance of this rule in compounded form to the same compounding of Simpson's rule as in **quad1**. (This method is sometimes used instead of Simpson.)

10.8 Show that the Cartesian product of Simpson's rule integrates functions of the form $f(x, y) = ax + by + c$ exactly over the unit square. Evaluations are at nine points, $\{0, 1/2, 1\} \times \{0, 1/2, 1\}$, and the integral is $(a + b)/2 + c$.

10.9 Compute the integral

$$\int_0^1 \int_0^1 \sin^2 \pi(x - y) \, dx \, dy$$

using product rules (midpoint or Simpson) with the same and different compounding on the x and y. Does different compounding on x and y make a difference?

10.10 The midpoint rule can be transformed using any distribution function F by evaluating at $F^{-1}\left(\frac{2i-1}{2n}\right)$ with n equally weighted points. Apply this *transformed midpoint rule* to the logistic distribution with $F(x) = 1/(1 + e^{-x})$. Compare your computation of the variance to your result in Exercise 10.2.

10.11 Construct a linear tranformation that takes the fundamental triangle with vertices at $(0, 0)$, $(1, 0)$, and $(0, 1)$ to the triangle with vertices at (a_1, b_1), (a_2, b_2), and (a_3, b_3).

10.12 Compare the triangular integration rules with a nested integration scheme following $\int_0^1 \int_0^x f(x, y) \, dy \, dx$ for the posterior in Example 10.2. Use both midpoint and Simpson versions of each.

10.13 Suppose X_i were IID Bernoulli with probability p, and let $U = \sum_{i=1}^{\infty} 2^{-i} X_i$. If $p = 1/2$, then U has the uniform distribution on $(0, 1)$. If $p \neq 1/2$, what is the support of the distribution of U? Given a real (or floating point) number y, describe an algorithm for evaluating its cumulative distribution function.

10.14 For a time, radiation counters were considered as potential devices for obtaining random variables. The physical model was that the counts were considered as a Poisson process with a constant rate λ. Discuss methods for obtaining either random bits or uniform random variables from this Poisson process. In reality, the inter-event time recorded by any counter might include "dead time" during which the system was recovering. Would this affect any method you have proposed?

10.15 Let X_n follow the multiplicative congruential formula $X_{n+1} = aX_n \bmod (2^k - 1)$, and let $Y_n = X_n \bmod 2^j$ with $j < k$. What can be said about the period of Y_n?

10.16 Write a Fortran routine to generate uniforms using RANDU (be careful of integer overflow). Test for uniformity in three dimensions using boxes and the chi-square test. Use 10^3 and 20^3 boxes.

10.17 Show that, for the uniform generator RANDU, $(X_{n+2} - 6X_{n+1} + 9X_n)/2^{31}$ is an integer.

10.18 Another measure of discrepancy for numeric sequences is the *star discrepancy* D_N^*, which is equivalent to the Kolmogorov–Smirnov distance between the empirical distribution function $F_N(x)$ of the sequence and the uniform distribution function $F(x) = x$ on $[0, 1]$. Show that $D_N^* \leq D_N \leq 2D_N^*$.

10.19 Show that, for the sorted sequence $\{x_i, i = 1, \ldots, N\}$,

$$D_N^* = \frac{1}{2N} + \max_i \left| x_i - \frac{2i - 1}{2N} \right|.$$

10.20 For the van der Corput sequence $\{\phi_2(i), i = 1, \ldots, N\}$, find D_N^* for $N = 2^L - 1$ and $N = 2^L$.

10.21 Using Halton sequences and the code **halton**, compute the posterior integral in Example 10.3 as with **chex103**.

10.22 Following the randomization scheme for Korobov sequences described in Section 10.7, find an error estimate using ten replicates for the problem in Example 10.3 as in **chex103**.

10.23 Find the variance of the median of five random variables from the logistic distribution directly by following Exercise 10.2 or 10.10 and integrating

$$\int_{-\infty}^{\infty} x^2 30 F(x)^2 (1 - F(x))^2 f(x)\, dx.$$

10.24 Evaluate the effectiveness of swindles for computing the variance of the median of five random variables from the $Normal(\theta, \sigma^2)$ distribution. Compare the direct approach with the first swindle's $\sigma^2/n + K^{-1} \sum_{k=1}^{K} \left[T_k - \overline{Y}_k \right]^2$ and the second swindle's $\sigma^2/n + K^{-1} \sum_{k=1}^{K} \left[T_k^2 - \overline{Y}_k^2 \right]$.

10.25 The Dirichlet density and the density of a transformation of the Dirichlet distribution makes good test problems for integration in many dimensions. The density function for the Dirichlet is

$$f(\mathbf{t}) = \frac{\Gamma(\sum_{j=1}^{d+1} \alpha_j)}{\prod_{j=1}^{d+1} \Gamma(\alpha_j)} \prod_{j=1}^{d} t_j^{\alpha_j - 1} (1 - \sum_{j=1}^{d} t_j)^{\alpha_{d+1} - 1}$$

with support only on the simplex $0 \le t_j \le 1, \sum t_j \le 1$. The transformation extends the support to R^d with the density

$$g(\mathbf{x}) = \frac{\Gamma(\sum_{j=1}^{d+1} \alpha_j)}{\prod_{j=1}^{d+1} \Gamma(\alpha_j)} \frac{e^{\sum_{j=1}^{d} \alpha_j x_j}}{(1 + \sum_{j=1}^{d} e^{x_j})^{\sum_{j=1}^{d+1} \alpha_j}}.$$

a) Verify the calculus for the transformed Dirichlet density $g(\mathbf{x})$. b) For $d = 2$, test the fixed rules for integration over a triangle (Section 10.4[A]) on the Dirichlet density $f(\mathbf{t})$. c) Compare other integration methods on these test problems.

References

Even though I have included here many papers not mentioned in the text, this list is by no means complete; the interested reader should expect to trace references further when in full pursuit of a particular topic. I would recommend two books without reservation: Knuth (1997) and Davis and Rabinowitz (1984). Both Ripley (1987) and Bratley et al. (1983) are more practical and readable. Neiderreiter's (1978) paper is notable for its extensive treatment of both Monte Carlo and quasi–Monte Carlo techniques. The more recent articles (e.g. L'Ecuyer 1988, 1990) on random number generators are more careful and show greater perspective than many of the earlier ones.

Milton Abramowitz and Irene Stegun (Eds.) (1970), *Handbook of Mathematical Functions*. New York: Dover.

D. F. Andrews, P. J. Bickel, F. R. Hampel, P. J. Huber, W. H. Rogers, and J. W. Tukey (1972), *Robust Estimates of Location*. Princeton, NJ: Princeton University Press.

C. Bays and S. D. Durham (1976), "Improving a Poor Random Number Generator," *ACM Transactions on Mathematical Software* 2: 59–64.

Paul Bratley, Bennett L. Fox, and Linus Schrage (1983), *A Guide to Simulation*. New York: Springer-Verlag.

H. S. Bright and R. L. Enison (1979), "Quasi-Random Number Sequences from a Long-Period TLP Generator with Remarks on Application to Cryptography," *Computing Surveys* 11: 357–70.

P. D. Coddington (1994), "Analysis of Random Number Generators Using Monte Carlo Simulation," *International Journal of Modern Physics C* 5: 547–60.

R. Cranley and T. N. L. Patterson (1976), "Randomization of Number Theoretic Methods for Multiple Integration," *SIAM Journal of Numerical Analysis* 13: 904–14.

Philip J. Davis (1975), *Interpolation and Approximation*. New York: Dover.

Philip J. Davis and Philip Rabinowitz (1984), *Methods of Numerical Integration,* 2nd ed. Orlando, FL: Academic Press.

K.-T. Fang and Y. Wang (1994), *Number-Theoretic Methods in Statistics*. London: Chapman & Hall.

A. M. Ferrenberg, D. P. Landau, and Y. J. Wong (1992), "Monte Carlo Simulations: Hidden Errors from 'Good' Random Number Generators," *Physical Review Letters* 69: 3382–4.

George S. Fishman and Louis R. Moore (1982), "A Statistical Evaluation of Multiplicative Congruential Generators with Modulus $2^{31} - 1$," *Journal of the American Statistical Association* 77: 129–36.

George S. Fishman and Louis R. Moore (1986), "An Exhaustive Analysis of Multiplicative Congruential Random Number Generators with Modulus $2^{31} - 1$," *SIAM Journal of Scientific and Statistical Computing* 7: 24–45.

Nancy Flournoy and Robert K. Tsutakawa (Eds.) (1991), *Statistical Multiple Integration* (Contemporary Mathematics Series, vol. 115). Providence, RI: American Mathematical Society.

M. Fushimi and S. Tezuka (1983), "The k-Distribution of Generalized Feedback Shift Register Pseudorandom Numbers," *Communications of the ACM* 26: 516–23.

John Geweke (1989), "Bayesian Inference in Econometric Models Using Monte Carlo Integration," *Econometrica* 57: 1317–39.

E. R. Golder (1976), "The Spectral Test for the Evaluation of Congruential Pseudo-random Generators," *Applied Statistics* 25: 173–80. [Corrections in Volume 25, p. 324 (Golder) and Volume 27, pp. 375–6 (Hoaglin and King).]

Gene H. Golub and J. H. Welsch (1969), "Calculation of Gauss Quadrature Rules," *Mathematics of Computation* 23: 221–30.

A. M. Gross (1973), "A Monte Carlo Swindle for Estimators of Location," *Applied Statistics* 22: 347–53.

J. H. Halton and G. B. Smith (1964), "Algorithm 247: Radical-Inverse Quasi-Random Point Sequence," *Communications of the ACM* 7: 701–2.

J. M. Hammersley and D. C. Handscomb (1964), *Monte Carlo Methods*. London: Methuen.

W. Hormann and G. Derflinger (1993), "A Portable Random Number Generator Well Suited for the Rejection Method," *ACM Transactions on Mathematical Software* 19: 489–95.

Loo Keng Hua and Yuan Wang (1981), *Applications of Number Theory to Numerical Analysis*. New York: Springer-Verlag.

Gershon Kedem and S. K. Zaremba (1974), "A Table of Good Lattice Points in Three Dimensions," *Numerische Mathematik* 23: 175–80.

Donald E. Knuth (1997), *The Art of Computer Programming* (vol. 2: Seminumerical Algorithms), 3rd ed. Reading, MA: Addison-Wesley.

V. I. Krylov (1962), *Approximate Calculation of Integrals* (trans. by A. H. Stroud). New York: Macmillan.

L. Kuipers and H. Neiderreiter (1974), *Uniform Distribution of Sequences*. New York: Wiley.

Pierre L'Ecuyer (1988), "Efficient and Portable Random Number Generators," *Communications of the ACM* 31: 742–9, 774.

Pierre L'Ecuyer (1990), "Random Numbers for Simulation," *Communications of the ACM* 33: 85–97.

P. A. W. Lewis, A. S. Goodman, and J. M. Miller (1969), "A Pseudo-random Number Generator for the System/360," *IBM Systems Journal* 2: 136–46.

T. G. Lewis and W. H. Payne (1973), "Generalized Feedback Shift Register Pseudorandom Number Algorithm," *Journal of the Association for Computing Machinery* 30: 456–68.

M. D. MacLaren and G. Marsaglia (1965), "Uniform Random Number Generators," *Journal of the ACM* 12: 83–9.

Dominique Maisonneuve (1972), "Recherche et Utilisation des 'Bons Treillis.' Programmation et Resultats Numeriques," in S. K. Zaremba (Ed.), *Applications of Number Theory to Numerical Analysis,* pp. 121–201. New York: Academic Press.

George Marsaglia (1968), "Random Numbers Fall Mainly in the Planes," *Proceedings of the National Academy of Sciences* 61: 25–8.

George Marsaglia (1972), "The Structure of Linear Congruential Sequences," in S. K. Zaremba (Ed.), *Applications of Number Theory to Numerical Analysis,* pp. 249–85. New York: Academic Press.

George Marsaglia (1985), "A Current View of Random Number Generators," in L. Ballard (Ed.), *Computer Science and Statistics: Proceedings of the Sixteenth Symposium on the Interface,* pp. 3–10. Amsterdam: North-Holland.

Makoto Matsumoto and Takuji Nishimura (1998), "Mersenne Twister: A 623-Dimensionally Equidistributed Uniform Pseudo-Random Number Generator," *ACM Transactions on Modeling and Computer Simulation,* 8: 3–30.

I. P. Mysovskikh (1980), "The Approximation of Multiple Integrals by using Interpolatory Cubature Formulae," in R. A. DeVore and K. Scherer (Eds.), *Quantitative Approximation,* pp. 217–43. New York: Academic Press.

Harald Neiderreiter (1978), "Quasi–Monte Carlo Methods and Pseudo-Random Numbers," *Bulletin of the American Mathematical Society* 84: 957–1041.

Harald Neiderreiter (1987), "Statistical Analysis of Generalized Feedback Shift Register Pseudorandom Generators," *SIAM Journal of Scientific and Statistical Computing* 8: 1035–51.

Harald Neiderreiter (1992), *Random Number Generation and Quasi–Monte Carlo Methods.* Philadelphia: SIAM.

Francois Panneton, Pierre L'Ecuyer, and Makoto Matsumoto (2006), "Improved Long-Period Generators Based on Linear Recurrences Modulo 2," *ACM Transactions on Mathematical Software* 32: 1–16.

Stephen K. Park and Keith W. Miller (1988), "Random Number Generators: Good Ones Are Hard to Find," *Communications of the ACM* 31: 1192–1201.

Stephen K. Park, Keith W. Miller, and Paul K. Stockmeyer (1993), "Technical Correspondence," *Communications of the ACM* 36: 108–10.

P. D. Proinov (1988), "Discrepancy and Integration of Continuous Functions," *Journal of Approximation Theory* 52: 121–31.

Daniel A. Relles (1970), "Variance Reduction Techniques for Monte Carlo Sampling from Student Distributions," *Technometrics* 12: 499–515.

Brian D. Ripley (1983), "Computer Generation of Random Variables: A Tutorial," *International Statistical Review* 51: 301–19.

Brian D. Ripley (1987), *Stochastic Simulation.* New York: Wiley.

Linus Schrage (1979), "A More Portable Fortran Random Number Generator," *ACM Transactions on Mathematical Software* 5: 132–8.

Gary Simon (1976), "Computer Simulation Swindles, with Applications to Estimates of Location and Dispersion," *Applied Statistics* 25: 266–74.

A. H. Stroud (1971), *Approximate Calculation of Multiple Integrals.* Englewood Cliffs, NJ: Prentice-Hall.

A. H. Stroud and D. H. Secrest (1966), *Gaussian Quadrature Formulas.* Englewood Cliffs, NJ: Prentice-Hall.

William H. Swallow and John F. Monahan (1984), "Monte Carlo Comparison of ANOVA, MIVQUE, REML, and ML Estimators of Variance Components," *Technometrics* 26: 47–57.

R. C. Tausworthe (1965), "Random Numbers Generated by Linear Recurrence Modulo Two," *Mathematics of Computation* 19: 201–9.

Shu Tezuka (1995), *Uniform Random Numbers: Theory and Practice.* Boston: Kluwer.

B. A. Wichmann and J. D. Hill (1982), "Algorithm AS 183: An Efficient and Portable Pseudorandom Number Generator," *Applied Statistics* 31: 188–90; 33: 123.

11

Generating Random Variables
from Other Distributions

11.1 Introduction

Chapter 10 provided an overview of Monte Carlo methods and dealt solely with the problem of generating from the uniform distribution. Since the uniform distribution is the fundamental distribution, we're now prepared to deal with the postponed problem of generating from other distributions. Given the results of Chapter 10, this problem should be viewed as transforming a source sequence of IID uniform random variables $\{U_i\}$ to an IID sequence of random variables $\{X_i\}$ with cumulative distribution function (cdf) F. A discussion of general methods for generating from continuous distributions forms Section 11.2. Specific algorithms designed for various distributions, such as the normal and Student's t, follow in Section 11.3. General methods for discrete distributions are discussed in Section 11.4, with specific cases in Section 11.5. Special problems, including random sampling from a population, are handled in Section 11.6. The problem of accuracy in Monte Carlo is tackled in Section 11.7.

Some general remarks are in order before pursuing the problem at hand. Algorithms for generating random variables should always be simple, fast, and exact. Simplicity is paramount, since users must often code and debug their own programs. Finding errors in random output is very difficult (see Exercises 11.14 and 11.20). If an algorithm is simple, most mistakes will bring consequences so severe that the error can be easily discovered. Speed is not so important, since the computational effort in generation is usually only a small fraction of the total effort in the Monte Carlo experiment. An algorithm should be exact in the sense that perfectly accurate arithmetic yields the exact distribution that is desired. In reality, of course, all generators will be approximations in the presence of finite precision arithmetic. This topic will be pursued in more detail in Section 11.7.

The algorithms given in this chapter will be presented in an informal form for simplicity. Their implementation as Fortran function subprograms is given in a number of demonstration programs; the list of these demonstrations begins on page 313. The reader should take note that coding a working algorithm often becomes more complicated as arithmetic shortcuts are sought. The working code sometimes appears in such a convoluted form that the original purpose of a step may be lost, so diligence is required.

303

11.2   General Methods for Continuous Distributions

Most distributions have characterizations that appear natural for generation. For example, the usual characterization of Student's t distribution is a normal divided by the square root of a chi-square divided by its degrees of freedom. Some characterizations lead to useful algorithms for generation, but others do not. For example, the distribution with cdf $F(x) = x^k$ on $[0, 1]$ could be generated from any number of methods. However, its characterization as the cdf of the maximum of k uniforms leads to a more effective algorithm for small k. When k becomes large, this algorithm slows considerably and so another approach should be sought. The methods presented in this section apply to almost any distribution, and algorithms following these approaches should be considered as potential competitors to methods relying on characterizations.

(A) *Transformations*

The probability integral transformation appears to solve the problem of random number generation in one fell swoop. If we wish to generate random variables from the distribution F, then transforming a uniform deviate U using the inverse cdf

$$X = F^{-1}(U)$$

leads to X having the distribution with cdf $F(x)$. Since the cdf is a monotone function,

$$\Pr(X \le x) = \Pr(F^{-1}(U) \le x) = \Pr(F(F^{-1}(U)) = U \le F(x)) = F(x) \quad (11.2.1)$$

for any cdf F. This method can be particularly effective for some distributions, such as the exponential:

$$F(x) = 1 - e^{-x} = u \iff e^{-x} = 1 - u \iff x = F^{-1}(u) = -\log(1 - u).$$

Since both U and $1 - U$ have the uniform distribution, X=-LOG(U) is the most common method of generating an exponential random variable. However, if code for computing $\log(1 - u)$ directly were available then such a route would be preferred for reasons of accuracy; see Section 11.6. The issue of accuracy arises because the function F^{-1} is rarely an arithmetic function. Although accuracy is not as serious a problem with such intrinsic functions as LOG, EXP, or SQRT, for most others the accuracy of the function approximation is a serious issue. More commonly, however, the evaluation of F^{-1} is so slow and cumbersome that other methods are preferred. Using an inverse incomplete gamma function is inappropriate for generating a chi-square random variable.

Occasionally, the distribution function $F(x)$ is not so difficult to evaluate yet the inverse F^{-1} is unavailable or very slow. Then the probability integral transformation or the inverse of the cdf can be viewed as solving a nonlinear equation. The first step is to generate U from the uniform distribution; then solve the nonlinear equation $F(x) - U = 0$ for x. The solution X has the distribution F.

(B) *Acceptance/Rejection*

Acceptance/rejection (A/R), invented by von Neumann in the early days of computing, is one of the most useful general tools in random number generation. Again X with the distribution F is sought, but suppose a random variable with cdf $G(x)$ is much easier to generate. Suppose also that, for all x, we can find β to satisfy a bound on the densities

$$\beta f(x) \le g(x) \quad \text{for } 0 < \beta < 1. \tag{11.2.2}$$

The function $g(x)/\beta$ is sometimes called an *upper envelope* for the density $f(x)$. Obviously, F must be absolutely continuous with respect to G; that is, if $g = 0$ then $f = 0$. The algorithm for generating X with distribution function F then follows.

   Algorithm AR1
   (1) Generate X from G.
   (2) Generate U from uniform$(0, 1)$.
   (3) If $Ug(X) \le \beta f(X)$ then deliver X (accept X as a random variable);
        else go to (1) (reject X and repeat).

The proof of the algorithm shows the strengths of A/R. First compute

$$\Pr(\text{accept } X) = \Pr\left(U \le \beta\frac{f(X)}{g(X)}\right) = \int \left[\beta\frac{f(x)}{g(x)}\right] g(x)\, dx = \beta,$$

since $f(x)$ is a density with the same support as $g(x)$. Then the distribution function of the output random variable X can be computed as a conditional probability:

$$\Pr(X \le x \mid \text{accept}) = \frac{\Pr(X \le x \text{ and } U \le \beta f(X)/g(X))}{\Pr(\text{accept})}$$

$$= \int_{-\infty}^{x} \frac{[\beta f(w)/g(w)]g(w)\, dw}{\beta}$$

$$= \int_{-\infty}^{x} f(w)\, dw = F(x). \tag{11.2.3}$$

Note that the middle step is computing the probability of U conditional on X, and then integrating X.

   The strategy with acceptance/rejection is to choose G that is easy to generate from and whose density $g(x)$ is close to f in shape. Since the scale factor β is also the acceptance probability, small β means a lot of rejections and so large β is preferred. Note that β itself is not required for the algorithm, only the ratio $r(x) = [\beta f(x)/g(x)]$, so that sometimes the computation of complicated normalization constants in the densities can be avoided. Moreover, sometimes the ratio $r(x)$ is itself difficult to compute, but bounding functions $b(x)$ and $B(x)$ can be found such that

$$b(x) \le r(x) = [\beta f(x)/g(x)] \le B(x). \tag{11.2.4}$$

If these bounds are tight and the functions $b(x)$ and $B(x)$ are much easier to compute than $r(x)$, then the algorithm can be speeded up using the following steps.

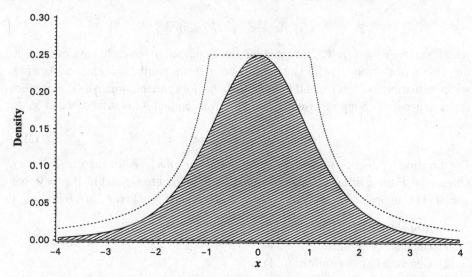

Figure 11.1. Upper envelope for acceptance/rejection. Solid line is rescaled t density with five degrees of freedom; dashed line is upper envelope density function $g(x)$.

Algorithm AR2

(1) Generate X from G.
(2) Generate U from uniform $(0, 1)$.
(3a) If $U \le b(X)$ then deliver X (quick accept).
(3b) If $U \ge B(X)$ then go to (1) (quick reject).
(3c) If $Ug(X) \le \beta f(X)$ then deliver X (accept X);
  else go to (1) (reject X and repeat).

Here step (3c) is the same as step (3) in AR1. Acceptance/rejection, including the use of inner and outer bounds, can be applied to discrete distributions as well as continuous ones.

Figures 11.1 and 11.2 show the use of acceptance/rejection for generating from a Student's t distribution with five degrees of freedom (Algorithm C2 in the next section). In Figure 11.1, we see the rescaled density $\beta f(x)$ with the upper envelope density $g(x)$ lying above it. One view of acceptance/rejection is to produce a point uniformly distributed in the striped region under the target density's curve, so that the marginal density of X is as desired. Notice that the two curves follow each other's shapes, but not particularly well. In Figure 11.2, however, we see the effectiveness of the inner and outer bounds. The region below the inner bound is shown in solid gray, and the outer bound cuts off most of the clear region below the envelope curve $g(x)$ so that the (unnormalized) density $\beta f(x)$ is computed only in the region between these two bounds.

The number of trials needed before acceptance obviously follows a geometric distribution with probability β; hence the expected number of trials is $1/\beta$, the inflation factor in the envelope $g(x)/\beta$. The use of inner and outer bounds doesn't change this, but it speeds up each trial. When β is near 1, the inner bound $b(x)$ becomes more important; as β decreases, the quick-reject outer bound $B(x)$ becomes more important.

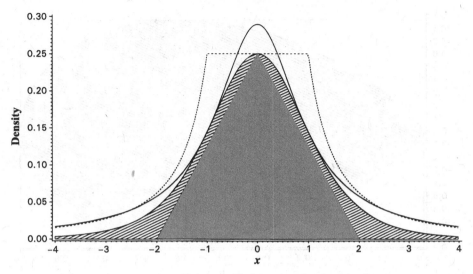

Figure 11.2. Inner and outer bounds for acceptance/rejection. Dashed line is the upper envelope density; solid line is quick-reject upper bound. Triangular lower bound forms solid quick-accept region.

(C) *Ratio of Uniforms*

The ratio of uniforms method is essentially a particular form of acceptance/rejection where the tails of distributions are made more manageable, often leading to short and simple algorithms for many distributions, including discrete ones. The key is a simple result by Kinderman and Monahan (1977).

Theorem: *If the point (U, V) is uniformly distributed over the region*

$$C_h = \{(u, v) : 0 \le u \le h^{1/2}(v/u)\},$$

then the ratio $X = V/U$ has a density proportional to $h(x)$.

Proof. Let the area of the region C_h be K. Then the joint density of $(X, Y) = (V/U, U)$ is given by $g(x, y) = y/K$ for $0 \le y \le h^{1/2}(x)$ and zero otherwise. Merely integrating out y produces the marginal density of X, which is $(2K)^{-1}h(x)$, so that $2K$ is the normalization constant. If $h(x)$ is itself a density, then the area of C_h is $1/2$.   □

This result goes nowhere if we cannot generate points uniformly over the region C_h. If C_h fits nicely into a region (e.g. a rectangle) where uniformly distributed points can easily be generated, then this approach may show some promise. Sometimes the boundary of the region C_h can be found in terms of u and v by solving $u = h^{1/2}(v/u)$, usually for v in terms of u. However, the parametric form $(u(x), v(x))$ is much easier to work with:

$$u(x) = h^{1/2}(x) \quad \text{and} \quad v(x) = xh^{1/2}(x). \tag{11.2.5}$$

Typically, the extrema of this boundary can be computed easily:

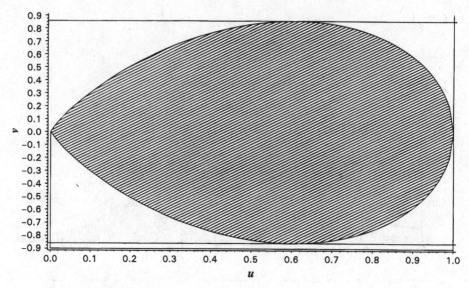

Figure 11.3. Ratio of uniforms for normal with outer box and region C_h (striped).

$$u^* = \max_x u(x) = \max_x h^{1/2}(x),$$

$$v_+^* = \max_x v(x) = \max_x x h^{1/2}(x),$$ (11.2.6)

$$v_-^* = \min_x v(x) = \min_x x h^{1/2}(x).$$

Often C_h fits snugly into the box with vertices $(0, v_+^*)$, $(0, v_-^*)$, (u^*, v_-^*), (u^*, v_+^*), and a very simple acceptance/rejection algorithm follows.

Algorithm ROU
(1) Generate $U \sim$ uniform$(0, u^*)$.
(2) Generate $V \sim$ uniform(v_-^*, v_+^*).
(3) $X = V/U$.
(4) If $U^2 \le h(X)$ then deliver X; else go to (1).

The acceptance probability is then the ratio of the areas of the region C_h and the enclosing box $u^*(v_+^* - v_-^*)$. As with acceptance/rejection, inner and outer bounds on $b(x) \le h(x) \le B(x)$ can speed up the algorithm by avoiding the computation of $h(x)$. For the normal distribution, the region C_h has an egglike shape and is shown in Figure 11.3 as a striped egg fitting snugly in a rectangular box. The effectiveness of the inner and outer bounds can be seen in Figure 11.4. The algorithm given later in the next section (Algorithm A3) for the normal distribution epitomizes the ratio of uniforms method, and the details of the inner and outer bounds are described there.

11.3   Algorithms for Continuous Distributions

For many distributions, several methods have been proposed but only a few have stood the test of time. Some methods appear here in order to illustrate other algorithms, although they may be inferior to current methods. Sometimes comparisons between

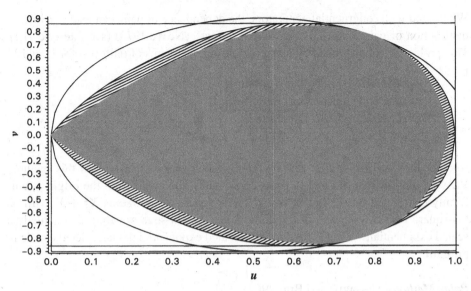

Figure 11.4. Ratio of uniforms for normal with quick-accept region (solid), remainder of region C_h (striped), and quick-reject outer bound.

algorithms are made difficult because of trade-offs between function calculation and the number of uniforms, where the relative speeds depend on both hardware and software and change considerably over time. Nonetheless, trade-offs that give up simplicity will always be painful.

The generation from a family of distributions, such as the gamma family, presents another challenge: finding an algorithm that can be general enough to work for an entire family of distributions. However, often an algorithm can be tailored for a particular member of a family after some setup – computing some constants that depend on the parameter – after which the tailored algorithm may be much more efficient. The balance in the trade-off between setup and speed depends then upon how fast the parameter changes in an application.

The list of distributions handled in this book is far from complete. I would recommend the monograph by Devroye (1986) to the interested reader; the book is quite comprehensive and contains much more than could be listed here.

(A) *Normal Distribution*

Fast, accurate, and simple algorithms are available for generating random variables from the normal distribution, but many packages still use the approximation $X = \sum_{j=1}^{12} U_j - 6$, where U_j are IID uniforms. This method is unacceptable, primarily because it is not exact where simple, exact algorithms are available. Additionally, this method is much slower than its competitors.

Box–Muller (1958)
The Box–Muller transformation is the earliest method for generating normal random variables, actually producing pairs of independent normals. It is not in common use because the library routines that are called (SIN, COS, SQRT, LOG) render it rather slow.

When used with congruential generators, the dependence of pairs can lead to a bizarre distribution of pairs known as the "Neave effect" (Neave 1973) (see Exercise 11.1). This problem can be avoided by using two different streams of uniforms for U and V.

  Algorithm A1 (Box–Muller) (**gnbxml**)
 (1) Generate U, V independent uniform$(0, 1)$.
 (2) Deliver $X = \cos(2\pi U)\sqrt{-2\log V}$
    and $Y = \sin(2\pi U)\sqrt{-2\log V}$.

Another look at Box–Muller reveals the characterizations that lead to this method. Viewing the bivariate normal in polar coordinates, the angle from the origin is uniformly distributed on $(0, 2\pi)$ as is $2\pi U$. The square of the radius $X^2 + Y^2$ will be chi-square with two degrees of freedom. Since the chi-square with 2 df is actually a scaled exponential, $-2\log V$ produces the scaled exponential deviate. See the code in **gnbxml**.

Polar Method (Marsaglia and Bray 1964)

The polar method is actually an accelerated version of Box–Muller that avoids the two trigonometric function calls. See the code in **gnpolr**.

  Algorithm A2 (Polar) (**gnpolr**)
 (1) Generate U, V independent uniform$(-1, 1)$.
 (2) $W = U^2 + V^2$.
 (3) If $W > 1$ then go to (1).
 (4) $Z = \sqrt{(-2\log W)/W}$.
 (5) Deliver $X_1 = UZ$ and $X_2 = VZ$.

The key here is that steps (1)–(3) produce the point (U, V) uniformly distributed on the unit circle. Then $U/\sqrt{W}$ is equivalent to the sine and $V/\sqrt{W}$ to the cosine of a random angle. Moreover, the angle is independent of W, which has a uniform distribution (see Exercise 11.3). One possible improvement is to generate an exponential random variable Y by another route and compute

 (4*) $Z = \sqrt{2Y/W}$.

Ratio of Uniforms

The ratio of uniforms algorithm for the normal distribution is a good example of this general method at its best. The analysis is not difficult, and the resulting algorithm is both simple and fast.

  Algorithm A3 (Ratio of Uniforms) (**gnrouo**)
 (1) Generate $U \sim$ uniform$(0, 1)$.
 (2) Generate $V \sim$ uniform$(-v, +v)$, where $v = \sqrt{2/e}$.
 (3) Let $X = V/U$ and store $Z = X^2$.
 (4a) (Quick accept) If $Z \le 5 - (4e^{1/4})U$ then deliver X.
 (4b) (Quick reject) If $Z > (4e^{-1/4})/U - 3$ then go to (1).
 (4c) If $Z \le -4\log U$ then deliver X; else go to (1).

This algorithm also illustrates the effect of labor-saving steps on the clarity of a simple algorithm. Although the ratio of uniforms method is quite simple, as is Algorithm A3, the relationship between the two may not be apparent to the reader.

The translation begins by examining the region C_h with $h(x) = \exp[-x^2/2]$ (the unnormalized density),

$$C_h = \{(u, v) : 0 \le u \le h^{1/2}(v/u) = \exp[-v^2/(4u^2)]\}$$
$$= \{(u, v) : x^2 = (v/u)^2 \le -4\log u\}, \tag{11.3.1}$$

allowing the main inequality to be restated in terms of the deviate X. The inner and outer bounds arise from inequalities on $\log u$:

$$(1 + \log c) - cu \le -\log u, \tag{11.3.2}$$

$$-\log u \le 1/cu - (1 - \log c). \tag{11.3.3}$$

These, too, may appear cryptic, but both arise from the simple inequality that the tangent line lies above the concave log function:

$$\log y \le y/d + (\log d - 1),$$

with the tangent taken at d. Taking $y = u$ and $d = 1/c$ leads to the lower bound (11.3.2); using $y = 1/u$ and $d = c$ yields (11.3.3). The area of the inner bound (11.3.2) is largest when $c = e^{1/4}$ (see Exercise 11.4), and note that the constant $4e^{1/4} = 5.1361$ would be computed in advance and stored. The same $c = e^{1/4}$ is used for the outer bound using inequality (11.3.3) for the original version of the algorithm in **gnrouo**. Knuth (1997) found the best value of $c = e^{1.35}$ for the quick-reject outer bound (11.3.3) numerically (see Exercise 11.5), leading to the improved version **gnrouk**.

Figure 11.3 showed the region C_h for the ratio of uniforms method as the striped egg-shaped region, fitting snugly in the rectangular box just described. The region determined by the inner bound was shown as the gray solid region in Figure 11.4 covering most of the striped region C_h, so the inner bound is rather tight. The Knuth outer bound – though the best of its family – does not work as well as the inner bound, but it still cuts off a sizable portion of the corners of the box.

The ratio of uniforms approach is really a form of acceptance/rejection, with the probability of acceptance being the ratio of the area of C_h $\left(\sqrt{\pi/2}\right)$ to the area of the outer box $\left(2\sqrt{2/e}\right)$,

$$\Pr(\text{accept}) = \frac{\sqrt{\pi/2}}{2\sqrt{2/e}} = \sqrt{\frac{\pi e}{16}} = .73;$$

the expected number of trials is 1.37. The inner and outer bounds reduce dramatically the number of evaluations of nonarithmetic functions, since for each trial with **gnrouk** we have

$$\Pr(\text{reaching (4c) or evaluating "log"}) = .17.$$

The probability of accepting quickly, branching on (4a), is large (.66). Not only does the ratio of uniforms lead to a simple algorithm, the fast and effective quick accept/reject bounds make it one of the fastest algorithms for generating from the normal distribution.

Leva (1992) found tight quadratic bounds, which improve matters further; this led to a slightly more complicated (but faster) algorithm in **gnroul**.

Algorithm A4 (Ratio of Uniforms – Leva Bounds) (**gnroul**)

(1) Generate $U \sim \text{uniform}(0, 1)$.
(2) Generate $V \sim \text{uniform}(-v, +v)$, where $v = \sqrt{2/e}$.
(3) Let $X = V/U$, $Z = U - S$, $Y = |V| - T$, and $Q = Z*Z + Y*(a*Y - b*Z)$, where the constants are $S = .449871$, $T = -3.86595$, $a = .19600$, and $b = .25472$.
(4a) (Quick accept) If $Q \le 0.27597$ then deliver X.
(4b) (Quick reject) If $Q > 0.27846$ then go to (1).
(4c) If $V^2 \le -4U^2 \log U$ then deliver X; else go to (1).

(B) *Exponential Distribution*

As discussed earlier, the exponential distribution has a closed-form expression for the inverse of its cdf. The transformations $-\log U$ and $-\log(1 - U)$ can be used for generating from the exponential distribution; our discussion on preferring the latter will be postponed until Section 11.7. Although these transformations are both fast and accurate, one other algorithm is particularly noteworthy because it can generate from a "transcendental" distribution (such as the exponential) using only arithmetic operations.

Algorithm B1 (von Neumann 1951) (**gevonn**)

(0) (Initialize) $K = 0$.
(1) Generate $U_1, U_2, \ldots$ as long as they decrease, until $U_{n+1} > U_n$.
(2) If n is even, then deliver $Y = U_1 + K$.
    If n is odd, then $K = K + 1$ and go to (1).

At first glance, this algorithm looks so weird that the output could follow any distribution. However, we can dispel the mystery by simplifying matters as follows.

Algorithm B2

(1) Generate $U_1, U_2, \ldots$ as long as they decrease, until $U_{n+1} > U_n$.
(2) If n is even, then deliver $X = U_1$; else go to (1).

The key to Algorithm B2 is the distribution of U_1 when successive uniforms are decreasing. Begin by defining the event that n uniforms occur in decreasing order:

$$E_n = \{U_n \le U_{n-1} \le \cdots \le U_1\}.$$

Then the distribution function for U_1 upon stopping in step (1) can be written as

$$\Pr(U_1 \le u, E_n, E_{n+1}^c) = \Pr(U_1 \le u, E_n) - \Pr(U_1 \le u, E_{n+1})$$

$$= \frac{u^n}{n} - \frac{u^{n+1}}{(n+1)!}, \tag{11.3.4}$$

since E_{n+1} is a subset of E_n (the superscript c denotes complement). Since we "accept" U_1 when n is even, it follows that

$$\Pr(U_1 \le u, \text{accept}) = \sum_{n \text{ even}} \Pr(U_1 \le u, E_n, E_{n+1}^c)$$

$$= \sum_{n \text{ even}} \left[\frac{u^n}{n!} - \frac{u^{n+1}}{(n+1)!} \right] = 1 - e^{-u}.$$

Taking $u = 1$ gives the acceptance probability

$$\Pr(\text{accept}) = 1 - e^{-1}$$

and so the distribution of X out of Algorithm B2 has the density $e^{-x}/(1 - e^{-1})$ on the range $(0, 1)$, which is a truncated exponential distribution. The exponential distribution follows the same shape throughout its support, so now we need only spread the distribution over the positive real line by copying the distribution to each unit length interval with the correct probability. If Y has the exponential distribution, then the probability content of each unit interval is simply

$$\Pr(k < Y \leq k + 1) = e^{-k} - e^{-k-1} = e^{-k}(1 - e^{-1}) \quad k = 0, 1, 2, \ldots;$$

this is simply the probability function of a geometric random variable with probability of "success" equal to e^{-1}, which is the probability of rejecting in Algorithm B2. As a result, the counter K in Algorithm B1 has the geometric distribution, which gives the correct probability content for each interval, and U_1 conditional on accepting has the correct distribution for the remainder. Again comparing with a true exponential deviate Y, we can check:

$$\Pr([y] < Y \leq y) = e^{-[y]} - e^{-y} = \Pr(U_1 \leq y - [y], \text{ accept}) \times \Pr(K = [y])$$

$$= \frac{1 - e^{-(y-[y])}}{1 - e^{-1}} \times e^{-[y]}(1 - e^{-1}). \qquad (11.3.5)$$

Although this algorithm is notable, it is substantially slower than the transformations because so many uniforms are needed. Marsaglia (1961), Sibuya (1962) (see Exercise 11.6), and others have suggested some clever modifications to speed up this method. This von Neumann algorithm can be extended to other distributions (Forsythe 1972) and generalized (Monahan 1979).

(C) *Student's t and Cauchy*

Student's t is the first *family* of distributions to be discussed. The algorithm based on its characterization demonstrates some of the difficulties in writing a single algorithm for a family.

> *Algorithm C1* (Student's t with k degrees of freedom)
> (1) Generate $Z_0, Z_1, Z_2, \ldots, Z_k$ IID normal$(0, 1)$.
> (2) Sum the squares: $S = \sum_{j=1}^{k} Z_i^2$.
> (3) $Y = Z_0/\sqrt{S/k}$.

As k grows large, the distribution of Y converges to the normal, yet the effort grows without bound. Replacing pairs of squares of normals by exponentials ($-2 \log U \sim \chi_2^2$) can only cut the work in half. Obviously, we need a better way to generate chi-square random variables, but the same problem must be faced there. Using the gamma algorithms presented later will not improve upon those designed specifically for the t.

    When designing an algorithm for a family indexed by a parameter α, two features must be considered. First, the effort for generating a random variable should not grow unboundedly in the parameter. Second, often an algorithm can be tailored for a particular member of a family (this is known as *setup*), usually by calculating some constants that are functions of the parameter α. The frequency of the change in the parameter will govern the trade-off between setup and efficiency, and the particular application will dictate that rate of change. For the Student's t family of distributions, the indexing parameter is the degrees of freedom. In the following algorithms, that parameter is considered to be a continuous variable – that is, not limited to the integers. The acceptance/rejection algorithm for the t family is the best example of its application to a family and also shows the trade-offs between setup and efficiency.

The t distribution has the density $f_\alpha(x) = c_\alpha u_\alpha(x)$, where

$$c_\alpha = \Gamma\left(\frac{\alpha+1}{2}\right)\Big/\left[\sqrt{\pi\alpha}\,\Gamma\left(\frac{\alpha}{2}\right)\right] \quad \text{and} \quad u_\alpha(x) = \left(1+\frac{x^2}{\alpha}\right)^{-(\alpha+1)/2},$$

which looks quite complicated. Nonetheless, for $\alpha \geq 1$, we can show that the unnormalized density $u_\alpha(x)$ lies below a simple rescaled density function:

$$u_\alpha(x) \leq \min(1, |x|^{-2}) \equiv 4g(x),$$

leading to the envelope inequality $\beta f_\alpha(x) \leq g(x)$ with $\beta = 1/(4c_\alpha)$. For acceptance/rejection, then, we need to generate from the density

$$g(x) = (1/4)\min(1, |x|^{-2}), \tag{11.3.6}$$

which can be done rather easily: Generate $Y \sim \text{uniform}(-1, 1)$; with probability 1/2 return $X = Y$, else return $X = 1/Y$. The main acceptance/rejection test takes on the simplified form

$$U \leq \beta\frac{f(X)}{g(X)} = \left(\frac{1}{4c_\alpha}\right)\frac{c_\alpha u_\alpha(X)}{g(X)} = \frac{u_\alpha(X)}{\min(1, |X|^{-2})} = \frac{u_\alpha(X)}{4g(X)}.$$

This does not involve the ugly constant c_α, which therefore need not be computed. Pushing further, the density kernel $u_\alpha(x)$ can be avoided using the inner (quick-accept) bound

$$1 - |x|/2 \leq u_\alpha(x)$$

and the upper bounds

$$u_\alpha(x) \leq [2u_\alpha(1)]u_1(x) \leq [2u_\infty(1)]u_1(x) = 2e^{-1/2}/(1+x^2). \tag{11.3.7}$$

The setup version of the acceptance/rejection algorithm for the t distribution takes the following form.

    Algorithm C2 (Simplified TIR from Kinderman, Monahan, and Ramage 1977)
    (**gttir**)
(0) (Setup) Compute $d_\alpha = 2u_\alpha(1) = 2(1+1/\alpha)^{-(\alpha+1)/2}$.
(1) Generate $V \sim \text{uniform}(0, 1)$ and $U \sim \text{uniform}(0, 1)$.
(2) If $V \leq 1/2$, then set $X = (1/4)/(V - (1/4))$ and $W = U/X^2$;
    else $X = 4 * V - 3$ and $W = U$
    (now $X \sim g(x)$ and $W = U * (4g(X)) \sim \text{uniform}(0, 4g(X))$).
(3) If $W \leq 1 - |X|$ then deliver X.

(4) If $W > d_\alpha/(1 + X^2)$ then go to (1).

(5) If $W \leq u_\alpha(X)$ then deliver X; else go to (1).

The non-setup version of Algorithm C2 simply replaces d_α with $d = 2e^{-1/2}$, which works for all α. However, further improvements exploit details avoided here for simplicity – namely, that the inner bound applies only for $|X| < 1$ and that the upper bound is useful only for $|X|$ in the interval $[(2u_\alpha(1) - 1)^{1/2}, (2u_\alpha(1) - 1)^{-1/2}]$. One of the critical concerns of an algorithm for the range $\alpha \geq 1$ is that the performance not degrade for large values of α. Indeed, the amount of computation does not vary greatly with α, and the expected number of trials is confined to a narrow range:

$$1.27 \leq 1/\beta = 4c_\alpha \leq 1.60.$$

In examining the upper bounds, one may also consider using the Cauchy distribution for the upper envelope $g(x)$. However, the Cauchy density is not as easily computed as a uniform and a multiply or divide (see Exercise 11.8).

The ratio of uniforms method leads to the simplest and fastest algorithm for the t distribution. As before, drop the constant c_α and let $h(x) = u_\alpha(x) = (1 + x^2/\alpha)^{-(\alpha+1)/2}$. Then the boundary of the enclosing box can be easily computed:

$$u^* = \max_x h^{1/2}(x) = \max_x (1 + x^2/\alpha)^{-(\alpha+1)/4} = 1,$$

$$v_+^* = -v_-^* = \max_x x h^{1/2}(x) = \max_x x(1 + x^2/\alpha)^{-(\alpha+1)/4} \tag{11.3.8}$$

$$= \sqrt{2\alpha}(\alpha + 1)^{-(\alpha+1)/4}(\alpha - 1)^{(\alpha-1)/4},$$

with $v_+^* = -v_-^*$ defined to be 1 for $\alpha = 1$ (Cauchy). Note that $v_+^* \to \sqrt{2/e}$ as $\alpha \to \infty$ (see Exercise 11.9). Construction of inner and outer bounds is more difficult. The comparison $u \leq h^{1/2}(x)$ can be reworked to

$$g(u) = \alpha(u^{-4/(1+\alpha)} - 1) \geq x^2. \tag{11.3.9}$$

Kinderman and Monahan (1980) derived the bounds

$$5 - au \leq g(u) \leq e/u - 3,$$

where $a = 4(1 + 1/\alpha)^{(\alpha+1)/4}$ and $e = 4(1 + 1/\alpha)^{-(\alpha+1)/4}$, but the latter inequality holds only for $\alpha \geq 3$. These results lead to the following algorithm.

> *Algorithm C3* (TROU from Kinderman and Monahan 1980) (**gtrou**)
>
> (0) (Setup) Compute $c = -(\alpha + 1)/4$, $a = 4(1 + 1/\alpha)^{-c}$, $e = 16/a$, and $v_+^* = -v_-^*$ from (11.3.8).
>
> (1) Generate $U \sim \text{uniform}(0, 1)$.
>
> (2) Generate $V \sim \text{uniform}(v_-^*, v_+^*)$ and form $X = V/U$.
>
> (3) If $aU \leq 5 - X^2$ then deliver X.
>
> (4) For $\alpha \geq 3$: if $X^2 \geq e/U - 3$ then go to (1).
>
> (5) If $U \leq (1 + X^2/\alpha)^c$ then deliver X; else go to (1).

Although Algorithm C3 is quite simple, the condition on the quick-reject step (4) is annoying and begs to be dropped. Another drawback is that the setup step (0) is quite extensive, with two exponentials and a square root; a non-setup version could be useful in some applications (see Exercise 11.11).

Finally, two special cases of the Student's t family demand special recognition. The first is the case $\alpha = 1$, which gives the Cauchy distribution with density $f(x) = \pi^{-1}(1+x^2)^{-1}$. The ratio of uniforms method was inspired by the following algorithm.

> *Algorithm C4* (Synthetic Tangent Algorithm for the Cauchy Distribution)
> (1) Generate $U \sim$ uniform$(0, 1)$.
> (2) Generate $V \sim$ uniform$(-1, +1)$.
> (3) If $U^2 + V^2 > 1$ then go to (1); else deliver $X = V/U$.

The synthetic tangent algorithm is also suggested by the modified polar method for the normal distribution, since the ratio of two standard normal deviates has the Cauchy distribution. Although the inverse distribution function has a closed form for the Cauchy case, $F^{-1}(u) = \pi^{-1} \tan^{-1}\big((u - \frac{1}{2})\big)$, the synthetic tangent algorithm may be faster in some circumstances.

The second special case of the t distribution is the case $\alpha = 3$, with the density $f(x) \propto (1+x^2/3)^{-2}$. This distribution has both a mean and a variance, but it still has long tails. Using $h(x) = (1+x^2/3)^{-2}$ and applying the ratio of uniforms method, the region C_h is the ellipse with boundary

$$(u - 1/2)^2 + v^2/3 = 1/4,$$

which leads to a simple algorithm (see Exercises 11.12 and 11.14).

> *Algorithm C5* (Student's t with 3 df)
> (1) Generate $U \sim$ uniform$(0, 1)$.
> (2) Generate $V \sim$ uniform$\big(-\sqrt{3/4}, \sqrt{3/4}\big)$.
> (3) If $(U - 1/2)^2 + V^2/3 > 1/4$ then go to (1); else deliver $X = V/U$.

(D) *Gamma, Chi-Square, and Chi*

The gamma family has two parameters, a shape parameter α and a scale β, so the density can be written as

$$f(x) = \frac{\beta^{-\alpha}}{\Gamma(\alpha)} x^{\alpha-1} e^{-x/\beta} \quad \text{for } x, \alpha, \beta > 0. \tag{11.3.10}$$

To cement the definition of the parameters, the mean is $\alpha\beta$ and the variance is $\alpha\beta^2$. The chi-square distribution with k degrees of freedom fits into this family with $\alpha = k/2$ and $\beta = 2$, and the chi is the square root of a chi-square. The gamma family is closed under summation when the scale parameter is the same: if $X \sim$ gamma(α_1, β) and $Y \sim$ gamma(α_2, β) and both are independent, then the sum $X+Y \sim$ gamma$(\alpha_1 + \alpha_2, \beta)$. Two special cases are also available: If Z is normal$(0, 1)$ then $Z^2 \sim \chi_1^2 =$ gamma$(1/2, 2)$, and gamma$(1, \beta)$ is the exponential distribution. Using normals and exponentials, a deviate from gamma$(k/2, \beta)$ for integer k can be generated; however, the effort goes up linearly with k. On the other end, generating from the gamma with small shape parameter faces some difficulties since the density is un-bounded for $\alpha < 1$.

The following ratio of uniforms algorithm for the chi distribution satisfies most de-mands in a single program. The execution time is bounded as a function of α; chi-square and gamma variates can be easily obtained (a square root takes longer than a square); and the parameter range extends down to $\alpha = 1/2$, which includes χ_1^2. Even with its setup, it is faster than its competitors. The density of the chi distribution with γ degrees of freedom is

$$f(x) = [2^{1-(\gamma/2)}/\Gamma(\gamma/2)]x^{\gamma-1}\exp[-x^2/2], \qquad (11.3.11)$$

so that X^2 is χ_γ^2 or gamma$(\gamma/2, 2)$. Let $\eta^2 = \gamma - 1$, so that the relocated random variable $Z = X - \eta$ has the density

$$g(z) = c_\eta h_\eta(z), \quad \text{where } h_\eta(z) = (1 + z/\eta)^{\eta^2}\exp[-(x^2/2) - z\eta]. \qquad (11.3.12)$$

The ratio of uniforms region lies within the usual box, with $u^* = 1$ as well as the more complicated

$$v_+^*(\eta) = e^{-1/2}(1/\sqrt{2} + \eta)/(1/2 + \eta),$$
$$v_-^*(\eta) = \max(-\eta, -e^{-1/2}(1 - 1/[4(\eta^2 + 1)])), \qquad (11.3.13)$$

which were established numerically.

Algorithm D1 (Monahan 1987) (**gchirv**)
(0) (Setup) Compute $\eta = \sqrt{\gamma - 1}$ and $v_+^*(\eta), v_-^*(\eta)$ given by (11.3.13).
(1) Generate $U \sim$ uniform$(0, 1)$ and $V \sim$ uniform$(v_-^*(\eta), v_+^*(\eta))$, and form $Z = V/U$.
(2) If $Z < -\eta$ then go to (1).
(3) (Quick accept)
    (a) $r = 5/2 - Z^2$.
    (b) If $Z < 0$ then $r = r + Z^2/[3(Z + \eta)]$.
    (c) (Test) If $U < r/(2e^{1/4})$ then deliver $X = Z + \eta$.
(4) (Quick reject) If $Z^2 > (4e^{-1.35})/U + 1.4$ then go to (1).
(5) (Regular test) If $2\log U < \log h_\eta(Z)$ then deliver $X = Z + \eta$; else go to (1).

The inner bounds for step (3) rely on logarithm bounds that differ on the two sides of zero. The quick-reject outer bound is actually the one found by Knuth for the normal distribution. Such a bound should not be a surprise because (a) at $\gamma = 1$, the χ is the half-normal, and (b) as $\gamma \to \infty$, the relocated distribution of Z converges to the nor-mal. To reemphasize the use of Algorithm D1, observe:

(i) to generate gamma(α, β), call D1 with $\gamma = 2\alpha$ and deliver $\beta(X * X/2)$;
(ii) to generate χ_k^2, call D1 with $\gamma = k$ and deliver $X * X$.

(E) *Logistic and Laplace*

These two distributions can be easily generated using transformations. In the logistic case, the distribution function takes the form $F(x) = 1/(1 + e^{-x})$, so that its inverse is rather simple: $F^{-1}(u) = \log(u/(1-u))$. Exercise a little care to ensure that the same uniform is used, since the code

```
LOG(RAN(1)/(1.-RAN(1)))
```

may have unpredictable consequences. An optimizing compiler might translate the code with only one call to the uniform generator, and the result would be a random variable with the logistic distribution. However, most compilers will translate the code to make two calls to the uniform generator, and the resulting distribution is the Laplace, or double exponential (see Exercise 11.20). Another characterization of the Laplace distribution is that of an exponential random variable with a random sign, following the density

$$f(x) = (1/2)e^{-|x|}.$$

This route should be followed if a random sign can be easily attached.

(F) *Beta, F, and Dirichlet*

The relationship between the beta and F distributions is well known, but it is the relationship of each to the gamma that is the key to their generation. Take the beta distribution with parameters α and β, with density

$$f(x) = \frac{\Gamma(\alpha+\beta)}{\Gamma(\alpha)\Gamma(\beta)}x^{\alpha-1}(1-x)^{\beta-1} \quad \text{for } 0 \le x \le 1, \ \alpha, \beta > 0. \tag{11.3.14}$$

If $U \sim \text{gamma}(\alpha, 1)$ and $V \sim \text{gamma}(\beta, 1)$ are independent, then $X = U/(U+V)$ has the beta distribution. The F distribution is characterized by independent chi-square random variables. If $U \sim \chi_m^2 = \text{gamma}(m/2, 2)$ and $V \sim \chi_n^2 = \text{gamma}(n/2, 2)$, then $Y = (U/m)/(V/n)$ has the F distribution with m and n degrees of freedom. In both the beta and F, the scale factor of the gamma cancels out.

Because Algorithm D1 can generate the chi distribution with degrees of freedom as low as 1, it can also cover the gamma distribution for any shape parameter $\ge 1/2$ satisfying most applications of both the beta and F. To generate the beta, call Algorithm D1 twice: once with parameter $\gamma = 2\alpha$ and the second time with $\gamma = 2\beta$. Squaring the first output produces U, squaring the second gives V, and the ratio $X = U/(U+V)$ produces the desired beta deviate. To generate the F, again call Algorithm D1 twice – first with $\gamma = m$ and then with $\gamma = n$. Taking the ratio of the two outputs before squaring saves a multiply, and the term n/m can be stored as a constant if repeated calls are to be made. Note that, in both beta and F cases, if repeated calls are needed then the setup can be exploited only by repeatedly calling with one parameter setting and then the other.

The Dirichlet distribution is a multivariate generalization of the beta. To follow this generalization, begin by visualizing the beta as really bivariate, with the second component $(1-x)$ the complement from 1. Because of the constraint that the components must sum to unity, the density exists in one dimension only. For the k-dimensional Dirichlet distribution, the first k components are all nonnegative and less than 1, and the shadow $(k+1)$th component is the complement from 1. Each component has a shape parameter α_i, $i = 1, \ldots, (k+1)$. The density exists only in k dimensions and can be written as

$$f(\mathbf{x}) = \frac{\Gamma(\alpha_1)\Gamma(\alpha_2)\cdots\Gamma(\alpha_k)\Gamma(\alpha_{k+1})}{\Gamma(\alpha_1 + \alpha_2 + \cdots + \alpha_k + \alpha_{k+1})}$$

$$\times x_1^{\alpha_1-1} x_2^{\alpha_2-1} \cdots x_k^{\alpha_k-1} \left(1 - \sum_{j=1}^{k} x_j\right)^{\alpha_{k+1}-1}; \qquad (11.3.15)$$

hence $\mathbf{x}$ is still restricted and so the sum of the components is less than 1. The algorithm for generating the Dirichlet follows a characterization that shows most clearly the generalization from the beta. Let $U_1, U_2, \ldots, U_k, U_{k+1}$ be independent gamma random variables each with shape parameter α_j, $j = 1, \ldots, (k+1)$. Then the k-dimensional vector $\mathbf{x}$ whose components are

$$x_j = U_j \Big/ \sum_{i=1}^{k+1} U_i \qquad (11.3.16)$$

has the k-dimensional Dirichlet distribution with parameters $\alpha_1, \alpha_2, \ldots, \alpha_k, \alpha_{k+1}$.

(G) *Noncentral Chi-Square, F, and t*

These three noncentral distributions are related, but not to each other. Well, that doesn't make sense, but it caught your attention enough to be careful with their characterizations. The noncentral t has a different characterization than the others. If $Z \sim$ normal$(\mu, 1)$ and $U \sim \chi_k^2$, then the ratio

$$Y = Z/\sqrt{U/k}$$

has the noncentral t distribution with k degrees of freedom and noncentrality parameter μ. This distribution should be generated by following this characterization precisely. The noncentral t gives the distribution of the usual t statistic under an alternative hypothesis.

The noncentral chi-square and noncentral F follow another characterization. Let Z_i IID normal(μ_i, σ^2) for $i = 1, \ldots, k$. Then the sum of squares

$$Q = \sum_{i=1}^{k} Z_i^2$$

has the noncentral chi-square distribution with k degrees of freedom and noncentrality parameter $\lambda = \sum_{i=1}^{k} (\mu_i^2/\sigma^2)$, although others (e.g. Searle 1971, p. 49) include a 2 in the denominator. The noncentral chi-square has the density

$$f(x) = e^{-\lambda/2} \sum_{j=0}^{\infty} \left(\frac{(\lambda/2)^j}{j!}\right) \frac{2^{-k-2j}}{\Gamma(k+2j)} x^{k+2j-1} e^{-x/2}, \qquad (11.3.17)$$

which can be viewed as a Poisson weighted sum of central χ_{k+2j}^2 densities. This characterization leads to one route for generating the noncentral chi-square: generate a Poisson random variable J with parameter $\lambda/2$ (be careful with how you've defined the noncentrality parameter! – see Algorithm C2 for the Poisson) and then, given J, generate a χ^2_{k+2J} random variable for the result. For another method, which is likely to be superior, see Exercise 11.19.

The noncentral F is usually characterized as $Y = (U/m)/(V/n)$, where U is a noncentral χ^2_m and V is central χ^2_n. Following this characterization is the obvious route for generation. The noncentral F gives the distribution of the F statistic in an analysis of variance situation under an alternative hypothesis. Doubly noncentral t and F distributions have also been defined, but their applications are more limited. In both cases, the denominator χ^2 is changed from central to noncentral in the definition, and the generation method should follow the characterizing definition.

(H) *Pareto and Weibull*

The Pareto and Weibull distributions have nothing in common except for similar generation methods: they can both be generated using inverse cdf transformations. The Pareto with shape parameter α and location parameter w has the density

$$f(x) = \alpha w^\alpha x^{-\alpha-1} \quad \text{for } x > w.$$

The distribution function has a simple form $F(x) = (w/x)^\alpha$ for $x > w$; the inverse is just as simple,

$$F(x) = u = (w/x)^\alpha \iff u^{1/\alpha} = w/x \iff x = w/u^{1/\alpha}.$$

The density of the Weibull looks nastier, but its cdf has a very simple form:

$$F(y) = 1 - \exp[-|(y - \mu)/\sigma|^\alpha],$$

where μ is a location parameter, σ a scale parameter, and α a shape parameter. If Z has the standard exponential distribution, then $Y = \mu + \sigma Z^{1/\alpha}$ has this Weibull distribution. So the Weibull distribution can be generated by transforming an exponential deviate. In this way, the Weibull is a generalization of the exponential different from the gamma, using a power transformation instead of using the distribution of sums.

(I) *Multivariate Normal and t; Wishart*

As noted previously, characterizations are often the key to finding algorithms for generating random variables. While the multivariate normal has so many characterizations, two of the more fundamental results suffice. If the components x_i of the p-dimensional vector $\mathbf{x}$ are IID normal$(0, 1)$, then jointly $\mathbf{x} \sim \text{normal}_p(\mathbf{0}, \mathbf{I}_p)$. Any linear transformation $\mathbf{y} = \mathbf{Ax} + \mathbf{b}$ retains multivariate normality: $\mathbf{y} \sim \text{normal}_q(\mathbf{b}, \mathbf{AA}^T)$. So, in order to obtain a random vector $\mathbf{y} \sim \text{normal}_p(\boldsymbol{\mu}, \boldsymbol{\Sigma})$, begin by generating components x_i $(i = 1, \ldots, p)$ IID normal$(0, 1)$, and transform $\mathbf{y} = \mathbf{Ax} + \mathbf{b}$ with $\mathbf{b} = \boldsymbol{\mu}$ and $\mathbf{A}$ such that $\mathbf{AA}^T = \boldsymbol{\Sigma}$. The Cholesky decomposition presents the best method for determining $\mathbf{A}$. For if we factor the covariance matrix $\boldsymbol{\Sigma} = \mathbf{LL}^T$ and simply let $\mathbf{A} = \mathbf{L}$, then $\mathbf{y}$ will have covariance matrix $\boldsymbol{\Sigma}$. Since $\boldsymbol{\Sigma}$ must be nonnegative definite, a modification of Cholesky decomposition will work even if it is singular (recall Exercise 3.13).

The care just exercised for the normal is also important for the multivariate t. If $\mathbf{x}$ has the multivariate t distribution in p dimensions – with location vector $\boldsymbol{\mu}$, dispersion matrix $\boldsymbol{\Sigma}$, and k degrees of freedom, denoted $\mathrm{MV}t_p(\boldsymbol{\mu}, \boldsymbol{\Sigma}, k)$ – then marginally each component x_i has the univariate Student's t distribution; even so, the multivariate t cannot be generated in that manner. The multivariate t is characterized (see DeGroot 1970, p. 59) by the vector $\mathbf{x} = (\sqrt{k/Z})\mathbf{y}$, where $\mathbf{y} \sim \mathrm{normal}_p(\boldsymbol{\mu}, \boldsymbol{\Sigma})$ and independently $Z \sim \chi_k^2$, so that each component shares the same random scaling. Notice that, following the usual characterization of the univariate Student t, each component would have a different scale and the joint distribution would not be multivariate t. The method for generation then follows this characterization directly, by generating the multivariate normal vector $\mathbf{y}$ as well as a χ or χ^2 variable for the scaling.

The Wishart distribution has the following characterization. Let $\mathbf{x}^{(i)}$ $(i = 1, \ldots, n)$ be IID $\mathrm{normal}_p(\mathbf{0}, \boldsymbol{\Sigma})$ vectors; then the unnormalized sample covariance matrix

$$(n - 1)\mathbf{S} = \sum_{i=1}^{n}(\mathbf{x}^{(i)} - \bar{\mathbf{x}})(\mathbf{x}^{(i)} - \bar{\mathbf{x}})^{\mathrm{T}}$$

has the Wishart distribution with $n - 1$ degrees of freedom and dispersion matrix $\boldsymbol{\Sigma}$. Clearly the Wishart is a generalization of the chi-square but with a scale matrix $\boldsymbol{\Sigma}$. Following this characterization is certainly one route for generation, but the effort for generating grows substantially as the degrees of freedom grow large. The Bartlett (1933) decomposition provides a much faster route. Without loss of generality, let $\mathbf{W}$ have the Wishart distribution with $\boldsymbol{\Sigma} = \mathbf{I}_p$ and k degrees of freedom, and compute the Cholesky factor $\mathbf{L}$ so that $\mathbf{L}\mathbf{L}^{\mathrm{T}} = \mathbf{W}$. Then the $n(n + 1)/2$ components of $\mathbf{L}$ are independent random variables with

$$L_{ii} \sim \chi_{k+1-i} \quad \text{for } i = 1, \ldots, p$$

and

$$L_{ij} \sim \mathrm{normal}(0, 1) \quad \text{for } j = 1, \ldots, i - 1 \text{ and } i = 2, \ldots, p.$$

This method provided the motivation for Algorithm D1 for the chi distribution with a small setup cost because of the constantly changing shape parameter. To obtain the general form of the Wishart distribution, the transformation $\mathbf{A}\mathbf{W}\mathbf{A}^{\mathrm{T}}$ yields a Wishart-distributed matrix with the same degrees of freedom but with dispersion matrix $\mathbf{A}\mathbf{A}^{\mathrm{T}}$. Again, a Cholesky factorization $\boldsymbol{\Sigma} = \mathbf{A}\mathbf{A}^{\mathrm{T}}$ provides the means for a general form of the Wishart distribution. See also Smith and Hocking (1972).

11.4 General Methods for Discrete Distributions

All three of the general methods presented for generating from continuous distributions have discrete analogs. The ratio of uniforms should be the surprise, but again it leads to fast, simple algorithms. One theoretical point to be noted is that all discrete distributions can be viewed as distributions on the integers. Discrete distributions are probability measures on countable sets of points, and "countable" invokes a correspondence with the integers. All of the methods presented here, then, will consider the problem of generating a random variable with the support $\{1, 2, 3, \ldots\}$ and with probabilities $\{p_1, p_2, p_3, \ldots\}$, where in some circumstances one or many of these probabilities may be zero.

(A) *Discrete Inversion*

In the continuous case, the transformation $F^{-1}(U)$ could, theoretically, permit generation from any continuous distribution. The practical computation of such a function, however, prohibits its use in many cases. In the case of a discrete distribution, the cdf $F(x)$ is a step function, so if we define the inverse correctly then the same approach can be used. However, instead of trying to define the inverse of a step function, just consider the problem of generating an integer with a particular probability.

Define $q_1 = p_1$, $q_2 = p_1 + p_2$, and in general

$$q_j = q_{j-1} + p_j = \sum_{i=1}^{j} p_i \leq 1.$$

Now generate a uniform random variable U, and determine the random index J such that

$$q_{J-1} < U \leq q_J.$$

Such an index is unique, and J is a discrete random variable with the desired distribution, since

$$\Pr(J = j) = \Pr(q_{j-1} < U \leq q_j) = q_j - q_{j-1} = p_j.$$

This table lookup to find the right index can be done in a simple-minded fashion, either starting from $j = 1$ and incrementing or employing the discrete bisection search outlined in Exercise 8.7 (see the code **gdinv**). If the support of the distribution is the integers $\{1, 2, \ldots, n\}$, then the bisection search can determine J in only $O(\log n)$ operations.

The case of an infinite support creates problems when the cumulatives q_j get close to 1. So very near 1 and with p_i very small, either many q_j will be equal, suggesting that the corresponding probabilities are negligibly small, or some q_j may jump all the way to 1, which would make the remaining cases impossible. With neither outcome satisfactory, good numerical practice would dictate that the tail probabilities should be mapped near 0, not near 1 where only a few numbers are available to represent the difference. If the tail sums $r_j = 1 - q_j = \sum_{i=j+1}^{\infty} p_i$ were available, then the remaining problem would be to do the search over an infinite (or very large) number of indices j. This remains an unsurmountable problem in general, but it leads to an interesting algorithm in the case of the geometric distribution.

The probability function for the geometric distribution is given by $p_j = p^j(1 - p)$, $j = 0, 1, 2, \ldots$. Then the cumulatives are $q_j = 1 - p^{j+1}$ and the tail sums are $r_j = p^{j+1}$. Comparing a uniform random variable U to the list of tail sums, $r_{j-1} > U \geq r_j$ might be easier to view under a log transformation:

$$\log r_{j-1} = j \log p > \log U \geq (j + 1) \log p = \log r_j.$$

Dividing through by $\log p$ leaves a simple problem of computing the greatest integer:

$$j < \frac{\log U}{\log p} \leq j + 1.$$

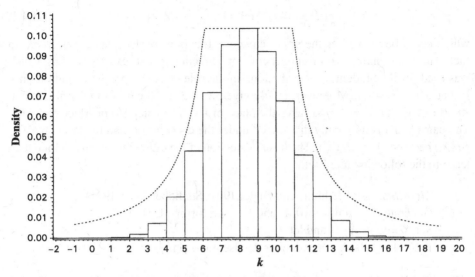

Figure 11.5. Discrete ratio of uniforms. Dashed line is upper envelope $g(x)$, with binomial probability function with $p = .40$ and $n = 20$.

Since the transformation $-\log U$ produces an exponential deviate, this method for generating geometric random variables merely rescales an exponential and takes the integer part $J = \lfloor \log U / \log p \rfloor$.

(B) *Acceptance/Rejection*

The acceptance/rejection method presented earlier for the continuous case is virtually unchanged in notation; the only difference is that the densities are now with respect to counting measure. In practice, however, the greater change is that few discrete distributions can be generated easily. The discrete uniform on $\{0, 1, \ldots, n-1\}$ can be easily generated by taking the greatest integer in a rescaled uniform $J = \lfloor nU \rfloor$. The geometric distribution can be generated by the algorithm just mentioned.

(C) *Ratio of Uniforms*

Here is the real surprise in the discrete analogs to the general methods. Just two steps simplify matters considerably, and the resulting algorithms are short, simple, fast, and not too difficult to follow. The first step is simply to make the target distribution continuous with a step function density constant on unit intervals, so that $f(x) = p_j$ when $j = \lfloor x \rfloor$. The second step, which also applies to the continuous case, is to view the ratio of uniforms method as strictly acceptance/rejection using a particular type of upper envelope. Recall that the enclosing region was usually inside of a box with vertices $(0, v_+^*)$, $(0, v_-^*)$, $(1, v_+^*)$, $(1, v_-^*)$ and that often the distribution was relocated. Suppose for simplicity that $v_+^* = 1$ and $v_-^* = -1$, and consider the distribution of $X = a + sV/U$, where the pair (U, V) are uniformly distributed within the box. Then X has the density called the "table mountain hat" (see Figure 11.5),

$$g(x) = (4s)^{-1} \min(1, s^2/(x - a)^2), \tag{11.4.1}$$

which could be viewed as the upper envelope function for acceptance/rejection. In fact, with $a = 0$ and $s = 1$, this upper envelope function $g(x)$ is exactly (11.3.6), which was used for the Student's t distribution. In the role of envelope, the condition on g is that $\beta f(x) \le g(x)$. Moreover, $U^2/4s$ given $X = x$ has the uniform distribution on $(0, g(x))$, so that $Y = U^2/4s$ takes the place of $Ug(X)$ in step (3) of Algorithm AR1. The pair (X, Y) is uniformly distributed under the curve $g(x)$, and the test $Ug(X) \le \beta f(X)$ becomes $Y \le \beta f(X)$. The discrete version of the ratio of uniforms method then leads to the following algorithm.

> *Algorithm DRU* (Ahrens and Dieter 1991; Stadlober 1989, 1991)
> (1) Generate $U \sim \text{uniform}(0, 1)$ and $V \sim \text{uniform}(-1, 1)$.
> (2) Set $X = a + sV/U$ and let $J = \lfloor X \rfloor$.
> (3) If $U^2/4s \le \beta f(X)$ then deliver J; else go to (1).

Here the constants a, s, and β are chosen to satisfy the envelope criterion $\beta f(x) \le g(x)$ as efficiently as possible – that is, β near 1. If the envelope bound is effective at the peak, where $g(x)$ is flat, then $\beta f_{\max} = (4s)^{-1}$, so $\beta = (4sf_{\max})^{-1}$ and the comparison in step (3) takes the form

> (3) If $U^2 \le f(X)/f_{\max}$ then deliver J; else go to (1).

As before, upper and lower bounds lead to quick accept/reject steps to speed up the algorithm. As in the continuous case, the ratio of uniforms method leads to simple algorithms that are competitively fast for discrete distributions, such as the binomial, Poisson, and hypergeometric.

(D) *Walker's Alias Method*

As previously noted, few discrete distributions can be generated easily, with the discrete uniform as one exception. Walker's method utilizes the discrete uniform in a greedy/borrowing scheme. Suppose the support for the target distribution $\{p_j\}$ is the integers $\{1, 2, 3, \ldots, n\}$. If we simply generated a discrete uniform random variable J on these n integers, then $p_j \ge 1/n$ for some j and $p_j < 1/n$ for other j. Some have too much probability, others not enough. Walker's method is to construct for each oversupplied ($p_j \le 1/n$) index j an alias a_j so that the excess on j is given to the alias. The mathematical foundation is a theorem stating that every finite discrete distribution can be written as an equiprobable mixture of 2-point distributions. Each 2-point distribution puts probability q_j on j and the remainder on an alias a_j. The algorithm is lightning fast, but it requires setup to construct the tables of probabilities and aliases $\{q_j, a_j\}$.

> *Algorithm Alias* (Walker 1977)
> (1) Generate $J \sim \text{discrete uniform}(1, n)$.
> (2) Generate $U \sim \text{uniform}(0, 1)$.
> (3) If $U \le q_j$ then deliver J; else deliver the alias a_J.

Table 11.1. *Probabilities and alias list from
Walker's method for the
binomial$(5, .4)$ distribution*

j	q_j	a_j	p_j
1	.4666	2	$.0778 = (.4666)/6$
2	1.0000	0	$.2592 = (1 + .5334 + .0218)/6$
3	.9782	2	$.3456 = (.9782 + .1568 + .9386)/6$
4	.8432	3	$.2304 = (.8432 + .5392)/6$
5	.4608	4	$.0768 = (.4608)/6$
6	.0614	3	$.0102 = (.0614)/6$

Steps (1) and (2) suggest a "reusing" of uniforms that has been avoided until now. The usual way of generating a discrete uniform is $J = 1 + \lfloor nU \rfloor$, but the remainder is uniformly distributed on $(0, 1)$. This suggests the following replacement steps.

(1) Generate $V \sim$ uniform$(0, 1)$ and multiply $W = nV$.
(2) Compute the integer part $J = 1 + \lfloor W \rfloor$ and the fraction $U = J - W$.

The algorithm given by Walker to construct the tables $\{q_j, a_j\}$ is frightfully and unnecessarily slow, taking $O(n^3)$. A faster setup procedure by Kronmal and Peterson (1979) takes only $O(n)$ but requires a bit more storage. The procedure is conceptually simple: give the excess to the needy.

Algorithm ASU (Alias Setup) (Kronmal and Peterson 1979)
(1) Initialize $q_i = np_i$, $i = 1, 2, \ldots, n$.
(2) Create two lists, $N = \{i : q_i \geq 1\}$ (needy) and $E = \{i : q_i < 1\}$ (excess).
(3) Repeat until E is empty:
    (a) Choose an element k of N and j of E.
    (b) Set alias for j: $a_j = k$ and remove j from the list E.
    (c) Adjust the probability: $q_k = q_k - (1 - q_j)$.
    (d) If $q_k < 1$ then switch k from list N to list E.

At every repetition of step (3), an element is deleted from one of the two lists. This algorithm with the two lists is easy to implement even in Fortran (see the code **walkst**). Table 11.1 is from the implementation in the code **walker** for the binomial$(5, .4)$ distribution; it shows the relationships among the two sets of probabilities p_j and q_j and the alias list a_j. Notice than the three needy $\{2, 3, 4\}$ take from the three excess $\{1, 5, 6\}$ and that one cell (2) has $q_2 = 1$ and no alias.

11.5 Algorithms for Discrete Distributions

With the exception of the geometric and negative binomial, the best (simple and fast) algorithms for the most popular distributions are discrete ratio of uniforms algorithms. In the three cases outlined in this section – binomial, Poisson, and hypergeometric – the algorithms require the computation of $\gamma(k) = \log \Gamma(k+1) = \log k!$. The best approach is write a separate routine for $\gamma(k)$. For smaller values of k, table $\gamma(k)$; for larger values, the use of the quickly converging Stirling's formula reduces the effort to little more than the computation of a log, since

$$\gamma(k) = \log \sqrt{2\pi} + (k+1/2)\log k - k$$
$$+ (12k)^{-1} - (360k^3)^{-1} + (1260k^5)^{-1} - (1680k^7)^{-1} + \cdots \quad (11.5.1)$$

(see Exercise 11.26).

The discussion of accuracy will be postponed to Section 11.6, but there is one issue peculiar to these problems. In most of these distributions, computing the probabilities for values in the tails is quite difficult – facing either a long series of multiplications (with its rounding error) or cancellation in the logs. Since these probabilities drop to zero quickly, the distribution should be cut off before the rounding or cancellation becomes serious. Stadlober (1989, 1991) and Ahrens and Dieter (1991) discussed this problem for the discrete ratio of uniforms algorithms.

(A) *Geometric and Negative Binomial*

The algorithm given previously for the geometric distribution, $J = \lfloor \log U / \log p \rfloor$, is certainly difficult to beat for speed and simplicity. However, recognizing that $-\log U$ generates an exponential deviate would open the door for using another method for the exponential to create Y, and then $J = \lfloor -Y / \log p \rfloor$ would give an equivalent result.

The usual characterization of the negative binomial distribution is the number of failures until k successes. Because the geometric gives the number of failures until the first success, summing k independent geometric random variables will suffice. For most applications, k is small and there is no need for a more complicated algorithm. However, for k large, consider the following result. Let $X \sim \text{Gamma}(\alpha, \beta)$, and let $J \mid X = x \sim \text{Poisson}(x)$; then, marginally, J has the negative binomial distribution. The joint density of X and J is

$$(\beta^{-\alpha}/\Gamma(\alpha))x^{\alpha-1}e^{-x/\beta} \times e^{-x}x^j/j!,$$

so that integrating out x gives

$$\frac{\beta^{-\alpha}\Gamma(j+\alpha)}{j!\,\Gamma(\alpha)}\left(1+\frac{1}{\beta}\right)^{-(j+\alpha)} = \binom{j+\alpha-1}{j}\left(\frac{\beta}{1+\beta}\right)^j\left(\frac{1}{1+\beta}\right)^{\alpha};$$

this is the probability of j failures until α successes, where $\text{Pr}(\text{success}) = 1/(1+\beta)$.

(B) *Binomial*

One very simple algorithm for the binomial (n, p) distribution is to mimic n Bernoulli trials: generate $U_1, U_2, \ldots, U_n$ IID uniform $(0, 1)$ random variables, and let J be the number that are less than the success probability p. Obviously this method becomes very slow as n grows large. A second simple algorithm for the binomial is discrete inversion. This method will remain effective for large n as long as np remains relatively small. If the setup effort is to be made to table the probabilities p_j and cumulatives

q_j, the same effort could be put to create the alias and probability tables for Walker's alias method, which would run much faster. As a result, the discrete inversion is only practical in a non-setup mode, and then only for np small.

For the general case, the discrete ratio of uniforms method leads to a relatively simple and fast algorithm. The keys to the general algorithm DRU are the constants a, s, and β, which enforce the envelope inequality $\beta f(x) \leq g(x)$. With the maximum of $f(x)$ occurring at $x = m \equiv \lfloor (n + 1)p \rfloor$, the envelope bound is effective there, although the tail comes into play with the scale factor s. The efficiency of the algorithm in terms of the expected number of trials $\beta^{-1} = 4sf(m)$ must be traded off with satisfying the envelope inequality. Numerical experimentation has led to the following simple approximation for s:

$$s(n, p) = c_1\sqrt{np(1 - p) + 1/2} + c_2, \tag{11.5.2}$$

where $c_1 = \sqrt{2/e}$ and $c_2 = 3/2 - \sqrt{3/e}$. The best value for the center point a is near the mean of the distribution, $a = np + 1/2$. The main comparison (3) should be written in terms of logarithms:

$$2 \log U \leq \log f(J)/f(m) = \gamma(m) + \gamma(n - m) - \gamma(J) - \gamma(n - J)$$
$$+ (J - m)\log(p/(1 - p)), \tag{11.5.3}$$

where the right-hand side is the variable T in the algorithm. Upper and lower bounds on $2 \log u$ give quick-accept/reject bounds:

$$u - 1/u \leq 2\log u \leq -3 + 4u - u^2 \tag{11.5.4}$$

(see Exercise 11.28), and the following algorithm can now be presented.

> *Algorithm BRUs* (Stadlober, simplified, $p \leq 1/2$) (**gbrus**)
> (0) Initialize $a = np + 1/2$, take $s(n, p)$ from (11.5.2), $r = \log(p/(1 - p))$, $g = \gamma(m) + \gamma(n - m)$.
> (1) Generate $U \sim \text{uniform}(0, 1)$ and $V \sim \text{uniform}(-1, 1)$.
> (2a) Set $X = a + sV/U$ and let $J = \lfloor X \rfloor$.
> (2b) $T = (J - m)r + g - \gamma(J) - \gamma(n - J)$.
> (3a) (Quick accept) If $U(4 - U) - 3 \leq T$ then deliver J.
> (3b) (Quick reject) If $U(U - T) > 1$ then go to (1).
> (3c) If $2 \log U \leq T$ then deliver J; else go to (1).

(C) *Poisson*

The Poisson process provides a convenient characterization of the Poisson distribution. Shortcuts to this characterization lead to an efficient algorithm for moderate values of the mean of the Poisson distribution. For large values of the mean parameter, however, this algorithm slows and once again a discrete ratio of uniforms method produces a faster algorithm.

In the Poisson process, the inter-arrival times are independent exponential random variables, and the number of arrivals in the time interval $[0, T]$ follows the Poisson distribution with mean parameter T. If the exponentials have mean 1, then the probability of no arrivals in the interval $[0, T]$ is the same as the first exponential deviate exceeding T and hence

$$\Pr(0 \text{ arrivals in } [0, T]) = p_T(0) = e^{-T}.$$

Then $p_T(j)$, the probability of j arrivals in $[0, T]$, follows the recursion

$$p_T(j) = \int_0^T \Pr(j - 1 \text{ arrivals in } [s, T]) e^{-s} \, ds = \int_0^\infty e^{-s} p_{T-s}(j - 1) \, ds,$$

since the time S of the first arrival has the density e^{-s}. Posing the Poisson formula

$$p_T(j) = e^{-T} T^j / j!,$$

which holds for $j = 0$, the recursion proof hinges on the step

$$e^{-T} \frac{T^j}{j!} = \int_0^T e^{-s} e^{-(T-s)} \frac{(T - s)^{j-1}}{(j - 1)!} \, ds.$$

Following this characterization, the algorithm suggests generating independent exponential random variables Y_i and stopping when $Y_1 + Y_2 + \cdots + Y_{J+1} > T$. Since the exponentials can be generated easily by the transformation $Y_i = -\log U_i$, the stopping rule in terms of the Y_i can be rewritten in terms of the U_i as

$$U_1 \times U_2 \times \cdots \times U_{J+1} < e^{-T},$$

and so the sum of exponentials is converted into a product of uniforms.

> *Algorithm C1*
> (0) Initialize $c = e^{-T}$.
> (1) Set $J = 0$ and $p = 1$.
> (2) Increment $J = J + 1$, generate $U \sim \text{uniform}(0, 1)$, and multiply $p = p * U$.
> (3) If $p \geq c$ then go to (1); else deliver $J = J - 1$.

Since the expected number of uniforms is one greater than the mean parameter, this algorithm becomes very inefficient when that mean grows large. Many algorithms have been proposed over the years for the Poisson, and most are long and very complicated in order to retain efficiency as the mean parameter grows large. The ratio of uniforms algorithm for the Poisson again has a bounded execution time as the parameter grows large, and it is simpler than most.

The ratio of uniforms algorithm given here for the Poisson distribution follows the general form DRU. The maximum of the probability function $p_\mu(j)$ occurs at $j = m = \lfloor \mu \rfloor$. The best simple centering parameter is $a = \mu + 1/2$, and the scale parameter s follows the same functional form as with the binomial (11.5.2) since the variance of the Poisson is also μ:

$$s(\mu) = c_1 \sqrt{a} + c_2. \tag{11.5.5}$$

The main comparison can be written in terms of logarithms:

$$2 \log U < \log f(x)/f(m) = (k - m) \log \mu + \gamma(m) - \gamma(k), \tag{11.5.6}$$

where $k = \lfloor x \rfloor$, and upper and lower bounds are used as in (11.5.4) for quick-accept/reject steps. The right-hand side of (11.5.6) is T in the following algorithm.

Algorithm C2 (Ahrens and Dieter 1991; Stadlober 1989, simplified) (**gprua**)

(0) Initialize $a = \mu + 1/2$, take $s(\mu)$ from (11.5.5), $g = \log \mu$, $m = \lfloor \mu \rfloor$, $q = mg - \gamma(m)$.

(1) Generate $U \sim \text{uniform}(0, 1)$ and $V \sim \text{uniform}(-1, 1)$, and set $X = a + sV/U$.

(2) If $X < 0$ then go to (1); else $J = \lfloor X \rfloor$.

(3) Set $T = Kg - \gamma(K) - q$.

(4) (Quick accept) If $T \geq U(4 - U) - 3$ then deliver J.

(5) (Quick reject) If $U(U - T) \geq 1$ then go to (1).

(6) If $2 \log U \leq T$ then deliver J; else go to (1).

(D) *Hypergeometric*

The hypergeometric distribution arises in sampling without replacement, and this characterization leads to a simple algorithm related to the sampling algorithm B2 in Section 10.6. With the hypergeometric, the random variable J is the number of red balls selected out of a sample of n from an urn with N total balls, of which M are red. As before, as n and N grow large, the simple characterizing algorithm performs poorly, and a ratio of uniforms method can handle the general case.

Simple sampling without replacement suggests the following scheme: draw the first ball from the urn with probability $p = M/N$. If this first ball is red, set $J = 1$ and reset for the new situation with $n_{\text{new}} = n - 1$, $N_{\text{new}} = N - 1$, and $M_{\text{new}} = M - 1$; otherwise, only n and N are updated and J is still zero.

Algorithm D1 (Hypergeometric by Sampling)

(0) Initialize $N_{\text{cur}} = N$, $M_{\text{cur}} = M$, $n_{\text{cur}} = n$, $J = 0$.

(1) Generate $U \sim \text{uniform}(0, 1)$. If $U > M_{\text{cur}}/N_{\text{cur}}$ then go to (3) (not a red ball).

(2) (Get red ball) Increment $J = J + 1$ and update $M_{\text{cur}} = M_{\text{cur}} - 1$. If $M_{\text{cur}} = 0$ then deliver J.

(3) Update $N_{\text{cur}} = N_{\text{cur}} - 1$ and $n_{\text{cur}} = n_{\text{cur}} - 1$.

(4) If $n_{\text{cur}} = 0$ then deliver J; else go to (1).

The ratio of uniforms algorithm approaches the problem as a discrete distribution with probability function

$$p_j = \frac{\binom{M}{j}\binom{N-M}{n-j}}{\binom{N}{n}} \quad \text{for}\quad \max(0, n - N + M) \leq j \leq \min(n, M). \qquad (11.5.7)$$

Notice that, without loss of generality, the parameter range can be reduced (see Exercises 11.30 and 11.31) to $n \leq N/2$ and $M \leq N/2$. The theory requires that the mean $\mu = nM/N$ be at least 1. Since contrary cases suggest another algorithm (see Exercise 11.32), this condition is not very restrictive. The algorithm again follows the same discrete ratio of uniforms format DRU. The centering point again is $a = \mu + 1/2$, and the scale factor s again follows the same variance expression:

$$s(n, N, M) = c_1\sqrt{\text{variance}(J) + 1/2} + c_2, \qquad (11.5.8)$$

with c_1 and c_2 as before. The mode occurs at $m = \lfloor(n+1)(M+1)/(N+2)\rfloor$, and the main comparison step takes the form $2\log U < \log p_j/p_m$, where the right-hand side can be expressed as

$$\gamma(m) + \gamma(M-m) + \gamma(n-m) + \gamma(N-M-n+m)$$
$$- \gamma(j) - \gamma(M-j) - \gamma(n-j) - \gamma(N-M-n+j), \quad (11.5.9)$$

for which tables of the function $\gamma(k)$ are essential.

   Algorithm D2 (Stadlober 1989) $(nM > N)$ **(ghrua)**
(0) Initialize $p = M/N$, $q = 1 - p$, $a = np + 1/2$,

$$\sigma = \sqrt{(N-n)npq/(N-1)} + 1/2,$$

$s = c_1\sigma + c_2$ from (11.5.8), $m = \lfloor(n+1)(M+1)/(N+2)\rfloor$, and

$$g = \gamma(m) + \gamma(M-k) + \gamma(n-m) + \gamma(N-M-n+m).$$

(1) Generate $U \sim \text{uniform}(0,1)$ and $V \sim \text{uniform}(-1,1)$, and set $X = a + sV/U$.
(2) If $X < 0$ then go to (1); else set $J = \lfloor X\rfloor$.
(3) $T = g - \gamma(J) - \gamma(M-J) - \gamma(n-J) - \gamma(N-M-n+J)$.
(4) If $U(4-U) - 3 \le T$ then deliver J.
(5) If $U(U-T) \ge 1$ then go to (1).
(6) If $2\log U \le T$ then deliver J; else go to (1).

Stadlober also presented another algorithm (HRUE), which has a more complicated formula for s and is a bit faster.

11.6   Other Randomizations

Generating the uniform distribution is the fundamental problem in Monte Carlo. Once that obstacle is overcome, generating from the various distributions appears rather straightforward. But before closing, a few other problems remain that are best described as randomizations. For problems in the design of experiments, these randomizations are straightforward. For example, to obtain a random Latin square design, merely take a standard Latin square and permute the treatment, row, and column labels. The fundamental randomizations are then the random permutation and the random sampling. An additional case – a random contingency table – is interesting in its own right and will illustrate the kind of thinking required to handle similar problems.

(A)   *Random Permutations*

There are two easy methods for generating a random permutation of the integers 1 to n. If a sorting routine is available that will sort on one variable and carry another variable along for the ride, then the following method is a breeze to use.

Algorithm A1 (Permutation by Sorting)
(1) For $i = 1, \ldots, n$, generate $U_i \sim \text{uniform}(0, 1)$ and let $A_i = i$.
(2) Sort the pairs (U_i, A_i) on U_i with A_i in parallel.

The sorted pairs (U_i, A_i) give the order statistics from an IID sample of uniforms, and the A_i are the anti-ranks, which are a random permutation under the IID assumption. The data management commands of higher-level statistical languages, such as SAS, perform such sorting routinely. The SAS code would be simply

```
DATA ONE ;
   SEED=5151917 ;
   DO A=1 TO N ;
   U=RANUNI(SEED) ;
   OUTPUT ;
   END ;
RUN ;
PROC SORT DATA=ONE ;
   BY U ;
RUN ;
```

and the variable A would have a random ordering of the indices 1 to n. The second method is not any more complicated and follows a method suggestive of random sampling.

Algorithm A2 (Permutation by Shuffling)
(1) Initialize $A_i = i$, $i = 1, \ldots, n$.
(2) For $i = 1, \ldots, n$:
    (a) Generate $J \sim \text{discrete uniform}(i, n)$.
    (b) Exchange A_i with A_J.

For the analogy to sampling without replacement, consider a row of numbered balls A_i in order. At the first step, select a ball at random and, to make room for it in the first position, exchange places with the first ball. At the second step, now only select from the balls in positions 2 through n. At the start of step i, the first $i - 1$ positions have balls already selected, and the last $n - i$ balls remain in the pool.

(B) *Random Sampling*

In taking a random sample from a population, the application may dictate what methods may be possible. Whereas small problems will be relatively easy, difficult problems can arise in problems that are straightforward but very large. In large problems, usually the objective is to sample records from a long computer tape. Since tape can only be read from start to finish, a method for sequential sampling is required. For modest problems, a sample of indices can be created ahead of time; in the reservoir sampling problem – when the population size is unknown initially – one pass is used to construct the indices and a second to pull off the desired records.

The first method considered is the simplest method for constructing a sample of size k of the integers 1 to n. Since the first k indices from a random permutation would suffice, the shuffling scheme Algorithm A2 can be run and stopped after k steps.

Algorithm B1 (Sampling by a Stopped Shuffle)
(1) Initialize $A_i = i$, $i = 1, \ldots, n$.
(2) For $i = 1, \ldots, k$:
 (a) Generate $J \sim$ discrete uniform(i, n).
 (b) Exchange A_i with A_J.

Notice that, for sequential sampling, this approach would require a sorting of the resulting indices $\{A_i, i = 1, \ldots, k\}$.

The second method is the standard sequential sampling method, which was suggested by the hypergeometric algorithm D1. This method requires only a single pass through the list of records, but it requires both k and n to be known.

Algorithm B2 (Standard Sequential Sampling)
(0) Initialize $j = k$.
(1) For $i = 1, \ldots, n$:
 (a) Generate $U \sim$ uniform$(0, 1)$.
 (b) If $U \le j/(n - i + 1)$ then select i and set $j = j - 1$.

For many problems, Algorithm B2 is unbeatable. A higher-level language poses little challenge, as you can see from the SAS code for the DATA step in sampling 200 individuals from a population of 1000.

```
DATA SAMPLE ;
  RETAIN I 0 J 200 ;
  SET POPULATION ;
  SEED=5151917 ;
  I=I+1 ;
  IF( RANUNI(SEED) < J / (1000-I+1) ) THEN DO ;
    OUTPUT ;
    J=J-1 ;
                                END ;
  RUN ;
```

A variant of the sequential sampling problem uses a known number k of samples to be taken with the size n of the population left unknown. This situation arises not only when the number of available records is unknown but also in the frequent case where a subpopulation is to be sampled. As a record is read (off tape), the candidacy in the subpopulation is determined. Moreover, in some circumstances, the space (on disk) available to hold a subset of the population may be much larger than the number k to be taken but much smaller than the entire population. These circumstances suggest the use of a technique known as *reservoir sampling*. The simple version skips certain details that may be important in some applications.

Algorithm B3 (Idealized Reservoir Sampling)
(1) (Initialize table) For $i = 1, \ldots, k$, generate $U_i \sim$ uniform$(0, 1)$ and form pairs (i, U_i).
(2) Find $U_m = \min U_i$.
(3) (Go through remainder of file) For $i = (k + 1)$ to end-of-file:
   (a) Generate U_i.
   (b) If $U_i > U_m$ then replace (m, U_m) in list with (i, U_i) and find new minimum index m.

At the end of the file, the uniforms are the k largest order statistics and the corresponding indices are a random sample of size k from the integers 1 to n. In this simplified form, the probability aspects are clear. However, the problems in applications are clearer in a related form where a reservoir is created.

Algorithm B4 (Applied Reservoir Sampling)
(1) (Initialize table) For $i = 1, \ldots, k$, set indices $A_i = i$ $(i = 1, \ldots, k)$ and set reservoir length $m = k$.
(2) (Go through remainder of file) For $i = (k + 1)$ to end-of-file:
   (a) Generate $J \sim$ discrete uniform$(1, i)$.
   (b) If $J \leq k$ then (output record i) increment reservoir length $m = m + 1$ and replace $A_J = m$; else skip record i.
(3) Sort indices A_i, $i = 1, \ldots, k$.
(4) (Reservoir pass) Select records from sorted index list A_i from reservoir.

Knuth (1997) attributed this algorithm to Alan G. Waterman. In its probability aspects, this algorithm resembles the shuffling algorithms A2 and B1 (but see Exercise 11.34). In Algorithm B4, records are explicitly placed in the reservoir, which acts as a larger sample from the entire population. In practice, records would be taken from tape in step (2b) and put on disk, later to be resampled with the short list in step (4).

All of these sampling algorithms (except for the stopped shuffle, Algorithm B1) require a uniform deviate for every member of the population. Another approach to sampling without replacement is to sample with replacement and oversample so there will be enough. The efficiencies of oversampling techniques rely on (a) the data structures available to check for previous membership if only one pass is taken or (b) analysis of the number to be oversampled if the duplicates are discarded afterwards. Operationally, the simplest route is to oversample, sort, and make a pass to delete duplicates and count extras. Then sampling the extras for deletion leaves the correct sample size. For further analysis, see Devroye (1986, pp. 635ff). For comparisons of implementation details, see Vitter (1987).

(C)   *Random Contingency Tables*

One of the most important problems in statistics is the analysis of $r \times c$ contingency tables, usually testing for independence. While Fisher's exact test is the most commonly used statistic in the 2×2 table, a variety of test statistics have been proposed.

A more important factor, however, is that only approximate null distributions are commonly available; rarely are any exact null distributions known. One computationally intensive approach for finding exact critical values or p-values would be to generate all realizations of the data. In the case of an $r \times c$ contingency table, the number of cases grows very large very quickly. Another route would be to find efficient exact counting algorithms, although the type of data and statistic limit the possibilities severely. A third route is to use Monte Carlo to estimate the exact null distribution by generating a sample of realizations of the data; this approach is not limited by the choice of a statistic. For an $r \times c$ contingency table, this means generating all tables having fixed marginals. Though imposing, the task is easier than you think.

Let R_i denote the row totals and C_j the column totals, so we have $N = \sum R_i = \sum C_j$ observations. The method follows a ball-and-urn scheme with labeled balls.

> *Algorithm C1* (Random Contingency Table) (Agresti, Wackerly, and Boyett 1979)
> (1) Fill an array A with R_1 elements equal to 1, R_2 elements equal to 2, ..., R_r elements equal to r.
> (2) Randomly permute all the elements in the array A.
> (3) Take the first C_1 elements of A for column 1, the next C_2 elements for column 2, ..., and fill the row that matches the array label.

Let us restate the algorithm more formally.

> *Algorithm C1* (Restated)
> (1) $t = 0$.
> (2) For $i = 1, \ldots, r$ do
>   For $k = 1, \ldots, R_i$ do $t = t + 1$, $A(t) = i$.
> (3) Permute the elements of A.
> (4) Initialize $N_{ij} = 0$ for $i = 1, \ldots, r$ and $j = 1, \ldots, c$.
> (5) $t = 0$.
> (6) For $j = 1, \ldots, c$ do
>   For $k = 1, \ldots, C_j$ do $t = t + 1$, $i = A(t)$, $N_{ij} = N_{ij} + 1$.

11.7 Accuracy in Random Number Generation

This discussion has been postponed a couple of times in order to gain some perspective on random number generation. From a naive viewpoint, accuracy problems can often be clubbed into submission by using double precision arithmetic. This route may solve some problems, but other problems are wished away and lie lurking to spring a trap. Proper numerical practice dictates finding where the traps lie and knowing when to worry. For problems in Monte Carlo, the goal is always the computation of some sort of integral, and the main problem is that a discrete set of floating point–representable numbers $\mathcal{F}$ is trying to approximate the continuous real line $\mathcal{R}$.

This discussion follows a paper by the author (Monahan 1985) and probes in a few different directions. The first question to be addressed is the best way to approximate a continuous distribution on a discrete, finite set $\mathcal{F}$. Next, once the ideal approxima-tion is posed, a useful measure of distance or error can suggest the discretization error faced in Monte Carlo integration. Since analysis quickly leads to intractable expres-sions, some general heuristic guidelines will be discussed.

Given our discussion of computer arithmetic in the second chapter, the best way to approximate a number x on the real line is to represent it with the closest value in the set of floating point numbers $\mathcal{F}$. In other words, round to the nearest number $\mathrm{fl}(x)$ that is a member of $\mathcal{F}$. For generating a continuous random variable X on the real line with cdf F, the best approximation (here called the "ideal" approximation) would be the discrete distribution F^*, which is the cdf of the discrete random variable $\mathrm{fl}(X)$. The ideal approximation can be achieved in some interesting cases. The order statistics from an ideal approximation F^* yield an ideal approximation for the order statistics of F. The exponential distribution can be generated ideally following a minor modifica-tion of the von Neumann algorithm (Monahan 1979). Obviously, the most important case is generating the uniform distribution ideally.

Whereas the interval $[0, 1]$ is fundamental in probability, the fundamental interval in base-b floating point arithmetic is $[1/b, 1]$, since all of the points in $\mathcal{F}$ in that inter-val are equally spaced. The points in $\mathcal{F}$ in the intervals $[b^{-j-1}, b^{-j}]$ are also equally spaced, and in order to generate the ideal uniform distribution, the interval $[0, 1]$ should be viewed as the union of intervals of the form $[b^{-j-1}, b^{-j}]$ for $j = 0, 1, \ldots, (E-1)$, where E is the limit of the exponent. The remaining interval is $[0, b^{-E}]$, for which only the endpoints are members of $\mathcal{F}$. The ideal approximation for the uniform distri-bution on the intervals $[b^{-j-1}, b^{-j}]$ has equal weight on the b^{d-1} interior points and half-weight on the endpoints, emulating the trapezoid integration rule. This distribu-tion can be obtained by generating a discrete uniform integer M on $[0, b^{d-1} - 1]$ and adding 1 with probability $1/2$, which is then relocated to the desired interval. To obtain the uniform distribution on $[0, 1]$, an index J to the intervals must be generated cor-rectly, that is, via a geometric distribution with probability $1/b$. When J exceeds the exponent range ($J \geq E$) then, with probability $1/2$, deliver 0 or b^{-E}. (Note that the soft underflow in the IEEE standard would affect this somewhat.)

Algorithm A (Ideal Uniform Distribution)
(1) Generate a random integer M on $[0, b^d - 1]$.
(2) With probability $1/2$, add 1 to M to get M^*.
(3) (Float) $W = (b^{d-1} + M^*)/b^d$.
(4) Generate geometric random variable J with probability $1/b$,

$$\Pr(J = j) = b^{-j}(1 - 1/b) \quad \text{for} \quad j = 0, 1, 2, \ldots.$$

(5) If $J < E$ then return $X = W * b^{-J}$; else with probability $\frac{1}{2}$ return $X = 0$ or $X = b^{-E}$.

Algorithm A differs from the usual route, $Y = M/b^d$, in two ways: normalization and centering. The usual practice is stochastically smaller than it should be and zeros out the new high-order digits uncovered by the normalization shift due to leading-zero digits.

Other measures can be proposed (see e.g. Exercise 11.36) to measure the discretization error, yet the distance between two cdfs,

$$e(F, G) = \int_{x_{-\infty}}^{x_\infty} |F(x) - G(x)| \, dx, \tag{11.7.1}$$

best captures the probability that is different and the distance to be moved to correct, where $x_{-\infty}$ and x_∞ are the smallest and largest elements in $\mathcal{F}$. The bias in integrating a function h can then be bounded by

$$\left| \int h(x) \, dF(x) - \int h(x) \, dG(x) \right| \le e(F, G) \sup |h'(x)| \tag{11.7.2}$$

if the function h is differentiable and vanishes for large x. Because floating point arithmetic follows $|\text{fl}(x) - x| \le U|x|$ for the machine unit $U = b^{1-d}/2$, the bias for an ideal approximation can be bounded by

$$\left| \int h(x) \, dF(x) - \int h(x) \, dF^*(x) \right| \le U \int |x h'(x^*)| \, dF(x), \tag{11.7.3}$$

where x^* lies between x and $\text{fl}(x)$. This expression suggests that the best place for the function h to misbehave is near the origin, where the floating point number system is most accurate.

The length of this chapter is in contrast to the naive approach – that the inverse cdf G^{-1} is the only route needed for generating random variables with cdf G. The analysis of accuracy from transformation methods faces two kinds of error. The first type of error is the approximation error of a nonarithmetic function. If $\hat{H}(x)$ approximates the transformation $H(x)$ with relative error w, then the error in the resulting distribution G is $e(G_H, G_{\hat{H}}) = w/(1 + w)$, and if the absolute error in $\hat{H}$ is w then $e(G_H, G_{\hat{H}}) = w$. The analysis of the discretization error is a bit more subtle because H is really mapping from $\mathcal{F}$ to $\mathcal{F}$, and the accuracy varies across the different points. For example, if $U \sim \text{uniform}(0, 1)$ then $X = 2U - 1 \sim \text{uniform}(-1, 1)$ with $H(u) = 2u - 1$. Mapping the many points near $u = 0$ into the few points near $x = -1$ is no cause for concern. However, the few points near $u = 1/2$ are mapped to the many points around $x = 0$ where $\mathcal{F}$ is most accurate. Consequently, if U followed the ideal approximation to the uniform $(0, 1)$ distribution, the error in $X = 2U - 1$ would be substantial. Clearly, attaching a random sign would be preferable. The two transformations for the exponential distribution carry this point further. Taking $-\log U$ maps the many points near the origin to the long tail of the exponential, which is proper. However, the few points near $u = 1$ are mapped to the many points near $x = 0$, which is quite inadequate since the mode of distribution is there. The other transformation, $-\log(1 - U)$, will (if properly computed) cover the region near the origin well, but it will fail to cover the long tail adequately. Since the von Neumann algorithm will generate the ideal approximation for the exponential distribution, this route should be taken if accuracy is a major concern.

In using other methods for generating random variables, a random variable obtained using acceptance/rejection can only be as accurate as the envelope distribution. The ratio of uniforms method, however, can be an improvement. The discretization takes the uniform distribution in a rectangle to a distribution on an irregular latticelike set, where many points in the (u, v)-plane can be mapped into any part of $\mathcal{F}$.

Using more accurate algorithms for generating random variables certainly slows down computations. Simply going to double precision will yield only a modest improvement. The more important problem is that of overflows, which are mostly the result of transformations hitting 0 or 1. Good numerical practice usually exploits the many points in $\mathcal{F}$ near the origin, and so transformations like $-\log U$ are commonly used. Although encountering $U = 0$ will lead to an error, the ideal algorithm will face this problem with a very low probability b^{-E}. Following the usual route hits zero with probability b^{-d}, and moving to double precision can only square this b^{-2d}. I believe it is worth the effort to generate the uniform distribution ideally, attaching a random sign to cover $(-1, 1)$. Most other problems do not warrant as much concern.

Programs and Demonstrations

gnbxml   *Box–Muller algorithm*
The Box–Muller algorithm for generating from the standard normal distribution is implemented in the function subprogram **gnbxml** and checked using Kolmogorov–Smirnov and Anderson–Darling goodness-of-fit statistics. An implementation of the Bratley–Fox–Schrage (1983) version of the Lewis–Goodman–Miller uniform generator is used as the source of uniforms. The normal distribution function is computed using **cdfn** and **cdfc** from Chapter 7; the log of the normal distribution function is computed using **alnphi**. Notice that only one (large) sample is taken.

gnpolr   *Marsaglia and Bray's polar method*
Marsaglia and Bray's algorithm is implemented in the function subprogram **gnpolr** and checked in the same manner as **gnbxml**.

gnrouo   *Ratio of uniforms method for normal, original version*
gnrouk   *Ratio of uniforms method for normal using Knuth's outer bounds*
gnroul   *Ratio of uniforms method for normal using Leva's improved bounds*
The ratio of uniforms method for the normal distribution is implemented in these three versions and checked in the same manner as **gnbxml**.

gevonn   *Von Neumann exponential algorithm*
The von Neumann algorithm for the exponential distribution is implemented as a function subprogram, using the Bratley–Fox–Schrage uniform generator (as with **gnbxml** and others) and checked using the Kolmogorov–Smirnov and Anderson–Darling goodness-of-fit statistics.

gttir   *Acceptance/rejection for Student's t distribution*
The acceptance/rejection method described as Algorithm C2 is implemented as the function subprogram **gttir** and checked using the Kolmogorov–Smirnov and Anderson–Darling goodness-of-fit statistics. The Student's *t* distribution function is computed using **ttail**.

gtrou   *Ratio of uniforms for Student's t distribution*
The ratio of uniforms method described as Algorithm C3 is implemented as the function subprogram **gtrou** and checked in the same manner as **gttir**.

ggchi   *Ratio of uniforms for chi, gamma, and chi-square distributions*
The ratio of uniforms method for the chi distribution described as Algorithm D1 is implemented as the function subprogram **gchirv** and checked using the Kolmogorov–Smirnov and Anderson–Darling goodness-of-fit statistics. The chi random variables are transformed to gamma deviate with unit scale, and the distribution function for the gamma is computed using the incomplete gamma codes **pgamma** and **qgamma**.

gdinv   *Discrete inversion*
The general discrete inversion algorithm described in Section 11.4 is demonstrated using several binomial distributions. The discrete bisection search is done using the function **ifind**. This implementation is checked using a chi-square goodness-of-fit test. Factorials and gamma function evaluations are computed using **slgamk**.

walker   *Walker's alias method*
Walker's alias method for finite discrete distributions is demonstrated for several binomial distributions. An implementation of the Kronmal and Peterson (1979) setup algorithm in **walkst** is used to compute the q_j and aliases a_j. This implementation is checked using the chi-square goodness-of-fit test.

gbrus   *Discrete ratio of uniforms for the binomial distribution*
Stadlober's discrete ratio of uniforms algorithm for the binomial distribution is implemented in the function subprogram **gbrus** and checked using the chi-square goodness-of-fit test. The function subprogram **slgamk** computes $\ln k!$ with a combination of tables and Stirling's approximation.

gprua   *Discrete ratio of uniforms for the Poisson distribution*
A simplified version of the discrete ratio of uniforms algorithm (described as Algorithm C2 in Section 11.5) for the Poisson distribution is implemented in the function subprogram **gprua** and checked using the chi-square goodness-of-fit test. The function subprogram **slgamk** computes $\ln k!$ with a combination of tables and Stirling's approximation.

ghrua   *Discrete ratio of uniforms for the hypergeometric distribution*
Stadlober's discrete ratio of uniforms algorithm (described as Algorithm D1 in Section 11.5) for the hypergeometric distribution is implemented in the function subprogram **ghrua** and checked using the chi-square goodness-of-fit test. The function subprogram **slgamk** computes $\ln k!$ with a combination of tables and Stirling's approximation.

Exercises

11.1   Using the uniform generator $x_{n+1} = 5^3 x_n \bmod 2^{13}$ (Kruskal 1969), compute pairs of normals via Algorithm A1 and plot the pairs. Do you find anything unusual?

11.2   *"Mox–Buller"*. Suppose we make a modification of the Box–Muller Algorithm A1 as follows.
   (1) Generate U, V independent uniform$(0, 1)$.
   (2) Deliver $X = \cos(2\pi U)\sqrt{-2\log V}$
      and $Y = \sin(2\pi V)\sqrt{-2\log U}$.

Find the marginal distributions of both X and Y; then generate and plot a sample from the joint distribution. Are X and Y uncorrelated?

11.3 In Algorithm A2, find the joint distribution of W and $U/\sqrt{W}$.

11.4 In Algorithm A3, restate the quick-accept bound $X^2 \leq 4(1 + \log c) - 4cU$ and determine the boundary and area of the quick-accept region of the (u, v)-plane. Show that this region has maximum area when $c = e^{1/4}$.

11.5 As in Exercise 11.4, restate the quick-reject bound $X^2 \geq 4/(cU) - (1 - \log c)$ and find the area as a function of c outside the region computed in that exercise but still inside the box with vertices $\left(0, \pm\sqrt{2/e}\right)$ and $\left(1, \pm\sqrt{2/e}\right)$. Does the maximum of this area occur at $c = e^{1.35}$?

11.6 Von Neumann's method for the exponential distribution has been extended in some interesting ways, two of which show some remarkable improvement in speed. In the first one (due to Marsaglia 1961), let M have the geometric distribution with parameter e^{-1}, $\Pr(M = m) = (1 - e^{-1})e^{-m}$, and let N have the Poisson distribution with zero removed: $\Pr(N = n) = 1/[n!(e - 1)]$. Show that $X = M + \min(U_1, \ldots, U_N)$ has the exponential distribution. Following this result, write an algorithm using inversion for the two discrete distributions and compare it to an implementation of the von Neumann algorithm. Sibuya (1962) generalized to M geometric with $\Pr(M = m) = (e^{\mu} - 1)/e^{\mu(m+1)}$ and well as N (with the zero removed) Poisson with parameter μ, $\Pr(N = n) = \mu^n/(e^{\mu} - 1)n!$. Show that this also will lead to X having the exponential distribution. Implement Sibuya's method with $\mu = \log 2$, so that the geometric is a shift count, and compare it to the other two.

11.7 Compare Algorithm C2 for the t distribution and its non-setup version with $d = 2e^{-1/2}$. Use two scenarios, one where α is constant and another where α changes with each call.

11.8 Write an acceptance/rejection algorithm for the t distribution using a Cauchy envelope and bounds (11.3.7). Compare setup and non-setup versions as in Exercise 11.7. Consider also the Devroye bound

$$\left(1 + \frac{x^2}{\alpha}\right)^{-(\alpha+1)/2} \leq \left(1 + \left(\frac{\alpha+1}{2\alpha}\right)x^2\right)^{-1}.$$

Prove this inequality and include it in your implementation of the Cauchy algorithm.

11.9 Verify that (11.3.8) gives the correct bounds for v_+^* and v_-^*, and give the limits as $\alpha \to 1$ and $\alpha \to \infty$. Where does v_+^* achieve its maximum?

11.10 Verify the bound (11.3.9).

11.11 Devise simpler bounds v_+^*, v_-^* (or use the maximum) and derive a non-setup version for Algorithm C3. Compare its performance.

11.12 Derive and verify Algorithm C5 for t_3. Find $\Pr(\text{accept})$.

11.13 Show that the distribution function for the Student's t distribution with three degrees of freedom is

$$F(x) = \frac{1}{\pi\sqrt{3}}\left[\frac{x}{2(1 + x^2/3)} + \sqrt{3}\tan^{-1}\left(\frac{x}{\sqrt{3}}\right)\right] + \frac{1}{2}.$$

11.14 Suppose we made an error in implementing step (2) of Algorithm C5 for t_3 by generating $V \sim \text{uniform}(-3/4, 3/4)$, forgetting the square root. Find the power of the Kolmogorov–Smirnov test for $N = 1000$ by simulating from the wrong distribution and testing goodness-of-fit using the distribution function of Exercise 11.13.

11.15 Derive the chi density in (11.3.11) as a transformation of a gamma random variable with density given by (11.3.10).

11.16 Find the normalization constant c_γ in the relocated chi density given by (11.3.12). Find the limits of c_γ as $\gamma \to 1$ and $\gamma \to \infty$.

11.17 Compare the performance of the t algorithms C2 and C3 with an algorithm based on the characterization of a normal divided by a χ, using Algorithm D1 to generate χs.

11.18 Let U and V be independent uniform$(0, 1)$ random variables. What is the distribution of $\log(U/(1 - V))$? Are you surprised?

11.19 Show that, if X and Y are independent exponential random variables, then $X - Y$ has the Laplace distribution.

11.20 Generate random variables using the code

```
Y=LOG( RAN(1)/(1.-RAN(1)) )
```

and test whether the output is logistic or Laplace.

11.21 Derive the density for the beta and Dirichlet, given by (11.3.14) and (11.3.15), arising from the characterization of a gamma random variable U divided by a sum of gammas.

11.22 The characterization of the noncentral chi-square from $Q = \sum Z_i^2$, where $Z_i \sim$ normal(μ_i, σ^2), suggests another route. Derive an algorithm and compare its performance with the Poisson mixed chi-square approach suggested in the text.

11.23 Given the characterizations of both the F and beta distributions in terms of gamma random variables, find the relationship between the F and beta.

11.24 Show directly that, if Y has the standard exponential distribution, then $J = \lfloor \lambda Y \rfloor$ has the geometric distribution.

11.25 For the binomial distribution with $n = 4$ and $p = 1/4$, compute the probabilities $\{q_j\}$ and aliases $\{a_j\}$ for Walker's alias method using Algorithm ASU.

11.26 Write a routine to compute $\gamma(k) = \log k!$ using (11.5.1) with error less than 10^{-6}. Reduce the computations by tabling the values of $\gamma(k)$ for small k.

11.27 (Ahrens and Dieter 1974) For generating the binomial, write the probability p in its binary expansion $p = .p_1 p_2 \cdots_{\text{base } 2} = \sum_{i=1}^{\infty} p_i 2^{-i}$. Consider the following algorithm.
   Algorithm CO (Count Ones)
   (0) Initialize $m = n$, $J = 0$, $i = 0$.
   (1) Increment $i = i + 1$, and generate $k \sim$ binomial$(m, 1/2)$.
   (2) If $p_j = 1$ then $m = k$; else $J = J + k$ and $m = m - k$.
   (3) If $m = 0$ then deliver J; else go to (1).
   Show that this generates the binomial distribution. (This algorithm will fly if the computer has a machine instruction to add the number of ones in a string of random bits of length m that is binomial$(m, 1/2)$. If your computer has such a machine instruction, you might consider comparing this algorithm's performance with **gbrus**.)

11.28 Verify the log inequalities in (11.5.4).

11.29 Write a routine to generate the binomial$(4, 1/4)$ distribution using inversion, and compare its performance with an implementation of Walker's method from Exercise 11.25.

11.30 Let $p(j \mid M, N, n)$ be the hypergeometric probability function given in (11.5.7). Verify the following relationships:

$$
\begin{aligned}
p(j|M, N, n) &= p(j \mid n, N, M) \\
&= p(n - j \mid N, N - M, n) \\
&= p(M - j \mid N, M, N - n) \\
&= p(n - N + M + j \mid N, N - M, N - n).
\end{aligned}
$$

11.31 Show how the formulas in Exercise 11.30 can be used to reduce the parameter range to $n \leq N/2$ and $M \leq N/2$.

11.32 If the hypergeometric mean is less than 1, discuss alternative methods for generation. (*Hint:* Consider inversion with probabilities computed recursively from 0.)

11.33 In Algorithm B3 for sampling, the minimum index m must be recomputed every time $U_i > U_m$. How much work will this entail?

11.34 In Algorithm B4 for sampling, compute for each record i the probability that it will remain in the sample.

11.35 In Algorithm B4 for sampling, what is the expected length of the reservoir?

11.36 For a continuous distribution function F, what discrete distribution G on $\mathcal{F}$ minimizes the Kolmogorov–Smirnov distance $\sup_x |F(x) - G(x)|$?

11.37 For $e(F, G)$ defined by (11.7.1), find a bound for the ideal approximation F^* in terms of $E\{|X|\}$.

11.38 Let $Y = M/b^d$, where $M \sim$ discrete uniform$[0, b^d - 1]$. Find the mean and variance of Y. Find the error from (11.7.1) from the uniform$(0, 1)$ distribution.

11.39 For the output of Algorithm A in Section 11.7, find its mean and variance.

11.40 Write an algorithm for generating from the density proportional to $r^d e^{-r}(1 + e^{-r})^{-2}$ using either acceptance/rejection or ratio of uniforms.

11.41 Let **A** be a positive definite, symmetric, Toeplitz matrix. Discuss how to exploit the Levinson-Durbin algorithm (Section 4.5) to generate multivariate normal vectors with covariance matrix **A**.

References

Whereas some readers may find this chapter comprehensive, the author sees it merely as an overview. Given the availability of Devroye's volume, some of the more esoteric distributions and algorithms of historical interest have been omitted here in favor of pursuing the goal of simplicity and currency. In the process, the work of some individuals has not been mentioned even though their contributions deserve it – for example, Cheng's work on the gamma distribution, Schmeiser's on the Poisson, and Mark E. Johnson's work on simulating multivariate distributions.

Alan Agresti, Dennis Wackerly, and James M. Boyett (1979), "Exact Conditional Tests for Cross-Classifications: Approximation of Attained Significance Levels," *Psychometrika* 44: 75–83.

J. H. Ahrens and U. Dieter (1974), "Computer Methods for Sampling from Gamma, Beta, Poisson, and Normal Distributions," *Computing* 12: 223–46.

J. H. Ahrens and U. Dieter (1991), "A Convenient Sampling Method with Bounded Computation Times for Poisson Distributions," in Peter R. Nelson (Ed.), *The Frontiers of Statistical Computation, Simulation and Modeling,* pp. 137–49. Columbus, OH: American Sciences Press.

M. S. Bartlett (1933), "On the Theory of Statistical Regression," *Proceedings of the Royal Society of Edinburgh* 53: 260–83.

George E. P. Box and Mervin E. Muller (1958), "A Note on the Generation of Random Normal Deviates," *Annals of Mathematical Statistics* 29: 610–11.

Paul Bratley, Bennett L. Fox, and Linus E. Schrage (1983), *A Guide to Simulation*. Berlin: Springer-Verlag.

Morris H. DeGroot (1970), *Optimal Statistical Decisions*. New York: McGraw-Hill.

Luc Devroye (1986), *Non-Uniform Random Variate Generation*. New York: Springer-Verlag.

George Forsythe (1972), "Von Neumann's Comparison Method for Random Sampling from Normal and Other Distributions," *Mathematics of Computation* 26: 817–26.

Albert J. Kinderman and John F. Monahan (1977), "Computer Generation of Random Variables Using the Ratio of Uniform Deviates," *ACM Transactions on Mathematical Software* 3: 257–60.

Albert J. Kinderman and John F. Monahan (1980), "New Methods for Generating Student's *t* and Gamma Variables," *Computing* 25: 369–77.

Albert J. Kinderman, John F. Monahan, and John G. Ramage (1977), "Computer Methods for Sampling from Student's *t* Distribution," *Mathematics of Computation* 31: 1009–18.

Donald E. Knuth (1997), *The Art of Computer Programming* (vol. 2: Seminumerical Algorithms), 3rd ed. Reading, MA: Addison-Wesley.

Richard A. Kronmal and Arthur V. Peterson, Jr. (1979), "On the Alias Method for Generating Random Variables from a Discrete Distribution," *American Statistician* 33: 214–18.

Joseph B. Kruskal (1969), "An Extremely Portable Random Number Generator," *Communications of the ACM* 12: 93–4.

J. L. Leva (1992), "A Fast Normal Random Number Generator," *ACM Transactions on Mathematical Software* 18: 449–53.

George Marsaglia (1961), "Generating Exponential Random Variables," *Annals of Mathematical Statistics* 32: 899–902.

George Marsaglia and T. A. Bray (1964), "A Convenient Method for Generating Normal Variables," *SIAM Review* 6: 260–4.

John F. Monahan (1979), "Extensions of von Neumann's Method for Generating Random Variables," *Mathematics of Computation* 33: 1065–9.

John F. Monahan (1985), "Accuracy in Random Number Generation," *Mathematics of Computation* 45: 559–68.

John F. Monahan (1987), "An Algorithm for Generating Chi Random Variables," *ACM Transactions on Mathematical Software* 13: 168–72.

Henry R. Neave (1973), "On Using the Box–Muller Transformation with Multiplicative Congruential Pseudo-random Number Generators," *Applied Statistics* 22: 92–7.

Shayle R. Searle (1971), *Linear Models*. New York: Wiley.

Masaaki Sibuya (1962), "Exponential and Other Random Variable Generators," *Annals of the Institute of Statistical Mathematics* 13: 231–7.

W. B. Smith and R. R. Hocking (1972), "Algorithm AS 53: Wishart Variate Generator," *Applied Statistics* 21: 341–5.

Ernst Stadlober (1989), "Sampling from Poisson, Binomial and Hypergeometric Distributions: Ratio of Uniforms as a Simple and Fast Alternative," Mathematisch–Statistische Sektion 303. Forschungsgesellschaft Joanneum, Graz, Austria.

Ernst Stadlober (1990), "The Ratio of Uniforms Approach for Generating Discrete Random Variables," *Journal of Computational and Applied Mathematics* 31: 181–9.

Ernst Stadlober (1991), "Binomial Random Variate Generation: A Method Based on Ratio of Uniforms," in Peter R. Nelson (Ed.), *The Frontiers of Statistical Computation, Simulation and Modeling*, pp. 93–112. Columbus, OH: American Sciences Press.

Jeffrey S. Vitter (1987), "An Efficient Algorithm for Sequential Random Sampling," *ACM Transactions on Mathematical Software* 13: 58–67.

John von Neumann (1951), "Various Techniques in Connection with Random Digits," in *Monte Carlo Method* (AMS 12), pp. 36–8. Washington, DC: National Bureau of Standards.

Alastair J. Walker (1977), "An Efficient Method for Generating Random Variables with General Distributions," *ACM Transactions on Mathematical Software* 3: 253–6.

12

Statistical Methods for Integration and Monte Carlo

12.1 Introduction

One of the advantages of Monte Carlo methods, as highlighted in Chapter 10, is that the whole array of statistical tools are available to analyze the results and assess the accuracy of any estimate. Sadly, the statistical analysis of many Monte Carlo experiments has been absent, with others poorly done. Quite simply, statisticians do not always practice what they preach. One rationalization with some validity is that the statistical tools for analyzing these data are beyond the mainstream of statistical methodology; one of the goals of this chapter is to remove this as a possible excuse. Some of the fundamental statistical tools are reviewed in Section 12.2. Density estimation, long an object of theoretical discourse, becomes an important tool in expressing the results of Monte Carlo studies; a brief discussion of the highlights of density estimation is included in this section. The most common statistical tests for these data involve testing whether a sample arises from a specified distribution; a brief discussion of goodness-of-fit tests forms Section 12.3. Importance sampling, discussed briefly in Chapter 10, presents a class of statistical problems with weighted observations. This requires some minor modifications of common statistical tools that are outlined in Section 12.4. An attendant problem with importance sampling is concern for the distribution of the weights; tests on the behavior of the distribution of weights are discussed in Section 12.5.

The other goal of this chapter is to introduce some specialized integration tools. In Section 12.6, Laplace's method provides an asymptotic approximation for moments of a posterior based mainly on the large-sample normal approximation to the posterior. Random and mixed quadrature methods for integrating posterior distributions are outlined in Sections 12.7 and 12.8.

12.2 Distribution and Density Estimation

In most Monte Carlo studies, the results come in the form of independent and identically distributed (IID) observations $(Y_1, Y_2, \ldots, Y_n)$ with distribution function F and, if continuous, density f. The estimation of the distribution function F is really the easiest problem, but the related problem of estimating percentile points can be a bit tricky. Density estimation is quite a formidable problem and requires some special techniques. But all of these methods rely on one fundamental tool: the empirical distribution function

343

F_n. The empirical distribution function is a random step function aiming to estimate F, and it can be viewed as an average of indicator functions:

$$F_n(y) = \frac{1}{n} \sum_{i=1}^n I(Y_i \leq y). \tag{12.2.1}$$

Since $\Pr(Y_i \leq y) = F(y)$ and each Y_i is independent, it follows that $F_n(y)$ is an average of independent Bernoulli trials with probability $F(y)$; in large samples,

$$F_n(y) \approx N\big(F(y), F(y)[1 - F(y)]/n\big)$$

from the central limit theorem. Notice that this result holds for each y, but clearly $F_n(y_1)$ and $F_n(y_2)$ are dependent, with $\text{cov}(F_n(y_1), F_n(y_2)) = F(y_1)[1 - F(y_2)]/n$ for $y_1 \leq y_2$. Fast computation of $F_n(y)$ at any particular y requires an initial sorting of the data to form the order statistics:

$$Y_{(1)} \leq Y_{(2)} \leq \cdots \leq Y_{(n)}.$$

Then evaluating $F_n(y)$ requires finding the placement of y in this ordered list, for which the discrete bisection search algorithm (Exercise 8.7) requires $O(\log n)$ work to compute for each y. Ties in the Y_i rarely present a problem, except in the Smirnov test.

Estimation of a percentile point – that is, finding c_q such that $F(c_q) = q$ for a probability q – can be a little trickier, depending on whether or not nq is an integer. One approach would be to take the inverse of the step function $F_n(y)$, which gives

$$\hat{c}_1 = \begin{cases} Y_{(j)} & \text{if } nq = j \text{ (an integer)}, \\ \frac{1}{2}(Y_{(j)} + Y_{(j+1)}) & \text{if } nq \text{ is not an integer}, \end{cases}$$

where $j = [nq]$. Although any value in the interval $(Y_{(j)}, Y_{(j+1)})$ could serve as the inverse, taking the average of the endpoints follows the convention for the sample median. Another simple estimate is just linear interpolation of $F_n(y)$:

$$\hat{c}_2 = (1 - u)X_{(j)} + uX_{(j+1)}, \tag{12.2.2}$$

where again $j = [nq]$ and $u = nq - j$. Notice that these two coincide for $nq = j$. Still another estimate generalizes the convention for the sample median as

$$\hat{c}_3 = \begin{cases} \frac{1}{2}(Y_{(j)} + Y_{(j+1)}) & \text{if } nq = j \text{ (an integer)}, \\ Y_{(j+1)} & \text{if } nq \text{ is not an integer}. \end{cases}$$

Notice the difference between $\hat{c}_1$ and $\hat{c}_3$: the cases are reversed with respect to whether or not nq is an integer. Notice also that the estimate $\hat{c}_1$ is asymmetric. That is, if we changed the signs of the Y_i and changed from q to $1 - q$, then only the sign of $\hat{c}_3$ changes (as it should) whereas the change in $\hat{c}_1$ would be more than just a sign change. The estimate $\hat{c}_1$ behaves differently just because of the left continuous definition of a distribution function. Because values of q near 1 are the most common cases, the use of extreme value statistics motivates the following estimate by Weissman (1978):

$$\hat{c}_4 = \hat{a} \log_e(k/d) + Y_{(n-k+1)}, \tag{12.2.3}$$

where $\hat{a} = k^{-1} \sum_{i=1}^k Y_{(n-i+1)}$, $q = 1 - d/n$, and k is a parameter to be chosen (but bigger than d). The motivation for $\hat{c}_4$ is to use the shape of the tail in a sparsely populated, thinly tailed distribution. Following a Monte Carlo study, Boos (1984) recommended the use of $\hat{c}_4$ for light-tailed distributions with n large but the linear interpolant $\hat{c}_2$ for heavy-tailed distributions. Summarizing briefly for $q \geq .95$: for tails lighter than exponential (such as normal), use $k/d = 4$; for approximately exponential tails, use $k/n = .2$ for $n \leq 500$ and $k/n = .1$ for larger n; see Boos (1984) for details.

Demonstration **rho0** aims to compute the upper and lower 5th percentile points for the distribution of the sample correlation coefficient for a sample size of 12 when the true correlation $\rho = 1/2$. Here, $n = 1000$ and $q = .05$ and $.95$, so nq will be an integer. For the Weissman estimate, $q = .05$ means $d = 950$, and $d = 50$ for the upper point where $q = .95$. Since light tails are expected and n is quite large, k is chosen to be 200. The results for $q = .95$ are $\hat{c}_1 = \hat{c}_2 = .801313$, $\hat{c}_3 = .802152$, and $\hat{c}_4 = .794659$; for $q = .05$, we find $\hat{c}_1 = \hat{c}_2 = .037543$, $\hat{c}_3 = .038485$, and $\hat{c}_4 = .036463$.

Before leaving percentile points, remember the statistical maxim that an estimator is useless without an assessment of its accuracy. The large-sample result is that

$$\hat{c}(q) \approx N\left(c(q), n^{-1}q(1-q)/f(c)^2\right),$$

which provides an additional motivation for probability density estimation.

Several methods have been proposed to estimate the density function $f(y)$ from a sample $Y_1, Y_2, \ldots, Y_n$ – methods that trade off statistical properties, aesthetics, and computational ease. The first and most common method is the kernel density estimator. This method can be viewed as smoothing out the lumps of probability in the empirical distribution function $F_n(y)$. The density estimate takes the form

$$\hat{f}_1(y) = \frac{1}{n} \sum_{i=1}^{n} k\left(\frac{y - Y_i}{h}\right)\bigg/ h, \tag{12.2.4}$$

where $k(u)$ is the kernel function. Choosing $k(u)$ to be a density function centered at 0 leads to a nonnegative estimate $\hat{f}_1(y)$ that integrates to 1 and makes the analysis easy; the theoretical gains of allowing a kernel to become negative don't balance the value of the estimate being a probability density. The scale factor h affects the smoothness or bumpiness of the estimate. Taking h larger spreads the lumps of probability in $F_n(y)$ more, but taking h too big will hide the shape. Taking h smaller reduces bias, but taking it too small leads to an unappealing, bumpy estimate. In Figure 12.1 are kernel density estimates of the distribution of the exchange rates ($n = 15$) from Example 10.3 with three values of h. Clearly $h = .2$ is too small and the estimate too bumpy; also $h = .8$ may be too large, as some bumps are completely smoothed out. Slight undersmoothing is preferred; Silverman (1986, p. 41) puts it well: "the reader can do further smoothing 'by eye,' but cannot easily unsmooth."

The mathematics surrounding the choice of h balances bias and variance. The reduction of bias with smaller h follows from

$$E[\hat{f}_1(y)] = \int \frac{k((y-t)/h)}{h}\, dF(t) = \int F(y - hv)\, dK(v) \to F(y) \text{ as } h \to 0$$

using integration by parts. The "optimal" smoothing parameter in terms of integrated MSE, that is,

$$E\left\{\int |\hat{f}(y) - f(y)|^2\, dy\right\},$$

has $h = O(n^{-1/5})$, but the constant depends on function f – which is being estimated. There are theoretical methods for automatically selecting h; one route is to use some

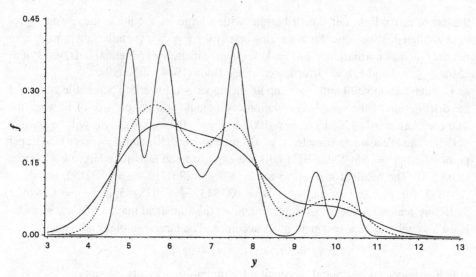

Figure 12.1. Kernel density estimate using normal kernel and exchange rate data (15 observations). Smoothing parameter h-values are .2 (solid, bumpy), .5 (dashed), .8 (solid, smooth).

simple statistics. After rescaling the kernel to have unit variance, Silverman (1986) recommends

$$h = .9 \min(\text{standard deviation}, \text{interquartile range}/1.34)n^{-1/5} \qquad (12.2.5)$$

based on considerations of the normal, t, and log-normal distributions. Another route is to use cross-validation, but this approach can be prohibitively costly for large sample sizes because the effort is more than $O(n^2)$. Since large samples are common with Monte Carlo, this route is impractical.

Although there is little theoretical basis for choosing a kernel k, a serious drawback of kernel density estimates is the computational burden in many practical problems – when n is large and the number of y values (say, M) is also large – since the estimate requires $O(Mn)$ work. Choosing a kernel with finite support may lose little theoretically and aesthetically yet gain considerably in reducing the constant. A finite support kernel with some theoretical advantages is the Epanechnikov kernel:

$$k(u) = \begin{cases} (3/4\sqrt{5})(1 - u^2/5) & \text{if } |u| \le \sqrt{5}, \\ 0 & \text{if } |u| > \sqrt{5}. \end{cases} \qquad (12.2.6)$$

A personal favorite is the density of the sum of three uniforms, a piecewise quadratic function with finite support that resembles the normal but without some of its theoretical attributes. The density of the sample correlation coefficient problem mentioned earlier in demonstration **rho0** is estimated using kernel methods in **rho1** and shown in Figure 12.2.

Two other methods for estimating a density function rely on the approximation mathematics from Chapter 7. The orthogonal series method is one of the older methods (Cencov 1962), not the most popular but certainly worth mentioning. Suppose we expand the density in a Fourier series, following the mathematics in Section 7.5:

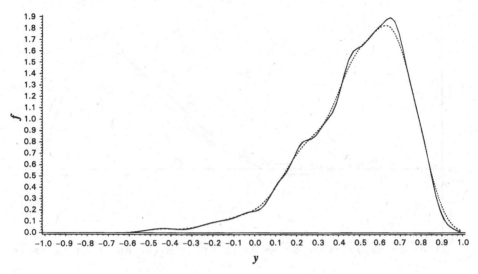

Figure 12.2. Kernel density estimates of density of sample correlation coefficient using $n = 1000$. Solid line uses $h = .6 * \text{stdv}/n^{0.2}$; dashed line uses $.9 * \text{stdv}/n^{0.2}$.

$$f(y) = \sum_{0}^{\infty} c_j \phi_j(y),$$

where $\{\phi_j(y), \ j = 0, 1, 2, \ldots\}$ are a series of complete orthonormal functions on the appropriate domain – such as sines and cosines or Legendre polynomials for $(-1, 1)$ and Hermite polynomials for $(-\infty, \infty)$ – and, perhaps, with a weight function $v(y)$. Then the Fourier coefficients can be estimated by

$$\hat{c}_j = \frac{1}{n} \sum_{i=1}^{n} v(Y_i)\phi_j(Y_i); \qquad (12.2.7)$$

it is easy to show (Exercise 12.4) that they are unbiased and that the variance vanishes as $n \to \infty$. The density estimate is then just the Fourier series with estimated coefficients truncated at k:

$$\hat{f}_2(y) = \sum_{j=0}^{k} \hat{c}_j \phi_j(y).$$

The integrated MSE is easy to find for orthogonal series estimates,

$$E\left\{\int |\hat{f}(y) - f(y)|^2 \, dy\right\} = \sum_{0}^{k} \text{var}(\hat{c}_j) + \sum_{k+1}^{\infty} c_j^2,$$

so the choice of k comes down to balancing the variance (first piece) and bias (second piece). An alternative to truncating at k is to taper the series based on smoothness assumptions that dictate a rate of decay of the coefficients c_j. The orthogonal series estimates often become negative, and integrating to 1 requires $\hat{c}_0 = 1$ in some cases. They are not the most appealing estimates, but they are very easy to compute and evaluate. The density of the sample correlation coefficient problem mentioned earlier in

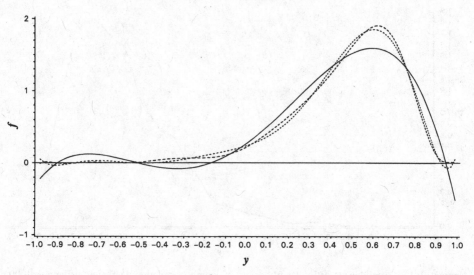

Figure 12.3. Orthogonal series density estimates of density of the sample correlation coefficient using $n = 1000$. Solid line uses four terms; dashed lines use eight and twelve terms.

demonstrations **rho0** and **rho1** is estimated using orthogonal series methods in **rho2** and shown in Figure 12.3.

Whereas the orthogonal series method can be viewed as a straightforward approximation of a function with a Fourier series, the spline method can be viewed as a spline interpolation of the distribution function. In this version of spline density estimation (due to Wahba 1975), choose a set of points or "knots" $\{t_j, \ j = 1, \ldots, m\}$ where the distribution function has been evaluated, $F_n(t_j) = F_j$ for $j = 1, \ldots, m$. What this actually requires is that we set up bins or intervals with the knots as endpoints (t_{j-1}, t_j) and then count the number of observations in the bins. Now let $S(y)$ be the cubic spline that interpolates the points $\{t_j, F_j, \ j = 1, \ldots, m\}$, ignoring for the moment the "extra" condition required. The density estimate is then simply the derivative of the spline,

$$\hat{f}_3(y) = S'(y). \tag{12.2.8}$$

Because the interpolatory splines have a certain built-in smoothness, the smoothing in the sense we are using here is governed by the number of points or knots used. As the sample size grows, the number of knots must also grow in order to reduce bias and ensure consistency. Using too many knots will lead to a bumpy derivative function. Again, the optimal rate for the number of knots is $O(n^{1/5})$. The "extra" condition can be obtained either by (i) using a natural spline with zero derivatives (of the density) at the endpoints or (ii) estimating the density at the endpoints by some other means, such as the kernel method. The first method is appropriate only if the domain (t_1, t_m) extends beyond the range of the realized sample. It is not possible to ensure that $\hat{f}_3(y)$ remain nonnegative, but it is easy to check (Exercise 12.3). The spline's coefficients can be computed in $O(m)$ operations by solving a tridiagonal system of equations. Computing the value of the density at a point can be computed in constant time, once the interval has been found. Finding the interval can take either $O(\log m)$ work if the

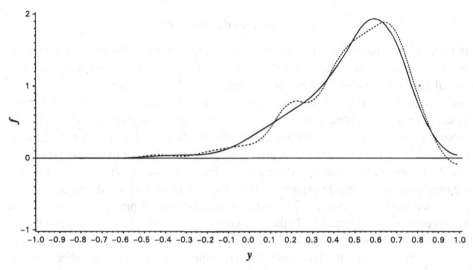

Figure 12.4. Spline density estimates of density of the sample correlation coefficient using $n = 1000$. Solid line uses eight bins; dashed line uses twelve.

knots are irregularly spaced or constant work if the knots (or a transformation of them) are regularly spaced. Because of the speed of the computation, the spline method is very effective for plotting densities. Moreover, other functionals (percentile points, means, etc.) of the distribution can be easily obtained from the interpolant $S(y)$. The density of the sample correlation coefficient problem mentioned earlier in demonstrations **rho0–rho2** is estimated using spline methods in **rho3** and shown in Figure 12.4.

Finally, a very different sort of density or distribution estimation arises when, instead of a sample of observations, a sample of conditional densities is available. In Bayesian problems, the conditional densities of a parameter may be available in closed form as $f(y \mid \mathbf{t}^{(i)})$ or $F(y \mid \mathbf{t}^{(i)})$ when most of the parameters follow a conjugate family. A similar situation arises when using the Monte Carlo swindle shown in (10.7.4). The problem is to express the density or distribution of Y from the average of these conditional densities or distributions. Often n is quite large, and plotting at many points y_j ($j = 1, \ldots, M$) may render computing the averages

$$\hat{f}(y_j) = \frac{1}{n} \sum_{i=1}^{n} f(y_j \mid \mathbf{t}^{(i)}) \tag{12.2.9}$$

prohibitively costly for large M. To reduce the overall burden $O(nM)$, reduce the number of points y_j in (12.2.6) and use cubic splines on the distribution function averages:

$$\hat{F}(y_j) = \frac{1}{n} \sum_{i=1}^{n} F(y_j \mid \mathbf{t}^{(i)}). \tag{12.2.10}$$

Then, to obtain density estimates $\hat{f}(y_j)$ for plotting, use the derivative of the spline interpolant of $\{(y_j, \hat{F}(y_j)), j = 1, \ldots, M\}$ as with the spline density estimates.

12.3   Distributional Tests

In many circumstances (and usually in debugging), we want to test whether the output of our program has the distribution that we claim it should. This would be a direct empirical test in the case of random number generation – say, for checking that a piece of code produces independent uniform or normal random variables. In other situations, where checking the entire simulation may be intractable, we may wish to check only pieces of it to gain some confidence in the whole. The most common situation has Y_i ($i = 1, \ldots, n$) IID $F(y)$, where n is usually large. First, we want to test the hypothesis that the sample comes from the idealized distribution G; that is, $H : F = G$. Second, we may want to investigate departures from independence, but this discussion will be postponed until a later chapter. In contrast to usual statistical practice, testing the first hypothesis is quite reasonable. In the real world, F can only be close to G, and the result is that we seldom reject the hypothesis in small samples because the tests are never very powerful against omnibus alternatives; in large samples, we always reject since F is never the same as the idealized G. In Monte Carlo situations, however, the sample size is usually large; hence no parameters of G need to be estimated and, if we reject H, we conclude the existence of an error in the code or in a theorem.

It is not by accident that we express the idealized distribution G in terms of its distribution function. Most of the tests rely on computations from it. Knowing only the density function makes life difficult; problems arising from these computational obstacles will be noted along the way.

(A) *Pearson's Chi-Square*

The oldest and most common test for goodness of fit is the Pearson chi-square test. Although founded on the discrete case, continuous data can be handled effectively by making it discrete. In the univariate case, construct disjoint intervals I_j that cover the support of the distribution; if $Y \in I_j$ then use $X = j$ as the discretized random variable. In higher dimensions, the intervals become boxes or bins. The chi-square statistic takes the form

$$Q = \sum_{j=1}^{M} \frac{(N_j - E_j)^2}{E_j},$$

where N_j is the count of the number of observations when $X = j$ and where E_j is the expected number when the hypothesis $H : F = G$ is true. Under the IID hypothesis, the distribution of the N_j is multinomial with $n = \sum N_j$ trials and probabilities E_j/n. The theory behind the test relies on the central limit theorem applied to the multinomial distribution, and the statistic Q becomes the one-sample Hotelling's T^2 test: in large samples, $Q \sim \chi^2$ with $M - 1$ degrees of freedom. The selection of cells (or intervals or bins) determines whether the "large sample" criterion obtains, and that issue involves both computation and the underlying distribution of Y. The best situation has equiprobable cells – that is, constant E_j and $M = O(n^{2/5})$. In the other direction, the chi-square statistic is robust enough to work with anything but really drastic departures, since large n can cover a multitude of sins.

Suppose the underlying distribution is discrete; then, if $Y = j$, it is natural to use $X = j$. However, when the cell probabilities are very small, the smallest cells should be aggregated. For the tail of the Poisson distribution, it is common to construct a cell so that $X = M$ if $Y \geq M$. When the underlying distribution is continuous, then the intervals should be constructed so that the probabilities for these intervals are the same. This requires computing a number of percentile points of the distribution, so establishing equiprobable intervals is impractical for some distributions. In such cases, use equal spacing of intervals (to obviate the need for code such as **jfind** to place Y in the proper interval) and then collect the tails in two separate cells.

The common rule of thumb for cell selection is for E_j to be at least 5, but this is quite conservative. Cochran (1954) recommended all E_j at least 1 and 80% at least 5. Roscoe and Byars (1971) gave much less restrictive guidelines, which work as long as the cells are approximately equiprobable. In the other direction, where cell selection is completely at one's discretion and n is large, Mann and Wald (1942) offered guidelines for how many cells to use:

$$M = 4 \left\{ \frac{2n^2}{c_\alpha^2} \right\}^{1/5}$$

for testing at level α, where c_α is the usual normal α critical value. Citing studies that suggest this guideline is conservative, Moore (1986) recommended the convenient $M = 2n^{2/5}$ for testing at level $\alpha = .05$.

(B) *Kolmogorov–Smirnov*

One of the most common tests for goodness of fit measures a distance between the empirical distribution function $F_n(y)$ and the hypothesized distribution function $F(y)$,

$$D_n = \sup_y |F_n(y) - F(y)|.$$

Only the two-sided statistic will be considered, since one-sided alternatives are not relevant in the Monte Carlo context. For continuous random variables, the Kolmogorov–Smirnov (KS) statistic is distribution-free, since transforming the data by $U_i = F(Y_i)$ does not affect D_n. In fact, the KS statistic is computed in this context; by evaluating the distribution function F only at the observations and then sorting, we have

$$D_n = \max_i \{ i/n - F(Y_{(i)}), \ F(Y_{(i)}) - (i-1)/n \}.$$

There is no need for the algorithms to yield the small-sample distribution of D_n. The KS test is not very powerful and hence not useful in small samples, but it is convenient in the large-sample Monte Carlo problems. Here the large-sample distribution is given by $\lim_{n \to \infty} \Pr(\sqrt{n} D_n \leq t) = Q(t)$, where

$$Q(t) = 1 - 2 \sum_{j=1}^{\infty} (-1)^{j+1} \exp[-2t^2 j^2] = \frac{\sqrt{2\pi}}{t} \sum_{j=1}^{\infty} \exp\left[-\frac{(2j-1)^2 \pi^2}{8t^2} \right]. \qquad (12.3.1)$$

The first sum works for large t and fails to converge for small t; the rare second expression behaves in a complementary fashion. Stephens (1970) gave an improved version of the convergence as

$$\left(\sqrt{n} + .12 + .11/\sqrt{n}\right)D_n \to Q(t).$$

The critical values of $Q(t)$ to remember are $Q(1.358) = .95$ and $Q(1.628) = .99$.

Smirnov (1939) constructed a two-sample version of this test using the distance between two empirical distribution functions:

$$D_{mn} = \sup_z |F_m(z) - G_n(z)|.$$

This test is useful when there are two ways (of different efficiency) to simulate the same process yet there is a need to check one simulation against the other. In the two-sample situation we have X_i ($i = 1, \ldots, m$) as an IID sample from F and Y_i ($i = 1, \ldots, n$) as another IID sample from G; we want to test $H : F = G$. The statistic D_{mn} is a little harder to compute, but not much more than sorting. In fact, the computational step resembles a merge sort (see Section 14.3). Begin by sorting both series, $X_{(1)} \le \cdots \le X_{(i)} \le \cdots \le X_{(m)}$ and $Y_{(1)} \le \cdots \le Y_{(i)} \le \cdots \le Y_{(n)}$. Then start with $S = 0$ and compare the smallest in each list. If the X is smaller then remove it from the list of Xs and decrease S by n (it may become negative); if the Y is smaller, remove it from the list and increase S by m. Once either of the lists is exhausted, $D_{mn} = S^*/(mn)$ where $S^* = \max|S|$. Of course, we could instead decrease by $1/m$ and increase by $1/n$ and so avoid dividing by mn, but then we couldn't do the counting in integers. The large-sample distribution of D_{mn} is similar to the one-sample case:

$$\sqrt{\frac{mn}{m+n}} D_{mn} \to Q(t).$$

See the demonstration code in **dks2s**.

(C) *Anderson–Darling*

Another goodness-of-fit statistic arises from the use of a different distance – namely, a weighted Cramer–von Mises distance between the empirical distribution function and the hypothesized:

$$A^2 = n \int_{-\infty}^{\infty} \frac{[F_n(y) - F(y)]^2}{F(y)[1 - F(y)]} \, dF(y)$$

$$= -n - \frac{1}{n} \sum_{i=1}^{n} (2i - 1)\{\log F(Y_{(i)}) + \log[1 - F(Y_{(n+1-i)})]\}. \quad (12.3.2)$$

As with the KS statistic, the Anderson–Darling statistic is a distance and thus requires sorting of the data and computation of the distribution function only at the observations Y_i. The Anderson–Darling presents some computational difficulties for values in the tails, since either F or $1 - F$ may be very small or near unity. For small values of F, the logarithm may accentuate any relative error effects, and accuracy may be lost when computing $\log(1 - F)$ unless a series expansion is employed because

$$\log(1 - F) \approx -F.$$

These problems suggest at a minimum some care in the coding and, for special cases (e.g. the normal; see **alnphi** in Chapter 7), special coding of $\log F$ and/or $\log(1-F)$. For power considerations, Stephens (1970, 1986) recommended A^2 over other goodness-of-fit statistics. The asymptotic distribution for A^2 is reached for even small values of n, and the upper .05 and .01 critical values are 2.492 and 3.857, respectively.

(D)   *Quasirandom Sequences*

Finally, in most situations we reject the hypothesis H only for large values of the statistic, because they are measuring a distance. Moreover, the power of these tests is not usually sufficient to find any but the most blatant errors. However, we should also be concerned when these goodness-of-fit statistics are too small. Rather than perfect data, this rare phenomenon normally indicates insufficient randomness or some lack of independence in the data. Recall that the quasirandom sequences discussed in Section 10.6 produced uniform-looking observations that filled up space too regularly. If one were to use these methods to generate uniform variates, and further to generate from other distributions (e.g. the normal), then the resultant observations $\{Y_i, i = 1, \ldots, n\}$ would fit the correct distribution yet do so too well. If we computed these goodness-of-fit statistics on these data, we would get distances that were too small – well, much too small. Using quasirandom sequences to generate data is a powerful way to detect errors, since we should expect a distance that would be clearly below typical upper critical values and even below lower ones as well.

Example 12.0: *Perfect Fit of the Normal Distribution*
The demonstration program **perfect** uses the Halton sequence (10.6.3) with bases 2 and 3 to generate uniformly distributed points in the unit square. It then employs the Box–Muller transformation (Section 11.3, Algorithm A1 and **gnbxml**), which produces a sequence of variables that fit the normal distribution too well. For $n = 16,384$ (certainly large enough to detect differences), the KS statistic is $\sqrt{n}D_n = .1554$ and the Anderson–Darling $A^2 = .021898$, well below the usual upper critical values and well below the lower .05 critical values of .520 and .283, respectively. However, the lower .01 critical values are in reach: .441 for $\sqrt{n}D_n$ and .201 for A^2. These results give us confidence that the algorithm was coded correctly.

12.4   Importance Sampling and Weighted Observations

Importance sampling is a powerful tool for Bayesian analysis of high-dimensional problems that require Monte Carlo integration, but it presents some difficulties in the analysis of the results. In the typical situation, information about the posterior distribution is sought in the form of posterior means and variances as well as percentile points of distributions and density estimates of some parameters. While the observations may be independent and identically distributed, they come with unequal weights, which force some modifications to the tools discussed in the previous two sections. The first step is to analyze the analog of the sample mean.

Commonly in Bayesian problems, the unnormalized posterior distribution $p^*(\mathbf{t})$ is too difficult to generate from, and so observations $\mathbf{T}^{(i)}$ ($i = 1, \ldots, n$) are generated from another distribution with density $g(\mathbf{t})$ that is absolutely continuous with respect to $p^*(\mathbf{t})$. In order to estimate the posterior mean of some function $h(\boldsymbol{\theta})$ of the parameter vector $\boldsymbol{\theta}$, the integration step is a modification of (10.7.1):

$$E_{p^*}\{h(\boldsymbol{\theta})\} = \frac{\iint h(\mathbf{t})p^*(\mathbf{t})\,d\mathbf{t}}{\iint p^*(\mathbf{t})\,d\mathbf{t}}$$

$$= \frac{\iint h(\mathbf{t})[p^*(\mathbf{t})/g(\mathbf{t})]g(\mathbf{t})\,d\mathbf{t}}{\iint [p^*(\mathbf{t})/g(\mathbf{t})]g(\mathbf{t})\,d\mathbf{t}} = E_g\{h(\boldsymbol{\theta})w(\boldsymbol{\theta})\}, \qquad (12.4.1)$$

where $\boldsymbol{\theta}$ has density $g(\mathbf{t})$ and the *weight function* is

$$w(\mathbf{t}) = p^*(\mathbf{t})/g(\mathbf{t}).$$

In order to estimate the integrals, we sample $\mathbf{T}^{(i)}$ ($i = 1, \ldots, n$) IID from $g(\mathbf{t})$ and then compute the ratio of means:

$$\frac{\frac{1}{n}\sum_{i=1}^{n} h(\mathbf{T}^{(i)})w(\mathbf{T}^{(i)})}{\frac{1}{n}\sum_{i=1}^{n} w(\mathbf{T}^{(i)})} = \frac{\frac{1}{n}\sum_{i=1}^{n} W_i Y_i}{\frac{1}{n}\sum_{i=1}^{n} W_i}. \qquad (12.4.2)$$

Owing to the large samples regularly used in Monte Carlo, the analysis of this ratio would lean on a large-sample normal approximation, provided the usual requirements of the central limit theorem (CLT) hold. Relabeling $W_i Y_i = Z_i$, the CLT suggests the analysis of

$$\begin{bmatrix} \bar{Z} \\ \bar{W} \end{bmatrix} \approx N\left(\begin{bmatrix} \mu_z \\ \mu_w \end{bmatrix}, \frac{1}{n} \begin{bmatrix} \Sigma_{zz} & \Sigma_{zw} \\ \Sigma_{wz} & \Sigma_{ww} \end{bmatrix} \right), \qquad (12.4.3)$$

where $\mu_z = \iint h(\mathbf{t})p^*(\mathbf{t})\,d\mathbf{t}$ and $\mu_w = \iint p^*(\mathbf{t})\,d\mathbf{t}$. Not only do we want to estimate the ratio of means μ_z/μ_w with the ratio of sample means $\bar{Z}/\bar{W}$ as its natural estimate, we need an assessment of accuracy.

One route to take is the usual large-sample asymptotics, or the delta method. Rewriting the ratio of sample means using the algebraic substitution $\bar{Z}/\mu_z = 1 + (\bar{Z} - \mu_z)/\mu_z$, we have

$$\frac{\bar{Z}}{\bar{W}} = \frac{\mu_z}{\mu_w} \times \frac{\bar{Z}/\mu_z}{\bar{W}/\mu_w} = \frac{\mu_z}{\mu_w} \times \frac{1 + (\bar{Z} - \mu_z)/\mu_z}{1 + (\bar{W} - \mu_w)/\mu_w}$$

$$\approx \frac{\mu_z}{\mu_w} \times \left[1 + \frac{\bar{Z} - \mu_z}{\mu_z} \right]\left[1 - \frac{\bar{W} - \mu_w}{\mu_w} \right]$$

$$\approx \frac{\mu_z}{\mu_w} \times \left[1 + \frac{\bar{Z} - \mu_z}{\mu_z} - \frac{\bar{W} - \mu_w}{\mu_w} \right],$$

provided, of course, that certain conditions are satisfied. This result suggests the following normal approximation:

$$\frac{\bar{Z}}{\bar{W}} \approx N\left(\frac{\mu_z}{\mu_w}, \frac{1}{n\mu_w^2}\left[\Sigma_{zz} - 2\frac{\mu_z}{\mu_w}\Sigma_{zw} + \frac{\mu_z^2}{\mu_w^2}\Sigma_{ww} \right] \right),$$

where the means (μ_z and μ_w) and variances (Σ_{zz} etc.) are with respect to g, the importance distribution. This approximation leads to a standard error for the ratio of means of the form

$$\frac{1}{\sqrt{n}\,\bar{W}}\left[S_{zz} - 2\frac{\bar{Z}}{\bar{W}}S_{zw} + \frac{\bar{Z}^2}{\bar{W}^2}S_{ww}\right]^{1/2},\qquad (12.4.4)$$

where

$$S_{zw} = \frac{1}{n-1}\sum_{i=1}^{n}(Z_i - \bar{Z})(W_i - \bar{W})$$

and similarly for S_{zz} and S_{ww}. Since this result relies heavily on $(\bar{W} - \mu_w)/\mu_w$ being small, let's look more closely at this quantity. Its variance takes the form $\Sigma_{ww}/n\mu_w^2$, which needs to be close to zero – say, $1/100$ or smaller. The usual estimate of this variance is approximately $S_2 - 1/n$, where

$$S_2 = \sum W_i^2 / \left(\sum W_i\right)^2.\qquad (12.4.5)$$

The quantity S_2 can be a useful indicator of the behavior of the weighting random variable. Its reciprocal can be interpreted as an effective sample size for these weighted observations, for if the weights were fixed then the variance of $\bar{Y}$ would be $S_2 \, \mathrm{var}(Y)$. The relationship to the coefficient of variation of the weights $\Sigma_{ww}^{1/2}/\mu_w$ should not be surprising.

A second route uses the same large-sample normal result (12.4.3) but relies on Fieller's theorem (1954) for confidence limits on the ratio of two normal means. Fieller's result provides a confidence interval for μ_z/μ_w of the form $(\bar{Z}/\bar{W} + c_1, \bar{Z}/\bar{W} + c_2)$, where c_1 is the negative and c_2 the positive root of the quadratic equation in ϕ:

$$\left(\bar{W}^2 - \frac{t^2}{n}S_{ww}\right)\phi^2 - 2\phi\frac{t^2}{n}\left(\frac{\bar{Z}}{\bar{W}}S_{ww} - S_{zw}\right)$$

$$-\frac{t^2}{n}\left[S_{zz} - 2\frac{\bar{Z}}{\bar{W}}S_{zw} + \frac{\bar{Z}^2}{\bar{W}^2}S_{ww}\right] = 0,\quad (12.4.6)$$

where t is the usual Student's t critical value. Notice that ensuring a positive coefficient for ϕ^2 is the same condition on the W_i as before, that is,

$$\bar{W}^2 - \frac{t^2}{n}S_{ww} > 0 \quad \text{or} \quad t^2 > \frac{S_{ww}}{n\bar{W}^2}.$$

Also notice that the bracketed part (which we hope is positive) of the constant term in (12.4.6) is the same bracketed term in the standard error formula in (12.4.4). To a first-order approximation, these two approaches are identical.

Example 12.1: *Log-Series Posterior*
The log-series posterior from Example 10.1 was analyzed in **quad1–quad3**; here a simple importance sampling scheme from the normal approximation to the posterior is used again in **quad4**, and the results from 100 samples (T_i, W_i) are stored in **quad4.wgt**. Some simple analysis gives the statistics

$$\begin{bmatrix} \bar{Z} \\ \bar{W} \end{bmatrix} = \begin{bmatrix} 3.7617 \\ 7.2076 \end{bmatrix} \text{ and } \begin{bmatrix} S_{zz} & S_{zw} \\ S_{wz} & S_{ww} \end{bmatrix} = \begin{bmatrix} 1.134947 & .310150 \\ .310150 & .617505 \end{bmatrix}$$

after rescaling the weights by 10,000 and with $Z_i = W_i T_i$. The estimate of the posterior mean is $\bar{Z}/\bar{W} = .5219$; following the calculations from (12.4.4), the standard error for this ratio is

$$\frac{1}{\sqrt{n}\bar{W}} \left[S_{zz} - 2\frac{\bar{Z}}{\bar{W}} S_{zw} + \frac{\bar{Z}^2}{\bar{W}^2} S_{ww} \right]^{1/2} = \sqrt{.979408}/72.076 = .01373.$$

Following now the Fieller route and using $t^2 = 1.96^2$ for $n = 100$, the quadratic equation (12.4.6) is

$$51.9258\phi^2 - .0009\phi - .0376 = 0,$$

which has roots $c_1 = -.02690$ and $c_2 = .02692$. The two methods are nearly identical, since

$$S_{ww}/n\bar{W}^2 = 1.012 \times 10^{-4}.$$

Before proceeding to modify all of the results in Sections 12.2 and 12.3 for weighted observations, more than a moment's reflection on importance sampling is appropriate. Geweke (1989) gave the conditions that ensure the central limit theorem will apply to yield (12.4.3). In addition to the fundamentals of importance sampling, such as absolute continuity of p^* with respect to g, Geweke's conditions require the existence of the variances Σ_{zz} and Σ_{ww}. Showing these analytically is often impractical, especially in high dimensions, and the additional assumption of bounded weights suggested by Geweke may be unnecessarily restrictive. To underscore how easy it is to run into problems, let $p^*(t) = \exp\{-t^2/2\}$ and let $g(t) = \phi(t - a)$, the standard normal density centered at a. Then the weight function $w(t) = \exp\{a(a - 2t)/2\}\sqrt{2\pi}$ is clearly unbounded even though $E(W^2) = \sqrt{2\pi}\exp\{3a^2\}$, which gets worse the further the importance distribution g moves from the posterior p^*. Mismatching the scale is even worse: if $g(t) = \phi(t/c)/c$, then $w(t)$ will be unbounded for $c < 1$ and $E(W^2)$ will be infinite if $c^2 < 1/2$. Figures 12.5 and 12.6 show $p^*(t) = \phi(t)$ and $g(t) = \phi(t/c)/c$ with $c = .8$ and 1.2, as well as the weight functions $w(t)$.

The result of some of this analysis is that bounded weights are good, a small coefficient of variation of the weights is good, and infinite variance of the weights is a major disaster. When only examination of the observed weights W_i ($i = 1, \ldots, n$) is possible, one signal for a problem is one or a few of the weights dominating the sum. Since the CLT relies on the average of a large number of independent quantities – with no few of them dominating the sum – this signal indicates that the CLT may not be working. A natural measure is $S_1 = \max\{W_i\}/\sum W_i$. Although both S_1 and S_2 are good indicators of what may be going on, they do not lead to useful tests on the behavior of the weights (this is discussed further in Section 12.5). The simple normal cases, while showing how easy it may be to make a grave error in the use of importance sampling, also reveal its strengths.

The strength of importance sampling is in oversampling relatively rare events. Its prevalence in simulating nuclear power plants stems from the fact that failure rates are

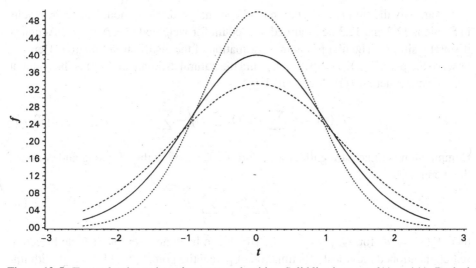

Figure 12.5. Target density and two importance densities. Solid line is target $f(t) = \phi(t)$. Dashed lines have different scales $g(t) = \phi(t/c)/c$ with $c = .8$ and 1.2.

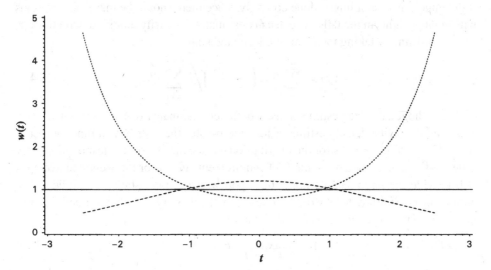

Figure 12.6. Importance sampling weight functions with $c = .8$ and $c = 1.2$.

very low, and nothing would be learned about the system if no failures arose. So values that lead to problems are sampled more frequently, but those observations hold very small weight. As a result, low probability or tail events occur more often but with small weights. In choosing the scale parameter c too small in the preceding normal examples, the tails of the distribution are being seriously undersampled; choosing $c > 1$ bounds the weights and the undersampling of the middle and permits oversampling in the rare-event tails. In general, a safe route is either to sample from a distribution with heavier tails and a larger variance or to sample from a Student's t instead of a normal; see also Hesterberg (1995).

So far, only the simple expectation has been analyzed. How should all of the results in Sections 12.2 and 12.3 be modified to account for weighted observations? Actually, it's pretty simple. The first problem is estimation of the distribution function. Here we observe the pairs W_i, Y_i ($i = 1, \ldots, n$), and the natural estimate of $F(y)$ is the mean of an indicator function $I(Y_i \leq y)$, which is

$$F_n(y) = \frac{1}{n} \sum_{i=1}^{n} W_i I(Y_i \leq y) \Big/ \frac{1}{n} \sum_{i=1}^{n} W_i. \tag{12.4.7}$$

Computation is rather straightforward: sort the Y_i carrying the W_i along and compute the increments,

$$F_k = \sum_{i=1}^{k} W_i \Big/ \sum_{i=1}^{n} W_i; \tag{12.4.8}$$

then $F_n(y) = F_k$ for $Y_{k-1} < y \leq Y_k$, which can be done with the discrete bisection search mentioned previously. Estimation of percentile points should be done with linear interpolation using $\hat{c}_2$ of (12.2.2), since the jumps of the distribution function come in different sizes. There should be no need for the extreme-value method $\hat{c}_4$ of (12.2.3) if the importance sampling is done correctly, since there should be many observations with small weights in the tails. The density estimates are easily modified, with the kernel method simply taking the form of a weighted sum,

$$\hat{f}_1(y) = \sum_{i=1}^{n} W_i k\left(\frac{y - Y_i}{h}\right) \Big/ h \sum_{i=1}^{n} W_i. \tag{12.4.9}$$

The orthogonal series estimates use coefficient estimates that are weighted averages, and the spline density estimator just interpolates the distribution function $F_n(y)$ from (12.4.7) as before. As for the distributional tests, the chi-square test requires very little modification, since the same CLT requirements given for the weighted averages will provide the large-sample normality upon which the chi-square test relies. The Kolmogorov–Smirnov tests would require two changes. One is that the definition of the distance requires some revision in computation,

$$D_n = \sup_y |F_n(y) - F(y)| = \max_k \{F_k - F(Y_{(k)}), \; F(Y_{(k)}) - F_{k-1}\}, \tag{12.4.10}$$

with F_k from (12.4.8); the other change is prompted by the effective sample size. Recall the role of n in the final statistic $\sqrt{n} D_n$; in (12.4.10), the effective sample size is not n. My recommendation would be to use $1/S_2$ from (12.4.5) in place of n when performing the Kolmogorov–Smirnov tests. Similar modifications are suggested for the two-sample test. Finally, the Anderson–Darling test is modified to

$$A^2 = -1 - \sum_{i=1}^{n} (F_i - F_{i-1})(F_i + F_{i-1}) \log F(Y_{(i)})$$

$$- \sum_{i=1}^{n} (F_i - F_{i-1})(2 - F_i - F_{i-1}) \log(1 - F(Y_{(i)})),$$

but a sample size adjustment should not be necessary.

12.5 Testing Importance Sampling Weights

As mentioned in the previous section, analysis of the importance sampling distribution and the weight function is often too difficult for practical verification of the conditions for the central limit theorem. We need the CLT in order to assess the accuracy of the importance sampling estimates. Recall that the first moment of the weights must exist or else nothing at all is possible. If the variance does not exist, then we can rely neither on the CLT nor on the existence of other expectations, such as posterior variances. The author (Monahan 1993) examined two approaches for testing whether the importance sampling distribution has first and second moments.

The first approach examines the tail behavior of the distribution of weights, modeling the distribution function as

$$1 - F(w) = Cw^{-1/\beta}(1 + Dw^{-1} + o(w^{-1})) \quad \text{for } w > 0. \tag{12.5.1}$$

Note that only nonnegative x are considered because the weights are nonnegative. Taking $\beta = 1$ gives the tail behavior of a Cauchy random variable, which just barely does not have a mean. Taking $\beta = 1/2$ corresponds to the tail of a Student's t random variable with two degrees of freedom, which barely does not have a variance. The hypotheses and alternatives of finite mean and variance can be written in terms of the parameter β as follows.

(infinite mean) $H_1 : \beta \geq 1$ versus $A_1 : \beta < 1$ (finite mean)

(infinite variance) $H_2 : \beta \geq \frac{1}{2}$ versus $A_2 : \beta < \frac{1}{2}$ (finite variance)

The motivation for setting up the tests in this way is that we should not be willing to use the asymptotic results unless these hypotheses are rejected. Hill (1975) proposed an estimator for the parameter β using the largest order statistics:

$$\hat{\beta} = \frac{1}{k} \sum_{j=1}^{k} \log(W_{(n-j+1)}) - \log(W_{(n-k)}), \tag{12.5.2}$$

where $W_{(j)}$ is the jth smallest order statistic from a sample of size n importance sampling weights. Haeusler and Teugels (1985) and Hall (1982) showed that if $k = o(n^{\beta/(\beta+1/2)})$ then the estimator $\hat{\beta}$ is asymptotically normal,

$$\sqrt{k}(\hat{\beta} - \beta) \to N(0, \beta^2).$$

Pursuing this approach further, a test for infinite mean can be constructed as

reject H_1 (infinite mean) in favor of A_1 (finite mean) if $\hat{\beta} < 1 - z_\alpha/\sqrt{k}$,   (12.5.3)

where z_α is the usual upper α normal critical value. A test for infinite variance can be constructed as

reject H_2 (infinite variance) in favor of A_2 (finite variance) if $\hat{\beta} < \left(1 - z_\alpha/\sqrt{k}\right)/2$,

$$\tag{12.5.4}$$

so that the critical value for $\hat{\beta}$ is just cut in half. Again, notice that these tests are set up with the null hypotheses being undesirable, and rejection should give some confidence that the conditions for the CLT may be satisfied. The study previously mentioned shows that $k = 4n^{1/3}$ works and that the sample size $n = 2500$ appears to be sufficient. A second approach uses the two importance sampling indicators S_1 and S_2:

$$S_1 = \max W_i \Big/ \sum_{i=1}^{n} W_i, \qquad S_2 = \sum_{i=1}^{n} W_i^2 \Big/ \Big(\sum_{i=1}^{n} W_i\Big)^2.$$

Establishing the distribution of these statistics when the null hypothesis is true is very difficult, since it depends so much on the underlying distribution of weights. Nevertheless, as a test for infinite mean,

reject H_1 (infinite mean) in favor of A_1 (finite mean) if $(\log n)S_1 < (-\log \alpha)^{-1}$

$$(12.5.5)$$

appears to work reasonably well although not as well as (12.5.3). Testing infinite variance using S_2 just doesn't work well at all.

Example 12.2: *Variance Components Problem*

The variance components problem with the exchange rate data was detailed in Example 10.3. Importance sampling – using some variation of the large-sample normal approximation to the posterior – is the standard approach for solving these kinds of Bayesian problems. The first step is find the mode $\mathbf{t}_m$ of the log posterior $\log p^*(\mathbf{t})$ and its Hessian $\mathbf{H}$. Then one of these two importance distributions are employed: either

$$g_1(\mathbf{t}) = (2\pi)^{-p/2}|\mathbf{H}|^{1/2}\exp\{-\tfrac{1}{2}(\mathbf{t} - \mathbf{t}_m)^{\mathrm{T}}\mathbf{H}(\mathbf{t} - \mathbf{t}_m)\}, \qquad (12.5.6)$$

the p-dimensional normal approximation to the posterior; or a multivariate Student's t approximation with k degrees of freedom,

$$g_2(\mathbf{t}) = \frac{\Gamma((k + p)/2)|\mathbf{H}|^{1/2}}{\Gamma(k/2)(p + k)^{p/2}\pi^{p/2}}$$

$$\times \left\{1 + \frac{1}{p + k}(\mathbf{t} - \mathbf{t}_m)^{\mathrm{T}}\mathbf{H}(\mathbf{t} - \mathbf{t}_m)\right\}^{-(p+k)/2}. \qquad (12.5.7)$$

To generate from g_1, first compute the Cholesky factorization of $\mathbf{H} = \mathbf{L}\mathbf{L}^{\mathrm{T}}$ and generate $\mathbf{Z}^{(i)}$ IID $N_p(0, \mathbf{I}_p)$; then form

$$\mathbf{T}^{(i)} = \mathbf{t}_m + \mathbf{L}^{-\mathrm{T}}\mathbf{Z}^{(i)}.$$

To generate from g_2, use the same Cholesky factorization and normal vectors $\mathbf{Z}^{(i)}$, but also generate the random variable $V_i \sim \chi_k$ (chi with k df) using **gchirv** from Chapter 11; then form

$$\mathbf{T}^{(i)} = \mathbf{t}_m + \big(\sqrt{p + k}/V_i\big)\mathbf{L}^{-\mathrm{T}}\mathbf{Z}^{(i)}. \qquad (12.5.8)$$

The demonstration **chex122a** uses g_1 as its importance sampling distribution; **chex122b** uses g_2 with $k = 5$ df, both with $n = 2500$ replications. In both cases, the tail parameter estimate is small: $\hat{\beta} \approx .71$ in the first case and $\hat{\beta} = .59$ in the second. With $k = 53$, both fail to reject infinite mean and variance, suggesting a problem in the tails.

12.6 Laplace Approximations

The central computational step in Bayesian analysis is the computation of information about the posterior distribution $p^*(\mathbf{t})$. Usually, the easiest pieces of information to obtain are moments of functions, the posterior means and variances in particular. Owing to the likelihood asymptotics from Chapter 9, there is a strong temptation to extend those further for Bayesian analysis. That is, approximate the log of the posterior as a quadratic with mode $\mathbf{t}^*$:

$$\log p^*(\mathbf{t}) \approx \text{constant} - \tfrac{1}{2}(\mathbf{t} - \mathbf{t}^*)^{\mathrm{T}}\mathbf{H}(\mathbf{t} - \mathbf{t}^*),$$

where $\mathbf{H} = -\nabla^2 \log p^*(\mathbf{t})$ at $\mathbf{t} = \mathbf{t}^*$. This, of course, is equivalent to saying that the posterior is approximately multivariate normal with mean vector $\mathbf{t}^*$ and covariance matrix $\mathbf{H}^{-1}$. Expectations of other functions could then be approximated by applying the delta method:

$$E[h(\mathbf{t})] \approx h(\mathbf{t}^*) \quad \text{and} \quad \text{var}[h(\mathbf{t})] \approx (\nabla h)^{\mathrm{T}}\mathbf{H}^{-1}(\nabla h). \tag{12.6.1}$$

Tierney and Kadane (1986) and Tierney, Kass, and Kadane (1989) derived better approximations by applying Laplace's approximation of the integral of a function with mode t^*:

$$\int e^{ng(t)} \, dt \approx e^{ng(t^*)} \int \exp\{-\tfrac{1}{2}(t - t^*)^2(ng'')\} \, dt = e^{ng(t^*)}(ng'')^{-1/2}\sqrt{2\pi},$$

which is accurate to terms $O(n^{-1})$ for a relative error of $O(n^{-1/2})$. Notice, however, that most posterior expectations arise as a ratio of integrals; that is, we usually want to compute

$$E_{p^*}[h(\boldsymbol{\theta})] = \frac{\iint h(\mathbf{t}) p^*(\mathbf{t}) \, d\mathbf{t}}{\iint p^*(\mathbf{t}) \, d\mathbf{t}}. \tag{12.6.2}$$

The trick is to apply Laplace's approximation to both the numerator and denominator and then take the ratio:

$$E_{p^*}[h(\boldsymbol{\theta})] \approx \frac{|\mathbf{H}^{**}|^{-1/2} \exp\{\log p^{**}(\mathbf{t}^{**})\}}{|\mathbf{H}^*|^{-1/2} \exp\{\log p^*(\mathbf{t}^*)\}}, \tag{12.6.3}$$

where $p^{**}(\mathbf{t}) = h(\mathbf{t}) p^*(\mathbf{t})$, $\mathbf{t}^*$ is the mode of p^*, $\mathbf{t}^{**}$ is the mode of p^{**}, and

$$\mathbf{H}^* = -\nabla^2 \log p^*(\mathbf{t}) \quad \text{at} \ \mathbf{t} = \mathbf{t}^*,$$

$$\mathbf{H}^{**} = -\nabla^2 \log p^{**}(\mathbf{t}) \quad \text{at} \ \mathbf{t} = \mathbf{t}^{**}.$$

The gain in using (12.6.3) is that the first-order error terms cancel with the ratio and hence the relative error drops to $O(n^{-2})$. For each function $h(\mathbf{t})$ whose expectation is sought, the mode of the log of the modified posterior, $\log p^{**}(\mathbf{t}) = \log p^*(\mathbf{t}) + \log h(\mathbf{t})$, needs to be found. This requires a new optimization for each function, but (1) the posterior mode $\mathbf{t}^*$ should be close and (2) a single Newton or Newton-like step should suffice, owing to Chapter 9 asymptotics.

Example 12.3: *Laplace Approximation to Log-Series Problem*
In Example 10.1, posterior mean and variance were computed on a posterior based on a sample from the log-series distribution

$$p^*(t) = t^{16}(1-t)/[-\log(1-t)]^{10}.$$

In **quad1**, the posterior mean was computed as .527057; the variance was .0187, using Simpson's rule with 20 intervals. For the Laplace approximation (found in **laplace1**), two searches for modes were performed using the Illinois method: one for $\log p^*(\mathbf{t})$, the other for $\log p^{**}(\mathbf{t}) = \log t + \log p^*(\mathbf{t})$. Following (12.6.3), the posterior mean was approximated by .5251 and the posterior variance by .0186. Using just the modal approximation (12.6.1), the mean is .5272 and variance $1/42.036 = .0238$, not nearly as close as the Laplace approximation.

Example 12.4: *Laplace Approximation for Extended Example from Chapter 9*
In Example 10.2, the likelihood from the extended example from Chapter 9 was modified by reducing the sample size to create a more interesting posterior for integration. Using product Simpson's rule in **chex102s**, the posterior mean vector and covariance matrix was computed as

$$E[\theta] = \begin{bmatrix} .271831 \\ .125142 \end{bmatrix} \quad \text{and} \quad \text{cov}[\theta] = \begin{bmatrix} .004474 & -.000645 \\ -.000645 & .002242 \end{bmatrix}.$$

With two parameters, six searches are required for the five posterior moments; the results are found in **laplace2**. The Laplace approximation method gave the following:

$$\hat{E}[\theta] = \begin{bmatrix} .271660 \\ .125327 \end{bmatrix} \quad \text{and} \quad \widehat{\text{cov}}[\theta] = \begin{bmatrix} .004466 & -.000645 \\ -.000645 & .002236 \end{bmatrix},$$

while the modal approximation gave

$$\mathbf{t}^* = \begin{bmatrix} .265782 \\ .110980 \end{bmatrix} \quad \text{and} \quad \mathbf{H}^{-1} = \begin{bmatrix} .004816 & -.000606 \\ -.000606 & .002195 \end{bmatrix}.$$

The Laplace approximation gave a remarkable improvement over the modal approximation.

One of the obvious requirements is that the function $h(\mathbf{t})$ be nonnegative over the region where the posterior mass lies. For the two examples just discussed, the parameter space is constrained and so this requirement is obviously satisfied. For contrary cases, one suggestion is to add a large constant to $h(\mathbf{t})$ to keep it positive and then subtract the constant off later. The alternative approach is to approximate the moment-generating function of the function of interest, so that the function is now $\exp\{sh(\mathbf{t})\}$; then $\log p^{**}(\mathbf{t}) = \log p^*(\mathbf{t}) + sh(\mathbf{t})$. Now compute the Laplace approximation for a few values of s near 0 and approximate the derivative at the origin numerically to get the moment. This latter approach is preferred, according to Tierney et al. (1989).

12.7 Randomized Quadrature

Fixed integration methods (e.g., Simpson's rule, Gauss–Hermite) exploit the smoothness of the integrand and give rapid convergence. The difficulty in assessing their accuracy, however, is a serious drawback. On the other hand, Monte Carlo integration does not even use continuity of the integrand and converges comparatively slowly, yet the usual statistical tools can be employed to assess accuracy. If only the best attributes of both could be combined ....

Consider computing $h(t)$ on the unit interval using a Riemann sum with a random starting point:

$$\hat{I}(h) = n^{-1} \sum_{i=1}^{n} h\left(U + \frac{i-1}{n}\right), \qquad (12.7.1)$$

where $U \sim \text{uniform}(0, 1/n)$. Then this integral estimate is unbiased,

$$E[\hat{I}(h)] = \int_0^1 h(t)\,dt$$

for all functions $h(t)$, and gains improved convergence through a smaller variance, usually $O(n^{-2})$. Applied statisticians would recognize this approach immediately as *systematic sampling*. Randomized methods can be exact for certain functions, give small variance for certain kinds of smoothness, and can be assessed for accuracy using standard statistical methods. As discussed in Section 10.7, Cranley and Patterson (1976) suggested using random starting points for Korobov rules. This can now be seen as just a multivariate version of (12.7.1):

$$\hat{I}(h) = \sum_{i=1}^{N} h(\{\mathbf{U} + (i/N)\mathbf{g}\}), \qquad (12.7.2)$$

where $\{\cdot\}$ means to take the fractional part and where the components of $\mathbf{U}$ are independent uniform$(0, 1)$ random variables. Now $E[\hat{I}(h)] = \int_0^1 \cdots \int_0^1 h(\mathbf{t})\,d\mathbf{t}$ for any function $h(\mathbf{t})$. In general terms, randomized quadrature works because the quadrature rule gives a good estimate of the integral. If the function is smooth, then the values of the function at the abscissas are negatively correlated (they must give nearly the same integral estimate each time) and so the sum has a much smaller variance than mere random sampling. As the function gets noisier, the improvement diminishes and the variance approaches that of random sampling.

Siegel and O'Brien (1985) suggested a random integration rule for the interval $[-1, +1]$. Let R have the density $3r^2$ on the unit interval. Then the integration rule

$$T(R) = w_0(R)h(0) + w_1(R)h(-R) + w_1(R)h(+R), \qquad (12.7.3)$$

where $w_0(R) = 2 - 2/(3R^2)$ and $w_1(R) = 1/(3R^2)$, is unbiased for all functions h. That is,

$$E[T(R)] = \int_{-1}^{1} h(r) \, dr,$$

and this is exact (zero variance) if $h(r)$ is a cubic polynomial. Notice the similarity in form and principle to the antithetic variates discussed in Section 10.7.

Genz and Monahan (1998) generalized this approach for integrating functions weighted with $|r|^{d-1} \exp\{-r^2/2\}$. The first-order rule takes the simple symmetrized, antithetic variables form

$$T_1(r) = \tfrac{1}{2}h(-R) + \tfrac{1}{2}h(R),$$

where $R \sim \chi_d$, which is exact only for linear h. The third-order rule $T_3(R)$ is similar to Siegel–O'Brien (12.7.3) but with $R \sim \chi_{d+2}$ and with weights $w_0(R) = 1 - d/R^2$ and $w_1(R) = d/(2R^2)$. This method is exact for cubic functions h with respect to the weight function and is unbiased for all h:

$$E[T_3(R)] = \frac{2^{-d/2}}{\Gamma(d/2)} \int_{-\infty}^{\infty} h(r)|r|^{d-1} \exp\left\{-\frac{r^2}{2}\right\} dr. \qquad (12.7.4)$$

Integration on the surface of a sphere with fixed quadrature was discussed in Section 10.4. These rules may appear unsatisfactory because the assumptions of smoothness are not intuitively obvious, and it is difficult to add more points without some reliance on further smoothness. Here randomization of these rules follows some of the spirit of compound rules: add more points without assuming further smoothness. The integration rule with abscissas $\mathbf{v}^{(k)}$ and weights u_k can be randomized using a random orthogonal matrix $\mathbf{Q}$. If $\mathbf{Q}$ has the right distribution, then

$$E\left[\sum_{k=1}^{m} u_k h(\mathbf{Q}\mathbf{v}^{(k)})\right] = \int_{U_d} h(\mathbf{z}) \, d\mathbf{z},$$

where U_d is the surface of the unit sphere in d dimensions. Stewart (1980) gave an algorithm for generating $\mathbf{Q}$ with the right distribution, a uniform distribution (invariant Haar measure) over orthogonal matrices. The basic theory is to generate a $d \times d$ matrix $\mathbf{X}$ with each entry X_{ij} independent standard normal and then compute the QR factorization $\mathbf{X} = \mathbf{QR}$ following the methods of Chapter 5. Stewart gave a very efficient algorithm using Householder transformations (Sections 5.5 and 5.6) for annihilating a vector: first construct the transformation $\mathbf{H}_1$ to annihilate a bivariate normal vector $\mathbf{x}^{(1)}$, and rotate the last two coordinates of the $\mathbf{v}^{(k)}$. Then construct transformation $\mathbf{H}_2$ on a trivariate vector $\mathbf{x}^{(2)}$ to rotate the last three coordinates, continuing on to finish with the vector $\mathbf{x}^{(n-1)} \sim N_d(0, \mathbf{I}_d)$ to construct $\mathbf{H}_{n-1}$. Multiplying by $\mathbf{Q} = \mathbf{H}_{n-1} \cdots \mathbf{H}_2\mathbf{H}_1$ can then be done sequentially on the vectors $\mathbf{v}^{(k)}$. Heiberger (1978) gave a similar algorithm with a different ordering; see Tanner and Thisted (1982) for corrections.

Example 12.5: *Random Rotation on the Unit Sphere*

The demonstration program **spkblh** uses Stewart's algorithm with Householder transformations, as just outlined, to rotate the antipodal (Section 10.4) integration rule on the unit sphere for integrating the kernel of the Langevin distribution (see Watson 1983, p. 101):

$$\frac{1}{|U_d|} \int_{U_d} \exp\{-k(\boldsymbol{\mu}^{\mathrm{T}}\mathbf{z})\}\, d\mathbf{z} = I_{d/2-1}(k)\frac{(2\pi)^{d/2}}{k^{d/2-1}},$$

where $I_j(x)$ is the modified Bessel function. Relevant results are tabled in Abramowitz and Stegun (1970): their Table 9.8 lists $e^{-k}I_0(k)$, $e^{-k}I_1(k)$, and $k^{-2}I_1(k)$; their Table 10.8 shows $\sqrt{\pi/(2k)}I_{n+1/2}(k)$.

12.8 Spherical–Radial Methods

The same spirit of exploiting the advantages of fixed quadrature and randomized methods motivated Monahan and Genz (1997) to propose a mixed method for the general Bayesian integration problem. The common asymptotics suggests that the posterior distribution should be approximately normal around the mode, with the inverse of the Hessian approximating the covariance matrix of the parameters. However, as noted in Sections 12.4 and 12.5 with importance sampling, putting too much trust in the asymptotics is dangerous and renders the CLT importance sampling results unreliable. We desire an approach that could exploit the multivariate normality without failing completely when the posterior is far from normal.

Their approach begins with the same step: compute the posterior mode $\mathbf{t}^*$ and Hessian matrix, $\mathbf{H} = -\nabla^2 \log p^*(\mathbf{t})$ at $\mathbf{t}^*$. Then compute the Cholesky factorization of $\mathbf{H} = \mathbf{B}\mathbf{B}^{\mathrm{T}}$ and change variables from $\mathbf{t}$ to $\mathbf{x}$ via $\mathbf{t} = \mathbf{t}^* + \mathbf{B}^{-\mathrm{T}}\mathbf{x}$. The desired integrals now take the form

$$\int \cdots \int h(\mathbf{t}) p^*(\mathbf{t})\, d\mathbf{t} = \int \cdots \int g(\mathbf{x})q(\mathbf{x})\, d\mathbf{x},$$

where $g(\mathbf{x}) = h(\mathbf{t}^* + \mathbf{B}^{-\mathrm{T}}\mathbf{x})$ and $q(\mathbf{x}) = |B|p^*(\mathbf{t}^* + \mathbf{B}^{-\mathrm{T}}\mathbf{x})$. Integration over $\mathbf{x}$ is now also over $\mathcal{R}^d$; the main change is that the new variable $\mathbf{x}$ is centered at the origin and scaled. The spherical–radial transformation is the next key step, essentially a change to polar coordinates. Again we change variables from $\mathbf{x}$ to $\mathbf{x} = r\mathbf{z}$, where r is the radius and $\mathbf{z}$ is a point on the surface of the unit sphere in d dimensions U_d. Now the desired integrals look like

$$\int \cdots \int h(\mathbf{t}) p^*(\mathbf{t})\, d\mathbf{t} = \int \cdots \int g(\mathbf{x})q(\mathbf{x})\, d\mathbf{x}$$

$$= \int_0^\infty \int_{U_d} g(r\mathbf{z})q(r\mathbf{z})\, d\mathbf{z}\, r^{d-1}\, dr; \qquad (12.8.1)$$

don't forget the r^{d-1}. The value of changing to $(r, \mathbf{z})$ is that the most common failure of the normal approximation to the posterior appears in the tails, isolated here to the radius r.

The spherical integration for a given r, the inner integral, calls for the randomization of spherical rules discussed in Section 12.7. Generate random orthogonal matrices $\mathbf{Q}^{(j)}$, $j = 1, \ldots, q$; then the inner integral is estimated using the average of the q replicates

$$G(r) = \frac{1}{q} \sum_{j=1}^{q} \left\{ \sum_{k=1}^{m} u_k g(r\mathbf{Q}^{(j)}\mathbf{v}_k) q(r\mathbf{Q}^{(j)}\mathbf{v}_k) \right\}, \tag{12.8.2}$$

since the inner sum is an unbiased estimate of

$$\int_{U_d} g(r\mathbf{z}) q(r\mathbf{z}) \, d\mathbf{z}.$$

Now that the inner integral (together with most of the d dimensions) has been taken care of, two approaches are considered for the outer integral: fixed and random. The randomized quadrature method for $\mathcal{R}^1$ described in Section 12.7 was derived for this particular problem. Here we generate $R \sim \chi_{d+2}$ and then compute

$$T_3(R) = w_0(R)G(0) + 2w_1(R)G(R)\exp\{R^2/2\}, \tag{12.8.3}$$

with the weights as before, so $w_0(R) = 1 - d/R^2$ and $2w_1(R) = d/R^2$. This third-degree randomized integration rule for the radius has proved to be quite effective in high-dimensional (d in hundreds) problems, but not as good as fixed rules in more modest problems ($d \approx 3, \ldots, 12$).

The best approach for integrating posteriors in modestly high dimensions is a mixed spherical–radial method: employ the randomized spherical integration rule as expressed in (12.8.2), but use a fixed method (e.g. Simpson) for the radial part. Here the radial integration uses abscissas r_i and weights w_i. The mixed spherical–radial method takes the form

$$\sum_i w_i r_i^{d-1} G(r_i) = \sum_i w_i r_i^{d-1} \frac{1}{q} \sum_{j=1}^{q} \left\{ \sum_{k=1}^{m} u_k g(r_i\mathbf{Q}^{(j)}\mathbf{v}_k) q(r_i\mathbf{Q}^{(j)}\mathbf{v}_k) \right\}. \tag{12.8.4}$$

The integration in the radial direction does not depend on normal-like tails, and the randomization appears in the high-dimension spherical integration. If the multivariate normal approximation to the posterior works well, then this approach can exploit it; if the approximation is poor, this mixed method can still soundly perform the integration and give reliable standard errors. An important byproduct of the mixed method are some effective diagnostics based on an analysis of the variance expression. Let us denote as Y_{ij} the term in braces in (12.8.4); then a standard error can be constructed in a straightforward manner. Estimate the variance of $G(r_i)$ in the usual way:

$$S_i^2 = \sum_{j=1}^{q} \frac{(Y_{ij} - \bar{Y}_i)^2}{q(q-1)}; \tag{12.8.5}$$

then the variance can be estimated as

$$\sum_i w_i^2 r_i^{2d-2} S_i^2. \tag{12.8.6}$$

Experiments have shown this variance estimate to be reliable.

The diagnostics from the mixed spherical–radial method can assess the quality of the multivariate normal approximation to the posterior. If the approximation is good, then the variances of $G(r_i)$ will be small and the plot of, say, $\log G(r_i)$ versus r should look like $-r_i^2/2$. Departures from normality (say, heavy tails) will be manifest in the

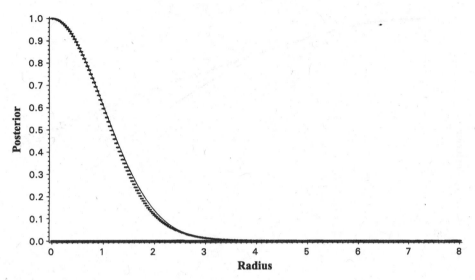

Figure 12.7. Spherical–radial method on blood-type problem. Plot of posterior with normal (solid line) and standard errors (slammed against axis) as a function of radius.

(tail) behavior of $G(r_i)$. The variances of $G(r_i)$ should be small for very small r, since the posterior should be flat at its mode. The variances of $G(r_i)$ will also be small for very large r as the posterior tails off to zero. In between, the variance estimates S_i^2 reflect the spherical symmetry of the posterior. These two plots can assess the quality of the normal approximation via tail behavior and spherical symmetry; a combined plot of (a) the weighted $w_i r_i^{d-1} G(r_i)$ versus r (compared to the χ_d kernel $r^{d-1} \exp\{-r^2/2\}$) and (b) the weighted standard error contribution $w_i r_i^{d-1} S_i$ will show both effects at once.

Example 12.6: *Spherical–Radial Integration of Posterior from Modified Blood-Type Example*
The posterior from the extended example of Chapter 9, with modified data as in Example 10.2 to make the problem more interesting, is integrated using spherical radial integration methods (see the code in **mixed1**). Since $d = 2$, the spherical integration (really just a circle) is coded using just sines and cosines; the radial integration with Simpson's rule is truncated at $r = 8$. The estimated relative error in the normalization constant is just .0002, and the posterior mean vector and covariance matrix are computed as

$$E[\boldsymbol{\theta}] = \begin{bmatrix} .271783 \\ .124921 \end{bmatrix} \quad \text{and} \quad \text{cov}[\boldsymbol{\theta}] = \begin{bmatrix} .004442 & -.000643 \\ -.000643 & .002217 \end{bmatrix}.$$

The diagnostic plots for the spherical–radial method are given in Figures 12.7–12.9. Figure 12.7 gives the $G(r)$ and S_i, and it is clear that near the mode the posterior is very close to normal. Figure 12.8, plotting $\log G(r)$ versus r along with $-r^2/2$, shows how the posterior normality deteriorates farther from the mode. The combined plot in Figure 12.9 shows the effect on the posterior, with the weighted radial part very close to the target χ_2 density. Note that, in all three plots, the errors are very small compared to the signal.

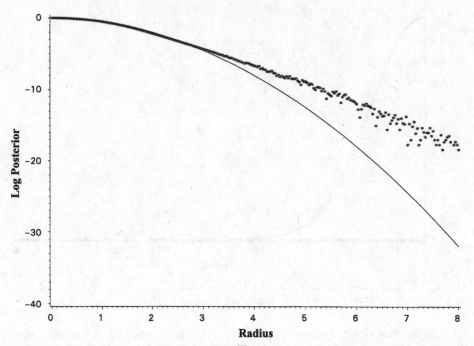

Figure 12.8. Spherical–radial method on blood-type problem. Plot of log posterior as a function of radius; solid line is $-r^2/2$.

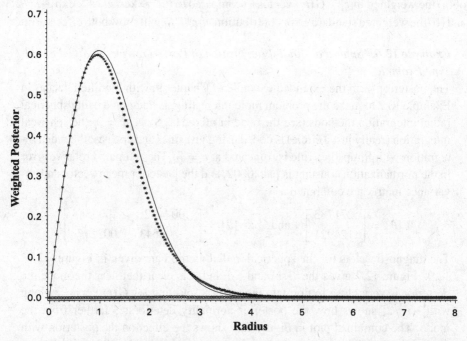

Figure 12.9. Spherical–radial method on blood-type problem. Plot of weighted posterior and chi density with 2 df; weighted standard errors still against axis.

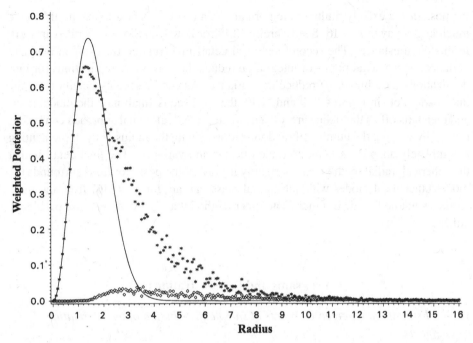

Figure 12.10. Spherical–radial method on variance components problem. Plot of weighted posterior and chi density with 3 df; weighted standard errors no longer small.

Example 12.7: *Spherical–Radial Integration of Posterior from Variance Components Example*

The posterior from the variance components example was previously analyzed in Examples 10.3 and 12.2; here the posterior is integrated using spherical–radial methods in the demonstration **mixed2**. Although the dimension $d = 3$ is still small, this problem presents some difficulties because the first two components must be positive. The range for the radial integration is extended to $r = 16$ and many more points are used, yet the relative standard error in the normalization constant is still at .0035.

As can be seen from the diagnostic plot Figure 12.10, the posterior is very close to normal near the mode (small values of r), but the tails are heavier than normal owing to the plot of $r^{d-1}G(r)$ tailing off much more slowly than the χ_3 density. More importantly, the error grows quickly and swamps the signal for large r. A possible cause for the error to grow so quickly is that the parameter space boundaries are wrecking the spherical symmetry. One possible remedy is to put more randomizations (bigger q) to reduce the error for larger values of the radius r.

Two technical details in the mixed spherical–radial method remain to be addressed. The radial integration can be handled well using Simpson's rule, but with a larger range than one might expect. Using r in standardized coordinates, one might think that $r = 2$ is two standard errors and large. But as d grows, the volume in the higher dimension grows also, and like r^{d-1}, so we're really integrating the χ_d density kernel if the posterior is exactly multivariate normal. As a result, it's best to extend the range much larger, say to $r = 16$. See Exercise 12.18 for how well Simpson's rule can work in this circumstance. The second technical detail involves the trade-off in bias and variance. More radial points of integration reduce the bias; more replications (or randomizations, or a bigger q) reduce the variance. As can be seen especially from the diagnostic plots in Figures 12.9 and 12.10, the variance is small near the mode, rises, and then tails off as the radius grows. The mixed spherical–radial approach can be improved by varying the number of randomizations q with the radius or by implementing a completely adaptive scheme to trade off bias and variance. The final detail is that the spherical–radial method can work only if most of the posterior mass surrounds the mode; other local modes with substantial mass that are far ($r > 16$) from the main mode cannot be found. But there's no other method that can work on those problems, either.

Programs and Demonstrations

rho0 *Estimation of percentile points of sample distribution of the correlation coefficient*
The correlation coefficient r for a sample size of 12 is generated using normals (**gnroul**) and χ (**gchirv**) random variables for $n = 1000$ observations. The four percentile point estimates $\hat{c}_j$ ($j = 1, \ldots, 4$) described in Section 12.2 are computed.

rho1 *Demonstration of kernel density estimation of the correlation coefficient*
Sample correlation coefficients ($n = 1000$) are generated as in **rho0** and kernel density estimates are computed using the density of the sum of three uniforms as the kernel; results are stored in **rho1.out**. Plotted later to form Figure 12.2.
eknlde – computes kernel density estimates for kernel with finite support.
ds3uns – computes density of the sum of three uniform variables scaled to interval $(-1, 1)$.
ifind – discrete bisection search described in Exercise 8.7.

rho2 *Demonstration of orthogonal series density estimation of the correlation coefficient*
Sample correlation coefficients ($n = 1000$) are generated as in **rho0** and orthogonal series density estimates are computed using Legendre polynomials; results are stored in **rho2.out**. Plotted later to form Figure 12.3.
ortpe – uses Clenshaw's method to evaluate finite Fourier series of a function.
ortpv – evaluates orthogonal polynomials.
weight – evaluates orthogonal polynomial weight functions.

rho3 *Demonstration of spline density estimation of the correlation coefficient*
Sample correlation coefficients ($n = 1000$) are generated as in **rho0** and spline density estimates are computed using the natural cubic spline interpolant to the empirical distribution function; results are stored in **rho3.out**. Plotted later to form Figure 12.4. Uses spline routines **splstn**, **strids**, **splev**, **spled**, and **jfind**.

dks2s *Demonstration of Smirnov two-sample nonparametric test*
First a textbook example of the Smirnov test statistic is computed, then several samples including ties are generated and the results from **dks2s** compared with the textbook approach to computation using sorts with parallel vectors.
dks2s – computes Smirnov two-sample nonparametric test statistic.
hsort – heapsort sorting algorithm.
hksort – heapsort sorting algorithm with an integer vector sorted in parallel to the vector of keys.

perfect *Demonstration of the use of quasirandom sequences to check generation code*
Generates pairs from Halton sequence with bases 2 and 3 and performs Box–Muller transformation; then checks by computing Kolmogorov–Smirnov and Anderson–Darling goodness-of-fit test statistics via **alnphi** and **cdfn**.
ncremnt – arbitrary base counter for Halton sequence.
expand – converts base counter vector in reverse order to get Halton sequence.

quad4 *Importance sampling for log-series posterior*
As described in Example 12.1, the log-series posterior from Example 10.1 is integrated using importance sampling from the normal approximation. The importance sampling weights are stored in **quad4.wgt**. The statistics necessary for analysis as described in Section 12.4 are also computed.

chex122a *Posterior integration of variance components example using normal importance sampling*
chex122b *Posterior integration of same example using importance sampling from multivariate t*
As described in Example 12.2, the posterior from variance components example from Chapter 10 is integrated using the normal approximation to the posterior in **chex122a**, whereas **chex122b** uses a multivariate t approximation with 5 df. Both use 2500 replications, and the weights are stored in files **chex122a.wgt** and **chex122b.wgt**. The tail behavior of the distribution of weights is analyzed as outlined in Section 12.5.

laplace1 *Application of Laplace approximation to log-series posterior*
As described in Example 12.3, the Laplace approximation is employed to compute the posterior mean and variance. The 1-dimensional searches are performed using the Illinois method.
illini – "Illinois" search algorithm.

laplace2 *Application of Laplace approximation to posterior from modified blood-type example*
As described in Example 12.4, the Laplace approximation is employed to compute the posterior means, variances, and covariance for the data of Example 10.2. Most of the code is a modification of **chex94rp**.

spkblh *Randomized quadrature on the surface of a sphere*
As described in Example 12.5, the kernel of the Langevin distribution on the surface of a sphere is integrated using the randomized quadrature of Section 12.7. The antipodal integration rule on the sphere is rotated using a random orthogonal matrix computed following Stewart's algorithm.
spkblh – randomized quadrature on the surface of a sphere.

mixed1 *Spherical–radial integration of posterior from modified blood-type example*
As described in Example 12.6, the posterior mean vector and covariance matrix for
the modified blood-type example are computed using spherical–radial integration.
The spherical integration, actually on a circle since $d = 2$, is coded simply with
sines and cosines; the radial integration uses Simpson's rule, truncating the range at
$r = 8$. The information for the diagnostic plots is written in **mixed1.dgn**.

mixed2 *Spherical–radial integration of variance components example*
As described in Example 12.7, the posterior mean vector and covariance matrix for
the variance components example, examined previously in Examples 10.3 and 12.2,
were computed using spherical–radial methods. A randomized antipodal spherical rule is used for the spherical integration; again Simpson is used for the radial,
but with truncation at $r = 16$. The diagnostic information is written in the file
mixed2.dgn.

Exercises

12.1 Discuss the computation of a kernel-type estimate of a distribution function.

12.2 Figures 10.1–10.4 display the log-series posterior from Examples 10.1 and 12.1. Using
the methods of Section 12.4 and the importance sampling weighted observations in
quad4.wgt, estimate the posterior density and compare it to the true density shown in
the figures.

12.3 Investigate the tail behavior of the importance sampling weights in **quad4.wgt**.

12.4 Using the results in **quad4.wgt**, estimate the .05 and .01 upper percentile points.

12.5 Write a routine to check a spline density estimate for nonnegativity.

12.6 Show that the estimates of the Fourier coefficients in orthogonal series density estimation (12.2.7) are unbiased.

12.7 Generate a sample of $n = 400$ observations from the t_3 distribution (Section 11.3, Algorithm C5). Estimate the upper .05 and .01 percentile points using estimates $\hat{c}_1$, $\hat{c}_2$, $\hat{c}_3$, $\hat{c}_4$,
and compare to the true values.

12.8 Generate a sample of $n = 400$ observations from the t_3 distribution, compute an estimate
of the tail parameter β using (12.5.2), and test for infinite mean and variance at $\alpha = .05$.

12.9 Generate a sample of $n = 400$ observations from the logistic distribution, compute an
estimate of the tail parameter β using (12.5.2), and test for infinite mean and variance
at $\alpha = .05$.

12.10 Write a routine to compute the Kolmogorov–Smirnov distribution function $Q(t)$ defined in (12.3.1).

12.11 Find the .10, .05, and .01 upper percentile points of $Q(t)$ from Exercise 12.10.

12.12 Modify the demonstration **perfect** for generating from the t_3 distribution (Algorithm
C5 again) and generate a sample of $n = 400$.
(a) Estimate the density using any of the methods in Section 12.2.
(b) Test for goodness of fit using chi-square, Kolmogorov–Smirnov, or Anderson–
Darling.
(c) Estimate the upper .05 and .01 percentile points as in Exercise 12.7.

12.13 Compare the results from Exercise 12.7 for estimating the percentile points of the t_3 distribution to those using importance sampling from the Cauchy (t_1) distribution together with weighted versions of the estimates $\hat{c}_1, \hat{c}_2, \hat{c}_3, \hat{c}_4$.

12.14 Apply the Laplace approximation method to estimate the posterior means using the reparameterized form of the extended example from Section 9.9 and **chex94rp**. Recall that the transformation made the likelihood much closer to normal.

12.15 Use the randomized Riemann sum (12.7.1) for finding the posterior mean and variance of the log-series posterior used in Example 12.1. Assess the accuracy of the posterior mean using the standard error for the ratio estimate from (12.4.4).

12.16 Compare the randomized Riemann sum (12.7.1) and a Simpson analog with alternating weights, one twice the other. Find the variances for each method for the following functions on $(0, 1)$: (a) $\exp(x)$; (b) $\cos(\pi x)$; (c) $1/(1 + 5x^2)$.

12.17 Integrate the function $f(x) = 1/(1 + x^2)$ on $(-1, 1)$ using the Siegel–O'Brien randomized quadrature method.

12.18 Integrate the kernel of the χ density $r^{d-1} \exp\{-r^2/2\}$ on $(0, \infty)$ for various values of d.
  (a) Find a truncation point. How does it depend on d?
  (b) How many points are required using Simpson's rule to get the relative error below 10^{-4}?

References

Milton Abramowitz and Irene A. Stegun (Eds.) (1970), *Handbook of Mathematical Functions.* New York: Dover.

Dennis D. Boos (1984), "Using Extreme Value Theory to Estimate Large Percentiles," *Technometrics* 26: 33–9.

N. N. Cencov (1962), "Evaluation of an Unknown Distribution Density from Observations," *Soviet Mathematics* 3: 1559–62.

William G. Cochran (1954), "Some Methods for Strengthening the Common χ^2 Tests," *Biometrics* 10: 417–51.

R. Cranley and T. N. L. Patterson (1976), "Randomization of Number Theoretic Methods for Multiple Integration," *SIAM Journal on Numerical Analysis* 13: 904–14.

E. C. Fieller (1954), "Some Problems in Interval Estimation," *Journal of the Royal Statistical Society B* 16: 175–85.

Alan Genz and John Monahan (1998), "Stochastic Integration Rules for Infinite Regions," *SIAM Journal of Scientific Computation* 19: 426–39.

John Geweke (1989), "Bayesian Inference in Econometric Models Using Monte Carlo Integration," *Econometrica* 57: 1317–39.

E. Haeusler and J. L. Teugels (1985), "On Asymptotic Normality of Hill's Estimator for the Exponent of Regular Variation," *Annals of Statistics* 13: 743–56.

P. Hall (1982), "On Some Simple Estimates of an Exponent of Regular Variation," *Journal of the Royal Statistical Society B* 44: 37–42.

Richard M. Heiberger (1978), "Algorithm AS127: Generation of Random Orthogonal Matrices," *Applied Statistics* 27: 199–206.

Tim Hesterberg (1995), "Weighted Average Importance Sampling and Defensive Mixture Distributions," *Technometrics* 37: 185–94.

B. W. Hill (1975), "A Simple General Approach to Inference about the Tail of a Distribution," *Annals of Statistics* 3: 1163–74.

H. B. Mann and A. Wald (1942), "On the Choice of the Number of Class Intervals in the Application of the Chi-Square Test," *Annals of Mathematical Statistics* 13: 306–17.

J. F. Monahan (1993), "Testing the Behavior of Importance Sampling Weights," *Computing Science and Statistics* 24: 112–17.

John Monahan and Alan Genz (1997), "Spherical-Radial Integration Rules for Bayesian Computation," *Journal of the American Statistical Association* 92: 664–74.

David S. Moore (1986), "Tests of Chi-Squared Type," in R. B. D'Agostino and M. A. Stephens (Eds.), *Goodness-of-Fit Techniques,* pp. 63–95. New York: Marcel Dekker.

J. T. Roscoe and J. A. Byars (1971), "An Investigation of the Restraints with Respect to Sample Size Commonly Imposed on the Use of Chi–Square Statistic," *Journal of the American Statistical Association* 66: 755–9.

A. F. Siegel and F. O'Brien (1985), "Unbiased Monte Carlo Integration Methods with Exactness for Low Order Polynomials," *SIAM Journal on Scientific and Statistical Computing* 6: 169–81.

B. W. Silverman (1986), *Density Estimation for Statistics and Data Analysis.* London: Chapman & Hall.

N. V. Smirnov (1939), "On the Estimation of the Discrepancy between Empirical Curves of Distribution for Two Independent Samples" (in Russian), *Bulletin of Moscow University* 2: 3–16.

Michael A. Stephens (1970), "Use of the Kolmogorov–Smirnov, Cramer–von Mises and Related Statistics without Extensive Tables," *Journal of the Royal Statistical Society B* 32: 115–22.

Michael A. Stephens (1986), "Tests Based on EDF Statistics," in R. B. D'Agostino and M. A. Stephens (Eds.), *Goodness-of-Fit Techniques,* pp. 97–193. New York: Marcel Dekker.

G. W. Stewart (1980), "The Efficient Generation of Random Orthogonal Matrices with an Application to Condition Estimation," *SIAM Journal on Numerical Analysis* 17: 403–9.

Martin A. Tanner and Ronald A. Thisted (1982), "Remark ASR42. A Remark on AS127. Generation of Random Orthogonal Matrices," *Applied Statistics* 31: 190–92.

Richard A. Tapia and James R. Thompson (1978), *Nonparametric Probability Density Estimation.* Baltimore: Johns Hopkins University Press.

Luke Tierney and Joseph B. Kadane (1986), "Accurate Approximations for Posterior Moments and Marginal Densities," *Journal of the American Statistical Association* 81: 82–6.

Luke Tierney, Robert E. Kass, and Joseph B. Kadane (1989), "Fully Exponential Laplace Approximations to Expectations and Variances of Nonpositive Functions," *Journal of the American Statistical Association* 84: 710–16.

Grace Wahba (1975), "Interpolating Spline Methods for Density Estimation I: Equi-Spaced Knots," *Annals of Statistics* 3: 30–48.

Geoffrey S. Watson (1983), *Statistics on Spheres.* New York: Wiley.

I. Weissman (1978), "Estimation of Parameters and Large Quantiles Based on the k Largest Observations," *Journal of the American Statistical Association* 73: 812–15.

13

Markov Chain Monte Carlo Methods

13.1 Introduction

One of the main advantages of Monte Carlo integration is a rate of convergence that is unaffected by increasing dimension, but a more important advantage for statisticians is the familiarity of the technique and its tools. Although Markov chain Monte Carlo (MCMC) methods are designed to integrate high-dimensional functions, the ability to exploit distributional tools makes these methods much more appealing to statisticians. In contrast to importance sampling with weighted observations, MCMC methods produce observations that are no longer independent; rather, the observations come from a stationary distribution and so time-series methods are needed for their analysis. The emphasis here will be on using MCMC methods for Bayesian problems with the goal of generating a series of observations whose stationary distribution $\pi(\mathbf{t})$ is proportional to the unnormalized posterior $p^*(\mathbf{t})$. Standard statistical methods can then be used to gain information about the posterior.

The two general approaches covered in this chapter are known as Gibbs sampling and the Metropolis–Hastings algorithm, although the former can be written as a special case of the latter. Gibbs sampling shows the potential of MCMC methods for Bayesian problems with hierarchical structure, also known as random effects or variance components. The key ingredient in Gibbs sampling is the ability to generate from the conditional distribution of each variable given the others; in the case of three components, generating from $f(x \mid Y = y, Z = z)$, $f(y \mid X = x, Z = z)$, and $f(z \mid X = x, Y = y)$. Under favorable conditions and starting values (X_0, Y_0, Z_0), the algorithm is simply as follows.

> *Algorithm BGS* (Basic Gibbs Sampling)
> For $i = 1, \ldots, n$ do
>   Generate X_i from $f(x \mid Y = Y_{i-1}, Z = Z_{i-1})$
>   Generate Y_i from $f(y \mid X = X_i, Z = Z_{i-1})$
>   Generate Z_i from $f(z \mid X = X_i, Y = Y_i)$

Then the triple (X_i, Y_i, Z_i) forms a Markov chain whose stationary distribution is the joint distribution $f(x, y, z)$. This algorithm is easy to use whenever the likelihood and prior permit easy generation from the conditional distribution of one parameter given all of the others. Note that any or all of the three components (X, Y, Z) may be multivariate.

Example 13.1A: *Variance Components with Normal Variables*

The simplest but most important random effects problem is the common variance components problem in normal variables visited previously in Chapter 10. Recall the change in notation from the standard:

$$Y_{ij} \sim N(\theta_i, \; \phi = \sigma_e^2), \quad j = 1, \dots, n_i;$$

$$\theta_i \sim N(\beta = \mu, \; \gamma = \sigma_a^2), \quad i = 1, \dots, p.$$

Our previous analyses constructed the likelihood for only the three fixed parameters (relabeled as $\beta = \mu$, $\phi = \sigma_e^2$, and $\gamma = \sigma_a^2$) by integrating out the random effect parameters θ_i, but these parameters will be retained here. Convenience suggests a prior on the fixed parameters of the following form:

$$\beta \sim N(b_0, \phi_0),$$

$$\phi \sim \text{inverse gamma}(a_1, b_1),$$

$$\gamma \sim \text{inverse gamma}(a_2, b_2),$$

with each component independent. The posterior then takes the form

$$p^*(\mathbf{t}, b, f, g) \propto g^{-(a_2 + p/2) - 1} \exp\left\{ -\frac{b_2 + \frac{1}{2}\sum_i (t_i - b)^2}{g} \right\}$$

$$\times f^{-(a_1 + N/2) - 1} \exp\left\{ -\frac{b_1 + W/2 + \frac{1}{2}\sum_i n_i(\bar{y}_{i\cdot} - t_i)^2}{f} \right\}$$

$$\times \exp\left\{ -\frac{\frac{1}{2}(b - b_0)^2}{\phi_0} \right\}. \tag{13.1.1}$$

The conditional distribution of the four (the first multivariate) parameters given all the others can be easily written:

$$(\theta_i \mid \beta = b, \; \phi = f, \; \gamma = g) \text{ independent } N(\theta_i^*, \gamma_i^*),$$

where $\gamma_i^* = 1/(n_i/f + 1/g)$ and $\theta_i^* = (n_i \bar{y}_{i\cdot}/f + b_0/g) * \gamma_i^*$;

$$(\beta \mid \boldsymbol{\theta} = \mathbf{t}, \; \phi = f, \; \gamma = g) \sim N(\beta_0^*, \phi_0^*),$$

where $\phi_0^* = 1/(1/\phi_0 + p/g)$ and $\beta_0^* = (b_0/\phi_0 + \sum t_i/g) * \phi_0^*$;

$$(\phi \mid \boldsymbol{\theta} = \mathbf{t}, \; \beta = b, \; \gamma = g) \sim \text{inverse gamma}(a_1^*, b_1^*),$$

where $a_1^* = a_1 + N/2$ and $b_1^* = b_1 + W/2 + \frac{1}{2}\sum_i (\bar{y}_{i\cdot} - t_i)^2$; and

$$(\gamma \mid \boldsymbol{\theta} = \mathbf{t}, \; \beta = b, \; \phi = f) \sim \text{inverse gamma}(a_2^*, b_2^*),$$

where $a_2^* = a_2 + p/2$ and $b_2^* = b_2 + \frac{1}{2}\sum_i (t_i - b)^2$.

See the demonstration program **chex131**. The reader should take warning that even though this approach may appear to be simple, the problem is particularly troublesome and will be revisited. See also Exercises 13.17, 13.18, and 13.19.

The keys for understanding MCMC methods are the Markov property and the finite discrete Markov chain. Our discussion begins with an introduction to Markov chains in Section 13.2, followed by the main theory behind Gibbs sampling in Section 13.3 and the Metropolis–Hastings algorithm in Section 13.4. Section 13.5 consists of a discussion of applicable time-series methods, and diagnostics are discussed in Section 13.7. The adaptive acceptance/rejection algorithms of Gilks and colleagues are described in Section 13.6.

13.2 Markov Chains

A series of random variables $\{Y_i, i = 1, \ldots, n\}$ has the *Markov property* if the conditional distribution of Y_i, given all the previous observations $Y_1, \ldots, Y_{i-1}$, depends only on the most recent observation Y_{i-1}. Saying this another way: The distribution of the future given the past and present depends only on the present. If Y_i has a finite discrete sample space (say, the integers $\{1, \ldots, m\}$) then this distribution can be written in terms of transition probabilities,

$$\Pr(Y_i = k \mid Y_1, \ldots, Y_{i-1}) = \Pr(Y_i = k \mid Y_{i-1} = j) = P_{jk}. \tag{13.2.1}$$

Hence this transition distribution can be expressed by an $m \times m$ matrix $\mathbf{P}$ with entries P_{jk} whose rows sum to 1. If the probability distribution of Y_0 is given by vector $\boldsymbol{\pi}^{(0)}$, then the distribution of Y_i can be written as $\boldsymbol{\pi}^{(i)} = (\mathbf{P}^{\mathrm{T}})^i \boldsymbol{\pi}^{(0)}$. (The reader should recognize the relationship with the power methods of Chapter 6.) If $\mathbf{P}$ has the correct properties then the largest eigenvalue of $\mathbf{P}$ is one with (a) right eigenvector $\mathbf{1}$ (column of ones), since $\mathbf{P}\mathbf{1} = \mathbf{1}\mathbf{1}$, and (b) left eigenvector $\boldsymbol{\pi}$ (i.e., $\mathbf{P}^{\mathrm{T}}\boldsymbol{\pi} = \mathbf{1}\boldsymbol{\pi}$), so that $\lim(\mathbf{P}^{\mathrm{T}})^i = \boldsymbol{\pi}\mathbf{1}^{\mathrm{T}}$. As a result, the distribution $\boldsymbol{\pi}^{(i)}$ converges to the stationary distribution $\boldsymbol{\pi}$ (with $\boldsymbol{\pi} = \mathbf{P}^{\mathrm{T}}\boldsymbol{\pi}$) at a rate that depends on the second largest eigenvalue of $\mathbf{P}$. Using Result 4 from Chapter 6, $(\mathbf{P}^{\mathrm{T}})^i$ can be written as $\mathbf{1}\boldsymbol{\pi}^{\mathrm{T}} + \gamma^i \mathbf{V}^{(i)}$, where $|\gamma| < 1$ and $\|\mathbf{V}^{(i)}\|$ is bounded. Then $\boldsymbol{\pi}^{(i)} - \boldsymbol{\pi} = \gamma^i \mathbf{V}^{(i)}\boldsymbol{\pi}^{(0)}$ and the convergence to the stationary distribution is geometric.

Just what are those "correct properties" that the transition matrix $\mathbf{P}$ must have? They are: irreducibility, aperiodicity, and recurrence. *Irreducibility* means that there is just one system; not one system moving around in the first half of the sample space and another in the second half (giving $\mathbf{P}$ two unit eigenvalues). If the Markov chain is not irreducible then it can get stuck in one part and never get to the other. As its name suggests, a periodic chain cycles through some states in a regular fashion; *aperiodicity* precludes this possibility. *Recurrence* means that the expected time to start in state i and return back to state i is finite. Although this may have not special intuitive meaning, its consequence is that the stationary distribution exists. With an infinite number of states, recurrence precludes the series from running off to infinity, never to return.

The main consequences of a Markov chain having these properties are threefold. First is that a stationary distribution exists and Y_i converges in distribution to it. The second is the ability to apply the strong law to the series in spite of its dependence:

$$\frac{1}{n} \sum_{i=1}^{n} g(Y_i) \to E\{g(Y)\}, \tag{13.2.2}$$

where Y has the stationary distribution. A series having this property is called *ergodic*. The third desirable property is a version of the central limit theorem, which depends on the geometric rate of convergence and works out as

$$\sqrt{n}\left(\frac{1}{n}\sum_{i=1}^{n} g(Y_i) - E\{g(Y)\}\right) \to N(0, \eta_g^2), \tag{13.2.3}$$

where the asymptotic variance term η_g^2 depends on the function g and the stationary distribution. The applicable time-series methodology is discussed in Section 13.5.

Now two other items require attention before proceeding. First, the Markov property can be relaxed to any finite degree of dependence by expanding the sample space. If the distribution of Y_i depends on both Y_{i-2} and Y_{i-1}, then expand the definition of the series $\{Y_i\}$ to two dimensions; the Markov property will then hold. The second item concerns using sample means to estimate expectations, exploiting (13.2.2). The first few observations Y_i have distribution $\pi^{(i)}$, not their limiting distribution π, and we want means with respect to π. In practice, starting the chain means a single value Y_0, not a distribution $\pi^{(0)}$, and different starting values will directly affect the first part of the series and also the average $n^{-1}\sum g(Y_i)$. As a result, the initial startup or "burn-in" of a series is often discarded from the average for estimating properties of the stationary distribution. How much of the series to discard – or at what point convergence of $\pi^{(i)}$ to π has been achieved – depends on the rate of convergence, which can be difficult to quantify in practice.

Generalizing the finite discrete Markov chain to the continuous case introduces some obvious difficulties and, of course, some subtle ones. First extend to the multivariate case, with sample space $\mathcal{R}^d$. The transition matrix $\mathbf{P}$ becomes a transition kernel $p(\mathbf{x}, \mathbf{y})$ (from $\mathbf{x}$ to $\mathbf{y}$) for computing probabilities as

$$\Pr(\mathbf{Y} \in A \mid \mathbf{X} = \mathbf{x}) = \int_A p(\mathbf{x}, \mathbf{y})\, d\mathbf{y}.$$

The stationary distribution of the chain must then satisfy the integral equation

$$\pi(\mathbf{y}) = \int p(\mathbf{x}, \mathbf{y})\pi(\mathbf{x})\, d\mathbf{x}. \tag{13.2.4}$$

The "correct conditions" for the Markov process to be ergodic are similar to the discrete case, but with some details. Irreducibility as applied to MCMC is not usually a problem, save for getting stuck in one part of the space and not being able to get out. Recurrence is rephrased in terms of sets with positive probability being visited infinitely often. The reader is referred to Tierney (1994, 1995), Meyn and Tweedie (1993), or Chan and Geyer (1994) for details.

13.3 Gibbs Sampling

Gibbs sampling is often the easiest MCMC method to implement and explain. However, its applicability can be limited to certain classes of problems. The problems that are conducive for Gibbs sampling are those where the conditional distributions of variables (given the others) can be easily constructed from the posterior distribution. That is, take the unnormalized posterior distribution $p^*(\mathbf{t})$ and examine each component, say $\mathbf{t} = (t_1, t_2, \ldots, t_d)$. Notice that the conditional distribution of θ_j given all of the other components is proportional to $p^*(\mathbf{t})$:

$$p(t_j \mid \boldsymbol{\theta}_{-j} = \mathbf{t}_{-j}) \equiv p(t_j \mid \theta_1 = t_1, \ldots, \theta_{j-1} = t_{j-1}, \theta_{j+1} = t_{j+1}, \ldots, \theta_d = t_d)$$

$$\propto p^*(t_1, \ldots, t_d),$$

although the only variable of interest is t_j.

Leaving behind Bayesian analysis for a moment, consider the following joint density with X discrete and Y continuous (see also Casella and George 1992):

$$f(x, y) = \binom{n}{x} y^{x+\alpha-1}(1-y)^{n-x+\beta-1} \quad \text{for } x = 0, 1, \ldots, n \text{ and } 0 \le y \le 1.$$
$$(13.3.1)$$

To obtain the conditional density of x given y, treat y as fixed in $f(x, y)$; then we find

$$f(x \mid y) \propto \binom{n}{x} y^x (1-y)^{-x}$$

or that $(X \mid Y = y)$ is binomial(n, y), with the deleted constants only part of the normalization. Going the other way, to derive the conditional density of y given x, treat x as fixed in $f(x, y)$; then we find

$$f(y \mid x) \propto y^{x+\alpha-1}(1-y)^{n-x+\beta-1}$$

or that $(Y \mid X = x)$ is beta$(x + \alpha, n - x + \beta)$. A Gibbs sampling algorithm following

For $i = 1, \ldots, n$ do
    Generate Y_i from $f(y \mid X = X_{i-1})$
    Generate X_i from $f(x \mid Y = Y_i)$

will produce a series of pairs (X_i, Y_i) whose stationary distribution is given by $f(x, y)$ in (13.3.1). Notice that the alphabetic order was reversed, generating Y first from the old X whereafter the new X would use the new Y. Checking the integral equation (13.2.4), with (X, Y) corresponding to $\mathbf{y}$ (new) and (u, v) corresponding to $\mathbf{x}$ (old), we have

$$p(u, v; x, y) = f(x \mid y)f(y \mid u)$$

$$= \binom{n}{x} y^x (1-y)^{n-x} \times \frac{\Gamma(\alpha+\beta+n)}{\Gamma(u+\alpha)\Gamma(n-u+\beta)} y^{u+\alpha-1}(1-y)^{n-u+\beta-1}.$$

Hence, using $f(u, v)$ (from 13.3.1) as $\pi(\mathbf{x})$, the right-hand side is

$$\int p(\mathbf{x}, \mathbf{y})\pi(\mathbf{x}) \, d\mathbf{x}$$

$$= \iint_0^1 p(u, v, x, y)f(u, v) \, dv \, d\mu(u)$$

$$= \iint_0^1 \binom{n}{x} y^x (1-y)^{n-x} \times \frac{\Gamma(\alpha+\beta+n)}{\Gamma(u+\alpha)\Gamma(n-u+\beta)} y^{u+\alpha-1}(1-y)^{n-u+\beta-1}$$

$$\times \binom{n}{u} v^{u+\alpha-1}(1-v)^{n-u+\beta-1} \, dv \, d\mu(u).$$
$$(13.3.2)$$

The innermost integral is just the beta kernel, and it cancels the ratio of gamma functions to yield

$$= \int \binom{n}{x} y^x (1-y)^{n-x} y^{u+\alpha-1} (1-y)^{n-u+\beta-1} \times \binom{n}{u} d\mu(u)$$

$$= \binom{n}{x} y^x (1-y)^{n-x} y^{\alpha-1} (1-y)^{\beta-1} \times \int \binom{n}{u} y^u (1-y)^{n-u} d\mu(u);$$

summing over u produces exactly $\pi(\mathbf{y}) = f(x, y)$, verifying (13.2.4). (See also Exercises 13.1 and 13.2.)

Example 13.2: *Ramus Heights (a.k.a. Jaw)*

In a classic repeated measures problem, Elston and Grizzle (1962) give four measurements on each of $n = 20$ boys of the size of the jaw at four ages. Denote the measurement of boy i at age x_j ($x_j = 8, 8.5, 9, 9.5$) as $Y_j^{(i)}$ with $i = 1, \ldots, n$ and $j = 1, \ldots, p$. Since parameterizing with the inverse covariance matrix will make some things easier, the model has $\mathbf{Y}^{(i)} \sim N_p(\boldsymbol{\mu}, \boldsymbol{\Omega}^{-1})$ but perhaps with a regression model for the mean vector $\boldsymbol{\mu}$; that is, $\boldsymbol{\mu} = \mathbf{X}\boldsymbol{\beta}$. The likelihood for these data can be written as

$$f(\mathbf{Y} \mid \boldsymbol{\beta}, \boldsymbol{\Omega}) \propto |\boldsymbol{\Omega}|^{n/2} \exp\left\{-\tfrac{1}{2} \operatorname{trace} \boldsymbol{\Omega} \mathbf{E}^*\right\}, \tag{13.3.3}$$

where $\mathbf{E}^* = \mathbf{E} + n(\bar{\mathbf{Y}} - \mathbf{X}\boldsymbol{\beta})(\bar{\mathbf{Y}} - \mathbf{X}\boldsymbol{\beta})^{\mathsf{T}}$ and $\mathbf{E} = \sum_{i=1}^{n} (\mathbf{Y}^{(i)} - \bar{\mathbf{Y}})(Y^{(i)} - \bar{\mathbf{Y}})^{\mathsf{T}}$. The prior on the inverse covariance matrix $\boldsymbol{\Omega}$ is Wishart with p degrees of freedom and scale matrix $\mathbf{C}^{-1}$. A flat prior is used for $\boldsymbol{\beta}$. Consequently, the posterior can be written as

$$p(\mathbf{b}, \mathbf{O}) \propto |\mathbf{O}|^{(n-1)/2} \exp\left\{-\tfrac{1}{2} \operatorname{trace} \mathbf{O} \mathbf{E}^{**}\right\}, \tag{13.3.4}$$

where $\mathbf{E}^{**} = \mathbf{E}^* + \mathbf{C}$. The conditional distribution of $\boldsymbol{\Omega}$ given $\boldsymbol{\beta} = \mathbf{b}$ is clearly Wishart, with scale matrix $(\mathbf{E} + \mathbf{C} + n(\bar{\mathbf{Y}} - \mathbf{X}\mathbf{b})(\bar{\mathbf{Y}} - \mathbf{X}\mathbf{b})^{\mathsf{T}})^{-1}$ and $n + p$ degrees of freedom (we are talking about the inverse covariance matrix $\boldsymbol{\Omega}$). For the other conditional distribution, some algebra is needed (Exercise 13.4) to show that $\boldsymbol{\beta}$ given $\boldsymbol{\Omega} = \mathbf{O}$ is $N_p\big(\tilde{\boldsymbol{\beta}} = (\mathbf{X}^{\mathsf{T}}\mathbf{O}\mathbf{X})^{-1}\mathbf{X}^{\mathsf{T}}\mathbf{O}\bar{\mathbf{Y}}, (n\mathbf{X}^{\mathsf{T}}\mathbf{O}\mathbf{X})^{-1}\big)$. In the demonstration **chex132**, $\mathbf{C} = \mathbf{I}_4$ and a simple linear regression model is used for $\mathbf{X}\boldsymbol{\beta}$ ($\boldsymbol{\beta}$ is 2-dimensional).

Clearly, Gibbs sampling can be easy to use if the conditional distributions work out into nice forms, as in Examples 13.1 and 13.2. In the following example, however, things don't seem to work out for one of the parameters.

Example 13.3A: *Pump Example*

George, Makov, and Smith (1993) discussed a hierarchical prior from a Poisson model for the number of failures Y_j for pump j with operating time x_j. The model for the data is $Y_j \sim \text{Poisson}(\phi_j x_j)$, where the rate parameters ϕ_j come from a gamma distribution (with parameters α and β) and use conjugate priors for these hyperparameters: exponential(1) for α; Gamma$(c, 1)$ for β. The likelihood is proportional to $\prod(f_j x_j)^{y_j} \exp\{-\sum f_j x_j\}$, and the (prior) distribution of the random effects parameters ϕ_j takes the form $b^a f_j^{a-1} \exp\{-bf_j\}/\Gamma(a)$. The density for α (resp. β) is chosen proportional to e^{-a} (resp. $b^{c-1}e^{-b}$).

Consider the case of Example 13.3, where the joint posterior of $\boldsymbol{\theta} = (\phi_1, \ldots, \phi_J, \alpha, \beta)$ is

$$p^*(f_1, \ldots, f_J, a, b) = \prod_j (f_j x_j)^{y_j} \exp\left\{-\sum_j f_j x_j\right\}$$
$$\times \prod_j \left[\frac{b^a f_j^{a-1} \exp\{-bf_j\}}{\Gamma(a)}\right] \times e^{-a} \times e^{-b} b^{c-1}.$$

However, first considering ϕ_1, we have

$$p(f_1 \mid \boldsymbol{\theta}_{-1} = \mathbf{t}_{-1}) \propto p^*(\mathbf{t}) \propto f_1^{a+y_1-1} \exp\{-f_1(b+x_1)\};$$

in general,

$$p(f_j \mid \boldsymbol{\theta}_{-j} = \mathbf{t}_{-j}) \propto p^*(\mathbf{t}) \propto f_j^{a+y_j-1} \exp\{-f_j(b+x_j)\} \quad \text{for } j = 1, \ldots, J.$$

Then

$$p(a \mid \boldsymbol{\phi} = \mathbf{f}, \beta = b) \propto p^*(\mathbf{t}) \propto b^{Ja} e^{-a} \prod_j \frac{f_j^a}{\Gamma(a)} = \frac{\left(e^{-1} b^J \prod_j f_j\right)^a}{\Gamma(a)^J}$$

and finally

$$p(b \mid \boldsymbol{\phi} = \mathbf{f}, \alpha = a) \propto p^*(\mathbf{t}) \propto b^{Ja+c-1} \exp\left\{-b\left(1 + \sum f_j\right)\right\}.$$

This leads to the conditional distributions given previously:

$$(\phi_j \mid \alpha = a, \beta = b) \sim \text{Gamma}(y_j + a, x_j + b),$$
$$(\alpha \mid \phi_j = f_j, j = 1, \ldots, J) \sim f(a) \propto \left(e^{-1} b^J \prod_j f_j\right)^a / \Gamma(a)^J,$$
$$(\beta \mid \alpha = a, \phi_j = f_j, j = 1, \ldots, J) \sim \text{Gamma}\left(Ja + c, 1 + \sum f_j\right).$$

Generating from two of these three looks easy. But one of them appears rather intractable, and if you look back in Chapter 11 for methods to generate from that density, you'll be disappointed. The distribution for α looks difficult, but even though some of the other prior distributions were modified, none of these conditional distributions would be easy either. Notice that there is very little leeway here. The range of prior distributions that permit a concise expression of the list of conditional distributions is quite limited. The form of the density for α, however, does permit generation from a clever scheme that is particularly suited to this kind of problem in Gibbs sampling. Gilks and Wild (1992), Gilks (1992), and Gilks, Best, and Tan (1995) have devised adaptive acceptance/rejection methods that are discussed in Section 13.6. An alternative approach for this problem is discussed in Section 13.4.

The theory behind Gibbs sampling hinges on using the product of conditional distributions of each variable (given the others) as the transition kernel of a continuous Markov chain. Using the general case for three variables (as in Algorithm BGS in Section 13.1) in order to check (13.2.4), we have

$$\int_3 \int_2 \int_1 \pi(y_3 \mid y_1, y_2)\pi(y_2 \mid y_1, x_3)\pi(y_1 \mid x_2, x_3)\pi(x_1, x_2, x_3)\,dx_1\,dx_2\,dx_3$$

$$= \pi(y_3 \mid y_1, y_2)\int_3 \pi(y_2 \mid y_1, x_3)\int_2 \pi(y_1 \mid x_2, x_3)\int_1 \pi(x_1, x_2, x_3)\,dx_1\,dx_2\,dx_3$$

$$= \pi(y_3 \mid y_1, y_2)\int_3 \pi(y_2 \mid y_1, x_3)\int_2 \pi(y_1 \mid x_2, x_3)\pi(x_2, x_3)\,dx_2\,dx_3$$

$$= \pi(y_3 \mid y_1, y_2)\int_3 \pi(y_2 \mid y_1, x_3)\int_2 \pi(y_1, x_2, x_3)\,dx_2\,dx_3$$

$$= \pi(y_3 \mid y_1, y_2)\int_3 \pi(y_2 \mid y_1, x_3)\pi(y_1, x_3)\,dx_3$$

$$= \pi(y_3 \mid y_1, y_2)\int_3 \pi(y_1, y_2, x_3)\,dx_3$$

$$= \pi(y_3 \mid y_1, y_2)\pi(y_1, y_2) = \pi(y_1, y_2, y_3). \qquad (13.3.5)$$

The main theoretical concerns for Gibbs sampling are starting values and ensuring irreducibility. Specifically for Gibbs sampling, Roberts and Polson (1994) gave results ensuring geometric convergence. In practice, the conditions are usually met but not easily verified. The most common exceptions are cases where a set of conditional distributions can be constructed but no distribution exists. For Bayesian applications, this usually means an improper posterior distribution arising from improper priors. An oft-cited example (e.g. Casella and George 1992) follows.

Example 13.4: *Conditionals from Improper Density*
Consider the two conditional exponential densities $f(y_1 \mid y_2) = y_2 e^{-y_1 y_2}$ and $f(y_2 \mid y_1) = y_1 e^{-y_1 y_2}$ for $0 < y_1, y_2 < \infty$. Plugging in these conditionals in order to solve (13.2.4), we have

$$f(y_1, y_2) = \int_2 \int_1 f(y_2 \mid y_1)f(y_1 \mid x_2)f(x_1, x_2)\,dx_1\,dx_2$$

$$= \int_2 \int_1 y_1 e^{-y_1 y_2} x_2 e^{-y_1 x_2} f(x_1, x_2)\,dx_1\,dx_2$$

$$= \int_2 y_1 e^{-y_1 y_2} x_2 e^{-y_1 x_2} f(x_2)\,dx_2.$$

Now integrate y_1 out of both sides to get the fixed point integral equation with just the second variable:

$$f(y_2) = \int_2 \frac{x_2}{(x_2 + y_2)^2} f(x_2)\,dx_2,$$

for which $f(y_2) \propto 1/y_2$ is a solution. The only problem is that $1/y_2$ is an improper density. See also Exercise 13.6 and further discussion in this section.

The reader may recall our efforts in Chapter 10 to reduce the dimension of the variance components example (Example 10.3), first to the three structural parameters by integrating out the random effects, then alluding to the possibility of integrating out the mean parameter in order to reduce to the dimensions of the two variance components. In stark contrast, this example resurfaced as Example 13.1 in its full-blown parameterization, the random effects included with the structural parameters. In this form, the conditional distributions are easy. If the random effects parameters were to be integrated out, as in Chapter 10, Gibbs sampling would be very difficult to do.

This situation is common in MCMC problems, where including random effects parameters or latent variables makes life easier. Let us consider this problem in detail. Suppose we partition the parameter vector $\theta = (\phi, \gamma)$, with ϕ representing random effects (or latent variables or nuisance parameters) and γ the structural parameters of interest. Writing the joint (unnormalized) posterior as $p^*(\mathbf{t}) = p^*(\mathbf{f}, \mathbf{g})$, the posterior for γ is proportional to $\int p^*(\mathbf{f}, \mathbf{g}) \, d\mathbf{f}$. In Gibbs sampling, if we are able to generate from the joint density proportional to $p^*(\mathbf{f}, \mathbf{g})$, then the "integration" can be done by just ignoring the first part of the parameter vector and dealing with only the marginal distribution of γ. Though it may at first seem like cheating, the mechanism for introducing this type of parameter is often the only trick that makes Gibbs sampling tractable; it goes by the name of *data augmentation* (see Tanner and Wong 1987).

The variance components example (Example 13.1) just mentioned also has a dark side. In an attempt to minimize the effect of the prior, some researchers have used parameters that make the prior improper: $a_1 = b_1 = 0$, so that the prior on ϕ (error variance) is proportional to $1/f$; $a_2 = b_2 = 0$, so that the prior on γ (treatment variance) is proportional to $1/g$; and $\phi_0 = \infty$, so that the prior on the mean β is flat. However, the resulting posterior is improper (see the continuation of Example 13.1 that follows). Of course this is troubling, but not so surprising. The surprising and more disturbing aspect of the improper posterior is that the Gibbs sampling algorithm can generate a sequence of observations that show no sign of the inherent impropriety. Perhaps no one would knowingly do such a thing, but this posterior distribution's improperness is difficult to detect (Hobert and Casella 1996). See also Exercises 13.17, 13.18, and 13.19.

Example 13.1B: *Variance Components (cont.)*

To see that this improper prior leads to an improper posterior, simplify by assuming a balanced problem, $n_i = n$. Then, starting from (13.1.1), integrate out the t_i to obtain an expression for $p^*(b, f, g)$ that is similar to (10.6.6):

$$g^{-1} \times f^{-(N-p)/2-1} \exp\left\{-\tfrac{1}{2}W/f\right\} \times (f + ng)^{-p/2} \exp\left\{-\tfrac{1}{2}B/(f + ng)\right\}$$
$$\times \exp\left\{-\tfrac{1}{2}(\bar{Y}.. - b)^2(g/p + f/N)\right\}.$$

Now, for fixed values of f and b, the joint density behaves like $1/g$ for small g whose integral diverges.

13.4 Metropolis–Hastings Algorithm

The other MCMC method can be viewed as a dependent version of the acceptance/ rejection method of generating random variables from Chapter 11. Recall that, for generating from a distribution of density $f(x)$, the method is to generate X instead from a distribution of density $g(x)$ and to accept this X with a probability that depends on the ratio of densities $f(x)/g(x)$. The algorithm would "throw away" some of the variables generated from a region where f was smaller than g in order to compensate. In the case of generating from the posterior distribution with density proportional to $p^*(\mathbf{t})$, the normalization constant can be ignored; the main problem is finding a bounding distribution, so that $p^*(\mathbf{t})/g(\mathbf{t})$ is bounded above.

The Metropolis–Hastings (MH) algorithm (Metropolis et al. 1953; Hastings 1970) generates a transition that is accepted or rejected in such a way that the stationary distribution of the Markov process has the desired form. Beginning with starting vector $\mathbf{X}^{(0)}$, the algorithm takes the following generic form.

For $i = 1, 2, \ldots, n$ do
  Generate $\mathbf{Y}^{(i)}$ from the transition density $q(\mathbf{X}^{(i-1)} = \mathbf{x}; \mathbf{y})$
  Generate U_i IID uniform$(0, 1)$
  If $U_i \le \alpha(\mathbf{X}^{(i-1)}, \mathbf{Y}^{(i)})$ then $\mathbf{X}^{(i)} = \mathbf{Y}^{(i)}$ (accept); else $\mathbf{X}^{(i)} = \mathbf{X}^{(i-1)}$ (reject)

This algorithm, with appropriate choices for q and α, will generate a series $\{\mathbf{X}^{(i)}\}$ whose stationary distribution is the desired $\pi(\mathbf{x})$. Taking some care with the nonzero probability of no change, we see that the acceptance probability comes from satisfying (13.2.4) and takes the form

$$\alpha(\mathbf{x}, \mathbf{y}) = \min\left\{\frac{\pi(\mathbf{y})q(\mathbf{y}; \mathbf{x})}{\pi(\mathbf{x})q(\mathbf{x}; \mathbf{y})}, 1\right\}. \tag{13.4.1}$$

With α determined, all that is left is the choice of the transition distribution q.

In spite of appearances, the choice of q is quite arbitrary. Keep in mind, of course, the goal of generating from the posterior distribution, so that the stationary distribution $\pi(\mathbf{t})$ is proportional to $p^*(\mathbf{t})$. Of the common choices for q, the first one is a simple random walk – that is, $\mathbf{y} = \mathbf{x} + \mathbf{z}$, where $\mathbf{z}$ independently has density q_r, so that $q(\mathbf{x}; \mathbf{y}) = q_r(\mathbf{y} - \mathbf{x})$. If the density q_r is chosen to be symmetric, as usual, then the acceptance probability simplifies to $\alpha_r(\mathbf{x}, \mathbf{y}) = \min\{\pi(\mathbf{y})/\pi(\mathbf{x}), 1\}$. This choice is simple, and it is particularly effective when q_r gives sufficiently wide dispersal to the candidates. The trade-off here is that low dispersal will give high acceptance rates but may not move enough to traverse the entire space, whereas high dispersal may mix well but reject so often as to be ineffective.

A second common choice of q is to ignore $\mathbf{x}$ altogether and generate from $q_i(\mathbf{y})$, sometimes called the "independence chain" (Tierney 1994). The obvious choice for $q_i(\mathbf{y})$ is an approximation to the posterior density $p^*(\mathbf{t})$. An acceptance leads to an independent "restart" and reduces the overall dependence, with its obvious advantages. The reader should note its similarity to importance sampling (Section 12.4), which would produce an independent series but with weighted observations.

Example 13.5A: *Metropolis–Hastings for Log-Series Posterior*
Recall the posterior from the log-series problem (Example 10.1) with unnormalized posterior

$$p^*(\mathbf{t}) \propto t^{16}(1 - t)/(-\log(1 - t))^{10} \quad \text{for } 0 < t < 1.$$

Three different candidate densities are used in the following demonstrations:

mh1 – $q(x; y)$ is a random walk with $Z \sim \text{uniform}(-.1, .1)$;
mh2 – $q(x; y)$ is a random walk with $Z \sim \text{uniform}(-.2, .2)$;
mh3 – independence chain $q(x; y) = q_i(y)$ and $Y \sim \text{uniform}(0, 1)$.

An interesting approach is to implement the Metropolis–Hastings algorithm to update one variable (perhaps multivariate) at a time. The mathematical background to support this arises from using, say, two steps to do the Markov transition for two (sets of) variables. Suppose that the transition kernel $p_1(x_1, y_1 \mid x_2)$ has the conditional distribution of Y_1 given $Y_2 = x_2$ as its stationary distribution, $\pi(y_1 \mid Y_2 = x_2)$. Let a second transition kernel $p_2(x_2, y_2 \mid x_1)$ have the conditional distribution of Y_2 given $Y_1 = x_1$ as its stationary distribution, $\pi(y_2 \mid Y_1 = x_1)$. Then the result of these two transitions (product of these kernels) has the joint density $\pi(y_1, y_2)$ as its stationary distribution. Note that the second step would be implemented conditional on y_1, not x_1. Checking (13.2.4), we have

$$
\int_2 \int_1 p_2(x_2, y_2 \mid y_1) p_1(x_1, y_1 \mid x_2) \pi(x_1, x_2) \, dx_1 \, dx_2
$$

$$
= \int_2 p_2(x_2, y_2 \mid y_1) \int_1 p_1(x_1, y_1 \mid x_2) \pi(x_1 \mid x_2) \, dx_1 \pi(x_2) \, dx_2
$$

$$
= \int_2 p_2(x_2, y_2 \mid y_1) \pi(y_1 \mid x_2) \pi(x_2) \, dx_2
$$

$$
= \int_2 p_2(x_2, y_2 \mid y_1) \pi(x_2 \mid y_1) \, dx_2 \pi(y_1) = \pi(y_2 \mid y_1) \pi(y_1) = \pi(y_1, y_2).
$$

Generalizing this result leads to the *single-component* Metropolis–Hastings algorithm.

For $i = 1, 2, \ldots, n$ do
  For $j = 1, \ldots, p$ do
    Generate $Y_j^{(i)}$ from transition density $q(X_1^{(i)}, \ldots, X_{j-1}^{(i)}, X_{j+1}^{(i-1)}, \ldots, X_p^{(i-1)}; y_j)$
    Generate U_i IID uniform$(0, 1)$
    If $U_i \leq \alpha(X_1^{(i)}, \ldots, X_{j-1}^{(i)}, X_j^{(i-1)}, \ldots, X_p^{(i-1)}, Y_j^{(i)})$ then $X_j^{(i)} = Y_j^{(i)}$ (accept);
    else $X_j^{(i)} = X_j^{(i-1)}$ (reject)

At each step j of this single-component MH algorithm, the goal is to generate from a chain whose stationary distribution is the conditional distribution of component j given all of the others, that is, $X_1^{(i)}, \ldots, X_{j-1}^{(i)}, X_{j+1}^{(i-1)}, \ldots, X_p^{(i-1)}$. One obvious solution is to generate directly from such a distribution if it is easy to do so. Another solution is to generate the new candidate in such a way that the acceptance probability is 1, which leads to

$$
q_i(X_1^{(i)}, \ldots, X_{j-1}^{(i)}, X_{j+1}^{(i-1)}, \ldots, X_p^{(i-1)}; y_j) \propto \pi(X_1^{(i)}, \ldots, X_{j-1}^{(i)}, y_j, X_{j+1}^{(i-1)}, \ldots, X_p^{(i-1)}).
$$

The reader should recognize that both solutions are the same and have already been discussed as Gibbs sampling. This provides further mathematical foundation for Gibbs sampling and also suggests the use of MH as an alternative route when, as in Example 13.3, one of the component distributions is somewhat intractable.

Example 13.3B: *Pump Example (cont.)*

As noted previously, Gibbs sampling is tempting because two of the three components lend themselves easily to generating from the conditional distributions. However, one (α) remains intractable:

$$(\phi_j \mid \alpha = a, \beta = b) \sim \text{Gamma}(y_j + a, x_j + b),$$

$$(\alpha \mid \phi_j = f_j, j = 1, \ldots, J) \sim f(a) \propto \left(e^{-1}b^J \prod_j f_j\right)^a / \Gamma(a)^J,$$

$$(\beta \mid \alpha = a, \phi_j = f_j, j = 1, \ldots, J) \sim \text{Gamma}\left(Ja + c, 1 + \sum f_j\right).$$

The single-component Metropolis–Hastings algorithm suggests (a) using the usual Gibbs steps for ϕ and β while (b) updating α using a MH step. In the demonstration **chex133**, a random walk candidate density is used for α, with $Z \sim \text{uniform}(-.5, .5)$.

The relationship among the three Monte Carlo alternatives gives an insight to how MCMC methods work. The fundamental task is to generate from random variables from a desired density $f(x)$; when direct generation from $f(x)$ is difficult or impossible, these alternatives are considered. In acceptance/rejection, X is generated from a candidate density $g(x)$ and accepted with a probability proportional to the ratio $f(x)/g(x)$. This ratio f/g must be bounded above, and a good density g has f/g tightly bounded above and below, yielding a uniformly large probability of acceptance. In importance sampling, the observation X generated by $g(x)$ is weighted by the same ratio $f(X)/g(X)$, where the weight compensates for the difference. The region where f/g is small is sampled more often under g than f, and observations from there are downweighted; where f/g is large, g does not sample often enough and the weight is large. Although an upper bound on f/g is not required, difficulties can arise when the ratio is unbounded; these were examined in Sections 12.4 and 12.5. What importance sampling accomplishes by weights, Metropolis–Hastings does by employing dependence. Using an independence sampler $g(y)$, MH accepts a new candidate Y if the ratio $f(Y)/g(Y)$ is relatively large. The probability of acceptance is

$$\alpha(x_{\text{old}}, y) = \min\left\{1, \frac{f(y)/g(y)}{f(x_{\text{old}})/g(x_{\text{old}})}\right\}.$$

Consider what happens when $Y \sim g$ and $f(Y)/g(Y)$ is large. In acceptance/rejection, that Y will be accepted with a high probability. In importance sampling, the observation Y will have a large weight. In independence MH, the observation will be accepted and then kept for a long time because – in subsequent trials – we have that $x_{\text{old}} = Y$, $f(x_{\text{old}})/g(x_{\text{old}})$ will be large, and α will be small. When f/g is unbounded, the series may stay in one place for a long time, losing geometric ergodicity and other desirable convergence properties (Tierney 1995).

13.5   Time-Series Analysis

The inference from MCMC methods comes from standard statistical analysis of observations from the stationary distribution of interest. Some of the less standard statistical techniques were discussed in Chapter 12. The analysis of most of these techniques is straightforward, but the series generated by MCMC methods are not independent and a review of time-series methodology is in order.

Let $\{Y_t, t = 1, \ldots, n\}$ be an ordered series of observations. Most statistical inference in time series is based on *covariance stationarity*. In this type of stationarity, the mean is constant and the covariance between any two observations depends only on the time difference; that is, for all t, $E[Y_t] = \mu$ and $\text{cov}(Y_t, Y_{t+h}) = \gamma(h)$. The result of MCMC methods, however, are series that have *strong stationarity*. For strong stationarity, the marginal distribution of each observation Y_t is the same $\pi(y_t)$, and the joint distribution of a set of observations is *not* time-dependent; that is, $\text{Pr}((Y_{t+1}, Y_{t+2}, \ldots, Y_{t+p}) \in A)$ does not depend on t. Only if the variance exists does strong stationarity imply covariance stationarity. Any statistical inference that deals with indicator or other bounded variables – such as estimation of the distribution function or density – will not be affected by the absence of a second moment. Obviously, the techniques of Section 12.5 for testing for infinite mean and variance will come in handy here; see Exercise 13.18. Hereafter, though, the existence of the second moments will be assumed.

The most important results in time-series analysis deal with the most fundamental statistical tools, the estimation of mean and variance with the sample mean and variance estimate. Define the sample mean and covariances as follows:

$$\bar{Y}_n = \frac{1}{n} \sum_{t=1}^{n} Y_t, \qquad \hat{\gamma}_n(h) = \frac{1}{n} \sum_{t=1}^{n-h} (Y_t - \bar{Y}_n)(Y_{t+h} - \bar{Y}_n).$$

Fuller (1996, chap. 6) and Anderson (1971, chap. 8) gave the following results.

Result 1: $E[\bar{Y}_n] = \mu$.

Result 2: $\text{var}[\bar{Y}_n] = \frac{1}{n^2} \sum_{i=1}^{n} \sum_{j=1}^{n} \gamma(|i - j|) = \frac{1}{n} \sum_{h=1-n}^{n-1} \left(1 - \frac{|h|}{n}\right) \gamma(h)$.

Result 3: $\lim_{n \to \infty} n \, \text{var}[\bar{Y}_n] = \sum_{h=-\infty}^{\infty} \gamma(h) = \eta^2$.

Result 4: $E[\hat{\gamma}_n(0)] = \sigma^2 \left(1 - \frac{\eta^2}{n\sigma^2}\right) + O(n^{-2})$, where $\sigma^2 = \gamma(0)$.

The main result is that, yes, the sample mean is a fine, unbiased, consistent estimate of the population mean. However, the usual way of reporting its standard error – namely, $(\hat{\gamma}_n(0)/n)^{1/2}$ – is not correct. If the series has strong positive autocorrelation ($\gamma(h)/\gamma(0)$ near unity), then the standard error can grossly underestimate the uncertainty in the sample mean. The usual variance estimate $\frac{n}{n-1} \hat{\gamma}_n(0)$ is biased, but the bias diminishes as $1/n$. Recall that $\gamma(0) = \text{var}[Y_i] = \int (y - \mu)^2 \pi(y) \, dy = \sigma^2$.

There are three basic routes for estimating η^2 consistently. The most common route in the time-series literature (see e.g. Fuller 1996) is to model the process using the ARMA family, estimate the parameters, and construct the estimate of η^2 from those estimates. For mild dependence, a first-order autoregressive AR(1) model, $E\{Y_t - \mu \mid Y_{t-1}\} = \rho(Y_{t-1} - \mu)$, may be appropriate; then η^2 is estimated by

$$\hat{\gamma}(0)\frac{1 + \hat{\gamma}(1)/\hat{\gamma}(0)}{1 - \hat{\gamma}(1)/\hat{\gamma}(0)} = \hat{\gamma}(0)\frac{\hat{\gamma}(0) + \hat{\gamma}(1)}{\hat{\gamma}(0) - \hat{\gamma}(1)}. \tag{13.5.1}$$

More commonly for these applications, modeling the series $\{Y_t\}$ is unnecessary (as well as difficult) and so a less parametric route is preferred. A straightforward approach is to use a truncated estimate based on Result 3 and the covariance estimates $\hat{\gamma}_n(h)$:

$$\hat{V}_1 = \sum_{h=-g_n}^{g_n} \hat{\gamma}_n(h),$$

where g_n grows slowly with n. Although this can be improved using weighted observations or "windows," a more effective nonparametric route uses frequency domain tools. Define the spectral density function $s(\lambda)$ as the Fourier transform of the covariance sequence:

$$s(\lambda) = \sum_{h=-\infty}^{\infty} \gamma(h)e^{-i2\pi\lambda h}.$$

The spectral density parcels out the variance in the series as a function of frequency $\lambda \in [0, \frac{1}{2}]$. For our purposes, the frequency $\lambda = 0$ corresponds to the mean, and $s(0) = \eta^2$ of Result 3. As described in Section 14.7(A), the common route for estimating the spectral density uses the periodogram computed using the fast Fourier transform (FFT). Denote the discrete Fourier transform for the centered series as $a_j = \sum_{t=1}^{n}(y_t - \bar{y}_n)e^{i2\pi jt/n}$; then the estimate of the spectral density at frequency $\lambda = j/n$ will use smoothed values of the periodogram $I_n(j/n) = (2/n)|a_j|^2$:

$$\hat{s}\left(\frac{j}{n}\right) = \sum_{k=-d}^{d} w_k I_n\left(\frac{j+k}{n}\right) \Big/ \left(2\sum_{k=-d}^{d} w_k\right).$$

For estimating at $\lambda = 0$, this estimate simplifies to

$$\hat{s}(0) = \sum_{k=1}^{d} w_k I_n\left(\frac{k}{n}\right) \Big/ \left(2\sum_{k=1}^{d} w_k\right) \tag{13.5.2}$$

because of symmetry in the periodogram $I_n(-j/n) = I_n(j/n)$. We also have $I_n(0) = 0$ from centering the series by the sample mean $\bar{y}_n$. The cutoff d should slowly grow with n; Geweke (1992) used equal weights and $d \propto n^{1/2}$.

Example 13.5B: *Metropolis–Hastings for Log-Series Posterior (cont.)*
Recall that, in demonstration **mh1**, $q(x; y)$ is a random walk density with $Z \sim$ uniform$(-.1, .1)$ and the series is analyzed in different ways. The sample size is relatively large, $n = 2^{14} = 16{,}384$; the sample mean $\bar{Y}_n = .52086$, $\hat{\gamma}(0) = .01803$, and the first-order autocorrelation $\hat{\rho} = \hat{\gamma}(1)/\hat{\gamma}(0) = .92652$. Following (13.5.1), a standard error for $\bar{Y}_n$ is

$$\left(\frac{\hat{\gamma}(0)}{n} \times \frac{1 + \hat{\gamma}(1)/\hat{\gamma}(0)}{1 - \hat{\gamma}(1)/\hat{\gamma}(0)}\right)^{1/2} = \left(\frac{.01803}{16{,}384} \times \frac{1 + .92652}{1 - .92652}\right)^{1/2} = .00537.$$

Following the spectral density approach using $d_n = 128$ and $\hat{s}(0) = .39419$, we have the standard error calculations $\sqrt{\hat{s}(0)/n} = \sqrt{.39419/16{,}384} = .004905,$

which differs by less than 10% (since the first-order autoregressive model fits quite well). The reader should note for reference that, in demonstration **quad1**, the midpoint rule achieved six good digits with just 20 evaluations.

Another view of the effect of autocorrelation on the inference is that the information available is not the same as if the same n observations were independent. This loss of information can be expressed in terms of the effective reduction in sample size. If the observations were independent, then $\mathrm{var}(\bar{Y}_n)$ would be estimated by $\hat{\gamma}_n(0)/n$, but since the observations are autocorrelated, n should be replaced by $n^* = n\hat{\gamma}_n(0)/\hat{s}(0)$. If an AR(1) model were used – which would be appropriate for modest levels of correlation – the effective sample size would be $n^{**} = n[1 - \hat{\gamma}(1)/\hat{\gamma}(0)]/[1 + \hat{\gamma}(1)/\hat{\gamma}(0)]$, adjusting by the reciprocal of the factor in (13.5.1). Notice that in the foregoing example, where $\hat{\gamma}(1)/\hat{\gamma}(0) \approx .92$, these calculations yield $n^{**} = 625$. This suggests that the information in 16,384 dependent observations is roughly equivalent to 625 independent observations from the same distribution.

If the situation suggests that the dependence is so small as to be negligible, then a white noise test can be done to check. The periodogram values can be used in one test for independence. If the Y_t are IID then the sequence of values $\{c_k, k = 1, \ldots, m - 1\}$, where

$$c_k = \sum_{j=1}^{k} I_n\left(\frac{j}{n}\right) \bigg/ \sum_{j=1}^{m} I_n\left(\frac{j}{n}\right), \tag{13.5.3}$$

has the same distribution as the order statistics from a uniform$(0, 1)$ sample of size $m-1$, where $m = [(n-1)/2]$. The statistic $D = \max_k\{|(k/(m-1)-c_k|, |c_k-(k-1)/(m-1)|\}$ then has the same distribution as the Kolmogorov–Smirnov test statistic discussed in Section 12.3. Fuller (1996) attributed this white noise test to both Bartlett and Durbin.

The simulation community takes a very practical approach to the analysis of dependent data of this sort with a technique known as *batching*. Here the series $\{Y_t, t = 1, \ldots, n\}$ is broken into subsets (or batches) $\{X_j^{(i)}\}$, where $i = 1, \ldots, k$ and $j = 1, \ldots, m$ so that $km = n$ and $t = m(i-1)+j$. The advantages of batching are varied. For something as simple as estimating the mean of Y_t, the sample batch means that $\bar{X}^{(i)}$ will have a distribution closer to normal and hence t-based confidence intervals are sound. In addition, the dependence across i will be smaller, so that first-order corrections for $\mathrm{var}[\bar{Y}_n]$ – such as fitting an AR(1) model to $\{\bar{X}^{(i)}\}$ and using (13.5.1) – should be all that is needed. More commonly, the dependence may be sufficiently small that no adjustments are needed. For statistics (e.g. variances) that depend on the batching, such batch statistics as $S_i = (m-1)^{-1} \sum_j (X_j^{(i)} - \bar{X}^{(i)})^2$ see some replication, with low to negligible dependence. Since the gain from replication marginally declines, Schmeiser (1990) suggested using small k (10 to 20) and large m to reduce any bias. Large m is especially important, since the biases in S_i are $O(m^{-1})$ from Result 4.

Example 13.5C: *Metropolis–Hastings for Log-Series Posterior (cont.)*
Once again in demonstration **mh1**, $q(x; y)$ is a random walk density with $Z \sim$ uniform$(-.1, .1)$ and the sample size is $n = 2^{14} = 16,384$. Here the batch statistics are computed with $k = 32$ and $m = 512$. The variance of the batch means that $\bar{X}^{(i)}$ is estimated as .0007932, and the standard error for $\bar{Y}_n$ is just

$\sqrt{.0007932/32} = .00498$, which nearly matches the spectral standard error computed previously. Note that the mean of the batch variances S_i is .017295, each with bias $O(m^{-1})$, as compared with the entire sample variance estimate .0180312, bias $O(n^{-1})$, and variance $\sigma^2 = .018720$ computed in **quad1**.

With the smaller sample size k from batching, the simple runs test (see e.g. Brownlee 1965, pp. 231ff) can be employed to check for both independence and stationarity. In the runs test, the statistic R counts the number of runs of observations above or below the median, applied here to the sequence of batch means $\{\bar{X}^{(i)}, i = 1, \ldots, k\}$. When the data are independent and identically distributed, $(2R - k)/\sqrt{k}$ is approximately standard normal for modest values of k. Too few runs is the main concern here, due either to a trend in the mean from slow convergence to stationarity of the batch means $\bar{X}^{(i)}$ or to positive autocorrelation (lack of independence) in the batch means. A strictly monotone sequence would give the minimum of two runs.

Finally, some early work in MCMC methods suggested a technique called *thinning* to reduce autocorrelation by only taking every kth observation. This is not a good idea, since information is thrown away and the variance of the sample mean can only go up (MacEachern and Berliner 1994). The gain is some reduction of autocorrelation, but taking k large enough to eliminate the autocorrelation would also eliminate most of the data. The goal of avoiding the need for sophisticated time-series methods would be better achieved by batching and using simple time-series tools or by generating replicate series (described further in Section 13.7).

13.6 Adaptive Acceptance/Rejection

As seen with Example 13.3, the simplicity and speed of Gibbs sampling comes to a screeching halt when just one of the conditional distributions does not take a well-known form. One alternative, as mentioned in Section 13.4, is to use the single-variable Metropolis–Hastings in its original form for that variable. A more courageous path is to employ the tools from Chapter 11 for generating from the conditional density.

Acceptance/rejection is the most widely used approach (ratio of uniforms is a special case) and also the most promising as a general algorithm. Generating from density $f(x)$ requires a bounding density $g(x)$ such that $\beta f(x) \leq g(x)$. The algorithm is to generate X with density $g(x)$ and accept it with probability $\beta f(X)/g(X)$. Acceptance/rejection is effective when β is large, generation from g easy, and the ratio f/g simple to compute. Improvements in efficiency are gained if easily computed upper or lower bounds (b, B) are available:

$$b(x) \leq \beta \frac{f(x)}{g(x)} \leq B(x).$$

For generating several variates from a single member of a family, some initial computation (setup) can lead to fast, efficient algorithms.

Using acceptance/rejection for generating from a conditional distribution for Gibbs sampling sounds foolhardy at first. Even finding the mode of the density requires some computation, let alone finding a bounding density $g(x)$. Spending time on a setup

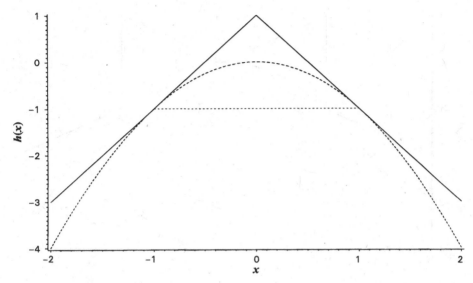

Figure 13.1. Adaptive acceptance/rejection algorithm with only two evaluations of log of density. Upper envelope using tangents; inner bound using secants.

seems hopeless since the parameters of the distribution will change from iteration to iteration. In the case of the parameter α in Example 13.3, we have $f(x) \propto c^x/\Gamma(x)^J$, and c will change each time. But there's some hope in that acceptance/rejection does not require knowledge of all of the normalization constants.

Gilks and Wild (1992) noticed that many of the peculiar distributions arising in Gibbs sampling from standard statistical models had a property that could be exploited in a very clever way toward their generation. In many cases, the log of the density was a concave function; that is, $\log(f(x)) = \alpha + h(x)$ is concave (e^α is the normalization constant for e^h). If we have two evaluations, $h_1 = h(x_1)$ and $h_2 = h(x_2)$, then the secant line is below $h(x)$. Lower bounds can help to avoid computing h, but upper bounds – specifically, an upper envelope function $g(x)$ – are required for acceptance/rejection. However, if the secant line is continued indefinitely then, outside the interval (x_1, x_2), this secant line lies above $h(x)$. Additionally, any tangent line will also lie above $h(x)$. With as few as two points, a piecewise linear function $H^*(x)$ can be found such that $h(x) \leq H^*(x)$ using the two tangent lines, although two evaluations of the derivative $h'(x)$ are also needed. With as few as three points, a piecewise linear function $H^*(x)$ can be found that lies above $h(x)$ by extending the two secant lines; this requires only three evaluations of $h(x)$. See Figures 13.1 and 13.2. More points x_j, although costing the computation of $h(x_j)$, will bring this upper approximant $H^*(x)$ closer to $h(x)$; see Figure 13.3. Since $h(x) \leq H^*(x)$, it follows that $f(x) \leq \exp\{\alpha + H^*(x)\}$ and that an upper envelope function $g(x)$ can be constructed proportional to $\exp\{H^*(x)\}$; see Figure 13.4.

Break the real line into intervals $S(i)$, $i = 1, \ldots, N$, using (a) n points x_i, where $h(x)$ (and perhaps $h'(x)$) is evaluated and (b) intersections of tangent lines or extended secant lines. Then, for $x \in S(i)$, $H^*(x) = c_i + d_i x$. Let $w_i = \int_{S(i)} \exp\{c_i + d_i x\}\, dx$, so that $\int \exp\{H^*(x)\}\, dx = \sum w_i$. Then the envelope density is $g(x) = \exp\{H^*(x)\}/\sum w_i$,

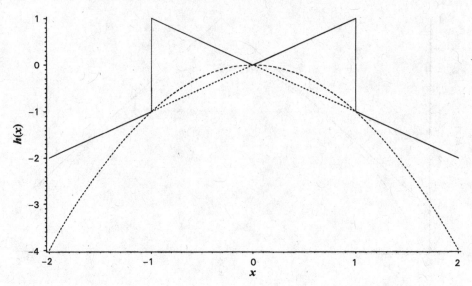

Figure 13.2. Adaptive acceptance/rejection algorithm with three evaluations of log of density. Upper envelope using tangents; inner bound using secants.

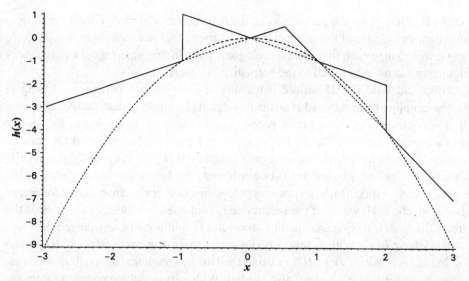

Figure 13.3. Adaptive acceptance/rejection algorithm. Secant (no derivative) algorithm with four evaluations of log of density.

the scaling probability is $\beta = \exp\{-\alpha\}/\sum w_i$, and the main acceptance check $U \leq \beta f(x)/g(x)$ is rewritten as

$$U \leq \frac{f(x)}{\exp\{\alpha + H^*(x)\}}$$

or, in log form,

$$\log(U) + c_i + d_i x \leq h(x).$$

Generating from $g(x)$ takes two steps. First, sample the interval $S(i)$ with probability $w_i/\sum w_i$; then, generate an exponential variate with density proportional to

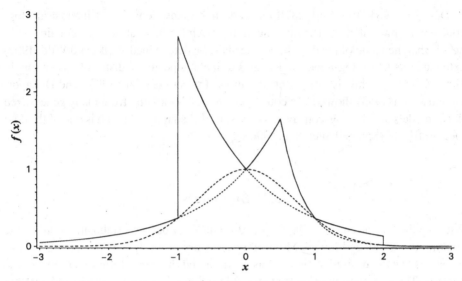

Figure 13.4. Adaptive acceptance/rejection algorithm. Secant algorithm with four evaluations transformed to original scale.

$\exp\{H^*(x)\} = \exp\{c_i + d_i x\}$ on interval $S(i)$. Exponential random variables on an interval can be found by transforming $-\log(\text{uniform})$ (see Section 11.2(A)). The secant line segments form a lower bound function $h^*(x)$ over the range of xs that can be used to avoid computing $f(x)$, providing the quick-accept test

$$\log(U) + c_i + d_i x \leq h^*(x).$$

The most nagging detail arises with the endpoints. If the region is unbounded on the left, then the slope of the secant connecting the two leftmost points (or the tangent at the leftmost point) needs to be positive; likewise, if unbounded on the right, the rightmost secant must have a negative slope so that the $\exp\{H^*(x)\}$ is integrable. If these secant lines are going in the wrong direction, then more points need to be added just to get the algorithm started, so judicious choice of the starting points is quite important. The demonstration code **gilks** uses the secant version and avoids evaluation of derivatives.

In the context of Gibbs sampling, a success or acceptance means the task for generating from this $f(x)$ is over. Although acceptance/rejection means sampling until a success, each failure produces a new point $(x_j, h(x_j))$, a snugger fit for h^* and H^*, and greater likelihood for success without having to compute h again. Hence each failure improves the probability of the next success and reduces its marginal cost.

Gilks and Wild (1992) originally developed the tangent method that uses both $h(x)$ and $h'(x)$ for drawing tangent lines to form $H^*(x)$ and secant lines for $h^*(x)$. Gilks (1992) then presented the secant approach just described, whose improvements mimic the advantages of the secant search method over Newton's method (Chapter 8). Gilks et al. (1995) gave a unified approach for handling nonconcave $\log(f(x))$ with a single-component MH step. Leydold (2000) proposed an adaptive acceptance/rejection approach using the Ratio of Uniforms method.

Devroye (1984; 1986, pp. 287ff) showed that many densities of interest are log-concave; he presented a different general approach for generation whose main weakness is that the mode of the distribution needs to be determined. Gilks and Wild (1992) extended this list of log-concave densities to include posterior distributions arising in Gibbs sampling. This list was extended further by George et al. (1993), and Dellaportas and Smith (1993) showed that conditional posteriors arising from many generalized linear models are also log-concave. As a result, this adaptive method is one of the core tools in BUGS (Spiegelhalter et al. 1996).

13.7   Diagnostics

With the theory currently available, it is difficult for a user to establish that all of the conditions are satisfied for MCMC methods to work properly – namely, that the sample series has the desired stationary distribution and the central limit theorem can be applied. The two main worries are that the initial effects have not dissipated and that the full range of the stationary distribution is not being visited. This, of course, assumes that the problem was properly posed; attempts have been made to sample from improper posteriors (Hobert and Casella 1996). As statisticians are adept at inference from a sample, the hope has been to use diagnostics to detect violations. The successes are modest and, as Cowles and Carlin (1996, p. 903) have put it: "Clearly,... automated convergence monitoring (as by a machine) is unsafe and should be avoided."

The Markov chain Monte Carlo method suffers from three main handicaps. First of all, the output is random and (as alluded to in Chapter 12) it is difficult to detect errors in random output. To find errors, both the sample size and the error must be large. Simplicity has additional value since the mistakes will be big and easy to find. The second handicap is that the output is autocorrelated and so the sample size needed to find errors must be amplified. The third handicap, rarely mentioned, follows from the ease of generating output using MCMC methods. For other numerical techniques, the user must know properties of the likelihood or regression surface, as well as likely values of the parameters, in order to get most software to work and give any useful results. For MCMC, an extremely naive user can generate a lot of output without even understanding the problem. The lack of discipline of learning about the problem that other methods require can lead to unfounded optimism and confidence in the results.

Only a few of the many methods for monitoring MCMC output are summarized here. All of these methods use sound, common-sense statistical methodology for the analysis of MCMC output.

(A) *Plot the Data*

The basic tool of applied statistics pays dividends here. A simple time plot of Y_t versus t can be used to detect initial transient effects and convergence to stationarity. Plots similar to a random walk can show lack of stationarity or poor mixing of the chain, where observations may cluster in regions for a long period of time before moving to

another region. Stem-and-leaf plots give a good view of the distribution and can detect
unusual tail behavior or outliers.

(B) *Gelman and Rubin*

Gelman and Rubin (1992a,b) took a very common-sense approach: if you're worried
about whether the series has converged to the stationary distribution, then (i) generate
replicate series with starting values more disperse than the stationary distribution and
(ii) test whether the means of the series are the same. The output then takes the form
of an analysis of variance: we observe Y_{ij} for $j = 1, \ldots, n$ from series i $(i = 1, \ldots, m)$
with $E(Y_{ij}) = \mu_i$. Convergence to the stationary distribution would mean that the μ_i
are all equal. The usual ANOVA sums of squares are

$$W = \sum_{i=1}^{m} \sum_{j=1}^{n} (Y_{ij} - \bar{Y}_{i\cdot})^2 \quad \text{and} \quad B = n \sum_{i=1}^{m} (\bar{Y}_{i\cdot} - \bar{Y}_{\cdot\cdot})^2,$$

but the usual test for equality of means that uses $F = [B/(m-1)]/[W/(m(n-1))]$
would not be appropriate. Using the results from Section 13.5, notice that the denominator $W/(m(n-1))$ is a biased estimate of σ^2,

$$E\left[\frac{W}{m(n-1)}\right] = \frac{n}{n-1}\left[\sigma^2 - \frac{1}{n}s(0)\right] + O(n^{-2}).$$

Note also that $B/(m-1)$ is a direct estimate of the variance of sample means from
replicates and is a clean (unbiased) estimate of $s(0) = \eta^2$. Consequently, the usual F
statistic is aimed not at 1 but rather at $\eta^2/\sigma^2 + O(n^{-1})$. Nonetheless, the combination
of these two pieces forms a better estimate of σ^2, reducing the bias to $O(n^{-2})$:

$$\hat{V} = \frac{n-1}{n}\frac{W}{m(n-1)} + \frac{1}{n}\frac{B}{m-1}. \tag{13.7.1}$$

Dividing by the within-variance estimate $W/(m(n-1))$, Gelman and Rubin then constructed the convergence diagnostic

$$\hat{R}^{1/2} = \left(\frac{n-1}{n} + \frac{1}{n}F\right)^{1/2} \tag{13.7.2}$$

as the "estimated potential scale reduction" in variance as the sample size $n \to \infty$ (see
Gelman and Rubin 1992b for a slightly modified version). For n large, $\hat{R}$ behaves like
$1/(1 - n^{-1}s(0)/\sigma^2) \sim [1 + n^{-1}s(0)/\sigma^2]$. Because testing the equality of means has
value in its own right, the Gelman and Rubin approach should be extended by (a) esti-
mating $\text{var}(\bar{Y}_{\cdot\cdot})$ using $\hat{S}(0)$ from Section 13.5 and (b) testing by comparing $B/\hat{s}(0)$ to
χ^2_{m-1}.

Two major issues have been raised with the Gelman and Rubin approach. First, they
recommend choosing starting values for the replicate series from a distribution more
dispersed than the stationary distribution. The stationary distribution is not known,
however, so this may be difficult in practice. A second issue is that their analysis con-
siders only one variable at a time in a technique with many variables. It is not obvious
which variable to analyze; analyzing many or all would be time-consuming and raise

issues of multiple comparison. One advantage of this approach is that it can be used with any MCMC method. A computational advantage of the Gelman–Rubin technique is that replicate chains are trivial to run in parallel, so the real time for computation can be kept modest with little effort.

Example 13.5D: *Metropolis–Hastings for Log-Series Posterior (cont.)*
In demonstration **mh3**, $q(x; y)$ is chosen so that $Y \sim \text{uniform}(0, 1)$, and here the series was restarted $m = 16$ times, each of length $n = 1024 = 2^{10}$. Here $B = 1.0181$ and $W = 297.9053$, so that the bias-corrected variance estimate $\hat{V}$ is computed as

$$\hat{V} = \frac{1023}{1024} \times \frac{297.9053}{16(1023)} + \frac{1}{1024} \times \frac{1.0181}{15}$$

$$= \frac{1023}{1024} \times .0182005 + \frac{1}{1024} \times .06787 = .018249,$$

which is still an underestimate. Note that $B/(m-1)$ estimates η^2 as .06787, which appears much larger than the average of the spectral estimates from the m series, .04934. However, since the test statistic $B/\hat{s}(0) = 20.63$ is smaller than its .05 level critical value $\chi^2_{15}(.05) = 25.00$, the replicate series means do not appear to be significantly different. The convergence diagnostic is

$$\hat{R}^{1/2} = \left(\frac{1023}{1024} + \frac{1}{1024} \times 3.73 \right)^{1/2} = 1.001332,$$

whose proximity to 1 suggests that convergence was reached with $n = 1024$ observations.

(C) *Geweke*

Geweke (1992) took a simple, direct approach to the issue of convergence. To test whether the mean at the beginning of the chain may be different from the end, just modify the simple t-test to take care of autocorrelation. Estimate the mean at the beginning by $\bar{Y}_A$ using n_A observations from the first part of the data; estimate the mean at the end by $\bar{Y}_B$ using n_B observations from the last part of the data. Using spectral methods as described in Section 13.5, estimate the variance of the difference by $\hat{s}_A(0)/n_A + \hat{s}_B(0)/n_B$. Then construct an analog to Welsch's t statistic,

$$Z = \frac{\bar{Y}_A - \bar{Y}_B}{(\hat{s}_A(0)/n_A + \hat{s}_B(0)/n_B)^{1/2}}, \tag{13.7.3}$$

and compare Z to the $N(0, 1)$ critical values. Geweke suggested taking n_A as $n/10$ from the very beginning of the series and $n_B = n/2$, the last half of the data. In addition, Geweke referred to the ratio $\sigma^2/s(0)$ as the "relative numerical efficiency" of MCMC, but this ratio is just σ^2/η^2 or the ratio of variances for the $\bar{Y}_n$ of an independent series to a stationary one. The Geweke approach does not require replicates and can be applied to any MCMC method, but it is essentially a univariate approach in a multivariate problem.

Example 13.5E: *Metropolis–Hastings for Log-Series Posterior (cont.)*
Again, in demonstration **mh2**, $q(x; y)$ is a random walk density with $Z \sim$ uniform$(-.2, .2)$. The sample size is $n = 2^{14} = 16,384$, and the series is broken into the first $n_A = n/8 = 2048$ observations and the last half $n_B = 8192$. Here $\bar{Y}_A = .522045$, $\bar{Y}_B = .523012$, $\hat{s}_A(0) = .1534$, and $\hat{s}_B(0) = .1426$. The computed test statistic is $Z = -.1006$, which gives no indication of differences in the means in the two pieces – suggesting quick convergence.

(D) *Heidelberger and Welch*

In a similar spirit as Geweke but in a more sophisticated fashion, Heidelberger and Welch (1983) constructed an approximate Brownian bridge to investigate transient initial effects. Define

$$T_k = \sum_{i=1}^{k} Y_i \quad \text{and} \quad \bar{Y} = n^{-1} \sum_{i=1}^{n} Y_i.$$

Then, as $n \to \infty$, the function

$$B_n(t) = \frac{T_{[nt]} - [nt]\bar{Y}}{(n\hat{S}(0))^{1/2}} \quad \text{for } 0 \le t \le 1 \tag{13.7.4}$$

converges in distribution to the Brownian bridge. Among the various goodness-of-fit statistics available, Heidelberger and Welch used the Cramer–von Mises statistic to measure departures from the assumptions. In simulations they showed that this approach can detect transient trends unless the trend extends throughout the data. For MCMC problems, this may not work well if the series never reaches convergence.

(E) *Raftery and Lewis*

In light of the importance of distribution and density estimation in the analysis of MCMC data, Raftery and Lewis (1992) took another very practical approach: viewing all analysis as the estimation of probabilities. Using the mechanics of a two-state Markov chain, they considered analyzing only binary variables in order to estimate the convergence parameters. From this, they could estimate both the extent of the transient initial effects (a.k.a. burn-in) and the sample size required to achieve a specified level of accuracy. This method, too, is univariate, but with a complicating twist: whereas the diagnostics may change in examining other variables, here they would also change in examining several probabilities from the same variable.

(F) *Dickey–Fuller*

This test (and its descendants) is commonly used in economic data to test for a random walk with the alternative of stationarity. In MCMC, this test can be used to see if the serial correlation is so large that stationarity is suspect and the series may be following a random walk. In its simplest form (Fuller 1996, chap. 10), the test statistic is

$$n(\hat{\rho} - 1) = n\left(\frac{\hat{\gamma}(1)}{\hat{\gamma}(0)} - 1\right);$$

the random walk hypothesis is rejected if $n(\hat{\rho} - 1)$ is smaller than the asymptotic critical values $c_{.05} = -14.1$ and $c_{.01} = -20.6$. Rejection corresponds to modest correlations, whereas correlations near unity suggest a random walk or at least raise the flag for further examination.

Programs and Demonstrations

chex131   *Demonstration of Gibbs sampling for normal variance components*
Gibbs sampling is employed to generate from the posterior distribution of Example 13.1 using the data from Chapter 10 (demonstration **chex103**).

chex132   *Demonstration of Gibbs sampling on Example 13.2 (Ramus Heights)*
Gibbs sampling is employed to generate from the posterior in Example 13.2 using the data from Elston and Grizzle (1962). Sampling from the Wishart distribution requires both normal (**gnroul**) and chi (**gchirv**) random variables.

chex133   *Demonstration of single-component Metropolis–Hastings*
As described in Example 13.3B (Pump Example), a Metropolis–Hastings step is used to handle the difficult parameter (alpha).

mh1, mh2, mh3   *Demonstrations of Metropolis–Hastings on log-series posterior from Example 10.1*
The Metropolis–Hastings algorithm is employed to generate from the 1-dimensional log-series posterior of Example 10.1. Three different candidate distributions are used in the three programs: the first two use random walk; the last one is an "independence" sampler.
mh1 – $q(x; y)$ is a random walk with $Z \sim$ uniform$(-.1, .1)$.
mh2 – $q(x; y)$ is a random walk with $Z \sim$ uniform$(-.2, .2)$.
mh3 – $q(x; y) = q(y)$ and $Y \sim$ uniform$(0, 1)$.

gilks   *Demonstration of adaptive acceptance/rejection algorithm*
The adaptive acceptance/rejection algorithm of Gilks (1992), which uses extended secants for construction of the upper envelope, is employed to generate from the standard normal distribution. Output tested as in **gnrouk**, etc.
gilks – implementation of adaptive acceptance/rejection using secants.

Exercises

13.1   Redo the calculations in (13.3.2) with the ordering of X and Y reversed in the Gibbs sampling. That is, generate X first (given v) and then Y given X.

13.2   Redo the calculations in (13.3.2) with the order of X and Y chosen at random: X first with probability p, and Y first with probability $1 - p$.

13.3 Analytically integrate out the random effects parameters ϕ_i in Example 13.3 (Pump), reducing the posterior to two dimensions. Compute the posterior moments by using numerical integration with a product Simpson's rule.

13.4 In Example 13.2 (Jaw), show that the conditional distribution of $(\beta \mid \Omega = O)$ is normal with mean vector and covariance matrix as given.

13.5 In Example 13.2 (Jaw), what would the conditional densities look like if the prior on β were multivariate normal with mean vector β_0 and covariance matrix Σ_0? Is there any proper prior that would lead to simple conditional densities?

13.6 In Example 13.4, the conditional densities are $f(x \mid y) = ye^{-xy}$ and $f(y \mid x) = xe^{-xy}$. Algorithmically, the Gibbs sampler in this situation would be

$$V_i, W_i \text{ IID exponential}(1), \quad X_i = V_i/Y_{i-1}, \ Y_i = W_i/X_i.$$

(a) Express X_n or Y_n in terms of V_i, W_i $(i = 1, \ldots, n)$ and Y_0.
(b) Can anything be said about the convergence or divergence of X_n or Y_n?

13.7 Give a transformation of a uniform$(0, 1)$ random variable that produces a random variable with density proportional to $\exp\{c + dx\}$ over the interval (a, b).

13.8 Show that the density for α in Example 13.3, proportional to $c^x/\Gamma(x)$, is log-concave.

13.9 Analyze the output from the demonstration **chex131**, computing the diagnostics from Section 13.7. Compare the results to the numerical integration in **chex103**.

13.10 Analyze the output from the demonstration **chex132**, computing the diagnostics from Section 13.7. Compare the results to the numerical integration results from Exercise 13.4.

13.11 For the log-series posterior from Example 10.1, used again in Example 13.5, find the parameters of the beta density that closely approximates $p^*(t)$. Use multiple regression with $\log(t)$ and $\log(1 - t)$ as explanatory variables.

13.12 Mimic the Metropolis–Hastings demonstration **mh3** using the "independence chain" candidate density $q(x; y) = q(y)$, which is the beta density from the solution of Exercise 13.11.

13.13 Redo the Metropolis–Hastings demonstration **mh3** using the same uniform importance sampling density, but now compute replicates by restarting with a sample from the beta density from the solution of Exercise 13.11. Since $q(y)$ should be nearly proportional to $p^*(t)$, it should start with a nearly stationary distribution – but can you tell?

13.14 For the log-series posterior Example 13.5, find a candidate density $q(x; y)$ such that $\alpha(x, y)$ is nearly constant and nearly 1.

13.15 Extend the demonstration **mh1** using Fortran and single precision by expanding the sample size to $n = 2^{20}$ or beyond, noting the effects of rounding error (which should slowly deteriorate the results).

13.16 Following Exercise 13.15, compute the convergence diagnostic $\hat{R}^{1/2}$ from (13.7.2) using varying sample sizes (e.g., $2^{16}, 2^{17}, \ldots$).

13.17 Repeat the demonstration **chex131** with the improper prior parameters mentioned in Section 13.3: $a_1 = b_1 = 0$, $a_2 = b_2 = 0$, and ϕ_0 large (say, 100 or more). This imbalanced problem does show some strange behavior.

13.18 Test the output from Exercise 13.17 for infinite variance using the methods described in Section 12.5.

13.19 Balance may have something to do with observing unusual behavior in the variance component problem with improper priors. Rework demonstration **chex 131** but with the balanced data from Box and Tiao (1973, second example), with $B = 41.6816$, $W = 358.70135$, $n_i \equiv 5$; use group means of 6.2268, 4.6560, 7.5212, 6.0796, and 3.8252:

   (a) with prior $a_1 = b_1 = 0$, $a_2 = b_2 = 0$, $b_0 = 0$, and $\phi_0 = (10^6)^2$ (Gelfand et al. 1990, Prior I);

   (b) with prior $a_1 = b_1 = 0$, $a_2 = 1/2$, $b_2 = 1$, $b_0 = 0$, and $\phi_0 = (10^6)^2$ (Prior II).

13.20 Compute the runs test on the batch means from demonstration **mh1**.

13.21 For the second half of the series generated in the demonstration **mh2**, compute the periodogram white noise test by computing the Kolmogorov–Smirnov test on the series $\{c_k\}$ in (13.5.3).

13.22 Apply Gibbs sampling to the pump problem (Example 13.3) by using the code **gilks** to generate from the distribution of α. Compare the results with the single-component Metropolis–Hastings method results from **pump1** and the numerical results from Exercise 13.3.

13.23 Using the output from Exercise 13.6, test for both infinite mean and variance using the methods described in Section 12.5. Also test for stationarity using the Dickey–Fuller test from Section 13.7(E).

References

The paper by Casella and George (1992), originally titled "Gibbs for Kids," gives a clear introduction to Gibbs sampling. Following the same spirit, Chib and Greenberg (1995) explain Metropolis–Hastings as a form of acceptance/rejection. The 1992 Valencia Meeting proceedings and the November 1992 issue of *Statistical Science* contain some of the early discussions of diagnostics; the latter includes also a debate over multiple series versus one long run. The book *Markov Chain Monte Carlo in Practice* (Gilks, Richardson, and Spiegelhalter 1996) contains survey papers by many of the innovators and serves as a good overall reference.

T. W. Anderson (1971), *The Statistical Analysis of Time Series*. New York: Wiley.

George E. P. Box and George C. Tiao (1973), *Bayesian Inference in Statistical Analysis*. Reading, MA: Addison-Wesley.

Paul Bratley, Bennett L. Fox, and Linus Schrage (1983), *A Guide to Simulation*. New York: Springer-Verlag.

K. A. Brownlee (1965), *Statistical Theory and Methodology*, 2nd ed. New York: Wiley.

George Casella and Edward I. George (1992), "Explaining the Gibbs Sampler," *American Statistician* 46: 167–74.

K. S. Chan and C. J. Geyer (1994), Discussion of "Markov Chains for Exploring Posterior Distributions" (by L. Tierney), *Annals of Statistics* 22: 1747–58.

Siddhartha Chib and Edward Greenberg (1995), "Understanding the Metropolis–Hastings Algorithm," *American Statistician* 49: 327–35.

Mary Kathryn Cowles and Bradley P. Carlin (1996), "Markov Chain Monte Carlo Convergence Diagnostics: A Comparative Review," *Journal of the American Statistical Association* 91: 883–904.

P. Dellaportas and A. F. M. Smith (1993), "Bayesian Inference for Generalized Linear and Proportional Hazards Models via Gibbs Sampling," *Applied Statistics* 42: 443–59.

Luc Devroye (1984), "A Simple Algorithm for Generating Random Variates with a Log-Concave Density," *Computing* 33: 247–57.

Luc Devroye (1986), *Non-Uniform Random Variate Generation.* New York: Springer-Verlag.

R. C. Elston and J. F. Grizzle (1962), "Estimation of Time Response Curves and Their Confidence Bands," *Biometrics* 18: 148–59.

Wayne A. Fuller (1996), *Introduction to Statistical Time Series,* 2nd ed. New York: Wiley.

Alan E. Gelfand, Susan E. Hills, Amy Racine-Poon, and Adrian F. M. Smith (1990), "Illustration of Bayesian Inference in Normal Data Models Using Gibbs Sampling," *Journal of the American Statistical Association* 85: 973–85.

Andrew Gelman and Donald B. Rubin (1992a), "A Single Sequence from the Gibbs Sampler Gives a False Sense of Security," in J. M. Bernardo, J. O. Berger, A. P. Dawid, and A. F. M. Smith (Eds.), *Bayesian Statistics 4,* pp. 625–31. Oxford, U.K.: Oxford University Press.

Andrew Gelman and Donald B. Rubin (1992b), "Inference from Iterative Simulation Using Multiple Sequences," *Statistical Science* 7: 457–511.

E. I. George, U. E. Makov, and A. F. M. Smith (1993), "Conjugate Likelihood Distributions," *Scandinavian Journal of Statistics* 20: 147–56.

J. Geweke (1992), "Evaluating the Accuracy of Sampling-Based Approaches to the Calculation of Posterior Moments," in J. M. Bernardo, J. O. Berger, A. P. Dawid, and A. F. M. Smith (Eds.), *Bayesian Statistics 4,* pp. 169–93. Oxford, U.K.: Oxford University Press.

Charles J. Geyer (1992), "Practical Markov Chain Monte Carlo," *Statistical Science* 7: 473–511.

W. R. Gilks (1992), "Derivative-Free Adaptive Rejection Sampling for Gibbs Sampling," in J. M. Bernardo, J. O. Berger, A. P. Dawid, and A. F. M. Smith (Eds.), *Bayesian Statistics 4,* pp. 641–9. Oxford, U.K.: Oxford University Press.

W. R. Gilks, N. G. Best, and K. K. C. Tan (1995), "Adaptive Rejection Metropolis Sampling within Gibbs Sampling," *Applied Statistics* 44: 455–72.

W. R. Gilks, S. Richardson, and D. J. Spiegelhalter (Eds.) (1996), *Markov Chain Monte Carlo in Practice.* London: Chapman & Hall.

W. R. Gilks and P. Wild (1992), "Adaptive Rejection Sampling for Gibbs Sampling," *Applied Statistics* 41: 337–48.

W. K. Hastings (1970), "Monte Carlo Sampling Methods Using Markov Chains and Their Applications," *Biometrika* 57: 97–109.

P. Heidelberger and P. D. Welch (1983), "Simulation Run Length Control in the Presence of an Initial Transient," *Operations Research* 31: 1109–44.

James P. Hobert and George Casella (1996), "The Effect of Improper Priors on Gibbs Sampling in Hierarchical Linear Models," *Journal of the American Statistical Association* 91: 1461–73.

Robert E. Kass, Bradley P. Carlin, Andrew Gelman, and Radford M. Neal (1998), "Markov Chain Monte Carlo in Practice: A Roundtable Discussion," *American Statistician* 52: 93–100.

Josef Leydold (2000), "Automatic Sampling with the Ratio-of-Uniforms Method," *ACM Transactions on Mathematical Software* 26: 78–98.

Steven N. MacEachern and L. Mark Berliner (1994), "Subsampling the Gibbs Sampler," *American Statistician* 48: 188–90.

N. Metropolis, A. W. Rosenbluth, M. N. Rosenbluth, A. H. Teller, and E. Teller (1953), "Equations of State Calculations by Fast Computing Machines," *Journal of Chemical Physics* 21: 1087–92.

S. P. Meyn and R. L. Tweedie (1993), *Markov Chains and Stochastic Stability.* New York: Springer.

A. E. Raftery and S. Lewis (1992), "How Many Iterations in the Gibbs Sampler?" in J. M. Bernardo, J. O. Berger, A. P. Dawid, and A. F. M. Smith (Eds.), *Bayesian Statistics 4,* pp. 763–73. Oxford, U.K.: Oxford University Press.

Brian D. Ripley (1987), *Stochastic Simulation.* New York: Wiley.

Gareth O. Roberts and Nicholas G. Polson (1994), "On the Geometric Convergence of the Gibbs Sampler," *Journal of the Royal Statistical Society B* 56: 377–84.

Bruce Schmeiser (1990), "Simulation Experiments," in D. P. Heyman and M. J. Sobel (Eds.), *Handbooks in Operations Research and Management Science* (vol. 2: Stochastic Models), pp. 295–330. Amsterdam: North-Holland.

David Spiegelhalter, Andrew Thomas, Nicky Best, and Wally Gilks (1996), *BUGS: Bayesian Inference Using Gibbs Sampling*. Cambridge, U.K.: Cambridge Medical Research Council Biostatistics Unit.

M. A. Tanner and W. H. Wong (1987), "The Calculation of Posterior Distributions by Data Augmentation," *Journal of the American Statistical Association* 82: 528–49.

Luke Tierney (1994), "Markov Chains for Exploring Posterior Distributions" (with discussion), *Annals of Statistics* 22: 1701–62.

Luke Tierney (1995), "Introduction to General State-Space Markov Chain Theory," in W. R. Gilks, S. Richardson, and D. J. Spiegelhalter (Eds.), *Markov Chain Monte Carlo in Practice*. London: Chapman & Hall.

14

Sorting and Fast Algorithms

14.1 Introduction

The theme of this chapter is a simple one: there may be better, faster ways of computing something than you may ever have thought of. One of the maxims of computer science is that just a few programs use most of the resources. Early in the history of computing, people recognized that much of the computing resources went into the common task of sorting a list of numbers. If this task could be done faster, then everything could be done better. A concentrated effort on improving sorting algorithms led to several breakthroughs, all following the principle known as "divide and conquer." In simple terms, to solve a large task, break it into smaller tasks of the same kind. Cleverly done, the resulting algorithm can be more efficient than anyone would have expected, earning the jargon adjective "fast." The principle of divide and conquer will be discussed in the next section, followed by a discussion of fast algorithms for sorting. Section 14.4 comprises statistical applications of divide and conquer. Another great breakthrough, the fast Fourier transform (FFT), will be discussed in Section 14.5. Using the FFT to compute convolutions will be discussed in Section 14.6, followed by some interesting applications of the FFT to statistics in Section 14.7. This chapter will close with some topics that are important but don't really fit elsewhere: algorithms for constructing permutations and combinations.

14.2 Divide and Conquer

The general principle of divide and conquer is to break a difficult task into subtasks, solve the subtasks, and then put the solutions together to solve the original task. This principle has led to some algorithms that give incredible improvements over naive approaches to the same problem. To assess just how much of an improvement these fast algorithms are, we must find some form of measurement. A simplistic approach would be to time an algorithm and its competitor. However, this may not enable us to generalize the results and so predict which would work better on any given problem.

In computer science, performance analysis is based on *computational complexity*. Hence the common route is to count some part of the task – an operation count similar to that in Chapters 3–6 with regard to numerical linear algebra. Back then we usually counted "flops" or floating point operations, which technically included fetching some numbers, multiplying and/or adding, and storing the result. Here, in examining sorting or similar operations, we can focus on a single task – such as a comparison, "Is x bigger than y?" or an exchange, "Put x into y and y into x" – just as we could have limited a flop to a multiplication. Concentrating on a single relevant task allows a more precise analysis, which (if properly done) can explain how well an algorithm will perform in a variety of problems. To emphasize: We must pick some part of the task that is relevant and can be counted precisely.

The mathematical expression of divide-and-conquer algorithms usually comes down to a simple recursive form:

$$T(N) = aT(N/b) + cN + d, \tag{14.2.1}$$

where $T(N)$ is the number of operations required to perform a task of size N by breaking the task into a subproblems of size N/b with $cN + d$ operations needed to put the subproblem solutions together to solve the original problem. Technically, we are referring to operation count, but practically, we're thinking time – hence the notation $T(\cdot)$. The solution to this recursive equation depends only on the relationship between the constants a and b:

$$a < b \implies T(N) = \frac{cb}{b-a}N + \frac{db}{b-a} = O(N),$$

$$a = b > 1 \implies T(N) = cN \log_a N + NT(1) + d\frac{N-1}{a-1} = O(N \log N). \tag{14.2.2}$$

These expressions can be verified by plugging in the solution and doing a little algebra; see Exercise 14.1.

Often, the number of operations depends on the input. In these situations, both the worst case and best case may well be easy to construct. Moreover, by placing a probability distribution over the possible inputs, an expected time or number of operations can be computed. This is often the case in sorting or computing order statistics, and the most useful probability distribution is one that is uniform over the possible permutations of the data. Another stochastic variation arises with random algorithms, that is, algorithms that explicitly employ some randomization. Here the expected time or number of operations (and variance, of course) should be computed when comparing algorithms.

The use, implementation, and comparison of these divide-and-conquer algorithms can depend on the computing environment. Some high-level languages do not permit recursive coding of algorithms; in particular, Fortran did not until recently. Nonetheless, clever coding can often obviate this defect; the accompanying code shows some examples. Likewise, ingenious data structure techniques (Section 1.4) can make some implementations easy. For example, it's easy to add or delete an element to a set that is stored as a linked list rather than as a simple linear list. But it's much slower to traverse a linked list than a sorted linear list when trying to find a particular element. Access to auxiliary storage can make a big difference in performance, and that access depends highly upon the environment (i.e., hardware, software, and language). For the algorithms considered here, we will limit the discussion to linear lists and a few variants, but none that require any special tools or auxiliary storage that is not explicit.

14.3 Sorting Algorithms

The simplest situation for sorting has but a single linear list of N numbers, and the desired result is the list in order – the *order statistics*. In the more general case, the values to be sorted are called "keys" and, along with those keys, an index or pointer must be carried along in order to retain the ability to access other information. In statistics, a vector of observation indices is carried along with the data to be sorted (keys); upon completion, this auxiliary vector holds the vector of antiranks. As a mundane example, the keys may be last (family) names, and a pointer to a location of other information (e.g., phone numbers, street addresses) is carried along. So if we want to find someone's phone number, we just traverse the sorted list (recall the speed of discrete bisection search); if we find the name in location j then pointer(j) holds the location of j's phone number.

One of the simplest sorting algorithms, known as *bubble sort,* is also one of the most commonly reinvented wheels. Its coding is very simple, but it is still possible to mess up.

Algorithm Bubblesort
```
DO J=2, N
DO I=1, J-1
IF( KEY(I) > KEY(J) ) THEN exchange KEY(I) and KEY(J)
END DO  ! LOOP ON I
END DO  ! LOOP ON J
```

The name "bubblesort" arises from the largest elements "bubbling to the top." As can be clearly seen from the simple coding, this algorithm requires $O(N^2)$ comparisons (IFs). The number of exchanges depends on the data – if the list of keys is already sorted, then there are no exchanges; if in reverse order, then about $\frac{1}{2}N^2$ exchanges are needed. If we compute an expectation with all permutations of the ordering equally likely, then the expected number of exchanges is still $O(N^2)$.

The surprise with bubblesort is that the fast algorithms for sorting can do so much better. Three $O(N \log N)$ algorithms will be presented here, and while there may be large constants hiding under those $O(\cdot)$s, all three algorithms are dramatically better than the forgettable bubblesort. The first of these is *mergesort,* which is a direct implementation of divide and conquer. In order to sort a list of length N, first sort two lists of length $N/2$ and apply the algorithm recursively, down to sorting lists of length 1 or 2. The pivotal task is putting the solutions to the two $N/2$ subproblems together – merging two sorted lists. But this task is relatively easy: compare the smallest elements in each list and then pull off the smaller to start the merged list. Each step consists of comparing the smallest remaining elements in the two lists and attaching it to the end of the merged list being formed (see Example 14.1). With auxiliary storage, this can be implemented simply with three pointers. The number of comparisons required depends on the data. In the best case, all of the elements in one list are smaller than the other, and after $N/2$ comparisons that exhaust one list we simply attach the other list at the end. At worst, we need $2N - 1$ comparisons to merge.

Mergesort may be analyzed as follows:

$$T(N) = 2T(N/2) + O(N),$$

so that $T(N) = O(N \log_2 N)$. Regardless of how bad the constants may be in $O(\cdot)$, for N large enough, mergesort will be faster. Mergesort is difficult to code without auxiliary storage and very difficult to code in Fortran. However, we have established a benchmark.

Example 14.1: *Mergesort*
The following table summarizes the merging of two sorted lists. At each step, only the underlined elements are compared.

First sorted list	Merged list	Second sorted list
<u>21</u> 23 33 40		<u>16</u> 28 38 44 59
	16	
<u>21</u> 23 33 40		<u>28</u> 38 44 59
	16 21	
<u>23</u> 33 40		<u>28</u> 38 44 59
	16 21 23	
<u>33</u> 40		<u>28</u> 38 44 59
	16 21 23 28	
<u>33</u> 40		<u>38</u> 44 59
	16 21 23 28 33	
<u>40</u>		<u>38</u> 44 59
	16 21 23 28 33 38	
<u>40</u>		<u>44</u> 59
	16 21 23 28 33 38 40	
		44 59
	16 21 23 28 33 38 40 44 59	

The next fast algorithm also directly applies the strategy of divide and conquer. Instead of breaking the list exactly in half, the aptly named *quicksort* uses an element of the set to break the list into three sets: those smaller, those equal, and those larger. Which element of the set? Well, any one will do for the most part – why not the first one? For most circumstances this will work very well, except (in the *worst* case!) when the list is already sorted. That's not good since it occurs so often. Hence the usual approach is to select an element of the set at random for the splitting. The analysis of the average effort works out as

$$T(N) = \frac{2}{N} \sum_{j=1}^{N-1} T(j) + O(N), \qquad (14.3.1)$$

whose solution is $T(N) = O(N \log N)$.

Algorithm Quicksort (KEY, BEGIN, END)
(1) Generate $J \sim$ discrete uniform(BEGIN, END).
(2) Partition list into $S_1 = \{$ those $< \mathrm{KEY}(J) \}$, $S_2 = \{$ those $= \mathrm{KEY}(J) \}$, and $S_3 = \{$ those $> \mathrm{KEY}(J) \}$, with sizes k_1, k_2, k_3 (respectively), reordering the

elements of list KEY so that the elements of S_1 have the smallest indices, S_2 in middle, S_3 at end.

(3) If($k_1 > 1$) then Quicksort(KEY, BEGIN, k_1).

(4) If($k_3 > 1$) then Quicksort(KEY, $k_1 + k_2 + 1$, END).

It should be obvious that quicksort can easily be coded recursively. Nevertheless, both the partition step (2) and the recursion stack can be coded without explicit recursion; see the demonstrations **partit** and **qsort**. A skeptical eye may be wary of the constant in $O(N \log N)$, but experience confirms that quicksort is appropriately named.

Heapsort, the third of these fast algorithms, does not employ the divide-and-conquer strategy but instead employs the data structure known as a "heap." A *heap* is a binary tree with the property that the nodes (or "fathers") are not smaller than their two sub-nodes (or "sons"). At first glance, having to code something as exotic as a binary tree might be sufficiently dissuasive. But without losing the efficiencies that the tree structure provides, a binary tree can be stored in a linear list, where node k has sons $2k$ and $2k + 1$. The important structure for this problem – comparisons of fathers and sons – is unhampered by this device. The largest element in the set is at the root of the tree (location 1) or, inverting, at the "top of the heap." The heapsort algorithm is easily described in two parts: create the heap; then successively remove the largest, replacing it with another, and reestablish the heap. The main step is to "heapify" (establish the heap property), which is accomplished by comparing a new node with the larger of its sons and, if out of order, exchanging and continuing to heapify the remainder of the list. The construction of the heap starts with the bottom nodes that have sons; then heapify the rest of the list, moving up the heap (down the list) to the top of the heap. This construction takes only $O(N)$ operations. Now the last element of the list is exchanged with the top (so the largest is now in location N), and the list from 1 to $N - 1$ is heapified. The element at the top is now exchanged with the last element of the list; the list is shortened by one and again heapified. The heapify step only takes $O(\log N)$ steps, so the total effort for heapsort is only $O(N \log N)$ in the best case, worst case, *and* average case. Knuth (1998, pp. 144ff) gave a detailed outline that is easily coded; see also the demonstrations **hsort** and **hksort**.

In some areas of statistics, the order statistics are superfluous and inference is based on the ranks. As mentioned earlier, we may accompany the vector of keys with an index vector – say **A**, with $A_j = j$ ($j = 1, \dots, N$) initially. If every exchange of the keys, say X_j and X_k, is accompanied by an exchange of the A_j and A_k, then (upon completion of the sorting) the vector **A** holds the *antiranks*. That is, suppose the original data are $\{X_j, j = 1, \dots, N\}$; if the jth antirank is $A_j = k$, then the kth order statistic follows $X_{(j)} = X_k$. The *ranks* can be found by inverting this permutation:

```
DO J=1, N
K=A(J)
R(K)=J
END DO  ! LOOP ON J
```

Hence the kth rank indicates which order statistic belongs to the kth observation.

14.4   Fast Order Statistics and Related Problems

The divide and conquer strategy can be effectively applied to some purely statistical problems with outstanding success. Moreover, in the field of robust statistics, the computational complexity $T(N)$ of an estimator can be just as critical a statistical property as power or variance; an estimator that cannot be computed in $O(N)$ or $O(N \log N)$ may have little practical value no matter how great its statistical properties. In this section, we'll look at some examples of estimators where the use of divide and conquer leads to improved computational complexity and makes the use of these estimators practicable.

The first problem is the sample median, or any order statistic from a sample of size N. When N is even, the usual definition is $M = \frac{1}{2}(X_{(N/2)} + X_{(N/2+1)})$. You may recall from Section 12.2 that the percentile point estimators $\hat{c}_1, \hat{c}_2, \hat{c}_3$ employ consecutive order statistics. Hence our problem should really be considered that of finding the kth and $(k + 1)$th order statistics from a sample of size N. One straightforward approach would be to just sort the data. If the data need to be sorted anyway then there is no possible gain, since the $O(N \log N)$ cost will have to be paid anyway. But if the data aren't going to be sorted, the question becomes whether we can compute consecutive order statistics from a sample of size N in less than $O(N \log N)$ time. The answer, quite surprisingly, is "Yes!" An algorithm (FIND) due to Hoare (1961) is an analog of quicksort and a direct application of divide and conquer.

> *Algorithm FastOS* (K, X, BEGIN, END) (Find kth order statistic of sample of size N)
> (1) Generate J $\sim$ discrete uniform(BEGIN, END)
> (2) Partition list into $S_1 = \{$ those $<$ KEY(J) $\}$, $S_2 = \{$ those $=$ KEY(J) $\}$, and $S_3 = \{$ those $>$ KEY(J) $\}$, with sizes k_1, k_2, k_3 (respectively), reordering the elements of list KEY so that the elements of S_1 have the smallest indices, S_2 in middle, S_3 at end.
> (3) If($K \leq k_1$) then FastOS(K, X, BEGIN, k_1).
> (4) If($k_1 < K \leq k_1 + k_2$) then return $X(J)$ as kth order statistic.
> (5) If($K > k_1 + k_2$) then FastOS($K - k_1 - k_2$, X, $k_1 + k_2 + 1$, END).

Essentially, with a single partition, the problem has been changed from finding one order statistic from a list of length N to finding a possibly different order statistic from a smaller list. A pessimistic analysis of the complexity of FastOS is

$$T(N) \leq cN + \frac{1}{N} \max_k \left\{ \sum_{N-k+1}^{N-1} T(j) + \sum_{k}^{N-1} T(j) \right\}, \qquad (14.4.1)$$

since the partitioning takes only cN effort. The solution to (14.4.1) can be shown (Exercise 14.4) to be a mere $O(N)$. The order-of-magnitude calculations can hide a nasty constant, indicating only that FastOS is an improvement over sorting for N large enough. But suspend your skepticism until you try it out. See the demonstration **fstmed** for computing medians; it can be easily modified to find any consecutive pair of order statistics.

The Hodges–Lehmann (1963) estimator, defined as

$$\hat{\mu} = \text{median}\{(X_i + X_j)/2,\ 1 \leq i \leq j \leq N\}, \tag{14.4.2}$$

is another location estimator whose computation can be improved using the strategy of divide and conquer. Johnson and Kashdan (1978) suggested this approach, but the author (Monahan 1984) employed a randomized strategy similar to quicksort. Again, the strategy is to cut the set, which in this case has $O(N^2)$ elements, without constructing all the elements – and to do it quickly. The unique feature of this problem is that the partitioning of the $O(N^2)$ elements can be done in $O(N)$ time. Envision the upper triangular matrix of values whose (i, j) element is $X_{(i)} + X_{(j)}$ (but don't create it). Select a partition element c and begin by comparing c to the $(1, N)$ element (which is $X_{(1)} + X_{(N)}$). If c is larger (or equal) then move down a row, and if c is smaller then move left a column, until the diagonal is reached. By following the path of comparisons, the elements of the set that are less than c and greater than or equal to c can be stored by just storing the row limits, requiring only $O(N)$ operations and $O(N)$ storage for each partition step. A modification of the quicksort strategy using random row medians is implemented in the demonstration **hlqest**. Robinson and Sheather (1988) implemented further improvements, including a fast initial partition and a generalization to any consecutive order statistics for constructing confidence intervals.

Demonstrations are also given for three other related problems. The first is the two-sample variation of the Hodges–Lehmann estimator

$$\hat{\Delta} = \text{median}\{X_i - Y_j,\ 1 \leq i \leq M,\ 1 \leq j \leq N\} \tag{14.4.3}$$

in the demonstration **hl2qst**; see also McKean and Ryan (1977). The other two demonstrations are for one-sample scale estimators. One is a median,

$$S_1 = \text{median}\{(X_{(j)} - X_{(i)}),\ 1 \leq i < j \leq N\}, \tag{14.4.4}$$

demonstrated in **abdfmd**; the other is a trimmed estimator,

$$S_2 = \text{sum of } k \text{ smallest } \{(X_{(j)} - X_{(i)}),\ 1 \leq i < j \leq N\}, \tag{14.4.5}$$

implemented in **abdftr**. All four of these estimators appear to take $O(N^2)$ or $O(MN)$ in time and space, and all four follow similar divide-and-conquer and partitioning strategies to reduce the effort to $O(N \log N)$, which is proportional to sorting. For an alternative approximate approach for computing the location estimators, see Exercises 14.6, 14.7, and 14.8.

14.5   Fast Fourier Transform

The most important computational breakthrough of modern mathematics is the fast Fourier transform (FFT). In this section we concentrate on the mathematical detail, postponing applications until the next two sections. Essentially, the discrete Fourier transform is a matrix multiplication with a structure that permits the nesting of the same steps. Here divide and conquer takes a different tack, but it follows the same recursive analysis. Although most of the steps involve transparently simple arithmetic, a constant distraction is the change in indexing. Throughout this and subsequent sections, all vectors and matrices are indexed from 0 to $N - 1$ instead of from 1 to N.

The discrete Fourier transform (DFT) of a vector $\mathbf{x}$ can be described as a matrix multiplication $\mathbf{Tx}$. The (j, k) element of the matrix $\mathbf{T}$ is $T_{jk} = w^{jk}$, where $w = \exp\{-2\pi i/N\}$ and i is the usual imaginary number $i = \sqrt{-1}$, so that

$$a_k = \sum_{j=0}^{N-1} w^{jk} x_j. \tag{14.5.1}$$

In Chapter 3 we counted as N^2 the number of flops for multiplying a matrix by a vector of length N. By exploiting the special structure of this matrix, the fast Fourier transform (Cooley and Tukey 1965) can do the job in merely $O(N \log N)$. One important property of w, an Nth root of unity, is that $w^{kN+m} = w^m$ for any integers k and m. The second important property is that the sum

$$\sum_{k=0}^{N-1} w^{jk} = N\delta(j) = \begin{cases} 0 & \text{if } j \bmod N \neq 0, \\ N & \text{if } j \bmod N = 0. \end{cases} \tag{14.5.2}$$

From these relationships, one can show that the (j, k) elements of the inverse matrix $\mathbf{T}^{-1}$ are w^{-jk}/N:

$$(\mathbf{T}^{-1}\mathbf{Tx})_m = \frac{1}{N}\sum_{k=0}^{N-1} w^{-mk} a_k = \frac{1}{N}\sum_{k=0}^{N-1} w^{-mk} \sum_{j=0}^{N-1} w^{jk} x_j$$

$$= \frac{1}{N}\sum_{j=0}^{N-1} x_j \sum_{k=0}^{N-1} w^{(j-m)k} = \frac{1}{N}\sum_{j=0}^{N-1} x_j N\delta(j - m) = x_m.$$

Since the inverse is closely related to the DFT, a similar algorithm should work for both.

The "fast" in FFT can be seen from assuming that N is composite, $N = N_1 N_2$. Consider the following algebraic steps arising from a rewriting of the indices, $j = j_1 N_2 + j_2$ and $k = k_1 + k_2 N_1$, where $j_1, k_1 \in [0, N_1 - 1]$ and $j_2, k_2 \in [0, N_2 - 1]$:

$$a_k = \sum_{j=0}^{N-1} w^{jk} x_j = \sum_{j=0}^{N-1} w^{j(k_1+k_2N_1)} x_j;$$

$$a_{k_1+k_2N_1} = \sum_{j_1}\sum_{j_2} w^{(j_1N_2+j_2)(k_2N_1+k_1)} x_{j_1N_2+j_2}$$

$$= \sum_{j_1}\sum_{j_2} w^{j_1k_1N_2+j_2(k_2N_1+k_1)} x_{j_1N_2+j_2} \quad (\text{since } w^{N_1N_2j_1k_2} = 1)$$

$$= \sum_{j_2} w^{j_2(k_2N_1+k_1)} \sum_{j_1} (w^{N_2})^{j_1k_1} x_{j_1N_2+j_2}.$$

Now observe that each of the N_2 inner sums is a DFT of length N_1, and if we table them as

$$G(k_1, j_2) = w^{j_2 k_1} \sum_{j_1} (w^{N_2})^{j_1 k_1} x_{j_1 N_2 + j_2}$$

then each of the N_1 outer sums becomes

$$a_{k_1 + k_2 N_1} = \sum_{j_2} (w^{N_1})^{j_2 k_2} G(k_1, j_2),$$

which are DFTs of length N_2. In the divide-and-conquer parlance, we perform a DFT of length $N = N_1 N_2$ by performing N_2 DFTs of length N_1 to get $G(k_1, j_2)$ and then N_1 DFTs of length N_2, or

$$T(N) = T(N_1 N_2) = N_2 T(N_1) + N_1 T(N_2). \tag{14.5.3}$$

For the simple case of even N, taking $N_1 = 2$ yields the familiar

$$T(N) = (N/2)T(2) + 2T(N/2), \tag{14.5.4}$$

whose solution is $T(N) = O(N \log N)$. The remainder of this section dwells on the gory details; first-time readers should skip to the next section for something more interesting.

The effectiveness of the FFT (and some details of its coding) become apparent by looking in detail at the case $N = 2^m$, the "power of 2" algorithm. Later we will see that this is all we really need. Again do some rewriting of the indices:

$$j = j_1 2^{m-1} + j_2 2^{m-2} + \cdots + j_\nu 2^{m-\nu} + \cdots + j_{m-1} 2 + j_m$$

$$= j_1 2^{m-1} + j_1^*$$

$$= j_1 2^{m-1} + j_2 2^{m-2} + j_2^*$$

$$\vdots$$

Here $j_\nu \in [0, 1]$, and j_ν^* subsumes the remaining indices and covers $[0, 2^{m-\nu} - 1]$. Now repeat this with k, but in the reverse order:

$$k = k_1 + k_2 2 + \cdots + k_\nu 2^{\nu-1} + \cdots + k_{m-1} 2^{m-2} + k_m 2^{m-1}$$

$$= k_1 + 2k_1^*$$

$$= k_1 + 2k_2 + 2^2 k_2^*; \tag{14.5.5}$$

here $k_\nu \in [0, 1]$, and k_ν^* subsumes the remaining indices and covers $[0, 2^{m-\nu} - 1]$.

Now begin with the full summation over j, and then step through one at a time:

$$a_k = \sum_{j_m} \cdots \sum_{j_1} w^{k(\sum j_\nu 2^{m-\nu})} x_{\sum j_\nu 2^{m-\nu}};$$

$$a_{k_1 + 2k_1^*} = \sum_{j_1^*} \sum_{j_1} w^{(k_1 + 2k_1^*)(j_1 2^{m-1} + j_1^*)} x_{j_1 2^{m-1} + j_1^*}$$

$$= \sum_{j_1^*} w^{(k_1 + 2k_1^*) j_1^*} \sum_{j_1} w^{k_1 j_1 2^{m-1}} x_{j_1 2^{m-1} + j_1^*}$$

$$= \sum_{j_1^*} w^{(k_1 + 2k_1^*) j_1^*} (x_{j_1^*} + w^{k_1 2^{m-1}} x_{j_1^* + 2^{m-1}}).$$

Notice that the even (0) and odd (1) values of k simplify (respectively) to

$$a_{0+2k_1^*} = \sum_{j_1^*} (w^2)^{j_1^* k_1^*} (x_{j_1^*} + x_{j_1^* + 2^{m-1}})$$

and

$$a_{1+2k_1^*} = \sum_{j_1^*} (w^2)^{j_1^* k_1^*} (x_{j_1^*} - x_{j_1^* + 2^{m-1}}) w^{j_1^*}.$$

No previous mention was made of the indexing needed to store and retrieve $G(k_1, j_2)$, and this issue will be further postponed except to mention here the storage of intermediate results in $X_{j_1^*}^{(k_1)}$:

$$X_{j_1^*}^{(0)} = (x_{j_1^*} + x_{j_1^* + 2^{m-1}}) \quad \text{and} \quad X_{j_1^*}^{(1)} = (x_{j_1^*} - x_{j_1^* + 2^{m-1}}) w^{j_1^*}.$$

Next consider the summation on j_2 using $X^{(k_1)}$:

$$\begin{aligned}
a_{k_1 + 2k_2 + 2^2 k_2^*} &= \sum_{j_2^*} \sum_{j_2} (w^2)^{(k_2 + 2k_2^*)(j_2 2^{m-2} + j_2^*)} X_{j_2 2^{m-2} + j_2^*}^{(k_1)}, \\
&= \sum_{j_2^*} w^{2(k_2 + 2k_2^*) j_2^*} (X_{j_2^*}^{(k_1)} + w^{k_2 2^{m-1}} X_{j_2 2^{m-2} + j_2^*}^{(k_1)}), \\
&= \sum_{j_2^*} w^{4 k_2^* j_2^*} X_{j_2^*}^{(k_1, k_2)},
\end{aligned}$$

where

$$X_{j_2^*}^{(k_1, 0)} = (X_{j_2^*}^{(k_1)} + X_{j_2^* + 2^{m-2}}^{(k_1)}) \quad \text{and} \quad X_{j_2^*}^{(k_1, 1)} = (X_{j_2^*}^{(k_1)} - X_{j_2^* + 2^{m-2}}^{(k_1)}) w^{2 j_2^*}.$$

Each step, a transform of length 2, can be summarized by the updates

$$X_{j_\nu^*}^{(k_1, \ldots, k_{\nu-1}, 0)} = (X_{j_\nu^*}^{(k_1, \ldots, k_{\nu-1})} + X_{j_\nu^* + 2^{m-\nu}}^{(k_1, \ldots, k_{\nu-1})}), \tag{14.5.6a}$$

and

$$X_{j_\nu^*}^{(k_1, \ldots, k_{\nu-1}, 1)} = (X_{j_\nu^*}^{(k_1, \ldots, k_{\nu-1})} - X_{j_\nu^* + 2^{m-\nu}}^{(k_1, \ldots, k_{\nu-1})}) w^{2^{\nu-1} j_\nu^*}. \tag{14.5.6b}$$

Since $j_{m-1}^* = j_m$ and $k_{m-1}^* = k_m$, the last step has

$$\begin{aligned}
a_{k_1 + \cdots + 2^{m-1} k_m} &= \sum_{j_m} w^{2^{m-1} j_m k_m} X_{j_m}^{(k_1, \ldots, k_{m-1})} \\
&= X_0^{(k_1, \ldots, k_{m-1})} + w^{2^{m-1} k_m} X_1^{(k_1, \ldots, k_{m-1})} = X^{(k_1, \ldots, k_m)}.
\end{aligned}$$

Hence, for the power-of-2 algorithm, each step consists of a long list of pairwise sums as well as an equally long list of pairwise differences scaled by w to some power. The issue of storage can no longer be ignored – where can $X_{j_\nu^*}^{(k_1, \ldots, k_\nu)}$ be stored? Since each step has all of those pairwise sums and differences, the two results could be stored over the two elements that contributed. If the rule is that the sums overwrite the first element and the differences overwrite the second, then $X_{j_1^*}^{(k_1)}$ is stored in $x_{j_1^* + k_1 2^{m-1}}$, $X_{j_2^*}^{(k_1, k_2)}$ is stored in $x_{j_2^* + k_1 2^{m-1} + k_2 2^{m-2}}$, and so on. At the end, $X^{(k_1, \ldots, k_m)}$ is stored in location

$$\text{rev}(k) = k_1 2^{m-1} + k_2 2^{m-2} + \cdots + k_\nu 2^{m-\nu} + \cdots + k_{m-1} 2 + k_m, \tag{14.5.7}$$

which is just exactly reversed from k in (14.5.5). That is: given k as defined in (14.5.5), if we reverse the order of the bits $k_1, \ldots, k_m$ with the operator $\text{rev}(k)$, then a_k is stored in location $a_{\text{rev}(k)}$. The power-of-2 algorithm then follows the calculations in (14.5.6a,b) and the storage steps just outlined; at the end, the elements are unscrambled using the bit-reversing operator $\text{rev}(k)$.

Two details remain. The biggest issue – what to do if $N \neq 2^m$ – is postponed until the discussion of the "chirp-z transform" (Section 14.6). The other issue is how to handle the inverse transform. Only two changes are needed for its computation: a negative sign in the exponent of w in (14.5.6b) and dividing by N at the end.

Example 14.2: *Discrete Fourier Transform of Length 8*
Let $\mathbf{x}$ be the vector $(1, 2, 3, 4, 5, 6, 7, 8)^{\mathsf{T}}$. Then the DFT can be computed as follows.

Storage	x_j	$X_{j_1^*}^{(k_1)}$	$X_{j_2^*}^{(k_1,k_2)}$	$X^{(k_1,k_2,k_3)}$
0	1	$X_0^{(0)} = 6$	$X_0^{(0,0)} = 16$	$X^{(0,0,0)} = 36$
1	2	$X_1^{(0)} = 8$	$X_1^{(0,0)} = 20$	$X^{(0,0,1)} = -4$
2	3	$X_2^{(0)} = 10$	$X_0^{(0,1)} = -4$	$X^{(0,1,0)} = -4(1+w^2)$
3	4	$X_3^{(0)} = 12$	$X_1^{(0,1)} = -4$	$X^{(0,1,1)} = -4(1-w^2)$
4	5	$X_0^{(1)} = -4$	$X_0^{(1,0)} = -4(1+w^2)$	$X^{(1,0,0)} = -4(1+w^2)(1+w)$
5	6	$X_1^{(1)} = -4$	$X_1^{(1,0)} = -4(1+w^2)$	$X^{(1,0,1)} = -4(1+w^2)(1-w)$
6	7	$X_2^{(1)} = -4$	$X_0^{(1,1)} = -4(1-w^2)$	$X^{(1,1,0)} = -4(1+w^2)(1+w^3)$
7	8	$X_3^{(1)} = -4$	$X_1^{(1,1)} = -4(1-w^2)$	$X^{(1,1,1)} = -4(1-w^2)(1-w^3)$

k	$\text{rev}(k)$	$\text{real}(a_k)$	$\text{imag}(a_k)$	w^k
0	0	36	0	1
1	4	-4	$4(1+\sqrt{2})$	$w = (1-i)/\sqrt{2}$
2	2	-4	$+4$	$w^2 = -i$
3	6	-4	$-4(1-\sqrt{2})$	$w^3 = -(1+i)/\sqrt{2}$
4	1	-4	0	$w^4 = -1$
5	5	-4	$4(1-\sqrt{2})$	$w^5 = (-1+i)/\sqrt{2}$
6	3	-4	-4	$w^6 = i$
7	7	-4	$-4(1+\sqrt{2})$	$w^7 = (1+i)/\sqrt{2}$

See the demonstration **fft2n**.

14.6 Convolutions and the Chirp-z Transform

Use of the FFT follows the same pattern as the continuous Fourier transform. The reader should keep in mind that the FFT is merely a fast computational algorithm for the DFT. The Fourier transform is great for computing convolutions – the transform of a convolution is the product of the transforms. This also applies to the DFT and is the key to all of the applications discussed here.

Let the notation $\mathbf{x} * \mathbf{y}$ define the elementwise product of two vectors; that is, $\mathbf{x} * \mathbf{y}$ is a vector whose jth element is $(\mathbf{x} * \mathbf{y})_j = x_j y_j$. Then the convolution of two vectors can be computed by computing the DFT for each vector, multiplying the transforms together elementwise, and then taking the inverse transform. Mathematically, this approach to convolutions can be written as $\mathbf{z} = \mathbf{T}^{-1}((\mathbf{Tx}) * (\mathbf{Ty}))$; the details are

$$z_u = \frac{1}{N} \sum_k w^{-uk} \left\{ \sum_s w^{ks} x_s \right\} \left\{ \sum_t w^{kt} y_t \right\} = \frac{1}{N} \sum_s \sum_t x_s y_t \sum_k w^{k(s+t-u)}$$

$$= \frac{1}{N} \sum_s \sum_t x_s y_t N \delta(s+t-u) = \sum_s x_s y_{u-s}.$$

Note that this is a *circular* or *periodic* convolution owing to (14.5.2), so that the final sum on s extends from 0 to $N - 1$. Therefore, if $u - s < 0$ then $x_s y_{N+u-s}$ is included in the sum.

In order to compute a noncircular convolution, the vectors $\mathbf{x}$ and $\mathbf{y}$ must be padded with at least $N - 1$ zeros to make those vectors at least $2N - 1$ in length. If we had two polynomials of degree $N - 1$, $p(z) = \sum_{j=0}^{N-1} x_j z^j$ and $q(z) = \sum_{j=0}^{N-1} y_j z^j$, then the product is a polynomial of degree $2N - 2$,

$$p(z)q(z) = \sum_{j=0}^{2N-2} \left\{ \sum_{k=0}^{j} x_k y_{j-k} \right\} z^j.$$

This is a common avenue to circumvent the periodicity inherent in Fourier transforms.

In the previous section we presented the power-of-2 algorithm, yet there are versions of the FFT for other composite values of N (see especially Singleton 1969). Our avoidance is due not only to sloth. First, as will be evident in the applications in the next section, often the length N can be chosen for convenience. The second reason is that, by employing the *chirp-z transform* (Bluestein 1970; Rabiner, Schafer, and Rader 1969) that follows, the power-of-2 algorithm can be used to compute the DFT for any value of N.

We begin with a little algebra: $(s - t)^2 = s^2 - 2st + t^2$, so that

$$st = s^2/2 + t^2/2 - (s-t)^2/2.$$

Now write the DFT for a vector $\mathbf{b}$ as follows:

$$a_s = \sum_{t=0}^{N-1} w^{st} b_t = \sum_{t=0}^{N-1} w^{s^2/2+t^2/2-(s-t)^2/2} b_t$$

$$= w^{s^2/2} \sum_{t=0}^{N-1} (w^{t^2/2} b_t) w^{-(s-t)^2/2}. \tag{14.6.1}$$

The sum can be viewed as a convolution of $x_t = w^{t^2/2} b_t$ and $y_t = w^{-t^2/2}$. Any convolution can be computed using three FFTs with enough padded zeros. The strategy here is to pad with enough zeros so that the length is a power of 2. If $2^{m-1} < N < 2^m$, then three FFTs are needed with length $2^{m+1} = N^*$ in order to compute the convolution. If $N = 13$, say, then pad with 19 zeros and use FFTs of length $N^* = 32 = 2^5$ to compute the convolution. One important detail is that this convolution must be circular, so that the vector **y** has entries stored as follows:

$$y_t = 1, \qquad\qquad t = 0;$$
$$y_t = w^{-t^2/2}, \qquad\quad t = 1, \ldots, N - 1;$$
$$y_t = 0, \qquad\qquad\, t = N, \ldots, N^* - N;$$
$$y_t = w^{-(N^*-t)^2/2}, \quad t = N^* - N + 1, \ldots, N^* - 1.$$

See the following example and the demonstration **chirpz**.

Example 14.3: Chirp-z Transform
Consider the DFT of a series of length 3 (can't be easier), $\mathbf{b} = (b_0, b_1, b_2)^\mathsf{T}$. Then the powers of w are $w^0 = 1$, $w^1 = -(1 + i\sqrt{3})/2$, and $w^2 = -(1 - i\sqrt{3})/2$. The DFT of **b** is then

$$a_0 = b_0 + b_1 + b_2,$$
$$a_1 = w^0 b_0 + w^1 b_1 + w^2 b_2,$$
$$a_2 = w^0 b_0 + w^2 b_1 + w^1 b_2.$$

In terms of (14.6.1), the vectors **x** and **y** can be written as

$$x_0 = b_0 w^0, \qquad y_0 = w^0 = 1,$$
$$x_1 = b_1 w^{1/2}, \qquad y_1 = w^{-1/2} = y_{-1},$$
$$x_2 = b_2 w^2, \qquad\, y_2 = w^{-2} = w^1 = y_{-2},$$

and the DFT looks like

$$a_0 = w^0 [x_0 y_0 + x_1 y_{-1} + x_2 y_{-2}]$$
$$= w^0 [(w^0 b_0)(w^0) + (w^{1/2} b_1)(w^{-1/2}) + (w^2 b_2)(w^{-2})],$$
$$a_1 = w^{1/2} [x_0 y_1 + x_1 y_0 + x_2 y_{-1}]$$
$$= w^{1/2} [(w^0 b_0)(w^{-1/2}) + (w^{1/2} b_1)(w^0) + (w^2 b_2)(w^{-1/2})],$$
$$a_2 = w^2 [x_0 y_2 + x_1 y_1 + x_2 y_0]$$
$$= w^2 [(w^0 b_0)(w^{-2}) + (w^{1/2} b_1)(w^{-1/2}) + (w^2 b_2)(w^0)].$$

For $N = 3$, the convolutions could be computed using FFTs of length 8, where y_{-1} would be stored in y_7 and y_{-2} in y_6. But if length 16 were used, y_{-1} would be in y_{15} and y_{-2} in y_{14}.

14.7   Statistical Applications of the FFT

Applications of the FFT in statistics range from the obvious and mundane to the surprising and clever. The intention of this section is to provide a sampling of this variety.

As the reader may anticipate, the more interesting cases arise when a computationally taxing problem can be solved by a completely different approach that exploits the ability to compute the DFT much faster than expected.

(A) *Time Series*

The first application of the FFT to statistical time-series analysis is the computation of the periodogram $I_N(f)$, which measures how much of the variation of a time series $\{y_t\}$ is attributable to activity at a particular frequency f. The periodogram is usually defined by

$$I_N(f) = \frac{N}{2}[A(f)^2 + B(f)^2],$$

where $A(f)$ and $B(f)$ are estimates of the periodic components of the series $\{y_t, t = 0, \ldots, N - 1\}$,

$$A(f) = \frac{2}{N} \sum_{t=0}^{N-1} y_t \cos(2\pi ft), \qquad B(f) = \frac{2}{N} \sum_{t=0}^{N-1} y_t \sin(2\pi ft).$$

An alternative definition of the periodogram has the series $\{y_t\}$ centered about its mean. Although the periodogram is defined for all frequencies $f \in [0, \frac{1}{2}]$, most applications would call for its evaluation only at several select frequencies. Use of the FFT would permit fast computation at N frequencies, but only at the Fourier frequencies $f_j = j/N$. The DFT of the series $\{y_t\}$ takes the form

$$a_j = \sum_{t=0}^{N-1} y_t \exp\left\{-\frac{2\pi ijt}{N}\right\} = \sum_{t=0}^{N-1} y_t \left[\cos\left(\frac{2\pi jt}{N}\right) + i \sin\left(\frac{2\pi jt}{N}\right)\right]$$

$$= \frac{N}{2}\left[A\left(\frac{j}{N}\right) + iB\left(\frac{j}{N}\right)\right],$$

$$I_N\left(\frac{j}{N}\right) = \frac{2}{N}|a_j|^2.$$

Notice also that, at these frequencies, it doesn't matter whether the series $\{y_t\}$ is centered or not (see Exercises 14.14 and 14.15). The FFT has had its biggest impact in the estimation of the power spectrum, where the ability to compute the periodogram quickly at many frequencies has promoted estimates that are smoothed periodograms computed at Fourier frequencies, as seen in Section 13.5.

The use of the FFT to compute convolutions also leads to faster methods for computing both autocorrelations,

$$r_k = \frac{1}{N-k} \sum_{t=0}^{N-k} y_t y_{t+k},$$

and cross-correlations,

$$v_{xy}(k) = \frac{1}{N-k} \sum_{t=0}^{N-k} x_t y_{t+k}.$$

Notice, of course, that $v_{xx}(k) = r_k$; also, each series would commonly be centered about its mean. All of the autocorrelations r_k, or cross-correlations $v_{xy}(k)$, can be computed using

$$[\mathbf{T}^{-1}(\mathbf{T}(\mathbf{x}) * \overline{\mathbf{T}(\mathbf{y})})]_k$$

$$= \frac{1}{N} \sum_j^{N-1} w^{kj} \mathbf{T}(\mathbf{x})_j \overline{\mathbf{T}(\mathbf{y})_j} = \frac{1}{N} \sum_{j=0}^{N-1} w^{kj} \left(\sum_s w^{sj} x_s \right) \left(\sum_t w^{-tj} y_t \right)$$

$$= \frac{1}{N} \sum_s \sum_t x_s y_t \sum_j w^{kj+sj-tj} = \frac{1}{N} \sum_s \sum_t x_s y_t N \delta(s - t + k) = \sum_{s=0}^{N-1} x_s y_{s+k}.$$

Unless there is inherent periodicity in the indexing, the circular convolutions that the FFT will compute must be avoided. The requirement here is that the series be padded by N zeros so that series of length $N^* = 2N$ are transformed, one multiplied by the conjugate of the other, and the product transformed back. If this is done, then $(N - k)v_{xy}(k)$ will be in location k for $k = 0, \ldots, N - 1$ and $(N - k)v_{xy}(-k) = (N - k)v_{yx}(k)$ will be in location $N^* - k = 2N - k$.

More than other areas of applications, the number of observations in a time series is often not subject to choice. As a result, N (or $2N$ in the case of correlations) will not be a power of 2 and so the chirp-z transform of Section 14.6 will be needed to compute the DFT efficiently. If the number of observations is subject to choice, then clearly choosing a sample size that is a power of 2 will have great computational advantages.

(B) *Characteristic Functions of Discrete Random Variables*

The characteristic function of a discrete random variable X is written as $\phi(t) = Ee^{itX} = \sum_x p_x e^{itx}$. If the support of the distribution is finite and limited to the integers $\{0, 1, \ldots, N - 1\}$, then the DFT of the probabilities $\{p_j\}$ will be the complex conjugate of the characteristic function of X evaluated at $t = 2\pi k/N$,

$$\phi\left(\frac{2\pi k}{N} \right) = \sum_{j=0}^{N-1} p_j \exp\left\{ i \frac{2\pi kj}{N} \right\} = \sum_{j=0}^{N-1} p_j w^{-jk} = \overline{a_k},$$

or the characteristic function evaluated at $t = -2\pi k/N$ will be the DFT of the probabilities. In the other direction, the probabilities are the inverse DFT of the series $\{a_k\}$, where $a_k = \phi(-2\pi k/N)$. However, if the support of the distribution is not bounded or if the support extends beyond $N - 1$, then

$$p_j^* = \sum_{m=0}^{\infty} p_{j+mN}$$

are the values of the inverse DFT of the series $\{a_k = \phi(-2\pi k/N)\}$. The probabilities from N and beyond are aliased back to integers within the range. See the demonstration **poisp**.

The problems with discrete random variables where the FFT can be exploited to speed up computation are all cases where the characteristic function is easily available, often because a sum of independent random variables is involved. In such cases, the usual approach is just to compute the characteristic function at the appropriate values and then compute the inverse FFT. We can anticipate two obstacles. First, if the support of the distribution is unbounded then there is an aliasing problem. The second problem is the effect of roundoff error. One check for the accuracy of the results from inverting a characteristic function to obtain a probability is that the computed probability should be real and nonnegative. If the imaginary parts are not small on a relative basis, then the computed probabilities are clearly suspect. In some circumstances, other tools are available to rescue the situation, as seen in the following example.

Example 14.4: *Ball and Urn Probabilities*

In an application that involved hashing, Ramakrishna (1987) used recurrence relationships to compute the probability $P(n, m, b)$ that n balls can be placed at random in m urns, each with capacity b balls, without overflowing: $P(n, m, b) = F(n, m, b)/m^n$. David and Barton (1962) gave an expression for $F(n, m, b)$ in terms of generating functions:

$$G_b(x) = 1 + x + x^2/2! + \cdots + x^k/k! + \cdots + x^b/b!,$$

$$G^*(x) = [G_b(x)]^m = \sum_{n=0}^{mb} F(n, m, b)\frac{x^n}{n!}.$$

The application has fixed m and b, so the values of $F(n, m, b)$ for various values of n can be found by inverting the characteristic function $G^*(e^{it})$ and multiplying the probabilities by $n!$. The characteristic function $G^*(e^{it}) = [G_b(e^{it})]^m$, and the $G_b(e^{it})$ can be found simply by computing the DFT of the probabilities $1/j!$ (Monahan 1987). But it's not quite that easy. Instead, construct $q_j = r^j/j!$ for $j = 0, \ldots, b$, and notice that the q_j are proportional to the probabilities for the Poisson distribution with mean r, truncated at b. Then the DFT of $\{q_j\}$ gives $G_b(re^{-i2\pi k/N})$ for $N > mb$, choosing N as a power of 2. Powering this up m times yields $G^*(re^{i2\pi k/N})$, and taking the inverse DFT will reproduce $q_j^* = F(n, m, b)r^j/j!$. The role of the scale r will become apparent only when considering which values of q_j^* will be large. Recall that the q_j were proportional to probabilities from a truncated Poisson distribution with mean r. For a reasonable truncation point b, the q_j^* will be proportional to the probabilities from a Poisson distribution with mean mr, which is approximately normal with mean mr and variance mr, so the standard deviation is $\sqrt{mr}$. Hence the largest values of q_j^* will be around mr and so, for j far from mr, the value of q_j^* will be relatively small and the roundoff error there much larger (relatively). If the interesting values of j are large, then r should be adjusted so that these values can be computed accurately. If there is no adjustment by r, then only values of j near m will be computed accurately and perhaps interesting values of j will be swamped by roundoff error.

The adjustment by the scalar r also brings the possibility of very large values and potential overflow. The self-controlled floating point calculations from Section 2.5 can be employed, writing a number as $D \times 2^I$ and storing the pair (D, I). Here, the complication is that we have complex numbers, so that the three pieces $(x, y, k) \equiv (x + iy) \times 2^k$ are needed. As a result, the FFT routine must be re-coded to handle this complicated arithmetic. However, because of the simple nature of the fundamental steps (14.5.6), this is not an insurmountable task. In the demonstration **chex144**, the computed value of $P(400, 30, 25)$ is given as .966968; Ramakrishna gave .9670.

Example 14.5: *Rank Tests*

Pagano and Tritchler (1983) showed how to construct the characteristic function for the null distribution of rank test statistics for the one- and two-sample problems. The one-sample problem is any statistic of the form

$$S_1 = \sum_{j=1}^{n} s(R_j)I(X_j),$$

where $s(R_j)$ is the score function; here $I(X_j) = 1$ if $X_j > 0$ and $I(X_j) = 0$ otherwise. The most common cases are $s(j) = j$ for the Wilcoxon test and $s(j) = \Phi^{-1}(j/(n+1))$ for the normal scores test. The characteristic function of the statistic S_1 is just

$$\phi_1(t) = e^{itT} \prod_{j=1}^{n} \cos(s(j)t),$$

where $T = \sum_j s(j)$. For the Wilcoxon case with $s(j) = j$, the support of the statistic is just the integers; hence, by forming

$$a_k = \phi_1(-2\pi k/N), \quad k = 0, \ldots, N-1,$$

for N a power of 2 larger than the largest value of the statistic, the distribution of the test statistic S_1 can be computed merely by computing the inverse FFT of $\{a_k\}$. See the demonstration **wlcx1s**. Notice that ties can be handled without any difficulty. If (say) the two smallest values of $|X_i|$ are tied, then multiply all of the scores by 2 and use $s(1) = s(2) = 3$ and $s(j) = 2j$ for $j > 2$; then the distribution for $2S_1$ is computed.

For other score functions, such as the normal scores, the distribution is discrete but the support is not the integers. The remedy suggested by Pagano and Tritchler is to discretize the scores using the modified

$$s^*(j) = \left[L \frac{s(j) - s_{\min}}{s_{\max} - s_{\min}} \right],$$

where $[\cdot]$ denotes the integer part, $s_{\min}$ and $s_{\max}$ mark the range of the $s(j)$, and L is some large multiplier (say, 1000). The test statistic S_1 using the modified scores $s^*(j)$ now has support on the integers, albeit with a much larger range. Nevertheless, the effort in computing the distribution is still roughly $O(n^2)$ and not combinatorial. The value of L can be varied to verify the lack of an effect.

For the two-sample problem, Pagano and Tritchler gave the characteristic function $\phi_2(t) = \psi(m, m+n, t)$ for the statistic

$$S_2 = \sum_{j=1}^{m\cdot} s(R_j),$$

where R_j denotes ranks from the combined $(m+n)$ sample. This characteristic function $\psi(j, k, t)$ can be computed by the recursion

$$\psi(j, k, t) = \exp\{its_k\}\psi(j - 1, k - 1, t)$$

$$+ \psi(j, k - 1, t) \quad \text{for } 1 \le j \le k = 1, 2, \ldots, \quad (14.7.1)$$

where $\psi(0, 0, t) = 1$ and $\psi(j, k, t) = 0$ for $j > k$. Each value of the characteristic function then takes $O(m(m + n))$ effort, choosing m to be the smaller of the two sample sizes. For an implementation to compute the distribution of the two-sample Wilcoxon test statistic with $s(j) = j$, see the demonstration **wlcx2s**.

As can be seen from these two examples, many combinatorial problems permit the calculation of the characteristic function of a discrete or discretizable random variable. Following the approach of Pagano and Tritchler (1983), many permutation tests that lead to counting combinations of subsets lead also to a recursion formula for a characteristic function of the form (14.7.1). Even if the calculation of the characteristic function may be quite involved, the alternative method for calculation usually entails enumeration of combinations. Although this topic will be covered in the next section, it is sufficient to recognize that such enumeration is usually exponential in its computational complexity, whereas the characteristic function approach is only polynomial. For further applications in the same vein, see Good, Gover, and Mitchell (1970) for $R \times C$ tables, Tritchler (1984a,b) or Spino and Pagano (1991) for permutation distributions, and Baglivo, Olivier, and Pagano (1992) for multinomials.

(C) *Convolutions of Continuous Random Variables by Discretization*

Since characteristic functions make convolutions easier to obtain and since discrete random variables are easier to deal with using the FFT, one route for obtaining the distribution of the sum of continuous random variables is to discretize the problem and then use the FFT to obtain the distribution of the sum. One strong advantage of this route is that the distributions are discrete: the probabilities should be positive and add to 1, and the imaginary parts should be zero. However, this route will work only if the discretization works well. Denote the continuous random variable by X with density $f(x)$ and denote the discretized random variable by X^*, whose support is restricted to the lattice $\{\delta j, j = 0, \ldots, N - 1\}$. Then $p_j = \Pr(X^* = x_j = \delta j)$ is approximating

$$\Pr\left((j - \tfrac{1}{2})\delta < X \le (j + \tfrac{1}{2})\delta\right) = \int_{x_j - \delta/2}^{x_j + \delta/2} f(u)\, du \approx \delta f(x_j). \quad (14.7.2)$$

To approximate the distribution of the sum of m independent random variables each with density $f(x)$, the approach is to compute the FFT of the sequence of probabilities $\{p_j\}$ to get $\{a_k\}$, then raise to the power m to get $(a_k)^m = b_k$, and then transform back the $\{b_k\}$ to obtain $\{q_j\}$. In this case the discrete probabilities $q_j = \Pr\left(\sum_{i=1}^{m} X_j^* = x_j = \delta j\right)$ are approximating

$$\Pr\left((j - \tfrac{1}{2})\delta < \sum_{i=1}^{m} X_i \le (j + \tfrac{1}{2})\delta\right).$$

If the random variables X_i are not identically distributed, then the exponentiation becomes a product: produce probabilities $p_j^{(i)}$ for random variable X_i, transform to get $\{a_k^{(i)}\}$, then $b_k = \prod_{i=1}^{m} a_j^{(i)}$, and then transform $\{b_k\}$ back to get $\{q_j\}$.

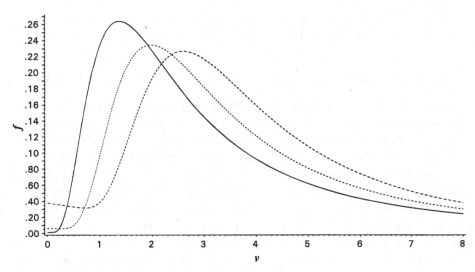

Figure 14.1. Discretization of continuous convolutions. Density of average of reciprocals of uniforms, with $m = 8$ (solid), 16, and 32 (dashed).

The key part of this approach is that the approximation (14.7.2) works well; everything else is details. However, this approximation does not work well in some important cases. For example, for the chi-square distribution, the probability at zero is

$$\int_0^{\delta/2} (2\pi)^{-1/2} e^{-x/2} x^{-1/2} \, dx,$$

which could be approximated by $\sqrt{\delta/\pi}$. This approximation works well when δ is small enough, but then $\delta f(x_j)$ will require special treatment for all small j; see Exercise 14.25. Distributions with infinite support pose two obvious problems. Truncation of the distribution at $(N-1)\delta$ requires the distribution to tail quickly to zero. If the distribution does not tail quickly to zero, or if the bound $(N-1)\delta$ isn't large enough, then any probability that the sum is greater than the upper bound will be aliased.

Example 14.6: *Distribution of Sums of Reciprocals of Uniforms*
In conducting research on the tests for infinite variance in Section 12.5, we sought the limiting distribution of

$$V_m = m^{-1} \sum_{i=1}^{m} \frac{1}{U_i},$$

where the U_i are IID uniform$(0, 1)$ random variables. To get a handle on the asymptotics, the distribution of $\sum_{i=1}^m (1/U_i - 1)$ was approximated for $m = 8$, 16, and 32 using the approach just described with $N = 2^{16} = 65{,}536$ and $\delta = 1/256$. The demonstration **tivmm1** constructs the $\{q_j\}$ for these three values of m and writes them into the file **tivmm1.dat**, using this discretization method and the extended precision version of the FFT. As can be seen in Figure 14.1, the density of $V_m - 1$ appears to approach a consistent shape, although the location of the distribution still shifts to the right as m increases. Notice how strong the aliasing effect has become for $m = 32$, as the density is clearly decreasing at the origin. The density for the sum at $x_j = \delta j$ is approximated by q_j/δ; rescaling by $1/m$ rescales the horizontal variable to $v = j\delta/m$ and the density to mq_j/δ.

(D) *Inverting the Characteristic Function of Continuous Random Variables*

The null distribution of many important statistics can be expressed as the sum of independent random variables. Since the sum of random variables can be conveniently expressed in terms of products of characteristic functions, the inversion of the characteristic function would be a natural approach for obtaining the distribution – either the density for plotting, or the distribution function for critical values. The fast Fourier transform also appears to be the natural computing tool for inverting characteristic functions. However, the ease of use in the discrete case does not carry over to the continuous case. Moreover, the problem of inversion of the characteristic function numerically is not that easy, even with such a tool as the FFT available.

The mathematics of the inversion of a characteristic function is rather simple. Denote the characteristic function of the random variable X by $\phi(t) = Ee^{itX}$. Then the inverse formula for the density can be expressed as

$$ f(x) = \frac{1}{2\pi} \int_{-\infty}^{\infty} \phi(t) e^{-itx} \, dt. \tag{14.7.3} $$

The density is usually not as useful as the distribution function, which takes the form

$$ F(x) = \frac{1}{2} - \frac{1}{2\pi i} \int_{-\infty}^{\infty} \frac{\phi(t)}{t} e^{-itx} \, dt. \tag{14.7.4} $$

The exploitation of the FFT follows from replacing the infinite integral with a finite one from $-T$ to T and then replacing the finite integral by a sum over evenly spaced points,

$$ f(x) = \frac{1}{2\pi} \int_{-T}^{T} \phi(t) e^{-itx} \, dt \approx \frac{\delta}{2\pi} \sum_{j=0}^{N-1} \phi(t_j) e^{-it_j x} \tag{14.7.5} $$

with $t_j = j\delta$. Evaluate $f(x)$ at evenly spaced values of x (say, $x_k = k\gamma$) and force the product of the two spacings $\delta\gamma = 2\pi/N$. Then (14.7.5) can be rewritten as

$$ f(x_k) \approx \frac{\delta}{2\pi} \sum_{j=0}^{N-1} \phi(j\delta) e^{-ijk2\pi/N}, $$

so that the DFT of scaled values of the characteristic function forms values of the density. The key is that the product of the two spacings follows $\delta\gamma = 2\pi/N$, which combines the relationship between the spacing δ of the t_j, the range $\pm T$ of the integration on t, where $2T = \delta N$, as well as the spacing γ of the x_k and their range $\pm G$, where $2G = \gamma N$. If the integration on t forces (a) the spacing δ because of smoothness and (b) the range $\pm T$ to reduce the truncation/aliasing error, then for fixed effort N this also forces the spacing of the x_k and their range. The "fast" in FFT permits N to be very large, and often both factors can be accommodated.

Observe that the periodicity in the DFT produces some simplifications for negative values of t and x. If we use $t_j = j\delta$, then $t_{N-j} = (N - j)(2T/N) = 2T - t_j = -t_j$.

Similarly, $x_{N-k} = -x_k$, so that the large indices can be used for negative values in the computation of the DFT. This obviates the need for shifting the distribution so that the support is all on positive values.

Although the inversion formula for the density is usually well behaved, the more useful distribution function is often quite troublesome. Notice that we're dividing by t in the integral (14.7.4); hence, in the sum we need to find something to replace $[\phi(t_j)/t_j]$ for $t_0 = 0$. If the distribution has a first moment, then the $j = 0$ term can be dropped from the sum (Bohman 1975) (note the prime for the missing zero term):

$$F(x) \approx \frac{1}{2} + \frac{x\delta}{2\pi} - \delta \sum_{j}{}' \frac{\phi(t_j)}{2\pi i t_j}.$$

Another approach is to find a distribution with known characteristic function $\psi(t)$ and distribution function $H(x)$, which leads to

$$F(x_k) \approx H(x) + \frac{\delta}{2\pi} \sum_{j=0}^{N-1} e^{-ijk2\pi/N} \frac{\phi(t_j) - \psi(t_j)}{t_j}; \qquad (14.7.6)$$

again, a special value would be sought for the case $t_j = 0$. If ψ and ϕ behaved similarly at the origin, then the difference divided by t may have a limit at zero that could be used in place of the $j = 0$ term. This will work in some cases using the normal distribution. However, not many other distributions will work, since few simple distributions have a distribution function and a characteristic function that are both easy to manipulate. The Cauchy characteristic function $e^{-\sigma|t|}$ behaves badly at the origin. The double exponential/Laplace characteristic function $\psi(t) = (1 + \sigma^2 t^2)^{-1}$ is nice and smooth at the origin, but notice that it tails off very slowly and would require T to be large.

The focus of this discussion has been what to do with the $j = 0$ term, but the point is that – beyond merely avoiding division by zero – the behavior of the characteristic function near the origin is important both for the behavior of the distribution and the numerical evaluation of the integral. In general, numerical inversion for the distribution function is difficult; see Exercises 14.22 and 14.23. One notable exception for a particularly useful case is postponed to Section 14.7(E), after an example of some mixed results.

Example 14.7: *Distribution of Sums of Reciprocals of Uniforms, Revisited*
As mentioned in Example 14.6, we seek the limiting distribution of

$$V_m = m^{-1} \sum_{i=1}^{m} \frac{1}{U_i},$$

where U_i are IID uniform$(0, 1)$ random variables. Given the insight gained from Figure 14.1, the limiting distribution could be established as $V_m - m \log m \xrightarrow{D} V$, where the random variable V is a stable law of order 1 with characteristic function

$$\phi_V(t) = \exp\left\{-\tfrac{\pi}{2}|t|\right\} \exp\{-it(\eta + \log t)\}, \qquad (14.7.7)$$

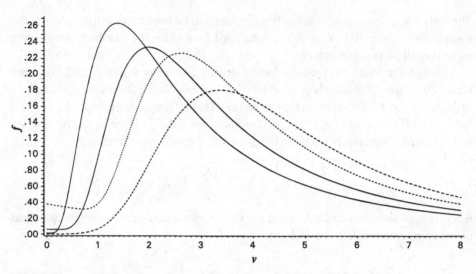

Figure 14.2. Limit density by inverting characteristic function. Density of average of reciprocals of uniforms, with $m = 8$ (solid), 16, 32 (both dashed), and limit (taller solid).

where $\eta = 1 - \gamma$ and $\gamma = .5772...$ is Euler's gamma. From Figure 14.1, most of the mass should be above -4 and tailing off very slowly. Clearly V does not have a first moment, so working with (14.7.6) for the normal distribution is hopeless. However, note that the amplitude follows the characteristic function of the Cauchy with scale $\sigma = \pi/2$. In the demonstration **chfniv**, the density is computed by following (14.7.5) with $N = 4096$, $\delta = 2\pi/256$, and the x-spacing $\gamma = 1/16$. The difference approach is followed for the distribution function, employing (14.7.6) with the Cauchy distribution and the scale mentioned previously. However, the behavior at the origin does not permit the use of a zero value at the origin (see Exercise 14.24), as was done here. As a result, the computed distribution function does not match the one computed by the sequential sum of density values multiplied by the x-spacing γ. Even so, the computed density in Figure 14.2 seems to fit well into the limiting distribution sketched in Figure 14.1.

(E) *Weighted Sums of Chi-Square Random Variables*

The null asymptotic distribution of some important statistics can be written as the weighted sum of independent chi-square random variables. Other problems arise that require the distribution of a quadratic form in normal random variables, which (after some manipulation) can be rewritten as a linear combination of chi-square variables. Imhof (1961) proposed inverting the characteristic function for this problem. Davies (1975, 1980) analyzed the truncation and integration error and proposed practical upper bounds effective for guaranteeing a desired level of accuracy.

Let $Q = \sum_{j=1}^{m} w_j X_j$, where w_j are weights (not required to be positive) and X_j are independent chi-square random variables with n_j degrees of freedom and noncentrality parameters δ_j. The characteristic function of Q is

$$\phi(t) = \prod_{j=1}^{m} (1 - 2iw_j t)^{-(1/2)n_j} \exp\left\{ i \sum_{i=1}^{m} \frac{\delta_j w_j t}{1 - 2iw_j t} \right\}. \tag{14.7.8}$$

Following (14.7.4), some complex mathematics, and the substitution $t = 2u$, we may express the distribution function of Q by the integral

$$\Pr(Q \le x) = \frac{1}{2} - \frac{1}{\pi} \int_0^\infty \frac{\sin(\theta(u))}{uR(u)} du, \tag{14.7.9}$$

where the angle $\theta(u)$ is

$$\theta(u) = \sum_{j=1}^{m} \left[(n_j/2)\tan^{-1}(2uw_j) + \frac{uw_j\delta_j}{1 + 4w_j^2 u^2} \right] - ux$$

and the term in the denominator is

$$R(u) = \prod_{j=1}^{m} (1 + 4w_j^2 u^2)^{n_j/4} \times \exp\{2u^2 \sum_{j=1}^{m} \frac{\delta_j w_j^2}{1 + 4w_j^2 u^2}\}$$

The integral (14.7.9) can then be approximated by the finite integral to an upper limit $U = (K + 1)\Delta$ using the midpoint rule, evaluating the numerator and denominator at $u = \Delta(k + \frac{1}{2})$ for $k = 0, \ldots, K$. See the demonstration **qimhof** and Exercise 14.27.

Davies (1975, 1980) also included an independent normal variate X_0 and allowed for the evaluation of $\Pr(Q + \sigma X_0 \le x)$. The inclusion of noncentralities makes the problem a little more complicated, but the noncentralities also make the problem easier. The difficulty here is the same as noted previously at the origin, and small m or n_j and $\delta_j = 0$ are much harder. Small values of x (corresponding to small probabilities) are also more difficult because the convergence of the terms is slow – Davies (1975) pointed out that this convergence can be surprisingly slow and require thousands of terms (K). Later, Davies (1980) fully analyzed the error terms, gave bounds, and presented code to automatically choose K and Δ to ensure a given level of accuracy. See Lu and King (2002) for improved bounds and guidelines.

14.8 Combinatorial Problems

The discussion of counting and combinatorial problems may not appear to fit well in this chapter. However, since these topics don't seem to fit in any other chapter, their sharp contrast to the preceding discussion makes its placement here useful. For as much as the motivation throughout this chapter has been to seek solutions that are surprisingly effective, this section examines a couple of the problems that can be the most tedious. Yet even as the number of steps may grow large quickly – say, as $n!$ or $\binom{n}{k}$ – all of the work is done in integers and so the steps are often quite fast. The number of steps, however, can grow so fast that these problems soon become intractable. As a result, predicting how long an algorithm will run is difficult, since the toy problems may run in the blink of an eye and so make timing impossible. It is therefore best to slowly increase the size of the toy problems, since they can suddenly appear to take forever.

For all of these problems (counting, subsets, permutations), the same framework is effective: an initialization, looping through to produce the next item and process it, and then a flag to signal the last item. Often these are coded as subprograms to produce the next item, which leads to the following program structure.

```
initialize
while (flag says it's not the last one) do
    first processing step
    ⋮
    last processing step
    call routine – get next item and flag
    end do
further code
```

These algorithms are most useful in statistical applications for implementing exact permutation tests. Permutation tests are designed so that, under the hypothesis of interest, a group of transformations of the observations does not change the distribution. For IID observations the order statistics are sufficient, and permutations of the order of the observations do not affect the distribution. Permutations of the responses (Ys) are usually the group of transformations, but in many cases the group of transformations can be simplified. The big advantage of permutation tests is that they do not require further distributional assumptions. Additionally, the test statistic itself is not restricted; the critical value is adjusted. Briefly put, the p-value under the permutation distribution is computed by counting the fraction of the permutations that produce a more extreme test statistic.

The drawback of permutation tests is that enumeration of all permutations is a burdensome task. Without some simplification, permutation tests are nearly impossible for all but small sample sizes, owing to the explosive growth of $n!$, the number of permutations. Just a few values make this point clear: $8! = 40,320$, $9! = 362,880$, $10! = 3,628,800$, $11! = 3.99 \times 10^7$, and $12! = 4.79 \times 10^8$. Without simplification, the sample size is therefore usually limited to one digit, since $10!$ exceeds one million. Some simplifications are worth noting. In the two-sample problem, the transformations are those that break the sample into two groups. So if m and n are the two group sizes, then the number of permutations is reduced by a factor of $m!\,n!$ to the combinatorial

$$\binom{m+n}{m}.$$

So if $m = 10$ and $n = 5$, then the number of permutations to be enumerated is cut from the impossible 1.31×10^{12} to a very practical 3003 (see Example 14.9 and **t2perm**). For testing the equality of two binomial probabilities, the transformations simplify to all 2×2 tables with fixed marginals, also known as Fisher's exact test.

Permutation tests' advantage of the lack of distributional assumptions makes them highly desirable – especially in clinical trials, where the sample sizes are small and the need for power is great. But for many practical sample sizes they are often computationally intractable, save some notable exceptions: the Pagano–Tritchler algorithm (and its successors) for rank tests mentioned in the previous section, and the network algorithms of Mehta and Patel (1986) for $r \times c$ contingency tables and related problems. As a result, the strong temptation is to follow the fundamental principle of statistics: don't take a census (enumerate all permutations or combinations); instead, sample from the population. The only disadvantage of sampling is that it can reduce the power slightly by adding randomness in the calculation of the p-value.

(A) *Counting in Base B*

Counting in a base arose in the reverse operator rev$(\cdot)$ in the FFT and in the radical inverse function for quasi–Monte Carlo integration in Chapter 10; see the routine **ncrmnt** in the demonstration **halton**. Other applications are similar; the general case involves generating every possible list of numbers $\{a_j, \ j = 1, \ldots, K\}$, where each number is bounded ($u_j \le a_j < U_j$), so that the total number of possibilities is $\prod_j (U_j - u_j + 1)$. For counting in base B, we have $u_j = 0$ and $U_j = B - 1$; there are B^K possibilities. The case $B = 2$ can be used to generate all 2^K possible subsets of k elements by using $a_j = 1$ for inclusion and $a_j = 0$ for exclusion.

A simple algorithm mimics counting: begin with all $a_j = u_j$ (their lower bound) and then increment a_1 each time until it hits its upper bound U_1. If any a_j hits its upper bound, then reset a_j to its lower bound and "carry" – that is, increment a_{j+1}. Once the cascade of "carrys" extends to the last a_K incremented to its upper bound, set the flag that the list is completed.

(B) *Subsets of Size K from N*

This problem can be viewed in a similar way to the counting problems, except that here we have a list of length K and each a_j is unique and bounded by N. The easiest way to ensure this is to force an ordering on a_j, such as $a_1 < a_2 < \cdots < a_K$. Then an easy algorithm is to follow the counting problem, with each a_j bounded below by a_{j-1}. The upper bound $U_j = N - K + j$ follows from the endgame with $a_K = N$, $a_{K-1} = N - 1$, ..., $a_j = N - K + j$.

In some applications, each subset needs to be assigned a unique integer, preferably from 1 to the maximum $\binom{n}{k}$. Knott (1974) suggested the function

$$v(\mathbf{a}) = 1 + \sum_j \binom{a_j - 1}{j}$$

and presented a method for inversion: create a subset from an integer. Although this numbering scheme following $v(\mathbf{a})$ does not preserve lexicographic order, a modification of it will:

$$v^*(\mathbf{a}) = \binom{N}{K} - \sum_j \binom{a_j^*}{j},$$

where $a_j^* = N - a_{K+1-j}$. See the demonstration **nxtkon**, which produces combinations in lexicographic order.

Example 14.8: *Null Distribution of Wilcoxon Two-Sample Statistic*
For the two-sample problem with sample sizes m and n, the Wilcoxon test statistic is the sum of the ranks in the first (m, smaller) sample, where the ranks are

those from combining the two samples. In other words, the statistic is the sum of a subset of size m of the $m + n$ ranks. The null distribution holds all subsets of size m of the ranks to be equally likely; hence, in the simple case (with no ties), the test statistic is just the sum of the indices in the subsets. The demonstration **nxtkon** generates all of the equally likely subsets, computes the index sum, and tables the counts of the sums to obtain the null distribution. Compare this distribution (in counts) to that generated by the demonstration **wlcx2s** discussed in Example 14.5.

Example 14.9: *Two-Sample Permutation Test*

As mentioned earlier in this section, the permutation test for the two-sample problem has the permutation distribution assigning equal probabilities to all subsets of size m out of $m + n$ observations. Because the permutation test provides the appropriate level for any test statistic, the possible power advantages of the usual Student's t-test when the distribution is normal are not jeopardized by the loss of level if the distribution is nonnormal. In the demonstration **t2perm**, a problem with sample sizes $m = 10$ and $n = 5$, the sample t statistic is computed. Then all subsets of sizes m and n are constructed from the combined sample, the t statistic computed for each, and a count made of the cases whose t statistics are greater than that of the original sample. The fraction of those cases (divide the counts by the number of subsets) gives the (one-sided) p-value of the test.

(C) *All Permutations*

Since the enumeration of all permutations has limited usefulness, this discussion will be brief. An algorithm by Wells (1961) constructs the sequence of permutations using transpositions, so only two entries are exchanged at each step. This algorithm is short and easily coded; the version in **permnx** is a translation of the Algol implementation by Boothroyd (1967). A more complicated algorithm by Shen (1963) produces the sequence of permutations in lexicographic order.

The problem of inverting permutations was addressed in Section 14.3 when we discussed computing ranks. Another aspect of permutations is assigning a unique integer to each permutation, similar to the $v(\mathbf{a})$ just given for combinations. Knuth (1997) gave an algorithm (shown next) for computing such a function $\mu(\mathbf{a})$ of a permutation $\mathbf{a}$ of length n; it is coded as **kperm** in the demonstration **permnx**. The basis of such a function is a mixed-radix number system, with bases $j!$ for $j = 1, \ldots, (n-1)$ and digits $c_j \in \{0, 1, \ldots, j\}$, so that $\mu(\mathbf{a}) = \sum_{j=1}^{n-1} c_j j!$.

    Algorithm Kperm (Compute Permutation Index)
(1) Initialize $\mu = 0$
(2) For $j = n, n-1, \ldots, 2$ do
        find largest of $a_1, \ldots, a_j$ and call it a_s
        $c_{j-1} = s - 1$
        $\mu = j\mu + c_{j-1}$
        exchange a_j and a_s
    end do;

This algorithm can be easily inverted to form a permutation.

>   *Algorithm Iperm* (Compute Permutation from Index)
>   (1) Initialize $k = \mu(\mathbf{a})$ and $a_j = j$, $j = 1, \ldots, n$
>   (2) For $j = 2, \ldots, n$
> $c_{j-1} = k \bmod j$ and $s = c_{j-1} + 1$
> $k = (k - c_{j-1})/j$
>   interchange a_j and a_s

Before considering using Algorithm Iperm to generate permutations, random or otherwise, notice that $n! - 1$ must be expressible in fixed point arithmetic.

Example 14.10: *Permutation Test for Trend*

The observations in the first sample for Example 14.9 were from ten months of my telephone bill. I may want to know if it's increasing, so I'm looking to test for a correlation between those values y_t and the time index t. Following Cox and Hinkley (1974, ex. 6.2, pp. 184ff), the relevant test statistic is simply $\sum t y_t$ and the transformations – under the hypothesis that these observations are IID – are permutations of the responses y_t. In the demonstration **ptrend**, the many (but not too many) permutations are constructed by **permnx**, the test statistic is computed for each permutation, and the p-value is computed. This task took about two minutes; increasing the sample size to 12 required four hours.

Programs and Demonstrations

hsort   *Demonstration of heapsort algorithm*
Samples of various sizes (up to 14,400) from various distributions are sorted using the heapsort algorithm. The results are checked in a direct fashion by ensuring that, in the sorted list, the values are in nondecreasing order. Uniform random variables are generated using the Lewis–Goodman–Miller algorithm.
hsort – sorts vector using the heapsort algorithm.

hksort   *Demonstration of heapsort algorithm with parallel sorting*
In the same way as **hsort**, samples are sorted with the heapsort algorithm. As observations are exchanged, elements of another vector are exchanged in parallel.
hksort – sorts vector using the heapsort algorithm and moves another vector in parallel.

bsort   *Demonstration of bubblesort algorithm*
In the same way as **hsort**, samples are sorted using the slow bubblesort algorithm. The results are checked in a direct fashion by ensuring that, in the sorted list, the values are in nondecreasing order.
bsort – sorts vector using the bubblesort algorithm.

partit　*Test of partitioning algorithm*
Samples of various sizes (up to 14,400) from various distributions are partitioned
into those less than, equal to, or greater than a partition element, which is one element of the sample. The results are checked in a direct fashion.
partit – partitions vector into those less than, equal to, or greater than the partition
element.

qsort　*Demonstration of quicksort algorithm*
In the same way as **hsort**, samples are sorted using the quicksort algorithm. The results are checked in a direct fashion by ensuring that, in the sorted list, the values
are in nondecreasing order. Uses two copies of Lewis–Goodman–Miller algorithm
for generating uniforms: one (**rang**) is for generating test data; the other (**ran**) is
required by **qsort**.
qsort – sorts vector using the quicksort algorithm.
partit – partitions vector into those less than, equal to, or greater than the partition
element.

fstmed　*Test of fast median algorithm*
Samples of various sizes (up to 14,400) of uniformly distributed random variables are
generated, and the sample median is computed using the quicksort analog **fstmed**.
The results are checked directly by ensuring that $k_a + k_e \geq k_b$ and $k_b + k_e \geq k_a$,
where k_a, k_e, k_b are (respectively) the number of observations above, equal to, or
below the computed sample median. Uses **partit** and two uniform generators, as in
the previous demonstration.
fstmed – fast algorithm for computing sample median.

hlqest　*Test of fast computation of Hodges–Lehmann location estimator*
The Hodges–Lehmann location estimator, defined in (14.4.2), is computed in two
ways. First the pairwise sums are formed, and the median is computed using **fstmed**.
These results are then compared with the output of the fast algorithm **hlqest**, which
follows a modification of the quicksort divide-and-conquer strategy. Uses two uniform generators: one is for generating test data; the other is required by **hlqest**.
hlqest – fast Hodges–Lehmann algorithm described in Section 14.4.

hl2qst　*Test of fast computation of two-sample Hodges–Lehmann location estimator*
The two-sample Hodges–Lehmann location estimator, defined in (14.4.3), is computed in two ways. First the pairwise differences are formed, and the median is
computed using **fstmed**. These results are then compared with the output of the fast
algorithm **hl2qst**, which follows a modification of the quicksort divide-and-conquer
strategy. Uses two uniform generators: one is for generating test data; the other is
required by **hl2qst**.
hl2qst – fast Hodges–Lehmann two-sample algorithm described in Section 14.4.

abdfmd　*Test of fast computation of robust scale estimator S_1*
The scale estimator S_1, defined in (14.4.4) and related to the Hodges–Lehmann location estimator, is computed in two ways. First the pairwise differences are formed,

and the median is computed using **fstmed**. These results are then compared with the output of the fast algorithm **abdfmd**, which follows a modification of the quicksort divide-and-conquer strategy. Uses two uniform generators: one is for generating test data; the other is required by **abdfmd**.

abdfmd – fast algorithm to compute scale estimate S_1 as described in Section 14.4.

abdftr   *Test of fast computation of robust scale estimator S_2*
The scale estimator S_2, defined in (14.4.5) and related to trimmed means, is computed in two ways. First the pairwise differences are formed and sorted, and S_2 is computed from the sorted pairwise differences. These results are then compared with the output of the fast algorithm **abdftr**, which follows a modification of the quicksort divide-and-conquer strategy. Uses two uniform generators: one is for generating test data; the other is required by **abdftr**.

abdftr – fast algorithm to compute scale estimate S_2 as described in Section 14.4.

fft2n   *Demonstration of fast Fourier transform*
The discrete Fourier transform of a series of length 8 is computed using the "power of 2" algorithm **fft2n**. The results can be compared to those given in Example 14.2.

fft2n – "power of 2" fast Fourier transform algorithm.

chirpz   *Demonstration of chirp-z algorithm for computing the fast Fourier transform*
The discrete Fourier transform of a series of length 7 is computed using the chirp-z algorithm **chirpz**. The chirp-z approach allows for the DFT of any length series to be computed efficiently using only a power-of-2 algorithm. The results can be compared to a direct computation of the DFT.

chirpz – implementation of the chirp-z algorithm for computing the FFT.

fft2n – "power of 2" fast Fourier transform algorithm.

poisp   *Demonstration of inversion of characteristic function using FFT*
The Poisson characteristic function with rate $\lambda = 4$ is inverted using the FFT algorithm **fft2n**. The results are compared to directly computed probabilities and sums to show aliasing.

fft2n – "power of 2" fast Fourier transform algorithm.

chex144   *Demonstration of FFT for discrete convolutions*
The ball-and-urn overflow probability problem described in Example 14.4 as a convolution is computed using the FFT. Because of the size of the series and the extreme range of the numbers, an extended arithmetic modification was needed, similar to the self-controlled floating point methods of Section 2.5.

fft2ne – modification of "power of 2" fast Fourier transform algorithm for extended range arithmetic.

adjst – normalization routine for extended range arithmetic; similar in spirit to **adjust**.

combo – computes the basic FFT step in extended range complex arithmetic.

dlgama – computes log of gamma function (double precision version).

wlcx1s   *Demonstration of Pagano–Tritchler method for distribution of rank tests using FFT*
As described in Example 14.5, the Pagano–Tritchler method for computing the null distribution of rank tests by inverting the characteristic function using the FFT is demonstrated for the case of the one-sample Wilcoxon statistic. The results are compared to a direct approach.
wlcxpt – computes distribution of the one-sample Wilcoxon statistic when ties are present.
fft2n – "power of 2" fast Fourier transform algorithm.

wlcx2s   *Demonstration of Pagano–Tritchler method for distribution of rank tests using FFT*
As described in Example 14.5, the Pagano–Tritchler method for computing the null distribution of rank tests by inverting the characteristic function using the FFT is demonstrated for the case of the two-sample Wilcoxon statistic. The results can be compared to a direct approach implemented in **nxtkon** for computing subsets.
fft2n – "power of 2" fast Fourier transform algorithm.

tivmm1   *Demonstration of convolutions of continuous random variables by discretization*
As described in Example 14.5, in seeking to understand the limiting distribution of the average of the reciprocal of uniform random variables, the distribution of $1/U - 1$ was discretized and the distribution of the sums of 8, 16, and 32 was computed by transforming the discretized distribution to obtain the characteristic function, raising that to a power to get the characteristic function of the sum, and then transforming back. Because of the size of the series and the extreme range of the numbers, an extended arithmetic modification was needed, similar to the self-controlled floating point methods of Section 2.5. Uses the extended range arithmetic routines **fft2ne**, **adjst**, and **combo** as in the demonstration **chex144**.

chfniv   *Demonstration of inversion of characteristic function to get density and cdf*
As described in Example 14.7, the characteristic function for the limiting distribution for the properly normalized average of reciprocal uniforms $\phi_V(t)$ given by (14.7.7) was inverted to obtain the density and the cdf. The density worked out well and was compared to the results of **tivmm1** in Figure 14.2. The distribution function values do not work out – even using the comparison scheme (14.7.6) with the Cauchy distribution – owing to difficult behavior of $\phi_V(t)$ at the origin.
fft2n – "power of 2" fast Fourier transform algorithm.

qimhof   *Demonstration of Imhof's method for deriving the distribution of sums of chi-square variables*
As described in Section 14.7(E), Imhof's method for inverting the characteristic function of sums of independent chi-square random variables is implemented in the routine **qimhof**. It was tested using cases from Davies (1980), stored in **qimhof.dat**.
qimhof – computes the distribution function of the sum of independent chi-square random variables.

nxtkon   *Demonstration of subset generation and subset index*

As described in Example 14.8, all subsets of size 4 of the integers $1, \ldots, 12$ are generated using the code **nxtkon**, and the indices are summed. The distribution of the sum of the indices matches that of the Wilcoxon two-sample test statistic, and these should be compared to the output **wlcx2s**. The subset index $\nu(\mathbf{a})$ is also computed.

nxtkon – generates the next subset of size k out of n.

kkombo – computes the subset index $\nu(\mathbf{a})$.

ibicof – computes binomial coefficients in integer form, mostly using table lookup.

t2perm   *Demonstration of permutation test for the two-sample problem*

As described in Example 14.9, the permutation test for the two-sample problem involves combining the two samples, enumerating all subsets, and comparing the computed test statistic with that of the original sample.

nxtkon – generates the next subset of size k out of n.

rbicof – computes binomial coefficients in floating point form, most using table lookup.

permnx   *Demonstration of permutation algorithm, index, and index inversion*

All permutations of size 4 are computed using the code **permnx**, a translation from Algol of code by Boothroyd (1967) of the Wells (1961) algorithm. For each permutation, the index function $\mu(\mathbf{a})$ is computed following Algorithm Kperm; then the index is inverted to match the original permutation using Algorithm Iperm.

permnx – implementation of Wells's algorithm to generate permutations.

kperm – computes the permutation index $\mu(\mathbf{a})$.

iperm – inverts the permutation index $\mu(\mathbf{a})$ to construct a permutation.

ptrend   *Demonstration of permutation test for correlation*

As described in Example 14.10, the permutation test for correlation with a time index involves enumerating all permutations, computing the inner product with the observations (from Example 14.9, **t2perm**) with the permutation vector, and comparing with the inner product from the original data.

permnx – implementation of Wells's algorithm to generate permutations.

Exercises

14.1   Verify (14.2.2). Try $T(N) = eN + f$ in the first case and $T(N) = gN \log N + eN + f$ in the second case; solve for g, e, and f.

14.2   Write a routine to compute the one-sample Wilcoxon statistic

$$\sum_{i=1}^{N} \text{rank}(|X_i|) \times \text{sign}(X_i).$$

14.3   Write a routine to compute the two-sample Wilcoxon statistic, the sum of the ranks of observations in one of the samples, with the ranks found from combining the samples. (See Section 14.7(B).)

14.4 Verify that the computational complexity of the fast order statistics algorithm FastOS is $O(N)$ by solving (14.4.1).

14.5 Compare the speed of **fstmed** for computing the sample median to the approach of sorting the sample using quicksort or heapsort. Design an experiment with different values of n.

14.6 An alternative method for finding the median is to find the root of the equation

$$g(a) = \sum_{i=1}^{N} |X_i - a| = 0.$$

  (a) What root-finding methods might be appropriate for this problem?
  (b) Can you take care of the problem of multiple roots as a function of N being even or odd?
  (c) Code a routine following this approach and compare it to **fstmed**.

14.7 The Hodges–Lehmann location estimator (14.4.2) arose from inverting the one-sample Wilcoxon statistic, that is, the root of the equation

$$w(\mu) = \sum_{i=1}^{N} \text{rank}(|X_i - \mu|) \times \text{sign}(X_i - \mu) = 0.$$

Following Exercise 14.6, code a routine that uses root-finding techniques for computing μ and compare this approach to **hlqest**.

14.8 Following Exercises 14.6 and 14.7, express the two-sample Hodges–Lehmann estimator $\hat{\Delta}$ as the root of a test statistic and compare this approach to **hl2qst**.

14.9 Modify **fstmed** to compute any consecutive pair of order statistics.

14.10 Write a divide-and-conquer algorithm to compute the 25% trimmed mean, the average of the middle half of the data.

14.11 Verify (14.5.2).

14.12 Complete the details in Example 14.1 by calculating the real and imaginary parts of $X^{(k_1, k_2, k_3)}$.

14.13 Can the DFT of length $17 = 2^4 + 1$ be computed using the chirp-z transform with FFTs of length $32 = 2^5$?

14.14 The periodogram $I_N(f)$ evaluated at Fourier frequencies $f = k/N$ is unaffected by whether or not the data are centered by the mean. Demonstrate this (mathematically) by showing that

$$a_j^* = \sum_{t=0}^{N-1} (y_t - \bar{y}) \exp\left\{-\frac{2\pi i j t}{N}\right\}$$

is the same as

$$a_j = \sum_{t=0}^{N-1} y_t \exp\left\{-\frac{2\pi i j t}{N}\right\}$$

for all $j \neq 0$.

14.15 Compare the mathematical results of the previous exercise with the practical results obtained by following the spirit of Exercise 5.13: compute the FFT of the series $y_i = 2^{12} + i$ ($i = 1, \ldots, 8$) and compare the results with the output of **fft2n**.

14.16 Invert the characteristic function of the binomial distribution $\phi(t) = (1 - p + pe^{it})^n$ for $n = 20$ and $p = 1/4$ using the FFT and methods of Section 14.7(B).

14.17 For a complex number written in three pieces as $(x, y, k) \equiv (x + iy) \times 2^k$, write code to raise this complex number to an integer power.

14.18 For a complex number written in three pieces as $(x, y, k) \equiv (x + iy) \times 2^k$, write code to raise this complex number to the power $-1/2$.

14.19 Use the discretization approach (see Section 14.7(C)) to compute the distribution of the sum of m independent uniform$(-1/2, 1/2)$ random variables. Compare your approximation of the density to that of the normal (with the same variance) for samples of size $m = 3, 5, 12$.

14.20 Use the discretization approach to compute the distribution of the sum of m independent logistic random variables. Compare your approximation of the density to that of the normal (with the same variance) for samples of size $m = 3, 5, 12$.

14.21 Invert the characteristic function of the normal distribution $\phi(t) = \exp\{-t^2/2\}$ to obtain the density, using (14.7.4) and the FFT. Compare the computed density with that of the normal.

14.22 Invert the characteristic function of the normal distribution $\phi(t) = \exp\{-t^2/2\}$ to obtain the distribution function using a direct approach. What value would you use for $\phi(t)/t$ at $t = 0$?

14.23 Invert the characteristic function of the normal distribution $\phi(t) = \exp\{-t^2/2\}$ to obtain the distribution function, using (14.7.6) and the FFT; use the Laplace/double exponential distribution for $\psi(t)$ and $H(x)$. Compare your results with **cdfn**.

14.24 For the characteristic function $\phi_V(t)$ given by (14.7.7), find the limit of $\phi_V(t)/t$ as $t \to 0$.

14.25 For small values of k and δ, compare approximations to the integral of the chi-square density near zero,

$$\int_a^b (2\pi)^{-1/2} e^{-x/2} x^{-1/2} \, dx,$$

for the following cases: $a = 0$ and $b = \delta/2$; $a = \delta/2$ and $b = 3\delta/2$; and the general case $a = \delta\left(k - \frac{1}{2}\right)$ and $b = \delta\left(k + \frac{1}{2}\right)$. Use various approximations for $e^{-x/2}$ for x near zero.

14.26 (Silverman 1982) Recall that the kernel density estimator (12.2.4) is a convolution,

$$\hat{f}(y) = \frac{1}{n} \sum_{i=1}^{n} k\left(\frac{y - Y_i}{h}\right) \Big/ h.$$

If the observations Y_i are rounded and/or discretized, show how to use the FFT to compute the kernel density estimate at many points using the FFT.

14.27 Show that the inversion formula (14.7.4) applied to the characteristic function of the sum of independent chi-square random variables given by (14.7.8) can be expressed as the integral in (14.7.9).

14.28 Describe a method to enumerate all 2×2 contingency tables with fixed marginals.

14.29 Show that the maximum value of $\mu(\mathbf{a})$ given by Algorithm Kperm is $n! - 1$.

14.30   What is the largest value of n such that $n! - 1$ can be expressed as a fixed point integer?

14.31   Relate the inversion of $\mu(\mathbf{a})$ (Algorithm Iperm) to Algorithm A2 of Section 11.6 for random permutations.

References

I learned about sorting, data structures, and fast algorithms by reading Knuth (1998) (but an earlier edition!) and Aho, Hopcroft, and Ullman (1974) while many of these subjects were new and evolving. Although the list of statistical applications may appear to be long, these tools have not been as widely accepted in statistics as in other fields.

Alfred V. Aho, John E. Hopcroft, and Jeffrey D. Ullman (1974), *The Design and Analysis of Computer Algorithms.* Reading, MA: Addison-Wesley.

Jenny Baglivo, Donald Olivier, and Marcello Pagano (1992), "Methods for Exact Goodness-of-Fit Tests," *Journal of the American Statistical Association* 87: 464–9.

L. I. Bluestein (1970), "A Linear Filtering Approach to the Computation of the Discrete Fourier Transform," *IEEE Transactions on Audio and Electroacoustics* 18: 451–5.

Harald Bohman (1975), "Numerical Inversions of Characteristic Functions," *Scandinavian Actuarial Journal,* pp. 121–4.

J. Boothroyd (1967), "Algorithm 29: Permutation of the Elements of a Vector," *Computer Journal* 10: 311.

J. W. Cooley, P. A. Lewis, and P. D. Welch (1967), "Historical Notes on the Fast Fourier Transform," *IEEE Transactions on Audio and Electroacoustics* 15: 76–9.

J. W. Cooley and J. W. Tukey (1965), "An Algorithm for the Machine Calculation of Complex Fourier Series," *Mathematics of Computation* 19: 297–301.

D. R. Cox and D. V. Hinkley (1974), *Theoretical Statistics.* London: Chapman & Hall.

F. N. David and D. E. Barton (1962), *Combinatorial Chance.* New York: Hafner.

R. B. Davies (1975), "Numerical Inversion of a Characteristic Function," *Biometrika* 60: 415–17.

Robert B. Davies (1980), "ASS 155: The Distribution of a Linear Combination of Chi-Squared Random Variables," *Applied Statistics* 29: 323–33.

I. J. Good, T. N. Gover, and G. J. Mitchell (1970), "Exact Distribution for χ^2 and for the Likelihood-Ratio Statistic for the Equiprobable Multinomial Distribution," *Journal of the American Statistical Association* 65: 267–83.

C. A. R. Hoare (1961), "Algorithm 63 (PARTITION) and Algorithm 65 (FIND)," *Communications of the ACM* 4: 321–2.

J. L. Hodges and E. L. Lehmann (1963), "Estimates of Location Based on Rank Tests," *Annals of Mathematical Statistics* 34: 598–611.

J. P. Imhof (1961), "Computing the Distribution of Quadratic Forms in Normal Variables," *Biometrika* 48: 419–26.

D. B. Johnson and S. D. Kashdan (1978), "Lower Bounds for Selection in $X + Y$ and Other Multisets," *Journal of the ACM* 25: 556–70.

Gary D. Knott (1974), "A Numbering System for Combinations," *Communications of the ACM* 17: 45–6.

Donald E. Knuth (1997), *The Art of Computer Programming* (vol. 2: Seminumerical Algorithms), 3rd ed. Reading, MA: Addison-Wesley.

Donald E. Knuth (1998), *The Art of Computer Programming* (vol. 3: Sorting and Searching), 2nd ed. Reading, MA: Addison-Wesley.

Lu, Zeng-Hua and Maxwell L. King (2002), "Improving the Numerical Technique for Computing the Accumulated Distribution of a Quadratic Form in Normal Variables," *Econometric Reviews* 21: 149–65.

J. W. McKean and T. A. Ryan (1977), "Algorithm 516: An Algorithm for Obtaining Confidence Intervals and Point Estimates Based on Rank in a Two-Sample Location Problem," *ACM Transactions on Mathematical Software* 3: 183–5.

Cyrus R. Mehta and Nitin R. Patel (1986), "FEXACT: A Fortran Subroutine for Fisher's Exact Test on Unordered $r \times c$ Contingency Tables," *ACM Transactions on Mathematical Software* 12: 154–61.

John F. Monahan (1984), "Fast Computation of the Hodges–Lehmann Location Estimator," *ACM Transactions on Mathematical Software* 10: 265–70.

John F. Monahan (1987), "An Alternative Method for Computing Overflow Probabilities," *Communications in Statistics A* 16: 3355–7.

A. Nijenhius and H. S. Wilf (1978), *Combinatorial Algorithms.* New York: Academic Press.

Marcello Pagano and David Tritchler (1983), "On Obtaining Permutation Distributions in Polynomial Time," *Journal of the American Statistical Association* 78: 435–40.

L. R. Rabiner, R. W. Schafer, and C. M. Rader (1969), "The Chirp-z Transform Algorithm and Its Applications," *Bell System Technical Journal* 48: 1249–92.

M. V. Ramakrishna (1987), "Computing the Probability of Hash Table/Urn Overflow," *Communications in Statistics A* 16: 3343–53.

Ian Robinson and Simon Sheather (1988), "Fast Computation of the Hodges–Lehmann Estimator and Its Associated Confidence Limits," *American Statistical Association Proceedings of the Statistical Computing Section,* pp. 187–91.

Mok-Kong Shen (1963), "Algorithm 202: Generation of Permutations in Lexicographical Order," *Communications of the ACM* 6: 517.

B. W. Silverman (1982), "Kernel Density Estimation Using the Fast Fourier Transform," *Applied Statistics* 31: 93–7.

R. C. Singleton (1969), "An Algorithm for Computing the Mixed-Radix Fast Fourier Transform," *IEEE Transactions on Audio and Electroacoustics* 17: 93–103.

Cathie Spino and Marcello Pagano (1991), "Efficient Calculation of the Permutation Distribution of Trimmed Means," *Journal of the American Statistical Association* 86: 729–37.

David Tritchler (1984a), "On Inverting Permutation Tests," *Journal of the American Statistical Association* 79: 200–7.

David Tritchler (1984b), "An Algorithm for Exact Logistic Regression," *Journal of the American Statistical Association* 79: 709–11.

Mark B. Wells (1961), "Generation of Permutations by Transposition," *Mathematics of Computation* 15: 192–5.

Author Index

Subject Index

Printed in the United States
by Baker & Taylor Publisher Services